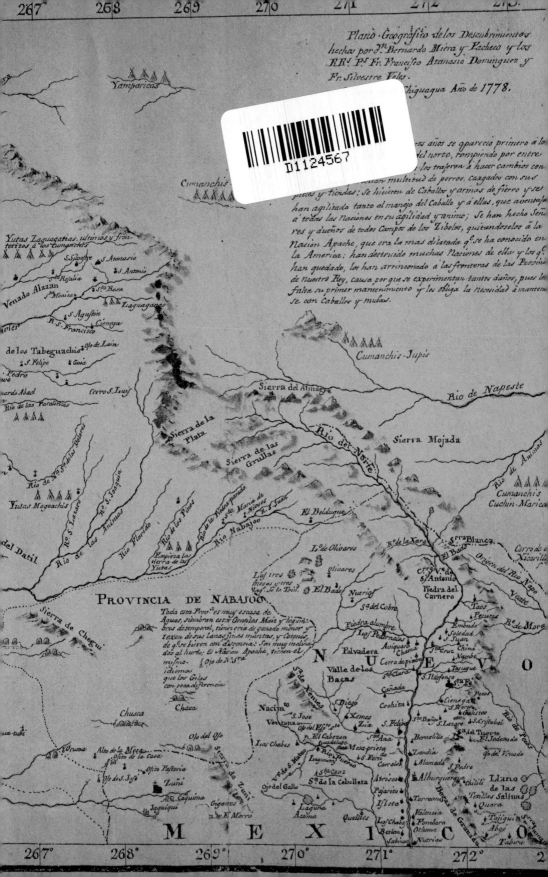

NAVAJO WARS

MILITARY CAMPAIGNS
SLAVE RAIDS
and REPRISALS

Frank McNitt

The University of New Mexico Press

For
Roland F. Dickey
with lasting friendship
and appreciation

Preface

In writing this book my principal concern has been to determine the underlying causes of the hostilities that led to almost continuous warfare between the Navajo Indians and white colonizers of the province and territory of New Mexico. Inevitably, a corollary concern was with the treaties that punctuated the temporary lulls between periods of fighting. The effort has engaged the better part of eight years and a search of some thirty thousand documents found in Spanish, Mexican, and American archives. The imbalance between the first two eras and the third is due to the vast imbalance between the available archival materials. Unfortunately, almost nothing exists today to document the Navajo side of the case.

No appreciable importance, I think, need or should be attached to the fact that the Navajo's adversary first was a Spanish subject of a foreign king, then a citizen of the Republic of Mexico, and finally—usually, although not always—an Anglo-Saxon citizen of the United States. I must admit it took me a long time to realize that differences among the three, as individuals or as instruments of the policies of three widely divergent governments, were, in the end, immaterial. This may be explained briefly by saying that a pattern established in the first century of Spanish colonization remained all but unchanged throughout the entire period of warfare, ending only with Navajo subjugation and removal to captivity at Bosque Redondo.

The pattern, I hope, will be a recognizable dominant theme of the book. At the risk of overgeneralization, key elements of the pattern are these: Navajos of the seventeenth century were an acquisitive, adaptable people with a keen propensity for raiding upon the property of their neighbors. The Spanish colonizers, subjected to Navajo raids, retaliated by visiting on these Indians the ancient slaving practices of Mediterranean Europe. They might as well have attempted to put out a fire with gasoline. It was this situation more than the nearly universal cause of Indian warfare elsewhere—land encroachment—that perpetuated a condition of hostility.

Land encroachment became a serious, though not dominant, issue in New Mexico only after the arrival of Americans in large numbers, that is to say, after 1846. Having a heritage of slavery of their own, Americans contributed to a prolongation of the pattern by piously decrying the practice of slaving while doing nothing effective to end it. Treaties entered into with the Navajos by agents of the three governments shared a common fault that made the treaties, if anything, contributory to renewed and intensified hostilities. This fault was the assumption that Navajos, because they were regarded as a "barbarous" people, had neither rights nor feelings worthy of consideration. After one or two rays of hope at the start, treaties drafted by Americans became progressively worse than anything conceived under Spanish rule. So unquestionably certain were the Americans of their right to seize land or anything else owned by Indians that, by 1861, the matter had been so resolved that Navajos were allowed but one option: they could choose between unconditional surrender and extermination. It is necessary to emphasize that the literal meanings of the words actually were intended.

The wonder of it is that the Navajos not only managed to survive but continued increasing in numbers until now they are the largest and most progressive tribe of Indians in the United States. A reservation school district survey completed in January 1971 showed a Navajo population of 130,811, excluding those who live in towns or cities.

The conclusions I have reached are my own and are not necessarily shared by any of the persons whose generous assistance has contributed substantially to this book. To David M. Brugge of Ganado, Arizona and and John P. Wilson of the Museum of New Mexico in Santa Fe I am most especially indebted. Entire sections of the book would have been impossible without their assistance. In giving freely of his anthropologist's knowledge of the Navajos and his own research with documents of the Spanish and Mexican eras, David Brugge has contributed enormously. With special skills in Southwest archaeology and history, John Wilson aided in many ways that will not be apparent to the reader, not least in clearing up misconceptions of the Roque de Madrid expedition to Dinetah in 1705 and providing documentation of the activities of the Manuel A. Chaves battalion of volunteers in 1860.

J. Lee Correll, successor in the Land Claim Office to the late Richard Van Valkenburgh, and still with the Navajo Tribe in a research capacity, cleared up many areas of doubt and generously furnished copies of letters, photographs, and transcripts of Navajo testimony before the Land Claim Commission in Washington. I am indebted to Marc Simmons of Cerrillos, New Mexico for the translation of fifteen Spanish and Mexican documents forming the historical basis of the origins of the Diné Ana'aii and their most notable leader, Sandoval. To Myra Ellen Jenkins and Ward Alan Minge I am grateful for permission to use and quote from their translations of Spanish and Mexican documents originally introduced as evidence in Navajo Land Claim hearings on the part of Acoma and Laguna Indians. Dr. Jenkins, who is state historian and senior archivist at the New Mexico State Records Center and Archives in Santa Fe, on several occasions gave me the benefit of her richly informed knowledge of Spanish New Mexico. Albert H. Schroeder of the National Park Service in Santa Fe, an authority on historical matters relating to Apache Indians as well as the Spanish colonial period, offered friendly advice and comment in addition to furnishing copies of his maps submitted before the Navajo Land Claim hearings.

I would like to acknowledge as well the assistance of Mrs. Sara D. Jackson, formerly with the National Archives and now with the National Historical Publications Commission in Washington D.C., and of Elmer O. Parker, Michael Chamberlain, Mrs. Mary M. Johnson (retired), James D. Walker, Mrs. Aloha South, William E. Lind, Dale Floyd, and Richard E. Spurr, all of the National Archives; of Miss Ruth E. Rambo, formerly of the Library of the Museum of New Mexico, and of Mrs. Sally Wagner and Mrs. Lucille Stacy, who were in charge of that library's collection of historical photographs; of Mrs. Margaret C. Blaker, archivist of the Smithsonian Institution; and of Kenneth W. Rapp, assistant archivist, and Mrs. Marie T. Capps, map and manuscript librarian, at the United States Military Academy.

I am indebted to Dr. William Fletcher Thompson, director of research for the State Historical Society of Wisconsin, for materials relating to Henry L. Dodge, as I am to Dodge's great-granddaughter, Mrs. Frank H. Spearman of Santa Barbara, California and to Miss Kathy Fisher of Keota, Iowa for other information about the Navajo agent. For photographs and other materials I wish to thank Mrs. Alys H. Freeze, head of the Western History Department of the Denver Public Library, and Mrs. Enid Thompson, librarian of the Colorado Historical Society. Finally, most helpfully in recent months I have been aided by Archibald Hanna, curator of the Western Americana Collection of the Beinecke Library, Yale University; and by Miss Margaret J. Sparks, research li-

brarian of the Arizona Pioneers' Historical Society in Tucson. Joe Ben
Wheat, curator of anthropology at the University of Colorado Museum,
went to considerable trouble to provide photographs of Massacre Cave
in Canyon del Muerto taken by Earl H. Morris. Dr. Harwood P.
Hinton of the University of Arizona offered valuable critical and editorial
assistance in the treatment of the 1860 operations of the Chaves battalion, and allowed me to withdraw a manuscript submitted to *Arizona
and the West* and related to that episode for inclusion in this book. I
am grateful, as well, to Robert O. Dugan, librarian of the Huntington
Library, for permission to quote frequently from the diaries of Richard
E. Kern. A part of Chapter 6, "Campaigns of 1847-49," appeared as
"Navajo Campaigns and the Occupation of New Mexico, 1847-1848" in
the July 1968 issue of *New Mexico Historical Review*. I would like to
thank Eleanor B. Adams, the editor, for permitting me to use that material here.

Over the years it had become unthinkable to go near to or pass
through Gallup, New Mexico without stopping to see M. L. Woodard.
No matter how busy he might be, he would take me back to his office
and there, his face aglow and his eyes shooting sparks of excitement,
show me his latest acquisitions: a prized and out-of-print book for his
fine private collection that sagged the shelves of one wall, or, as on the
last time, a new old artifact (a *yeibichai* mask) for his fabulous
Navajo museum downstairs. And then we would sit and talk. In more
ways than he would live to know, he contributed much to this book.

Frank McNitt

Contents

ILLUSTRATIONS

Part One

"The mountains thereabout [the vicinity of Acoma] apparently give promise of mines and other riches, but we did not go to see them as the people from there were many and warlike. The mountain people come to aid those of the settlements, who call the mountain people Querechos."

—Antonio de Espejo, 1583

1

Spanish Contact

Coronado's progress through the summer and fall of 1540, from his defeat of the Zunis at Hawikuh to his conquest of the pueblos of the Rio Grande, may at some point have been observed by the Navajos or at least discussed by them in their rancherias, which sometimes were close to diversionary lines of the Spaniards' march. Horses mounted with full equipage, their riders white-skinned under their beards, some carrying harquebuses and many wearing armor or chain mail, were entirely new to the country. Passage of so strange a caravan across vast lengths of land, seemingly uninhabited from pueblo to pueblo, could not have been unremarked.

It may be assumed that the Navajos were aware of Coronado, if he was not of them. Pedro de Castañeda, the chronicler who shared with Coronado the events of the journey, made no references to any Indians who can be identified as Navajos. Long months after the suppression of Hawikuh, and well beyond the east banks of the Pecos, Coronado himself in May of 1541 noted the presence of "Querechos," a nomadic tribe of buffalo hunters whom he described as occupying skin-covered lodges. These almost certainly were Plains Apaches.

One authority has maintained that none of the Spanish explorers who followed Coronado until Oñate in 1598 knew anything about the Navajos. The point is controversial, turning on vague historical documentation and incomplete archaeological evidence. Spanish accounts from the second half of that century of discovery refer by name, and with reasonable consistency, to the Pueblos of New Mexico. To the less sedentary tribes of the same region they refer with a casual imprecision that can only anguish a pinpointing historian. Thus are the nomadic warriors ranging from Tusayan to east of the Pecos called Querechos, Corechos, Vaqueros, Chichimecos, and Cocoyes.

In their indiscriminate use of these names the Spaniards frequently referred to different branches of the same tribe, and even to different tribes, by the same name. At Acoma in 1583, Pérez de Luxán observed that the pueblo was built defensively on a mesa top because "of the war this pueblo has with the Querechos Indians, who are like Chichimecos" —the last a Spanish term for any Indians who might be described as barbarians. At Awatovi shortly afterward, Luxán observed that Hopis of that village, on the Spaniards' approach, "sent away the warriors that had been assembled in the mountains. These people are called Querechos." But remaining with the Hopis still, he added, were "many Chichimecos whom they call Corechos." This confusion of names may not be as difficult to fathom as it seems. Querechos in both cases probably were Apacheans, possibly some among them who might later be identified as Navajos, and the "barbarians" called Corechos may have been a different band or branch of the same stock. The Querechos found near Awatovi and Acoma may have been Navajos either trading or raiding away from Dinetah (their homeland)—that region centering upon Largo and Gobernador canyons in northwestern New Mexico, where the earliest known Navajo presence in the Southwest dates back to about 1540 or two decades earlier. In any event, almost certainly the Querechos mentioned by Luxán were mountain warriors distantly related to the tipi-dwellers encountered by Coronado.

From the shadows of complete obscurity or uncertainty, Navajos and their Apache cousins began to assume separate, historical identities near the end of the 1500s. This was inevitable as the first tentative Spanish colonization of the upper Rio Grande Valley brought the two races into closer contact, perhaps neutral and mutually curious at first, then openly and increasingly and bitterly hostile.

Borrowing from the Pueblos, Spaniards applied more specific terms to these "mountain people": Cocoyes, a name of short duration; and a corruption in varying forms of *Ápachu*, a Zuni word meaning "enemies" and used by the Zunis in speaking of the Navajos. Its sound fell strangely on the Spanish ear, and the word appears in early documents as *Apiche* or *Apad* and finally as *Apache de Nabajú* or its variant, *Navajo Apaches*. Confusingly enough, the Spaniards for a century more usually referred to Navajos, without distinction, as Apaches.

A contact of sort appears to have been established in the closing months of the sixteenth century when Fray Alonso de Lugo was sent to convert the savages of the province of Jemez and "all the Apades and Cocoyes of its sierras and neighborhood." Don Juan de Oñate, the colonizer of New Mexico, added a few more pebbles of evidence when he wrote to the viceroy in 1599 that "Querechos, or Vaqueros . . . live in tents of tanned hides, among the buffalo; the Apiches, of whom we have also seen some, are infinite in number" and live as Pueblos "in towns, and they have one, eighteen leagues from here, of fifteen plazas." Finally, there were the Cocoyes, "a very numerous people who dwell in jacal huts and who farm. I have detailed information on them and of the large settlements at the source of the Rio del Norte, and of those to the northwest and west toward the South Sea." [1]

There can be no doubt that the Querechos mentioned by Oñate were the same Plains Apaches encountered by Coronado. The "Apiches" found in a town "of fifteen plazas" some forty-five miles from Oñate's headquarters at San Gabriel del Yunque are not identified with equal certainty. Spanish exuberance with numbers accounts for fifteen plazas when more likely there were two; the Indians may have been pueblo-dwelling Jicarillas on the eastern slopes of the Sangre de Cristo Mountains. But the reference to the Cocoyes is a telling one: jacal huts—in other words, mud and stake dwellings—may be equated with Navajo forked-stick hogans; and, among the nonsedentary tribes, only the Navajos were farmers.

The first printed reference to "Apaches de Nabajú appeared in 1626, in Fray Gerónimo de Zárate Salmerón's *Relación*, which said these Indians could be found by ascending the Chama River. Four years later the name appeared again, in the *Memorial* of Fray Alonso de Benavides, who wrote that northward from the "rancherias of the jurisdiction of Xila—one encounters the Province of the Apaches of Navajo. Although they are of the same Apache nation as the foregoing, they are subject and subordinate to another chief captain, and have a distinct mode of living. . . . [They] of Navajo are very great farmers, for that [is what] 'Navajo' signifies—'great planted fields.'" Benavides thereafter referred to the Navajos as Navajo Apaches, or simply as Apaches.

The natural confusion of the earliest Spanish writers, assailed by foreign tongues, confronted by many different Indian tribes in an entirely strange land, is compounded by a tendency on their part toward sometimes outrageous exaggeration. In order to impress either Church or King, clergy and military alike were apt to bend the truth to their various purposes. Thus Benavides, informing his superiors of the problems the Navajos presented to missionaries and military, wrote: "There [in the Navajo province] the population is so dense that in less than eight days, on one occasion, they assembled more than thirty thousand

1. Forbes 1960, p. 91; and R. Gwinn Vivian 1960, pp. 183–84.

to go to war, for they are a very bellicose people. This is a very conservative estimate, because the sargento mayor of the Spanish soldiers
told me that once when he had fought them in a war he had seen more
than two hundred thousand, as near as he could estimate."

Boundaries became as nebulous as a mirage when Spanish documents
define the country roamed by nonsedentary tribes: "The Apaches occupy all frontiers and surround us completely," was a conclusion often
reached. Coronado and Castanéda, Espejo and Luxán, Gaspar Castaño
de Sosa, and Juan de Oñate, among the early explorers who left journals
or reports, told only when and where certain tribes were encountered
and how the Indians were painted, clothed, or armed. To a handful of
missionaries—Benavides, Zárate Salmerón, Posada—was left the task of
recording where the Apachean and Navajoan Athapaskans had their
rancherias, and where they roamed and raided.

Archaeological research has established an early concentration of
Navajos in the region referred to today as Dinetah—the homeland of
the Diné ("the People"), as Navajos call themselves. Spanish documents of the early 1600s inferentially support this evidence, but also
refer specifically to other Navajo concentrations outside of the Dinetah
perimeter: to the fringes of neighboring Pueblo occupation on the Rio
Grande, from Taos southward "for fifty leagues," or 130 miles; less
specifically, to rancherias a day's journey or a bit more from Santa Clara
Pueblo, to areas in the Chama Valley and not far from but "beyond"
Jemez; to "Casafuerte" and the rancherias of Quinia and Manases, two
leaders of the tribe, "another fifty leagues or more" beyond the province
of Navajo. This area of Navajo habitation or frequent occupation is
extended considerably farther by the early Spanish writers when they
mention, again inferentially, regions far beyond, even to the Hopi
mesas, where Navajos roamed, traded, and raided. Less than a century
later they were reported raiding on the Great Plains in what is now
western Kansas.

Benavides, who was father custodian in New Mexico from 1625 to
1629, wrote in the *Revised Memorial* that Apaches were found about
fifty leagues "along" the Rio Grande and "toward the west." The
Navajo nation, he added, "is on the frontier of the settlements of New
Mexico" and the Navajo population "becomes greater as we go toward
the center of their land, which extends so far in all directions that . . .
it alone is vaster than all the others . . . In journeying westward
through this nation, one never reaches the end of it."

Spanish hyperbole again, here probably not Benavides's intention to be interpreted literally, but rather his way of stressing the need for additional clergy. However, if the core of his meaning is admissible, and "the center of their land" may be regarded as Dinetah, he seems to have been saying that Navajos often or sometimes were found in considerable numbers far beyond the limits of their recognized homeland. Because trading was second in importance for Navajos only to raiding, such a premise is reasonable.

Only occasional distinction was made between Navajos and Apaches by Fray Alonso de Posada, who served as missionary to New Mexico's Pueblos from 1650 to 1660. Writing of that decade some years later, Fray Alonso referred to both tribes as Apachas. He observed that their clothing was made from dressed skins and that they wore leggings above their moccasins and jackets that they prided themselves in keeping clean. Their sole weapon was the bow and arrow. In describing the country frequented by Navajos, Fray Alonso said that if one traveled seventy leagues (about 180 miles) in a northwesterly direction from Santa Fe, the trail would cross "the mountains called *Casafuerte* or Navajo" and bring the traveler to the Grande (or San Juan) River. Country immediately to the north of the river was claimed by the warlike Utes.[2]

Casafuerte, meaning "fortified house" or "fortress," appears to have emerged as a specific place name in Navajo country at about this time. In 1673 Juan Domínguez de Mendoza was directed to make a campaign of reprisal against the Navajos "in the jurisdiction of Rio Grande [San Juan River], Casa Fuerte Navajo" and all other regions necessary. Two years later Mendoza again commanded a punitive expedition with orders to march to the cordilleras of Navajo and to Casa Fuerte.[3] Commenting upon the second, abortive Pueblo revolt of 1696, Governor Diego de Vargas wrote that the Pueblo Indians had fled into the mountains, some joining the Navajos and others going as far as "the fertile and beautiful lands of Casa Fuerte and Cuartelejo."

From the frequency of the reference and the manner in which the term is phrased, it appears certain that Casafuerte was a stronghold occupied persistently by Navajos during the last half of the seventeenth century. Modern writers have debated the whereabouts of this place, Fray Alonso's translators observing that Posada probably had reference to the Chusca Mountains ranging southward from the Four Corners

2. Tyler and Taylor 1958, pp. 303–4. The distance of a league used in this work is 2.6 miles.
3. R. Gwinn Vivian 1960, p. 190.

region of northwestern New Mexico. They add that the words *casa fuerte* suggest a stronghold and speculate that Shiprock peak and the small, fortresslike mesas surrounding it might well have acquired that name.

If Fray Alonso was estimating distance by crow-flight, his seventy leagues would be enough to drop a soldier in the foothills of the Chuscas. To the Spanish eye, the dark brown volcanic combs reaching out from the base of nearby Shiprock might have created images of fortress walls of similar formidable height in Spain. Westward another sixteen miles, Spanish troops would have entered the beautiful valley of Tse-lichee-daskan, or red rock mesas, and there confronted a sentinellike plug of basalt, almost black, thrusting upward through the crust of earth and above its encircling collar of talus.

But for Governor Vargas remarking the "fertile" as well as beautiful lands of Casafuerte, this indeed might be the place. The prairie surrounding Shiprock could not have been much less arid in the 1600s than it is today, however, and if the red rock valley to the west once was fertile, it is not so now. Without disproving this region, because in all other respects it does answer the descriptions of Casafuerte, another possibility claims attention. This is the dominant peak of the Chuscas some miles south of Shiprock—the eminence once called Cayetano, now Beautiful Mountain, capped by a symmetrical crown of palisaded stone cliffs and, above them, a green apex of fir trees. Petroglyphs carved into boulders along the canyon and valley on the eastern approach testify to an Anasazi occupation centuries before the Navajos arrived. Climbing upward toward the peak, the valley broadens and today is one of the most fertile cultivated by Navajos anywhere. Historically, the mountain had always been a Navajo defensive site, and it continued to be one until the final Navajo resistance was made there in 1913. Beautiful Mountain most nearly fits the conditions imposed on Spanish Casafuerte.

Most significant, if Casafuerte is indeed one of the two places considered here, is the time—about sixty years—by which it would advance the Navajo occupation of the Chusca Mountains. A recent archaeological survey of Chusca Valley found no evidence of Navajo occupation before 1750.[4] A similar survey of the mountains might provide earlier dates of occupation.

4. Some 1,700 sites in Chusca Valley were surveyed during seven months of 1962–64 by Stewart and Barbara Peckham, John P. Wilson, Joel Shiner, and Alan Brew, of the Museum of New Mexico. Of these sites about 1,500 were pre-Pueblo and Pueblo, the remainder Navajo.

Don Bernardo de Bustamente, a soldier who campaigned against the Navajos with Roque de Madrid in 1714, later recalled that the province of Navajo was entered "at the Castillejos" some thirty-one miles west of Jemez, and lay about fifty-two miles northwest of Zuni. He had been told that the province in length measured 180 miles.[5] Castillejo, or "small castle," probably was used in this context to describe a defensive site well known to Spanish soldiers in 1714 but perhaps less important or less forbidding than Casafuerte. Don Bernardo indicates that Navajos occupied a series of such sites—mesa tops, most likely—from thirty miles beyond Jemez to within fifty-two miles of Zuni.

The Vargas document appears to suggest that part of the Navajo tribe had separated from those at Dinetah and occupied one or two regions far to the west, and there had been joined by fleeing Pueblos in 1696. The Bustamente testimony, though taken some years after the campaigns described, extended the region of Navajo occupancy in 1714 south of Dinetah, possibly to the region of Big Bead Mesa and from there west to the lower Chusca Valley.

One other observer at the beginning of the second century of Navajo-Spanish contact deserves to be heard. In August 1706, Governor Don Francisco Cuervo y Valdez defined the province of Navajo as extending as much as 260 miles southward from the land of the Utes and Comanches, bounded on the east by (among other places) Taos, the old pueblo of Chama, the pueblos of Santa Clara, San Ildefonso, Cochiti, and Zia, the villages of Bernalillo and Albuquerque, and the region of "Zivolleta" (where the village of Cebolleta later was established), and on the west by the Colorado River. All of its vast area, Governor Cuervo believed, was inhabited by innumerable Indians of the Navajo nation.[6]

A state of nearly constant warfare—of raids, and campaigns in reprisal—had existed between Navajos and Spaniards for a century before Governor Cuervo defined these boundaries. Spaniards had pursued the tribesmen from the Rio Grande to Zuni and beyond, from the San Juan River to the vicinity of Laguna and Acoma and historic El Morro. At the beginning of the eighteenth century, the Spaniards' knowledge of country occupied by Navajos had been gained firsthand—by the officers who, at Cuervo's orders, had led three expeditions against the tribe in 1705; by the captains who had crossed the cordilleras in 1675, following and fighting the Navajos to the mountains called Casafuerte. Clearly, from Dinetah the Navajos had spread far "in all directions" during the seventeenth century.

5. Hill, *Navaho Culture Changes*, p. 406.
6. Hackett 1937, pp. 381–82.

From the days of first contact with the Navajos until the early 1700s, Spanish accounts reiterate that these were mountain people who raided and farmed. By 1650, if not earlier, Navajo raids increasingly concentrated on driving off Spanish and Pueblo horses. Sheep were acquired in raids probably beginning about 1690, as a result of Navajo contact with Pueblo refugees. Alone among the surrounding tribes, the Navajos became committed to raising stock. Navajos continued to be mountain people for half a century more, until their growing herds of captured livestock forced them down to graze the valleys and plains. There, of course, they became more vulnerable to attack.

A Tewan myth related by Adolph Bandelier, as credible as any myth, suggests that Navajos were familiar with the pueblo of Yunque Yunque before Don Juan de Oñate settled there and made it his capital in 1599. (His first headquarters, established a year before, were on the east bank of the Rio Grande opposite San Juan Pueblo and named San Juan de los Caballeros.) According to the myth, a division occurred between the summer and the winter people, traveling south from Cibobe, the former, Tewan people settling at Yunque Yunque, the others establishing themselves across the Rio Grande near San Juan Pueblo. In time it was agreed that a bridge should be built over the river, and this the medicine priests proceeded to do "by laying a long feather of a parrot over the stream from one side, and a long feather of a magpie from the other." On this bridge the people began to cross. But as they were midway an evil sorcerer caused the feathers to overturn, "and many people fell into the river, where they instantly became changed into fishes. For this reason the Navajos, Apaches, and some of the Pueblos, refuse to eat fish to this day." [7]

Be this as it may, the Spanish colonists had not been settled in long before their pueblo town, San Gabriel del Yunque, felt the scourge of Navajo attacks. An additional eighty soldiers were said to have reinforced the settlement in 1600, but the number of men Oñate could muster was not enough to discourage Indian raids. Located as it was at the junction of the Chama River and the Rio Grande, at the very mouth of the Chama Valley, San Gabriel invited Navajo attack over the Chama trail to Dinetah. These attacks were further encouraged by Oñate's frequent absence on trips of exploration, which left only a small garrison to defend San Gabriel.

Father Lázaro Ximénez wrote in 1608 that "los yndios apaches" constantly raided the horse herds and the people of San Gabriel, and there

7. Bandelier 1890, *Final Report*, p. 60.

were neither soldiers nor arms enough to withstand the attacks.[8] Oñate
was directed by the viceroy to provide necessary defenses, but the colonists, who felt they had suffered enough, petitioned the viceroy to allow them to return to New Spain. Months passed before a reply was
received; when it came, the settlers were directed to hold fast. New
Mexico was not to be abandoned.

There is general agreement today that the "apaches" who harassed
San Gabriel were Navajos. Largely as a result of their depredations, the
little pueblo was forsaken in favor of a new capital built by Oñate's
successor, Governor Don Pedro de Peralta, in the spring of 1610 upon
Indian ruins thirty miles to the south, in treelesss rolling foothills of
the Sangre de Cristo Mountains. A Spanish document of 1679 says that
because San Gabriel was desolated by Navajos, the capital was moved
to a place named Santa Fé de Granada—a name soon shortened to
Santa Fe.[9]

Removed from the doubtful security of river settlements, Franciscan
friars as well as settlers became the victims of unpredictable attack. At
one of the Jemez pueblos, which they alternately raided and visited for
trade, Navajos in 1639—possibly in collusion with the people of Jemez
—killed Fray Diego de San Lucas.[10] At Hawikuh, in 1672, Fray Pedro
de Arvila y Ayala was dragged from his church and stripped naked, and
at the foot of a cross in the churchyard his head was crushed with a
bell. Modern writers have disagreed on not only the date when this occurred but also whether the friar's murderers were Apaches or Navajos.
Hodge cites Bandelier and Bancroft as his authorities for the year 1672
but questions the former's implication that Navajos were to blame.

Unrest among many of the Pueblos under the encomienda system
and Christianizing efforts of the friars, together with a frequent shifting
in relationships between Pueblos and Navajos, kept the new colony in
a state of turmoil. During the 1640s, Pueblos and Navajos alternated
between fighting each other and forming alliances to drive out the colonists. According to one authority, Pueblo herders employed by Spanish
encomenderos from time to time turned over large herds of horses to
Navajos. Conversely, Navajos all but halted trade between the pueblos
of Zuni and Hopi and the Rio Grande settlements. Reprisals against
the Navajos deepened the enmities. Zuni was attacked in 1658 by In-

8. Worcester 1951, pp. 103–4. Hammond and Rey (1953, p. 1059) observe that
"these Apaches were undoubtedly Navajo."

9. Worcester 1951, p. 104, n.

10. Benavides's *Revised Memorial*, ed. Hodge, Hammond, and Rey 1945, p. 277.

dians described as Apaches but who may have been Navajos, and in the next year other pueblos similarly were raided.

Fray Alonso de Posada may have been describing western Apache bands as well as Navajos when he observed of the period 1650–60 that "the Apachas" considered all mountain ranges in and surrounding New Mexican provinces as their own property. These Indians were so constantly at war with them that the Spaniards usually carried arms. Spanish horses were stolen day and night, cornfields were ravaged, and Pueblos lived in fear of attacks in which the men were killed "atrociously," the women and children carried off as captives.

Fray Alonso is not alone in presenting a picture of Navajo rapine, but the impression conveyed here inevitably is a distortion because of its one-dimensional view of a complex, mutually hostile relationship. The Spanish colonist was neither so innocent of provocation nor so helpless as Posada suggests. Granted that acquisitive Navajos would have preyed on Pueblo fields and the herds of the settlements in any case, it must be said that Spanish conduct toward the Indians (like the conduct of Mexicans and Americans later) tended to inspire, not discourage, any increase in the tempo and destructiveness of the Navajo raids.

Enslavement of Indians was forbidden by Spanish law, yet the law was not enforced, and under one guise or another a slave trade flourished in New Mexico. To a limited degree, the seizure of captive children and women from enemies undoubtedly was practiced by the Apachean tribes before Coronado's time, and the custom—not unknown to Mediterranean peoples centuries before—was deliberately nurtured by the Spaniards as a means for commercial gain as well as for supplying plentiful free labor. For more than two hundred years the slave trade reached out from Santa Fe and lesser towns; it was felt by every free tribe of Indians residing in or bordering on the province. David Brugge's study of Catholic Church baptismal records shows that, of all tribes, the Navajos suffered most from Spanish raids. A central thesis of the present book is that a direct link existed between continuing slaving forays and prolonged Navajo warfare upon the settlements; that in proportion to captives lost to the raiders, Navajo attacks on pueblos and white settlements increased or diminished. To this day, however, the subject remains controversial. As one distinguished authority has described it,

> Since the Vargas Reconquest [1692–93] the Spaniards had begun collecting Indian captives of various plains and desert tribes, both by capture and by ransom. The idea was to civilize and

christianize them, not to have them be unpaid slaves or servants of their masters. They were not traded by their owners like animals, as African slaves were in other parts of English and Spanish America. Generally they were freed when they married fellow captives, and by law all children of these people were born free.[11]

Not all authorities place the start of the slave trade that late, or see its motivation as solely benevolent. In an introduction to a report on his excavations at Gran Quivira, archaeologist Gordon Vivian observed that "Civil governors [of New Mexico] were a greedy and rapacious lot whose single-minded interest was to wring as much personal wealth from the province as their terms allowed. They exploited Indian labor for transport, sold Indian slaves in New Spain, and sold Indian products . . . and other goods manufactured by Indian slave labor. . . . Governor Rosas (1637–41) was the first to establish a large workshop in Santa Fe for production of items, particularly cloth, for export. Both Pueblos and 'Utaca' captives worked long hours there under conditions of virtual slavery."

Rosas was not the first, but he was one of numerous governors of the province who used or misused the repartimiento—a variant of the encomienda system—for his own profit and otherwise exploited Indian labor. Theoretically, at least, the system established by royal decree in 1509 and practiced thereafter in Spanish colonies of the New World was designed to be as benevolent as it was practical. Not to be confused with outright slavery, an encomienda (only a few of which were granted in New Mexico) might be a pueblo or any other collective group of Indians persuaded into any service that could result eventually in tribute to the royal crown. The repartimiento, whose benefits might extend to other Spaniards as well as to the encomenderos, was a system of forced but paid labor. In return for their labor, the heathen Indians would receive minimal payment while enjoying advancement into civilized society and conversion to Christianity. Unfortunately, the encomenderos entrusted with making the system work too often regarded their Indians as a ready and malleable pool of cheap labor.

The clergy, whom he maligned and held in open contempt, accused Governor Juan de Eulate, a predecessor of Rosas, of many violations of

11. Chávez, 1956, p. 70. Use of the word "ransom" by modern connotation could be misleading. Navajo women and children captured by Ute war parties often were taken to Spanish settlements and there sold to (or bought, i.e., ransomed, by) Spanish townspeople. The transaction usually was by barter, as silver coin was a rarity in the province. France V. Scholes notes that "an Apache slave was worth four oxen."

the spirit and letter of laws applied to the province by royal decree. Between 1618 and 1625—the period of his term as governor—Eulate is said to have forced Indians to work for him and his associates without pay. He was accused or organizing slave raids upon nomadic Indians and forcing the captives into service as day laborers or sending them to Nueva Vizcaya to be sold as slaves. It is said as well that he issued permits to soldiers of the presidio in Santa Fe to "seize orphans in the converted pueblos and used them as house servants." [12]

The repartimiento system not only permitted the servitude of large numbers of Indians at the least possible cost to operators of these feudal enclaves, but provided as well that the same or other Indians furnish the raw goods for manufacture, such as hides, or finished articles for ready sale—salt, piñons, cloth, leather footwear, and stockings. The wage customarily paid by an encomendero was half a *real* (or about half a cent) a day or its equivalent in goods. This changed in 1659 when Don Bernardo López de Mendizábal became governor of the province. Curiously, because Don Bernardo may easily have been the greediest of a long succession of avaricious governors, he doubled the wage of the reduced Indians to one *real* a day, plus food, and then defaulted in payment of wages to hundreds of Indians whom he had impressed into his own service of processing and manufacturing goods.

While his predecessors had made handsome profits in the acquisition or sale of Indian slaves, Governor López apparently was determined to use his three-year term of office to make a fortune. His various ventures in this direction are related by France V. Scholes on the basis of the manuscript trial records of López and, among others, his successor, Governor Dionisio de Peñalosa Briceño y Berdugo, found by Dr. Scholes in the Archivo General y Público de la Nación in Mexico City.[13]

One of more than one hundred complaints against him charged that López, after arriving in Santa Fe, took possession of eighteen "Apache" captives that his predecessor, former Governor Juan Manso de Contreras, claimed as his own rightful property. The captives, who may have been Navajos, had been taken in a raid by two Spaniards and a war party of Pueblo warriors from Picuris. Over the protests and denials of Manso, López said that he had bought the captives (or some of them) from the Picuris in exchange for cows.

Don Bernardo was the son of a family well placed in service to the

12. Scholes 1936, pp. 146–49. The encomienda system is examined at length by Barber (1932).
13. Scholes 1937, 1941.

crown and had been well enough educated in canon law at the Royal University of Mexico to know the law and the means of circumventing it. About forty years old, possessed of an angry temper, an acid tongue, and a lust for bedding women second only to his lust for gold, he was at no pains to conceal his secular disdain for the clergy. It brought him into conflict with Fray Juan Ramírez, who in his appointment as custodian had traveled to the province with Don Bernardo in early summer 1659. The better he came to know the governor the more reason Fray Juan found to dislike him; the friar became one of Don Bernardo's principal accusers before the audiencia that tried him in 1663 at Guadalajara. Less than two months after López arrived in Santa Fe, Ramírez declared in his formal complaint, the governor sent more than seventy Apache (or Navajo?) men and women to be sold for slave labor in the mines of El Parral. And even as he wrote this indictment, he said, an army of forty Spaniards and eight hundred Pueblo auxiliaries was four days out, marching into Indian country under the direction of López to seize more captives.

Ramírez observed that "this inhuman practice" of the slave trade was "a thing which his Majesty and the señores viceroys have forbidden." But his deeper and more ardently expressed indignation centered on the fact that in sending out his small palace guard and the largest available force of Pueblo auxiliaries, López had stripped the settlements of defense against heathen Indian marauders. "The kingdom," Fray Juan wrote on September 8, 1659, was "full of heathen who have entered the pueblos of Las Salinas, the camino real, and the farms of El Río, and the pueblos of Hemes, San Ildefonso, and San Felipe. In these pueblos they have killed some Christian Indians and have carried off others alive to perish in cruel martyrdom. They have also driven off some herds of horses and mares." [14] Fray Juan Ramírez did not then, as a few authorities do not to this day, find any connection between the López slave raids and the intensified attacks upon the royal road to Mexico and the pueblos that furnished auxiliaries to López's troops.

His need for Pueblo auxiliaries to strengthen his tiny force of presidial soldiers on one occasion led Governor López to plot murder. Ties of friendship, strained only by infrequent overflows into aggression, for years had found Navajos in close association with the Pueblos of Jemez. Navajos frequently visited the pueblo either to trade hides for grain or cloth or to attend ceremonial feasts and dances. If there was any way for him to destroy this alliance, Don Bernardo stood to gain the sup-

14. Worcester 1941, pp. 10–11.

port of Jemez warriors in future forays. In a complaint subsequently introduced during the governor's trial, Captain Andrés Hurtado asserted that López arranged for certain of the Jemez to cooperate in an unprovoked, surprise attack upon a large gathering of visiting Navajos. Fifteen of the Navajos were slaughtered. Following this episode, Hurtado declared, Governor López "executed a follow-up raid on the camp of the nomads nearby during which ten men and thirty women were captured." [15]

Don Bernardo's claims upon slaves were not exclusive. Traffic in Indian slaves not only was enjoyed by the upper levels of secular authority but also extended at this time or soon after into every home of moderate means—even, if in lesser degree, to the Franciscan clergy. By no means did all of the clergy become involved, but enough of them were dependent upon Indian labor that the line between benevolent Christian effort and outright exploitation often was scarcely discernible.

In 1661, while serving as alcalde mayor of the Zuni and Hopi jurisdictions, Captain Diego de Trujillo testified that Pueblos of Walpi, after capturing nine "Apaches," gave one (whether a woman or child is not stated) to the resident friar, one to Trujillo himself, and offered the other seven in trade. In a complaint against López entered later, Trujillo said he told the Hopis he would have to consult the governor to determine if López wished to buy the unallotted captives. Fearing they would be cheated in such an arrangement, the Pueblos objected. Trujillo consequently acted upon the friar's advice: he bought the captives but reserved "three of the best" for the governor should Don Bernardo decide he wanted them.

Trujillo might better have done nothing. When López learned of the arrangement he stripped the alcalde mayor of his office, humiliated him in other ways—and commandeered all of the captives for himself.

The rapacity of Governor López was no different from but only more vigorous than that of governors who preceded and followed him. Governor Peñalosa, a man of less imagination than López, would dissemble to a point and then ingenuously admit all. So it was that during his own trial, when he was accused on specific evidence of attempted or actual seizure of two girls eight or nine years old from the pueblos of Cochiti and Zia—girls he was accused of desiring to impress as servants in the Casa Real—Peñalosa denied the charges. He denied as well having taken a crippled girl from Taos and sending her as a gift to the viceroy's wife. Why, he asked, should anyone believe he would stoop to

15. Scholes 1935, p. 85; 1937, p. 398.

such things when it was known "he had so many Apache captives that he gave away more than a hundred!" [16]

Early in the seventeenth century civil governors of New Mexico learned that for military operations of any importance they were largely dependent upon Pueblo auxiliaries. Soldiers of the presidial force—never more than a hundred, and half that number more often—at best formed a nucleus armed haphazardly with harquebuses, swords, dirks, pikes, lances, and even bows and arrows. Helmets of metal, caps and hats and jerkins of cloth or leather, some chain mail and spurs with barbarously pronged rowels, and horse armor of embossed leather—none of it government issue, and all of it in need of repair—made up the equipment of the presidio's troops.

Just when Pueblos first were impressed into service against the Navajos, and the circumstances under which they agreed to campaign, have not been fully determined. In his relation of how eight hundred Pueblo auxiliaries marched with forty Spanish soldiers into undefined Indian country in autumn of 1659, Fray Juan Ramírez implied that this was by no means the first time Pueblos had joined in war as allies of the Spaniards. Because with each year the Spanish grip upon Pueblo affairs reached deeper and grew tighter, it might be assumed that the Pueblo auxiliaries were not always eager volunteers. The presence of Franciscan friars on many of the campaigns suggests a measure of clerical influence or persuasion. Often, however, this would not have been necessary, since Navajo depredations upon their villages would have made the Pueblos eager to join the Spaniards in reprisal.

One of the first specific references to a campaign against Navajos by such a combined force is contained in the *Servicios* of Juan Domínguez de Mendoza, said to have been the ablest and most experienced citizen-soldier in the province when the little army set forth in 1675.[17] Scholes has noted that from about 1640 to 1690 Domínguez held every military rank open to a citizen volunteer and served the province four

16. Scholes 1941, pp. 37–38.
17. *Servicios personales del Maestro de Campo Don Juan Domínguez y Mendosa*, MS 19258, Biblioteca Nacional, Madrid, quoted in R. Gwinn Vivian (1960, p. 190) from manuscript furnished by France V. Scholes. During the administration of Gov. Juan de Samaniego y Xaca (1653–56), after Navajos ambushed Jemez Pueblo, taking 35 captives and leaving 19 Pueblos dead, Domínguez led a punitive expedition in pursuit. He "surprised the Navahos during a native ceremonial, killed several Navahos, imprisoned 211, and released the captives, including a Spanish woman." It is not stated if Pueblo auxiliaries accompanied Domínguez on this occasion.

times as lieutenant governor; the proud family to which he belonged was the wealthiest in the province.

In September 1675 the gathering forces rendezvoused at Zia Pueblo for the expedition, described vaguely in antique Spanish as leading across the cordilleras of Navajo to Casafuerte. To Zia, Domínguez brought forty harquebusiers. Here he was joined by three hundred Pueblos. On the campaign he is reported to have killed fifteen Navajos and recovered from captivity six Pueblo Indians and the daughter of a Spanish citizen. Large quantities of Navajo corn were destroyed and thirty-five Navajos were brought back as slaves.

Three years later, after increasing attacks by the nomad tribes led the Spaniards to question their own ability to hold the young province, Juan Domínguez again outfitted a campaign against the Navajos and again was aided by Pueblo auxiliaries. In July 1678 he started for Navajo country with fifty mounted Spanish troops, four hundred "Christian Indians," and two "infidel" Utes who recently had appeared at Taos and volunteered for the campaign, no doubt as guides. Following his return by way of the Chama Valley, Domínguez related that he had killed a number of the enemy, captured fifty men, women, and children, rescued two women held by Navajos, taken thirteen horses, and laid waste a sizable quantity of Navajo crops.

The number of captives taken and rescued in these two campaigns (eighty-five Navajos and nine Pueblos and Spanish citizens) fairly represents the approximate ratio of captives taken by the two sides during the next 190 years; the figures as well give evidence of the relative importance attached by Spaniards and Navajos to taking captives into bondage.

Spanish reliance on Pueblo auxiliaries in time was to be followed by Spanish inducements to the Navajos to aid in fighting Apaches, but in the late 1600s the weakness of Spanish arms in New Mexico, indicated by the collaborative campaigns against Casafuerte, was demonstrated clearly in the Pueblo uprising that started on August 10, 1680. (Navajos took little part in the Pueblo Revolt, for reasons best known to themselves and now long obscured, perhaps related to repeated Pueblo participation in Spanish forays against them.) In less than one month the Spanish settlements and mission churches lay abandoned, and the Spaniards had withdrawn to a point below present El Paso, Texas.

On his reconquest of New Mexico in 1692, a year in advance of the return of the colonists, Governor Diego de Vargas heard rumors that a number of the pueblos planned to ambush his column. If there was such a plan, nothing came of it. From Jemez, where he found the people living on the high mesas—for protection, they said, against the Navajos—Vargas proceeded to Acoma, Zuni, and Walpi, receiving at each pueblo assurances that the Indians would submit peacefully to the return of Spanish rule. Nowhere, it appears, did his expedition encounter Navajos, although they were mentioned frequently. At Acoma he heard that Apaches intended to kill him and all of his people. Pueblos of Acoma professed to dread such warfare, saying the Navajos were their only friends. Vargas found the Hopi mesa at Walpi heavily defended and was told that Navajos had warned the Hopis that the returning Spaniards would carry off all of the Hopi women, children, and livestock.

Following the reoccupation of Santa Fe by the Spaniards in December 1693, some bands of Navajos formed tentative alliances with the Jemez and other Pueblos, together fighting the colonists in a series of minor skirmishes. It was during the period of this second revolt, culminating in 1696, that many of the Indians of Rio Grande pueblos sought refuge in Navajo country. Where the tribes mingled and lived together, as on the Chacra Mesa, Navajo protection was rewarded handsomely: Pueblo weavers taught Navajo women the craft that flourished on Navajo looms into an art; Pueblo pottery was imitated in form and polychrome paint (but crudely; in time the imitation declined and was forgotten); ceremonial customs of the Pueblos, including symbolic paintings, dance masks, and other paraphernalia, were borrowed and transformed into things wholly Navajo.

Navajo and Pueblo partners in this alliance benefited materially; unfortunately, the era of harmony was brief. For more than a decade after the reconquest, according to the testimony of Governor Cuervo, Navajos continued with "audacity . . . their reckless depredations upon the frontiers and pueblos" of New Mexico. Early in the first year of his term as governor, Cuervo set in motion what may have been the most relentless and effective campaigns made against Navajos to that time. Pueblo warriors again served as auxiliaries, their presence in large numbers and their knowledge of Navajo country being more important to the successful outcome than Spanish accounts acknowledge.

The first of these strikes was made late in March 1705 in what appears to have been a reflexive action after two large Navajo war parties plundered the corrals of San Juan, Santa Clara, and San Ildefonso pueblos. Powder and lead were issued to Captain Roque de Madrid and a

pursuit was organized. Navajos were undeterred by this reprisal, however, and in August, with the hope of ending their harassment, Governor Cuervo directed Captain Madrid to lead a much stronger force
into the Navajo heartland and devastate it.

Gathering Pueblo auxiliaries to his command as he marched upriver
from San Juan Pueblo, Madrid forded the gorge of the Rio Grande near
Taos, turning westward into the mountains at Piedra del Carnero. The
country was broken, heavily forested, and for the most part difficult.
Madrid's diary reflects the hardships that he and his troops and Indian
allies overcame, emphasizing that he dared to go where no Spaniards
ever before had been. The exact nature of his Pueblo force, numbering
more than one hundred warriors, at least, remains somewhat conjectural. It included Pueblos of Tesuque, Picuris, and Taos, as well as
some *genízaros* from Jemez. Because his reference to involvement of
"Tewa nations" seems more inclusive than not, others may have joined
him from Santa Clara and San Juan, and possibly still others from
Nambe and San Ildefonso.

Distances traveled each day were accounted for in an approximation
of leagues between often recognizable landmarks, Madrid's observations
on time, distance, and terrain ample enough to permit a fairly close tracing of his column's progress. An ultimate assessment of this campaign
must await the publication of John P. Wilson's translation of Roque de
Madrid's lengthy *diario* on which these comments are based; in the
meantime it is enough to say that, after watering his horse herd on the
San Juan River, Madrid turned south. Emerging from the "Sierra de las
Grullas," or San Juan Mountains, he met the Navajos in their Dinetah
stronghold in several encounters between August 11 and 14.

A baroque prelude to the fighting occurred a few days earlier. With
startling insouciance, Madrid relates how, after the capture of two Indian women (one a Navajo, the other of Jemez), he had them subjected
to physical abuse to make them reveal the whereabouts of Navajo
rancherias; the women finally, still refusing to tell him anything, died
in an agony of torture.[18]

In a region of mesas and cañadas, the valleys or canyons barren and
cut by dry arroyos, the troops came upon and burned the first Navajo
rancherias discovered on the march. A few Navajos were killed before
they could escape, as the others did, to the heights of nearby mesas.

18. Madrid, 1705, unpublished journal. Although the journal was written in the
first person, Wilson notes, there is little doubt that it was kept by Antonio Alvarez
Castrillón, Madrid's "Secretary of War."

Several skirmishes occurred under similar circumstances, the small army pressing south, cutting down and destroying one cornfield after another. The hot August sun was a pale disk where rolling clouds of smoke hung over burning hogans, the sun slowing the column near midday as the horses began to suffer visibly from thirst.

The most serious encounter, beginning on August 11, 1705, and continuing at dawn the next day, occurred at a place Captain Madrid called "los Peñoles." On his approach to the towering mesa Madrid saw a number of his Pueblo auxiliaries in the act of killing a Navajo woman. When he stopped them, the woman cried out a plea to be baptized—possibly in the hope that this would save her life. The favor was performed; the Pueblos then, without hindrance, killed her.

> Another one was captured with her daughter [Madrid related]. I continued with my assaults until reaching los Peñoles. There I found the Apaches up above. I and all my companions experienced considerable affliction and grief at seeing the horses so weak and unsteady from thirst, and without remedy for their distress, as to be unable to punish the enemy, who made a great mockery of us, yelling from the top of the hills upon seeing the manner in which our horses moved among the rocks, smelling and neighing.[19]

For three days more the troops remained in the vicinity, moving half a league from los Peñoles in the evening of August 12, and, next day, another four leagues to a new camp "upstream." From this place Madrid operated against the Navajos until his foe had vanished completely from the region. A march of four days and twenty-six leagues—about sixty-seven miles—brought the returning troops and their Indian auxiliaries to Zia Pueblo. At least thirty-nine, possibly "many more," Navajos had been killed and a number of women and children captured. The sole casualty of Madrid's force was a wounded Pueblo warrior.

Unless additional evidence is found, the exact location of the mesa Madrid referred to as los Peñoles may never be known. As nearly as can be determined, Navajos were first seen when the troops, emerging from Compañero Canyon, crossed Tapicito arroyo or creek and entered the broad plain of the Cañada Larga immediately east of Largo Canyon.

19. Reeve 1958, pp. 218–21. In basing his account upon Fray Silvestre Vélez de Escalante's "Extracto de Noticias," a section of which is published in *Documentos para la Historia de Mexico*, Reeve miscalculated the distances Madrid's forces marched, and placed the encounter described here two days farther to the south, at Big Bead Mesa. John P. Wilson's translation of the Madrid journal indicates clearly that all of the action against the Navajos occurred in the Dinetah region.

As his column moved south, Madrid came upon los Peñoles among other and lower mesas, probably near the southern head of Cañada Larga and about one day's march due north of Torreon and the tip of Chacra Mesa.

The punishment they suffered from Madrid's small army was severe enough to cause the Navajos to ask for peace, but their overtures were brushed aside. Governor Cuervo ordered out a third campaign in September. The troops and Pueblo auxiliaries on this occasion turned westward into Navajo country from the vicinity of Taos. The force found Navajo rancherias and saw many Navajos on mesa summits, but the Indians melted away before they could be reached. A single casualty was reported, a Navajo killed by Pueblos. Discouraged from continuing the pursuit further into the mountains, the troops returned by way of Pedernal Mountain, two leagues from Abiquiu.

Soon afterward Navajo delegations came to the settlements with new requests for peace, bringing as evidence of good faith a number of women and children they had captured, livestock they had run off, and various trade articles with which they hoped to ransom some of their own people held as slaves.

A truce of sorts was arranged. In August of the following year Governor Cuervo reported to the king of Spain that since the final campaign of 1705 the frontier had remained tranquil and that a Navajo leader, whom he identified as Perlaja, a man of evident influence, had sent several delegations of his people to ask for peace. Cuervo noted that Navajos moved freely about in the settlements to trade, and from this he concluded that they seriously wished hostilities to end.

For nearly three years the Navajos avoided conflict with the frontier settlements, even coming to Santa Fe in March 1708 to ask that peaceful relations be continued. Governor Joseph Chacón Medián Salazar y Villaseñor, who had succeeded Francisco Cuervo the year before, gave assurance of his similar desire for peace. As the year wore on, however, western bands of Navajos were said to have attacked villages of the Hopis, and other raids were reported along the Rio Grande. By February 1709 enough of the western Navajos were at war to bring down full-scale Spanish reprisals on the tribe. In that month Navajos raided the vicinity of Santa Clara Pueblo. Captain Roque de Madrid went in pursuit with a company of militia, on the first of six punitive campaigns made within the year before the Navajos again appealed for peace. A Navajo attack on June 8 against Jemez Pueblo resulted in another punitive campaign. The engagements of this period all appear to have centered in the eastern province, with numbers of Pueblos offering their assistance to the Spaniards.

An unprecedented period of peace, lasting more than fifty years, followed the campaigns of 1709. During this time, known Spanish documents record not a single Navajo raid upon a Spanish settlement. Occasional depredations by Navajos against their Pueblo neighbors to the south and east resulted in punitive expeditions by Spanish and Pueblo forces, but the Navajos clearly and most earnestly wished no war with the Spaniards. Indeed, their desire for peace went deeper: they wanted Spanish protection against a deadly alliance.

Perhaps as early as 1709 the Navajos had begun to feel the pressure of combined Ute and Comanche attacks from the north across the San Juan River. There can be no certainty in accounting for the alliance. In their occasional forays northward and onto the plains, Navajos may have baited these tribes into striking back. Perhaps the Navajos, enriched with growing herds of stolen livestock, simply provided a tempting prize to a hungry foe. Comanches at this time had not moved southward to the llano estacado of present Texas, but roamed the prairie near the head of the Arkansas River. With the Utes, directly to their west, they ranged in a menacing arc above Dinetah. The alliance continued into the 1750s, coinciding almost exactly in time with the period during which Navajos maintained peace with the Spaniards.[20]

Always known to the Spaniards as mountain people, the Navajos withdrew to higher, more inaccessible elevations of the mesas. Here they built fortified sites of stone—large circular emplacements, houses, parapet walls, towers and lookout points—from which they could defend themselves against surprise or heavy attack. These sites extended southward from Gobernador and Largo canyons to the Chacra and Big Bead mesas. Encumbered with livestock, the Navajos found it necessary to disperse, to divide into smaller rancherias, and to move, year by year, to the south and west.

Spanish militiamen engaged in fighting Navajos in the early 1700s naturally were concerned only with events that touched immediately upon their own lives. These citizen soldiers left only fragmentary records, the pieces of which must be fitted together to document this half-century. One of the men whose testimony was secured by Governor Don Joaquín Codallos y Rabal was Antonio Montoya, who accompanied several expeditions into Navajo country. Montoya observed that Navajos were at war with Spaniards during the regime of Governor

20. Schroeder (1963, p. 10) dates the Ute-Comanche alliance from 1713.

Chacón (1707–12), but were at peace throughout the administration of Governor Don Juan Domingo de Bustamente (1722–31). He believed the Navajos had turned to peace because they were under frequent attack by Utes and Comanches. Twice, Montoya accompanied expeditions that started from Jemez; he spoke of finding Navajo country far to the west, among mountains and mesas. In other references that seem to describe Dinetah, he spoke of Navajos living in houses of stone and mud on mesa tops and mountains. To the best of his knowledge, the Navajos in 1745 numbered between three and four thousand "old and young." [21]

Possibly because the Utes and Comanches diverted their attention, the Navajos caused no trouble among the pueblos until early 1713. Then, during the administration of Governor Juan Ygnacio Flores Mogollón, they descended upon the herds of San Ildefonso Pueblo. Fifteen of the raiders were tracked returning homeward with the stolen animals through the Chama Valley. Captain Alphonso Rael de Aguilar counseled immediate pursuit, but Governor Mogollón, beset by advisers some of whom cautioned against starting another Navajo war, vacillated. He waited until October 22 before directing Captain Cristóbal de la Serna to take 50 presidial soldiers, 20 militia, and 150 Pueblos into Navajo country. Serna was cautioned not to use force if the Navajos showed a willingness to surrender captured stock and Pueblo captives.[22]

Captain Aguilar has been reported as saying that the Navajos, troubled then by Ute attacks, surrendered some three hundred sheep. Other references to the Navajos' concern at the time was made by one of Serna's militiamen, Blas Martín, who said that he and the troops entered Navajo country after gathering at Jemez and observed the Navajos occupying defensive heights in anticipation of attack by Utes and Comanches. Years later, on a third expedition he accompanied during the regime of Governor Gaspar Domingo de Mendoza (1739–43), Martín said his company marched through the Chama Valley to the San Juan River and, four leagues from that stream, came to Dinetah and again found the Navajos in the same mesa-top fortifications. No protest was raised against the Spaniards' passage; on the contrary, Martín said, the Navajos welcomed them.

21. "Original Depositions Sent to . . . Count of Fuenclara, Viceroy . . . by Sergeant Major Don Joachim Codallos y Rabal, Governor and Captain General of New Mexico," Bancroft Library, trans. in Hill, *Navajo Culture Changes*, pp. 400–402. The Montoya testimony was taken in 1745.
22. Reeve 1958, pp. 226–27.

Spanish reprisals were severe after the Navajos raided Jemez in March 1714, killing one of the principal men of that pueblo. With a small force of soldiers and militia and 212 Pueblos Captain Roque de Madrid reached Navajo country by way of the Chama Valley and turned south. In several engagements he reported killing about 30 Navajos, capturing 7 others, and seizing 200 fanegas of corn and 110 sheep. On their return the party stopped at Jemez.

Another expedition moved against the Navajos in October 1716. What prompted the campaign is not recorded, but Acting Governor Felix Martínez directed Captain Serna to march against the tribe with about four hundred men, the majority of whom were Pueblos. Once more, Jemez was the starting point. Antonio de Ulibarri, who accompanied the command, recalled that they had penetrated the province some twenty leagues when, at a place called Los Peñolitos, a battle was fought. No Spanish casualties were mentioned. Six Navajos were said to have been killed.

Testimony taken later from several men who participated in these campaigns indicates that between 1709 and 1716 Navajos were encountered in Dinetah and westward from Jemez for a distance of about eighty miles. There is enough evidence to support a belief that archaeological surveys may, in time, show more than a limited occupation by Navajos of the region directly north of Mount Taylor in the first decade of the eighteenth century.[23] Other records leave no doubt that Navajos were living on the eastern slopes of Mount Taylor by 1750. For this, the missionary efforts of a small band of Franciscan fathers were responsible.

23. Brugge (1968, p. 34, table 5, p. 38) notes that the greatest numbers (24) of baptisms of Navajo captives between 1700 and 1745 were recorded in parishes between Santa Fe and Albuquerque (19), in Albuquerque (1), and west of Albuquerque (4), while only 9 baptisms were recorded in the same period north of Santa Fe. He observes, "There is a strong indication in these figures that in spite of the spectacular nature of cultural development in the Dinetah during this period it was not the center of the greatest Navajo population."

2

Cebolleta and the Diné Ana'aii

As reliable an observer of Indians as any of his time, Benito Crespo, bishop of Durango, visited New Mexico in 1730. He traveled northward from El Paso del Norte and called at all of the pueblos except Hopi, Zuni, Acoma, and Laguna. His object was to determine how the missions of the province fared and what might be done to improve their situation. Of three pueblos he failed to visit, he did obtain information: all was well at Zuni and one resident minister, Crespo felt, was sufficient for the pueblo's eight hundred persons; Acoma and Laguna shared one friar, and, since they were separated by only four short leagues, he considered one friar enough.

This the bishop wrote to Viceroy Juan Vázquez de Acuña on September 8, 1730, while stopping at Bernalillo. He added that if they were given zealous workers, missionaries would greatly advance the cause of Christianity because "the place of the pagans, called Cebolletas," was within seven leagues of Laguna Pueblo.[1]

Cebolletas, or Cebolleta, was then not a settlement but a locality known well to Pueblos, Navajos, and Apaches, situated almost directly north of Laguna and approached over mesas and across valleys by a steadily ascending trail. Cebolleta is on a mountain stream of the same name, then but not now flowing at surface level, between sheer cliffs and dark green slopes of the Mount Taylor range immediately to the west. Red rock mesas like rusting hulks of ships loom up from the prairie that rolls off and down to the east. Entrance from the south is gained by crossing broken, rocky terrain leading out to high grassland and then to a natural gateway, a formidably black and towering basalt plug with a sloping base of loose slag and shale. A person toiling north from Cebolleta on the very old trail to Jemez and Zia finds himself soon among fallen rock and never far from the stream bed of the Rio Puerco.

1. Adams 1954, p. 98.

Big Bead Mesa lies twenty-five miles distant as the crow flies. Bishop Crespo's "Cebolletas" is the "Zivolleta" mentioned in 1706 by Governor Cuervo as one of the boundary places of the province of Navajo. The name derives from wild onions once gathered there.

Bishop Crespo informed the viceroy that a numerous people called Navajos were found on the Rio Grande between the pueblos of Santa Ana and Santa Clara, and that these Indians were ripe for instruction, because they were a farming people who already worshipped the holy cross. If his information on the last point was faulty, the bishop compounded his error by adding that conversion of the Navajos would be easy, as the mission of Jemez was only five leagues from the point where the Indians were concentrated.

The bishop's reference to "the place of the pagans, called Cebolletas" and his observation immediately following regarding a numerous people called Navajos to the north might suggest that he was discussing two different tribes. Some authorities believe this to be the case and maintain that the pagans of Cebolleta in fact were Apaches, who are known to have raided and visited in the area at the time. Others, on the basis of Governor Cuervo's testimony and military reports of some two decades before Bishop Crespo's visitation, feel reasonably certain that the bishop's pagans were Navajos.

What is more important is that Bishop Crespo's recommendation that missionary work be done among the Navajos eventually was acted upon. This speaks more for Franciscan fervor than for Navajo desire for baptism. Earliest attempts to Christianize the Navajos, beginning with Fray Alonso de Lugo in the early 1600s and continuing with efforts by Benavides and other friars some thirty years later, all failed.

Harassment by Utes and Comanches along their northern borders made the Navajos more yielding to evangelical harvest when Fray Carlos Delgado and Fray José Yrigoyen journeyed to the rancherias of Dinetah in 1744. The willingness of some Navajos for their children to be baptized, in return for a few trinkets and promises that they would be given livestock and clothing, encouraged the efforts of these and other missionaries during the next four years. A location for a mission at Cebolleta appears to have been chosen in early November 1748 by Fray Juan Miguel de Menchero, and subsequently a second mission site was found at Encinal, several leagues to the southwest across a saddle of the mountains.

How many Navajos moved south to the Cebolleta region and when they moved are not known. Fray Juan Sanz de Lezaún, who was named to direct the mission at Encinal, later recalled the method employed in building the missions and the unhappy consequences that set in almost at once. Noting that he was in charge at Encinal and Father Manuel Vermejo was the friar at Cebolleta, he observed that godly labor among the heathen had proceeded at both places for five months, and that the Navajos finally had repented their sins. All had been lost, however, because the governor had sent the Indians of Laguna to Cebolleta to work his fields and build a church and pueblo, and had sent the Indians of Acoma in similar manner to Encinal. The Pueblos, feeling "heavily oppressed," created such a schism among the Navajos that the latter ceased to cooperate with the missionaries and revolted.

The bloodless revolt evidently occurred in March 1750. An investigation was ordered by Governor Tomás Vélez Cachupin and councils with dissident Navajos were held at Cebolleta on April 16 and at Encinal the next day. Testimony of Navajos at both places indicated that the Indians shared the same grievances: they were firmly opposed to being colonized and forced to live in pueblos, they had never asked that missionaries be sent to them, they had told Father Menchero from the beginning that "they were grown up, and could not become Christians or stay in one place because they had been raised like deer." They would allow some of their newborn children to be baptized, and later perhaps their children, when grown, might build pueblos and have a mission. At Encinal, one complaint was that Father Menchero had not given them all of the things he had promised, "which included many mares, horses, mules, cows, and sheep, and clothing." [2]

The missions of Cebolleta and Encinal appear to have been abandoned soon afterward, the Franciscans making no further attempt for another 150 years to Christianize the Navajos. In growing numbers, however, the Navajos came to occupy the region, until in 1754 the governor of New Mexico observed that Navajos in large part had abandoned their homes in Dinetah and fled south to Cebolleta and the vicinity of Zuni.

Navajo claim to the Cebolleta-Encinal region was challenged from two directions in the twenty years following abandonment of the missions. Laguna Indians, exercising what may have been a prior right, continued to cultivate fields in the vicinity of those places. [3] More dis-

2. *New Mexico Documents* 2: 1095–1123, Bancroft Library, trans. in Hackett 1937, pp. 432–38.

3. Judgments favoring Laguna and Acoma pueblos were handed down following land-claim hearings in 1957 and afterward. Archaeological evidence offered by Dr. Florence Hawley Ellis indicates that a small site on the southeast side of the

turbing to the Navajos was an encroachment of Spanish sheepherders and cattle ranchers, who were granted land titles on the Rio Puerco and westward to Encinal and other grazing areas in the Mount Taylor foothills. Land grants were issued during the terms of six governors, from 1753 until 1772, drawing increasing resistance from the Navajos, who were themselves grazing livestock in those areas.

One of the more troublesome incidents, and the one best documented, arose when Governor Pedro Fermín de Mendinueta in December 1786 authorized the alcalde of Laguna to measure off a league of five thousand Castilian varas lying west of the region called Encinal. If adjoining settlers did not object, grazing rights to the land were to be issued to Baltasar Baca and two of his sons.[4] Certain stipulations were imposed. The Bacas were enjoined from injuring the ranches and fields of their Acoma and Laguna neighbors, "and much less the un-Christianized Apaches of the Navajo province." The land was not to be planted but used for grazing only, and the Bacas were not to reside there. Baltazar Baca, soon to become notorious for his corruption as alcalde mayor of Laguna, winked away the conditions under which the land had been given and probably cared not a jot when his activities at Encinal infuriated the Pueblos and Navajos. Among other achievements credited to either himself or one of his sons was the fathering with a Navajo woman of a son, Francisco Baca, who in time became a leader of Cebolleta Navajos.

Perhaps this encroachment aroused Apache resentment as well; in any case, the Navajos and southern Apaches formed an alliance in 1772, two years later raiding the Rio Grande pueblos and along the Puerco frontier until the settlers were forced to withdraw. Spanish defense was makeshift; in addition to a token presidial force, in 1772 only 250 persons in the province are said to have had firearms worthy of loading, and most of these were old shotguns. Unable to muster more than eighty regular troops, Governor Mendinueta called on widely scattered inhabitants to come together for common defense in a series of fortified towns; further, he warned that all settlers must arm themselves and be prepared to fight. The use of Pueblo auxiliaries was declared a neces-

---

present pueblo of Laguna, and several neighboring sites, were settled by Puebloans of uncertain origin in the late fourteenth century. These first settlers appear to have been joined by Queres Indians June 4, 1699, when the pueblo was named San José de la Laguna (Jenkins 1961, p. 51, n.).

4. An account of this grant, from its Spanish origins through litigation of recent times, is found in Jenkins 1961.

sity.[5] In September 1774 Mendinueta informed the viceroy that two expeditions against the Navajos had been made by militia and Pueblos. Twenty-one of the "barbarians" had been killed and forty-six taken captive. The Spanish command admitted four of their people killed and thirty-one wounded.

Depredations continued into the following month, the governor reporting that on October 5 a fairly large war party of Navajos attacked some ranches near Laguna. Four of the persons living there were killed, two were carried off as captives, and a number of sheep were slaughtered. The Navajos were pursued and overtaken and in the ensuing fight lost two warriors. Of the pursuing party, twenty-two were said to have been wounded.[6]

Navajo raids subsided in the decade following. The southern Apaches and Comanches, meanwhile, so terrorized northern New Spain and the Spanish settlements of New Mexico that in 1778 Comandante General Teodoro de Croix called a meeting of military leaders at Chihuahua to formulate a defensive strategy. Recognizing the Apaches as the most formidable enemy to be dealt with, the men drafted a plan by which the Spaniards would form alliances with any or all tribes, including the presently hostile Comanches, to fight marauding Apache bands. The task of making the plan work fell to Lieutenant Colonel Juan Bautista de Anza, who the same year was appointed governor of New Mexico. With Pueblos already enlisted in his cause because they suffered equally from the constant raids, Anza concentrated first on the Comanches, directing campaigns against them so effectively that within a few years the tribe was subdued and by 1786 was providing auxiliaries for expeditions against the Apaches.[7] During this period the only noteworthy aggression by Navajos occurred in 1782, when they succeeded in driving the Lagunas from the vicinity of Cebolleta.

Governor Anza used threats, bribery, and cajolery to break the Navajo-Apache alliance in the summer of 1785. An acceptable Navajo tribal leader who would join him against the Apaches was to be flat-

5. Schroeder 1963, p. 11; Jones 1962, pp. 88–89. In 1772 the equipment of each presidial soldier was said to include a broadsword, lance, shield, musket, and pistols. Pueblo auxiliaries were equipped with a pistol, shield, and lance in addition to their bows and arrows (*Reglamento e Instrucción para los Presidios que se han de formar en línea de frontera en la Nueva España por el Rey N.S. en cédula de 10 de Septiembre, 1772*).

6. Myra Ellen Jenkins and Ward Alan Minge, "Record of Navajo Activities Affecting the Acoma-Laguna Area, 1746–1910," Defendants' Exhibit for U.S. Indian Claims Commission, September 1961, Cases 226–27, New Mexico State Records Center and Archives (1961), p. 7 (hereafter, Jenkins-Minge).

7. Jones 1962, pp. 92–95; Moorhead 1968, pp. 147–49.

tered with the title "general" and offered various supplies and emoluments. To all Navajo auxiliaries he extended the same inducements hitherto available to his Pueblo allies: all of the booty or loot they could seize when the fighting ended, only excepting horses. For each Apache head cut off and brought in there was to be a reward upon delivery, and for each Apache captive a bounty of 100 pesos. Scarlet cloth and medals were offered as additional incentives. The governor at the same time threatened the Navajos with seizure and punishment if any but war parties ventured south of the Rio San José into Apache country; he also prohibited trade or communication of any sort between Navajos and people of the settlements.

In response to Anza's inducements, a Navajo war party appeared early in June at Laguna, informing the alcalde mayor that they were ready to campaign against Apaches but wished the aid of eighty Pueblo warriors. More than that number accompanied them when they started out June 16. On reaching the Sierra Azul they fought a battle in which more than forty Apaches were killed. Navajo losses were light. In reward for the success of the campaign, the Navajos were permitted to resume trade with people on the river. The Navajos made two other campaigns against the Apaches without important results, but Anza believed the campaigns had the virtue of instilling in the Navajos a desire for war against this foe, an attitude he wished to keep alive.[8]

Fourteen Navajos, among them a recognized leader of the tribe known as Antonio el Pinto, came to Santa Fe afterward with the alcalde mayor of Laguna to talk with the governor. El Pinto, a headman of considerable wealth and influence, who with one other man was said to have been instrumental in breaking off the Apache alliance, admitted his former close ties with the Apaches but promised that, much as he had been opposed to the Spaniards before, "he would be devoted and faithful in the future." If Governor Anza found El Pinto's change of heart credible, a successor to Teodoro de Croix did not. For the remainder of the year the new acting comandante general, Colonel Joseph Antonio Rengel, regarded the Navajo leader with suspicion and doubted the friendship many of the tribe professed to hold for the Spaniards. On February 4, 1786, he advised the viceroy that the Navajos were not entirely committed to breaking with the Apaches and yet did not refuse it because the friendship of the Spaniards was more to their interests than that of the Apaches—and they wished to enjoy the one without losing the other.[9]

8. Thomas 1932, p. 260.
9. Ibid., p. 264.

Not important in itself, but emphasizing both the Navajo attitude toward the colonizer and frequent Navajo inability to act in concert as a tribe, was an episode reported in March 1786, only a few weeks after Rengel's observation to the viceroy and at a time when the Navajos were said by their leaders to be at peace. A band of Navajos descending the bare sandy slopes west of the Rio Grande fell upon the ranches of Albuquerque, killing two persons, stealing twenty-seven horses, and destroying twelve other horses.

Regardless of Rengel's suspicions, the comandante general and Anza were committed to involving the Navajos, by any means possible, in war with the Apaches. They sent presents to important men of the tribe and arranged for the Navajos to meet Governor Anza in council on March 22 at Vado del Piedra, a crossing of the Puerco between Cebolleta and Jemez. Before the day arrived a rumor spread that the council was a trap to lure the Navajos to an ambush and massacre; only one Navajo appeared at the place and time designated, all of the others having scattered into the mountains. Out of an atmosphere of mutual distrust, Anza somehow persuaded the Navajos, through a lone emissary and an interpreter sent out to their rancherias, that the rumor was false and the Spaniards meant them no harm. Several days later eighty Navajos appeared and a council was held.

Anza made a mistake—one that would be repeated by far less able Mexican and American officials—when he told the Navajos that they would have to accept his choice of one leader or "general" to govern the tribe and another to be "lieutenant general." To these positions Anza appointed Don Carlos and Don Joseph Antonio, sons of old Navajos who had cooperated with the Spaniards in the past. Because this arrangement obviously pleased the governor and meant nothing at all to them, the Navajos assented. Antonio el Pinto, their most respected and influential leader, was not considered for a position of authority; either then or soon afterward, his loyalty doubted, he was confined to jail for some months in Santa Fe. Translations from the Spanish account imply only that during the council the Navajos were responding under duress. Before the council ended the Navajos agreed to Anza's most important demand—that they join the Spaniards in war upon the southern Apaches—and agreed further to make a campaign entirely on their own the following July against their one-time allies. Two Comanches who accompanied Anza to the council are said to have threatened the Navajos with extermination by the Comanche nation if they failed to make good their promises. In return for the Navajo concessions,

Anza offered the Navajos a curious pledge to protect them against their enemies—Utes, and of course Comanches—should protection be needed.

A month before the Navajos were to start against the Apaches, "General" Don Carlos, accompanied by his lieutenant general, seven other Navajos, and an interpreter, visited the governor in Santa Fe. Don Carlos said that he had visited all of the rancherias of his dependency and had been assured that the tribe, having "deposed" El Pinto—entirely unlikely—now recognized his leadership and agreed to make war on the Apaches.

In spite of these assurances, no more than twenty-six Navajos allowed themselves to be enlisted in July 1786 along with twenty-two of the hated Comanches, some Pueblo auxiliaries, and a few Spanish troops, all under the command of Salvador Rivera (for a foray that was supposed to have been entirely Navajo). The expedition, which appears to have deteriorated into a slave raid, succeeded in killing one Apache woman and capturing fourteen other women and children and undoubtedly inspired the Apaches to redouble their own acts of aggression. Otherwise, Rivera's foray was notable only as a rare instance when Navajos and Comanches campaigned with instead of against each other.

Antonio el Pinto, who had been jailed a second time on suspicion of sympathy for the Apaches, was released on April 4, 1788, by Anza's successor, Governor Fernando de la Concha. Perhaps because of El Pinto's influence, perhaps because of Apache reprisals, more Navajos volunteered when Concha mounted a large expedition against the Gila and Mimbres Apaches in 1788. Even the presence of a few Comanche auxiliaries did not deter them.

Concha left Santa Fe August 22 with seventy-four presidial troops, eight Comanches, and eight Jicarilla Apaches. By the time he was ready to start out from Laguna Pueblo his force had increased to about five hundred, including militia and Pueblos from Acoma, Taos, Zia, Santa Ana, and Jemez.[10] Between the Rio Puerco and Laguna, Concha was met by El Pinto and fifty-two Navajo warriors, all of whom signified their wish to join him. From them Concha selected Antonio el Pinto and nineteen of his band. The others he thanked for their good will, presented with gifts, and told to go back; the cost of feeding so many for two months would have put too heavy a strain on his meager treasury.

In his diary of the campaign Concha makes frequent reference to

10. Concha Diary, ed. Feather, pp. 287–304. Some six months before this campaign, Moorhead notes, New Mexico's single garrison, at Santa Fe, numbered 120 officers and men (1968, p. 88).

El Pinto, whose familiarity with the country soon became apparent. The governor, who had left Santa Fe without an appointed guide, assigned that responsibility to the Navajo, while Francisco García (who had been appointed tribal interpreter at Anza's 1786 council with the Navajos) accompanied the troops as interpreter.

The Gila Mountains lay before them in the morning of September 9 when Concha, who was about to break camp, asked El Pinto what hour he considered best for the column to advance. El Pinto objected strenuously to crossing the mountains, Concha noted, warning the governor that he would lose his supply train and horse herd on the steep, rugged slopes. Concha would not be deterred and El Pinto in the end agreed to continue as guide.

In a mountain valley the next evening they surprised an Apache rancheria. Eighteen Apache warriors were killed and four Apaches, probably women, were captured. El Pinto, fearing that Concha wished him killed, was persuaded against his will to lead the vanguard of the expedition deeper into Apache country. Two days later, in the Mimbres Mountains, Concha saw several Apaches on high ridges watching his column's slow approach. One of the Apaches recognized El Pinto and yelled at him bitterly, accusing him of betraying his Apache friends by bringing these enemies against them. He challenged El Pinto to come within range, saying the Apaches would fill his body with arrows and leave him dead. When the echoes of the shouted harangue died away the substance of the Apache's words was explained to Concha. With a nice logic, the governor decided that this baiting of El Pinto was advantageous, "as much because of the fear which our knowledge of the area inspires in [the Apaches] as because of the hatred against Navajos which it has produced."

Concha's motley command saw other Apaches and, although it did not engage them again, a detachment of Taos Indians succeeded in capturing a Mimbres girl and three horses. Concha, who may or may not have wanted El Pinto dead, decided that his campaign had proceeded far enough. He allowed El Pinto, with the Apache captives, to start home with Navajos of his band and a number of the Pueblos. Concha himself arrived in Santa Fe on October 6, 1788.

El Pinto was rewarded sometime later by the governor, who bestowed on him the title of general, with its implied leadership of the Navajo tribe and possibly also with the 200-peso stipend the title had carried when it was conferred, two years before, on the now-forgotten Don Carlos. El Pinto's efforts in the 1788 and other Gila campaigns, unfortunately, also were recognized by the Apaches. In the fall of 1793 a reprisal attack fell on El Pinto's rancherias in the vicinity of Big Bead Mesa. Gathering a force of twenty-four Navajos, two Jemez Indians, and two Spaniards occupied as interpreters, El Pinto pursued the raiders. Somewhere on the slopes or plateaus of Mount Taylor he overtook the Apaches. El Pinto killed two invaders himself, but was badly wounded in the arm by an arrow. The wound would not heal, and, in spite of all that could be done for him, Antonio el Pinto died on October 26.[11]

From the region of Chacra Mesa or the Chusca Mountains (there is no certainty as to which), Navajos and Utes formed a war party to attack the Comanches in the winter of 1792. After traveling for some days they surprised a Comanche camp, unguarded except by old men and boys while the warriors hunted buffalo. The war party destroyed the camp completely and either killed or carried off as captives the people in it. A formidable Comanche war party soon afterward descended upon a Ute village and demolished it.

Governor Concha feared that if the Comanches embarked on war against the Navajos the province of New Mexico would suffer severe damage; to attack the Diné in their own country the Comanches would have to pass through the settlements and disrupt the tranquil lives of the citizens.[12] In an attempt to reconcile the tribes, he asked Navajo leaders to bring their Comanche captives to Santa Fe and surrender them to a delegation of Comanches, who also would be summoned to the capital. The Comanches appeared to be willing, pending the outcome of the meeting in Santa Fe, to stop attacking the Navajos.

Whether the meeting ever took place has not been established, but Concha's efforts to establish harmony between these implacable enemy tribes met with no visible success. Separated though they were by Spanish settlements along the Rio Grande, Navajos continued to range eastward onto the buffalo plains to hunt or raid, and Comanche war parties marauded at will west of the Rio Grande.

In 1796 the Navajos again made peace with the southern Apaches—an alliance that lasted eleven years—and resumed depredations in a se-

11. According to Richard Van Valkenburgh, El Pinto was known to Navajos as Hashke Lik'izhi (Spotted Warrior) or Sabildon (Talks Like Shooting) (Brugge, *Navajo Times*, May 19, 1966).

12. May 6, 1973: Fernando de la Concha to the Viceroy Condé de Revilla Gigedo, Santa Fe, #1234, Spanish Archives, New Mexico State Records Center and Archives (hereafter, SA, NMSRCA), trans. in Simmons 1967, pp. 25–27.

ries of minor raids against Spanish settlements and the pueblos of Jemez and Laguna.[13]

Shortly before the resumption of these hostilities but in the same year, Lieutenant Colonel Don Antonio Cordero, a veteran of the New Mexico presidial forces who participated in a number of campaigns against the Apaches, compiled notes on Apachean bands. Like so many others before him, Cordero included Navajos as one branch of the Apache nation. His brief reference to the Navajos gives important insight into the condition of the tribe and the region it occupied at the close of the eighteenth century.

> This tribe is the farthest north of all of their nation. It inhabits the mountain range and the mesas of Navajo which gives them their name. They are not nomadic like the other Apaches, and they have fixed domiciles [rancherias of hogans, in geographical regions] of which there are ten, namely: Sevolleta, Chacoli, Guadalupe, Cerro-Cabezon, Agua Salada, Cerro Chato, Chusca, Tunicha, Chelle and Carrizo. They sow corn and other vegetables. They raise sheep and they manufacture coarse cloth, blankets and other textiles of wool which they trade in New Mexico. In past times they were enemies of the Spaniards: at present they are faithful friends and are governed by a general who is appointed by the governor: they suffer some inconveniences which are caused by their compatriots the Chiricaguis and Gileños, who are their neighbors on the south; on the north they are bound with the Yutes, on the west with the Moquinos, and on the east with the province of New Mexico.[14]

The light raids of the four years preceding 1800 provided a deceptive, pastoral overture to the start of the new century. In nearly fifteen years of war with other tribes and peace with the Spaniards, the Navajos had accumulated in wealth and numbers a strength greater than they had ever known before. They would need it, for their real struggle with the white colonizers was just beginning. With only brief intervals of peace, the fighting that started at this time lasted for sixty-five years. Arrayed in turn against the forces of Spanish, Mexican, and American governments, this "wild tribe" survived calculated destruction only by a metro-

13. Schroeder 1963, p. 11; and Worcester 1951, p. 115.
14. Matson and Schroeder 1957, p. 356. The ten areas Cordero mentions actually embraced four regions of contiguous Navajo occupation: Cebolleta, Salado Creek (a small tributary of the Rio Puerco), Guadalupe Canyon, and Cabezon Peak; Chaco Canyon and the Chacra Mesa; the Chusca-Tunicha mountains, Chusca Valley, and Carrizo Mountains; and Canyon de Chelly.

nomic war-and-treaty device until ultimately this device was rejected. Whereas in the past the Navajos had found only slaving forays a legitimate cause for reprisal, now they would experience, and strike back fiercely against, the beginning tides of land encroachment. They would begin to pay dearly in land, as well as with their women and children, for stolen Spanish livestock.

From the earlier advance to the Rio Puerco, the Spanish now made a more determined attempt to push their frontier west into grazing country held by the Navajos. On January 31, 1800, Governor Fernando Chacón issued a grant to thirty stock raisers and residents of Albuquerque permitting them to move their herds of sheep and cattle to Cebolleta, and there establish a town. On March 16 the settlers moved in. Navajos who had been grazing their own sheep and horses over the land protested at once. The settlers started building a wall around their village and refused to move. Snow still covered the higher mountain peaks when the Navajos struck first in a persistent series of raids designed to drive the newcomers out.

In response to these attacks, Governor Chacón intervened personally, departing May 13 from Santa Fe to lead a force of five hundred troops, militia, and Pueblo auxiliaries to the Chusca Valley deep in Navajo country. He was preparing to attack when twenty of the tribe's principal headmen advanced to meet him and ask for peace. Only on the third day, after the Navajos had made restitution for their raids, was the appeal granted.[15]

Early in 1804, six leaders of the Cebolleta Navajos appeared before Governor Chacón in Santa Fe to request that the lands of Cebolleta be returned to them and that the settlers be removed. But they were turned away by the governor, who remarked later that, although the Navajos on several occasions had lived in the region of Cebolleta, the lands of that place had never belonged to them; what was important now was the fact that Cebolleta was occupied by thirty Spanish settlers. This number might be greater, Chacón explained, but that the available water would not support more people. He observed that for the protection of their property the settlers had built walls fortifying their homes and plaza. Walls of stone, still partly standing, can be found today in the center of the old town among twisted tamarisk trees.[16]

15. June 21, 1800: Chacón to Comandante General Pedro de Nava, #1492, SA, NMSRCA, Jenkins-Minge, p. 17.

16. Anastacio Márquez, whose family has lived in Cebolleta since 1800, once recalled his great-grandmother, Clara Chávez, relating stories of how, at the first warning of Navajo attack, the people would close up their homes surrounding the forti-

In Chacón's view, if Cebolleta were turned over to the Navajos, they would use it only to spy on the Spaniards' movements and then, when the fancy struck them, abandon it to plunder the herds and flocks in the valleys nearby. At his meeting with them in the Chusca Valley in 1800, Chacón had told the Navajos that were they to live at Cebolleta, or close to Spanish settlers, nothing but strife would result. The Navajos had agreed, and agreed also—or so Chacón thought—to accept new boundaries of grazing lands that he prescribed for them. He congratulated himself because in the intervening four years further uprisings had been avoided.

Soon, however, Navajos—from Cerro Cabezon to Encinal and Cubero—responded to their exclusion from Cebolleta with a new outbreak of raids. In April alone, nine sheepherders were killed, one youth was taken captive, and much livestock was stolen. An influential Navajo leader known as Segundo appeared at Laguna protesting that the people for whom he could speak wanted peace, and that it was only the poor and hungry of the tribe who were making trouble. Raids spread from Jemez to settlements of the lower Puerco, but the worst was reserved for Cebolleta. During the night of April 24, more than two hundred Navajos swarmed into the plaza. Three houses were broken into and sacked; twelve horses and fifty cattle were driven off. Leaving the villagers shaking with terror, the war party then fell upon a sheepherders' camp. They killed three of the pastors, took a young boy captive, and added the sheep to their stolen herd. The alcalde mayor of Laguna led a force in pursuit the following day and succeeded in recovering a part of the livestock.[17]

As spring turned to summer and the raids continued, Spanish authorities resolved not to heed such individual appeals for peace as made by Segundo but to wage a campaign of unprecedented strength into all parts of Navajo country. Until the forces at Chacón's disposal could be reinforced with troops sent from Sonora in late fall, the governor pro-

---

fication and gather within the walled plaza with as much of their livestock as could be crowded in. Márquez said the people of Cebolleta once grazed "maybe 30,000 or 35,000 sheep and 2,000 cattle" on 175,000 acres of land, and his father, Fermín Márquez, at one time owned 7,000 sheep. When his great-grandmother was a girl the land was unfenced and Cebolleta Creek, now cutting an arroyo 30 feet deep, ran at ground level. In one Navajo raid, Márquez said, his uncle (then a boy) was captured and the boy's father killed. The boy later escaped and was recovered by the Márquez family in Chihuahua (personal interviews, October 1966 and June 1967).

17. May 16, 1804: Chacón to Comandante General Nemecio Salcedo, #1730, SA, NMSRCA, Letter no. 1, trans. J. M. Martínez; and *Diary of Events*, trans. Brugge.

posed that a summer expedition be undertaken by a company of five hundred men, fifty to be regular soldiers of the Santa Fe presidio and the balance to be militia and Pueblo auxiliaries. The force was led by Lieutenant Don Antonio Vargas. Details of the operation are entirely lacking. Late in August, however, Chacón reported to Comandante General Nemecio Salcedo in Chihuahua (Salcedo, although stationed there, being responsible for the military defense of the northern province) that Vargas had hurt the Navajos severely. This apparently was the case, although the punishment Vargas claimed to have inflicted scarcely suggests that he had emerged from a hard-pitched battle. Of fifty-seven Navajos said to have been left dead on the ground, only seventeen were warriors; forty, presumably, were women, children, or old men. Vargas also brought back a number of horses and cattle and five captive "slaves."

Citizens of Cebolleta, meanwhile, continued to feel the scourge of Navajo raids. Having seen in dismay that the high stone walls and houses squaring off their plaza failed utterly as a fortress—had, in fact, been breached again and again—men of the village looked for other means to protect their women and children. They found it one league directly north of the village: a vast cave in the deep canyon, its mouth well concealed by underbrush and tall fir trees, opening one hundred yards to the west on an elevation slightly above the canyon trail. A secure hiding place that could easily accommodate a hundred persons or more, the cave also had two constant springs of clear water.

On one of the first occasions when the cave provided shelter, according to village tradition, the men of Cebolleta vowed that if their women and children survived unharmed, the cave would be dedicated as a shrine. The attack on the village is said to have been one of the heaviest the settlers had experienced, but after long hours of fighting the Navajos withdrew. No harm had come to the families of the men, hidden in the canyon above, and soon afterward the cave was dedicated as the shrine of the Virgen de Nuestra Señora de Lourdes, Los Portales.[18]

The heaviest attack ever made upon Cebolleta came on August 3, 1804, when a war party numbering between nine hundred and a thousand Navajos stormed the village. For a time it appeared that this fourth summer of the village might be its last; had it not been for the presence of a detachment of soldiers, the mountain settlement might well have been wiped out. The list of casualties among the defenders,

18. Azize Michael of Bibo (formerly called Cebolletita) took me to this cave in May 1965. Anastacio Márquez said the Navajos knew of the cave's existence but were not aware of its use as a refuge.

remarkably small, suggests that a majority of the Cebolleteño women and children had removed in time to the shelter of the cave. The dead included a corporal of the garrison, one male villager, and a "Christian" Indian; the injured, four soldiers, ten male villagers, and one woman. Navajos were said to have lost twenty-two warriors killed and forty-four wounded. No mention is made of livestock having been run off. If this in fact was the case, it is an instance so rare as to suggest that the Navajos attacked with the sole purpose of destroying Cebolleta once and for all.

What the raid failed to do was nearly accomplished by the alcalde mayor of Laguna. This last in the series of attacks shocked the villagers so much that the alcalde mayor proposed Cebolleta be abandoned. When he learned of this, General Salcedo advised Governor Chacón that "by separate order of today, I will tell you what must be done relating to the precise necessity of keeping this site of Cebolleta colonized. . . ." [19] In response, Chacón sent Lieutenant Don Nicolás Farín with thirty soldiers to take up station at Laguna Pueblo for the immediate protection of the frontier. Farín was informed shortly after his arrival at Laguna that large numbers of reinforcements were being sent to New Mexico from Sonora under command of Lieutenant Colonel Antonio Narbona. Upon their arrival, Farín was directed to join his detachment of soldiers (as well as Pueblo auxiliaries he apparently was raising at this time among the warriors of Laguna, Acoma, and Isleta) with Narbona's command in a two-pronged winter campaign into Navajo country. This time no mercy was to be shown the enemy until they were thoroughly defeated. Farín was instructed to establish a garrison at Cebolleta, once the campaign was concluded, for the protection of that frontier.[20]

The young officer given overall command was experienced in campaigning in moderate to hot climates against Apaches in Mexico, but this was to be his first encounter with Navajos. Nine years before, as a youthful ensign, Antonio Narbona had served as adjutant to Captain José Zúñiga when the latter was ordered to explore a trade route from Sonora to Santa Fe. Fighting Apaches became a secondary object of the

19. September 16, 1804; Salcedo to Chacón, #1754, SA, NMSRCA, Jenkins-Minge, p. 20.

20. Farín's importance to the winter campaign probably was greater than the two documents available at this writing suggest. Certain ambiguities in the orders that sent him to Laguna, and followed upon his arrival there, make his exact role in the campaign uncertain (October 5, 1804: Salcedo to Chacón, #1763, SA, NMSRCA, trans. Rosario O. Hinojos; November 20, 1804: Chacón [?] to Farín, #1774, SA, NMSRCA, trans. M. Baca).

expedition, and upon the return Lieutenant Narbona was entrusted with the custody of a warrior, four other Apache captives, and five pairs of ears—trophies of proof that, by custom of the time, would bring reward to the bearer if presented to the governor or another suitable officer.[21]

The winter 1804–5 campaign got off to an abortive start. Not all of the factors that handicapped him are known, but when Narbona left Zuni his command marched headlong into a blizzard that for more than two days and nights buffeted them continuously. Nearly exhausted, floundering about in snowbound, mountainous country, the mounted troops and infantry finally stumbled upon a Navajo rancheria on December 3. Narbona could not be sure where he was, except that his guides told him he was "at the foot of the sierra of the Cañon de Chelly." With the odds in strength greatly on his side, the encounter was a sorry little episode, soon over. A Navajo warrior was killed on the spot, another was mortally wounded, and a woman and two little girls were taken as captives. One week later Narbona had pulled his command back to the edge of Navajo country, as far back as Laguna Pueblo. From here, "filled with embarrassment and shame" over the outcome, Narbona confessed to Governor Chacón that he was ready to pull out completely and go home: "Should your Excellency decide that I may return to my province, I need the sum of five hundred pesos in order to accomplish it and supply my whole troop with provisions. I shall be most grateful to your Excellency if you would have the kindness to order that [the money] be given to me. . . ."[22]

Coupled with this failure was the gloom occasioned at about the same time by the abandonment of Cebolleta. Worn down by incessant raids, the villagers at last had moved away. Chacón at once informed Narbona that his proposal was unthinkable: pressure against the Navajos must be renewed. In this position Chacón was supported firmly a month later when he was advised in turn by General Salcedo that the war must be fought "from the sierras of the Rio Puerco to the Cañon de Chelly." Salcedo was severely critical of Narbona's December campaign and of the outlook generally. He insisted that Chacón order the Cebolleta colonists to return to their village. A thinness of documentation unfortunately casts doubt on the sequence of events at this time.

21. Zúñiga Journal, ed. Hammond 1931, pp. 52, 62. Spaniards are said to have adopted the practice from the Aztecs. In June of 1969 a unit of American troops in Vietnam was reported to have returned from battle with ears cut from North Vietnamese dead as body-count proof.
22. December 10, 1804: Narbona to Chacón, #1778, SA, NMSRCA, trans. J. M. Martínez; summary in Jenkins-Minge, p. 21.

Cebolleta, it is clear, was soon reoccupied by its frightened settlers;
Narbona moved his headquarters forward to Zuni, and in January he
started once more toward the awesome fortress of Canyon de Chelly.
Coinciding with this movement, according to Bancroft, another column
led by Lieutenant Vicente López was on the march to the north and
east where it "also defeated the foe at Chacá"—which would mean in
the vicinity of either Chacra Mesa or Chaco Canyon.[23]

On this occasion there was no complaint of snowstorms; Narbona
did not mention the weather at all. And yet the high and broken country his troops passed through was locked in winter, a monochrome of
black and white until they reached the red rock cliffs near the eastern
head of Canyon de Chelly. Narbona's command numbered slightly more
than three hundred troops brought from Sonora, joined with a company
of Opata Indian auxiliaries from the village of Bacuachi and reinforced
by Zuni guides and citizen militia. The militia was led by men whose
family names were old in the province: Captain Don Lorenzo Gutiérrez,
Lieutenant Don Bartolomé Baca, and the young Antonio Armijo.

Snow lay deep among the rocks and trees where, on the brink of a
gorge, the command halted. It was the morning of January 17, 1805.
The breathtaking descent was accomplished while Don Bartolomé Baca
stood guard on the rim with a detachment of militia. The main force
safely down, Baca moved westward along the summit. His orders were
to follow the rim, clearing the dense brush of any Navajos he found.
He encountered several groups of Navajos and fought his way through
them, killing three warriors and capturing a Pueblo ally from one of the
Hopi villages.

Narbona meanwhile advanced down the canyon over a level floor of
snow. Sheer cliffs of dark pink stone stained with darker vertical streaks
from snow and rain runoff hemmed him in left and right, towering
eight hundred feet toward the sky. Large numbers of Navajos appeared
and vanished, showering arrows upon the head and flanks of the
column. Many of them soon were discovered holding a defensive
position on a fortified high point of rocks. The fighting continued
through the afternoon, ending in early darkness of winter when the
soldiers managed to drive the defenders from their emplacement. The
invading forces then camped on the canyon floor, building fires with
limbs torn from nearby clumps of pin oaks and fruit trees.

Musket fire reverberated thunderously in the gorge in the morning
of the eighteenth. By noon the last shots had been fired; the battle-

23. Bancroft 1962, p. 285, n. 6.

stained soldiers and their Opata and Pueblo allies gathered around fires for a feast. Sheep and goats drawn from a captured herd of 350 head were slaughtered, quartered, and spitted, the balance reserved to feed the troops and their prisoners on the return to Zuni.

The count of dead and captured Navajos went on. Ninety warriors (apparently including old men) and twenty-five women and children had been killed. Narbona would take back with him as captives three warriors and thirty women and children; among the captives, with his wife and two children, was the headman Segundo, who in April had appeared at Laguna as spokesman for the peace faction of his people. Although Narbona had captured thirty Navajo horses, eighty-five of his own had become so worn out that he was compelled to destroy them. His own casualties were light: Lieutenant Don Francisco Piri, who commanded the Opata auxiliaries, was dead of pneumonia, and sixty-four among his militia, soldiers, and Indians were wounded.

He had scouted the canyon from its timbered eastern approach to its red sandstone mouth. Should it be necessary for troops to return and battle Navajos here again, Narbona advised that they bring a larger force than his and a greater supply of ammunition. He had come with more than ten thousand cartridges, but his guns had consumed almost all of them.[24]

Historians and others have debated for a half-century the possibility that during the engagement of January 17–18 there occurred the physically documented but undated massacre of a number of Navajo women, children, and old men who had concealed themselves from Spanish troops in a cave high in the canyon wall. Archaeologist Earl H. Morris once related a story of that episode as told to him by a Navajo, explaining that the hiding place of the Navajos was revealed when one of their old women, who as a girl had been held captive by the Spaniards, excitedly taunted a party of troops below "as men who walked without eyes." The troops fired into the cave from a promontory, bullets ricocheting murderously from the cave's sloping wall.[25]

Narbona makes no mention of such an action, which would not be surprising had his command been responsible. There are some who believe, however, that Spanish documents not yet discovered may prove that the massacre occurred sometime after 1805. Until and unless

24. The text of Narbona's report, translated by David M. Brugge, appears in Appendix A.

25. Morris 1925, p. 263. Although Morris believed that from this episode the north branch of Canyon de Chelly was named Canyon del Muerto, there is evidence

such documents are found, the weight of evidence suggests that Narbona could well have been responsible. Ammunition expended in his December campaign, in which only two Navajos were shot, must have been negligible. The unusually large number of women and children killed, together with the inordinate expenditure of nearly ten thousand cartridges, are mute evidence of some extraordinary military contingency.

Of the Navajos captured, Narbona distributed eleven as slaves to members of his command—some to remain in New Mexico, some to be taken to Sonora; the others he kept. Possibly reminded of a similar occasion nine years before, he entrusted the ears cut from the dead Navajo men to a corporal with instructions to carry them to Governor Chacón.[26]

The punishment they received during the winter campaign induced the Navajos to ask for peace. In March, in the final days of his long administration as governor, Chacón drew up a series of proposals as a basis for a treaty. Thereafter he turned over the matter to his successor, Joaquín Real Alencaster.

Cristóbal and Vicente, at the time regarded by Spanish authorities as the designated first and second generals of the Navajo nation, appeared before the new governor at Santa Fe in early April to offer renewed appeals for peace and to make urgent demands that the lands of Cebolleta be returned to them. As evidence of good faith they returned two captive children, one taken from the village of Cebolleta and the other from Alameda. Alencaster told the headmen in the strongest terms that the lands they requested never would be given up, and that the Navajos must not make such claims again. The governor then informed them that the authority to end hostilities rested not with him but with the

to the contrary. Observing that this name does not appear in contemporary or later Spanish reports, David L. DeHarport (1960, pp. 95–96) says that during an archaeological survey of the canyon in 1882, James Stevenson of the U.S. National Museum found two mummies in a cist of a cave and in "commemoration of this find . . . named the tributary Cañon de los Muertos, or 'of the dead.'" The cave itself was named Mummy Cave some fifteen years afterward, following a survey by Victor Mindeleff. Massacre Cave is located approximately one-half mile nearer the head of Canyon del Muerto, on the north face of the canyon wall. At the time of Narbona's campaign the three major branches of the gorge all were known as Canyon de Chelly. Although Narbona said he entered Canyon de Chelly and there engaged the Navajos, it is conceivable, therefore, that the action occurred in Canyon del Muerto.

26. January 24, 1805: Narbona to Chacón, #1792, SA, NMSRCA.

comandante general, Don Nemecio Salcedo. He proposed that another meeting be held in twenty-five days at Jemez, after Salcedo's views of the Navajos' requests had been learned. In addition to an end to the fighting, Cristóbal and Vicente had asked for the return of Navajo captives, including the family of Segundo taken at Canyon de Chelly, and that Josef Antonio García—a man whom they trusted—be named their interpreter. When he communicated these requests to Salcedo shortly afterward, Alencaster suggested that in addition to Antonio García it might be useful to the authorities to have a second interpreter, both men acting also as informers "as to the good behavior of the [Navajos], in whose peace we are very much interested." [27]

On May 12, 1805, Alencaster signed a treaty at Jemez with Cristóbal and Vicente, who agreed to a condition that also had been proposed by Chacón: that the Navajos relinquish all claims to the lands of Cebolleta. They agreed as well that the tribe should surrender all captives and make no alliance with any tribe hostile to the Spaniards, but aid the latter against any foe, and that any Navajo accused of committing a crime would be surrendered by the tribe for punishment. For his part, Alencaster agreed that the Navajos would be permitted "commerce, stock-raising, and planting of fields and other enterprises"—vaguely worded concessions that ceded little, if anything, over which he held control.

Considerably more important, the governor agreed to the release of Segundo and sixteen other Navajo captives, with the stipulation that "in case of there being other prisoners among them or among us they will be handed over reciprocally." The release of Segundo and other captives was perhaps unparalleled in Navajo-Spanish relations (although it may have been an unfair way to quiet Navajo claims to the Cebolleta region). Had Alencaster actually carried out the balance of his promise, it would have been a first step toward a permanent peace.

Finally, Alencaster warned the Navajos that violation of the treaty by them would be considered a formal declaration of war and would result in immediate attack and extermination of the entire nation.[28]

Cristóbal and Vicente managed to return some Spanish livestock, but otherwise they were unable to enforce the treaty terms. Too many Navajos wanted the lands of Cebolleta. Proof of this came in October when forty or more Navajo families moved into the Cebolleta area,

27. April 12, 1805: Alencaster to Salcedo, #1810, SA, NMSRCA, trans. Baca.
28. May 15, 1805: Alencaster to Salcedo, #1828, SA, NMSRCA, trans. Brugge and Martínez.

settled down as if to stay, and began helping themselves to corn from the villagers' fields. Once more there was talk of the Cebolleteños abandoning their homes. José Manuel Aragón, the alcalde of Laguna, was one of those who recommended capitulation. He regarded the town as useless to the province and not worth endlessly continuing massacres and robberies. There was no evidence, however, that the settlers did leave their village a second time; only minor disturbances were reported in the next decade, settlers on the frontier and Navajos alike complaining of occasional depredations. Small detachments of troops went out to prevent quarrels from flaring into serious conflict, but the official policy seems to have been to make concessions in order to preserve peace.

Segundo apparently gained favor with the Spaniards at this time. On one occasion he was mentioned with approbation by Alencaster after he had returned a fugitive Indian from Jemez and again professed his desire to support the terms of the 1805 treaty. In reply to a complaint by the governor about a Navajo alliance with Mescalero and Gila Apaches, Segundo said that during the war of 1805 there had been friendship between the tribes but that since then Gileños had stolen Navajo horses and the former alliance no longer existed. Recently, in fact, he said, Navajos had captured four Mescalero slaves, killed fifteen of their men and women, and lost but one of their own warriors. So convincing was Segundo's account that Alencaster said he was willing to believe Segundo told the truth.[29]

Hostilities between Navajos and Apaches continued for an indefinite period, Navajo war parties crossing the Rio Grande in 1809 to attack Mescaleros in the Rio Abajo, then raiding southern Apaches in the San Mateo and Mogollon mountains, and in turn suffering raids in reprisal.

Their traditional and bitterest enemies, the Comanches, possibly in retaliation for raids onto the buffalo plains and possibly with some encouragement by Spaniards, attacked Navajos on the southern slopes of Mount Taylor so fiercely in the summer of 1816 that there seemed no alternative to abandoning the rancherias completely. The Navajos' suspicion of Spanish complicity was not eased when a Comanche war party, moving without hindrance through Spanish settlements and the Jemez outpost, descended upon them in August—the attack coinciding with raids on Navajo livestock by Spanish settlers of the Rio Abajo. The Navajo headman Salvador, with two companions, went to Jemez to protest. When he was notified of Salvador's complaint, Governor Pedro

29. November 3, 1807: Alencaster to Salcedo, #2089, SA, NMSRCA, trans. Brugge.

María de Allande authorized the alcalde of Jemez to go to the Navajo rancherias with interpreter Antonio García and assure them that the governor considered them as his children and friends and regretted that the Comanches had harmed them.[30]

Professions of friendship were not enough. A month later José Vicente Ortiz, alcalde of Laguna, learned that about fifteen Navajos had come to the pueblo, saying they were leaving their homes at Encinal, San José, and Cubero to join with others of the tribe at Canyon de Chelly. They were moving far to the west, they said, because of their fear of Comanche attacks. They asked that someone appeal in their behalf to the governor requesting a paper ordering that no one settle upon their lands, a request that no doubt went unheeded.[31]

More Navajos than the fifteen who came to Laguna probably left at the same time, and it is possible that a gradual reduction of the tribe's numbers in the Mount Taylor–Cerro Cabezon region began then (autumn of 1816), families and clan groups moving to the Zuni Mountains, the Chusca Valley and Mountains, and Canyon de Chelly. Thirty years later only a small remnant of the tribe, and those renegades who had willfully split away from the Navajo nation, still remained near Encinal and Cebolleta.

The long interval of relative peace with the Spaniards ended in 1818. Records in the Spanish archives that have thus far come to light do not explain the cause of the trouble. Spanish aggression, when it occurred, almost never was recorded; Navajo raids, stemming from whatever cause, were recorded promptly. In any case, Navajo hostilities were resumed in February, Governor Allande observing in June that a general uprising was feared. At San Miguel, a small seasonal sheep camp west of Mount Taylor, two sons of the Navajo headman Vicente killed a Corrales man named Juan Alire and wounded four sheepherders. Spanish grazing on land the Navajos regarded as their own may have lighted the fuse. From San Ysidro to the north "a great unrest among the Navajo tribe" was reported.[32]

30. August 20, 1816: Ygnacio Vergara, alcalde of Jemez, to Allande, and Allande's reply, August 21, #2669, SA, NMSRCA, trans. Martínez.

31. September 26, 1816: Ortiz to Allande, #668, Spanish Archives, Bureau of Land Management, Santa Fe, trans. Brugge.

32. June 25, 1818: Allande to the alcalde of Jemez, #2727, SA, NMSRCA, trans. Martínez. Brugge notes that "Alire was killed in a dispute over gambling, probably a card game. . . . From my observations of Navajo gambling habits, they more readily accept losses than whites, and Spanish provocation is not unlikely" (personal communication).

Late in June, Alcalde José Ortiz of Laguna led a reconnaissance force of twelve men westward to San Miguel and into the Zuni Mountains and then back to the slopes of Mount Taylor. He reported seeing tracks he believed were those of livestock run off by Navajos. He noted also that in accordance with the governor's instructions he had offered the services of six men to the lieutenant of justice at Zuni for a campaign into Navajo country. Having no stomach for such a venture, the teniente de justicia sent the men home on the pretext that they were not adequately supplied with powder and bullets.[33]

Although Governor Allande insisted that he had positive information that the Navajos were preparing a general uprising and would strike the settlements from all directions, Ortiz was not so certain. If Allande wished him to make a campaign against the Navajos he would go, Ortiz said, although he thought the raids did not indicate an uprising by the tribe but rather were the actions of a few starving thieves. Instead of making war, Ortiz proposed taking a small escort into Navajo country where he would meet with the principal headmen and urge them to go to Santa Fe for councils with the governor.

However well intended, his advice came late. Allande already had sent a small party to talk with the Navajos and the results were discouraging. The interpreter Antonio García with eighteen men had gone to the Chusca region, there met with a number of Navajo headmen, and been told by the *capitáncillo* Joaquín that an uprising indeed was planned. Notifying Ortiz of this, the governor advised him to prepare to meet an attack. Meanwhile, a small contingent of troops would be sent to El Vadito, in the vicinity of Jemez, to await reinforcements by the full company of Captain Don Bartolomé Baca.

A surprising development that caused a lasting division of the Navajo nation occurred two days later. The sun was setting in the evening of July 20, 1818, when smoke signals appeared on the approach to Jemez. Fearing a hostile war party, Ygnacio Sánchez Vergara, the alcalde of the pueblo, hastily set about defending the village. His fears were dispelled when the headman Joaquín entered the pueblo asking for the house of the alcalde. Once in the alcalde's presence, Joaquín made it clear that he, his brother, and two nephews had come in peace to warn the Spaniards that the Navajos were preparing to make war on them. He had done everything in his power to keep the nation at peace, but his efforts had failed, Joaquín said; consequently, he had taken all of his

33. July 7, 1818: Ortiz to Allande, #2732, SA, NMSRCA, trans. Martínez.

people away, renouncing any further connection with the tribe. He was convinced that the Navajos would be so severely defeated in a war with the Spaniards that finally they would lose all of their proud and arrogant spirit.

No one could have fully comprehended at the time the importance of Joaquín's action. He led those who were loyal to him out of the Navajo tribe and committed them to a subservient, mercenary alliance with whatever authority governed New Mexico. The defection was a tribal sore that deepened with time as others, for a variety of reasons, joined the renegades, until their band numbered slightly more than two hundred. The split was hurtful and was to be permanent; only Joaquín's authority would wane, to be taken over in time by a more masterful renegade.

Joaquín informed the alcalde that what he now called the "rebels," or war faction, of the Navajos were gathering in the Carrizo Mountains, and that their war parties would be joined by Utes. As though to prove that his new loyalty to the Spaniards could be trusted, he said that on his journey to Jemez he had encountered five Navajos returning from a raid with a small number of stolen livestock, which he had attempted to recover, succeeding in capturing five of the animals. More convincing still, he said that if two troops of Spanish soldiers would take the field against the Navajos, he and his warriors would accompany and aid them.[34]

Navajo reaction to betrayal by Joaquín's band was immediate and unmistakable. The defectors' lives suddenly were in jeopardy and for their new loyalty and services they demanded protection. Allande's successor, Governor Facundo Melgares, was informed in October by Salvador García, alcalde of Zuni, that Joaquín had been at the pueblo but had departed—a disappointment, because "I wanted to bind him to us, and send him to your Lordship . . . so that Your Excellency might determine what was best [to do with him]. The same happened with a second Navajo informer who was being protected by Lieut. Don Dionicio Baca; when I wanted to carry out my plans, he told me that he would not cooperate until the order came giving him the protection he asked for." [35]

34. July 21, 1818: Vergara to Allande, #2736, SA, NMSRCA. The text of Vergara's letter, translated by Simmons, appears in Appendix B. Virtually nothing is known of Joaquín prior to this time; it is possible that he took his name from the former governor, Joaquín Real Alencaster.

35. October 25, 1818: García to Melgares, #2759, SA, NMSRCA, trans. Simmons.

Joaquín's band, referred to now by others of the tribe as Diné Ana'aii, or "Enemy Navajos," was compelled to move eastward, camping about Jemez or the river settlements. Even here they were not entirely safe as Navajo war parties harassed the Spanish frontier through the winter and spring of 1818–19.

Campaigns were made into Navajo country in February and March of 1819, the last resulting in the death of thirty-three Navajos and capture of fourteen others together with a small number of livestock. Portions of the tribe withdrew to the vicinity of the Hopi mesas during the conflict; possibly many of them thereafter made that region their permanent home. A peace treaty, not long to be honored, was signed on August 21, its most notable term being the appointment of Joaquín as Navajo general responsible for the behavior of the entire nation—an absurd condition, which the Spaniards should have realized was impossible. It was further stipulated that Joaquín would live as near as possible to Jemez, which may have been Joaquín's own idea, but the stipulation, like the rest of the eighteen treaty terms, was soon to be interpreted loosely.[36]

Occupation of the Cebolleta region by small remnants of the tribe— those remaining after the Comanche attacks of 1816—appears to have ended by 1821, and from that time the vicinity north of Cebolleta became a haven and point of concentration for the Diné Ana'aii. There is evidence that Joaquín soon began looking about in the region for fat farm land that he might cultivate and call his own. While engaged in a search for livestock that had been run off from Jemez, Joaquín inspected with the eye of a possible owner the rancho of Pedro Padilla lying north of Cebolleta. It did not suit his purposes, he decided, because the soil was not good for farming and during the spring runoff the Puerco would surely flood all of the arable land. Joaquín asked an intermediary to inform the governor that he would be grateful, therefore, if Melgares would allow him to cultivate land nearer Cebolleta and Laguna.

Now as later, however, the Diné Ana'aii were fated to be outcasts, shunned by their own tribe and used by the government at Santa Fe but held by both sides in suspicion or contempt. In July, 1821, the officer of a small garrison protecting Cebolleta wrote to Governor Melgares that he suspected the motives of the Navajos living nearby and doubted the sincerity of their desire for peace. He asked that his command be reinforced.[37]

36. Brugge (personal communication); Bancroft 1962, pp. 286–87.

37. July 9, 1821: Capt. Bartolomé Baca to Melgares, #2992, SA, NMSRCA, and in Jenkins-Minge, p. 33.

The concerns of a captain at Cebolleta, and his own concern over increasing hostilities with the Navajos, may have seemed more real to Governor Melgares than the eleven-year war for independence from Spain now nearing an end in Mexico. Bancroft has observed, "There is no indication that the great national struggle sent even a ripple of excitement to the northern interior." Less than one month after news was received in Santa Fe of Agustín de Iturbide's successful conclusion of the war with Spain, Melgares ordered another expedition sent out against the Navajos. A large force of militia and Pueblo auxiliaries from Acoma, Laguna, and Isleta started from Cebolleta for the Chusca Mountains under the command of Juan Armijo. It was the last campaign against the tribe under the nominal rule of Spain, and it was ill-fated. On October 4, one day after his departure and while still in the Cebolleta Mountains, Armijo lost a sizable part of his command through desertion. Bickering, insubordination, and other desertions among the militia drained his force throughout the march.

The sole engagement was fought near Ojo del Oso. The Navajos were taken by surprise and seven were killed before they knew the militia and hostile Indians were near.[38] The Navajos carried away several of their dead by force, but they were unable to prevent Amijo from cutting the ears from the other four bodies. Among the rest of the booty seized was a baby not yet weaned from its mother. Twenty days after its start the campaign ended.

38. October 23, 1821: Armijo to Melgares, #3060, SA, NMSRCA, trans. Brugge.

3

Juanico and Vizcarra

To the Spanish inhabitants of New Mexico, separated from the seat of government at Mexico City by hundreds of miles and an incalculable divergence of interests, problems attendant upon the creation of a newly independent republic seemed remote. The change, in fact, affected them little. To the Navajos, for two of the last three years engaged in war, the emergence of the Republic of Mexico meant nothing at all. The face of their foe was the same.

Don Facundo Melgares, in 1822 in his last year as governor, had not brought to that office a brilliant military record. Against the Navajos he seemed able only to conspire and temporize, and, when these measures failed, to fight again, never more than ineffectually.

Through the spring and summer of 1822 hostilities continued on both sides, the Navajos thoroughly committed to war and clearly holding the upper hand. A campaign sent out by Melgares in March resulted in the capture of one old man and a few horses. A second campaign of forty-five days, to have been led by the governor himself, was directed to rendezvous May 20 at Cebolleta; what came of it, if anything, is not known. The greatest success that government forces could claim was the death of thirteen Navajos at Jemez under circumstances unknown, sometime before early June.[1] From the river settlements of the Rio Abajo northward to Mora and Taos, Navajo reprisals were unusually ferocious. Governor Melgares evidently chose not to record these Navajo successes, but parish burial records of the Catholic Church show that during the first seven months of the year at least twenty-seven and perhaps as many as thirty-six persons died in Navajo raids.[2]

1. June 15, 1822: Alejo García Condé, Durango, Mexico, to Melgares, #65, Mexican Archives (hereafter, MA) NMSRCA, trans. Brugge. There is reason to believe that these Navajos were murdered during the Melgares regime, under circumstances described by Gregg as occurring at Cochiti and placed by Twitchell during the administration of Colonel Vizcarra.

2. Brugge 1968, pp. 54–55.

The fear inspired by Navajo attack was observed by an American in Santa Fe in vivid contrast to what he described as a pathetically ill equipped company of militia mustered by Melgares for defense. Of the Navajos, Thomas James remarked that they killed anyone they came upon, regardless of age or sex, and what they could not carry off they burned and destroyed. Grazing lands were stripped bare of livestock, he said, and from the south the Navajos marauded toward Santa Fe and swept on to Taos, desolating that quiet valley before finally disappearing into the mountains with their booty.[3] Of Melgares's citizen army, James wrote:

> The militia of Santa Fe when on parade beggared all description. Falstaff's company was well equipped and well furnished compared with these troops of Governor Melgares. Such a gang of tatterdemalions I never saw before or since. They were of all colors, with all kinds of dresses and every species of arms. Some were bareheaded; others were barebacked. Some had hats without rims or crowns, and some wore coats without skirts; others again wore coats without sleeves. Most of them were armed with bows and arrows. A few had guns that looked as if they had been imported by Cortez, while others had iron hooks fastened to the ends of poles, which passed for lances.
>
> The doughty governor, Facundo Melgares, on foot, in his cloak and *chapeau de bras*, was reviewing this noble army. He was five feet high, nearly as thick as he was long, and as he waddled from one end of the line to the other, I thought of Alexander, Hannibal and Caesar, and how their glories would soon be eclipsed. . . . At last, when all was ready, the governor sent them forth to the war and himself went to his dinner. In the meantime where was the enemy—the bloodthirsty Navajos? They had returned in safety to their own country with all their plunder and were even then far beyond the reach of Governor Melgares' troop of scarecrows.

A caricature, in some measure accurate, but a libel, in its implications, on the courage and ability the poorly armed militia often displayed. James wrote with the scorn and condescension that too frequently laced the observations of American newcomers to this hard land. In any case, Melgares directed that another campaign be made against the Navajos, the militia to rendezvous at Jemez August 16 "as well armed as possible and afoot rather than on horses." Although the troops were to have remained in the field forty-five days, less than a

3. Thomas James, *Three Years Among the Indians and Mexicans* (1846; reprint ed., Chicago: Rio Grande Press, 1962), pp. 184–85.

month after its start Melgares was outlining terms he would propose at a peace council with the Navajos.[4] Navajo raids that continued in the Rio Abajo during September failed to alter the governor's plans and on October 29 a treaty of peace was signed at Zia. Somewhat vague in its phrasing, the treaty called for a reciprocal exchange of captives, freedom for the Navajos to trade and travel in the province, and the appointment of Segundo as tribal general—provided that the Navajos accepted his leadership. No mention was made of the Diné Ana'aii leader Joaquín, whose place in favor apparently was in eclipse.

Melgares evidently did nothing to implement this second proposal for the mutual exchange of captives. Before the end of 1822 he was succeeded by another military man, but this time one of the ability of an Anza or Vargas. José Antonio Vizcarra, known well a few years later to American officers and traders traveling the Santa Fe Trail, has been described as "a man of commanding appearance, dignified, with perfect manners" and, typical of many Spaniards and Mexicans of the time, a superb horseman.[5] About his bearing and manners the Navajos could have cared little; they knew him to be a warrior, and that to them was all that counted—a warrior more at ease in a saddle than in the hard chair at the Palace of the Governors.

Two months after assuming office Vizcarra gave evidence that his regime would stand in stark contrast to that of his fumbling predecessor. He acted when winter frost was still deep in the ground, early in February 1823. His plan was to force the Navajos to accept what experience had taught was unacceptable—a virtual subjugation to Mexican rule to which war would be the only alternative. With a retinue of followers Vizcarra proceeded to Laguna Pueblo and there, on February 5, drew up an ultimatum embraced in four brief terms. These were presented one week later at a council of Navajos convened at the neighboring Laguna pueblo of Paguate, four miles south of Cebolleta. Although the Diné Ana'aii occupied this region and may have been represented, again no mention is made of them or their leader Joaquín. Only in the bleak phraseology of a military communiqué, a statement stiff in construction now antique and omitting all details of the grim

4. July 21, 1822: Circular letter from Melgares to all alcaldes, Governor's Letter Book, p. 17, #3034, SA, NMSRCA, trans. Jenkins and Johnson; and September 12, 1822: Governor's Letter Book, pp. 46–48, trans. Brugge.

5. Twitchell, *Facts of New Mexican History*, vol. 2, p. 23. In 1829 and afterward, Col. Vizcarra led Mexican forces patrolling the Santa Fe Trail between the Arkansas River and Las Vegas. Gregg (1954, p. 75) mentions encountering him below Point of Rocks in 1831.

reception that must have been accorded him, did Vizcarra reveal that it was the headman Juanico—and not Segundo—who appeared at Paguate as spokesman for the Navajos, and that the impossible terms that he came to force upon the Navajos were, for the most part, refused or deflected.

Vizcarra's terms demanded that the Navajos surrender all Mexican captives in their possession; Navajos held captive would be released in turn, "but only if they wish to go, for if they should wish to receive the beneficial waters of baptism it does not seem proper for Catholics to deny them." In short, Navajos held as slaves would be retained for their own salvation. The Navajos also must return all stolen livestock or other property seized since the October treaty of 1822; and finally, the Navajos must agree to be converted to Catholicism and submit to being resettled—in pueblos. The people who had been raised like deer must move to adobe hives. It is doubtful if Vizcarra knew that the first attempt to enclose Navajos in pueblos had been tried at or near this same place seventy-five years before.

Vizcarra's terms were discussed at the Paguate council February 12. Some agreement of dubious value was reached, both sides temporizing on certain points, and at length an arrangement was made in the name of Juanico and those of his tribe by two of Vizcarra's officers, Captain Bartolomé Baca and Don Antonio Sandoval.[6]

Before he left Paguate, Vizcarra reclaimed such Mexican captives as were found, but when Navajos asked for the return of their people held in the settlements he found less need for haste. He would keep his part of the agreement, he told them, when the Navajos had met all of his proposals. As to stolen property, Juanico said the Navajos were starving and could not further diminish their herds to pay for stolen livestock; however, he pledged that robberies would cease. In the matter of agreeing to conversion to Catholicism and living in pueblos, Juanico and the others were as evasive as Vizcarra had been on the issue of returning captives. Juanico asked for four months' time after the next moon before giving an answer, to permit him to determine the feelings of his people.

If the council at Paguate accomplished anything, it was to widen the gulf separating the two sides. Vizcarra almost at once drew up plans for a campaign; the Navajos soon returned to raiding. Between April 29

6. February 12, 1823: Record of the meeting held between Gov. Vizcarra and the Navajo tribe, Camp at Paguate, #183, MA, NMSRCA, trans. Brugge, and in Jenkins-Minge, p. 46.

and June 1, sixteen Mexicans were killed in the Rio Abajo, eight of
them during a single attack on the village of Sabinal.[7] It is doubtful if
these casualties influenced the governor's thinking, other than to give
further impetus to a preconceived plan of war: on June 17 Vizcarra announced that he would leave Santa Fe the next day at the head of a
punitive expedition into Navajo country.

Weeks of preparation must have been required to organize his command. Nothing to match it had been known in New Mexico before.
Troops of regulars and militia were drawn from every quarter, companies were formed from men of Rio Arriba and Rio Abajo, until
Vizcarra could number a force of about fifteen hundred troops—equal
in number to the Army of the West that Stephen Kearny presently
would lead from Missouri to overwhelm this same province. So great
an impression did the expedition make upon the citizens that its feats
became legendary, its success magnified in the telling, until, forty years
afterward, it was remembered, "Within the recollection of our oldest
inhabitants but one period of peace has been enjoyed, and this was
from 1824 to 1836, a period of twelve years [when] the world renowned
Viscaro entered [Navajo] country from different directions . . . whipped
them in many battles, and so completely subdued them that . . . a
treaty was held at Jemez . . . the result of which was twelve years of
profound peace and prosperity. . . ." [8] As so often with legends, this
one was largely illusionary. Nevertheless, although the campaign was not
as punishing as Narbona's Canyon de Chelly campaign, the hard realities about to face the Navajos were even more severe, a harbinger of
worse to come, when they would be driven and scattered and driven
again.

In his daily journal of the campaign Vizcarra makes no reference to
Pueblo auxiliaries, although possibly there were some. Almost inadvertently, however, he does reveal the presence in his command of one
Diné Ana'aii—"the Navajo Francisco"—whose presence probably meant
that others of this band also were with Vizcarra. It is the first record of
many when Diné Ana'aii campaigned against their own people.

Bancroft appears not to have known of the expedition and Twitchell
refers to it only obliquely; historians of more recent times have been
increasingly aware of its importance, but details of the campaign remained virtually unknown until Vizcarra's journal and the diary of a

7. Parish burial records show that six men were buried at Socorro on April 29, two
more at Belen on May 3, and eight victims of the Sabinal attack at Belen on May 31
and June 1 (Brugge 1968, p. 57).
8. Santa Fe *New Mexican*, October 28, 1864.

subordinate officer, Colonel Francisco Salazar, were translated and annotated by David M. Brugge in an effort that has restored the Vizcarra legend to reality.[9]

From the capital, which he left June 18, Vizcarra led his large command over a route to the Chusca Mountains that was to be followed almost step by step by the forces of Colonel John M. Washington twenty-six years later. Crossing the Rio Grande near Santo Domingo, Vizcarra traveled over a rough mesa trail to Jemez, from there struck the Rio Puerco of the East, and then marched in a northwesterly direction to Torreon and on to "Mesa Azul"—or Chacra Mesa—and, on the eighth day, made camp near the tall broken walls of "Pueblo del Ratón," easternmost of the Chaco ruins and now known as Pueblo Pintado. Nowhere on the route thus far is there reference by Vizcarra to having encountered Navajos or found evidence that they occupied the region. On the next day, June 26, the command followed the Chaco River, which Vizcarra refers to as "La Agua de San Carlos," past the ruins of "several pueblos . . . which were of such antiquity that their inhabitants were not known to Europeans," until camp was made at a place Vizcarra called "El Peñasco." The day's march, given as seven leagues or eighteen miles, would be three miles short of the distance from Pueblo Pintado to the south mesa ruin of Peñasco Blanco by the modern road, but by the shorter river course it is probable that Vizcarra's command did camp in the canyon below the latter ruin.

From El Peñasco the command followed the Chaco arroyo to a place Vizcarra called "Las Vueltecillas," where a party of fifty men under Captain Don Lorenzo Corsi was sent "to search for the Chieftain Antonio El Pinto"—possibly the son of the headman of that name who had been killed by Apaches in 1793. The soldiers scouted the vicinity of Juan's Lake, but to Vizcarra's disgust, "through the laziness of the corporal, there was no armed encounter; at a short distance they stopped to talk, and after loitering the party [under Corsi] returned." At eight o'clock that night, having marched twenty-three miles and while still in the Chaco arroyo, the troops camped at a place Vizcarra called "Aguaje de la Baca." [10]

9. "Vizcarra's Navajo Campaign of 1823," trans. and ann. Brugge, *Arizona and the West* 6: 3, pp. 223–44.

10. "Las Vueltecillas" may have been the wide bend in the Chaco near the Tsaya trading post, built in the 1870s. The search for El Pinto's Navajos occurred in almost the same region where Lt. J. H. Simpson (with Col. Washington's expedition) reported the first meeting with Navajos on August 29, 1849. The day's march of 23.4 miles could hardly have taken the command beyond the point where Coal Creek joins the Chaco below present Bisti.

On arrival in the Tunicha (or Chusca) Valley, Vizcarra's command was joined by two regiments of militia. A day was spent in camp, resting, the troops then beginning the ascent of the Chusca Mountains on July 4. They saw a few Navajos during the climb, probably scouting the army's advance, which appears to have been over the pass later taken by Colonel Washington in 1849 and named for him at that time. Vizcarra went into camp July 6 somewhere in the vicinity of the present Crystal trading post after a number of the troops became sick and four died from eating a poisonous herb. The sick or otherwise disabled, totaling 150 men, were directed to return to Jemez under command of Lieutenant Colonel Don Manuel Armijo.[11] Two days later came report of the army's first armed clash with Navajos. In the mountains not far from the pass, Captain Julián Armijo's troops, returning from escorting the disabled men as far as Chusca Valley, came upon a party of mounted Navajos evidently trying to escape. Fourteen Navajos of both sexes were killed, a girl was captured, and five Navajo horses were taken—all, apparently, without injury to Captain Armijo's force.

Colonel Vizcarra, meanwhile, had explored southward to "Laguna Colorado" and "Cienega del Peñasco Colorado," which in all likelihood were Red Lake and the valley immediately to the east, watered by Black Creek and separated from the lake by a massive red rock mesa. Red Lake and the valley in which it lies were the site of a historic meeting place for Navajos, later confusingly identified as Laguna Negra, or Black Lake, when American troops occupied the region. The confusion is heightened by the presence of another, smaller lake several miles to the north, known also as Black Lake.

For two days Vizcarra lingered in the vicinity, allowing his pack train to catch up and awaiting the return of a patrol sent with Captain Don Juan Cristóbal García to scout the region of the Carrizo Mountains fifty or sixty miles to the north. Captain García was able to report a skirmish, in which three of his men had been wounded.

Vizcarra's journal indicates that for at least one week, although probably longer, Navajos in the mountain region had been aware of the army's approach and, since then, had observed its daily movements. Against the advance of such a force it was characteristic of Navajos not to emulate the tactics of white soldiers but to baffle and confuse by being where they were not expected to be and, like morning fog, slipping

11. Armijo, who later was to serve as governor (1827–29, 1837–44, and 1845–46), was escorted as far as the Chusca Valley by two parties of 200 men each, who were ordered to scout the mountains on their return to the main command.

away to vanish in small groups, driving their livestock before them. Their tactics could be maddening to an adversary handicapped by unfamiliarity with springs or water holes, diminishing food supplies, and horses foundering from thirst and exhaustion, with only an occasional opportunity to fire at a scattered foe. Vizcarra does not mention that such was his predicament, but evidence of it can be found between his lines: in the heart of the Navajo country he discovered few Navajos; he discovered little more than fresh tracks indicating recent departure.

Vizcarra marched from his camp near Red Lake on July 11, skirting south of Canyon de Chelly but probing the heads of several of the lower branch canyons, dividing his command and sending out occasional diversionary parties. All the while he continued steadily west and south with a notion he would find Navajos in the vicinity of the Hopi mesas. For men and animals alike the march was punishing. Near the mouth of Canyon de Chelly on July 13 his men had to dig sand in the bed of the dry wash to get water. West of there the next day they encountered two Navajos near the command's afternoon camp; fifteen troops sent in pursuit managed to kill one and return with his horse. On July 15, somewhere in the vicinity of Low Mountain, the ascent became so rough that it was necessary to carry the baggage by hand. Here there was a skirmish in which one Navajo was killed by militia commanded by Captain Don Miguel Montoya. On the sixteenth, possibly in the vicinity of Polacca Wash, Vizcarra's forces engaged in a running fight and pursuit that by nightfall resulted in eight Navajos killed and the capture of "eight slaves."

From his camp on Polacca Wash, eight miles north of First Mesa, Vizcarra before dawn on July 17 sent 325 men under Captain Don José Francisco Baca to advance toward Walpi. He had heard, probably from a prisoner taken the day before, that Navajos with herds of livestock might be found there. Whatever the source, Vizcarra was informed on arriving at Walpi himself that if Navajos had been there they no longer were. Directing the troops to go into camp near a spring at the foot of the mesa, Vizcarra the same afternoon talked with the war captain of Walpi who "came at my call, and offered to take me to where the Navajos had their camp and their stock." This, he was informed, was at "Chellecito"—a remote canyon many leagues nearly due north over the almost impassable wilderness of Black Mesa and in the vicinity of Marsh Pass.

Vizcarra remained for three days at First Mesa, making one uneventful night patrol with fifty men toward Oraibi. Returning, he sighted three Navajos in the distance and pursued them but was left far behind. Then, impatient for the main baggage train to come up, Vizcarra with an escort of one hundred men started back toward Canyon de Chelly, where the pack train had been left. His phrasing for the journal entry relating his movements from July 21 through July 24 is possibly misleading, but it appears that on July 22 he came up with the baggage train, guarded by Colonel Don Francisco Salazar, probably in the vicinity of the canyon's mouth. Salazar assured him that nothing eventful had occurred since he had seen his commander last. Nothing, that is, "other than a party of fifty men he [Salazar] placed under the command of Lieutenant Don Juan Andrés Archuleta, following a track, had succeeded in attacking a rancheria of Navajos, killing five women and capturing nine slaves of both sexes, and taking twelve horses and mules and seventy head of sheep and goats." Nor was that all. Captain Don Miguel Montoya had had the lesser success of killing two women and capturing eight slaves of both sexes.

After these recent but modest achievements, Vizcarra could claim to have killed thirty-one Navajos, of whom at least eight were women, and to have taken twenty-six captives of both sexes—marketable in Santa Fe, depending on their condition on arrival, at about 100 pesos each. From the journal entry it is impossible to determine where the troops of Archuleta and Montoya killed the seven Navajo women; possibly in Canyon de Chelly or its vicinity.

On his return to First Mesa with the baggage train Vizcarra was told of other casualties inflicted on the enemy. During his absence "the Navajo Francisco" and four soldiers had left camp to gather wild onions; while so engaged they had encountered two Navajos, killing one and taking the other captive. "Francisco" is believed to be Francisco Baca, the emergent headman of the Diné Ana'aii who succeeded Joaquín. Vizcarra at once moved his command two leagues to a spring that would provide more water, presumably on Wepo Wash. Water for the animals of such an army, in this arid country, was an increasingly serious problem. More than three hundred sheep and goats said to be owned by the headman Segundo were separated from Hopi herds at First Mesa and distributed for extra rations to the troops. An attempt had been made to hide them, with Hopi assent, among the pueblo's herds.

Patrols went out in search of Navajos and of more adequate sources of water, Vizcarra himself leading fifty men north on a scout of Oraibi and Dinnebito washes. They found few Navajos and of these all escaped but one, who was shot. On the fourth day Vizcarra prepared to march against the Navajos said to be at Chellecito, then changed his mind when a Hopi who had been pressed into service as his guide said that there were no springs along his planned route and that he would have to hope for the unlikely event of rain in the dry season. (Vizcarra later found the story to be untrue—possibly intended to discourage him from finding the Navajos.) Thus for nine days of unrelieved and blistering sun, indecision, and a constantly diminishing supply of water the army remained on Wepo Wash.

Finally, on August 3, Vizcarra divided his command, directing Colonel Salazar to take 250 men northward across Black Mesa on a trail left by Juanico and other Navajos who were driving livestock before them. The rest of the command started with Vizcarra in the direction of Moencopi Wash.

Salazar's diary entries from August 3 to 18 are brief, giving no reference to the distance traveled each day but only an occasional place name or description by which his route can be determined. During the first four days, traveling as rapidly as the rough terrain allowed, his progress was, by his terms, uneventful. On the fifth day he descended from the northern rim of the mesa to the plateau stretching toward Monument Valley and went into camp "below the Cerro Elevado." [12] For the next two days, still following at least part of a trail left by Juanico's people, who appear to have divided into three bands, Salazar moved more slowly and evidently not far, his troops scouting an adjacent canyon and circling about the area of "Cerro Elevado" in hope of flushing Juanico's band.

Vizcarra, meanwhile, encumbered with the baggage train, toiled over approaches to Second and Third Mesas, rested at the spring marking the later site of Hotevilla, followed Moencopi Wash through Blue Canyon, and turned into Cow Springs Wash, making camp on the fourth day, August 6, above present Tonalea—"at the place where there are two stone pillars"—the unmistakable Elephant's Feet. Little progress was made the next day, the baggage train moving only eight miles while small parties went out in search of springs or pools of rainwater, scouting arroyos and nearby mesas to the west and east.

Traveling easterly on August 8 from the vicinity of White Mesa, the

12. In a country blessed with such a profusion of buttes, pinnacles, and mountains, it is obviously impossible to determine with certainty the location and identity of Salazar's "Cerro Elevado." I am inclined to believe this landmark was Aghathla Peak, eight miles north of Kayenta. The supposition is based on a number of considerations, but primarily on the evidence given by Salazar in relating his movements between August 11 and August 15.

troops surprised and attacked an Indian rancheria, killing four men and taking seven captives before discovering that they had mistaken a band of Paiutes for Navajos. One of Vizcarra's soldiers was killed and another wounded in the engagement. The captives were freed except for one man, whom Vizcarra held as a guide to tell them where the Navajos were. In early afternoon Vizcarra crossed what he believed to be the tracks of Juanico's horse herd and cattle and followed the trail until a heavy rain and early darkness forced him into camp.

After daylight on August 9 in the Klethla Valley, Vizcarra came on converging tracks indicating that Navajo sheep and goats had been joined by Juanico's horses and cattle. Fifty men on the freshest horses were sent at double time in advance, another seventy whose horses were worn out were placed as a rear guard, and Vizcarra followed the advance force with the remaining horses and infantry. At noon, having left Marsh Pass behind, the troops discovered a number of Navajos—among them Juanico—"on the ascent to a mesa."

No contemporary account exists that describes Juanico's appearance or offers any insight into his nature. Unquestionably, however, he emerged at this time not only as one of the influential men of his nation but as an important war leader (possibly ranking with the legendary Cayetano and the better-known headman Narbona, whose name was borrowed from the Spanish colonel). From his position above the Spanish troops, Juanico called out that he wanted to talk with the commander. Through the interpreter Miguel García, Vizcarra "replied in a few words that I had come to fight."

Sending a part of his infantry to make a flank approach from the right, Vizcarra led the rest of the troops in a frontal attack, the Navajos withdrawing slowly and firing back to allow time for their livestock to be driven off. Gaining the summit after forcing the defenders from a difficult pass, Vizcarra's men surrounded and captured a number of cattle and several small droves of sheep and goats. Not far beyond this point, while attempting to secure more animals, several of the soldiers were attacked by ten Navajos, soon joined by others as Vizcarra came up to lend support to the other side. Dismounting because of the rough ground, horsemen of both sides joined a brief hand-to-hand melee. The fight was broken off when the Navajos escaped, taking a gun snatched from an ensign's hands and five of the Mexicans' horses. Vizcarra said he saw no Navajo fall during the combat, but of his own force he numbered four wounded, including Lieutenant Don Manuel Sánchez.

His account of the engagement is graphic enough, but Vizcarra leaves only a confused impression of flight and pursuit over difficult rocky terrain of mesa and canyon—the Navajos losing eighty-seven cattle and more than four hundred sheep and goats, but probably escaping with the major part of their livestock. Exactly where the fighting and pursuit took place remains largely conjectural. Vizcarra says that before the day ended he traveled thirty leagues, or seventy-eight miles—an impossible distance under such circumstances—and camped the next night on his back trail "in an arroyo under a fallen cottonwood which was named the Spring of San Lorenzo." Brugge believes that the Navajos were fleeing north or northeastward, attempting to get their stock across the San Juan River, and that Vizcarra's camp the night of August 10 was on Oljetoh Wash. This conjecture, which in all respects is reasonable, could have taken Vizcarra a shorter distance than he thought but generally northward to Hoskinini Mesa, northwest of Kayenta, and from there down to some point on the Oljetoh.

Through the long day of August 9 when Vizcarra's command was engaged with Juanico's Navajos, Colonel Salazar and his smaller force were only a few miles distant, scouting what were or were believed to be Navajo tracks in the vicinity of Cerro Elevado and entirely unaware of the fighting and pursuit over the nearby mesas. In the morning of August 10, as Vizcarra prepared to begin his return over his own outward trail to the Hopi mesas and then to Canyon de Chelly, Colonel Salazar left Cerro Elevado, traveling north toward the San Juan. Within the lower reaches of Monument Valley he came upon a small cluster of dwellings and attacked at once, killing one warrior and taking "a bunch of twelve slaves, both children and adults." Only when the action was over did he learn that the Indians were not Navajos but Paiutes. As with Vizcarra on August 8, Salazar allowed the survivors their freedom. On leaving the Paiute camp he turned his force back the way they had come and, failing to find water, camped once more at Cerro Elevado.

Breaking camp at six o'clock the next morning, Salazar took an easterly direction, halting several hours before sunset "in a valley where I found a small lake of rain water," a vague description that might have placed him almost anywhere but in this case probably in the vicinity of the fertile fields of Dinnehotso.

Five miles east of this place, Salazar in the morning of August 12 came upon a broad trail of livestock—sheep and goats, horses and cattle —that from the signs had been traveling rapidly in the direction of the Bear's Ears, twin promontories north of the San Juan visible far in the distance. For the remainder of this day and part of the next Salazar's column followed in pursuit, making a dry camp in the afternoon of August 13 "under the mesas"—which, again, might have been anywhere in northern Arizona but probably was immediately south of the San Juan River.

Salazar makes it clear that he gave up the chase at this point, possibly knowing he would lose the trail on the shelf rock, shale, and mountainous terrain that loomed before him on the other side of the river. The next morning his command traveled south for perhaps forty miles, halting "at the mouth of a red canyon" that presumably was in the vicinity of the present Rock Point trading post. Starting from the mouth of the canyon next day the column had proceeded five miles when two Navajo girls and a boy were observed near a hogan and evidently captured. Other Navajos soon made their presence known, eight warriors daring to attack the Mexicans' vastly superior force and wounding one soldier. The skirmish was brief; the Navajos withdrew into rough country where Salazar had no desire to follow them. He continued, instead, halting on the Chinle Wash where, he said, it is joined by the "Arroyo del Carrizo"—probably the Lukachukai Wash.

Salazar was scarcely more than a mile distant from this place the next morning when he was attacked in force by Navajos who evidently had gathered after learning of the previous day's skirmish. His diary offers no estimate of their numbers but Salazar leaves no doubt that his party of 250 soldiers chose retreat to a standing fight and drew fire for the rest of the day. The Navajos struck his column frontally, on both flanks, and from the rear. Salazar's comment that he ordered the soldiers to take great care to maintain good order suggests that the withdrawal was verging on rout. Again and again Navajos rode through his ranks, scattering the troops about and seizing and riding away with several firearms and seven horses bearing full equipment. Four men of Salazar's rear guard were killed; he makes no estimate of Navajo casualties.

Near sunrise the next morning, before his troops could mount, the Navajos resumed their attack. The harassment continued after the column moved off, mounted warriors striking at the flanks and goading the Spaniards to break formation and chase them. Thus the retreat under fire went on until an hour before noon, when the Navajos withdrew. The weary troops went into camp well before sundown—an indication that their horses were near exhaustion—probably in the vicinity of present Many Farms. About noon the next day, August 18, with nothing more than three captives to show for his loss of four men and seven horses, Colonel Salazar rejoined the main command under Vizcarra near the mouth of Canyon de Chelly.

From this point onward the return journey appears to have been without incident. The army followed the south rim of Canyon de Chelly and camped for one day of rest in the vicinity of Red Lake, where some of the cattle taken from Juanico were distributed to the soldiers. On August 24, after negotiating the pass through the Chusca Mountains and reaching the valley below, Vizcarra discharged two regiments of militia to make their separate ways home to Rio Arriba and Rio Abajo. With the balance of the command he proceeded directly eastward for fifteen leagues until meeting the Chaco Wash at Fajada Butte. For the next two days he followed his outward route, resting briefly at Pueblo Pintado before continuing past the Chacra Mesa and down Torreon Wash. Below the present town of Cuba the command turned east on a trail leading across the Jemez Mountains by way of the Valle Grande. At sunset on August 31, after an absence of seventy-four days, the troops arrived at Santa Fe. The expedition was over.

Casualties accounted for by Vizcarra and Salazar, which cannot be regarded as entirely accurate, indicate that thirty-three Navajos, including at least eight women, were killed and thirty others were captured. Of livestock, the Navajos lost 801 sheep and goats, 87 cattle, and 23 horses and mules. Five Paiutes, mistaken for Navajos, were killed. Five Mexicans were reported killed, four died of sickness, and at least thirteen were wounded. Twelve Mexican horses were captured. No attempt was made to estimate the number of Navajo wounded.

4

Mexican Rule

An incident supposedly occurred at Cochiti at about this time that some years later, in the retelling, caught the attention of Josiah Gregg. That partisan but usually reliable observer could be no more than vague about the date or exact circumstances, noting only that "by repeated acts of cruelty and ill-faith" the New Mexican government inspired neighboring tribes of Indians, but especially the Navajos, into retaliatory acts of hostility. "On one occasion, a party consisting of several chiefs and warriors of the Navajoes assembled at the Pueblo of Cochití, by invitation of the government, to celebrate a treaty of peace; when the New Mexicans, exasperated no doubt by the remembrance of former outrages, fell upon them unawares and put them all to death." [1]

There can be no certainty in the matter, but this treacherous act occurred either two years before, during the regime of Governor Melgares or following a treaty Vizcarra made with the Navajos on January 20, 1824, at Jemez.[2] Except for minor depredations the Navajos remained at peace during 1824. This fact, coupled with the unusual fierceness of Navajo attacks upon the settlements in 1822, is evidence, although not conclusive proof, that the murder of Navajos related by Gregg did occur during the Melgares administration.

1. Gregg 1954, p. 199. Gregg himself is not specific, but Twitchell (*Facts of New Mexican History*, vol. 2, p. 42), in relating the same story virtually in Gregg's words, says the episode occurred "during the rule of Vizcarra" (see my n. 1, chap. 3).

2. "Tratados de paz, Jemez, Jan. 20, 1824," in Reeve 1971, no. 3, pp. 244–45. The single treaty document (despite the plural designation) is in the collection of the Archivo Histórico Militar Mexicano, Mexico, Secretaría de Guerra y Marina, D481.3/271. Comprising fourteen articles, the treaty was signed by Vizcarra, Jefe Político Bartolomé Baca, and, for the Navajos, only by Antonio el Pinto—probably a son of the headman killed by Apaches in 1793. The treaty was notable for two articles calling for a reciprocal exchange of Navajo and Spanish captives. A third article, however, referred the release of Navajo captives to the government in Mexico City. Article 6 required Navajo headmen to force fellow tribesmen to give up stolen property, and Article 7 declared that Navajos might "ask for the aid of local authorities" should property be stolen from them by Mexicans.

A situation that had been in the making since the defection of Joaquín in 1818—a deepening cleavage between the Diné Ana'aii and the Navajo nation—was accepted as irrevocable in early 1825. In his capacity as *jefe militar* for New Mexico, Colonel Vizcarra observed that the Navajo nation, vacillating between peace and war, ignoring the treaty he had made with them a year before, constituted one of the territory's gravest misfortunes. Two factions of the tribe were sharply defined in his mind: those who were on the side of government and arrayed against the ladrons (thieves), and those who were hostile and opposed. "Those who are with us," Vizcarra noted in reference to the Diné Ana'aii, "have come several times requesting auxiliary force and offering to hand over all of the thieves, formally acquainting us with proof that they were on our side. The proof is that they have killed seven of the other [faction] with such motive."

Vizcarra coined a homely definition that was to outlast him, one that prevailed well into the period of American occupation: henceforward the Diné Ana'aii would be known to authorities in Santa Fe as "those who are with us," and other Navajos, excepting occasional peace factions among the nation, would become "those against us." The tribal division that met with official approval from Vizcarra was to be encouraged by succeeding authorities, who would pay in coin or goods and offer other inducements to persuade the Diné Ana'aii to betray and even kill their kinsmen.

In barracks adjoining the Palace of the Governors three Navajo prisoners were a daily reminder to Colonel Vizcarra that his campaign against their people two years before had not accomplished its purpose. He had not succeeded in subjugating the Navajo nation. Navajos after a year of relative peace continued to raid the settlements. Within a short time he would be succeeded by Colonel Antonio Narbona—remembered well in the territory for his singular action at Canyon de Chelly. The presence of the three Navajo captives was an irritant. They had been brought in and turned over to him by the same party of Diné Ana'aii who had killed the seven Navajos. Vizcarra was aware that the captives were of no use to anyone, but instead were just an expense—being fed at the cost of one *real* each day.

With the celebrated Colonel Narbona coming so soon to replace him, Vizcarra determined that it would be well to campaign once more against the Navajos. He communicated this idea to the comandante general in Durango, Mexico, saying he would start out March 9 with troops of the Santa Fe garrison. These would be reinforced by citizen militia raised by the *jefe político*, Governor Bartolomé Baca (who at Canyon de Chelly had served well under Narbona as a lieutenant). The miserable Navajo captives living in the barracks at government expense suddenly inspired Vizcarra with an idea.

"I have resolved," he informed his superior in Durango, "that if in the expedition which I am going to undertake, some more prisoners are captured, I will take them all with me when I leave this territory so that they may be placed at Veracruz or another presidio, because I believe that little would be gained by giving them their freedom here. And if the other members of their Nation see them disappear, it may serve to stimulate [peace] and they will do no evil." [3]

Navajos were not to be found anywhere in the region where Vizcarra had been informed they would be numerous. Because of the shortage of his supplies and the great distance he would be obliged to travel in pursuit, as well as his inability to secure fresh horses as remounts, he decided not to follow them into the recesses of their country as he had done in 1823. Before he turned back, however, he was informed by Diné Ana'aii attached to his column that a number of Navajos were gathering in the vicinity of Abiquiu. Word of this he sent on by special messenger to Santa Fe, suggesting that Governor Baca find some means of seizing these "rebels."

The accuracy of the Diné Ana'aii information was proved when a force gathered by the alcalde of Abiquiu managed to capture forty-one Navajo men and women. All of these but three—"three of the bad ones, who were handed over to me" (for what purpose he did not explain)— Vizcarra set at liberty while returning to Santa Fe. Having extracted from the liberated captives information as to where the remainder of their band could be found, the colonel directed Brevet Captain José Caballero to take a detachment of thirty soldiers, together with seven Diné Ana'aii and one hundred militia, and follow in pursuit. Caballero's column surprised its quarry April 7, killing eleven Navajos, one of whom was said to have been their war captain. Following the tracks of a fleeing Navajo woman and boy, Diné Ana'aii succeeded in capturing twenty more of the same band. These captives, Vizcarra observed later (discarding his plan of taking them to Veracruz) were "placed at the disposition of the Señor Jefe Político [Governor Baca] so that he might distribute them to the inhabitants of the territory at his discretion." [4]

3. March 5, 1825: Vizcarra to Comandante General, Jefe Militar Letterbook, Letters #143–44–45, MA, NMSRCA, trans. Simmons.

4. April 18, 1825: Vizcarra to Comandante General, Jefe Militar Letterbook, Letter #196, MA, NMSRCA, trans. Simmons. Troops returning from the cam-

Traffic in Indian slaves was illegal under Mexican law, as it had been under royal Spanish decree, but it had been practiced for so long that it had become an ingrained custom of the territory. It was common for military commanders to refer openly to the captives they had taken as "slaves"; these same slaves might be apportioned like so many cattle among the troops or retained by the commander, or they might turn up later as servants in the homes of lay and clerical authorities. It was common, too, to disguise the practice in the euphemistic deceit that by exposure or conversion to Christianity the lot of Indian slaves was made immeasurably happier than the condition of the barbarians who remained at large. Nevertheless, it was a bizarre departure for one in Vizcarra's position to discuss candidly, in official correspondence, a plan for the distribution of captive slaves at the discretion of a civil governor. Only by such candor were the common folk led to understand that under Mexican rule slaving, even though illegal, was officially sanctioned as openly—or almost as openly—as the traffic in African slaves was sanctioned in the neighboring United States.

Removal of the final vestige of restraint was all that was needed to give impetus to the already flourishing but not often publicized business of citizen companies forming for slaving forays into Navajo country. This, coupled with a constant fostering of Diné Ana'aii leaders, almost always to the calculated harm of the Navajos, made a continually expanding warfare with the Navajos inevitable.

Only a few months after he replaced Vizcarra and Bartolomé Baca as New Mexico's military and political governor, Antonio Narbona in November of 1825 granted an audience to an American named George C. Sibley. One of the three commissioners appointed by President John Quincy Adams to mark out a trade route from the western frontier of Missouri "to the confines of New Mexico," Sibley observed nothing of the soldier in his host but remarked that Narbona was "a Gentleman of pretty good talents, quite a man of business. . . ." [5]

The new governor continued a pattern set by his predecessors when, early in his administration, he recognized Francisco Baca as leader of the Diné Ana'aii and acknowledged the renegades of that band as

paign on April 14 gave a slightly different version of the results, saying they had killed 11 Navajo warriors and 3 women, and taken 22 captives (Military Papers, Santa Fe Presidial Company, Enlistment Papers, MA, NMSRCA, Testimony of Juan de Abrego, Santiago Lucero, and Sgt. José Bustamente, trans. Brugge).

5. "Report of the Commissioners on the Road from Missouri to New Mexico, October 1827," ed. Buford Rowland, *New Mexico Historical Review* 14: 3, p. 220, n. 20.

friendly allies. Nothing at all is known of what happened to cause the downfall of the original defector; Joaquín, if he still lived, was cloaked in total obscurity. Native to the region of present San Fidel in the southern foothills of Mount Taylor, and fathered, it is said, by one of the Baca family granted land near Encinal in 1768, Francisco Baca was a literate or semiliterate half-breed who claimed his mother's lineage.[6] How clearly he perceived or agreed with the division between the Diné Ana'aii, whose leader he was, and the Navajo nation, whose leader he pretended himself to be, is uncertain.

Early in 1826, however, as the "Captain of the people of my Nation," Baca in a wandering recital made vague reference to various injuries and complaints and then specifically called on Colonel Narbona to take action against Pueblos of Zuni. The Zunis, it would appear, had "wrought havoc" and caused continuing suffering among Baca's people living, he said, in the "Sierra de Sandia." Baca's communication was written from Cebolleta, almost certainly in the hand of another although the signature is that of Francisco Baca. Its importance lies in what is revealed of the relationship between Baca and Governor Narbona, and a suggestion that at least a part of the Diné Ana'aii may have been occupying, rather than visiting, a region as far east as the Sandia Mountains.[7]

What Narbona may have done to chastise the Zunis, if anything, is not known. Two months later, in any event, his attention was diverted to that part of the Navajo tribe for whom Francisco Baca could not speak, when Don Antonio Chávez of Belen complained that the "enemy Navajos" had, on March 20, robbed him of eight horses and mules. In itself this amounted to little, but because the Navajos "have committed hostilities the entire winter against these jurisdictions," Chávez implored Narbona to send 150 infantry and horsemen to the defense of Belen.[8]

During the three years following, Navajos raided along the Rio Grande, striking repeatedly at Jemez but ranging from Abiquiu and the Valle Grande southward to Belen. Thousands of sheep and other livestock were run off; some of the pastors were carried away as slaves and others were killed. A token force of fifteen soldiers was sent in

6. Myra Ellen Jenkins, personal communication.
7. January 15, 1826: Francisco Baca to Narbona, Governor's Papers, Letters Received from Within New Mexico, MA, NMSRCA, trans. Simmons.
8. Chávez's complaint was forwarded by Pablo Baca of Belen in a letter to Narbona, March 24, 1826, ibid., NMSRCA, trans. Simmons.

March 1829 to patrol the frontier at Jemez. A lack of documentation obscures much of this period of Narbona's governorship, unfortunately, but the Navajos again were punished so severely that they made repeated requests for peace. A council was held, but of its outcome nothing is known.

Authorities at Jemez and Santa Fe were advised of a quarrel in May 1830 between Francisco Baca and a member of his band of Diné Ana'aii —a person called Cebolla—but Colonel Vizcarra, who again was the territory's commanding officer, dismissed the affair lightly. This is too bad, because the person called Cebolla was soon to become very important indeed.

The story, in such meager detail as Vizcarra offers, is simple enough. On May 7, it seems, four horses were stolen by Navajos from among "those which they have taken from the Californias"—an allusion, presumably, to horses driven from California and taken in a Navajo raid upon Diné Ana'aii. As a consequence, a feud had arisen between Cebolla and Francisco Baca. Vizcarra's interest was less than intense. He informed the civil governor, José Antonio Chávez, that hostilities generated by Francisco Baca amounted to no more than a private quarrel between Baca and the Diné Ana'aii called Cebolla. Vizcarra had no wish to intervene in the dispute but was inclined to consent to a request Baca had made that an interpreter be sent to reprimand Navajos guilty of the robbery. If he accomplished nothing more, the interpreter might return with useful information of what the Navajos were up to.[9]

For an introduction to Cebolla it would be difficult to devise a more fitting initial appearance: a controversial figure ambiguously engaged in a minor brawl. He was that and much more. Cebolla—soon to be known as Cebolla Sandoval, occasionally as Antonio Sandoval, and finally just as Sandoval—was ambitious, cunning, devious, and contradictory. As he attained power he became a plotter, a man who played any three sides against a shifting middle. He was an informer most often for the whites but occasionally, with a surprising loyalty—unless, again, the information was paid for—for the Navajos. Wherever trouble occurred, Sandoval was likely to be found. He would buy and sell slaves among his own people. He became a wealthy man whose services, for almost any murky or evil purpose, were for hire. He was a dealer, at a

9. June 11, 1830: Vizcarra to Chaves, Comandante Principal Papers, Letters Sent to Authorities Within New Mexico, MA, NMSRCA, trans. Simmons.

price, in Navajo scalps. He aspired to and soon would attain undisputed leadership of the Diné Ana'aii.[10]

Cebolla Sandoval was not quite ready for a leading part, however, when a campaign was made into Navajo country in March 1833. Five hundred citizen volunteers joined the Santa Fe regulars at Jemez, but the expedition failed to discourage Navajo raids. Records of the period fail to indicate direct Navajo resistance, only an intensification of raids, mainly against Zia and Jemez, when Mexican authorities pushed the frontier still farther to the west by opening Cubero to settlement. Nine miles west of Laguna, Cubero—like Cebolleta before its village was established—had been a region well known by the name but without a town. This changed in 1833 when Governor Francisco Sarracino authorized the settlement of Cubero by one Juan Chaves and sixty-one settlers from Albuquerque.[11] On a rocky elevation slightly above a usually dry wash tributary to the Rio San José, the wash fringed by cottonwoods but otherwise in a wide and quite sandy valley protected to the north by the shouldering foothills and peak of Mount Taylor, the settlers built a stone and adobe town. Strongly Indian in heritage—the ruins of a sizable Anasazi pueblo, no doubt related long before Coronado's time to Laguna or Acoma, lay only a mile to the north—it would achieve a matchless reputation as a hell-raising military post brothel, a haven for army deserters, murderers, renegades, slavers, and thieves.

Cubero was near enough to Cebolleta (only a few miles across Mount Taylor's lower slopes to the northeast) to be within country claimed, controlled, or occupied by Diné Ana'aii. Its establishment coincided with the abdication of Francisco Baca. As the settlers moved in, Baca made his land above San Fidel available to them, but for perhaps a year or more lingered on. Then it was reported that he had "taken his family away from Cebolleta, to parts unknown but far away." [12] The cause is uncertain, and although this occurred at the time of encroachment by Cubero settlers, it seems unlikely that their presence alone ac-

10. Of the early and other truly important headmen—El Pinto, Juanico, Narbona, and Cayetano—unfortunately far less is known. Cebolla's Navajo name, Haastin Tlth'ohchin, or Onion, was derived from the region (Cebolleta: "onion") where he lived. His later name was taken from that of José Antonio Sandoval, prefect of Albuquerque.

11. Jenkins 1961, p. 63, n. The locality and later the village of Cubero were named for Gov. Pedro Rodríguez Cubero (1697–1703) who treated with the Indians at "the place called Cubero, near the pueblo of Laguna."

12. August 14, 1834: Ambrosio Culaque, Jemez, to Sarracino, Governor's Papers, Letters Received from Within New Mexico, MA, NMSRCA, Jenkins-Minge, p. 56.

counted for Baca's departure. Three years more were to pass before Cebolla Sandoval would assume recognized leadership of the Diné Ana'aii, but possibly his ambition and growing power had some influence on Baca's decision to move away.

However this may be, their concern over Mexican settlement of Cubero, combined with continuing slaving raids into their country, stirred Navajos to redoubled acts of reprisal. As long as the slave raids and periodic punitive campaigns achieved desired results, the authorities in Santa Fe found no reason, regardless of the losses of individual sheep owners, to modify their policies or interrupt the cycle of aggression. Accordingly, another expedition against the Navajos made its departure from Santa Fe on October 13, 1834, this time under the leadership of Captain Blas de Hinojos, comandante general of the territory. The campaign lasted slightly more than one month and by Mexican accounts was successful: sixteen Navajos were reported killed, and three were brought back as slaves; fifteen horses and mules and three thousand sheep were seized.[13]

Early in the following year a party of Utes arriving at Jemez to trade let it be known that some of the wealthier Navajos had joined their people at Sleeping Ute and La Plata Mountains—possibly a reaction to increasing Mexican militancy. A short time after the Utes' departure Jemez was visited again, this time by a delegation of Navajos who, upon leaving, drove off fifty animals from the Jemez herds. They were pursued; eighteen of the stolen animals were recovered, and one Navajo was killed.

The raid on Jemez was followed by a second expedition led into Navajo country by Blas de Hinojos. A force of about one thousand men was raised, most of them citizen volunteers but including as well a sizable contingent of Pueblo warriors, among them a number of Jemez warriors and their war captain, Salvador. It was a heterogeneous army made up of almost every male citizen able to mount a horse and willing to fight. Captain Hinojos left Santa Fe on February 8, 1835, at the head of the main column. Of three divisions taking the field, a second was led by Don Juan Antonio Cabeza de Baca, a wealthy rancher and alcalde of the town of Peña Blanca. If Vizcarra's route of 1823 was followed, and this was now a familiar military road to Casafuerte, Hinojos apparently was delayed, for it took twenty days—about twice the normal time—for his divisions to reach the foot of Washington Pass.

13. December 31, 1834: Military Papers, Service Record of Blas de Hinojos, MA, NMSRCA, trans. Brugge.

Their approach was at a season when gusty winds carrying stinging clouds of sand scour the valley. Such forces of nature usually produce gloom in the most optimistic men. The troops marching with Hinojos, on the contrary, were a laughing, confident, and almost totally undisciplined band who advanced on the steep rocky face of the summit unaware of danger. Near the point where the pass narrows and bends through dark gray rocks they were ambushed. How many fell in the first few minutes is not known, but by Navajo account the Mexicans never before had suffered as many casualties. Taken unprepared and completely by surprise, they were felled like deer trapped in a box canyon. Blas de Hinojos and Cabeza de Baca were left with the many dead among the trees on the mountainside.

In testimony taken on his return to Santa Fe five weeks after the ill-starred departure, Juan Esquivel, one of the soldiers who survived, said nothing of the army's casualties. Of the Navajos' losses, he said thirty-five warriors were killed. Not in this engagement but elsewhere during the campaign, Esquivel reported, four Navajos were captured and 6,604 sheep, 108 cattle, and 14 horses were driven off.

Among Navajos the battle in the mountains became a legend handed down from one generation to the next for more than seventy-five years. Josiah Gregg, after hearing a reasonably fresh version, wrote:

> The valiant corps, utterly unconscious of the reception that awaited them, soon came jogging along in scattered groups, indulging in every kind of boisterous mirth; when the war-whoop, loud and shrill, followed by several shots, threw them all into a state of speechless consternation. Some tumbled off their horses with fright, others fired their muskets at random; a terrific panic had seized everybody. . . .

Twenty-one years afterward Navajo Agent Henry L. Dodge remarked that during his recent visits to different parts of their country the Navajos took "great pleasure in pointing out to me one of their Mountain passes in which they say they put to rout one thousand Mexicans and Pueblos and killed Capt Inohos & the Father of Don Tomas Baca the rich man of Penablanco and forced the Capt of the Pueblos of Jemez to jump off a precipice and kill himself." [14]

14. June 13, 1856: Dodge to Gov. David Meriwether, National Archives (hereafter, NA), New Mexico Superintendency of Indian Affairs (hereafter, NMS), microcopy T21, role 2; Military Papers, Santa Fe Presidial Company, Enlistment Papers, 1821–45, Mexican Archives; Gregg 1954, p. 200; and Brugge, Navajo Times, April 28, 1966. Still another version of this episode was told to me by Mrs. Richard

In spite of their own severe losses during the campaign, Navajos regarded the engagement near the pass as a victory. Not content with that, they soon retaliated. A war party that could not have numbered fewer than two hundred moved toward the Rio Abajo and on June 5 struck at the new settlement of Lemitar on the west bank of the Rio Grande. A thousand sheep and goats were driven off, the Navajos also taking with them one of the pastors; in a fruitless effort at pursuit, one Mexican was killed and two others were wounded. Two days later, townsmen at Socorro were rubbing night out of their eyes at cockcrow when the same war party descended on the village's outer limits, seized a shepherd, rounded up all livestock either corralled or grazing loose in the fields, and then paraded whooping at a gallop through the town plaza before turning to drive off the stolen animals.

Here, too, a pursuit was organized, a band of townsmen following the tracks as far as the Ojo de la Culebra. Upon nearing the spring and seeing that the Navajo war party gathered there far outnumbered them, the Mexicans reined in. At a distance they sat on their horses, watching, as smoke curled up over fires and the odors of roasting mutton fresh from the corrals of Socorro drifted toward them.[15]

One month later, in July 1835, the headman Narbona appealed for peace to the new governor and *jefe militar*, Colonel Antonio Pérez. An unusually gifted but controversial man, Pérez agreed to a council at San Miguel in Navajo country under conditions favorable to himself. If all went as planned the council was held in the lower plains of Mount Taylor on August 26, the governor arriving quite as ready to make war as to talk peace. Three days before his departure from the capital, Pérez announced that he would be accompanied by the entire strength of the Santa Fe garrison as well as six hundred militia. He was determined that "the peace repeatedly solicited by these aborigines" would result to the benefit of the territory and do honor to the soldiers under his command. An agreement appears to have been made for a mutual exchange of captives, but no document recording the council has been found.[16]

Wetherill, who heard the story from Navajos before 1910, while she was living in Chaco Canyon. By this account also, the engagement was a decisive Navajo victory.

15. June 7, 1835: J. F. Baca, Socorro, to Governor Pérez, Governor's Papers, Letters Received from Authorities Within New Mexico, MA, NMSRCA, trans. Brugge.

16. August 15, 1835: Pérez to Comandante Inspector General, Governor's Papers, Letters Sent to Comandante General, MA, NMSRCA, trans. Brugge.

Reference is found in July 1836 to a campaign led against hostile bands of Navajos by José Francisco Vigil, his force composed of volunteers from Abiquiu, Ojo Caliente, and the pueblos of San Juan and Taos. Before starting out, Vigil was advised that a number of headmen, including Narbona, José Tapia, Caballada Mucha, and El Negrito, and the Diné Ana'aii leader Cebolla Sandoval, had been at Zuni offering to cooperate with Governor Pérez in punishing warring elements of the nation. The bands of these headmen were at peace with the Mexicans and Vigil was admonished not to molest them. The outcome of the campaign is not known.[17]

The Vigil adventure could have been no more than a muted overture to expeditions sent against the Navajos that same fall and winter. The second of these was led by Colonel Pérez himself. Possibly because the governor was under harsh criticism at the time, through no fault of his own, the winter campaign of 1836–37 received little popular support from those who remained at home, and, when it ended, was immediately forgotten. It is doubtful if Navajos forgot that winter so easily, however.

At the outset, and under instructions of the comandante general of Chihuahua to bring an end to the devastating raids, Pérez raised the largest force ever gathered to invade Navajo country. Three divisions of two thousand men each started out on September 14, commanded by Lieutenants José Caballero, José Silva, and Francisco García (the last an aging veteran). No account of the country the troops penetrated has been found, although it is evident that the commands operated separately, the unusually cold early fall weather handicapping their movements and presaging an intensely bitter winter. After a month in the field, in the vicinity of Zuni, Lieutenant García died of the cold. His body was buried in the churchyard of the pueblo and his troops were united with those of José Caballero. A week or so later the campaign ended. Nineteen warriors and one woman had been killed, one captive taken, and a large quantity of livestock captured. Mexican casualties other than the death of Lieutenant García were not mentioned.

Despite the fall campaign, Navajo depredations continued unabated. Early in December Governor Pérez observed that an "icy cold . . . the worst of winter" gripped the territory, but he was determined nevertheless to take personal command of another expedition against the Navajos. There was no precedent for such a winter campaign except Colonel

17. July 21, 1836: Instructions given to José Francisco Vigil . . . Military Records, MA, NMSRCA, Jenkins-Minge, p. 59.

Narbona's action at Canyon de Chelly thirty-two years before. On December 9 Pérez started from Santa Fe with the nucleus of a force that was to number, not quite the 1,000 men he had hoped to raise, but 60 soldiers of the presidial company and 750 militia and auxiliaries, for the most part "those unhappy wretches that regularly report fatigue." If one recalls that Narbona had the advantage of 300 trained Sonoran troops to bolster his militia and Indian auxiliaries, and weather conditions not favorable but less harsh, the Pérez expedition was perhaps the most difficult undertaken against the Navajos until that time.[18]

The governor's small detachment of regulars proceeded to the village of Cubero and at that place Pérez awaited the gathering of his forces, five companies composed mainly of militia. A shortage of trained officers compelled him to entrust command of the companies to citizens: Julián Tenorio of Albuquerque; Fernández Aragón of Sandia, José Martínez of Bernalillo, José Francisco Vigil of San Juan (who had led the previous summer campaign), and José Gonzales of Taos. Deep snow covered the ground when Pérez departed from Cubero on December 16, 1836. Mounted troops went in advance, the horses breaking trail for infantry and a supply train that otherwise could barely have moved.

Pérez had not traveled far when he received word that Pueblos of Zuni had formed an alliance with the Navajos. Instead of following his original plan of marching in full strength against the Chusca stronghold, Pérez accordingly led the major part of his force toward Zuni, at Ojo del Gallo probably taking the familiar old trail by way of Agua Fria, El Morro, and Pescado Springs. At midnight on December 24, still some twenty-six miles distant from his objective, Pérez divided his command so that the pueblo could be surrounded and taken by surprise. The people of Zuni, although a part of them in fact sympathized with the Navajos, convinced Pérez that the pueblo's relations with the Navajos were hostile—an assurance that was reinforced when they turned over to him two Navajo captives who Pérez at once ordered be shot. The night's operation had been painful for the Mexicans as well. One of the militia froze to death and fourteen others suffered frostbite.

Before marching on Zuni, while in the vicinity of Ojo del Gallo, Pérez had detached a column of two hundred men under Fernández

18. September 16, 1836: Letter #60 from Governor's Papers, Letters Sent to Comandante General (Chihuahua), MA, NMSRCA, Jenkins-Minge, p. 60; November 1, 1836 and December 8, 1836: ibid., Letters #64–65, trans. Brugge; February 16, 1837: ibid., Letter #67, Jenkins-Minge, pp. 61–62.

Aragón with orders to proceed toward Ojo del Oso "where the Navajos regularly live for permanent water" and to attack and destroy any Navajos found there. After this diversionary movement Aragón was to rejoin the command "at the Quelites," or Calites Canyon, probably near the mouth of the canyon at the junction of Black Creek and the Rio Puerco of the West. Aragón's citizen troops faithfully carried out their orders. Marching in subfreezing weather, between the lower Chuscas and Ojo del Oso they attacked four Navajo rancherias, killing twenty warriors, capturing a woman and fourteen children, and rounding up 5,300 sheep and 80 mules and horses. Two of the militia were wounded by arrows, one fatally, and Juan Lucero—one of fifty-four men who sustained frostbite—lost two fingers on the left hand. The high rate of Navajo casualties indicates that the rancherias were attacked when the Navajos were asleep or otherwise completely off guard.

From Zuni, Pérez led the main command northward into the eastern foothills of the Chusca range. Here he found that the Navajos had fled, their fresh tracks in the snow showing they had scattered in many directions and in small numbers to frustrate pursuit. The prospect of crossing the Chuscas through deep drifts and night temperatures ten to twenty degrees below zero was bleak enough to have turned most commanders back. The freshness of the tracks persuaded Pérez to go on. He ordered a party of three hundred men under the command of Ensign Diego Saenz to follow the largest trail as it led across the mountains; the main command was to follow more slowly and meet Saenz at the Ojo del Carrizo.[19]

Seven days later the two columns met at the place agreed upon. The troops led by Saenz were haggard from exposure. Half of his command suffered from frostbitten hands and feet. One man lost an ear, another, three toes. Their tenacious pursuit had led them to three rancherias. They had killed eight warriors, captured two women and a child, and seized two thousand sheep and eighteen horses and mules.

The combined fall and winter campaigns of 1836–37 failed to endure in memory and never became legend, as had the less arduous Vizcarra campaign of 1823. But in terms of Navajo losses the combined expeditions of 1836–37 were the more punishing.[20] They served also to re-

19. There is no spring remembered today as Ojo del Carrizo, but from this and other early references it would appear to have been on the lower western slopes of the Carrizo Mountains and north of Canyon de Chelly. Pérez was then in the upper Chusca Valley, probably near Beautiful Mountain.

20. In the combined campaigns Navajos lost 49 warriors and 1 woman killed and 20 women and children captured, according to Pérez's account, as well as 8,837

emphasize a painful precedent. Again excepting the Narbona campaign, Navajos had been safe during winter from major Spanish or Mexican aggression, their enemy preferring, as they did themselves, to make war in the spring or summer. In the winter campaign led by Governor Pérez, the losses to his troops from frostbite were calculated against advantages to be gained from demoralizing surprise attack when escape from the enemy in deep snow would be most difficult. Relying mainly upon ragged militia and his own toughness and skill, Pérez drove a hard point. His campaigns were a harbinger, an example not soon to be followed with success by Mexican or American troops, but fateful when it was.

If any change in Navajo-Mexican relations was to be noted during the next three years, it would only be the increasing frequency of hostilities, Mexican slave raids drawing the usual Navajo reprisals in the form of occasional murders and stock thefts as far eastward as the grazing valleys near Las Vegas. Nor was the administration of Manuel Armijo, who took over the governorship after the assassination of Pérez in 1837, able to do more than aggravate the situation.

A campaign led personally by Armijo in the fall of 1838, ostensibly to punish the Navajos for their most recent depredations, remained in the field two months. Entering Navajo country by way of Jemez, Armijo's command of nearly one thousand men in three divisions attacked rancherias and fleeing groups of Navajos from the upper Chusca Valley as far south as the Gila River, where the fugitives found refuge with the Apaches. Armijo claimed that seventy-eight warriors were killed and that his command had captured fifty-six "slaves of both sexes," taken 226 horses, 2,060 sheep, 6 serapes, 160 buckskins, and other camp booty, and, after "destroying a great field that would have produced over six hundred fanegas of corn," driven the Navajos more than one hundred leagues from the Chusca stronghold. No account is given of his own losses except for a passing reference to Ensign Don Rafael Tapia, who was mortally wounded by a musket ball.[21]

---

sheep and 206 horses and mules. Mexican losses, probably more than reported, were given as three dead, one wounded, and 208 who suffered frostbite.

21. November 25, 1838: Governor's Papers, Letters Sent, Comandancia Letterbook, Letter #33, MA, NMSRCA, trans. Brugge. Capt. Don Francisco Martínez, who accompanied the expedition, said that "76 slaves of both sexes" were captured and the command recovered 1 Mexican captive from the Navajos—a commentary on the ratio of slaves captured by the opposing sides (Military Papers, 1842, Service Records, MA, NMSRCA).

Navajo peace overtures in the spring of 1839 were rejected by Governor Armijo on grounds that Navajos were not to be trusted. At the same time, Armijo warned the prefect of Albuquerque, Don José Antonio Sandoval, that illicit trade with the Navajos by people living in that jurisdiction must cease.

For reasons not clear, Armijo reversed his position of April and on July 15, 1839, entered into a peace treaty with the Navajos at Jemez. In a proclamation issued simultaneously, the governor announced that inasmuch as terms of peace, "for which we have been negotiating with the Navajos for some time," had been concluded that day, and because the Navajos had requested it, he had appointed one of their headmen to govern the tribe under the authority of Prefect Antonio Sandoval of Albuquerque.[22] The identity of the Navajo chosen by Armijo to govern the tribe is not revealed in Armijo's message. The fabled but little-known Cayetano, in Governor Armijo's view "one of the most important men of the [Navajo] Nation," was spokesman for the tribe at the Jemez council.[23]

After an introductory clause declaring that there now would be peace and commerce between the adversaries, a second article of the treaty provided that "in order to carry out the good faith which animates the agreeing parties, the Navajo chieftains have agreed to surrender our captives which are in their Nation . . . and have agreed also [that] those of their own remain among us as a just reprisal, acquired through an honorable war." The Navajo headmen agreed to use every available means to insure that their people would in no way disturb the peace of the Mexican inhabitants. Trade between Navajos and the settlements was to remain on the same terms as before the recent war.

The fifth article dealt firmly with a sensitive issue—one which, second only to the slave trade, again and again was to be a cause of warfare. Any Navajo who committed murder must be surrendered to Mexican authorities for punishment. In turn, if a Mexican sheepherder should kill a Navajo, thirty sheep would be paid to the family of the

22. July 15, 1839; Proclamation of peace treaty made at Jemez Pueblo with Navajo Nation, by Gov. Armijo, Governor's Papers, Letters Sent to Authorities Within New Mexico, MA, NMSRCA, trans. Simmons.

23. July 15, 1839: Treaty of Peace and Friendship Celebrated with the Navajo Nation by His Excellency, Governor of the Department of New Mexico, ibid., MA, NMSRCA, Jenkins-Minge, pp. 51–52. In a personal communication, J. Lee Correll informed me, "The earliest reference I have . . . to Cayetano is August 18, 1805 (SA #1867) at which time Cayetano was an adult. He was seeking to ransom a Navajo girl taken in the war of 1805 and he is referred to as 'not being poor' although he doesn't like paying the 100 peso ransom."

dead man and the murderer would be punished according to law. Indemnity payment of livestock to satisfy a charge of murder was possibly as old to the territory as the slave trade, but Armijo's insistence that a Navajo accused of murder be given up for punishment (which of course meant hanging) should be noted well. Repeatedly this demand would be made of the Navajos, but with a consistency that appears to have been perfect, the demand never met with compliance.

A curious solution to another aspect of slavery was offered in a clause stating that any Navajo woman who succeeded in escaping from the home of her master, on arrival in her own land should be allowed to remain free, and no demands would be made on her people to pay ransom.

For various reasons, possibly in part because of a failure to arrange a satisfactory exchange of captives, the Navajo appointed by Armijo as tribal leader was powerless to keep the nation at peace. On September 24 a male citizen was reported to have been killed in the vicinity of Cebolleta by a Navajo who also drove off a number of animals. Two campaigns were made simultaneously into Navajo country between October 13 and January 1840, resulting in the capture of more than 10,000 Navajo sheep and 145 horses. Sixteen Navajos were said to have been killed and two were brought back as captives.[24]

Troops on this occasion fought skirmishes in the vicinity of the Carrizo Mountains and Canyon de Chelly, penetrating as far as the "Mesa de la Calabaza," north of Black Mesa. Burial records of the Rio Abajo parishes of Tome and Belen show that Navajo warriors exacted a stiff price for the successes of Armijo's returning columns. Two Mexicans killed by Navajos were buried at Tome on December 3; sixteen others, most of them young male adults and evidently the victims of a massive Navajo attack, were buried the next day at Belen; and a single male Mexican, also the victim of Navajo attack, was buried December 7 at Tome.[25]

As the year ended Governor Armijo warned all of the Pueblos that the Navajo nation was at war and called upon all inhabitants of the territory to support his efforts to subjugate their common enemy.

Josiah Gregg had departed New Mexico for the last time, but only by a month or two, when Governor Armijo in July 1840 issued notice

24. Notations: MA, NMSRCA, Jenkins-Minge, p. 68; ibid., p. 69, "Excerpts from a Diary of the Campaign against the Navajos"; General Orders issued during campaign against the Navajos, October 18, 1839–January 9, 1840, trans. Brugge.
25. Brugge 1968, p. 62.

that import duties to be collected from a caravan of traders approaching from the United States would be used to pay the cost of another Navajo campaign. The oncoming train was a large one, and the war chest to be gained from it could have been substantial. Armijo's plan for continuing the war may or may not have been an influencing factor, but Navajos again appealed for peace, many of them gathering near the headwaters of the Rio Puerco while two of their number were sent by the headman Cayetanito as emissaries to intercede with authorities at Abiquiu.[26] The fact that the appeal was taken to Abiquiu rather than to the capital suggests that Navajos had reason to mistrust a direct approach to the governor. Negotiations failed, however, and Navajos on August 22 descended upon Sabinal, killed two men and a woman, wounded three others, and ran off ninety head of horses and mules. A week later Governor Armijo called for a thousand volunteer militiamen from Rio Arriba and the Rio Abajo, announcing at the same time plans for another Navajo campaign to start in September.

Cebolla Sandoval, who appears to have had a falling out with Armijo and may in consequence have temporarily aligned himself and his Diné Ana'aii followers with the main body of the tribe, was marked for special attention. A diversionary party of sixty residents of Cebolleta led by Juan Ramírez, presumably well acquainted with the country Cebolla occupied not far to the northwest, fell upon his rancherias and put his band to flight. Describing Cebolla as "very astute, and . . . largely responsible for [the failure to make] peace," Armijo indicated that while none of the band was killed, the citizens with Ramírez captured a number of women and children, recovered one of their own people held captive, and also seized livestock and a quantity of goods left abandoned in the hogans.[27]

Two columns of five hundred men each had set forth, meanwhile, and campaigned separately against the Navajos under the command of Captain Don José Salazar and Captain Don Francisco Vigil. The citizen auxiliaries and rural militia making up Salazar's force are said to have killed thirteen warriors and captured eight women and children, and brought back as prisoner the headman José Largo, who had rashly

26. July 19, 1840: Pedro León Luján, Abiquiu, to the Subinspector of the Rurales, Don Juan Andrés Archuleta, Military Records, 1840, Militia, MA, NMSRCA, Jenkins-Minge, p. 71. Cayetanito, here mentioned as a "chieftain," was a son of Cayetano.

27. October 3, 1840: Armijo to the Minister of War and Navy, Mexico, Governor's Papers, Letterbook of Communications Sent to Guerra y Marina, 1840–1841, Letter #10, Jenkins-Minge, p. 72.

come to Salazar's camp asking for a truce and cessation of the war.

Troops of Captain Vigil's command encountered the Navajos in the vicinity of a mesa whose summit was described as six hundred varas, or some eighteen hundred feet, above the valley plain, and its slopes so treacherous that no horse or mule could climb to the top. Navajos held the heights behind defensive walls of large rocks and placed warriors as lookouts to guard the one trail over which the enemy must approach. After scouting the position to test its strength, Captain Vigil concealed his command at a distance of four or five leagues and waited for the better part of a day and into the night in hope the Navajos would believe the soldiers had withdrawn in discouragement. Finally, one hour before midnight, the column was ordered to start out on foot for the mesa summit.

The Navajos were taken by surprise, eighteen of the soldiers breaching the defensive walls before the attack was discovered. Navajos who were not killed outright in the first assault, Governor Armijo noted later, "rather than see themselves prisoners, hurled themselves over the cliff and they all died. On this same mesa . . . in the year 1818 . . . Colonel Don Facundo Melgares maintained a siege of 40 and some days, and after all that time, he did not attain its surrender, because on top of it . . . they have permanent water." [28] Armijo neglected to mention where in Navajo country the Salazar and Vigil columns operated. The fortified summit stormed by Vigil's troops in some respects suggests Beautiful Mountain, although in altitude the mesa as mentioned here would be only slightly more than one-half that of the legendary fortress. (Assaulting the heights of Beautiful Mountain eighteen years later, Lieutenant Milton Cogswell would describe "the mesa of Cayatano" as rising about four thousand feet above the valley floor— overestimating by one-quarter. On or near the top he found several natural tanks containing water and, about a mile from the summit, a spring of fresh water.)

Vigil reported that his command killed twenty warriors and took "six slaves of both sexes," a number of horses, and more than two hundred fanegas of corn.

In the closing months of the year and early in 1841 numerous delegations of Navajos came to Jemez to ask for peace. Among the first of the emissaries was the headman called Anceluno, who also informed the prefect that the family of José Largo had recently moved to "Encinal de Sebolleta," where they had joined with the Diné Ana'aii, and

28. Ibid., Letter #11, trans. Brugge.

that a major part of the tribe now lived in the valley regions near Canyon de Chelly. Another delegation came on January 5 to ask if Armijo would discuss peace. The headman Narbona, they said, waited with thirty Navajos on the "Mesita Azul," or Chacra Mesa, but in three days more would come to Jemez and then proceed to Santa Fe to see the governor. Finally, on March 8, Francisco Sandoval, the rurale commander at Jemez, reported to Armijo that a very large number of Navajos had arrived at his house in the neighboring village of San Ysidro and then departed for Santo Domingo for a peace council. Their number included the headman Narbona, José Tapia, Hashke Juna (a son of Cayetano), and the Diné Ana'aii leader Cebolla Sandoval, as well as one hundred warriors.[29]

Armijo was sick at the time and unable to attend the council but was represented by Colonel Juan Andrés Archuleta, inspector of the rurales of the First District. Except for one clause, which declared that neither side in future should be allowed to take captive slaves, the treaty was substantially the same as others that had preceded it. Navajos must surrender all Mexicans held as captives, but Armijo's government would allow freedom only to those Navajo captives who managed to escape from their masters. Navajos accused of murder must be surrendered for punishment, but if a Mexican should murder a Navajo an indemnity of five hundred sheep would be paid to the family of the dead man.[30]

In a statement issued shortly after the treaty was signed, Prefect Don Antonio Sandoval's son Francisco, as commander of the rurales and justice of the frontier at Jemez, informed the territory that since the conclusion of the treaty the Navajos frequently had asked for the return of eight of their people held by the Mexicans, but that Armijo had refused their requests, saying that the conduct of the Navajos had not been good. Nevertheless, Francisco Sandoval went on, it was now desired that the inhabitants of the territory should contribute to a fund so that the Navajo slaves could be purchased from their Mexican owners; these Navajos then would be exchanged for Mexicans held by Navajos.[31]

Colonel Archuleta forwarded a copy of the document to Armijo on

29. Notations: MA, NMSRCA, Jenkins-Minge, pp. 73–74.
30. March 10, 1841: Copy of Peace Treaty . . . Governor's Papers, Letters Received from Within New Mexico, MA, NMSRCA, Jenkins-Minge, p. 75.
31. David Brugge, personal communication, relating to Francisco Sandoval letter, undated but filed with the March 10, 1841 treaty, MA, NMSRCA. A somewhat different interpretation is given by Minge in Jenkins-Minge, p. 68.

March 12, 1841, saying that the Navajos had agreed to all points and that the governor "could arrange and sign things when he was well, if it was his wish to do so." On the same day it was learned that the Navajos, in partial fulfillment of their agreement, had released four Mexican captives before leaving to return to their homes.

From San Ysidro came the first intimations of trouble. Francisco Sandoval advised Armijo that before departing the Navajos had expressed serious dissatisfaction with the outcome of the council. They would become even more dissatisfied, Sandoval observed, if the spoils taken from them at the time of the campaign of Captain Salazar were not returned to them. The terms of the Santo Domingo treaty evidently had not been explained to them in a way they fully understood. The headmen now complained that, although they had surrendered Mexican captives, they were convinced that Armijo had no intention of giving up Navajos held as slaves. They pointed out that on more than ten occasions Navajos had liberated Mexican captives, in compliance with treaty demands, but that as yet none of their people had been set free. They asked that Navajo captives be returned to them, either at Chaco Canyon or at Jemez.

Informing Armijo of this, Francisco Sandoval observed that in his opinion it would not be advisable to let citizens drive cattle or move other property over the trails between Jemez and Laguna, or from Jemez to settlements on the Rio Grande, until the question of releasing Navajo captives had been resolved. Even if a guard were furnished, he implied, it would only invite Navajo attack. As long as the Navajos were in their present angry mood, he recommended that no person should be allowed into their country for any reason.

So grave did he regard the situation, and so many were the unfortunate things that had happened to threaten the peace, that Sandoval felt it was no longer enough merely to tell the Navajos the truth. Implying that something should be done to satisfy the Navajos' demands, he said he hoped he would receive Armijo's decision within twelve days. In a postscript he noted that it was Cebolla Sandoval who had brought him the news of the Navajos' displeasure with the outcome of the treaty council, and added that the Diné Ana'aii leader might be held responsible for the way they felt.[32]

Regardless of any part he may have had in this, Cebolla Sandoval appears at this time to have regained favor with the Mexican authori-

32. March 14, 1841: Francisco Sandoval to Armijo, Governor's Papers, Letter Received from Within New Mexico, MA, NMSRCA, trans. Brugge and Simmons.

ties. His presence at Santo Domingo with Narbona and other headmen possibly meant nothing more or less than that he was now recognized as leader of the Diné Ana'aii, a man to be reckoned with. There is increasing evidence, beginning with the appeals for release of Navajo captives, that Cebolla Sandoval was unusually active in his efforts to cooperate with the Sandoval family of San Ysidro and Jemez and with the governor. That Armijo appreciated these efforts is borne out by a message of March 26 to Francisco Sandoval in which the governor said he was well pleased with Cebolla Sandoval's behavior and the efforts he was making to preserve the peace. Armijo wished that the Diné Ana'aii leader be told of the governor's good feeling toward him, and also that, should his continuing efforts toward peace prove effective, Armijo would accord him recognition equal to that once granted Francisco Baca. Cebolla was to be encouraged to exhort the Navajos to peace and explain to them why Armijo had not returned their captive people and that he would do so if the Navajos gave evidence of actually desiring peace.[33]

How effective Cebolla Sandoval proved to be as an arbitrator is uncertain. Others, in any case, also wanted peace. Two Navajos who said they had been sent by Narbona and the Navajo headman called Armijo appeared at Francisco Sandoval's home on April 6. They had come, they said, to determine what progress had been made toward the settling of differences; they asked that the governor be advised that the Navajo Armijo had gone among all of the rancherias of his region urging the people to remain at peace.[34] Francisco Sandoval assured them of the governor's good will and told them they should put aside their distrust. Their captive people would not be released, he said, but if the Navajos would comply with terms of the Santo Domingo treaty, the governor would "in no way . . . fail to keep his promises to them."

Further evidence of the Navajos' wish to avoid hostilities came in August 1841 when José Largo, free again after his capture by Salazar, appeared at Cebolleta with two other Navajos at the door of the justice

33. March 26, 1841: Armijo to the Commander of the Frontier at Jemez, Governor's Papers, Letters Sent to Authorities Within New Mexico, MA, NMSRCA, Jenkins-Minge, p. 77.

34. April 6, 1841: Francisco Sandoval to Armijo, Governor's Papers, Letters Received from Within New Mexico, MA, NMSRCA, trans. Simmons. The Navajo headman known as Armijo no doubt took or was given the governor's name. A member of the same eastern division of the Navajos of which Narbona was principal leader, Armijo occupied land in the Chusca foothills and valley in the vicinity of Ojos Calientes, or Bennett's Peak. Always protective of the interests of the Navajo nation, Armijo nevertheless was nearly always an advocate of peace.

of the peace. They brought with them eight horses and eighty sheep to turn over as payment, under terms of the treaty, for the death of a Cochiti Indian at the hands of a Navajo.

For nearly two years more the Navajos and Mexicans observed a state of armistice. If more than one or two Navajos held in bondage were surrendered by Governor Armijo, no record of it has been found. A growing division within the tribe between war and peace factions at least once gave rise to rumors that the Navajos were about to make war again. But for a short time longer an open resumption of hostilities was avoided.

Word of serious dissent among the Navajos was brought in early June 1843 by Cebolla Sandoval. An important segment of the tribe was gathering in the Zuni Mountains, at Ojo del Oso, and in the vicinity of the Chusca Mesa, their number representing a peace faction led by Zarcillos Largos, Juan Chaves, El Facundo, and other headmen. If Cebolla Sandoval's word could be relied upon, it was the purpose of these headmen "to separate themselves from the 'thieves'" and to accompany Mexican forces in a campaign against Navajos of the war faction. Those of the nation who favored peace acted in good faith, Cebolla Sandoval explained, and as proof of this he told how some of them had joined with his Diné Ana'aii in searching for the Indians (Navajos, presumably) who had stolen cattle from one José Chaves.[35] A division of the tribe into peace and war factions is wholly credible, but Zarcillos Largos in the role of a campaigner with Mexican troops against his own people is beyond belief.[36]

Tilting toward war, both sides continued on an unpredictable course into March of 1844, each new peace effort thwarted by an act of aggression. No sooner had the military governor, General Mariano Martínez de Lejanza, drawn up articles of a new treaty than Navajos on March 3 raided Abiquiu. Driving fourteen oxen and several head of cattle before them, they finally escaped their pursuers in the vicinity of Chacra Mesa. Four days later, in a renewed display of good will, Navajos of the peace faction brought into the settlements and surrendered

35. June 5, 1843: J. Sarracino, Inspector of Militia, to Acting Governor and Comandante General, Don Juan Andrés Archuleta, ibid., MA, NMSRCA, Jenkins-Minge, p. 79.

36. Zarcillos Largos (Long Earrings), called Nataallith, or Peace Chanter, by the Navajos, must by all historical accounts be regarded as one of the great leaders of the Navajo nation. Although referred to often as a war chief by American officers in the 1850s, he more often is found as a spokesman for peace. There is no evidence whatever that he ever took part in making war on other Navajos.

a number of Mexican captives. They were told that four Navajo captives held by Captain Don Francisco Vigil would be turned over to General Martínez, with an implied promise that when the general's proposals for a new treaty were agreed to, the four Navajos would be released. Records fail to show what disposition of the prisoners was made. Finally, on March 18, a delegation of Navajos arrived at Jemez prepared to enter peace talks and requesting that the council be held there rather than at Santo Domingo. Fears they expressed that at the latter place they might be attacked by Jicarilla Apaches were overcome, and the council was held at Santo Domingo on March 23 as planned.[37]

Names of the Navajo headmen who attended and signed the treaty are not known with certainty, although General Martínez in first and second drafts of treaty terms noted that those who had appealed to him for peace and then agreed to his conditions included Narbona, El Guero, Cabras Muchas, Juan Chaves, and Archuleta. There was no mention of Zarcillos Largos and Armijo, or of the Diné Ana'aii Sandoval.

Draft copies of the treaty are phrased in language more than ordinarily wooden and burdened with overtones of distrust, fear, and an implicit threat of immediate war if Navajos ever again should raid the settlements. The terms are monotonously repetitive: most important, Navajos would be required to surrender all Mexican captives, but Mexicans would not reciprocate. However, the freedom of Navajo slaves could be purchased with the payment of ransom.[38]

The council agreement at Santo Domingo followed closely the pattern of previous treaties, and because this was the last of the efforts at peace under Mexican rule, the nature of the efforts deserves some attention. Of eight treaties made with the Navajos since May 1805, copies of the terms of seven treaties have been found. Navajos were called upon in six of the known treaties to surrender all of the captives held by them. In the treaty of 1805, Alencaster agreed to surrender seventeen Navajo prisoners, and it was agreed that *in the future* captives of both sides would be exchanged reciprocally. In the treaty of 1819, Melgares made no reference to captives held by the Navajos but agreed to

37. Notations: MA, NMSRCA, Jenkins-Minge, pp. 84–88.

38. February 26, 1844: Proposals for treaty of peace with the Navajo Tribe, Governor's Papers, Letters Received from Within New Mexico, and Letters Sent, Letterbook of Miscellaneous Communications, 1844–1845, MA, NMSRCA, trans. Brugge.

return all Navajos *held in Santa Fe* upon fulfillment of all treaty terms by the Navajos. Otherwise, Navajo captives might gain their freedom if they managed to escape, or were ransomed, or if the Navajo nation first returned *all* Mexicans held as slaves. The last condition might, at the time, have seemed to be a reasonable or practical one, since the Navajos held only a comparatively few Mexican captives; the requirements of finding and returning them to the settlements would have been proportionately much less difficult. A considerable amount of evidence has been gathered bearing on the number of Navajos held in peonage or slavery; much less is known of the number of whites captured and held as slaves by Navajos. On the basis of available evidence, however, a ratio of approximately twenty Navajos to one white captive would be a conservative estimate.

Navajos on ten occasions did begin a token return of captives and then stopped when it became obvious to them that a like number of Navajos never would be returned from the white settlements. Instead of easing the hostilities both sides felt, the Mexican authorities' unilateral approach to ending the slave trade could only deepen the Navajos' bitter sense of frustration and resentment.

The Martínez treaty of 1844 was little more than a week old when Navajos—disregarding what had been said and done at Santo Domingo —demanded that certain of their people captured by Utes and sold as slaves to Mexicans be returned to them. Governor Martínez at first refused, then relented to the point of drawing on the department treasury for 111 silver pesos, which he ordered paid for the ransom of a captive Navajo girl and two other Navajo children who had been taken by one Don José Partalam. At the same time, Martínez drew another 175 pesos "for gratification" of Navajo headmen, presumably those who had accepted his treaty.

The governor's unusual generosity, it soon became apparent, was not properly appreciated. On July 11 it was learned that Utes had joined with Navajos in attacks upon the settlements. No one could have really been surprised. On the same day orders were given to Colonel Archuleta to enlist five hundred militia and lead his forces from Cubero against the Navajos. Results of the campaign are not known, but with the first early bite of fall, warnings were sent to civilians and to military authorities throughout the territory alerting them to the possibility of attack. Informed by the justice of the peace at Jemez that Narbona and Cayetano were joining with Utes for possible attack upon Jemez, the governor in early October directed the prefect of the district to prepare the pueblos of his jurisdiction. Martínez said he regretted that he was unable to supply reinforcements; for the moment, all available troops were committed to the northern frontier.[39]

A condition of general but undeclared warfare prevailed. Navajos raided at will and the Mexican authorities apparently were unable to rally forces strong enough to protect the settlements. Only the capital seemed secure. In early September 1845, other measures failing, a resort to negotiations was considered worth trying. Captain Don Francisco Sandoval, commanding the rurale forces at Jemez, was directed to discuss with the Navajos what conditions they would agree to; at the same time he was asked to send the leader of the Diné Ana'aii to Santa Fe for a talk with the commanding general "on various points of interest" to the government.[40]

Nothing more is known of a meeting between the general and Cebolla Sandoval, but an understanding of some sort must have been reached, for in the following spring it was reported that sixty citizens of Cebolleta had asked permission "to enlist in the enterprise proposed by the Navajo Chief Sandoval, to fight the barbarians"—meaning, of course, the Navajos. No payment was to be made for their services; their reward was to be any booty and spoils of war they could seize. Armijo's blessing was upon Sandoval's fratricidal venture because, in the general's words, "the war with the Navajos is slowly consuming the Department, reducing to very obvious misery the District of the Southwest." Details of Sandoval's campaign are not given; nothing more is known of the outcome than that Manuel Armijo, in his third term as governor, a month later expressed gratification over its success.

Sandoval continued to offer his services to the government and Armijo in early July said the Diné Ana'aii leader's faithfulness would be rewarded. He promised that Sandoval's wages would be paid promptly and in full—that is, if Armijo's treasury could afford it. As the governor knew well, ominous clouds were gathering from another direction. On the same day Armijo wrote praising Sandoval, Colonel Stephen Watts Kearny's Army of the West was five days out of Fort Leavenworth,

39. October 6, 1844: Governor's Papers, Letters Sent, Secretary of Government Letterbook, MA, NMSRCA, Jenkins-Minge, p. 89.

40. September 5, 1845: Governor's Papers, Letterbook of the Comandancia General of the Department of New Mexico, to Capt. Don Francisco Sandoval, at Jemez, MA, NMSRCA, Jenkins-Minge, p. 92.

marching to invade and overwhelm Armijo's beleaguered territory. Concluding his message referring to Sandoval's faithfulness, Armijo observed that "since the Department awaits invasion from the United States, there can be no movement of forces against the Navajos." [41]

The Navajos, however, found nothing to prevent them from moving against Mexicans. Even with an American army approaching his capital from the east, Armijo was compelled to turn his attention west. His orders of July 8 to the prefects of the Central, Northern, and Southeastern districts outlined a bleak situation. Notice had been received that Navajos threatened war against the frontiers of the Third District. The governor ordered the prefects to divide the district into three military sections, extending from Bernalillo to Socorro, under the command of Don Julián Perea, Colonel Don Ramón Luna, and Colonel Don José Chaves.

These commanders were entrusted with defending the frontier if Navajos attacked at any point on the river. They were to be given necessary support by the citizens.[42]

More than any of the official records show, Navajo hostility at this critical time weighed heavily to the advantage of Kearny's approaching army. Without doubt, the Navajo threat was a factor in Armijo's failure, when his final hour of decision arrived, to make even a pretense of resisting the American invasion. For a few days more, however, he had nothing to do but wait.

41. July 4, 1846: Armijo to Prefect of the 3d District, Governor's Papers, Letters Sent, Letterbook to Authorities Within New Mexico, MA, NMSRCA, Jenkins-Minge, p. 94.

42. July 8, 1846: Armijo to Prefects of the Central, Northern and Southeastern Districts, ibid., MA, NMSRCA, Jenkins-Minge, p. 94.

Part Two

"*Americans! you have a strange cause of war against the Navajos. We have waged war against the New Mexicans for . . . years. . . . We had just cause for all this. You have lately commenced a war against the same people. You are powerful. You have great guns and many brave soldiers. You have therefore conquered them, the very thing we have been attempting to do for so many years. You now turn upon us for attempting to do what you have done. . . .*"

—Zarcillos Largos, at Ojo del Oso,

November 22, 1846

5

The Treaty of Ojo del Oso

Although real enough, the forces of expansionism that for three centuries had brought sparse settlement to the province of New Mexico had been felt only in small shock waves. After Coronado's time, Spanish colonization had lacked thrust and energy; it had ebbed into the valleys of the Rio Grande, the Mora, the Pecos, and the Puerco, and there had stopped. To the nonsedentary Indian tribes, Spanish expansionism may at times have seemed shadowy or as equivocal as changing light. Land encroachment and slavery, by contrast, had both continuity and reality —the searching stare of a New Mexico sun at cloudless summer noon. In lesser or greater degree, then, expansionism and slavery were forces the Navajos had experienced and knew something about; they could not know how these same forces had been combining for years elsewhere and were now about to alter their way of life.

In August 1846, like thunderheads moving before curtains of rain, the sweeping shadow of these forces moved down the Mora Valley in the form of a marching army of fifteen hundred men. This was Kearny's Army of the West: the mounted Missourians of Alexander W. Doniphan in the vanguard, and then the plodding Missouri infantry—river-bottom farm boys, mostly, who regularly outmarched Major Meriwether Lewis Clark's still-trailing battalion of light artillery.

Below the stony hillside village of Tecolote the head of the long column turned west into a forested pass between mountains. At the summit of the defile of Apache Canyon, instead of Manuel Armijo's defending army, they found a deserted breastworks. Immobile in the gray mist were nine pieces of abandoned artillery, one cannon marked "Barcelona, 1778." The defenders had withdrawn, permitting Kearny to enter and occupy Santa Fe in the evening of August 18.[1] Not one shot had been fired.

1. Susan Magoffin, who with her husband James had been part of a trading caravan en route to Chihuahua, noted in her diary, "While all these men, the citizens of

Events of the next seven weeks, the time Kearny allowed himself to consolidate his seizure of New Mexico and establish the structure of temporary government, deserve closer attention than it is possible to give them here. The presence in Santa Fe of Indians from nearby pueblos was frequent enough to pass almost unremarked; delegations of Utes and Apaches came at Kearny's request to "promise good conduct in the future." But days went by before there was awakening awareness among Americans that they were being watched—spied upon might be more accurate—by Navajos who would not come in to talk with the commander. Lieutenant William H. Emory of the Topographical Engineers illustrated the myopia of the moment when, perhaps ten days after the army's arrival, he noted that a band of Navajos ("naked, thin, and savage looking fellows") moved in with Antoine Robidoux, who, as Kearny's interpreter, occupied quarters opposite those of Emory. They did nothing but eat, sleep, and drink, Emory observed, and they noticed nothing at all unless it was a cinnamon-colored naked little brat who played in the court. This one they stared at as though lusting to devour him.

Amusing, of course, but not true. These Navajos were there for a reason. They were noticing everything—everything, no doubt, from the way Emory combed his peculiar red whiskers to the meticulous way he buttoned himself into his blue tunic; from the number of volunteer troops quartered about the town to the nature and possible quality of their muskets, and the number and sorry condition of their gaunt horses. Conclusions were thereby formed that had direct bearing, a few weeks later, on Navajo raids in perilous proximity to Kearny's marching columns.

With the advantage of thirty years' hindsight, Captain Philip St. George Cooke could observe that the Navajos were "a numerous, and warlike tribe who dwell in fastnesses of the mountains westward of the Del Norte. . . ."; that they "are richer than the mass of the people, whose flocks and herdsmen they harry. . . ."; and that, thanks largely to Navajo depredations, the herds of sheep owned by New Mexicans had, since 1832, been decimated by eighty percent (the last an exaggeration).[2]

Santa Fé and the adjacent villages [Armijo's militia], were assembled in the canon, and their families at home left entirely destitute of protection, the Navijo Indians came upon them and carried off some twenty families" (Magoffin 1962, p. 110). Although there may be some substance to Susan's information, the success of the Navajo raid would appear to be greatly exaggerated.

2. Cooke 1878, pp. 47–48.

When rumors reached Santa Fe that Armijo had met General Ugarte and together they would march against the capital, Kearny determined to visit the Rio Abajo to quiet the minds of the people. With him on his departure September 2, 1846, he took seven hundred troops—a force strong enough to make an impressive show should any citizens below be considering revolt. The command traveled as far as the village of Tome, twenty-five miles below Albuquerque. While they were in the Rio Abajo, word spread through the ranks that Navajos had attacked settlements three miles to the rear, almost within sight and sound of the troops, killing one New Mexican and wounding another and running off a quantity of livestock. The incident moved Captain Cooke to remark later that the Navajos continually harassed the citizens but were careful not to ruin them utterly, instead leaving them the means of increasing their property for future Navajo plunder.[3]

Upon his return to Santa Fe a week later, Kearny advised superiors in Washington that citizens of the territory seemed to be satisfied with the change in government and that there was no need for the Americans to fear resistance or open revolt. What remained to accomplish, he said, was to protect the inhabitants against further depredations by Navajos and Utes.[4] To this end he had directed Colonel Doniphan to send three companies of mounted volunteers under command of Lieutenant Colonel Charles Ruff to garrison the village of Cebolleta until further orders, and to detach Major William Gilpin with two companies of the same regiment for the protection of Abiquiu and the upper approaches to the Rio Grande Valley. Events bearing on the performance of this order, which in fact resulted from the recent Navajo depredations, will be related presently. Kearny in the meantime moved several companies of Missouri Mounted Volunteers to positions near the Navajo and Ute frontiers for the protection of inhabitants. Peace treaties would be made with these tribes, he said, but if the Indians failed to comply with the terms, a force large enough to ensure complete success would march into their country to punish them.[5]

Kearny's decision to garrison Cebolleta and Abiquiu suggests that he was acting on the advice of seasoned New Mexican campaigners who knew that these villages controlled two or three principal Navajo ap-

3. Emory, ed. Calvin 1951, p. 80; and Cooke 1878; reprint ed., 1964), pp. 65–66.
4. September 16, 1846: Kearny to Adjutant General Roger Jones, NA, K209–210, AGO, LR, microcopy 567, roll 319.
5. Ibid., September 23, 1846: Orders No. 30.

proaches to the river settlements. Thus an important precedent was set. American officers for years to come, with no personal experience of the country or its Indian tribes, would rely upon the advice of those native to the region. In this way the wisdom or error of Spanish and Mexican custom was perpetuated, influencing civil and military policy of American authorities in very nearly all of their relations with the Navajos.

Summer of 1846 was ended; the days were growing shorter. His work was done, and General Kearny was ready to depart with his staff and three hundred dragoons for California. A framework of civil government for which he later would be censured had been established. Doniphan was to remain in command of military forces until the arrival of Colonel Sterling Price on September 28. To handle affairs of civil government Kearny appointed Charles Bent governor; Donaciano Vigil, secretary; Richard Dallam, marshal; Francis P. Blair, Jr.—then twenty-four years old and with a brilliant career ahead of him—U.S. district attorney; Charles Blumner, treasurer; Eugene Leitensdorfer, auditor of public accounts; and Joab Houghton, Antonio José Otero, and Charles Beaubien judges of superior court.[6] Earlier, Kearny had appointed a Wisconsin man as treasurer of Santa Fe to replace (but for a short time only) the ailing Francisco Ortiz.

This was Henry Lafayette Dodge, thirty-six years old and a son of Colonel Henry Dodge, under whom General Kearny had served when the First Regiment, U.S. Dragoons was established thirteen years before. Henry L. Dodge—never known to use his middle name—was the eldest son and fourth of the thirteen children born to Colonel Henry and Christiana McDonald Dodge.[7] He may have accompanied Kearny's army to Santa Fe, although there is no certainty about this. In 1832,

6. Ibid., September 22, 1846.

7. In editing the Simpson Journal (1964, pp. xlvii–xlviii), I erred by accepting Governor James S. Calhoun's word for it that Dodge's middle name was Linn, and the twice-repeated statement in Mexican War service records that he was born in 1817. According to Mrs. Frank H. Spearman, his great-granddaughter, Dodge "heartily *disliked* the name Lafayette and was known all his life as Henry L. Dodge or H. L. Dodge" (personal communication). Mrs. Spearman is authority as well for saying that Dodge and his wife Adele had four children: George, Mary, Christiana Adel, and Louis Fields Linn Dodge. I have found no record of his family's being with him in New Mexico. Kathy Fisher notes that Grandfather Israel Dodge "at the Battle of Brandywine, was wounded in the chest by a bayonet" and that the Marquis de Lafayette was wounded in the same battle. My other sources are: NA, Service Records, Mexican War, RG 94; NA, Volunteer Organizations, Muster Rolls, box 2550; and NA, Pension Records, Indian Wars, RG 15, WC970.

during the Black Hawk War, he had volunteered and served for eight months with Captain James H. Gentry's company, which was part of a regiment of Michigan militia commanded by Colonel Henry Dodge. It is said that Henry L. Dodge took part in the final battle of Bad Axe River and witnessed the defeat of the Sac and Fox chieftains Black Hawk and Keokuk. Although it would appear that he had received some training in law, his letters indicate only a rudimentary frontier education. No matter. A brother, Augustus Caesar Dodge, two years his junior, possessed an equally awkward command of grammar but was elected to the United States Senate from Iowa and later became minister to Spain. Colonel Henry, meanwhile, had been appointed by President Jackson as first governor of Wisconsin Territory and later served in both the House and Senate of the United States.

It was a sturdy family, taking its background from Henry Dodge's grandfather, Israel Dodge III, a New London, Connecticut veteran of the American Revolution. Israel in time moved his family to Sainte Genevieve, Missouri, a fur trading post on the Mississippi River opposite Kaskaskia. Henry L. Dodge was born there April 1, 1810, and there, at twenty-six, married Adele Becquet. For the next seven years or so they lived in Dodgeville, Wisconsin and at nearby Mineral Point where Dodge worked in the lead mines. When, and why, he was persuaded to move West remain a mystery. In July 1847 he enlisted in the Santa Fe Battalion of Mounted Volunteers, the muster rolls describing him as being five feet nine inches tall, with a florid complexion, gray eyes, and dark hair. Much more will be heard of him.

Whatever his legal experience, there is no indication that Dodge had any part in drafting what became known as the Kearny Code—a set of laws under which the territory was governed until 1886. Critics in Congress soon were protesting that Kearny had exceeded his authority in establishing a permanent form of civil government in New Mexico. Unpredictably, this criticism helped to set in motion and later gave encouragement to a conflict between civil and military authorities that endured with crippling effect for nearly two decades.

Such future concerns could not have been even remotely on Kearny's mind the afternoon of September 25, 1846, when he left Santa Fe at the start of his march to California. Captain Cooke was "haunted by the ghostly shapes of our starving horses," but no incident occurred until the command was on the west bank of the Rio Grande, seven miles below Albuquerque. Observing that they were opposite a pass frequently taken by Navajos, Cooke noted that only a few days before the Navajos had killed several New Mexicans and driven off about two thousand sheep.[8] Three days later, on October 2, in the vicinity of La Joya, the mayordomo of a neighboring ranch sent word cautioning Kearny to guard his horses and mules, as forty Navajos had crossed the river close by the night before. Another message received the same day advised Kearny that Colonel James Allen, who was to have led the Mormon Battalion of volunteers to California, had died. Kearny named Cooke to assume Allen's command and directed him to start back for Santa Fe next day and there await the arrival of the Mormon troops.

Navajo raids and excursions so close to his line of march, obviously intended to test him, succeeded in angering the commander. Kearny recalled that headmen of the Navajo nation had ignored his invitation to come to Santa Fe to discuss terms of peace with the New Mexicans; he had seen them instead continue to kill and rob the inhabitants who had been promised, and now should receive, protection from the United States. He therefore ordered Colonel Doniphan to lead a military expedition into Navajo country with the object of securing peace. All prisoners and stolen property held by Navajos must be given up and returned. To ensure the Navajos' future good conduct, Doniphan should, if he deemed it necessary, take hostages with him on his return to the river.[9]

Nooning on the river next day while waiting for the wagons to catch up, Kearny's command was approached by an express rider who brought word that about one hundred Navajos had attacked the town of Polvadera that morning, driving the inhabitants into their houses and running off all of their cattle and horses. As the town was on the river only twelve miles below, Kearny sent Captain Benjamin D. Moore with a company of dragoons in pursuit. On his return, Moore reported that the Navajos had abandoned the cattle to a pursuing party of New Mexicans but had escaped with the horses; he had arrived with his dragoons too late to help.[10]

A short distance above Socorro on October 5, Kearny addressed a proclamation to the inhabitants of the Rio Abajo—a message of some significance because it was an endorsement and extension of the type

8. Cooke 1878, p. 75. Emory notes, "At this ravine the Navajoes descended when they made their last attack; at the same moment the volunteers were ascending the other slope of the hill, on their way to garrison Cibolleta" (Emory, ed. Calvin, p. 81).

9. The orders, dated October 2, 1846, are found in Connelley 1907, p. 266.

10. Turner 1966, pp. 78–79.

of uncontrolled guerrilla warfare that had plagued the territory for two centuries under Spanish and Mexican rule:

> In consequence of the frequent and almost daily outrages committed by the Navajoes, upon the Persons & Property of the Inhabitants of the Rio Abajo, by which several lives have been lost, and many horses, mules & cattle stolen from them—and in consequence of the many applications made by them, to the undersigned, for permission to march into the Country of those Indians;
>
> Now be it known to all, that I, Brigadier General S. W. Kearny, Commanding the Troops in the Territory of New Mexico, hereby authorize all the Inhabitants (Mexican & Pueblos) living in the said District of Country, viz the Rio Abajo, to form War Parties, to march into the Country of their enemies, the Navajoes, to recover their Property, to make reprisals and obtain redress for the many insults received from them.
>
> The Old, the Women and the Children of the Navajoes, must not be injured.[11]

Kearny's plan of march was substantially changed next day by an unexpected meeting with Kit Carson, who was bearing dispatches from Lieutenant Colonel John Charles Frémont in California reporting (too optimistically) the subjugation of Mexican forces there. Pressing Carson into service as a guide, much against Carson's will, Kearny divided his command. Major Edwin Vose Sumner was directed to remain in New Mexico "at some point in the Rio Abajo Country, to be selected by himself," with Companies B, G, and I, First Dragoons. From this point onward Kearny would take only his staff and one hundred dragoons of two companies under Captain Moore.

Now 160 miles below Santa Fe, Kearny anticipated less difficulty with his baggage train, which had slowed his progress. Instead, there was more. Five days later, on the broken and sandy approach to the Gila, the wagons were abandoned.

Far in Kearny's rear the Mormon Battalion made slow progress. On October 26, the eighth day, in the vicinity of Los Lunas, Cooke learned that Navajos the evening before had run off five or six thousand sheep owned by Don Antonio José Otero, whose hacienda and ranch across the river at Valencia were among the richest in the Rio Abajo. Two of his shepherds had been killed, and Otero, who had been riding all

11. NA, K-196–1846, filed with K209–210, AGO, LR, 567–319.

night, had hired some Pueblos to pursue the raiders. At Los Lunas, Captain Cooke stopped at a ranchhouse of the Luna family, where he was informed that all of the able males of the village had started after the Navajos.[12]

Fearing for the safety of the women left alone at Los Lunas, Cooke sent a message reporting these incidents to Captain Henry K. Burgwin, whose two companies of dragoons had been detached from Kearny's command near Socorro and now were in camp eight miles distant, near Albuquerque. Receiving Cooke's message on October 27, Burgwin put his poorly mounted dragoons in motion. His object was first to aid the people of Los Lunas and then to provide escort for a caravan of American traders bound for Chihuahua.

Cooke, going on at the head of the Mormon Battalion, found upon nearing Socorro that Captain Burgwin's dragoons, half of them mounted on mules, were a mile or two behind him. He learned shortly that on Burgwin's approach to Los Lunas some villagers had galloped out to meet him with word that the Navajos had just robbed them and carried off a woman. At nearby Isleta Pueblo, at about the same time, the Navajos had seized a woman and five children and also had driven away livestock. Captain William N. Grier's company, only partially mounted, was detached from Burgwin's command and sent at once in pursuit. Some of the livestock was recovered on the way, the troops holding the trail for sixteen miles until all but Grier, Lieutenant Clarendon Wilson, and two soldiers were forced to stop because of their horses' exhaustion. Grier's small party proceeded toward a ravine and rode directly into an ambush. Where they had seen four Navajos riding in advance of them, fifty more suddenly appeared, mounted and ready to fight. Grier and his three companions opened fire immediately. According to Cooke's version of the affair, they killed two of the Navajos and retreated without injury "under a shower of arrows" until met by a few of the dragoons plodding toward them on foot. At this point the Navajos are said to have withdrawn.[13]

Another, probably more reliable account of the fight gives a different conclusion. Advancing to the support of the Chihuahua caravan, other troops under command of Captain William P. Walton, while encamped

12. October 26, 1846: Cooke Journal, NA, 246-K-1847, filed with K209–210, AGO, LR, 567–319. Cooke's journal entry describing the attack is omitted from his later *The Conquest of New Mexico and California*.

13. November 2, 1846: Cooke Journal, cited above.

near Isleta several nights later, heard "a great shouting and yelling and the firing of guns and ringing of bells." Tracing the sound to the pueblo, they discovered a crowd milling and dancing about three tall lances, the blades of which were adorned with the scalps of three Navajo warriors, the long, straight, black hair sweeping in the wind. Naturally curious, Walton's men were told that in his recent pursuit of the Navajo raiders Captain Grier and his small party had come upon the Indians in a canyon of the mountains. His men had killed and scalped three of the warriors, rescued the captive women, and recovered the stolen livestock. One of Grier's soldiers was said to have been slightly wounded as the captain "made good his retreat." [14]

Thus, under circumstances that Colonel Cooke either confused or preferred not to describe, Captain Grier engaged United States troops for the first time in armed conflict with the Navajos.

For the time, in the hazy weather of late September 1846, Colonel Doniphan had little to do but wait and watch the cottonwoods begin to turn golden. His command was dispersed—three companies on duty at Santa Fe, Companies A and E with Major Gilpin at Abiquiu, and the remaining three companies by last account in the vicinity of Cebolleta. This force and Gilpin's had started out with orders to protect the country from Navajo and Ute raids, recover any stolen property that might be found, and if possible induce ten or twelve headmen of those tribes to come under protective truce for a council in Santa Fe. When Colonel Price arrived to relieve him, Doniphan was to regroup his Missourians and move south on Chihuahua to join General Wool.

On the day before their departure for the Navajo frontier at Cebolleta, the Missouri Volunteers of Companies D, F, and G found themselves leaderless. Lieutenant Colonel Ruff resigned his volunteer commission September 17 in order to take a captaincy offered in the regular Mounted Rifles. Captain Monroe M. Parsons led the troops on foot to the grazing camp at Delgado's ranch on Galisteo Creek where they had left their horses, the men grumbling under the fourteen-pound weight of the guns and sabres they carried and the ignominy of horse soldiers put afoot. Nine days later Parsons was relieved by Congreve Jackson, captain of Company G, a man who some thought was given

14. Connelley 1907, pp. 271–72. Walton's command of about 300 men was proceeding south from Albuquerque under directions of Col. Doniphan, who was then on his way to the treaty council at Ojo del Oso.

more to brooding than action but who nevertheless was elected to Ruff's vacant command by a majority of the volunteers. On September 25 Congreve Jackson received his commission as lieutenant colonel.

As the troops marched downriver for the crossing at Albuquerque, they heard complaints of Navajo attacks and rumors that a number of the pueblos were going to send war parties in reprisal. At Laguna, where the command arrived and went into camp September 28, a grim ceremony was in preparation, to be performed over four Navajo scalps. These had been brought in the day before by Laguna warriors after their pursuit of Navajos who had descended on the pueblo, killed two children and a man, and driven off a number of sheep. The scene that night made a vivid impression on Marcellus Edwards, an eighteen-year-old private who only a few months before had been a hired boy in the county clerk's office in Marshall, Missouri.

Edwards recalled that the ceremony started in a distant part of the pueblo, his awareness of it coming with the faint, hollow thump of a drum. The monotonous beat ended and a stillness prevailed for some time, when presently some thirty warriors bedecked in their finest kilts and buckskins filed silently into the plaza and formed into facing columns of two ranks. Their long hair was tied up neatly, and each wore an eagle plume and tuft of downy feathers hanging down at the back of the head. From eyebrows to jawline their faces were painted red, their foreheads black, their throats and the undersides of their chins stark white.

Much louder now, the hammering on the drum resumed, and the dance began with the two ranks of warriors frequently facing about and in quickstep stamping and moving forward and back, each warrior brandishing his weapons, whether bow and arrows or club or long-barreled musket. To their left and right, facing inward upon the dancing men, were single lines of women dancers, also attired in their best robes and maintaining the same quick-stamping step forward and backward while holding up their arms as though pledging their support. A rhythmic chanting progressing from low growl to staccato yelp accompanied the dancing and the waving about of the Navajo scalps, streaming at the ends of sticks or long poles. The dance continued through the night, a fellow soldier, Private Jacob S. Robinson, observing that as the tempo increased in fury occasional shots were fired at the bobbing, weaving scalps.[15]

15. Edwards, ed. Bieber 1936, pp. 183–84; and Robinson 1932, pp. 35–36. At Cochiti Pueblo, Bandelier was informed that when enemy scalps were brought in

From Laguna a winding, rough trail led the troops northward to the Mexican village of Moquino where they made camp on September 30, close to the towering volcanic plug marking the southern approach to Cebolleta, four miles distant. Water was scarce, the grass poor, and when his few wagons were unloaded Colonel Jackson discovered that the quartermaster in Santa Fe had furnished his command with enough food to last a few weeks only. Angered by this carelessness, Jackson ordered Second Lieutenant George P. Gordon to take a small escort back over their route and return with an adequate supply of provisions and medicine. At the same time, possibly on information received from the Diné Ana'aii leader Sandoval, Jackson determined to move his camp on Gordon's return to a place in the mountains to the west. This, Jackson was told, was a region occupied until recently by Sandoval's people, who had deserted their hogans and cornfields when told by the villagers of Cebolleta that the soldiers were coming to kill them. Sandoval's presence in Jackson's camp is unexplained; perhaps it was a casual encounter, but more likely Sandoval already had arranged to make himself useful. In any case, he agreed to go to the country of the Chusca Navajos to determine if they would talk peace with these Bilagáana (Americans).[16] In the meantime, Jackson could only wait. His men appear to have avoided going into Cebolleta, then a village of some five hundred persons, instead passing the hours at poker or playing ball.

In Santa Fe, Colonel Doniphan on October 6 received General Kearny's orders directing him to lead his regiment on a military expedition into Navajo country. He was not specifically instructed to take punitive measures, but was to confine his operation to securing peace with the tribe and negotiating for the release of Mexican captives and stolen livestock. Preparations began at once. Lieutenant Gordon, who had arrived from the Moquino camp to requisition supplies, was given an express for Jackson, directing him to send out part of his force to ask the Navajos to attend a peace council. A skeptical observer, Captain William M. D. McKissack, the assistant quartermaster, noted Gordon's departure and this new turn of events without enthusiasm:

they were paraded and then taken to a kiva "where they report to all the people about the campaign. Finally, the war dance and war song are performed, and the crowd disperses. The scalps are preserved by the cacique at his own house, hung to a round shield" (Lange and Riley, p. 163).

16. Bieber (1936, p. 32) says that Sandoval returned in about ten days, reporting "that most of the chiefs were inclined toward peace but that they would prefer to have the white men come into their country to discuss the terms of an agreement."

"Col. Doniphan has received orders to proceed against the Navahoe Indians, who have been at war with the Mexicans for years & refuse to make peace. . . . Since our arrival in the country they have committed many depredations & will require severe punishment before they cease to molest the Inhabitants; but I fear another Florida War if the Indians desire to protract it; as they live in the mountains impracticable for roads & can only be pursued slowly with pack mules for transporting stores, ec." [17]

Major Gilpin arrived in Santa Fe a week later with a delegation of about sixty Capote and Moache Ute warriors and headmen. After receiving his orders from Kearny slightly less than a month before, he had left the major part of his command in garrison at Abiquiu and with eighty-five men proceeded two hundred miles north into Ute country, on his march collecting tribesmen willing to come in and talk peace with the new government. Doniphan met the Utes in council October 13, 1846, and two days later reached agreement with them on treaty terms. At the same time, Gilpin was advised of the impending Navajo campaign and the part he would take in it after his return to Abiquiu. Shortly afterward, Doniphan alerted the three companies of volunteers in Santa Fe and ordered them to fatten their horses at a grazing camp, near San Miguel, on the road to Las Vegas.[18]

Averaging about twenty-four miles a day with his loaded wagons, Lieutenant Gordon reached Jackson's camp at Moquino on October 10, the fifth day out of Santa Fe, his arrival nearly coinciding with the return of Sandoval.

Colonel Jackson moved at once to comply with his orders, selecting Captain John W. Reid to lead a party of ten volunteers from each of his three companies westward to the Chuscas. Reid's prospects on the eve of departure may have been a bit disturbing: detailed accounts of Navajo attack were fresh in memory and the country to be penetrated was entirely unknown to him; he could take only three pack mules provisioned for four days, and thereafter his men must live off the country. It was not an easy mission. An individual named John Thomas, of whom nothing is known, was provided as guide and interpreter, sharing these duties with Sandoval. Private Robinson, one of

17. October 6, 1846: McKissack to Maj. Gen. Thomas S. Jesup, NA, RAC, RG 92, Office of the QM General, Consolidated Correspondence, file 1794–1915, box 987.

18. October 20, 1846: Doniphan to Secretary of War Marcy, NA, RAC, RG 94, 295-D-1846, AGO, LR.

those who volunteered, observed that Sandoval was accompanied by his son—a fine youth, Robinson thought, about twelve years old.[19]

The camp at Moquino was abandoned October 12, Jackson departing first with the main part of the command for a point on the Rio San José within five miles of Cubero or, as Marcellus Edwards termed it, "bucket town." The new camp was in the vicinity of cornfields and numerous hogans, which the troops set about destroying to obtain firewood. This evidently was the place of the Diné Ana'aii that Jackson had been told about at Moquino.[20] Burning the deserted hogans was an unnecessary arrogance that no doubt accounted for a retaliatory raid some ten days later.

Captain Reid's party in the meantime was slowly making its way upward through Cebolleta Canyon. After emerging on the barren high tableland above Cebolleta their route followed a northwesterly course, the horses finding difficult footing in places where the ground was covered with black cinders and porous rock of ancient lava flow. Snow covered the still distant but sharply outlined top of Mount Taylor, towering at their left, as well as lesser peaks of the same sprawling range on their right. Turning more toward the lowering sun, in late afternoon air that was mild but at 8,500 feet thin enough to make them gasp when they had to dismount and walk, the party—near the end of the second day out from Moquino—descended toward Lucas Canyon and what Robinson described as a valley. Here they encamped the night of October 13 near the rancherias where Sandoval made his home. The Diné Ana'aii leader was a rich man, Robinson observed, owning five thousand sheep and perhaps one hundred horses that grazed undisturbed over an elevated plain possibly three thousand feet higher than the country at the base of the mountain. In Robinson's eyes, Sandoval's home was an oasis of green grass and fine trees, of springs and rivulets and waterfalls casting veils of spray, a place where corn and wheat grew in rich abundance.[21]

For two days more, Sandoval led Reid's command ninety miles to the northwest. They saw numerous round hogans with masonry walls and roofs of poles and dirt north and west of Lucas Canyon, probably in the vicinity of present Seven Lakes, and on the approach to Chusca

19. Robinson 1932, pp. 39–40.

20. Edwards, ed. Bieber 1936, p. 188. The place was given the name "Camp San José."

21. Robinson 1932, pp. 41, 56. From Robinson's description of the route taken it appears that Sandoval's home was on a high plain of the northern slopes of Mount Taylor, some 25 miles northwest of Cebolleta.

Valley. Ascending the Chusca Mountains, the troops made a frosty camp on the summit the night of October 15, at the edge of a beautiful lake and near the hogan of an aging Navajo headman. Sunlight on the clear morning of the sixteenth showed them a high region of rolling grassland and meadows fringed with dark groves of tall fir and spruce, palisaded to the south by majestic red rock mesas.

Setting out with ten of the old Navajo's people, the soldiers presently encountered a group of about thirty warriors accompanied by eight or ten women: a delegation sent to meet and conduct them to a place where hundreds of Navajos already were assembled and awaiting them. The apparel of this well-mounted escort excited Robinson's interest. The men wore curious caps, skinned-out heads of mountain lion and lynx; nearly all carried finely figured blankets. The meeting may have occurred in the lower valley of Red Lake, or near Vizcarra's "Laguna Colorado," but Robinson's description of topography from here on is too sketchy to permit determining with certainty just where Reid's party went. The troops, followed by eight hundred mounted warriors and perhaps as many women, two days later came to the camp of the principal headman, Narbona.

While Reid's attention was occupied with his reception by Narbona and other headmen, the soldiers found themselves in a jostling crowd of Indians who overran the camp in their curiosity and desire to inspect or touch the firearms and other equipment of the extraordinary white people. Within minutes the camp took on the shouting, laughing atmosphere of a trade fair, as the Navajos pressed forward to barter—a hunting shirt of buckskin for a cotton shirt, a braided lariat for a tin cup, a softly tanned hide for a slice of tobacco or a butcher knife or for straps or buckles.

The scene became wildly festive. Having traded for the last trinket, the Navajos turned to a chase—as many as five hundred young men leaping on their horses when rabbits were flushed from cover, the astonished Robinson deciding that at no fox hunt or steeplechase of his memory had he seen anything to equal the horses and horsemanship of the Indians. All sounds except sharp yelps were drowned in a drumming thunder of hooves as the brown and black and dappled horses careened and wheeled and swept in lines or clusters across the wide plain, the naked riders like burrs low on their backs, or leaning back and throwing up their arms in mock warfare, feathers and feathered-fur headgear streaming in the wind. Tiring of this, the young men amused themselves at another game—hurling lances divested of metal points.

If well aimed, the lances passed through buckskin hoops six or eight inches in diameter as these were thrown to spin over the ground.

The women of the camp paid little heed to these things but concentrated intently on their own game of dice, played on either a blanket or a flat rock, the thrower casting three marked bones. Circles of pebbles were used as counters; the bets were any article of personal adornment, or a buckskin. As evening came on a large circle formed for a dance. To the music—a resonant thump of one small drum, knuckles pounding a thin hide tightly stretched over the mouth of a black pottery jar—seven young women, each wearing a scarlet blanket, stood side by side and stepped solemnly first to the right and then to the left. Between dances some dignified male member of the assemblage would walk slowly into the center of the firelit ring to deliver an oration. Unable to understand what was said, the soldiers were impatient for the dancing to resume. Only one man was permitted to stand at the head of the young women and join their dance, and the same man was not allowed to dance twice.

Like other discerning Americans who came after him, Robinson did not fail to notice that Navajo women, or many of them, were pretty and that their feet were unusually small. His effort to glimpse their ankles was frustrated by a wrapping of deerskin strips, which he thought unattractive, about their legs. The strings of beads he had seen them offering earlier as bets in their dice game may have been of turquoise or bone or shell, but of silver jewelry there evidently was none; Robinson observed only that the women wore brass rings on their arms, the larger the rings the better.

Most impressive of all, he thought, were the parti-colored blankets the women wore, which, as distinguished from the common blankets woven in stripes of blue, black, and white, they refused to part with for any consideration. Men and women both let their hair grow long; the men tied theirs up in a queue or, like the women, bound it with wool string at the back in a bunlike *chongo*. In his summary of these people, Robinson observed that Navajos mingled little with New Mexicans or Indians of other tribes, but considered themselves much their superiors.

Events of the day had turned out so amicably, and so easily had Captain Reid's men joined with the Navajos in barter and games, that by evening most of their fears that they might suddenly be attacked had been dispelled. On the soldiers' arrival at the camp their horses had been taken, supposedly to better pasturage some five miles away.

His concern about their recovery continued to trouble Captain Reid, who still regarded his situation as precarious although the Navajos for the most part showed a desire to be friendly. He had been greeted by a number of the tribe's principal men, among these, and regarded with the most respect by his people, the aging Narbona. Nothing in the man's manner of dress seems to have set him apart from the others. The severe effects of rheumatism (or probably arthritis), which nearly incapacitated him, Reid noted, failed to prevent him from advancing to the meeting as custom demanded—astride his horse.

Captain Reid judged Narbona to be about seventy years old and held in great reverence by his people for the warlike exploits of his youth and early manhood. Reid thought that this once-imposing leader was a diminished skeleton of a man—mild, amiable, anxious before his death to make peace for his people with their old enemies as well as the "New Men," as he called the Americans.[22]

Captain Reid engaged in a council with Narbona and the other head-men that night, while most of the Missourians appear to have elected to remain at the dance, which continued until dawn. Most of the Navajos at the council seemed disposed toward peace, but some thought it contrary to their honor, as well as their interest, to make peace with Mexicans, although with the New Men they were willing to do so. Those who favored a general peace prevailed in the end. Before the council dispersed, Captain Reid obtained promises from the principal men that they would overtake him at Agua Fria, forty miles from Congreve Jackson's camp on the Rio San José, and accompany him to Santa Fe to conclude a final peace treaty. The night was passed in a variety of diversions, of which sleep apparently was not one.

With light of morning, Reid prepared to depart. The fears he had held for his horses were baseless; upon learning his intentions the Navajos at once rounded up the animals and drove them to where the troops waited with saddles and bridles. Leaving Narbona's camp on October 19 and again relying upon Sandoval as guide, Reid's command was warned to be on the alert for less peaceable Navajos who might steal their horses. On the return route, which evidently took a more

22. Letter from Capt. Reid to John T. Hughes, author of *Doniphan's Expedition* (1847, pp. 170–72) and appearing also in the Connelley reprint (1907, pp. 291–93). Evidently named for Lt. Col. Antonio Narbona, the Navajo leader had been a spokesman for the peace faction of his nation at least since 1833. Three years after this event his home was said to have been in the Chusca Valley, near the present Two Gray Hills trading post.

southerly course through the Wingate Valley, they encountered groups of Navajos driving flocks of sheep; returning, it was learned, to their homes, from which they had fled in fear that Reid's troops had come out to destroy them. During the last few days the command's supplies of food ran out, and the weather, bitterly cold, caused some suffering. On the seventh day, with one of their companions near death, they raised Jackson's camp near Cubero.

Here they found muttering among the men of increasing cases of illness, possibly scurvy. Jokes were made at the expense of a private who had so enjoyed himself at a fandango in one of the blind pigs of the nearby town that he had wandered about lost, until morning, on the way back to camp. But most of the talk was about a raid on the camp several days before Captain Reid's return, in which forty horses had been run off. The Navajos were blamed for this, in a broad sense correctly. Ladrons of Cubero were quite capable of such larceny, but more probably the horses were stolen by Diné Ana'aii in retaliation for Colonel Jackson's having allowed his troops to burn their hogans on October 13.

Congreve Jackson apparently was little concerned with cause and effect, but he did share a not uncommon feeling about the proper treatment of Indians. He directed Captain Parsons to take sixty men out on the trail of the stolen horses and to scalp any Navajo in possession of any of the animals.

Captain Parsons rejoined Colonel Jackson's main command November 2, finding the troops in a new camp in a canyon about five miles north of Cubero. With them his men brought twenty-seven horses they had managed to recover. Their own mounts were bony and lame, near exhaustion from days of hard riding. Marcellus Edwards observed that the soldiers who accompanied the Reid and Parsons details were sickened by such campaigning. It was his opinion that the use of twelve-month volunteers such as his outfit in a war against the Navajos would be futile: "If the government has to bring them to terms of peace by force, she must employ men for that purpose who must come prepared to undergo the greatest hardships before they can dislodge them from their mountain retreats." An inexperienced soldier and former clerk, Edwards was entirely right.

A minor incident had occurred three days before Parsons' return. A company of fifty New Mexicans, poorly armed and presenting a motley appearance, approached the Missourians' camp. It was their intention,

they said (perhaps inspired by General Kearny's proclamation sanctioning guerrilla war parties), to campaign against the Navajos. They asked
to speak with the commanding officer, but Jackson refused to see them.

The lull that had settled over Santa Fe following Kearny's departure
was over. Confusion set in and the expedition to Navajo country was
delayed. The arrival of Colonel Sterling Price, instead of bringing
Doniphan relief, added to his problems, for Price brought 1,220 men of
the Second Regiment of Missouri Mounted Volunteers and an additional battalion of mounted troops.

Navajos were committing daily raids upon the New Mexicans. He
would start in a few days for their country, Doniphan wrote the secretary of war late in October. He would go as far and take as many troops
as his limited resources would permit, "and doubt not will bring the
war to a close in 30 days—We deem this a very important duty as the
Government owes the New Mexicans protection." Doniphan's cheerful
estimate of a thirty-day campaign with limited resources was characteristic of the popular military evaluation of Navajos at the time. There
was much that each side must learn of the other.

The valley leading west from the Rio Grande is lush green where the
Chama flows, broad or narrowing depending on the sand hills and
cones and mesas enclosing it, and shaded in summer by cottonwoods
that appear to have grown there since the beginning of time. The old
road winds a gently ascending course following the river's south bank.
From pale tan near the mother river the soil turns increasingly reddish
with each mile, the ranch houses found here and there among cornfields
consequently darkening in hue as one progresses upriver. So the buildings of Abiquiu, facing on a broad plaza, have the color of old buckskin once rubbed with a ball of red paint.

For all its long heritage, of which he perhaps knew nothing or cared
little, Major Gilpin may have considered the village strategically situated for a defensive garrison. Possibly that also is why its site was
chosen by Tewa Indians for a pueblo, years before the Spanish came.

Here there is a narrow pass between a red rock mesa thrusting down
from the north and an opposing wedge of even higher and dark rock,
the few houses perched on a saddle of the latter, the Chama River
flowing between and below. Geography as well as the events of time
had stamped it almost irrevocably as an Indian town; neither the Missourians of his two companies nor troops of the commanders who

followed Gilpin could change that. Long since buried, the Tewa pueblo was replaced by another built by the Spaniards who presently found themselves a minority among their own Indian blood relatives—most of these originally Hopis, captured or secured by barter.[23] Lastly, though above Abiquiu the valley broadens again before it becomes a deep chasm leading to the red, yellow, and purple cliffs and buttresses of the Piedra Alumbre, the town was so situated that it commanded a close view of and held in short range virtually every Navajo and Ute war party that for two hundred years followed the Chama to the settlements of the Rio Grande.

It was here, then, that the 180 men of Companies A and E formed columns in the morning of October 22, 1846, ready after days of waiting to begin their march into Navajo country. Santiago (James) Conklin, a veteran of packtrain trade with the Navajos, was attached to the command as guide and Navajo interpreter.[24] Other auxiliaries included 20 New Mexicans from Taos, an equal number of Pueblos, and 25 peons to whom Major Gilpin entrusted his train of pack mules.

From Abiquiu, Gilpin's command traveled northwest to the San Juan, for much of the way following the Chama. The country is one of deep canyons, grassy plateaus and still higher meadows, and small lakes that reflect the peaks and ridges of mountains. If a diary was kept by any of the soldiers, it has not been found. The only existing contemporary account was written by John T. Hughes, a private in Doniphan's Company C, which was quartered first in the vicinity of Santa Fe and then at various points on the Rio Grande but never west of Socorro. Most of what is known of Gilpin's and Doniphan's expeditions during the ensuing weeks is derived from this source, Hughes obtaining the salient information upon the return of those officers. If a few of his dates are in error, his factual record is generally believed to be sound;

23. "After the Tewa pueblo at Abiquiu was colonized by the Spaniards a number of Indian captives, mostly Hopi (Moki), were settled there by the Spaniards. . . . Bandelier's information agrees with that of the Tewa informants. . . . 'The modern town of Abiquiu stands almost on the site of an ancient village. That town was peopled in part by "Genizaros", or Indian captives, whom the Spaniards had rescued or purchased from their captors. The Tehuas [Tewa] of Santa Clara contend that most of these Genizaros came from the Moquis [Hopi], and that therefore the old pueblo was called Jo-so-ge' " (Harrington 1916, p. 137).

24. Hughes (1847, p. 177 n.), named Conklin among these auxiliaries, using the Spanish equivalent of James, but evidently failed to recognize his identity and listed him only as Gilpin's "Mexican interpreter." Conklin was 46 years old at the time. By his own testimony he was born in Canada, raised in St. Louis, and had lived in New Mexico since 1825 ("Condition of the Indian Tribes," *Senate Reports*, 39th Cong., 2d sess., 1866–67, p. 337).

only in his descriptive passages of country he never saw, but only imagined, does he go wildly astray. The journals of Jacob Robinson and Marcellus Edwards agree on the point that winter had set in early, that even in October in the mountain regions the troops suffered hardships —especially, no doubt, during the long nights when, with inadequate blankets and ragged summer clothing, their beds often were in deep snow in below-freezing temperatures. So harsh were the conditions, indeed, that from accounts of the returning troops Hughes imagined a country eternally crowned with snow and equated Gilpin's march over the Chuscas with Hannibal's conquest of the Alps.

Scarcely as formidable as the Italian Alps, the San Juan Mountains are rugged enough. Gilpin's command probably encountered them in the vicinity of present Dulce and descended to the San Juan soon afterward, perhaps somewhere between Pagosa Junction and Blanco. Westward, the river valley is open and level enough to have offered few obstacles. The bands of Aguila Negra and Archuleta lived in country just south of the river, and possibly these were the Navajos who came to Gilpin's camp November 9. They told him of Captain Reid's council with Narbona and other headmen west of the Chuscas, Gilpin confusing or misunderstanding their report to mean that a final treaty had been entered into. From his camp, then near the confluence of the Animas and the San Juan, Gilpin persuaded one of the Navajos to carry a message to this effect to Doniphan, whom he knew to be on his way to meet Congreve Jackson at Cubero.

Colonel Doniphan had left Santa Fe with his staff October 26, having ordered Companies B, C, and H to proceed from the grazing camp at San Miguel by way of Galisteo and Manuel Delgado's ranch and meet him at Santo Domingo. Four days later, the command having joined, Doniphan continued downriver, reaching Albuquerque early in the morning of November 1. Hughes, a firsthand observer, noted that "such of the men as were able, and desired it, purchased wine, and beer, and *mezcal*, which is made of the maguey, and of which the Mexicans are very fond," and the same day forded the wagons across the river, making camp a few miles below on the west bank. While in camp at this place Doniphan received reports of the recent Navajo raids on Los Lunas and Isleta and of a rumored force of Mexicans marching north from El Paso, threatening the safety of the several hundred traders whose wagons were halted at Valverde on their interrupted journey to Chihuahua. Although at the time it appeared to place himself in danger, Doniphan directed Captain Walton to take the three companies of his command in support of other troops already on their way to Valverde. With only his staff and a few other men Doniphan the next day continued toward Jackson's Camp San José.

Stories he heard of Navajo raids were probably exaggerated, and Doniphan may have feared that his own small party invited attack.[25] More likely, he knew that the Navajos for the most part shared a desire to be friendly to Americans; except for the engagement with Captain Grier, they had avoided armed clashes with the Bilagáana. He knew, in any event, that at Laguna Pueblo, forty-six miles west, he would meet the command of Major Benjamin B. Edmonson—three companies of the Second Regiment of Missouri Mounted Volunteers that he had previously ordered to the relief of Jackson's troops. His progress for the next three days was without incident and he arrived in Jackson's camp near Cubero on November 5.

The prospect that greeted him was not encouraging. Food supplies had run out and for days, until fresh provisions had been brought to them by Major Edmonson's wagons, Jackson's men had lived on pumpkins and parched corn appropriated from stores abandoned by the Diné Ana'aii. Many of the men were sick, a few had died, and most had discarded the tattered uniforms and boots issued long months and miles in the past at Fort Leavenworth in favor of buckskins and moccasins.

After Doniphan had spent nearly a week in uncertain waiting upon the Navajos who had promised to follow Captain Reid in two days, Sandoval and a number of Navajo headmen appeared at the camp. They told Doniphan that in ten days many more of the tribe's principal men would meet him in council at Ojo del Oso. No further reference to Sandoval is made by the diarists but it is apparent that he remained with the troops or in close touch. Edwards says that after their meeting with Doniphan the Navajos "were dismissed with a few presents."

The Navajo carrying Major Gilpin's message written three days before on the San Juan came into Doniphan's camp November 12. The colonel sent him back with a reply: it was not true that Captain Reid had made a treaty with the Navajos—Reid had secured only an agreement to have them meet in council; this would be held at Ojo del Oso and Gilpin was directed to be at that place on November 20, bringing with him as many Navajo headmen as he could persuade to come. Doniphan then made plans to leave the sick with Captain Horatio H.

25. Lt. James W. Abert, hearing a warped account while at Atrisco on October 26, related that Navajos "devastated the whole valley, killing all the human kind they met. . . ." (Abert, reprint ed., 1962, p. 96).

Hughes at Cubero and on November 17 start for the council place with Lieutenant Colonel Jackson and about 150 troops. On the same day the men who had accompanied the expeditions of Captains Reid and Parsons were to start back for the river and their places be taken by fresh troops waiting at Laguna with Major Edmonson.

Doniphan's message was brought to Major Gilpin during his ascent of a pass over the Chusca Mountains, a difficult proposition in the best of seasons but made unusually so then because snow covered the switch-back trail at the higher elevations. To reach this place from his camp on the San Juan, Gilpin had proceeded without haste. Frequently encountering Navajos during his march, he traveled forty miles downriver on November 10 and 11 and then, in the vicinity of Shiprock peak, turned south into the broad Chusca Valley. It is unlikely that he found snow here, but three days more were required to travel fifty miles to the stony, barren slopes that mark the lower eastern approaches to the Chuscas. From the valley below to the summit his men toiled upward for three thousand feet, for much of that distance through snow.

A less persevering officer might have turned back, but with five days left before he was expected at Ojo del Oso, and no doubt with the assurances of James Conklin that most of the Navajos were yet to be found ahead, Gilpin continued. Doniphan relates that upon crossing the Chuscas, Gilpin made his way "by the Red Lake to the valley of the little Colorado"—which is only partly correct—and Hughes more accurately notes that the night of November 17 the command stayed at Canyon del Trigo (so named because here the Navajos cultivated extensive fields of wheat). Large numbers of Indians visited Gilpin's camp next morning, all expressing their wish to be friends. By evening the troops were encamped within sight of Canyon de Chelly.[26] Of its several gorges, it appears that Gilpin's command skirted Monument Canyon, the southern branch of Canyon de Chelly. From here he started early in the morning of November 19 for his rendezvous with Doniphan. He was accompanied by a few Navajo headmen and about thirty of his command, probably including Conklin, and reached Ojo del Oso by a forced march the following day. Most of his troops he left with Captain David Waldo, who followed more slowly and arrived at the meeting place November 22.

26. The Doniphan quotation is from his only known report of the expedition, an undated, three-paragraph message to Adj. Gen. Jones (*Senate Exec. Docs.*, 30th Cong., 1st sess., no. 1, pt. 1, p. 496). Canyon del Trigo, or Wheat Canyon, is situated near the head of Pueblo Colorado Wash, north and slightly west of the later site of Fort Defiance.

Located on the rising southern slope of the Wingate Valley, here several miles wide, Ojo del Oso—Bear Spring—for years had been a stopping place for Navajo war parties. In contrast to the red rock mesas forming a wall opposite, the spring occupied a gently tilted ground, the soil yellow and sandy, the covering of moderate-sized piñon and cedar, ranging according to the light from gold-flecked green to almost black. Before the time of the earliest Navajos, the spring had been used by Anasazi, whose ruined pueblos were discovered in low walls for the valley's entire length.[27]

Doniphan and the troops accompanying him arrived at Ojo del Oso the morning of November 21, finding Gilpin's small force waiting for them in the middle of an encampment of five hundred or more Navajos.[28] Thirteen inches of snow had fallen in the valley several nights before and at that elevation, over 6,500 feet, the weather was intensely cold. The troops had no tents; presumably they and the Navajos alike improvised brush shelters.

Zarcillos Largos, not a young man, as Hughes says, but then well into middle age, appears to have been the Navajos' principal spokesman. Preliminary talks only were held the first day, Doniphan explaining the purposes of his government in New Mexico and his own objectives in asking the headmen to meet with him. Hughes possibly had access later to a transcript or notes of what was said; he does, in any case, quote Zarcillos Largos as replying that while he admired the spirit and enterprise of the Americans, he "detested the Mexicans." During the council the following day, Hughes notes that a man he names as T. Caldwell, of whom nothing is known, served as interpreter.

Doniphan emphasized that Navajo attacks on New Mexicans must cease or the Navajos would face war with the United States. He pointed out that because his government had taken military possession of New Mexico, the laws of his country now extended over this territory and the lives, property, and rights of its inhabitants were assured protection under his flag. He had come to Ojo del Oso, he said, because it was his country's desire to enter into a treaty of peace with the Navajo nation, whose people then should have the same protection accorded the New Mexicans.

He had come with ample powers, he told the Navajos, to negotiate a

27. Called Shash Bitoh by Navajos, the spring was located about 14 miles east of present Gallup, New Mexico, on the later site of new Fort Wingate.

28. Hughes, upon whose account the following references to the council and treaty are based, said 500 Navajos were present. Doniphan reported that "large numbers of them, perhaps three-fourths of their tribe, collected at Ojo del Oso. . . ."

permanent peace, but if they refused to treat on honorable terms he had been instructed to make war against them. His tone became threatening. He warned them not to enter into a treaty unless they could do so in good faith, as "the United States made no second treaty with the same people; that she first offered the olive branch, and if that were rejected, then powder, bullet, and the steel."

Zarcillos Largos responded directly to Doniphan's threat, at the same time explaining the Navajo logic of recent raids on the Rio Grande:

> Americans! you have a strange cause of war against the Navajos. We have waged war against the New Mexicans for several years. We have plundered their villages and killed many of their people, and made many prisoners. We had just cause for all this. You have lately commenced a war against the same people. You are powerful. You have great guns and many brave soldiers. You have therefore conquered them, the very thing we have been attempting to do for so many years.
>
> You now turn upon us for attempting to do what you have done yourselves. We cannot see why you have cause of quarrel with us for fighting the New Mexicans on the west, while you do the same thing on the east.
>
> Look how matters stand. This is *our war*. We have more right to complain of you for interfering in our war, than you have to quarrel with us for continuing a war we had begun long before you got here. If you will act justly, you will allow us to settle our own differences.

If some of the phrasing is that of Hughes, the sense and bite of these words is not; this truly is Zarcillos Largos speaking. Among his listeners were aging veterans of this prolonged war: Juanico, whom Vizcarra had tried to hunt down in the wilderness above Marsh Pass; José Largo, who had been captured six years before in Salazar's campaign; Narbona, who remembered the Spanish conquest of Canyon de Chelly forty-one years before and now wanted peace; and Segundo, who once had counseled peace and then been captured in that 1805 campaign.

In reply Doniphan said that the war between the Americans and New Mexicans had ended—the New Mexicans had surrendered. It was the custom of his governmenut, he explained, when a people capitulated, to treat them as friends. The country and its citizens now belonged to the United States by conquest, so that in the future if the Navajos stole property from the New Mexicans they were stealing from Americans; if they killed New Mexicans they were killing Americans.

The high plane of this reasoning may have been beyond the Navajos' understanding. They had seen how Colonel Doniphan's troops behaved toward the conquered enemy in Santa Fe; possibly they were confused by the continuing sounds of warfare in the country below. In generations of war between the Navajos and Spaniards and then Mexicans, no quarter ever had been asked or given. The Navajos had no equivalent for the word "surrender." The concept of protecting a defeated enemy was as strange to them as it was to the New Mexicans. Perhaps because the forcefulness of Doniphan's personality made a deeper impression upon the Navajos than was conveyed in the interpreter's version of his words, Zarcillos Largos took a more conciliatory position. If the country in truth belonged to the Americans and the Bilagáana intended to hold and rule it, he said, the Navajos would cease their raids, for they had no quarrel with Americans nor any wish to have war with so powerful a nation.

The treaty that was signed after this exchange contained five articles, of which three were similar to or based upon terms long familiar to Navajos. The treaty provided for a lasting peace between the American people and the Navajo nation; for mutual trade (with an added provision that, with full protection, Americans, New Mexicans, Pueblos, and Navajos would have free access to the others' territory); and for all property taken by either party from the other since August 18, to be restored. The new terms—perhaps startling in their newness—declared that New Mexicans and Pueblos were included in the term "American people" (whereas the Navajos were not) and called for a mutual restoration of all prisoners, the several parties being pledged to redeem by purchase such captives as were not returned in equal exchange.[29]

Insofar as it proposed a mutual—if conditional—return of prisoners, the treaty in concept marked a step forward, but it fell short of Armijo's treaty of 1841 by failing to recognize and prohibit the evil of slave raiding. As Captain McKissack was one of the first to predict, the treaty was soon broken. Blame for this was laid entirely upon the Navajos, but the responsibility was not theirs alone. The treaty failed because no effort was made to implement it. Doniphan appears to have dismissed it from his mind in his desire to join General Wool and neglected even

29. For the United States the treaty was signed by Doniphan, Lt. Col. Jackson, and Maj. Gilpin, Navajo headmen who attached their cross-marks were Zarcillos Largos, Caballada Mucha, Alexandro, Cayetanito, José Largo, Narbona, Segundo, Pedro José, Manuelito, Tapio (José Tapia), Archuleta, Juanico, and—for the Diné Ana'aii—Sandoval and Savoietta (Cebolleta) García. Among those who notably did not sign were Cayetano, Armijo, and Aguila Negra.

to notify Governor Bent that a treaty with Navajos had been made.

The treaty failed also because, in spite of what Zarcillos Largos said about the numbers and power of American soldiers, a sizable faction of the Navajo tribe remained unimpressed. The importance of this last circumstance cannot be exaggerated. If the muskets and cannon of the Americans were superior to Navajo muskets and bows and arrows, the American horses were not. Most Navajos now and for some time to come regarded themselves superior to the Bilagáana in both numbers and fighting ability. They had no understanding whatever of the overwhelming resources the United States could bring against them.

Two of the younger headmen who signed the treaty but evidenced no feeling of awe at the Americans' strength were the brothers Cayetanito and Manuelito, said to be the sons of Cayetano. Cayetanito or K'aak'eh (Wounded), the younger of the two, was identified with the war faction of the tribe until, late in 1861 (a year after his father's death), he became a leading spokesman for peace.[30]

Standing nearly six feet six inches tall and of powerful frame, Manuelito was to become one of the great war leaders of the tribe. He had probably been born between 1818 and 1820 in the vicinity of the Bear's Ears in southeastern Utah. A member of the Bit'ahnii clan, he had won recognition as a warrior at an early age, in 1835 taking part in the rout of Mexican and Pueblo forces led by Captain Blas de Hinojos at Washington Pass and two years later in a devastating Navajo attack on Oraibi Pueblo. While still a youth in Anglo terms, he married a daughter of Narbona, then by Navajo custom moved to the region of her home, in this case southeast of present Tohatchi in the lower Chusca Valley. As his leadership in war became better known he was called by Navajos Nabaah Jilt'aa, or Warrior Grabbed Enemy.[31]

30. For at least 40 years before he died of causes not known but shortly prior to December 27, 1860, Cayetano was generally aligned against the whites. From the early period of American occupation his home was in the vicinity of Beautiful Mountain, then called Monte del Cayetana or Cayetano Mountain. Sometimes confused by the military with his son Cayetanito, his name was given a variety of spellings: Cyotanos, Caetanos, Cayatena, Quietanas, Ki-a-tan-a, and Ky-a-tan-a. The relationship between Cayetanito and Manuelito was brought to light in testimony of Manuelito's grandson, Eddie Nakai, before the Indian Land Claim Commission in 1961 (Navajo Tribe v. U.S. Docket 229, pp. 2516–2618). In the Hughes version of the Doniphan treaty, Cayetanito's name is spelled Kiatanito.

31. Testimony of Eddie Nakai, cited above; also J. Lee Correll, "Manuelito, Navajo Naat'aani," Navajo Times, September 9, 1965; and Van Valkenburgh and McPhee (1938, p. 7). Correll notes that Manuelito had two other brothers,

Colonel Doniphan concluded the Ojo del Oso council by distributing a few presents among the headmen and then gave orders for Captain Parsons and part of the command to begin their return next day to the Rio Grande. With Major Gilpin and his detachment and accompanied also by Lieutenant Colonel Jackson and three Navajo headmen, Doniphan continued south to Zuni. Hughes did not name the Navajos, but since Doniphan's object was to arrange a treaty between the Zunis and Navajos, it is likely that Zarcillos Largos and Narbona were two of those who went with him. The Americans were given a friendly welcome, but the Navajos were not. So hostile was their reception that a guard was ordered to protect them from harm while they remained at the pueblo. Mutual enmities, ancient and recent, were aired at a council over which Doniphan unhappily presided; at moments it appeared that violence might flare up before his eyes. The review of past grievances created an atmosphere of intense animosity, but Doniphan refused to abandon his purpose. Only because of his insistence, the semblance of a peace treaty was made November 26.

If any formal document or handful of notes recorded these proceedings, it remains undiscovered. In his brief, undated report to Adjutant General Roger Jones, Doniphan said he had made "a permanent treaty" with the Navajos, but was silent in respect to the compact made under duress at Zuni.

Major Gilpin departed with his troops at the conclusion of that council, Doniphan following the next day with Congreve Jackson and an escort of seven men. It was at precisely this time, although Doniphan had no way of knowing it, that all of the dubious accomplishments of Ojo del Oso fell apart.

The Englishman George Frederick Ruxton, traveling northward against the tide of American troops on the Rio Grande and stopping for a bit with the merchant caravan at Valverde, noted with disdain what he described as a slovenly lack of order and gross insubordination among the Missouri volunteers encamped in the vicinity. There may have been some cause for Ruxton's criticism. If so, and if the lack of discipline was common among all or most units on the river, it was no wonder that in the morning of November 26 one of the commands

---

K'ayelli (One with Quiver), and El Ciego (the Blind One). After marrying, Manuelito was known first by the name given by Navajos to the place where he lived: Ch'ilhaajini, or Black Weeds.

below Socorro discovered singular losses of livestock. A New Mexican pastor employed to guard the animals attached to the command was missing, and with him had disappeared seventeen government mules. Tracks leading in another direction showed where more than eight hundred sheep intended to supply the troops with mutton had been run off. Two Lafayette County volunteers, Privates James Stewart and Robert Spears, through the incredible carelessness of their commanding officer, were sent to recover the sheep and bring them back.

The bodies of Stewart and Spears, bristling with Navajo arrows, were found later six miles to the west. With laxness on their part matching the incompetence of their orders, they had started off without rifles or sidearms and had been unable to defend themselves. The heads of both men were thoroughly smashed with stones. A pursuit was organized, thirty men riding out with Lieutenant Linnaeus B. Sublette, but the party returned next day, their horses foundered with hard riding, to report complete failure.[32]

Evidence indicated that only a few Navajos were involved. Almost certainly they had not been present at the Ojo del Oso council. Proof is lacking, but in all likelihood the raid and murders were in retaliation for the shooting and scalping of three Navajos by Captain Grier a month before: almost invariably, such incidents were repaid in kind. Word of the affair spread rapidly and was the cause of consternation and headshaking: the two Missouri volunteers were the first American soldiers to be killed by Navajos. Their deaths were taken to mean that the Navajos did not intend to honor their treaty with Doniphan but wanted war.

Meanwhile, Doniphan and Gilpin met again at Laguna Pueblo and from there proceeded to the river, reaching Socorro December 12. For reasons known only to himself, Doniphan felt it unnecessary to notify the civil authorities at Santa Fe of the outcome of his expedition. His offhand neglect to communicate details of his treaty obligations or of any other responsibilities incurred during his expedition to Governor Bent marks the beginning of breakdown, the initial wedge between military and civil officers in New Mexico.

"I have been informed indirectly," Governor Bent advised Secretary of State James Buchanan, "that Col. A. W. Doniphan who in October

32. Accounts of the episode are related by Hughes (in Connelley 1907, p. 275), Ruxton (in Twitchell, *Facts of New Mexican History*, vol. 2, p. 219, n. 157), Robinson (1932, p. 63), and Drumm (in Magoffin 1962, p. 109, n. 40). Hughes says the incident occurred November 27, the Navajos running off 873 sheep.

last marched with his regiment against the Nabajo Indians has made a treaty of peace with them. Not having been officially notified of this treaty, I am not able to state the terms, upon which it has been concluded, but so far as I have been able to learn, I have but little ground to hope that it will be permanent." [33]

33. December 26, 1846: Charles Bent, Santa Fe, to James Buchanan, NA, Dept. of New Mexico, AGO, Old Letter Book No. 1, bound as 5.

6

Campaigns of 1847–49

Late winter in the first new year of American occupation found the forces of Colonel Price weakened by scurvy and thinly spread on two fronts. In the Rio Abajo two companies of the First Dragoons returning in late March to headquarters at Albuquerque from the insurrectionary battle of Taos (which does not concern us here) were alerted frequently—usually too late—to renewed attacks by Navajos. Assurances of Zarcillos Largos to the contrary, Navajo warfare against New Mexicans had not ceased.

In the months following the departure of Colonel Doniphan and the murder at Taos of Governor Bent and five others, Colonel Price found that raids on Spanish livestock commanded less of his attention than attacks on his grazing camps by allied New Mexican and Indian forces under the guerrilla leader Manuel Cortés. One observer of this scene, whose lack of protective bark was equaled by his youth and candor, was Philip Ferguson, a printer's apprentice when he enlisted in the Third Missouri Regiment. His diary entry of September 2, 1847, noted, "The Santa Fe Battalion started today on an expedition into the Navajo country, these Indians having violated their treaty with Colonel Doniphan by their robberies of the Mexicans. The three companies composing this battalion are made up principally of re-enlisted volunteers and are a very wild and reckless set. Nearly every man left drunk!"

A jaunty informality seems to have characterized the expedition. No official report of the campaign has been found and it is almost certain that Major Robert Walker, commanding the battalion, made none. In the carefree manner of its planning, Walker's campaign exemplified Colonel Doniphan's notion that Navajos could be whipped to their knees in thirty days, more or less, by any determined and well-led force. It was the first punitive expedition by American troops against the

Navajos but in the looseness of its organization bore some resemblance to earlier Mexican slaving raids. The weekly Santa Fe *Republican*, ignoring the liquorish departure, observed that since Doniphan's treaty of the previous November, Navajos on various occasions had marauded through the territory, killing many New Mexicans and driving off large numbers of stock, some of which was owned by Americans, and that there were troops enough on hand to make it unnecessary to tolerate such outrages. The *Republican* reported that Major Walker's volunteers had left with two months' provisions, "their search being through a country exceedingly rough and broken. . . . all of these men are hardened and inured to the service and are determined upon giving this set of marauders a chastizing which they will not soon forget." [1]

Walker's command probably included a number of New Mexican and Indian guides, although no mention of them is made in the *Republican* story, which comments only that Walker's junior officers were Captains John L. Hamilton, William H. Grove, and William B. Armstrong, their mounted troops accompanied by a detachment of artillery—a rare occasion when cannon were dragged into Navajo country. The artillery, detached from Captain Francis Hassendeubel's company serving with the First Dragoons at Taos, would not have included Henry Dodge, whose intimate acquaintance with Navajos began at a later time. [2]

Seven or eight days after its departure the battalion crossed the Rio Grande below Albuquerque and marched nearly due west. At Ojo de la Jara, a familiar landmark on the old Spanish trail between Acoma and Zuni, Major Walker left his wagons under strong guard and proceeded with pack animals and ten days' provisions. From Zuni the command pressed north through forested hilly country to Cienega Amarilla, then past the later site of Fort Defiance and on to Red Lake. From a base camp there, three detachments were sent out in different

1. Santa Fe *Republican*, September 10, 1847. Previous references have stated that the campaign was made early in 1847, an error traceable to the September 27, 1858 report of Superintendent James L. Collins to the Commissioner of Indian Affairs. This account is based upon articles published in the *Republican* of September 17 and 24, October 16, and November 27, 1847, and January 15, 1848.

2. Dodge enlisted July 15, 1847, at Santa Fe in Battery A, Light Artillery, Santa Fe Battalion of New Mexico Mounted Volunteers. His battery later was attached to Maj. Benjamin Lloyd Beall's 1st Dragoons, then at Taos. When he was discharged at Las Vegas on August 27, 1848, he requested that instead of bounty land he be given the alternative payment of $100, which he received in script (NA, RAC, RG 15, 1817-SC-1773).

directions. Captain Grove's command returned on the second day and
Captain Hamilton's on the third, both reporting they had failed to find
either Navajos or Navajo stock. A third party, fifteen men under Second
Lieutenant Thomas H. Coats, scouting westward to the head of Pueblo
Colorado Wash, was surprised and fired upon in close rocky terrain
by about twenty Navajo warriors. Determining that he had taken no
casualties, Coats led his men in a charge in which one Navajo was
killed and several were wounded. The other Navajos withdrew, leaving
a number of their horses to be captured or shot by the pursuing
soldiers.

Upon the return of Lieutenant Coats, discovering that his provisions
were exhausted, Major Walker marched toward Canyon de Chelly,
presumably on the advice of his guides and in the hope of capturing
Navajo sheep and finding other supplies of food. His command, now
numbering about 140 men or slightly less than half its full strength,
reached the mouth of Canyon de Chelly and penetrated the canyon six
miles. The stillness of the deep gorge, disturbed only by the sound of
their mounted progress, soon convinced the troops that further advance
was futile—the Navajos had long since abandoned the place and taken
their livestock with them. Walker's decision to leave most of his supplies at Ojo de la Jara and live off the fat of Navajo land was then
seen to have been a terrible mistake: because of the lateness of the
season, cornfields already had been stripped bare and no other crops
were to be found. Retracing their own tracks to the canyon mouth the
troops found that not quite all of the Navajos had vanished: on
rimrock high above, small figures against the sky, a few of the Indians
were watching Walker's withdrawal from well beyond the range of his
muskets.

This much and only a bit more the major related when he returned
with a small escort to Santa Fe for more supplies October 14. The
campaign, far from being a success, had nearly ended in disaster. Close
to the point of starvation while still camped at Canyon de Chelly,
Walker's men had begun the long march to Ojo de la Jara in a mood
verging on panic. One by one, they killed and ate their pack mules.
When the last mule was gone they subsisted on the meat of dogs—no
other game being found—and wild parsley. Their acute distress finally
was relieved by the arrival of a detachment that had been sent ahead
to Zuni for provisions, which the Zunis offered generously. His battalion, Walker said, was encamped in the Zuni Mountains awaiting his

return.[3] Shortly thereafter, as winter closed in, the battalion was assigned to duty at Socorro.

Indirectly, because Walker's battalion suffered more punishment than it inflicted, the campaign had one effect upon the Navajos that might have been beneficial in other circumstances. Late in November several headmen came to Santa Fe to ask for another council of peace. Neither they nor the official with whom they spoke is identified, although the latter may have been Colonel Edward W. B. Newby, then commanding the Ninth Military Department of New Mexico. Conditions for discussing peace were not suitable, the Navajos were told; they were directed to bring more of their principal men to Santa Fe, and also to bring with them and turn over all captive prisoners and all livestock taken by the tribe. No mention was made of a reciprocal surrender of Navajo captives. The headmen departed, saying they would comply with the proposals and return before the next full moon.

"We have no faith in their promise to do so," the *Republican* commented, "nor do we believe that a lasting peace can be made until they have felt the full force and power of the Government." G. K. Gibson, the newspaper's founder and editor, expressed the hope that officials in Washington would direct at least a battalion of troops into Navajo country to lay it waste and wage a war of destruction.

There is no evidence that a second Navajo delegation returned. In January 1848, however, another item in the same newspaper observed that the Navajos had been quiet for the last two or three months, or since troops had been sent to garrison the Rio Abajo. The Navajos continued at peace until the next April, when raids on New Mexican livestock were resumed.

Colonel Edward W. B. Newby appears to have been a competent officer whose term of eleven months in command of the Ninth Military Department has been neglected or overlooked entirely by historians. Bancroft mentions his name three times and Twitchell, demoting him in rank to lieutenant colonel, twice. For three reasons at least he deserves better treatment. He was the first of only two Ninth Department commanders to complain of having many more troops at his disposal than he needed. He was the first military officer to acknowledge and call to the attention of superiors in Washington the often

3. A search of files at the National Archives has failed to turn up any report of the campaign.

crippling rivalry between civil and military branches of territorial authority. Lastly, he led a campaign against the Navajos that resulted in a second American treaty with the tribe. Like Doniphan's treaty, it was never ratified; it was not much worse or better than the treaties that had preceded it.

Colonel Newby, not a professional soldier, was unaccustomed to the punctilious filing of reports. Only indirectly, by his oblique reference at a later date, is any light shed on the cause of renewed Navajo raids in the spring of 1848. Probably in March or early April (Newby is vague on the point), New Mexican raiders stole immense numbers of cattle and sheep from the Navajos.[4] He does not say so, but it is safe to assume that the Navajos retaliated with such force that Newby felt impelled to lead a punitive expedition against their traditional stronghold—the vicinity once known to Spaniards as Casafuerte. He would go with no thought of making peace, the *Republican* observed incorrectly, "but to give them a good flogging which they richly deserve for their many depredations." [5]

The command that started from Santa Fe May 1, 1848, comprised 150 men of the Third Missouri Mounted Volunteers and 50 Illinois Infantry, also mounted for this occasion. Newby proceeded to Jemez, where he obtained guides, and then on May 4 continued in a northwesterly direction. Late in the sixth day, in the broad plain of the upper Chusca Valley, the column came upon four or five Navajo horsemen moving leisurely not far in advance. Newby ordered a detachment of men on the best horses to overtake and seize the Indians, but soon saw from the ease with which the Navajos outdistanced their pursuers that it would be folly to march openly upon them. The superiority of their horses to his own surpassed every previous notion. Camp was made at the foot of Beautiful Mountain, referred to by Newby as "Monte del Cayatana," which he found an extremely rugged natural barrier to the inner Navajo country. The immediate presence of the Indians in large numbers was made known to the troops almost at once. Clouds of dust rising in the near distance indicated that the Navajos were gathering large herds of their livestock, but mainly sheep, and driving them westward to the mountain foothills and into a pass across the mountains.

Enough daylight remained to make Newby believe a determined pursuit could be successful. He accordingly directed Captain David D.

---

4. June 17, 1848: Newby to Jones, NA, RAC, RG 94, 90-N-1848, AGO, LR.
5. Santa Fe *Republican*, April 2, 1848.

Stockton of the Missouri Volunteers to take fifty men and follow the Navajos' trail with all possible speed, emphasizing that Stockton was "not to halt until he had overtaken them." [6] Others who heard the orders remembered the colonel as being even more emphatic and explicit: Stockton was instructed to pursue the Navajos "night and day until [he] overtook them—to secure their stock, and scour the country."

Leaving the main body of troops probably in the vicinity of present Sa-nos-tee, Captain Stockton appears to have followed Peña Blanca Creek on its course through the boulder-strewn, gradually climbing approach to the pass. Here, after proceeding some five miles, he ordered his men to halt and make camp. How faithfully he had carried out his instructions is open to question: there is evidence that many Navajos were observed nearby and a case might be made that he at least had "overtaken" them. There is evidence also that, regardless of what Colonel Newby had told him, Stockton wished to avoid trouble.

At daylight the next morning Stockton's men awoke to find Navajos to their right and left driving hundreds of sheep toward the pass. To their astonishment the captain gave no order to attack, but allowed the Navajos to escape with their stock. One of the Missourians, a private named Green, observed the captain's inertia with puzzled surprise. When a few of the volunteers set out on their own initiative and brought back eleven Navajo prisoners, all well armed and mounted, Green asked Captain Stockton for permission to take ten soldiers in an effort to capture a part of the sheep. Stockton refused the request, saying he was sure that the Navajos presently would bring the stock in themselves and voluntarily surrender.[7] Stockton, who appears to have lapsed into a paralysis of fear, did manage to send an express back to Newby informing the colonel of his situation.

Newby at once mounted his command and proceeded to Stockton's camp. Here he found only four or five of the Navajos captured earlier, the others having been allowed to ride off.

"I was astonished to find," Newby remarked later, "that the Prisoners were mounted, well armed, and running at large through the encampment." He was further surprised to discover that a number of Indians were within close range in the hills surrounding his position, that Stock-

---

6. June 17, 1848: Newby to Jones, cited above.

7. Private Green and 2d Lt. James M. Hunt of the Illinois regiment returned to Santa Fe on May 17, in advance of the main command. Green's comments are quoted from an account of the campaign published in the Santa Fe *Republican* of May 21, 1848.

ton's troops were scattered and variously at ease, and that most of the men were wandering about unarmed.

This informal scene was transformed a moment later when Newby ordered the remaining prisoners disarmed and dismounted. As hands reached out to seize their weapons, the Navajos wheeled their horses in flight, at the same time opening a fire of arrows and musket balls that was augmented by a fusillade directed on the camp from all sides by their companions in the hills. Forty or fifty rounds were expended by the troops from such cover as they could find before the Navajos broke off the fight and withdrew. Several Navajos were wounded and four were left dead. A pursuit was formed with such effect that Newby soon called a halt "for the purpose of disencumbering myself of the greater part of the prisoners"—how many there were, he does not say.

His report of the engagement then appears to telescope the remaining events of that day and the next into one. Another version, appearing soon afterward in the *Republican*, probably was more accurate: "The next morning Col. Newby proceeded on with his command, having sent out scouting parties, and met two or three of the chiefs coming in to make peace, he told them he did not want peace, but wanted to fight them—he also told them he would give them three days to bring in their people, and if they would then make peace to his satisfaction, he would then enter into a treaty with them." [8]

Newby waited nine days in camp at Beautiful Mountain for the peace delegation to come in. Then, on May 20, he signed a treaty with José Largo, Narbona, Zarcillos Largos, and five other headmen.[9] No account of the proceedings other than a treaty copy has been found. A possible division of feeling among the Navajos over making peace with the Bilagáana is suggested by the absence of Cayetano, whose home this region was and who also had failed to sign Doniphan's treaty. If, indeed, there had been ill-feeling on Cayetano's part in the past, there was understandable cause for hostility now: the four Navajos killed by Newby's command in all probability were members of Cayetano's band. From his viewpoint, furthermore, the seizure of Navajo prisoners and killing and wounding of others was unprovoked—a retaliation for Navajo raids on enemy Mexicans in a continuing war that, to Navajo minds, was none of the Americans' business.

The treaty opened with a declaration of "firm and lasting peace" be-

8. Ibid.
9. Others who signed were Chapitone, Archuleta, Juan Lucero, Segundo, and Pablo Pino. A copy of the treaty is enclosed with Newby's June 17 report to Jones, cited above.

tween Navajos and the people of the United States and New Mexico "during its occupation by the United States"—the last phrase, repeated twice, suggesting that, in Colonel Newby's mind at least, the Americans' stay in the territory might be of limited duration. An important provision of the Doniphan treaty was given greater emphas's in another article that provided for the restoration of all prisoners of both sides, the restoration to be complete regardless of the number of captives either party held.

Newby assured the Navajos that during their occupation of New Mexico the Americans would guarantee strict observance of the treaty by New Mexicans. His motive was sound, but it was a rash promise— one he was able to implement only in part. A mutual exchange of some captives was arranged, but in a matter of weeks a company of New Mexicans was raiding again in Navajo country.

The fifth and last article omitted the usual demand for restoration of all livestock taken by Navajos, possibly because, as Newby observed, New Mexicans very recently had taken "immense herds" of sheep and cattle from the tribe, but it did require the Navajos to surrender three hundred sheep and one hundred mules and horses as indemnity for expenses incurred by the campaign.

On June 17, following his return to Santa Fe, Colonel Newby reported the Navajos had fully complied with their part of the agreement, having delivered the stipulated number of animals and surrendered twelve captives. He may have overstated the case, for the *Republican* observed that in the evening of July 5 a delegation of Navajos appeared in the capital bringing a large herd of horses from which the army quartermaster would select about fifty—this completing the number the Navajos had agreed to give up. They also brought in two or three more captives and would have brought more, the *Republican* continued, "had it not been for a Mexican expidition which has been out against them, and drove a large party of Navijos from the country, or to such a distance that they were not able to come in."

Having violated the treaty by renewed aggression, the New Mexicans then consented to an equal exchange of captives. For the Navajos it was an emotional reunion. The writer of the *Republican* story noted that "the Navijos manifested great parental affection on meeting with their children and wives, which had been taken prisoners by the Mexicans. We have every reason now to believe that . . . all hostilities will cease unless the Mexicans are the first to transgress." [10]

Larger events in distant places made their inevitable imprint. The

10. Santa Fe *Republican*, July 8, 1848.

war with Mexico came to an end in the spring of 1848, bringing Sterling Price back to Santa Fe where he arrived with his staff on August 4. Within the week orders were issued directing Colonel Newby to concentrate at Las Vegas, preparatory to returning to Alton, Illinois to be mustered out. Troops of the Third Missouri regiment were gathered in camp at Taos late in August; they were to depart for home within a few days. Lieutenant Alpheus Wheeler, their acting quartermaster, was in town arranging for wagons and teams for the eastward journey, when the *Republican* reported in its August 24 issue that "a large party of Navijos came in the other day with more captives, and delivered them over" to Governor Donaciano Vigil. If a similar number of Navajo captives was surrendered by New Mexicans on this occasion, the *Republican* did not mention it.

Waves of troops marched through Santa Fe during most of August, all jubilantly celebrating the end of war. The hero of the moment, however, was neither a Missouri farmboy nor General Zachary Taylor but the Canadian-born "Skimmer of the Plains," Francis X. Aubry, whose travels between Santa Fe and Independence, "with a rapidity almost super-natural," each time surpassed his own previous record. In August, he was back again and basking in the glory of his last trip out: he had covered the distance of more than eight hundred miles in seven and a half days.

It was indeed a time of arrivals and departures. Following the Mercury of the Plains by only two days came a slower and more hardbitten traveler of beaver lines, the mulatto scout Jim Beckwourth, who brought nothing more than his own musky reputation and a packet of mail. Among the letters he carried were General Orders No. 25 issued the previous June from the office of the adjutant general, including the information that "Bvt. Lt. Col. Washington of the 3d Regt. U. S. Artillery, has been appointed Civil and Military Governor of New Mexico" and that he had received orders to march for Santa Fe by way of Chihuahua in the shortest possible time.[11]

John Macrae Washington received his orders while stationed with

11. Aubry's record-breaking—and horse-killing—travels across the plains in 1847–52 so captured the public imagination that a Missouri riverboat and a military post on the Arkansas River were named for him. His brief career, starting as a freighter of war supplies in 1847, ended in 1854 when, during an altercation over one of his feats, he was stabbed to death in Henry Mercure's Santa Fe store by Maj. Richard H. Weightman. The exploit referred to here, as well as Beckwourth's arrival with the mail, were reported in the Santa Fe *Republican*, August 9, 1848.

occupation forces in Monterrey, the capital of Nuevo León. The appointment probably came as much as a reward for long service—he was then about fifty years old—as for his experience in campaigning against Indians. He had won his captaincy in wars with the Creek Nation in 1833 and 1834; two years later he had fought against the Seminoles in Florida. With General Wool's army, he performed well enough in command of artillery in the battle of Buena Vista to be cited for gallantry, with the brevet rank of lieutenant colonel. At Monterrey, not too many miles from where the first shots of the war had been fired, he was a very long way from his family in Warrenton, Virginia.

He left Monterrey late in July, leading his column by way of Saltillo and Chihuahua to arrive in Santa Fe October 10. The force of 250 men he brought with him, together with the same number of dragoons already present in the territory under Major Benjamin Lloyd Beall, made up the total strength of his departmental command—or, if Colonel Newby had been correct, half the number of troops needed to protect the territory. In the view of Samuel Ellison, a Kentuckian who had served with him in Mexico, he was "a very positive, brave, & efficient officer." [12] Within a few weeks he was advised he must manage with the force he had, as reinforcements could not be sent across the plains in winter; he was not to expect relief until the following June.[13]

The winter of 1848-49 was unusually severe. The Navajos remained at peace, but from November through January depredations by Jicarilla Apaches threatened the territory. In spite of deep snow, Beall's dragoons were on constant patrol in the northern plains and mountains but managed, with "the most strenuous exertions and much suffering" to protect the mountain villages from serious injury.

In early February, as trouble with the Jicarillas subsided, Navajos ended an eight months' observance of Newby's treaty by raiding on the lower Puerco. Some six to eight thousand sheep were run off. The prefect of Valencia County called upon dragoons stationed at Albuquerque to support a party of civilians who already were assembled and waiting to move against the raiders. Eighteen enlisted men were sent out with a sergeant in the evening of February 6, but the combined

12. Espinosa 1937, p. 7. Ellison came with Washington to Santa Fe and remained there until his death in 1899. He served as interpreter and secretary to a number of succeeding military and civil governors of the territory, spent three terms in the territorial legislature, and for the last eight years of his life was territorial librarian.

13. October 13, 1848: Marcy to Washington, *House Exec. Doc.*, 31st Cong., 1st sess., no. 17, p. 263.

efforts of the two forces availed nothing. The raid was a prelude to others. The alcalde of Corrales a few weeks later appealed to the commander at Albuquerque for assistance in making a campaign against the Navajos. His request met with brusque refusal, Second Lieutenant O. H. P. Taylor replying that he could not spare enough troops for a campaign, that the alcalde had foolishly waited one week after the robberies occurred before asking help, and that, furthermore, any effective action would entail a campaign of one or two months by at least one hundred men. Lieutenant Taylor could spare at most twelve or fifteen men for three weeks.[14]

A Rhode Island man scarcely six years out of the Military Academy at West Point, Lieutenant Taylor was convinced that "no peace ever was or ever will be permanent with [the Navajos], they are very cowardly never standing to fight on equal terms." The opinion is worth noting as it would typify the attitude of most of Taylor's fellow officers until they gained more experience.

Renewed hostilities by the Jicarillas, joined by Utes, led Colonel Washington in March to call for the organization of four companies of volunteers. Most of those who responded were native New Mexicans anxious to serve, even without pay, to protect their homes. Their term of enlistment was six months. Henry Dodge was appointed captain of a company of eighty-five infantry and soon afterward was ordered to make his headquarters at Jemez. Seventy-eight mounted volunteers commanded by Captain John Chapman were sent to garrison Abiquiu. Two other companies were commanded by Captain J. M. Valdez and Captain A. L. Papin.[15] Colonel Washington planned to discharge the volunteers upon the arrival of regular troops from Fort Leavenworth, a plan he discarded as spring wore on and it became evident that a major campaign against the warring tribes might be necessary. Two months after the companies were formed he observed that their presence "has undeceived the neighboring tribes of hostile Indians in the idea . . . that they could war against one portion of the people and perhaps be assisted in it by the other"—an allusion, apparently, to the guerrilla activities of Manuel Cortés.[16]

14. February 3 and 28, 1849: Taylor to Bvt 2d Lt. John H. Dickerson, AAAG, Santa Fe, NA, RAC, RG 393, T-3-1849, LR.

15. NA, RAC, RG 94, Volunteer Organizations, Muster Rolls, Box 2550. Dodge's company, including two lieutenants, eight noncommissioned officers, and one musician, served creditably and without pay until it was mustered out at Santa Fe on September 23, 1849.

16. May 25, 1849: Washington to Jones, NA, AGO, LR, no. 363, microcopy 567, roll 420 (hereafter, 547–420.) Mountain villages isolated in the Sangre de

Henry Dodge's "Eutaw Rangers"—the name he gave his militia company—had been in service only a few weeks when Colonel Washington ordered Dodge to proceed at once to Laguna and Acoma, where a dispute over land and water rights threatened peace between the two pueblos.[17] Elsewhere, raiding bands of Apaches and Utes continued through spring to plague the territory, concentrating their attacks upon inhabitants of the northern villages. In early July, Colonel Washington informed the adjutant general that several persons had been murdered and a considerable quantity of stock run off, with evidence that Navajos and Comanches also were engaged in raiding in other areas. John Dillard's train of California-bound emigrants lost a few horses and mules to Comanches in the vicinity of Cerro Tucumcari and might have suffered worse losses but for the presence of a military escort led by Captain Randolph B. Marcy. The emigrant train rolled into Santa Fe in the evening of June 28, 1849, after traveling 819 miles from Fort Smith, Arkansas.

A junior officer lately attached to Marcy's staff, First Lieutenant James H. Simpson of the Topographical Engineers, was instructed to report for duty to Colonel Washington, subject to the colonel's orders until further notice.

Captain Dodge, meanwhile, had been occupied with problems of more immediate concern than water rights. Not long after he reached Jemez with his militia company, early in July a small party of Navajos murdered a herder named Vicente García near the pueblo and drove off a sizable herd of stock. Several of the Navajos were captured and returned to confinement at Jemez. On receiving the news in Santa Fe, Colonel Washington issued orders that contemplated a campaign of reprisal into the Navajos' lower Chusca Valley. Captain (now Brevet Major) William N. Grier was directed to proceed from Santa Fe to Jemez with a detachment of dragoons, place Dodge's militia under his command, and prepare to march after being joined by the mounted volunteers of Captain Valdez, then stationed at Taos.

Grier reached Jemez July 12, where he was informed that García's

Cristos between Taos and Santa Fe all have legends of frequent raids at this time by Apache and Ute war parties. The incidents, usually entailing one or two deaths, fields of crops devastated, and livestock stolen, were rarely reported in time for the military to take effective action.

17. April 22, 1849: Henry Dodge, "to whom it may conserne," NA, NMS T21-1. At Laguna, Dodge appointed "Louis Sericur, Stentiago Arigon, [and] Juan Ignacio Chavis" to "regulate all maters in differance." Dispute between the pueblos continued and two years later, as agent for Gov. James S. Calhoun, John R. Tullis altered Dodge's boundary line more favorably to the Acomas (April, 1851: Tullis to Calhoun, Abel 1915, pp. 339–41).

murder was the act of only a few Navajos, who were said to be in hiding a distance of eight days' travel to the southwest.[18] Five days went by without word from Valdez. As he waited, Major Grier's enthusiasm for the campaign cooled. To his mind, conditioned by the way things were done in the regular army, Dodge's Eutaw Rangers presented a scruffy appearance. To Dodge's force of sixty men, whom he regarded as *"not of the best,"* Grier could add only the twenty dragoons he had brought with him. He found that he had no stomach for marching into Navajo country with such a command, and that if he couldn't have better material, then he wanted more of it, "as numbers will sometimes pass for strength." [19]

Major Grier's concern, in the end, went for nothing. Continued pressure by hostile bands in the north forced Colonel Washington to change his plans and order Captain Valdez to remain at Taos. Even as Grier waited at Jemez another party of Navajos killed another New Mexican pastor and stole more sheep in the Rio Abajo, but the major was directed to return to Santa Fe; his command was neither strong enough nor composed of the right kind of troops to campaign effectively against the Navajos. Colonel Washington believed only a part of the tribe was disaffected and so thought it unlikely that an expedition against them would be necessary. Captain Dodge and his company, meanwhile, were to remain at Jemez.[20]

The reinforcements that Colonel Washington had been expecting for so long arrived in two contingents, all of the companies weakened and gaunt from the effects of cholera. An epidemic sweeping across the plains that summer had passed through their ranks while they were in barracks at Fort Leavenworth. On reaching Santa Fe nearly every man, to Washington's horrified gaze, seemed a skeletonlike apparition, although rest and food would allow most of them to march again in a few weeks. The first men were of Captain Croghan Ker's Company K, Second Dragoons, who appeared while Major Grier was still at Jemez. The captain brought word that straggling in his rear by ten days were four companies of the Third Regiment, U.S. Infantry, commanded by Brevet Lieutenant Colonel Edmund Brooke Alexander.

With the infantry but possibly sharing the luxury of a carriage were

18. July 9, 1849: Dickerson to Grier, NA, RAC, RG 393, D-41-1849, LS; and July 13, 1849: Grier to Dickerson, RAC, RG 393, G-1-1849, LR.

19. July 17, 1849; Grier to Dickerson, NA, RAC, RG 393, G-2-1849, LR.

20. July 17 and 19, 1849: Dickerson to Grier, NA, RAC, RG 393, D-43-1849, D-44-1849, LS.

two civilians: James S. Calhoun (who would describe himself as a native of Georgia), about forty-seven years old, and William E. Love, Calhoun's aide and the husband of Calhoun's daughter Carolina. They reached Santa Fe on July 22. Among other papers Calhoun found waiting for him was his appointment as first Indian agent in New Mexico, the commission having been forwarded to Santa Fe in April by Commissioner of Indian Affairs William Medill. Typical of a time when Indian agencies were offered as political plums, Calhoun had no experience in Indian affairs. The favor, however, was not lavish: his annual salary was a moderate $1,500, with an added allowance of $2,300 for expenses and contingencies.[21]

The arrival of Alexander's troops, which the cholera epidemic had delayed by a month, had been anticipated by Colonel Washington as the moment when he could be relieved of command. It had been his intention to turn over the Ninth Military Department and return to the States. Instead, at the end of July he explained that it seemed best for him to stay on, as continuing Indian depredations compelled the use of all troops then serving in New Mexico, including the four companies of volunteers. Colonel Washington felt that it was his duty not to withdraw any of the available force but to retain in the territory the two companies that otherwise he would have taken back East.

What hostile action on the part of the Navajos, if any, occurred during the intervening days is not known, but in less than a week Colonel Washington prepared to lead an expedition into Navajo country. On August 5 he advised the adjutant general that, because repeated depredations by Navajos had lately led also to the murder of citizens, he was determined to make a campaign against them.[22]

In terms of the small armies of ragged militia sent against the Navajos by Spaniards and Mexicans, the size of Colonel Washington's command was not large, but most of his troops were experienced veterans commanded by competent officers. They were well disciplined, well equipped, well provisioned, and well armed. Instead of the antique flintlocks of Vizcarra's day, they carried the model 1841 rifle, an accurate muzzle-loading percussion-lock firearm that had proved its great

21. Abel 1915, pp. xi–xii. Nothing can be found in Calhoun's official correspondence to suggest that his wife, the former Mrs. Annie V. Williamson, whom he married in 1830, accompanied him to New Mexico, and it appears that his two married daughters, Carolina Love and Martha Ann Davis, also remained at home.

22. July 30 and August 5, 1849: Washington to Jones, NA, AGO, LS, nos. 427 and 515, 567–420.

shocking power in the Mexican War. The invading force also was equipped with cannon—one six-pound field gun, a ponderous weapon trundled on its carriage behind horses, and three twelve-pound mountain howitzers that could be disassembled and packed on mules. Thirty days' rations for five hundred men were issued and a wagon train was assembled to carry the heavy baggage.[23]

The main part of the command left Santa Fe in the morning of August 16, Colonel Washington and his staff riding in advance of two companies of Second Artillery—a battery of fifty-five men commanded by Brevet Major Henry Lane Kendrick. With the colonel were James L. Collins, who had offered his services as Spanish interpreter, and James Conklin, whose experience made him as useful as interpreter and guide as he had been three years before to the Doniphan expedition. Also attached to the colonel's party, which camped that night at Cieneguilla, were Indian Agent Calhoun and his three civilian aides, Cyrus Choice, John G. Jones, and William Love.

A short distance to the east and rear, following the old wagon road to Algodones, Lieutenant Simpson and his aides rode with Colonel Alexander at the head of 123 men, four companies of the Third Infantry. In the published orders setting the columns in motion, Simpson was directed simply to make "such a survey of the country as the movements of the troops will permit." Vague and undemanding as the orders were, Simpson accepted his instructions with the zeal of an ardent neophyte about to be ordained to the priesthood. With sextant and thermometers he took daily readings of longitude, latitude, and temperature. When others sprawled out to rest in camp at night he made exacting notes of what had occurred each day, notes eventually to be gathered together and, with the diary of one of his aides to assist his memory, rewritten and published as Simpson's *Journal of a Military Reconnaissance*.

The diary was less that than a collection of random observations jotted down in pencil by Richard H. Kern and illustrated with equally abbreviated, sometimes whimsical sketches.[24] This versatile young man was preparing to follow the command by one day with the assistant quartermaster, Captain Thomas L. Brent, helping to drive a herd of

23. Except as otherwise noted, this account of Colonel Washington's campaign is based upon Simpson's *Journal*.

24. "Notes of a Military Reconnaissance of the Pais de los Navajos in the Months of Aug & Sept 1849," HM 4274, Huntington Library (hereafter cited as Kern Diary).

unbroken pack mules in the wake of the troops. No muleteer, Richard had been engaged by Simpson as the expedition's artist, and his brother Edward Kern as its cartographer; lithographs made from drawings by Richard and Edward's map—the first reliable one ever made of Navajo country—later appeared in the Simpson *Journal*.

After the second night's camp, at Santo Domingo, the command forded the Rio Grande and in a back-breaking ascent, the first nine miles through deep sand, crossed Borego Mesa. Before nightfall the columns descended into the valley where the pueblo of Jemez lay on the small river of the same name. The difficulty his wagons had had over the rough trail persuaded Colonel Washington to abandon both the wagons and the heavier part of the baggage and from this point forward to rely only upon pack mules. The command made camp near a cornfield just north of the pueblo and remained for three days, waiting to be joined by Pueblo auxiliaries and Brent's rebellious mules. On arrival at Jemez the command had at once been reinforced by Captain Dodge's militia, reduced to fifty men. The Indian auxiliaries reached the rendezvous before evening of the third day, fifty-four warriors from the pueblos of Santa Ana, Zia, San Felipe, Santo Domingo, and Cochiti, with their respective war captains: Quandiego of Santo Domingo, Salvadore of Santa Ana, Mariano Chávez of San Felipe, and—nominally in charge of them all—one named by Simpson as Hosea Beheale of Santa Ana. The name sounds Navajo. Possibly this was Hastiin Beheale, who had adopted the village of a Pueblo wife, or perhaps was a Diné Ana'aii.

Two others who joined the command here as guides were the Diné Ana'aii leader Sandoval and the amiable, always loquacious governor of Jemez, Francisco Hosta. In days ahead Hosta was to regale the troops with myths and legends and very nearly convinced Simpson that Anasazi ruins encountered on the way were vestiges of the era of Montezuma. Of Hosta, Richard Kern says nothing, except to note that his wife, Whart-te, was "an industrious woman," which would fairly describe nearly any Pueblo wife. At the end of his diary, however, on one page otherwise blank, appears

Hosta
Hoste
Francisco

and on the facing page, a pencil sketch of an Indian man in profile, the black hair in a bang across the eyebrows and then cut to shoulder length. One beady eye with an oriental tilt is set at the bridge of a huge beaked nose; below the flaring nostril a whispy mustache nearly hides a small pursed mouth. The face is lean and the jawline prominent. Hosta, if this is he, wears a necklace with a bird-shaped pendant.

With these additions to his command, Colonel Washington left Jemez August 22, moving less than six miles to the broad Salada valley and making camp south and a few miles west of the village of San Ysidro. When the march resumed next morning, a native of that village, Rafael Carravahal, joined the ranks as another guide. Although almost nothing is known of his past, it is clear that this seasoned and aging man possessed an intimate knowledge, gained from earlier expeditions against the Navajos, of the country the troops were to pass through. The command increasingly came to rely upon him as faith in Sandoval's good intentions diminished. No overt act of disloyalty to the command was charged against the Diné Ana'aii leader, but he was regarded with growing suspicion and on one occasion at least Simpson wondered if he had not deliberately guided the columns in a wrong direction. However this may be, the command had an overabundance of guides and needed only the additional reinforcements of John Chapman's eighty militia, who joined the column the same day, to reach full complement—some 395 men in all. Within three days that number was to be reduced by twenty, all of them deserters from Captain Chapman's company.

Cabezon Peak lifted its rounded dome to their left as the troops crossed the Rio Puerco, in Richard Kern's view "a miserable dirty & little stream of brackish water," and proceeded northwesterly over rolling sandy terrain. They raised the eastern prow of Chacra Mesa before entering the valley of Torreon and came, finally, at evening of August 26, to high windswept ground where the ruined walls of Pueblo Pintado stood alone a quarter of a mile above the winding Chaco River. "A prominent & lonely object" in the twilight, Richard noted, ". . . There can be no doubt of its having been [built] by a race living here in long past ages—Its style is so different from any thing Spanish. . . ." Simpson and the Kern brothers lingered next morning to measure and diagram the walls, later hurrying to rejoin the columns as they entered the deepening entrance to Chaco Canyon—in Richard's notes again, "An immense corridor with numerous side passages—finest rocks— passed several immense boulders . . . with many hieroglyphs cut in them."

As one ruin of the ancient Chaco civilization succeeded another,

Simpson became more fascinated by the moment, Kern's diary entries indicating a shared excitement of discovery. Thus next morning, on breaking camp near the base of Fajada Butte, Colonel Washington permitted Simpson to make a survey of other ruins in the canyon while he led the command out of the canyon westward, skirting the Chaco's south mesa.[25] With Carravahal as guide and Richard Kern assisting him, Simpson made the first survey of one of the two major centers of Anasazi occupation as well as one of the most important archaeological sites in the United States. The achievement—astonishing for an engineer hitherto interested in harbor improvements and lighthouses—mainly accounts for the enduring value of his journal.

Almost midway between the canyon and Chusca Valley, Simpson in the morning of August 29 encountered fifteen Navajos approaching on horseback, the first mentioned in his journal as having been seen on the march. They proved to be friendly and attached themselves to Simpson's party for the remaining distance to the troops' encampment.

In the evening the forces rejoined forty miles beyond Chaco Canyon, in the Chusca Valley east of but near the location of the present Naschiti trading post. Two versions of the reunion are given. On topping a rise obscuring the expanse of valley and sighting the camp seven or eight miles off, Simpson was cheered to see the tents flickering at that great distance like specks of light; pale smoke rising in the clear air suggested the fragrances of good things to eat. Richard Kern, on the other hand, his artist's eye fixed on the Navajos riding at his side and especially on one of the New Mexican militia mingling with them, observed that their escort greeted the sight ahead with a shout and brandishing of arms. The Spanish bravo in their midst was a spectacular claimant of attention. He had painted himself a ghastly vermilion; his face, his hands, every part of his clothing, and as if that were not enough, his mule as well.

Within a mile of camp, Kern observed, "a large band of Indians appeared to be coming between us & it & we came in at a round gallop." Here, more Navajos were found everywhere in a milling, talking, restless throng. A reason for this was soon clear. Three of their number had been seized by the troops as prisoners and a nearby cornfield had been plundered to feed the command's animals.

25. When the command divided in the morning of August 28, those accompanying Simpson, in addition to Richard Kern and Carravahal, were James Collins, Asst. Army Surgeon John Fox Hammond, eight New Mexican militia, and several Pueblo auxiliaries.

Later that day and again next morning before the command moved on, a delegation of Navajo headmen visited the camp to talk with Colonel Washington. They assured him that they did not wish to fight the Bilagáana but would observe the terms of peace outlined in Newby's treaty the year before. They said that in compliance with demands made upon them by Major Grier at Jemez the preceding month, they were now ready to surrender fifteen horses and mules as well as a number of sheep. Some women accompanied the Navajo men to these meetings but remained in the background. Their dress was two dark-hued blankets sewn together, tied at the waist with a woven sash or belt, sleeveless and V-necked, and modestly long except when, in the fashion of men, they bestrode a horse. Inevitably then the dress hiked up, revealing legs bundled in the deerskin leggings that Private Robinson once had found unappealing.

The troops proceeded northward from this camp. At one point during the day their progress was hindered by a downpour of rain and a violent hailstorm. Throughout the march the columns never were out of sight of Navajo horsemen—"Multitudes of Indians around us," Kern noted—the Pueblo auxiliaries galloping off to join with them. The glinting flash and barbaric color of mingled war gear, paint, and costume made an unforgettable picture. Several warriors wore helmet-shaped fur caps and many were naked except for breechcloths. One, affecting a thin, smeary white body paint, struck Simpson as being especially hideous.

Colonel Washington and his staff had gone ahead among the Indians but after a time halted to allow the main body of troops to catch up. The colonel issued an order for Sandoval to direct the Indians to get aside or move on and not block the column's progress. Soon, Simpson noted, "I could see the whole body of Indians (Pueblos and Navajos) moving in a cloud of dust in advance of us. A dark, portentous cloud was hovering at the time over the Tumecha mountains beyond, the forked lightning ever and anon darting vividly athwart it; the beautiful peaks of the Ojos Calientes lay quartering to the right; and in the rear could be seen the main command—first the packs, then the infantry, and last the artillery, (which, on account of some obstacle, had for the moment got behind,) coming forward." [26]

26. Simpson's "Tumecha mountains" of course were the Tunicha range (later called Lukachukai) lying between the Chusca Mountains to the south and Carrizo Mountains to the north. The distinction between them requires noting, but for the purposes of this work the entire range is referred to simply as the Chusca Mountains and the 100 miles of southward-sloping open plain to the east as Chusca

Simpson has nearly all of it. If he misses anything, it could be the still hot sweating heat of an August afternoon in this valley, the thin gray vertical sheets of rain trailing across the Chusca ridges, the convincing crash of thunder that followed upon each streaking glare of lightning—and the patches of blue sky and pools of brilliant gold and green and tan light bathing the high dry ground to the east.

At some point after encountering the Navajos, although neither Simpson nor Kern mentions it, the mountain howitzers were removed from the pack mules and made ready for action. The hauling of these guns, together with the more unwieldy six-pound cannon, through heavy sand no doubt accounted for the slowing down of Major Kendrick's battery. By afternoon, after traveling fifteen miles from their last camp, the troops came to a hill of bare sand and small stone about fifty feet high, up which the artillery was dragged with difficulty. Six miles more brought the command to a north fork of Tunicha Creek where the order was given to encamp. The place chosen was on the quite flat and bare, not very broad summit of a peninsula of land littered with potsherds, not far from the low ruined walls of an extensive Anasazi village and perhaps one mile south and east of the present Two Gray Hills trading post.

Several hundred Navajos ringed a portion of the camp as another delegation of headmen approached the tent of the expedition's commander. Colonel Washington addressed them bluntly, saying that it was his purpose to chastise them for the murders and robberies they had committed. The headmen replied that these were the actions of lawless men whom they were powerless to control. For the sake of peace, however, they said, they would make restitution by giving up livestock in numbers equal to that which had been stolen, they would turn over certain captives, and they would attempt to deliver up the murderer of Vicente García, the pastor killed a month before at Jemez. As he witnessed these proceedings Richard Kern noted that the headmen "said if we were their friends why did we take their corn," adding that there was nothing they could do but submit, although it was hard. They would not promise to attend a council Washington proposed to hold at Canyon de Chelly—they disavowed all connection with Navajos west of the Chusca Mountains—but they agreed to return and talk peace with Washington again next day.[27]

Valley. "Tunicha" is a Spanish adaptation of the Navajo word Tu-in-tsá ("abundant water").

27. Kern Diary, August 30.

As the troops went about camp chores before settling down that evening it became apparent that although corn grew in abundance in the valleys below and on either side of them, the horses and mules on picket line would find but poor pasturage on this stony plain above. The resentment of the Navajos, so recently expressed, was weighed against need. A decision was made: to insure against interference by the Indians, Colonel Washington sent an armed detail to the cornfields under command of Captain Dodge.

How much this infelicitous start affected the mood of events next day cannot be estimated. Soon after camp was stirring, however, Colonel Washington directed Major Kendrick to reconnoitre the mountain pass that must be crossed with the artillery. He would take with him Captain Dodge and a detachment of his militia, a number of Pueblo auxiliaries, and Carravahal as guide. Because of Kendrick's early start, this party was absent when the Navajo headmen returned at noon to council, their number now including Narbona, José Largo, Archuleta, and the younger Armijo and Pedro José. With them, as a sign of their good intentions, they brought and turned over to Colonel Washington a number of sheep, horses, and mules.

Other Navajos were crowding about, Richard Kern observed, as the Colonel and Agent Calhoun opened the parley with James Conklin acting as interpreter. The terms of the treaty Washington would submit to the tribe at Canyon de Chelly were explained to the headmen and agreed to by them without objection. On only one point was full assent lacking. The two elder headmen, Narbona and José Largo, said they would not appear at the Canyon de Chelly council but authorized Armijo and Pedro José to act for them in the same manner as they would do were they present.

The gathering might have dispersed without incident had not Sandoval, who thus far had been relegated to the rear as a silent observer, chosen to reassert some of his former authority. Perhaps it rankled when he compared his position as a guide for the Bilagáana to his former power as a capitan under Mexican governors. In any case he thrust himself forward and began haranguing several hundred Navajos who sat astride their horses, rifles and bows in hand, in an open ring before him. Simpson's impression at the moment was that Sandoval intended to explain further the purpose of the white man's government, but he soon perceived that something more serious than an oration was developing.

Sandoval's part in this, if any, is not clear, but during his harangue a horse found among the Navajos was identified as an animal stolen some months before from one of the command's New Mexican militia. When this was reported to Colonel Washington he demanded that the horse be returned at once. The order threw the camp into noisy confusion. Narbona and other headmen left the colonel's side, apparently intending to quiet their people and tell them what to do. Washington waited some minutes for their return. When they failed to come back he directed Lieutenant Lorenzo Torez with a detachment of the guard to seize the disputed horse and its rider, or, failing in that, to seize another horse equal to the one claimed. Then he strode from the tent to see that his order was obeyed. As there was no inclination on the Navajos' part to comply, Washington warned them that they would be fired upon if they resisted.

Calhoun, standing close by, believed the Indians numbered from three to four hundred, all mounted and armed. As Lieutenant Torez and the guard advanced upon them the Navajos turned their horses about and broke into a run. Washington immediately ordered the guard to open fire. Seconds later Brevet Major John J. Peck directed the crew of the six-pounder to swing the field gun into action. As rapidly as the cannon's range could be corrected and the lanyard pulled on reloading, three shots were hurled at the scattering horsemen. After the third round, when Navajos were observed filing into a ravine to the north, a mounted pursuit was ordered.

Narbona lay dead, his body bleeding from four or five wounds. He was left where he fell, disturbed only by a trophy hunter of the command who pressed his knife to the forehead and cut and ripped off the scalp of nearly white shoulder-length hair. Six other Navajos were said to have died, either at once or soon afterward of wounds.

Caught by surprise, then filled with panic by the roar and tearing metal charge of the cannon, the Navajos at first made no attempt to fire back. Only after they had scattered into small groups among the foothills did they try to defend themselves. Even then, still withdrawing, they attempted only to cut off and fire on isolated units of pursuing soldiers. When the disorganized and frantically haphazard engagement at last ended, the command found that it had taken no casualties other than a few horses killed and some of the pack mules lost, having bolted in fright.

Late in the afternoon, for reasons entirely obscure, Colonel Washington gave the order to break camp. After proceeding slightly more than four miles to the northwest, in a direction nearly opposite to that which he knew he must take to strike the mountain pass, he halted for the night. The packing and unpacking of so much equipment to travel so short a distance in the wrong direction must have been impelled by some crisis or need; but the reason passed without comment in the notes of Simpson and Kern and the later report of Agent Calhoun.

Sandoval was sent off in the evening, accompanied by Hosta and some of the militia, to find Major Kendrick's party and lead it back to the new camp. Night descends quickly on the Chuscas at the end of August. The evening star is no more than visible low over the shoulder of Beautiful Mountain, the horizon rim still glowing, when the valley foothills fill with darkness. In the gathering dusk Sandoval failed to find Kendrick's trail.

It was much later that night when the picket guard posted about the command's position opened fire on what they believed to be attacking Navajos. The shots were directed at nearly point-blank range—not at Indians but at Kendrick's men, who had found their own way to the encampment. Henry Dodge was thrown from his saddle when his horse reared away from the flash of a guard's musket. The whizzing ball came closer, he allowed, than any that ever had been fired at him before. Worse, the fellow who shot at him was discovered afterward to have been a member of his own company. Another soldier was similarly thrown from his horse and Carravahal came into camp bleeding from a flesh wound where a ball had grazed his arm. Sandoval and Hosta rejoined the column next morning, having met with Kendrick's Pueblo auxiliaries, who had been forced to stay out because their horses had foundered in the mountains.

If Colonel Washington was disturbed by the violent turn of events or felt misgivings about the successful outcome of the peace council, there is no indication of it in notes or reports written at the time by himself or others who accompanied him. From the start he had declared that it was his intention to make a campaign against the Navajos and to chastise them for their bad conduct. In his only reference to the affair, his words were coolly restrained. After marching for eight days and arriving at the Chusca Valley in the vicinity of cornfields, he remarked, he "first met with the Indians and on the next day a party of them was fired upon by our troops which resulted in killing and wounding several of them. Among the dead of the enemy left on the field was Narbona the head chief of the nation who had been a scourge to the inhabitants of New Mexico for the last thirty years." [28]

28. September 25, 1849: Washington to Jones, NA, AGO, LR, no. 514, 567–421.

Colonel Washington's appraisal of the headman of course is untrue. From 1833 every reference to Narbona but one presents him as an advocate of peace, first in his councils with the Mexicans and then in his several previous meetings with the Americans. True, Chusca Navajos had maintained intermittent warfare with the Spanish population, but without Narbona's encouragement or participation, and they had refrained from attacking the persons or property of Americans. As a consequence of Narbona's death, Navajos were to extend warfare to the Bilagáana.

During the next six days the troops negotiated the difficult climb through Ponderosa pine and immense blocks of rock at Washington Pass (named by Simpson in the colonel's honor) and then followed the Rio Negro (now Crystal Wash) a day westward into the shade of a tall pine forest. Turning northward to Tsaile Creek, they passed through upland glades and areas of heavy timber until they finally emerged into open sagebrush country that offered a startling view of Los Gigantes—buttresses and arches of red rock to the north that in extent and majestic size could be compared with nothing but an inconceivable clustering of Gothic cathedrals congealed into one magnificent formation of red stone. Very far to the west could be seen some of the rock combs and peaks and buttes of lower Monument Valley. Here the column turned west again, tracing the north rim of Canyon del Muerto. No attempt was made during this time to ambush the troops, nor was any incident reported more serious than the effort of a sole Navajo to drive off a straggling pack mule, a theft averted by the revolver shots of a junior officer. Most of the Navajos had fled into the valley or to hiding places in the mountains, although a few remained to scout the command's flanks and rear. Skirmishers were ordered outward in advance of the column, beginning with the ascent of Washington Pass, but as the Navajos offered no resistance the marches each day settled into uneventful routine.

On September 6 the troops reached their objective: the waterless sand flats where Chinle Wash bends to the western entrance of Canyon de Chelly. Adjacent cornfields supplied roasting ears for the men as well as forage for the animals. All fires were extinguished at dusk—a military expediency that Simpson reflected must have had some moral effect upon the Navajos who, unseen in the darkness, maintained a watchful guard on the camp. Other fires had been noticed by the command some hours before; near sundown, the troops descending to the valley had seen several hogans in flames. Richard Kern believed that these fires had been set by Navajos to signal the soldiers' approach, whereas Simpson merely noted that "It was somewhat exciting to observe . . . the huts of the enemy, one after another, springing up into smoke and flames, and their owners scampering off in flight." Possibly Kern was right.

On this day or the day before, but entirely unknown at the time to Colonel Washington, a party of Navajos killed an American, unquestionably in reprisal for the death of Narbona and others at Chusca Valley. A citizen named Charles Malone, carrying mail to the command from Santa Fe, was attacked in the vicinity of Chaco Canyon. Malone and his New Mexican guide were killed and the contents of the mail bags were scattered over the ground.[29]

Unaware of the incident, Colonel Washington was coolly receptive the morning after his arrival at Canyon de Chelly when Sandoval brought in two Navajos who professed a desire to talk peace. One identified himself as a brother of the late Narbona; the other, who at once assumed the role of spokesman for the two, was presented as Mariano Martínez, "the principal chief of the Navajos"—a flattering but inaccurate description of him unless the colonel's interpreter referred only to the principal headman of Navajos then in the vicinity. As simply Mariano he was destined to figure several times again in important affairs of the tribe, but always in the shadow of more influential men. At the moment, he made an imposing appearance in a sky-blue greatcoat similar to those worn by the officers, a narrow-brimmed tarpaulin hat with domed crown, and buckskin leggings and moccasins. A bow and quiver were suspended over his back, and at his waist he carried a pouch and knife. His face was sombre.

In the somewhat halting colloquy that followed, Colonel Washington asked the interpreter to tell Mariano that when a chief wished to talk with him he should make this known with a white flag and he would be escorted safely to camp; everyone else must remain a mile off or risk being shot. Mariano accepted this without objection. On his assurance that the Navajos wanted peace, Washington replied that they might easily obtain peace by complying with the terms of Colonel Newby's treaty, and that the sooner they did comply the better it would be for them. Mariano then was informed that the tribe must turn over, in payment for property stolen since the signing of Newby's treaty,

29. Abel 1915, p. 47; and Simpson *Journal*, 1964, p. 152. Calhoun, referring to this incident, said, "These murders were committed about the 5th of September last, near forty miles east of Tunicha, and one hundred fifty west of Santa Fe, by Navajo Indians. . . ."

1,070 sheep, 34 mules, 19 horses, and 78 head of cattle. To all but the last Mariano assented; as for the cattle, he protested that these must have been stolen by Apaches as he knew nothing about them. Washington refused to concede the point and Mariano at last agreed. If he could not bring in the same cattle, he said, others would be brought to replace the numbers stolen. It was then arranged that Mariano would return with other headmen in two days to enter into talk of a new treaty.

Early next morning a Mexican captive who said he wished to speak with the colonel visited the camp. The man, who appeared to be about thirty years old, evidently had learned that the new treaty would demand the return of all captives. He said that he had lived with the Navajos since his capture seventeen years before and insisted that he had no wish to be restored to his people. When questioned about his family and former friends, known to be living at Santa Fe, his manner indicated that he wished neither to speak nor hear about them. Simpson found him "a very active, intelligent-looking fellow" who in his speech, dress, and conduct was indistinguishable from a Navajo. Calhoun, who was present at the meeting, noted that this unusual visitor had been captured by a roving band of Navajos while herding sheep near Tecolote; that he now had two Navajo wives and three children, and that he belonged still to a Navajo whom Calhoun called Waro (probably the headman Herrero), to whom he had been sold originally.

His name, as the agent understood it, was Josea (Hastiin) Ignacio Anañe. All but the name of the captive may be accepted without question. Calhoun's spelling of Spanish names frequently was faulty; there is good reason to believe that the captive was Juan Anaya, who presently would serve as interpreter for Henry Dodge after the latter's appointment as Navajo agent and still later exert some influence in Navajo affairs.

If this is so, it is possible that Dodge's first meeting with Anaya occurred at this time, for immediately after the captive's appearance in camp Dodge joined a party formed by Simpson to make a reconnaissance of Canyon de Chelly. Meeting no resistance from Navajos encountered during the march but instead being greeted with friendliness, the column advanced about nine miles into the gorge before turning back.

Colonel Washington's feelings in the morning set for the treaty council must remain conjectural because neither he nor others who recorded the event touch on this sensitive point. The situation might be likened to any ceremonious occasion when, with preparations made for twenty, to the host's dismay only two guests show up. For this was Colonel Washington's embarrassing predicament. The council was attended by only Mariano Martínez and Chapitone, the headman of a San Juan band who had signed Colonel Newby's treaty in 1848. Armijo and Pedro José, both pledged before Narbona's death to be present, were absent. So also were all of the influential Navajos who might justly claim to reflect the views of important divisions of the tribe.

As military governor, and having traveled so far, Washington may have felt a bit let down, although no trace of annoyance is detected in his later report, which merely observes that "the principal chief of the Navijos [Mariano], who said his acts were binding upon the whole nation, entered my camp attended by subordinates and sued for peace." [30] The "subordinates," according to Simpson, Calhoun, and Richard Kern, were the headman Chapitone and three New Mexican captives who subsequently were restored to their own families. No other Navajos attending the affair are mentioned by name or rank, but it appears that a number of men, women, and children gathered to observe the proceedings from a distance. The council started at once after Mariano made a token surrender of livestock: 104 sheep and 4 mules and horses.

The meeting is said to have been held on a small knoll between the future site of the Sam Day trading post (later the Thunderbird ranch) and the mouth of the canyon. More sophisticated in its phrasing than any previous agreement with the Navajos, Washington's treaty also was infinitely more far-reaching in its demands upon the nation. Article three opened with the statement that the United States should have the exclusive right of regulating trade and intercourse with the Navajos and closed with the stipulation that, until the government should otherwise order, the territory of the Navajos would henceforth be annexed to New Mexico. Article nine further reinforced this seizure, saying that the United States should, at its earliest convenience, designate, settle, and adjust the Navajos' territorial boundaries and pass and execute in their territory such laws as might be deemed conducive to the Indians' prosperity and happiness.

As the land then ranged and claimed by Navajos approximated in size the New England states of Massachusetts, Connecticut, and New Hampshire, the order of annexation, with a future unilateral determination of boundaries, trade, and laws, ranked in scope somewhere between

30. September 25, 1849; Washington to Jones, cited above.

the bolder aspirations of Captain Kidd and lesser visions of Napoleon I.

In consideration of these concessions by the Navajos, Colonel Washington pledged his government to grant the Navajos such donations, presents, and implements and adopt "such other liberal and humane measures" as the government might deem proper. Although the Navajo people never accepted or complied with the treaty terms, the colonel's pledge was redeemed by Congress in the amount of $18,000. A second appropriation of $5,000 was voted in 1854.

Otherwise, the tribe was required to surrender the man or men who had killed Vicente García near Jemez, and to turn over in thirty days at that pueblo all stolen property and captives held by Navajos. No provision was made for a reciprocal return of Navajos held in bondage. Further, it was stipulated that Navajo land should be freely open to passage by American citizens, and for the construction of United States military posts, agencies, and trading houses. In another concession, Navajos were assured that if any member of the tribe was murdered or maltreated by a citizen of the United States, the guilty person would be arrested and punished according to law.[31]

No provision had been made to offer the Navajos presents or trade goods, but at the conclusion of the council about one hundred warriors spent the rest of the afternoon bartering with the troops. Simpson observed that the Navajos had few rifles but most were armed with bows and lances and many carried shields of buffalo hide or the reinforced hide of deer. His eye again was drawn to their splendid blankets—a major item in their barter—and to the helmet-shaped caps. Lance shafts were six to eight feet long, tipped with points that might once have been knife or sword blades. The bows were about four feet long or a bit less, some backed with sinew, and with a heavy pull; arrow shafts were about two feet long, tipped with points cut from hoop iron.

The purpose of his campaign now accomplished, Colonel Washington saw no reason to remain longer. Accordingly, camp was broken at seven o'clock the next morning and the column formed for a march to Zuni where, it was said, the pueblo a few days before had suffered from an attack by Apaches. The route the command followed took the troops on a circuitous ascent to the south rim of Canyon de Chelly and then through sun-shafted pine forests and hilly meadows in a southeasterly direction to Cañoncito Bonito, near the future site of Fort Defiance. Through the Cienega Amarilla and following the sometimes

31. The full text of the September 9, 1849 treaty may be found in Abel 1915, pp. 21–25; Kappler 1904, vol. 2, pp. 583–85; and Simpson *Journal*, 1964, pp. 258–61.

ephemeral course of Black Creek south into Calites Canyon the troops marched, arriving at evening of the sixth day at Zuni.

A mock war demonstration was staged on their approach to welcome them, men and boys of the pueblo on horseback and afoot stirring whorls of dust, their staccato yelping mingled with booming gunfire. The governor of Zuni summoned the colonel and his staff that night and in his rooms offered a meal of assorted breads, tortillas with chile, and melons and peaches. Here they learned that the reported attack on the pueblo by Apaches was a false rumor but that some trouble in recent days had been caused by a train of California-bound emigrants and by a small raiding party of Navajos who had been driven off, leaving one of their number dead. The emigrants had commandeered, in the name of the government, a quantity of the pueblo's food and a number of horses and mules. On leaving, they had turned over the trussed-up personage of the governor of Laguna, kidnaped from his village and carried along after he had refused the emigrants' similar demands for sheep and other supplies.

Having observed the body of the dead Navajo on the approach to the pueblo earlier, Richard Kern returned that night on a ghoulish mission, accompanied by Surgeon Hammond and one other. He had reproached himself since the episode of Chusca Valley for not having secured the head of the fallen Narbona, which, all in the interest of science, except for his thoughtless oversight he could have sent for measurement to a friend in Philadelphia. Now opportunity offered a second chance. With the aid of Hammond's special skill he was back soon with a grisly trophy.[32]

Colonel Washington discharged the Pueblo auxiliaries in the evening of his arrival at Zuni, commending them for their good conduct. His route of march next day followed the one taken two years before by Major Walker's Santa Fe Battalion. The same route for some years to come, until Major Kendrick pioneered a shorter wagon road through the Wingate Valley, would serve as the Americans' military road into Navajo country. The march was uneventful and would have passed unnoticed in all later accounts had it not been for Simpson's diversion-

32. Robert V. Hine, Edward Kern's biographer, documents the incident (1962, pp. 77, 80), noting that the Navajo's head was taken for Dr. Samuel G. Morton, a friend of the Kern brothers and fellow member of the Philadelphia Academy of Natural Sciences. Richard's own comment (Kern Diary, September 15), is brief: "Went after supper with Dr H & Tom C[hamplin?]—to procure the head of a Navajoe who had been found near this place trying to steal and was killed by the inhabitants. Succeeded & returned to camp about 10½ oclk."

ary exploration of the pueblo ruins and inscriptions, the latter beginning with Juan de Oñate's party in 1605, at El Morro. Here again, as at Chaco Canyon, Simpson relied upon the indispensable Richard Kern to assist him in making what was the first and therefore a most fascinating record of this landmark. Soon afterward, on reaching Ojo del Gallo and with the slate-blue heights of San Mateo looming to the north, Simpson memorialized a president by naming the peaks Mount Taylor.

From his camp two days later on the Rio San José, Colonel Washington discharged John Chapman's militia, condemning the conduct of those who had deserted. Evening of the next day brought the troops to the west bank of the Rio Grande at Atrisco, opposite Albuquerque. Here the expedition ended, units of the command separating to make their own way back to Santa Fe. Colonel Washington and his staff arrived first, on September 23. Two days later the infantry plodded in behind Captain George Sykes. Major Kendrick, with the artillery, came last, reaching Santa Fe September 26. Washington's troops had marched 587 miles in forty-two days. They had killed seven Navajos, including one of the tribe's most influential headmen. The command had suffered no losses other than a few horses and mules. Some livestock and several captives had been recovered. Also, a treaty had been made—the first of only two with the Navajos that the United States Senate would ratify.

Upon his return to Santa Fe, Agent Calhoun was of the opinion that the Navajo nation numbered not more than five thousand. Colonel Washington's estimate was considerably higher: from seven to ten thousand of whom between two and three thousand were warriors, almost invariably well mounted and usually well armed. The two were closer to agreement on the need for military posts in Navajo country. Washington recommended at least one, in either the Chusca Valley or the "Sienega Grande" (presumably the valley extending south from Cañoncito Bonito). Calhoun, more lavish in his disposition of troops neither present nor available, thought military posts or stations should be established in the Chusca Valley, at Canyon de Chelly, or near Jemez and Laguna pueblos, and at Zuni—where he also urged the location of an agency. He further emphasized, as he was to do frequently in months ahead, the desirability of confining the Navajos to a reservation of clearly drawn boundaries where they would be under military surveillance. This was necessary, he felt, because

"The Navajos commit their wrongs from a pure love of rapine and plunder. . . . [they] are hardy and intelligent, and it is as natural for them to war against all men, and to take the property of others as it is for the sun to give light by day." [33]

His judgment is a generalization too narrow in focus and too broad in its condemnation, but having elements of truth. From the first days of Spanish colonization the record of Navajo aggression against Pueblo villages and Spanish settlements (coupled with Pueblo and Spanish aggression against Navajos) offers incontrovertible evidence of raiding and acquisitive traits—most notably but not invariably among the poor, the hungry, and the young. What Calhoun and others for some time failed to perceive was an almost unique Navajo characteristic: tribal adherence to a rule of individual self-determination (within strict limits of their broad religious code) that made it difficult if not impossible for Navajos to achieve unanimity, or even a majority of tribal unity in action, whether for war or peace, until the very end of their military history. Loose allegiance might be given the headman of separate bands, but tribal custom did not require Navajos to accept unwanted leadership, nor was there any obligation or social pressure for the individual to accept a majority decision or viewpoint.

In their refusal to accept Colonel Washington's treaty, however, the Navajos were paradoxically (but understandably) almost unanimous. Mariano Martínez and Chapitone had performed nothing more than an empty gesture to satisfy the American intruders and induce them to leave as quickly as possible. Terms of the treaty, to the extent that they could be understood, were impossibly one-sided and opposed to Navajo interests. Reaction to Narbona's death, while in some measure known, is more difficult to assess. A small portion of the tribe may have been gradually persuaded to war while others wished to remain at peace. Those Navajos inclined toward war, however, were reasonably convinced that while the Americans were better armed than Spanish and Mexican troops and auxiliaries had been, they were not greatly to be feared.

The murder of the American mail carrier Charles Malone and his New Mexican guide already has been noted as a consequence of Narbona's death. A warring segment of the tribe imposed on the territory further retribution in a series of raids. Near Sandia Pueblo two days after Colonel Washington and his staff passed by on their return to Santa Fe, a small band of Navajos killed five New Mexicans and escaped with their property. A week later, within three miles of Santa Fe, a large party of Indians, not identified but almost certainly Navajos,

33. Abel 1915, pp. 32–33. Washington's comment on the tribe's number is found in his September 25 letter to Jones, cited above.

murdered another New Mexican, leaving his body bristling with sixteen arrows shot into his back and two into the chest. Complaints of Navajo depredations came at the same time from the governors of San Ildefonso and Santo Domingo pueblos. On October 5 Navajos attacked the Spanish village of Le Bugarito, northwest of Laguna, killing two men, wounding a third, and carrying off a woman captive.

In these early stages, as if to demonstrate their repudiation of peace with New Mexicans, Navajo aggression was not directed against the Bilagáana—that could wait—but against their traditional enemies. An appeal for arms and ammunition with which to fight off Navajo attacks was made to Agent Calhoun October 15 when he was visited in Santa Fe by the governor, the cacique, and the war captain of Zuni. Since Colonel Washington's command had stopped at the pueblo a month before, they said, Navajo harassment had caused them great suffering; although there were 555 men and youths able to bear arms to defend their village and its fields and herds, they had only thirty-two guns and fewer than twenty rounds of ammunition apiece. They assured Calhoun that if given the arms they could defend themselves against Navajo and Apache attack. Their confidence went further: if permitted to form an allegiance with other Pueblos, they would exterminate every Navajo caught south of the San Juan River.[34]

Lieutenant Simpson and Calhoun, meanwhile, had been engaged in duties related to the recent campaign. Both were absent from Santa Fe during the early part of October, Simpson surveying the vicinity of Cebolleta to determine a suitable location for a military post and Calhoun traveling to Jemez to await the arrival of Chapitone and other Navajos who, in compliance with the treaty, were to surrender the remaining captives and stolen property held by the tribe. That Chapitone was prepared to fulfill the agreement was testified to later by Calhoun, who reported that the Navajo headman and his followers were at the Laguna pueblo of Paguate, a few miles south of Cebolletita, on or about October 8. They had with them the captives and stolen property and were preparing to proceed to Jemez when they were frightened off by a probably accidental combination of events.

Calhoun's early arrival at Jemez, on October 7, 1849, was predetermined by his plan to meet there with the governors and war captains of twelve pueblos prior to his meeting with Chapitone. Although Calhoun shortly before had expressed the view that a combination of Pueblos could exterminate the Navajos, his council with the Pueblo leaders ostensibly was for no other purpose than to acquaint himself with them

34. Abel 1915, p. 50.

and the condition of their villages, and to hear any complaints they wished to make.

Chapitone's arrival at Paguate unhappily coincided with this council at Jemez and also with Simpson's survey for a military post in the neighborhood where Chapitone now found himself. Simpson's object was not hostile, but the fact that he was accompanied by Lieutenant John Buford and one company of the Second Dragoons may easily have disturbed the Navajo delegation. Chapitone would have continued to Jemez with the captives and property, Calhoun learned afterward, had he not been alarmed by stories of New Mexican traders that told of a gathering army of Pueblos, Spaniards, and American troops who were preparing to exterminate the Navajo nation.[35] Chapitone left his people at Paguate and went on to Jemez to determine if the rumors were true. Evidently he was persuaded that they were not, for he then sent word to Colonel Washington that the surrender of captives would be made at San Ysidro at the end of the month. What may have occurred after that to change his mind is not known, but the agreement was not kept.

Although he had been close to, if not a part of, these events, Simpson made no reference to Chapitone on his return to Santa Fe. His report to Colonel Washington was confined to the subject of his recent assignment. After a reconnaissance of the country, he recommended as the most suitable location the tiny settlement of Cebolletita, situated about two miles below Cebolleta on the road to Laguna.[36]

In support of this choice he said that the village lay astride several avenues of approach taken by Navajos to the Spanish settlements; that it offered an abundance of wood and water for troops, and forage for their animals; that three ranches in the vicinity had buildings suitable for military use, which might be rented. Although there was a shorter pack-mule trail, the distance by wagon road to Albuquerque was sixty-one miles. Finally, he said, another advantage of the locality was its proximity to Sandoval's Diné Ana'aii, in his term "the friendly Navajos." It was a position that offered reciprocal advantages: Sandoval's people would receive protection from the Americans, in return for which the Diné Ana'aii would supply information about the plans and movements of the Navajos.

35. Ibid., p. 49.
36. October 10, 1849: Simpson to Washington, Simpson *Journal*, 1964, pp. 244–45. In more recent times Cebolletita has been known as Bibo, named for a family of traders to the pueblos of Laguna and Acoma.

7

The Many Faces of Sandoval

Colonel Washington was relieved of command before he could garrison the Cebolleta region. His successor was Brevet Colonel John Munroe, also an artillery officer and, like Washington, dedicated to the principle that it was madness to try to fight well-mounted Indians without adequate cavalry. Munroe spoke with a Scotch burr. In the view of Samuel Ellison, he was "the best mathematician in the army, as well as the ugliest looking man." Like Calhoun, he was a Whig and "a very determined man in all his acts and doings. He would brew his pitcher of toddy at night, & take the first drink of it at noon the next day, after which hour he would not attend to any official business." [1]

Munroe was staying at the Astor House in New York when he was notified on June 26, 1849, that he was to prepare at once to go to New Mexico. His departure from Fort Leavenworth was postponed to allow time for the assembling of fresh troops to accompany him across the plains. Finally, on August 25, he set out with Companies D and E of the Second Dragoons commanded by Brevet Colonel Charles A. May and a detachment of recruits for the Third Infantry commanded by Captain William H. Gordon. Somewhere on the trail an unseasonable snowstorm enveloped them, causing some losses in men. The command nevertheless reached Santa Fe October 22 and Munroe assumed the duties of military governor next day. [2]

Although his recent survey had caused Lieutenant Simpson to recommend Cebolletita, Colonel Munroe decided to establish a military post at the larger mountain village instead; Captain Croghan Ker was directed to proceed to Cebolleta with Company K, Second Dragoons, and settle in quarters. Although the post was occupied almost continu-

1. Espinosa 1938, p. 7.
2. June 26 and July 28, 1849, and June 28, 1850: NA, Headquarters of the Army, Letter Book 7, LS.

ously from December 1, 1849 (upon Ker's arrival), until its abandonment two years later, it was not established officially until September 3, 1850.[3] Additional measures to restrain Navajo raiders were taken when Colonel Munroe ordered a second outpost to be established at San Ysidro. Captain Gordon proceeded to that place with Company H, Third Infantry, arriving November 18. Again, as if previously warned of Munroe's plan, Navajos rode into the village four days ahead of Gordon and drove off a sizable heard of livestock.[4]

During the last weeks of the year the Navajos were quiet. Calhoun was heartened to believe that the major part of the tribe might yet comply with the September treaty but at the same time expressed concern over mischief that might be caused by traders carrying guns and ammunition—as well as incendiary rumors—to the Chuscas and beyond. On December 16 he issued notice that traders going to the country of Navajos, Apaches, and Utes were engaged in unauthorized traffic. He realized that such mild warning would not be taken seriously, and doubted whether it would have any other effect than to make the traders a little more cautious. At Cebolleta, which soon would gain a reputation as sanctuary for thieves and departure point for illicit traders and slave raiders, the notice received more attention. On reliable authority, Captain Ker was informed that a number of persons from Cebolleta and the river were about to start with trains of goods for Navajo and Apache country. If possible, he was to intercept and stop them.[5]

Less mindful of illicit traders than of the herd of animals he was driving, probably beef cattle and some sheep, Henry Dodge at about the same time made his way southward from Santa Fe. The instructions he carried from Colonel Munroe required him to proceed to Cebolleta as subsistence agent in the quartermaster's department, and there "make all expenditures that may be necessary for the Post, such as the purchase of Corn, hiring Men to herd Animals &c.—"[6] The animals he drove he was charged with delivering safely to grazing land near the

3. The post was established by Orders No. 31, dated August 20, 1850, HQ, 9th Military Department, NA, RG 94, Post Returns, Cibolleta, N.M. Troops were withdrawn from Cebolleta in October 1851 by order of Col. E. V. Sumner, after establishment of Forts Defiance and Union.

4. November 18, 1849: Gordon to Lt. Lafayette McLaws, AAG, NA, RAC, RG 393, no file mark, LR; Abel 1915, p. 86.

5. December 28, 1849: Ker to McLaws, NA, RAC, RG 393, K-3-1849, LR.

6. December 18, 1849: Capt. A. W. Reynolds, AQM, to Dodge, NA, NMS T21-1.

mountain village where, in time, they would provide food for Ker's dragoons.

Whatever the reasons that may have prompted it, Munroe's choice of the stocky, gray-eyed young man was, for the most part, a good one. Perhaps no one else would have made such an utter botch of his correspondence, his accounts, and his quarterly returns, but perhaps no other man could have been more effective in this unrewarding job.

Dodge had been at Cebolleta a short time only when two incidents occurred that cast Sandoval of the Diné Ana'aii in equivocal new light. First it must be remarked that Sandoval's people, as had been their custom for years, passed freely and often through the village. Sandoval himself commanded recognition; he had the bearing and fine equipage that at once set him apart as a *rico*, a wealthy person of rank and importance. Even some of his followers came to be known by name to the dragoons, so often were they encountered there. So common was it to speak of them as "friendly Navajos" that it did not occur to Captain Ker and the others that Sandoval's motives might be more complex and his actions less transparent, and less friendly, than they assumed. Surprisingly, then, Sandoval acted unpredictably early in January 1850.

It began when word came from Pedro Pino, the governor of Zuni, informing Captain Ker that Navajos had carried off two Zuni women and stolen a number of horses and mules. Snow was already on the ground and heavy skies threatened more, but Ker ordered K Company to saddle. With a native of the village acting as guide he departed January 8, the column taking the tortuous pass leading north. Their route skirted the snow-drifted mountain slopes in a north and then westerly direction toward the Chuscas, where Ker believed he might find the captured woman and livestock.

Sandoval was seen in Cebolleta the next morning, stopping at the house of an American named Black, an acquaintance who may have been attached to the garrison. When informed by Black that the dragoons had left the day before to campaign against the Navajos, Sandoval became enraged, declaring that if it was Ker's purpose to kill Navajos, he could have saved himself trouble and miles of travel by killing him, the leader of the Diné Ana'aii.

Assistant Army Surgeon William A. Hammond, who had remained at the post, observed Sandoval leaving Black's house and soon afterward saw Sandoval's son mount his horse and ride rapidly off in the direction taken by the troops. A few moments later, Hammond said, Sandoval gave an obviously spurious explanation, saying he had sent his son in search of a medicinal plant. Hammond called out the guard and ordered Sandoval placed in irons, accusing him of sending his son to inform the Navajos of Ker's approach. He then allowed Sandoval six hours in which to have the youth followed and brought back. The son returned during the afternoon and admitted on questioning that he had been told to follow the dragoons' trail. Hammond suspected that other Diné Ana'aii had been sent as spies but as no other evidence was found he turned Sandoval free.[7]

Captain Ker in the same afternoon, one day's march from Cebolleta and in the vicinity of Sandoval's rancherias, had other reason to suspect that the column was being watched. A Navajo who had been sighted keeping pace with the dragoons at a distance was captured. The prisoner said he had been sent by Sandoval's son-in-law to warn Chalita (evidently a headman of the Chusca region) of the approaching troops.

Two Navajos encountered during the march the next day were persuaded to hasten on in advance of the column and inform their people that the troops were coming and that their commander wished to talk with them. On reaching the Chusca Valley two days later Ker sent a small detachment ahead with the guide to establish contact with the Navajos, but it soon became apparent that the Indians wanted only to keep at a distance. The guide then went on alone and for this brashness almost paid with his life. While trying to induce a party of Navajos to come into the Bilagáana camp, he was told to put down his rifle before saying more; when he complied, the Navajos immediately opened fire but failed to hit him. Sentinels placed about the troops' camp drew more Navajo fire the next morning. The attacking Indians were driven off with the loss of one warrior. At this point Ker abandoned his objective. Rations had run short and his men and their horses had suffered greatly from cold and struggling against a nearly continuous fall of snow.[8] In the meager and unsatisfying detail of the garrison's reports, this was the first episode involving the Diné Ana'aii leader.

Less than a week had passed after the dragoons' return to Cebolleta when Sandoval again appeared in the village. Although action against him as a spy was still contemplated, he came boldly to Ker's head-

7. January 22, 1850: Hammond to Ker, NA, RAC, RG 393, H-4-1850, LR.
8. January 22, 1850: Ker to McLaws, NA, RAC, RG 393, K-1-1850, LR. On his return to Cebolleta after an absence of fourteen days, Ker reported that "The Indians whom I captured & who I still retain in custody informs me that Sandival dispatched other messengers from this place to warn the Tribe of our Expedition."

quarters as a mediator for the Navajo tribe, declaring that he had learned that Navajos of the Chusca region so recently hostile to Ker now wished to make peace with the Americans. After conveying this information Sandoval left almost at once for Santa Fe, where he met with Colonel Munroe, presumably advising the military governor to the same effect.[9] Sandoval's behavior on these two occasions would appear to find him acting selflessly and in the interest of the Navajo nation; the documentation unfortunately is one-sided and superficial and so it is impossible to explain Sandoval's motives or behavior.

Through the early days of spring as Munroe worried over means for holding the thin frontier line with a force of some six hundred troops, Calhoun continued to impress upon his superiors in Washington the desirability of confining hostile tribes on reservations—an undertaking that then or in the foreseeable future was utterly impossible, as it would first have required the military defeat of some twelve thousand formidable warriors of four widely scattered tribes. He proposed reservations of fifty square miles for the Navajos, Apaches, Comanches, and Utes and explained that there would be no need to feed the Navajos as "they can take care of themselves." Again, a few days later, he urged the adoption of his reservation policy, adding that these "wild Indians" should be compelled to build pueblos and cultivate crops.[10]

While Calhoun was thus conjuring plans for placing them in pueblos on a reservation, Navajos in early spring of 1850 appear to have been occupied with trading parties coming to their country and perhaps also, because there are references to such activities at this time, with the forays of slave raiders. If depredations by ladrons of the tribe were committed they went unreported.

Lack of communication with the Navajos was due in part to what must be one of the more whimsical military episodes known to the territory. Captain Ker late in March marched away from Cebolleta with twenty-two dragoons and simply vanished. No one had the faintest idea where he had gone, or why. When his absence from the post eventually was recognized as desertion, Major Marshall Saxe Howe was ordered early in May to proceed at once with troops from Albuquerque to Cebolleta. Ker in the meantime reappeared, going at once to Santa Fe

9. January 29, 1850: Ker to McLaws, NA, RAC, RG 393, misfiled K-1-1849, LR; and February 3, 1850: McLaws to Ker, NA, RAC, RG 393, LS. Reporting Sandoval's visit to Santa Fe, McLaws said only that "Sandoval chief of the Puebla Navajos has called & paid his respects to the Governor."

10. March 25 and 30, 1850: Calhoun to C.I.A. Orlando Brown, Abel 1915, pp. 175, 178.

to face the inevitable. He gave a rambling account of escorting a convivial party of Indian traders to the Gila River, on the lame pretense he felt it was his duty to offer them (and, one supposes, their kegs of whisky) his full protection. Because of a shortage of officers in the department, Colonel Munroe did not convene a court martial but instead accepted Ker's resignation from the service.[11]

Major Howe remained at Cebolleta only a few days, but long enough to register his belief that the village had no strategic importance. Command of the post was passed down to Lieutenant John Buford, who took an instant dislike to Henry Dodge and simultaneously found his eyes and nose affronted by the quarters that he fell heir to. Located in stone and adobe buildings indistinguishable from pueblo dwellings and near the center of the village, the rooms, Buford observed, were old, cramped, and filled with bedbugs.

The arrival of spring, meanwhile, found Navajos striking along the northern frontier. Large numbers of sheep were stolen on the Puerco in May and horses and mules were taken a week later in a series of depredations near Abiquiu. At least one herder was wounded and seven others were unaccounted for. Other raids at about the same time resulted in a flurry of rumors, the word of each incident multiplying the number of outrages in the retelling until the true situation became hopelessly confused. At Cebolleta, Lieutenant Buford sifted the reports as best he could. Although some frightened villagers believed that the Navajo nation had gone to war, Buford concluded that relatively few war parties were out and even these were limited in size to four or five warriors. A Diné Ana'aii informant who recently had escaped from his Navajo captors told how a war party returning from a raid upon Corrales had brazenly driven their stolen sheep within ten miles of the Cebolleta garrison. Sandoval himself appeared in the village at about the same time, saying that Navajos had threatened to kill him and members of his band.

Not all of the tumult was talk. Buford personally verified the murder by Navajos of a New Mexican near Jemez and a Puebloan of Acoma and thefts of stock in both instances. Sandoval had gone off in pursuit hoping to pick up the tracks of the marauders.[12]

If one were to heed only the reports issuing from the frontier posts and Calhoun's office in Santa Fe, one might assume that during the

11. May 24, 1850: Munroe to Bvt. Maj. W. W. Mackall, AAG, Western Division, NA, RAC, RG 393, LS.

12. June 10, 1850: Buford to McLaws, NA, RAC, RG 393, B-10-1850, LR.

summer and fall of 1850 Navajo depredations continued very much as in the recent past. There are indications, however, that a June raid in which fifteen thousand sheep were lost on the Rio Puerco and a strike at Corrales a month later in which a pastor was killed were more incidental to than symptomatic of what actually concerned a major portion of the tribe.

A Comanche threat in late June to invade Navajo country, coupled with the arrival of fresh troops from the States that made it possible for Colonel Munroe either to strengthen or simply to maintain his frontier garrisons, may well have been of major influence, but there is reason to believe that this summer and fall were a time of significant withdrawal and of some limited tribal conflict over what policy should be followed in relation to the Americans.

This is indicated on the one hand by a resumption of Navajo attacks upon traditional enemies far within the frontier—the Pueblo villages of Zuni and Hopi—and on the other by an effort late in September of two principal headmen of the tribe to enter into peace talks with Calhoun and Colonel Munroe.

Attaching less importance to this overture than we do here, Calhoun observed only that the Navajos' request for a meeting came by way of Jemez and was brought to him by Hosta, and that Colonel Munroe had authorized Hosta to invite the Navajo headmen to Santa Fe and assure them of safe conduct.[13] If the Navajos did come in, the meeting can have accomplished nothing, as Calhoun does not mention it again.

Even the Puerco raiders of June gave evidence of withdrawal. Offering his aid once more to the Bilagáana, Sandoval sent members of his Diné Ana'aii to spy on the rancherias where the large flocks of stolen sheep had been taken, a three-day march from Cebolleta, and then relayed reports of an unwarlike, pastoral scene. The raiders had settled down to the planting of large fields of corn and wheat and showed no inclination to strike again at the frontier. On the strength of this information Lieutenant Buford asked permission to lead a campaign into Navajo country about the first of August, when corn and melons would be ripe and Navajos would be relaxing at home, enjoying the results of their labor. Sandoval assured him that should he be unable to kill and capture many of them, nothing could prevent him from driving back five times as many sheep and horses as the Navajos had stolen that year. Sandoval offered to join the campaign with twenty of his warriors, and Buford thought he might further augment his force of dragoons by

13. September 30, 1850: Calhoun to Brown, Abel 1915, p. 260.

taking ten or fifteen Cebolleteño volunteers.[14] Permission to make the campaign was granted; but as fate would have it, Buford had been transferred to command of Las Vegas by the time the orders came.

Word of Navajo attacks upon Zuni was first received in early August when Pedro Pino, together with the war captain and other principal men of the pueblo, visited Santa Fe to sign the Pueblo treaty drafted by Calhoun the previous month. Pedro Pino recalled with some bitterness General Kearny's promise of protection to be afforded peaceful tribes, and then told how war parties of fifty and then one hundred Navajos had attacked his village during the past four weeks. Three Zunis had been killed and some livestock run off. Pino spoke again of how poorly armed the men of his pueblo were, and again requested that guns and ammunition be given to them so that they might make war on the Navajos. Colonel Munroe refused to furnish firearms but did supply some powder and lead before the delegation started home.[15]

Hostilities between the two tribes continued through the summer of 1850. Late in September, after an engagement in which Zunis killed about thirty of their old foe, Calhoun was told that the Navajos were preparing to attack Zuni again. A few days later Colonel Munroe reversed his former position and directed that sixty flintlock muskets be sent by military train to Zuni, with an adequate supply of flints and six thousand buck-and-ball cartridges. These arms were intended only for the defense of the pueblo, and Pedro Pino was told he must agree to return the muskets on demand.[16]

Early in October, appearing in even greater force, Navajos again attacked the pueblo of Zuni and destroyed adjoining fields of crops. The raid was carried out boldly within sight of a detachment of dragoons serving as escort to the bishop of Durango. Almost simultaneously, a delegation of seven Hopis arrived in Santa Fe and in an audience with Calhoun complained bitterly of depredations made on their villages by Navajos.[17]

Pedro Pino had advised Calhoun that a temporary withdrawal of the major part of the Cebolleta garrison in the latter part of July followed closely upon the first Navajo attacks upon his pueblo; removal of troops

14. July 18, 1850: Buford to McLaws, NA, RAC, RG 393, B-20-1850, LR.
15. August 12, 1850: Calhoun to Brown, Abel 1915, pp. 249–51.
16. October 9, 1850: McLaws to Chandler, NA, RAC, RG 393, LS. The muskets reached Zuni on October 30, Pino the same day signing his mark to a receipt and pledging to return them on demand.
17. Abel, 1915, pp. 263–64.

from the outpost, Pino supposed, only gave the Navajos "a fair chance against us," and encouraged them to extend their June raids into a summer campaign. Calhoun and Colonel Munroe may have conceded that this was so, but it appears that depredations by Mescalero Apaches in the Rio Abajo and by Jicarillas in the Mora Valley and elsewhere made the temporary withdrawal of troops from Cebolleta necessary.

Garrison headquarters at Cebolleta had been maintained in the period Pino complained of only by a small guard and a few men on sick call. On September 3, Brevet Lieutenant Colonel Daniel T. Chandler tersely announced his arrival with a command of two companies where before there had been one. In the clamorous dislocation of trying to find accommodations for his men he had been too busy to note much else than that the price of forage was high and the village and its vicinity for the moment were quietly at peace. With Lieutenant Buford's former dragoon Company H, Colonel Chandler had brought his own Company I, Third Infantry—these troops with the inclusion of Assistant Surgeon William A. Hammond making a total complement of seven officers and sixty-four men. Their sudden descent upon the village could not have failed to strain Cebolleta's poor resources. One of Chandler's junior officers was to serve as assistant quartermaster, but before the end of the first day the colonel requested, in a message to department headquarters, that he be allowed to employ Henry Dodge as forage master and interpreter. In due time came the reply, "It is Colonel Munroe's desire that Captain Dodge in particular should be employed" for the tasks mentioned.

For the present there was trouble enough to occupy Chandler's attention. An almost immediate concern was the uncontrollable drinking of the officer placed in command of his dragoons; another was a continuing hostile presence of Navajos in the vicinity of Zuni.[18] Chandler had been at Cebolleta only a month when he asked to be allowed to make an expedition against Navajos harassing the pueblo, his force to include a number of Pueblo and New Mexican auxiliaries. Munroe agreed that Chandler might offer limited assistance to the Zunis but refused to authorize a campaign; he regarded Chandler's command, even with

18. Capt. William H. Saunders, who had succeeded Lt. Buford in command of Company H, 2d Dragoons, offers an example of the effects of acute alcoholism combined with opium—then frequently prescribed by frontier post surgeons as a palliative. Saunders's case is fully documented in NA files. Heitman, usually accurate, says Saunders resigned from the service June 30, 1851, and died July 6, 1857. Actually, Saunders submitted his resignation ten days after arriving at Cebolleta, was permitted to stay on, and died of chronic alcoholism July 6, 1851.

auxiliaries, inadequate for such an undertaking. Shortly afterward it appears that Chandler found it unnecessary to take any action in the direction of Zuni, as the Navajos abruptly broke off their summer attacks upon the pueblo and again raided eastward toward the Puerco and Rio Grande—the renewed hostility against the settlements coinciding closely with the apparent failure, already noted, of the peace overtures made by two of the principal Navajo headmen.

From the middle of summer, when he had offered to send members of the Diné Ana'aii with Lieutenant Buford on a campaign into Navajo country, Sandoval had been spoiling for a chance to increase his herds. An opportunity came at last in November when Ramón Luna, the prefect of Valencia County, appeared at Cebolleta demanding that Colonel Chandler assist him in punishing Navajos for their latest outrage.

A band of these Indians, by Luna's account, had stolen two thousand sheep from the herds of Andrés Romero and Anastacio García in the vicinity of Valverde, on the east bank of the Rio Grande about thirty miles south of Socorro. When he was informed of the robbery on November 16, Ramón Luna at once called upon the alcaldes of the county to furnish men for a citizens' expedition against the Navajos, directing that this force rendezvous the next day at Cubero and there wait upon his arrival with hoped-for reinforcements. At Cebolleta the colonel informed him that he was indeed sorry, but the horses of his garrison were in such miserable condition for want of forage that it would be impossible for the dragoons to be of any help. Luna thereupon proceeded with fourteen citizens already furnished to him by the alcaldes and shortly afterward was joined by forty men "raised at that time" by Chandler's permission. The prefect did not identify these forty men, although there is good evidence that they included a number of Diné Ana'aii, Sandoval himself, and thirteen or fourteen Cebolleteños.[19]

Whether Luna found an additional force waiting for him at Cubero, as planned, or encountered them later is unclear, but he continued to Red Lake where he "joined the balance of the volunteer company" and succeeded in capturing five hundred sheep. These, Luna said, were recognized as part of the herd stolen at Valverde.

19. January 20, 1851: Luna to Munroe, Abel 1915, pp. 284–86. Luna's report, which curiously makes no reference to the important presence of the Diné Ana'aii, is one of the rare firsthand accounts of New Mexican slave raids against Navajos.

With a command numbering 292 men Luna continued westward into Navajo country. Reaching Mesa de la Vaca, or Black Mesa, he divided his forces and scattered them in several directions. What happened then one can only imagine; Luna does not say, but the Navajos obviously took a clawing. Seven hundred fanegas of corn were confiscated and other booty included twenty-eight women and children and twenty-four men taken captive and more than five thousand head of sheep, horses, and oxen seized. Laden and handicapped by this plunder but having taken no casualties themselves, Luna's campaigners started on the return march. Navajos surrounded them constantly and harassed every mile of their progress. At the mouth of Canyon de Chelly six of Luna's men ventured from camp in disobedience of orders and were killed. Some days later, emerging from the Wingate Valley near San Miguel, under the slopes of Mount Taylor and within a short distance of Cebolleta, thirteen of the party who came from that village broke off from Luna's command. A few Diné Ana'aii may have been with them.

After campaigning nearly two months in distant places, these men, within a day's march of home, made camp with perhaps less than their usual precautions—probably with a large fire against the cold January night. No guard was posted when they rolled into their blankets to sleep.

A survivor of the party, variously identified as one of Sandoval's band or as a New Mexican, reached Cebolleta January 12. Richard Tolin, an Albuquerque man who temporarily was replacing Henry Dodge as interpreter at the post, later recalled that "a friendly Nabajo Indian arrived . . . and reported that thirteen Mexicans on their return to the Settlements from a Campaigne were surprised by the Indians during the night and their arms [were] taken away from them. . . . The Mexicans then ran in all directions." The friendly Navajo could not tell Tolin if any of his companions had escaped. Residents of the village asked Captain Saunders, in command during Chandler's absence, to take a detachment of dragoons across a saddleback pass in the mountains in an attempt to rescue any others who might have survived. Tolin glumly observed that snow blocked the trail to such depth that the dragoons refused to budge. A rescue party of citizens started out but straggled back in defeat next day.[20]

20. February 5, 1851: Tolin to Chandler, NA, RAC, RG 393, enclosure with C-12-1851, LR, Chandler to McLaws, same date. Saunders (February 2, enclosure with above) reported that on January 14 "a vague rumor reached here that some

At Los Lunas about a week after he had left the men at San Miguel, Ramón Luna received bad news. Six of the missing campaigners had been found, four of them wounded. Nothing at all had been heard of the other seven.

Little is known of Sandoval's part in the expedition. Such information as exists is derived from two sources. The Reverend Hiram Walter Read, who came to New Mexico in 1849 as chaplain at Fort Marcy and in early 1851 was at Cebolleta as a Baptist missionary, on a tour of the frontier to determine possible fields of fruitful endeavor, may have felt that he had discovered a challenging prospect for conversion. In a journal entry for March 11 he observed, "A famous half-tamed Nabajo Chief named Sandoval, who resides in this vicinity, came into town to-day to sell some captives of his own nation which he had recently took prisoners.—He sold one young man of 18 years of age for thirty (30) dollars." 21

Sandoval may have proceeded almost at once to Santa Fe, where the market for his booty would be brisker and the prices higher, for Calhoun on March 31 advised the commissioner of Indian affairs that "Sandoval, our Navajo friend near Cebolleta, returned about the 20th of the month from a visit to his Navajo brethren with Eighteen captives, a quantity of stock and several scalps having lost one man in the expedition." 22

---

conflict had taken place between the Navajo Indians and a party of Mexicans and Indians who left this vicinity about two months previous on an expedition. . . . as well as [I] can remember . . . I was informed by a Mexican—who represented himself as having just arrived at this Post—and as belonging to the expedition . . . that a small party of his band . . . were supposed to be somewhere on the Mountains, and either killed or frozen. . . . All the rumours relative to this Party . . . were so inevident and conflicting, as to render any prompt and decisive steps on my part impossible. . . ."

21. Read diary 1942, p. 133.

22. Abel 1915, p. 307. The date of Sandoval's return is uncertain, as Read saw him at Cebolleta on March 11. Although there is no direct testimony linking Sandoval and his people with Ramón Luna's campaign, the evidence so strongly supports such a conclusion that I accept it as fact. Two Navajos who came from the vicinity of Red Lake to Cebolleta in April told Colonel Chandler that "Sandoval in his last campaign against us, stole everything we had, our horses, wives, children & even the sheep skins we slept on. . . ." (April 19, 1851: enclosure of "Memorandum of 'talk' held with Navajo Indians," with Chandler to McLaws, NA, RAC, RG 393, C-36-1851, LR).

8

Navajo Naach'id

Henry Dodge was in Albuquerque when he was asked to provide escort for the Reverend Mr. Read on the missionary's visit to Cebolleta in March 1851. A sincerely pious man who could and did, as a matter of conscience, decline an invitation to accompany the Valdez family to a village fandango, Read also appears to have had a practical side. Observing him as he departed from Santa Fe on his journey to Cebolleta, a stranger would hardly have guessed his divine calling.

"I was mounted on my horse," Read confided that night to his diary, "gun in hand, a brace of pistols in the holsters on my saddle, wore a broad-brimmed white wool hat, short beaver-overcoat, buckskin pantaloons, and thick boots." [1]

Thus attired when he met Dodge in Albuquerque March 8, he found nothing worth remarking in Dodge's appearance or attire, although it did not escape him that this was a son of the influential "General Dodge" of Wisconsin. A small detachment of troops rode with them, together with a baggage wagon and ambulance, as they directed their course toward the Puerco. Six miles beyond that stream they went into camp, the missionary noting in his journal that, as they were now in Navajo country, a strong guard stood watch through the night. He slept on the ground, or rather tried to, "but could not on account of the cold, and the incessant howling of the wolves."

The next day was a Sunday, and Read would rather not have profaned it by resuming the journey but regretfully consented to the inevitable, "as I am traveling in company with others whose affairs I cannot control." In late evening, shortly before arriving at Cebolleta, the party came to some small settlements—probably Moquino and Cebolletita, where the missionary noted that the natives seemed to live in constant fear. For protection against Navajo attack they had

1. Read diary 1942, pp. 230–33.

built numerous stone forts on high points through the region and from these stood guard over their grazing livestock.

Cebolleta itself impressed the missionary dismally, although the officers of the post, three of whom had their families with them, welcomed him cordially. Observing that the village could claim some three hundred residents, apart from the garrison, Read noted for the later consideration and possible action of the Baptist Home Mission Society that the village was far up in the mountains, a tiny island of ignorant and indolent people surrounded by wild Navajos. He thought it worth not a fraction of what it cost to protect it. Two days later the missionary found an excuse to turn back from the frontier and continue his tour in the more civilized settlements of the Rio Abajo.

There is evidence that as late as the previous October Henry Dodge had been buying large quantities of goods in Santa Fe and Albuquerque to supply the needs of the officers' families as well as of the villagers at the frontier store he operated with Pinckney R. Tully. It is possible that he continued in this venture at this time, while also acting as forage master and interpreter for Colonel Chandler. Purchases for this remote general store were usually made from the houses of St. Vrain and McCarty or Messervy and Webb in Santa Fe and of Henry Connelly in Albuquerque, the values ranging from a few dollars at a time to $928.93. Even a partial listing taken from the invoices gives some idea how counters and shelves of a frontier store were stocked:

From St. Vrain and McCarty—"1 Doz pr Pantaloons, ½ Doz Looking Glasses, ½ Doz Red flannel Shirts, 1 Bbl Whisky 37 gall, 37 yds Prints Yellow, 49 yds Ticking"; from Messervy and Webb—"4 Pcs Wide Manta, 6 Pcs Narrow Manta, 1 Doz childs Shoes, 1 Doz Umbrellas, 1 Bunch Hawk Bells, 1 Doz Santos, 1 Box Wool Cards, 2 Boxes Seidlitz Powders, 1000 Needles, Hooks & Eyes, Silver Beads, Spanish cards, Gun Flints, 6 Boxes Percussion caps, 4 Doz Pewter Mirrors, 1 Doz Black Wool hats, 1 Doz White Wool hats, 3 Doz Checked Shirts"; from Henry Connelly—"8 pr White Blankets, 1 Doz Spades, 1½ lbs Clark beads red, 4 Axes, 42 lbs Copper kettles, 27 lbs Corn."[2]

Winter chill gripped the territory in the early months of 1851 when reports filtering to military posts and authorities in Santa Fe told of Navajo plundering and murder on a scale rarely known before. In the very midst of the alarms, James Calhoun found himself elevated to the

2. From invoices dated August 17 and 18, 1850; September 19, 1850; October (?) 1850, NA, NMS T21-1.

governorship, on March 3, by presidential appointment; Colonel Munroe (remaining as department military commander) ordered a fifteen-gun salute, and surrendered his quarters in the Palace of the Governors. In his early days in office Calhoun was inclined to take each new report of Navajo rapine at face value. The military, more experienced and less credulous, on occasion could be deceived. What may here be referred to as the Sarracino incident illustrates a common aspect of the times. The episode occurred immediately before Calhoun's accession to the governorship.

Major Marshall Saxe Howe, commanding at Albuquerque, was attending court-martial proceedings at that post the morning of February 1 when he was summoned from the hearing by Colonel Munroe. The time was eleven o'clock and Munroe's presence was no more than coincidental. After a few words with the colonel, Major Howe directed his bugler to sound assembly. Troops of Company K, Second Dragoons were ordered to form up and prepare to march at once. Don Francisco Sarracino, the prefect of Bernalillo County, had just arrived and through Colonel Munroe conveyed word that more than one hundred Navajo warriors, armed to the teeth and well mounted, that morning had swooped down on Pajarito, ten or twelve miles to the south, and driven off about a thousand sheep and a large number of horses, mules, and oxen. Valuable time was lost as Major Howe debated whom to place in command, but within an hour of assembly call Lieutenant Alfred Pleasanton led the detachment out toward the river. He was accompanied by the prefect Sarracino, who said he had six good guides awaiting them on the far side of the Rio Grande. These men, Don Francisco said, would take Pleasanton directly to the Navajos' trail.

The guides drew a picture of such pillage and desolation that Pleasanton was led to believe that all of the stock in the Rio Abajo had been driven off. He was surprised upon reaching the vicinity of Pajarito to have the guides point out to him fewer tracks than he had expected. He was more surprised when the guides, with a "Muy gracias," hastily rode off. Left to his own resources, Pleasanton followed the trail westward and soon observed that there were no sheep tracks at all and very few of horses or mules. He further noticed that the Navajos were on foot.[3]

At their camp in the valley of the Rio Puerco, Pleasanton's dragoons were joined at daylight next morning by eleven travel-stained horsemen.

3. March 28, 1851: Pleasanton to Lt. J. W. Alley, enclosure with March 28, 1851: Howe to McLaws, NA, RAC, RG 393, H-9-1851, LR.

The sombreros, buckskins and serapes, and horse equipage of all identified them even at a distance as New Mexicans, but the leader of the
party introduced himself as James L. Hubbell, an American who had
adopted the Spanish surname Santiago after long residence at Pajarito.
It quickly developed that they had been in pursuit of the same Navajos
since early the preceding morning, and that most of the stolen stock—
sixty-five cattle and ten mules—had belonged to either Hubbell or his
neighbor, Don Juan Gutiérrez. Besides these, the raiders had taken a
horse owned by Blas Chávez and thirteen oxen from the pasture of the
prefect's relative, Juan Antonio Sarracino. The stolen herd of one thousand sheep existed only in the prefect's imagination. And the band of
more than one hundred well-armed warriors? Hubbell had counted nine
Navajos, only two armed with guns.[4]

His pursuit had been a discouragement, Hubbell said, because it
so nearly succeeded and then failed. From a rise near the Puerco
his party had seen the dust they looked for, perhaps eight or ten miles
ahead, and forced their horses into a gallop. The distance between
them had been narrowed to a mile or two when the Navajos, noticing
Hubbell's approach, lanced all of the cattle except one cow and three
calves. The chase had continued, but when the Navajos perceived
that they were losing ground steadily, they lanced six of the slower
mules and horses. Near Mesa Prieta, looming to the east of Cebolleta,
Hubbell abandoned the pursuit. His horses were too exhausted to continue.

Hubbell's men joined with the dragoons on the return toward Albuquerque. What he could not understand, Hubbell said, was why Pleasanton had been so slow in starting. The raid had occurred at sunrise
and Sarracino and Hubbell had left Pajarito at the same time—or so
Hubbell thought—so that the prefect should have reached Albuquerque
at seven or eight in the morning. What had happened? Pleasanton

4. James Lawrence Hubbell was born in Newtown, Connecticut, later moved to
Salisbury in the same state. On July 30, 1846, at the age of 22, he enlisted at Ste.
Genevieve, Missouri, in the 2d Regiment, Missouri Mounted Volunteers. Described
as 5 feet 9 inches tall and of fair complexion, he was discharged on July 30, 1847 at
Santa Fe. A year later he settled in Pajarito. Here he married Julianita, a daughter of
neighboring rancher Don Juan Gutiérrez (McNitt 1962, p. 143). Among six chil-
dren by this marriage were two sons, Don Lorenzo Hubbell, whose trading post at
Ganado, Arizona, is now preserved as a national historic site, and a younger brother,
Charles, who also became a trader to the Navajos. During the Civil War, Santiago L.
Hubbell was stationed at Fort Craig and at Albuquerque as a captain of Company G,
1st Cavalry, New Mexico Volunteers. In the years following the war he was a
government contractor supplying beef cattle to military posts in New Mexico.

could not say; he knew only that the prefect had not reached the post until eleven.

Sarracino's behavior throughout had been strange. The prefect had allowed four hours to pass before even starting out to report the raid. Why? He had neglected to mention to Major Howe that Santiago Hubbell was leading a party of ranchers in pursuit. Why had he not mentioned this and why had he lied about circumstances of the Navajo raid? He was the first man, after taking Pleasanton across the river, to go home. Why? Pleasanton was convinced that the prefect was a coward first and a fork-minded lying rogue unworthy to hold small public office.[5]

While newspapers fanned a growing public criticism of what increasingly was regarded as military ineptitude in handling "the Indian problem," Governor Calhoun observed that Munroe's efforts were not meeting with success; he believed that, unless the executive department (meaning himself) intervened at once, the defenseless inhabitants might well be murdered in their beds by savages who beset them on all sides. With this in mind, he issued a proclamation on March 18, calling upon all able-bodied male citizens of the territory to form volunteer companies for service against Indians. No provision was made for payment, but Calhoun assured any who volunteered that the booty system of old would reward them: the volunteers might keep all property, including women and children, they captured.[6]

The day following appearance of the proclamation, Calhoun addressed a message to the governors and caciques of all pueblos, saying that the savage Indians who were daily murdering and robbing the people of New Mexico must be "exterminated" or so beaten as to prevent their coming into or near the pueblos. For this reason Pueblo leaders were to avoid any communication with Navajos; should Navajos come near, the Pueblos were to shoot them, taking their animals and other property and dividing it according to their laws or customs.[7]

5. March 30, 1851: Munroe to Adjutant General, with enclosure: Skinner to Howe, NA, AGO, LR, no. 427, 567-449. Munroe summarized the Sarracino episode and other similar incidents by observing that each case teemed with direct lies of intentional misrepresentation; the object, always, was to prepare the way for fraudulent claims upon the government for property supposedly stolen by various warlike Indians.

6. Enclosure with March 22, 1851: Calhoun to Lea, Abel 1915, pp. 299–301.

7. Ibid., March 19, 1851: Calhoun to the caciques and governors of pueblos, pp. 301–2.

As he doubtless intended it should be, Calhoun's sanctioning of the booty system was an irresistible lure. If the proclamation appealed mainly to adventurous scoundrels, it applied as well to hot-blooded patriots. Foremost among the latter was Manuel Antonio Chaves, who had been an Indian fighter since his first march against the Navajos at the age of sixteen. Now, exactly twice that age, Chaves could claim to have carried arms against the "savage" foes of his people for half his life. The ink of Calhoun's proclamation still smudged thumbs when Manuel Chaves, then in Santa Fe, offered to raise six companies of volunteers—a total force of six hundred men—provided that Governor Calhoun would furnish, on loan, one hundred pack mules for his train, six hundred rifles, and a sufficient amount of ammunition. His men would not expect pay, Chaves said, for the only compensation they wanted was the disposal of captives and livestock; for their part they promised to hunt down the Navajos "to their extermination or complete surrender."

A final stipulation made it clear that his volunteers would not be subject to the command of Colonel Munroe or any other officer of the regular army, but only to the superior orders of Governor Calhoun.[8]

Nothing, of course, could have been better calculated to irritate Colonel Munroe and dampen any feeling he may have had that it would be desirable to cooperate with Calhoun. The governor's proclamation was derogatory enough in its implications; publicity given to the proposals of Manuel Chaves could only underscore Calhoun's low opinion of Colonel Munroe and the Ninth Military Department. What Calhoun failed to take into account was that without the rifles that only Colonel Munroe could supply, Don Manuel's expedition was not likely to go far. The incident unquestionably deepened the rift between the department commander and Governor Calhoun, although they continued to maintain a formal courtesy in the exchanges of their official relationship. When it became certain that Munroe would deny him the rifles and ammunition, Calhoun appealed directly to President Millard Fillmore, entrusting his letter of March 29 to Henry Connelly, the wealthy merchant of Peralta, who was traveling to the States and would deliver the message to the president personally.

New Mexico would enjoy neither quiet nor prosperity, Calhoun advised President Fillmore, until hostile Apaches and Navajos were com-

8. Ibid., March 18, 1851: Manuel Chaves: "Proposals to Raise Six Companies of Volunteers for an Expedition to the Navajo Country," pp. 302–3.

pletely subdued. Were he provided with one thousand muskets he could effectually check the "depredations that are being daily committed in our very midst." [9] But alas, as the president knew, Calhoun's treasury was empty and he was utterly without munitions of war.

A few days later in his dual role as superintendent of Indian affairs, Calhoun informed Secretary of the Interior Alexander Stuart of the territory's bankrupt treasury and its desperate need of weapons of all kinds to make expeditions of reprisal against hostile Indians. If only the means were furnished him, Calhoun said, he was confident that in a few months he could secure a lasting peace with the warring tribes, locate them upon reservations, and compel them to build pueblos and cultivate the soil.[10]

Calhoun's concern was only deepened by the presence in Santa Fe of the governor of Jemez. Hosta complained of Navajo raids and appealed for powder and lead for the guns that he said his pueblo had in sufficient supply. Hosta's request, forwarded to Colonel Munroe, received an immediate rebuff: Munroe had reason to believe that the people of Jemez were friendly with Navajos and so he would not, without some clearer evidence of necessity, supply them with ammunition.[11]

Rifles and ammunition needed by Manuel Chaves before he could subdue or exterminate the Navajos were not forthcoming from Washington or anywhere else. It is doubtful if his plan to raise six companies of volunteers came to much, although Chaves may have generated enough fervor to induce at least a small party to take the field. There was sufficient reason already for Washington to refuse Calhoun's request for arms. Even as Henry Connelly was carrying Calhoun's message to President Fillmore, Colonel Munroe was calling in experienced junior officers and knowledgeable civilians to advise him upon mounting an expedition of regular troops into Navajo country.

Plans for the campaign were far enough advanced by April 1 for Colonel Munroe to inform the adjutant general that the troops would march in May, when the grass was up, provided that relations with neighboring tribes did not interfere.[12] With this letter Munroe enclosed a tracing of a map drawn with the help of "the old guide" Rafael Carravahal. Showing no fewer than six major routes by which

9. Ibid., March 29, 1851: Calhoun to Fillmore, p. 305.
10. Ibid., March 31, 1851: Calhoun to Stuart, p. 306.
11. March 31, 1851: Munroe to Calhoun, NA, RAC, RG 393, LS.
12. April 1, 1851: Munroe to Jones, NA, RAC, RG 94, AGO, M-161-1851, LR.

the invading force could reach Canyon de Chelly, as well as the location of important springs, the map also showed where Navajo cornfields—a vital source of supply for cavalry—might be found.[13]

In the days immediately following, Colonel Munroe built all of his preparations on a projected force of about four hundred men: four companies of dragoons, three of infantry, and one of artillery. A tentative date of May 15 was selected for the departure. As late as May 2 Munroe, perhaps intentionally, appeared to be undecided about the route he would follow, although his ultimate choice was to rendezvous at Laguna and from there proceed either through Wingate Valley to Ojo del Oso (a route still unexplored by the military) or by way of El Morro to Zuni. That he favored the latter route was indicated first when Henry Dodge was sent on April 14 to negotiate for a supply of corn at Zuni to be held in reserve for the troops at that pueblo. A depot for subsistence stores and more corn was established at Laguna, and additional subsistence stores were laid in at Albuquerque.[14]

On his return to Cebolleta, Dodge reported that he had succeeded in purchasing one thousand bags of corn and could obtain as much more if it were needed. He left a man at the pueblo to guard the supply pending Munroe's arrival. A few days before he reached Zuni, Dodge learned that a party of Navajos had wounded a Zuni man and stolen four horses within sight of the pueblo. About ten days afterward six Navajos approached the pueblo making signs of peace, but when Dodge went out to meet them accompanied by forty Pueblos, the Navajos turned and fled and would not allow Dodge to come close enough to talk with them. Had they desired to, Dodge believed, the Navajos could easily have driven off a number of the Zuni horses and mules, but they had noticeably avoided any display of enmity. During his stay at Zuni, Dodge was informed that Navajos were planting extensively at Canyon de Chelly, many of them were living west of there at Black

13. The main routes are: (1) Abiquiu to the San Juan via Canyon Largo; (2) Jemez to the San Juan via Cabezon, upper Puerco Valley, and Cerro de Huerfano; (3) the Chaco Canyon–Chusca route followed by Colonel Washington in 1849; (4) Jemez via Seven Lakes to the Lower Chusca Valley and Ojo del Oso, with alternate routes northward—one following the eastern slopes of the Chuscas to the San Juan, the other via Ojo de la Trinchera to Cañoncito Bonito and Canyon de Chelly; (5) Albuquerque to Ojo del Oso and beyond via Laguna and the Wingate Valley; (6) Albuquerque to Zuni via Ojo del Gallo and El Morro—the old Spanish trail and route of Maj. Walker's 1847 campaign. A number of subsidiary trails connecting these major routes also are shown.

14. October 10, 1851: Munroe to Jones, NA, AGO, LR, no. 383, 567–450.

Mesa, and *ricos* of the nation had moved north with their herds to the San Juan.

Dodge's information that many of the more prosperous Navajos had moved north to the river confirmed similar reports that Munroe had received from others in his effort to determine the places where his troops would find the largest numbers of the tribe. From Abiquiu, some weeks before, Brevet Major Lawrence P. Graham had reported that a large body of Navajos was encamped on the San Juan. Utes who came to his post had informed Graham that these Navajos "some time last winter seceded from the great body of the nation and are not now on friendly terms with them." [15]

How much importance Colonel Munroe attached to this information is uncertain, but events in the immediate future indicate that a schism of major proportions, stemming from a great tribal Naach'id (or traditional gathering of the nation), found Navajos bitterly divided on the issue of war or peace.[16] Dodge's account of the two opposing factions' appearance at Zuni in a span of ten days suggests that one element of the tribe wished to end hostilities with the Pueblos, possibly with the Bilagáana as well.

Word of Munroe's campaign plans, meanwhile, leaked out almost at once and spread to all parts of the Navajo country; various reactions were soon apparent. Sandoval appeared at Munroe's headquarters in April to ask that firearms be furnished to his Diné Ana'aii. He inquired also about the time set for the troops to march, saying that he would like to accompany the expedition with about twenty of his warriors. Colonel Munroe received him politely but with suspicion and remained noncommittal. Before agreeing to anything that Sandoval pro-

15. April 1, 1851: Graham to McLaws, NA, RAC, RG, 393, G-5-1851, LR.
16. The Navajo word *Naach'id*, which in modern translation loosely means "handling" or "managing" (Wall and Morgan 1958, p. 41), refers to a now obsolescent ceremonial-political gathering of nearly the entire tribe, which is said customarily to have been held during the winter. Some informants, according to David Brugge (1966, pp. 22c–23c), have said it was solely a ceremonial occasion, while "others have described it as having important political functions in the making of war and peace." Its derivation bears some trace of Plains Indian custom— the assemblage forming in a great camp circle—as well as a suggestion of Anasazi or historic Pueblo influence: a ceremonial hogan situated centrally in the camp circle with its floor excavated to some depth below ground level. Brugge mentions traditional references to a Naach'id held in the Dinetah region, possibly in the first half of the 1700s, and states that the last Naach'id of which there is present knowledge was held in the late winter or early spring of 1859. There is some evidence that the Naach'id under consideration here was held in the vicinity of Red Lake.

posed, he felt it was desirable to have the more informed opinion of Colonel Chandler.

Sandoval might ostensibly be at war with western bands of Navajos, Chandler accordingly was advised, but at peace and in communication with the *ricos* of the tribe on the San Juan. Munroe feared that if Sandoval were to give information of his movements to the San Juan Navajos, the military plans soon would be known to the entire tribe. He therefore cautioned Chandler to avoid giving Sandoval any hint of the proposed troop movements, but instead to learn everything he could regarding the Diné Ana'aii who, if they desired, could be of assistance to the department.[17]

Chandler's reply of April 23 was as complicated as warranted by Sandoval's contradictory, complex character. He informed Colonel Munroe, first, that raids had been made by Navajos upon Diné Ana'aii livestock, and that Sandoval and some of his people, as already known, in the past winter had campaigned against the tribe, Sandoval returning with Navajo scalps, captives, and livestock and boasting that he, personally, had killed one Navajo man.

Sandoval was undoubtedly at war with Navajos in the vicinity of Red Lake, Chandler believed, and always had seemed especially hostile to those living near Canyon de Chelly, but appeared to hold no animosity toward the *ricos* on the San Juan. They apparently had not, as other Navajos had, stolen from his herd of livestock. Chandler concluded that Sandoval would not be as hostile to the San Juan Navajos *"unless we make it his interest to be so."*

Sandoval could be trusted *"as a guide"* because he knew it to be to his interest to render service and remain on good terms with the government, Chandler continued, but he had no doubt that as soon as Colonel Munroe's troops began their march the Diné Ana'aii leader would send runners to the Navajos to inform them of the command's route and its strength. Chandler recommended that Sandoval and his warriors be armed and allowed to join Munroe's columns, where they could be watched. He added that although Navajos and Diné Ana'aii continually raided each other's herds there was no apparent desire on the part of either side—with an exception in the case of Sandoval—to kill one another. As for Sandoval, he said, Navajos were "extremely desirous of taking his scalp." He concluded, "Although . . . Sandoval does not seem so hostile to the Indians on the other side of the [San Juan] river, as those about Cheille & Laguna Colorado, yet he says they

17. April 17, 1851: McLaws to Chandler, NA, RAC, RG 393, LS.

all ought to be whipped badly, or they will not keep any treaty they may make."[18]

Several peace overtures were made by Navajos at this time, each offering further evidence bearing on the tribal Naach'id of the previous winter and making it clear that nearly all of the tribe who then had taken a position favoring war—mainly those bands concentrated in the region extending westward from Red Lake to Canyon de Chelly and beyond—now were changing their minds and, in concert with those Navajos gathered on the upper San Juan, wanted to make peace. Only a few bands remained in favor of making war. Word to this effect was received at Cebolleta on April 19 when two Navajos appeared at Colonel Chandler's headquarters saying that they had been sent by headmen of their region near Red Lake to ask for peace.

Some ten or twelve days before, they informed Chandler, a party of American traders had come to the vicinity of Ojos Calientes in the Chusca Valley. While bartering silver belts and red cloth for the Navajos' mules, the traders had told of a campaign that was to be made against them by about six hundred American soldiers.[19] People of their tribe were very much afraid that the Bilagáana intended to punish them severely for what they had done or not done—for stealing sheep and mules and for failing to accept the terms of treaties. They themselves were but *pobres*, the two said: insignificant and poor and chosen for this mission because it would not matter much to anyone if Chandler's soldiers killed them. The headmen had directed that one of the two should remain at Cebolleta while the other returned with the Bilagáana's reply. The man who was to return had been instructed also to make a smoke signal each day and so inform the tribe of his approach. Chandler accordingly held one of the Navajos as hostage while he directed the other to return and ask the headmen to come to Ce-

18. April 23, 1851: Chandler to McLaws, NA, RAC, RG 393, C-37-1851, LR.

19. This may be the first known reference to what evolved into the famous and often quite beautiful Navajo concha belt. Its origin as a foreign trade article (more likely of Mexican rather than American manufacture) might date from the late 1840s. Its fairly common use in 1856 was noted by Jonathan Letterman, post surgeon at Fort Defiance (1856, p. 290). He observed that over short buckskin or red baize breeches and jacket made of blanket or baize, a Navajo man might throw a blanket, "under and sometimes over which is worn a belt, to which are attached oval pieces of silver, plain or variously wrought." John Adair (1944, p. 6) comments that Atsidi Sani, who may have been the first Navajo to work iron, probably learned the trade about 1850 from a Mexican. Conflicting evidence, Adair says, makes it impossible to date the inception of silversmithing as a Navajo craft: the art may have originated with them as early as 1850 or as late as 1870.

bolleta to talk. From the information given him, he advised Colonel Munroe, the delegation might be expected to arrive in ten days. He requested that the department commander instruct him at once as to the course he should pursue.[20]

The ubiquitous Sandoval, who appears to have had a way of knowing just about everything that was happening, shortly afterward assured Colonel Chandler that he had been present at the Naach'id of the past winter. He confirmed the story brought to the post by the two Navajos and said that he was present at the great assemblage when a headman now on the San Juan had urged the tribe to remain at peace with the Americans.[21] While it is conceivable that Sandoval knew what was done at the Naach'id, it is unlikely that he was a participant. At the time of the tribal gathering he was campaigning in Navajo country with the forces of Ramón Luna.

Colonel Munroe's wishes in the matter of a peace council at Cebolleta were bluntly made known. If the Navajos did come in, Chandler was directed to tell them that the treaty made with their nation by Colonel Washington was in full force and was considered binding upon every member of the tribe. Until they complied with terms imposed by the treaty, no other treaty with them would be made or even discussed.[22]

A party of traders returning to Abiquiu at this time brought similar overtures from another direction. Major Graham informed Governor Calhoun that the traders recently had visited Navajos on the San Juan and found them anxiously desirous of peace. Six or seven of their headmen might be expected momentarily at Abiquiu, coming with the hope of making a new treaty. Graham was advised, as Chandler had been, that the 1849 treaty must be complied with before a new treaty could be made. Calhoun then sounded a sterner note than had characterized Munroe's instructions to Chandler. Should the delegation still wish to come to Santa Fe and leave hostages after pledging immediate compliance, it would be well for them, for if they did not, they would receive a beating "that will stop but little short of extermination." [23]

20. April 19, 1851: Chandler to McLaws and enclosure: "Memorandum of 'talk' held with Navajo Indians at Cebolleta, N.M.," NA, RAC, RG 393, C-36-1851, LR.

21. April 23, 1851: Chandler to McLaws, cited above.

22. April 25, 1851: McLaws to Chandler, NA, RAC, RG 393, AGO Letter Book 7, LS.

23. April 26, 1851: Graham to Calhoun (enclosure), NA, RAC, RG 393, G-7-1851, LR; and April 28, 1851: Calhoun to Graham, NA, Territorial Papers, microcopy T-17, roll 1.

The Navajos gave no indication of willingness to accept the 1849 treaty signed by Mariano Martínez and Chapitone. On April 30 six headmen of the Chusca–Red Lake regions arrived at Cebolleta, as Chandler had expected. They were sent back to their homes the following day, Chandler directing them to convey Colonel Munroe's position in the matter to their people. No further overture came from that quarter.

As the day neared for the start of his campaign, Colonel Munroe ordered Captain William H. Gordon, commanding at Taos, to be prepared to move his company to Abiquiu to relieve Major Graham, whose dragoons were to accompany the expedition. On the following day, May 2, Colonel Chandler was informed that Pueblos of Zuni would be acceptable as auxiliaries if it was thoroughly understood that they would receive no payment and would not be furnished with provisions, arms, or ammunition. Meanwhile, the delegation of headmen from the San Juan that Graham was expecting at Abiquiu arrived instead at Cebolleta. They were dismissed without a hearing and with the same admonition given the other delegations.

The hour for Colonel Munroe's columns to march came and passed. Troops at the outposts awaited orders to rendezvous at Laguna while the department commander kept his own council at Santa Fe. Into this vacuum filtered ominous word of a change in the Navajos' recent peaceable attitude. Although the *ricos* encamped on the upper San Juan remained quiet, others lower on the river in the vicinity of the Carrizo Mountains were said to be moving southward, on both sides of the Chuscas, and talking of making war on the settlements. An air of uncertainy seemed to prevail among many of the tribe. Several Navajo families living near Cubero expressed a desire to find shelter with Sandoval. Colonel Chandler directed them to come to Cebolleta; if he found they told the truth and had not been engaged in raiding, and if no objection was raised in Santa Fe, he would permit them to join the Diné Ana'aii.[24]

This mounting tension reached an apex in the warm night of June 15, 1851, when three murderous attacks occurred within a few miles of the mountain village. A man named Mulligan, employed as clerk by Henry Dodge, reached Cebolleta first—on foot, disheveled and bleeding profusely from a wound, and still clutching a revolver in one hand. He told of being attacked by a party of eight Navajos at a spring

24. June 2, 1851: Chandler to McLaws, NA, RAC, RG 98, C-55-1851, LR. Chandler's action was approved by Munroe and Calhoun on June 10.

on the western approach to the Puerco. The mule he had been riding also had been wounded in the fight and he had abandoned it. With only the revolver to defend himself, he had fired three times. One of the shots, he thought, had found a target. In any case he had managed to escape. Two of the same Navajos, it was learned later, the same night attacked but failed to kill a New Mexican who was traveling the Albuquerque road near the Puerco.

The third incident occurred several hours later within five miles of Cebolleta. One of the headmen of the San Juan Navajos, traveling with three companions, was accosted and stopped by a roving party composed of New Mexicans—possibly from Cebolleta—and members of Sandoval's Diné Ana'aii. The four travelers explained their purpose in being there: they wished to come in to see and talk with the Bilagáana officer Chandler.

Those in the party who ringed about them debated among themselves. They would conduct the Navajos to the officer's presence, they finally said, but only if the Navajos proved their good intentions by surrendering their arms. As soon as the Navajos gave up their weapons, the New Mexicans and Diné Ana'aii fell upon them furiously and killed three with clubs and stones. The fourth man somehow escaped in the darkness. Of the three left dead, one had signed treaties of peace with Newby and Washington—the headman called Chapitone.[25]

Not long afterward it was learned that Colonel Munroe, after some indecision, had postponed his carefully laid plans for a Navajo expedition. The presence of large number of Apaches in close proximity to settlements of San Miguel County, coinciding with a gathering of many Comanches and Apaches in the council grove at Bosque Redondo, Munroe explained, had compelled him to divert all of his disposable dragoon strength to patrol the eastern frontier.[26] Another, although unstated, deterrent may have been Munroe's imminent relief from command of the Ninth Military Department. Lieutenant Colonel Edwin Vose Sumner even then was marching westward with reinforcements from Fort Leavenworth.

25. June 18, 1851: Chandler to McLaws, enclosure with October 10, 1851: Munroe to Adjutant General, NA, AGO, LR, no. 383, 567–450.
26. Ibid.

9

Forts on the Frontier

In reporting the attack upon Chapitone, Colonel Chandler went so far as to say that the Navajos had been "treacherously murdered," but he ascribed no motive that would explain the act, and (despite one provision of the 1849 treaty) he found it unnecessary to investigate or bring the murderers to account. To what degree, therefore, the incident may have reflected Diné Ana'aii partisanship or concern in the peace-or-war struggle then dividing the Navajo nation is impossible to say. The attack apparently was not provoked, the identity of Chapitone must have been known to those who killed him, and the murderers probably knew that their savage action would have predictable repercussions. Colonel Munroe understood the implications; he remarked later that he had realized at once that the deed was calculated to provoke Navajos to retaliation.[1]

The first act of reprisal characteristically brought Navajo raiders down upon the pueblo of Isleta, which so far as is known, was innocent of any aggression. Although dragoon companies in the Rio Abajo were being reinforced and alerted to possible attack, the Navajos succeeded in driving off a sizable herd of the pueblo's livestock before any effective pursuit could be organized.[2]

1. June 18, 1851: Chandler to McLaws, enclosure with October 10, 1851: Munroe to Adjutant General, NA, AGO, LR, no. 383, 567-450.
2. The raid on Isleta, June 25 (Abel 1915, p. 364), moved the territorial legislature on June 30 to memorialize President Fillmore, requesting that he authorize the organization and arming of volunteer militia subject only to the command of Gov. Calhoun (ibid., pp. 366–68). On July 9, reiterating a previously stated conviction that regular troops were unable to offer protection to citizens of New Mexico, the legislature called upon Calhoun to use the powers of his office and raise volunteer companies to campaign against Navajos and Apaches. The legislators, predominantly New Mexicans, further asked that Calhoun distribute among the volunteers "in proportion to their numbers, an equal share of all the Captives, and other spoils that may be taken. . . ." (ibid., pp. 386–87).

A second blow, in some ways reminiscent of the Sarracino incident, was directed late one night in July against the party of Robert Nesbit and Hiram R. Parker, who were engaged in cutting hay under government contract for the army quartermaster. A scarcity of spring rain had left the ground cover of the lower valleys short and brown; for lush grass the partners had been forced to a higher elevation in the Jemez Mountains. At the Valle Grande, an emerald swatch surrounded by tall timber some forty miles from Santa Fe, a blockhouse of green cottonwood logs had been built. Connected to it at the rear was a corral of the same logs laid one on top of the other to a height of four or five feet. Here with a train of mule wagons purchased from Henry Dodge's associate, Pinckney Tully, the Nesbit-Parker outfit had been cutting a rich harvest.

A soaking rain fell on the mountain meadows through the afternoon of July 2, turning to a steady drizzle after nightfall. Because of the rain and darkness, Nesbit said later, a man posted on guard at the corral failed to detect any sign of danger until a Navajo's arrow pierced his neck. Almost at the same instant the guard pressed the trigger of his gun, the shot being enough to arouse the men asleep in the blockhouse. For two hours, Nesbit and Parker said, they and their beleaguered men "kept up a continued fight . . . on the three sides of the house, while another portion of the Indians were endeavoring to pull down the corral to get the animals out, which they succeeded in doing . . . a little after three o'clock—when they drove off all the animals, consisting of over one hundred head in all."

Navajos in the attacking party, they informed Colonel Munroe, numbered between 250 and 300 warriors. Affidavits were to be furnished, and in the circumstances they would request Munroe to inform them how to recover their animals or, failing that, apply for cash indemnification, as the loss was so great they it might ruin them.[3]

Another version of the incident was related shortly afterward by a party of eleven Pueblos of Jemez who by mere chance encountered a detachment of dragoons patrolling southward through the mountains from Abiquiu. They had been herding cattle in the vicinity the night of the attack, the Pueblos said. As the Navajos had withdrawn with the stolen horses and mules the Jemez had followed quietly, keeping themselves hidden. Finally, at a place where the Navajos had to de-

3. July 6, 1851: Nesbit and Parker to Munroe, enclosure with October 10, 1851: Munroe to Adjutant General, cited above.

scend a steep hill that left them exposed and at a disadvantage, the Jemez killed two of them and captured five mules. Two of the mules had been left on the road back to the Valle Grande; the other three had been restored to Nesbit and Parker. Lieutenant Beverly H. Robertson felt the matter worth investigating and persuaded one of the Pueblos to accompany his detachment to the hay camp.

He reported later that he found the blockhouse situated on a hill of gentle declivity, within fifty yards of a piece of woodland, the corral, which joined the house, being on that side. He spoke with the guard who had been wounded at the start of the attack, examined a part of the corral that the Navajos had torn down, and was shown where forty or fifty arrows had been fired at the blockhouse door to discourage any effort by the men inside to break out. There were no loopholes in the house, Robertson observed thoughtfully, and the only opening toward the corral (through which Parker had fired two shots from his revolver) was so high in the wall that one ball struck the topmost log on the opposite side of the corral.

"There were no guns fired at the Indians, except *one*, by the sentinel on Post," Robertson reported. "The sentinel said it was impossible, from the darkness of the night, to tell their exact number, but he believed there could not have been less than forty."

The guard's story, Robertson believed, fitted rather well with what the Jemez had told him—that the Navajos numbered perhaps thirty or forty warriors. Men employed by Nesbit and Parker at the hay camp also confirmed the Pueblos' accounting for stolen livestock: the Navajos had driven off six horses and forty-three mules, of which five had been recovered.[4]

From Bosque Redondo, meanwhile, Comanche bands that had gathered in council with the Jicarillas filtered north to the upper Canadian or northwest through Anton Chico toward Santa Fe. Except for the theft of a stray beef or two, no depredations were charged against them, and dragoon patrols assigned to watching them reported no conduct on their part that could cause alarm in settlements where the Comanches might appear to barter horses or trade for supplies. One

4. Ibid., July 7, 1851: Robertson to Graham, and July 17, 1851: Robertson to McLaws. In reporting this incident to the adjutant general, Munroe noted that although Nesbit and Parker had said they would furnish affidavits supporting their claims of loss, the papers never were received. "I am this particular in regard to this affair," Munroe commented, "because I believe it to be the intention of Nesbitt & Co. to petition Congress for a remuneration for their losses."

unfortunate incident occurred when horses were stolen from a band that came in friendship to Santa Fe to talk peace, but the matter was straightened out before ugly consequences developed.

An encampment of three hundred Comanche warriors near Santo Domingo, therefore, caused no especial alarm, although Captain Horace Brooks was directed on July 2 to leave Santa Fe with a detachment of artillery to keep an eye on their movements. In recent days, it was said, they had butchered a few beeves at Anton Chico and La Cuesta—their usual levy upon the Spanish settlements—but otherwise had harmed no one. Brooks reported a few days later that after trading at the pueblo for supplies the Comanches had crossed the river and taken a westerly direction. He believed at first they might have gone toward San Ysidro, but a patrol sent out on their trail was called back when it was learned that the Comanches had been seen south of Albuquerque.

At Cochiti, where he stopped with Major Henry L. Kendrick, Captain Brooks was informed that the Comanches were not wandering aimlessly about the country, but in fact were preparing to make a surprise attack upon Navajos of the Chusca region.[5]

The truth of this was established when a party of more than one hundred warriors separated from the main band July 4 and halted in the vicinity of Cebolleta, while an interpreter went ahead with a few men to ask Colonel Chandler's permission for them to pass through the village. Chandler understood the Comanches to say that they had lately left the columns of Colonel Sumner proceeding along the Arkansas toward Santa Fe, and that they were now on a war expedition into Navajo country. Although he gave the Comanches permission to pass, the war party failed to appear and Chandler learned afterward that they had been seen on the Albuquerque road returning to the river.[6] Later it was discovered that the shortage of grass and water, due to the extreme dry spell, caused them to abandon the campaign.

Comanches were still in the region the following week when a war party said to number about three hundred Indians surprised Edward Ownby's hay camp near the Ojo del Gallo and so savaged the hay cutters that only one man of fourteen was known to have escaped unhurt. As always in such affairs, early reports were wildly inaccurate; it was not until Lieutenant William Duncan Smith, patrolling westward from Cebolleta, reached Cubero late in the same day that anything like a

5. July 8, 1851: Brooks to McLaws, NA, AGO, LR, enclosure with no. 327, 567-450.
6. Ibid., July 5, 1851: Chandler to McLaws.

coherent story emerged.[7] Even then details were lacking and the identity of the attacking Indians was uncertain. Four men from the hay camp, all wounded in one or more places by arrows, were found at Cubero. They said the attack had occurred just before daybreak, while most in the camp were still asleep. What had happened to the others they could not say.

Although darkness had closed over the town, Lieutenant Smith delayed long enough to requisition a broken-down oxcart, the best that Cubero seemed to offer, which might be needed if more wounded men were found. Then, with the cart rumbling behind, he set out in the night with twenty dragoons of his detachment. By starlight, first at a trot and then slowing to a walk because his horses were jaded, Smith had progressed about ten miles when a fifth wounded man was discovered lying in a ditch. In such light as could be made it was found that the man had taken five or six arrow wounds. He said his name was Fitzgerald and that he was overseer of Ownby's camp—Ownby himself not having been present when the Indians attacked. Risking a chance that the Indians might still be in the vicinity, Lieutenant Smith divided his command, directing his sergeant to select such horses as were still able to go on and with a few men thus mounted continue the search until he reached the scene of the attack. Fitzgerald, although critically wounded, gave an account of what happened while they waited for the patrol to return.

One of his men had gotten up about an hour before dawn, he said, to hunt for deer—the camp's meat supply being low. "He made a fire to cook some coffee, before going out—there was one man on guard at the time. Shortly after, hearing a very loud Indian yell, I arose and saw that we were completely surrounded by about three hundred Indians, who had formed two belts around us." The circle of Indians nearest the camp had tied their horses to the brush and were on foot, those beyond remaining mounted. "Both parties immediately commenced firing upon us, before we had time to put on an article of clothing. The majority of our party were soon wounded, and believing their situation to be hopeless, they took to flight, but rallied and then fled again."

Fitzgerald said the Indians, surprisingly, made little effort to stop them but instead continued to close in upon himself and two others, one named Parker and the other Smith, who remained in the camp. Parker, he said, "was soon brought to the ground, and [Smith], in at-

7. July 13, 1851: Smith to Whistler; July 16, 1851: Ownby to Munroe; and Whistler to Chandler, NA, AGO, LR, enclosure with no. 383, cited above.

tempting to fight through was also brought down. I found my way through, got two more wounds, and crossed the creek where I hid. It was then day and I saw them mutilate and scalp Parker, and, apparently, go through the same operation with B. Smith—after which, taking everything transportable which was about, they burnt the wagon body &c, fired several shots, and left the place."

Much later that night the sergeant's patrol returned, bringing another wounded man they had found on the way. The bodies of Parker and Smith they had seen, as Fitzgerald described them, lying near the camp. With the two wounded survivors the dragoons then turned back toward Cubero, reaching the town shortly before daybreak. Several others who had escaped and hidden themselves in the nearby mountains had come in during the night, one bringing a New Mexican woman who had been at the camp and also was wounded. Three of the party remained unaccounted for and were presumed dead.

The recent presence of a Comanche war party near Cebolleta, in numbers approximating those seen at the Gallo, made it appear that these Indians may have swung back from the river and attacked Ownby's men. Lieutenant Smith was naturally curious. On questioning the overseer again, he learned that the Indians wore buckskin leggings and had painted their faces and bodies; all were adorned with feathers and were well mounted. In short, it was the usual description of a carefully organized war party. The description may have fitted the Comanches very well, but the lieutenant gathered other evidence.[8] During the night preceding the attack, citizens of Cubero informed him, one of Sandoval's Diné Ana'aii had encountered a hostile Navajo in the mountains north of the village. The Navajo, it was said, told Sandoval's partisan that three large war parties were approaching from the Chuscas. One would strike at Cubero, a second would attack in the vicinity of Cebolleta a day or two later, and the third would sweep toward the river.

Eight wounded survivors accompanied Lieutenant Smith's detachment back to Cebolleta. The return was painfully slow, most of the mounted company plodding on foot. A number of the dragoon horses were so worn out they were abandoned on the road, while the best of

8. Scalping was commonly practiced by Comanches; while occasionally a part of Navajo warfare, it apparently was so rare that not more than two or three specific references to Navajos taking scalps were found in some 30,000 military and civil documents examined during research for this work.

them, hardly able to hobble, had to be led. Shortly after their return, Colonel Chandler, then in Santa Fe, was apprised of what had happened. Lieutenant J. N. G. Whistler, in temporary command, sent a small force of men back to the Gallo to guard the hay stored there—some four hundred thousands pounds, destined for the Cebolleta garrison, which the Indians for some reason had neglected to destroy. He talked with the hay camp survivors and with Sandoval and all confirmed the story told by the people at Cubero.

The Diné Ana'aii leader told Whistler that some of his band had been out hunting when a party of Navajos came upon them and took away their horses, explaining that the Navajos had gone to war against the Americans and so needed all of the horses they could find. If Sandoval's information was accurate, about 700 warriors were now at large; of this number 260 took part in the attack on Ownby's camp.

Such was the state of affairs in the Ninth Military Department when Colonel Edwin Vose Sumner relieved Colonel Munroe of command on July 19, 1851.

Let it be said at once that if Colonel Sumner was not the most abrasive and difficult officer ever placed in command it was not for lack of his earnest effort. Let it be said also that a trait of character that in part led subordinates to call him "Bull-head Sumner" contributed to his most redeeming quality: he was—for practical if not humane considerations—unalterably opposed to arming volunteer militia for thinly disguised slave raids against Navajos or other Indians. In fairness it must further be said that the nickname was first bestowed with no hard feeling but some awe after a musket ball, striking him fairly in the head, caromed off and Sumner recovered with no apparent ill effects.

A native of Boston, Sumner was imbued with certain extreme manifestations of a Yankee heritage: an immoderate penuriousness and a conviction that, through him, God's will in all matters worthwhile would be done. It had not been his fortune to attend the United States Military Academy; his advancement would seem to have been won on staying power. After fourteen years in the infantry he had been transferred in 1833 to serve as captain under Colonel Henry Dodge in the second of the two newly formed regiments of dragoons. Eighteen years of duty as a dragoon officer on the western frontier and in the war with Mexico seemed only to have heightened his regard for the infantry. At the time of his return to New Mexico he was a campaigner as toughened as a pig's nose. He was in his fifty-fifth year.

A fair share of the military program he was to impose on New Mexico—and the Navajos—was not of his own conception, but originated in orders received from Secretary of War Charles M. Conrad before Sumner departed from Fort Leavenworth on May 26 for Santa Fe. He was instructed by Conrad to, among other things, enforce rigid economies, remove troops garrisoned in towns to frontier posts nearer to the Indians, and, as nearly as possible, inflict "severe chastisement" in one campaign against Navajos and in another against Utes and Apaches.[9] Aware of the limited force that Colonel Munroe would relinquish to the new commander, and in view of the expeditions Sumner was expected to make, Adjutant General Roger Jones offered Sumner a full regiment of the recently organized Mounted Riflemen. Sumner declined testily, saying that if he needed any more mounted troops he would not care to take the regiment offered him, "for although they can be made good riflemen, it will take a long time to make them good horsemen," and in any case, "I did say to you, Sir, that I did not wish any more troops sent to New Mexico than enough to fill the companies now there." [10]

Accordingly, when he started across the plains, Sumner took with him only 523 raw recruits and 10 officers—the last including a dragoon officer long favored in his eyes, who might be termed a military protégé: Brevet Major James H. Carleton.

Colonel Sumner's column raised the modest stone and adobe buildings of Lucien Maxwell's ranch on July 10 and a short while later, after leaving the Bent's Fort road and proceeding due west up a broad valley for one mile, came to the Rayado post occupied from spring of 1850 by two companies of dragoons. Situated on the south bank of the stream some three miles from the Sangre de Cristo foothills, the establishment, commanded by Captain Richard Stoddert Ewell, served both as hay camp and winter grazing ground for the department's surplus horses

9. April 1, 1851: Conrad to Sumner (Abel 1915, pp. 383–84). One notable means of economy that Conrad proposed—and that ultimately failed—was the planting of "kitchen gardens" by troops stationed at frontier posts. Sumner enforced the economy measures Conrad favored, with numerous innovations of his own, but from the outset ignored the Secretary's instructions to "act in concert with the Superintendent of Indian Affairs [Calhoun], whom you will allow to accompany you in the expeditions into the Indian territory, if he should deem it proper to do so, and to whom you will afford every facility for the discharge of his duties."

10. April 24, 1851: Sumner to Jones, NA, AGO, S-190-1851, LR, 567-452.

and mules. The setting offered magnificent sweeps of landscape and a mountain road to Taos, but there were certain disadvantages as well. Timber covering the nearer mesas, except those to the north, would shelter attacking Indians; the land and quarters, all owned by the obliging Maxwell, carried an annual rental fee of $3,400.[11]

Until he learned of this last contingency, Sumner may have considered the Rayado seriously as a location for his future headquarters. As it was, before continuing his march southward, he directed Captain Ewell to examine and report on a site that had appealed to him a day or so before—the vicinity near the crossing of the Canadian with the Bent's Fort road, six miles below the present town of Raton. Ewell's report was discouraging: the Canadian at this point was ephemeral; where it chose to emerge from the ground at all, the stream was sluggish and carried only water enough between steep banks to wet the pastern joints of a horse.[12]

Although he had traveled through the same country five years before with Kearny's Army of the West, Colonel Sumner examined the timbered river valleys and vast open plains lying between with a fresh and deepened interest. Santa Fe, he had firmly decided, would not be his departmental headquarters. Somewhere between Tecolote and San Miguel he turned off the main road to the capital and marched down the Pecos a distance in search of an eligible site. Nothing is found to tell how far down the stream he explored, but the evidence suggests he went no farther than Anton Chico. What he saw apparently did not please him. He reached Santa Fe with his footsore command on July 19.[13]

His first action and belligerent comment describing it are well known. He broke up the military post at Santa Fe—"that sink of vice and extravagance"—and moved the supplies and all troops except one company of artillery out of that sinful place to a site he had determined upon for a new depot and for his headquarters. Dispersal of the garrison and its resultant economic blow to the capital's mercantile life caused grumbling and cries of protest, but to this din Sumner was aloof.[14]

11. October 25, 1851: Maj. Thomas Swords to Maj. Gen. Thomas S. Jesup, *Senate Exec. Docs.*, 32d Cong., 1st sess., no. 1, pt. 1, pp. 235–41; and April 14, 1851: Bvt. 2d Lt. Parke to McLaws, enclosure with April 30, 1851: Munroe to Jones, NA, AGO, M-228-1851, LR, 567-449.

12. July 17, 1851: Ewell to Buell, NA, RAC, RG 393, E-3-1851, LR.

13. Swords letter to Jesup, cited above.

14. October 24, 1851: Sumner to Jones, NA, RAC, RG 393, AGO Letter Book 8, no. 81, LS.

Eight benefactors had appeared almost within hours of his arrival and offered him a twenty-year lease on a one-mile-square section of land for the token sum of five dollars. They said that Sumner might select at will from a land grant lying within Taos and San Miguel counties. It was stipulated further that while Sumner might select a section of his own choice, neither he nor any successor to his command could use the land for any purpose other than that of a military post; the premises were not to be "underlet" to anyone for any purpose whatever; and the land and all improvements on it would revert to the lessors at the end of twenty years.

The offer was made by Robert T. Brent, a member of the legislature from Santa Fe; Donaciano Vigil, who appeared for Gregorio Trujillo; James M. Giddings, a Kentuckian who had first come to New Mexico in 1835 and in 1851 was serving as probate clerk for Santa Fe County; George H. Estes; William Barclay (of Barclay's Fort); Herman von Grolman; Henry O'Neil; and Samuel B. Watrous, whose ranch buildings were found among cottonwoods at the junction of Sapello Creek with the Mora River, downstream only a short walk from Barclay's establishment.[15]

A proposal so alluringly generous must have been irresistible. Sumner lost no time in hastening the departure of troops toward the chosen location. Brevet Lieutenant Colonel Edmund Brooke Alexander, in response to Sumner's orders, abandoned the post at Las Vegas early on July 26 and in the evening of the same day arrived at the site of the new fort and headquarters on Coyote Creek. With him he brought his own Company G, Third Infantry, Brevet Major Philip R. Thompson's Company F and Carleton's Company K, First Dragoons. They were joined next day by Company D, Third Infantry and a detachment of recruits commanded by Second Lieutenant John C. Moore, who had marched from Santa Fe on July 23. Colonel Sumner is believed to have arrived on July 30, and in orders issued August 2, when construction was started, named the post Fort Union.[16]

15. July (?), 1851: Brent et al. to Sumner, NA, RAC, RG 393, Dept. of N.M., no. L3, Unentered Letters Received, box 40. I have departed from the spelling of three names as they appear in the original lease: Doniciano Vigil, Herman Grollman, and James B. Watrous. The document appears to be an important archival stray. Although the Fort Union military reservation was increased to 8 miles square in 1852, buildings of the first garrison occupied about 80 acres, or one-eighth of a square mile.

16. Post Returns, Fort Union, July, 1851; and AGO Memorandum: "Fort Union," dated September 12, 1929, NA, microcopy 617, roll 1305. Alexander noted

The site was a safe one hundred miles from Munroe's den of iniquity. Sumner directed that the first buildings of unbarked pine logs be laid out in an open square two miles west of the Bent's Fort branch of the Santa Fe Trail and closely situated under foothills of the Sangre de Cristos. Ruts of a new wagon road freshly furrowed the plain eastward across a grassy sweep of valley toward the timber and wild game that could be procured from the Turkey Mountains.

During the first week of August Colonel Sumner remained at the tent encampment, his hours consumed by a hundred details that demanded attention, but none so important as the planning of Fort Union's buildings and his forthcoming Navajo campaign. At Santa Fe, Major Kendrick of the Second Artillery anticipated a problem of the campaign when he inquired if Colonel Sumner expected him to take his company's camp women into Navajo country. His own wish was to leave them behind, to be sent along at a more convenient time.[17] Sumner's reply, if any was made, has not been found. But possibly harder to deal with were inquiries Sumner received from Governor Calhoun, with whom he had started quarreling almost from the moment of his arrival in the territory.

Perhaps forewarned by Colonel Munroe of Calhoun's tendency to assume an air of omniscience in military matters, Sumner curtly informed the governor he might accompany the Navajo expedition if he were determined to do so but made it clear that Calhoun's presence would be unwelcome. At the same time, Sumner declined to give any assurance that military escorts would be provided when Calhoun or one of his agents wished to travel in Indian country. Hostility between the two men deepened as Calhoun, in turn, tirelessly lectured Sumner on how to operate his department command.

Only three accounts of Colonel Sumner's Navajo campaign have thus far come to light. Two of them—the report of Sumner himself,

---

that on July 29 the two dragoon companies were "transferred to Dragoon Camp near this Post"—without further identifying the camp's whereabouts. The garrison, exclusive of dragoons, numbered 4 officers and 216 enlisted men present for duty. 2d Lt. Lewis H. Marshall had marched from Santa Fe in temporary command of Company D, 3rd Infantry. The other officer present was Asst. Surgeon Thomas A. McPartin. According to the AGO Memorandum, "July 26, 1851, date of first arrival of troops, is usually regarded by this Department as the date of the establishment of Fort Union."

17. July 31, 1851: Kendrick to Buell, NA, RAC, RG 393, K-2-1851, LR.

and the diary of James A. Bennett, a trooper in Company I, First Dragoons—give little more than a sketchy outline.[18] An excellent account of what befell the column on its westward march to Navajo country is found in one of the diaries of Richard H. Kern, who regrettably—for our purposes here—parted with Sumner at Zuni.

Sumner set out from Santo Domingo on August 17. His command approximated in size the force that had accompanied Colonel Washington two years before: four companies of dragoons, two companies of the Third Infantry, and one of the Second Artillery—some 350 men. A train of fifty wagons followed in the rear of the columns, loaded with supplies intended principally for the new military post Sumner proposed to establish in Navajo country. Henry Dodge rode with the command as sutler. He may have been placed in charge of the civilian teamsters; certainly he was responsible for about ten drovers and a large remuda of mules, sheep, and cattle also destined for the new fort.

After crossing the Rio Grande at Albuquerque the troops proceeded westward by way of Laguna and Cubero, Kern noting in his diary that "Capt Dodge prevailed on the Col. to go over the Mountain" on a trail to El Morro running a bit south of Colonel Washington's 1849 route.[19] Approaching Ojo del Gallo, near the point where Ownby's hay camp had been attacked by Navajos the previous month, Private Bennett remarked that he saw the bones of four of the victims but could not reach them, presumably because the bodies had fallen or been thrown into deep crevices of lava malpais that channels the region.

Navajos struck first at Sumner's column near Pescado Springs in the night of August 30. Their raid upon the mule herd was undetected until the chief arriero, Joaquín, came into camp to report that all of the mules but two had been run off. "Old Bull," as Sumner is characterized in the Kern diary, roared with displeasure. He aroused the troops by

18. October 24, 1851: Sumner to Jones, cited above, and "James A. Bennett: A Dragoon in New Mexico, 1850–1856," ed. Brooks and Reeve 1947, pp. 79–81. The third account appears in the 1851 journal of Pvt. Josiah M. Rice, published in 1970 as A Cannoneer in Navajo Country, ed. Richard H. Dillon. Rice adds helpful background information and his narrative tends to confirm what is unstated but implicit in Bennett: Sumner's Navajo campaign was a fiasco. Like Bennett, Rice wrote his journal long afterward and made serious errors; both journals must be approached with great care.

19. Kern Diary, 1851, vol. 1, H.M. 4277. Kern mapped and pictorially recorded the expedition of Capt. Lorenzo Sitgreaves from Zuni Pueblo to Camp Yuma near the junction of the Gila and Colorado rivers. Kern remained with Sitgreaves and most of his party at Zuni, awaiting the return from Cañoncito Bonito of Maj. H. L. Kendrick and an escorting detachment of thirty men of Company B, 2d Artillery.

having a bugler sound assembly and then ordered all remaining animals to be picketed within the limits of his camp. Most, if not all, of the mules were recovered next day under circumstances that suggest the Navajos permitted the animals to escape.

At Cañoncito Bonito, a place known to Navajos as Tséhootsoh (or Meadows in the Rocks), Colonel Sumner found what he regarded as an ideal site for a military post, a choice deplored by successive post commanders because on three sides the narrow canyon was hemmed in by almost vertical walls of rock and scrubby sand topped by a southward-tilting tableland that made the location not merely vulnerable but inviting to hostile attack. An attacking force could (and in time would) drop musket balls and arrows upon Sumner's fort below with about the ease that peas would be shelled into a pot upon a stove.

Hell's Gate, as it soon became known to troops garrisoned there, officially was named Fort Defiance.[20] The wagon train, infantry, and a detachment of Major Kendrick's artillery were left there with Major Electus Backus, a rugged campaigner then about fifty years old, who was ordered to start constructing a log fort at once. Supplies for the balance of the command were transferred to pack mules and, with two mountain howitzers unlimbered and packed with ammunition on the backs of mules, the march was resumed. Sumner's objective was the western entrance to Canyon de Chelly.

The Navajos, who for more than a week had known of Sumner's progress, remained out of sight until the command continued from Cañoncito Bonito. A warrior then came to the camp and was instructed by Sumner to carry a message back, asking two of the headmen known to be in the vicinity to come, with several others, to talk. Something in the colonel's words or manner failed to convince the Indians of his friendly purpose; when Sumner finally concluded that the headmen were not coming in, he ordered the troops thereafter to fire at the Navajos on sight. A vagueness coupled with annoyance is detected in his remark, "We killed and wounded a number of them, but I cannot say how many. They never faced us, or gave us an opportunity to inflict upon them any signal chastisement."

20. Bennett's journal indicates the troops arrived there on August 21, which seems improbable as they would have had to march about 250 miles in five days. Fort Defiance was established officially on September 18, 1851, by Orders No. 29, 9th Military Department. Van Valkenburgh (1941) says the site "was a favored Navajo rendezvous in the pre-American era. Medicine men here collected herbs known as Łe'eze', Horse Medicine, and the bubbling springs were shrines into which white shell and turquoise were thrown as payment or pleas for further blessings."

Sumner's annoyance may have stemmed as well from the fact that his command, reduced to about two hundred troops, was constantly flanked by Navajos who remained out of rifle range during daylight but closed in at night, harassing the picket lines and occasionally firing into the camp. After an enlisted man was wounded in the leg seriously enough to require carrying on a litter, trooper Bennett noted that Major George A. H. Blake of the First Dragoons each night ordered a trench to be dug inside his tent, in which he felt reasonably secure. While Sumner's report seems to imply that he was in command of the situation at all times and troubled only by the Navajos' unwillingness to stand still and be shot at, Bennett's testimony suggests both less and more than that.

His object, Sumner later explained, was to attack the Navajos wherever he encountered them and to destroy their crops. But in this he was disappointed, as few Indians were seen in the canyon and little damage was done to orchards and fields under cultivation. The troops penetrated De Chelly Canyon twelve or fourteen miles. Their progress was protected along the south rim of the gorge by a detachment of dragoons, some mounted and others on foot, sent in advance with Major Lawrence Graham.

Sumner judged the canyon to be a bit more than one hundred yards wide with perpendicular sandstone walls as much as six hundred feet high—errors in judgment on the conservative side. After marching about four miles the column came under attack from Navajos observed on the high north rim who loosed showers of arrows and musket balls followed by a frightening but not very dangerous avalanche of rocks. An attempt to scale the cliffs and get within range of the Indians was made by troops commanded by Brevet Major Philip R. Thompson and Captain Richard Ewell, but soon was abandoned as hopeless. Sumner said he halted his command at three o'clock in the afternoon. While the men and horses were resting he decided that, because the Indians on the canyon rim above were far out of reach of his firearms, it would be "prudent and proper to leave the Cañon." The withdrawal was made safely that evening.

Incidents of the day were recorded by Bennett and Private Josiah Rice of the Second Artillery in the candid prose of enlisted men communicating their thoughts to a diary instead of in the selective manner a commander of troops might use to report a not very successful military operation.

The morning began with a Navajo fusillade that succeeded only in wounding one horse, but badly enough that the animal had to be destroyed. More for moral effect than anything else, as few of his enemy could be seen, Sumner ordered a round fired by the two howitzers, followed by a volley of rifle fire. Soon afterward the troops raised camp and began the march into the canyon, a march that in Bennett's memory turned into an enjoyable picnic at first only slightly marred when a musket ball occasionally whizzed past. After traveling about two miles the command "feasted sumptuously" from a cornfield and watermelon patch, later destroying what they had not consumed. They had not gone much further, when, coming upon a burgeoning peach orchard, "we regaled ourselves and filled our pockets and sacks." They might have better prodded a hornets' nest; the air suddenly buzzed with musket balls fired from the rimrock and the men were forced to find shelter among rocks, where they remained the rest of the day.

A scene that Bennett found unforgettable came as night darkened the color and then closed out the massive shape of the canyon walls: lights of a thousand little fires glowed on the canyon rim. "The dark forms of the savages were seen moving about them," he observed. A council of the officers was called, at which it was decided that the Navajos so greatly outnumbered his command that Sumner would be justified in withdrawing. The horses accordingly were saddled at about ten o'clock and the column started back down the canyon in darkness.

The withdrawal was accomplished in almost absolute silence, Sumner communicating his orders in a whisper. During the morning's march the pace had been unhurried but now, in darkness and the unseen but threatening presence, Private Rice overheard Sumner urging a junior officer to "Hurry up a little faster, Mr. Griffin." Near the entrance to a small branch canyon, still some six miles from the mouth of this frightening gorge, the column almost stumbled upon a party of Navajos. Dogs were heard barking, or so Rice thought, an instant before a rustling wind of arrows and popping of muskets cut the silence. Bugler Tice took an arrow crease in one arm, a dragoon horse was struck in the neck, and Rice "got shot slap-dab through my topknot and never touched a hair." At midnight, with no more damage than this, the troops reached the canyon's welcome mouth.

The concluding episodes of Sumner's only campaign against the Navajos were related tersely by the colonel and in somewhat more detail by Private Bennett. After regaining the entrance to the canyon without loss, Sumner reported that he remained all of the next day encamped on the Chinle Wash and then started back toward Cañoncito Bonito.

That night a few Navajos stole between the picket guards, fired into the camp, and immediately vanished. One of Sumner's orderlies was wounded.

The day spent in camp could not have been a restful one, as Bennett noted that Navajos, as usual, surrounded them. One who was bold enough to attempt cutting a horse out of the picket line was shot in his tracks and then "very much mutilated by the soldiers." Of gravest concern, but a concern Sumner would not mention in his report, was the desperate condition of the horses. The dragoon mounts for the most part were animals bred in Missouri and imported across the plains; accustomed to grain and fodder and frequent watering almost never to be found in this territory, they had been poor things at the start of the campaign but now were worse. As Bennett put it: "Animals all starved out, dying by the dozens daily."

By the time the returning column reached Cañoncito Bonito the loss of horses and pack mules exceeded three hundred. Again, nothing in Colonel Sumner's report is found to confirm this, but Bennett remarked that upon leaving Fort Defiance on the long road to the river the troops moved off on foot, leading those horses that were still able to walk. Somewhere on the return route the command encountered the empty wagons of a supply train on its way from the new post back to Fort Union. "Some hope now if we get sick, we can ride in a wagon," Bennett observed. At Laguna Pueblo it was learned that the Navajos had been there before them and stolen a number of cattle.[21] At Albuquerque, Bennett and his fellow troopers attended a fandango and that night "we forgot all the troubles we have passed through and so we danced until morning."

If his expedition to Canyon de Chelly achieved little of consequence, Sumner's establishment of Fort Defiance in the heart of Navajo country almost at once had a profound effect. Ill chosen as the site was, the presence of the fort and its small garrison unquestionably in months ahead had a restraining influence upon hostile elements of the Navajo nation.

Before his departure from Cañoncito Bonito Colonel Sumner again divided his command. The garrison left with Major Backus included

21. This raid is not referred to elsewhere, but there were other depredations by Navajos during Sumner's absence. Calhoun reported a Navajo attack August 26 near Peña Blanca in which a New Mexican girl was killed and a flock of goats stolen. Two days later, Calhoun reported, he was visited by a delegation of Hopis who "complained that the Navajos had continued to rob them, until they had left them exceedingly poor, and wretched indeed did they look" (Abel 1915, pp. 413, 415).

Assistant Surgeon David. L. Magruder; Captain Ewell and Lieutenant Robert Johnston of Company G, First Dragoons; Lieutenant John P. Holliday's Company K, Second Dragoons; Lieutenant Charles Griffin, temporarily commanding the residue of Major Kendrick's Company B, Second Artillery; Lieutenant Henry B. Schroeder's Company F, Third Infantry; and Lieutenant J. N. G. Whistler, commanding a detachment of Company I, Third Infantry. In all, the major had at his disposal 295 noncommissioned officers and privates.[22]

The stores and livestock brought out with the troops were expected to maintain the garrison for about two months; additional supplies were to be sent in a train of thirty-six wagons in October. Major Backus was ordered to treat the Navajos "with the utmost vigor" until they showed a willingness to remain at peace. If the troops' presence should fail to discourage Navajos from raiding, Sumner believed, then "nothing will do it but their entire extermination."

22. Fort Defiance Post Returns, September, 1851, NA, microcopy 617, roll 301. The garrison also included "2 fifers, 2 ferriers & blacksmiths [and] 1 artificer"—in this case probably meaning either a mechanic or a carpenter. Backus noted that the new fort "is about 70 miles N. West from Zunia and about 190 miles a little north of west from Albuquerque."

10

A Council at Jemez

Upon his less than triumphant return through Santa Fe, Sumner was unable to conceal the fact that his loss of dragoon horses was staggering. Before continuing to his Fort Union headquarters he let it be known that he was considering replacing cavalry with infantry. Governor Calhoun, who had not been reticent in his criticism of Sumner's military policies, was horrified. It would be folly to suppose that fewer than two additional *mounted* regiments would be able to preserve quiet in the territory, Calhoun believed.

He informed Secretary of State Daniel Webster that desperation was abroad in New Mexico and suggested that his relations with the department commander were in such hostile array that one or the other of them should be relieved of duty. At the same time he advised Commissioner of Indian Affairs Luke Lea that he had access to Navajo and Ute funds appropriated by Congress but was powerless to use them, as Sumner denied him military escort to Indian country.[1]

His last statement was no longer quite true. The recently peaceable conduct of Capote and Wiminuche bands of Utes caused Sumner to relent enough to promise Calhoun a military escort to Ute country, but he would not consent to aiding any of the governor's schemes—either altruistic or warlike—involving the Navajos. These Indians had broken so many treaties, he declared, that he regarded it as useless to talk further with them at this time. He proposed that before any action was taken affecting the Navajos Calhoun discuss the matter with him early in November when he expected to be in Santa Fe. From this it is clear that Sumner had no inkling that two days later, at distant Fort Defi-

1. October 1, 1851: Calhoun to Webster, Abel 1915, pp. 430–31; ibid., Calhoun to Lea (same date), pp. 432–33. In ratifying treaties made in 1849, Congress had appropriated $18,000 to implement Articles 9 and 10 of the Navajo treaty and a similar amount for Utes.

ance, Major Backus would embarrassingly enter into a verbal treaty or agreement with Zarcillos Largos and Gordo—a contretemps that will be considered presently.

When Sumner came to Santa Fe in November 1851 he was presented by Calhoun with a petition signed by a group of citizens headed by Preston Beck, Jr., asking that they be allowed to form a volunteer company to aid in protecting the territory against marauding Indians. Sumner at once directed that seventy-five flintlock muskets, bayonets, and cartridge boxes be supplied to Governor Calhoun, but at the same time he imposed two conditions: the arms must be returned to him upon demand, and they were not to be used for campaigns into Indian country unless Beck's volunteers acted in support of regular troops.[2]

In conversation with Calhoun earlier, Sumner had expressed his opposition to citizen forays and made it clear he would use regular troops, if necessary, to forestall them. A prolonged, acrimonious quarrel grew out of this situation, and finally Preston Beck, Jr. declined to accept the arms under Sumner's terms. If the dispute had any importance it was only to emphasize once more that Calhoun was a firm advocate of citizen forays against Indians, and Colonel Sumner—regardless of how unpopular this made him—just as adamantly would oppose arming citizens without strict controls.

At Fort Defiance, where warnings of winter came on each night's colder air, Major Backus exhorted his troops to greater efforts in skills they had never learned or long forgotten. Under the curious and constant surveillance of the Navajos the men toiling at Cañoncito Bonito looked more like woodcutters, farmers, and herdsmen than soldiers. For every man trained early in the use of broadax, saw, and cradling or mowing scythe, ten were tyros. Overcoming their clumsiness with a dozen unaccustomed tools, the men worked with a will. Fort Defiance, a cluster of unbarked log huts arranged in open rows around a rectangular parade ground, began to take shape. The Navajos offered no resistance. A few of the headmen, among them Zarcillos Largos, even made tentative overtures of friendship. Major Backus was wise enough not to turn them away.

By early November quarters for five companies and three sets of

2. November 9, 1851: Calhoun to Sumner, with petition enclosure, NA, RAC, RG 393, N-12-1851, LR; and November 10, 1851: Sumner to Calhoun, NA, RAC, RG 393, AGO Letter Book 8, no. 107, LS.

officers' dwellings had been completed, as well as a hospital and commissary store. In a week more the quartermaster's office and storehouse and the stables were to be ready for use. Before the end of the month Backus expected to finish the remainder of the officers' quarters, each containing one room and a kitchen. Of the results obtained by labor details assigned to herding and hay cutting he could not say as much, though the fault was not theirs. All beef cattle and oxen except those retained in yoke had been slaughtered and the meat salted down. But the animals had been poor and the meat was indifferent—the worst, in fact, that Major Backus ever had seen issued to soldiers. As for the hay brought in from high and low grasslands near the post, he could say little at all except that it was not nearly enough. Perhaps fifty tons were stored away with prospect of gathering twenty tons more before snowfall; it could not sustain the dragoon horses and post mule herd through the winter. The hay was there for the cutting, all right, but the kind of scythes needed for the job had not been sent out from Fort Union.

Difficulties unforeseen by anyone continually arose, but Major Backus was not easily dismayed. "I have never seen a greater amount of labor performed in the same space of time," he said, "by the same number of men." But with 209 miles of slow trail between him and Albuquerque, facts must be faced. He did not see how he could subsist the dragoon mounts unless forage were freighted in. In past weeks twelve of the horses broken down during Sumner's Navajo campaign had died and many more were not expected to live.

There were other warnings of danger to the security of the fort. Provisions for his garrison were running desperately short: fresh meat, though poor, enough for fifteen days; salt meat for eight, coffee and sugar for eleven. Supplies of beans and rice were entirely gone, but he had enough bread and flour to last a month. Nothing had been heard from the promised supply train supposed to have been sent out in October, but his store of food would, he hoped, see them through.[3]

The major's optimism was ill founded. Only a few days before, the supply train on which he was counting so much had lain all but mired in the mud of the Rio Grande. Up to this point the train had been conveyed by Brevet Major Daniel H. Rucker, quartermaster at Fort Union. At the river Rucker washed his hands of the whole sorry business. He turned the train over to Colonel Chandler, whose command

3. November 5, 1851: Backus to 1st Lt. John C. McFerran, AAAG, NA, RAC, RG 393, B-17-1851, LR.

at Cebolleta had been broken up and dispersed at the conclusion of the Navajo campaign. As escort for the train and reinforcements for Fort Defiance, Chandler also took charge of some one hundred men of Companies C and I, Third Infantry.

Wagons were overloaded, the mules were ganted, and the oxen were in worse shape still. Chandler had been ordered to make haste, but he had no idea when he might reach Fort Defiance. All he could say with certainty was that between the river and Laguna it would be necessary to halt the train occasionally and graze the animals for a day or so at a time. Twelve days later he had progressed as far as Laguna, sixty miles from his starting point. He was met at the pueblo by Lieutenant Whistler with an escort of dragoons who had come out from Defiance to report a condition of extreme emergency: the garrison was close to the point of starvation.

Because his mules were better able to travel than the oxen, Chandler cut out the mule-drawn wagons and sent them on with Whistler. A snowstorm had combined with the heavy sand of the road to further delay his progress.[4]

The same snowstorm halted hay-cutting operations at Cienega Amarilla, eight miles south of Fort Defiance. Private Josiah M. Rice expressed the general feeling of despair when he wrote, "we were the Lost Tribe . . . no provisions coming to refresh us." The breaking point came at noon on November 17 when Major Backus led the major part of the garrison south to the cienega hay camp; forty-two men remained behind, ordered to hold on as long as possible and then evacuate the canyon after burning the fort buildings.

Early in the morning of November 18 word arrived that the mule train conducted by Lieutenant Whistler was only a few miles distant. With this reassurance, Major Backus started to return to the fort with the infantry and artillery, leaving the dragoons to graze their horses for two more hours before following in his rear. Soon afterward it was discovered that an uncontrollable fire had blazed up and was destroying the hay camp. Backus later estimated that forty or fifty tons of hay were lost, leaving only fifteen tons for his entire winter supply.

It was certain that the fire had not started by accident. Aware that his troops were near desertion or mutiny, Backus was unsure whether they or Navajos were responsible. He realized at once that without hay the dragoon companies could not be retained at For Defiance.

4. November 2 and 14, 1851: Chandler to Sumner, NA, RAC, RG 393, C-10-1851, C-11-1851, LR.

If Chandler's wagons brought salt, Backus decided, he would slaughter some of the oxen at once and put the meat down in barrels. In any case, he probably would be compelled to jerk some of the beef. Chandler was not bringing corn, so Backus reasoned that he must either let the dragoon horses starve or send them away; they were already unfit for service and half of them could carry a rider no more than ten miles a day. Captain Ewell was grazing the animals of both dragoon companies at Red Lake, but it was a temporary expediency at best. Backus resigned himself to sending Company K to Fort Conrad for the winter and Ewell's company to Laguna.

Relief from Chandler's train still had not reached him when Backus observed that "in the event of the failure of the ox train to bring up our supplies, we have not more than a sufficiency of provisions to enable us to reach the Rio Grande, and no means of transporting our Artillery and other public property." [5]

Chandler's oxen, meanwhile, had continued to make agonizingly slow progress after leaving Laguna, averaging no better than seven miles a day. Only fine weather favored his lumbering advance. When he made camp near Ojo de la Jara November 21, still a hundred miles short of his destination (one day after Major Backus had remarked on the possible necessity of abandoning the fort), Chandler realized that his oxen were so broken down that few if any of them would ever make the return trip.

Finally, on December 6, thirty-four days after leaving the Rio Grande, the train reached Fort Defiance. Almost at once it was discovered that a sizable part of the load had been lost to thieves.

Many of the flour sacks had been torn open; much flour had been wasted or destroyed. Boxes of provisions had been broken open, the contents looted. A board of officers would be appointed to investigate the matter, but Backus must have known that this routine formality would be all but pointless. The stolen food would not be recovered and the civilian teamsters and escorting recruits would not easily be made to testify against themselves. Noting the condition of the oxen, the major supposed it was fortunate that the train had arrived at all. If the mule train had not been ramrodded through in advance his garrison would have had to live on bread and water for two weeks. Even now, with 240 mouths to feed, the supplies brought in by Colonel Chandler furnished enough flour for four months but the salt meat would be exhausted in twenty-four days. If there was fodder enough to

5. November 20, 1851: Backus to McFerran, NA, RAC, RG 393, B-22-1851, LR.

sustain the cattle herd the garrison would have beef for about four months, but the prospects were not encouraging.

Again Major Backus faced the possibility of being forced to abandon the post. "If we meet with a single accident, we may be compelled to sacrifice our position," he advised department headquarters. He urged that a mule train loaded with salt meat be sent out to him at the earliest possible moment.[6]

Snow was falling heavily in the canyon as Backus wrote. His message was to be carried back by Colonel Chandler, who was to start next morning for the river, leaving behind a number of broken wagons and all but four yoke of oxen. The lightened train, carrying only the equipment of the departing dragoon companies and food and forage for the journey, was expected to reach the river in twenty-three days. Company K had already been sent on to Fort Conrad, but Captain Ewell's troopers were to escort Chandler as far as Laguna and there— the department commander willing—proceed to Los Lunas to seek winter shelter.

Sentiment in the territory during the first eleven months of 1851 had universally favored making war upon the Navajos. Peace overtures by the tribe had been rejected on four separate occasions in the spring by Colonel Munroe and Governor Calhoun, who, as previously observed, advised the headmen that there would be no talk of peace until Navajos complied with terms of the 1849 treaty. Calhoun had reiterated this position on July 30 when he informed the commissioner of Indian affairs that unless he was overruled in Washington he would not treat again with the Navajos. His energies thereafter had been bent toward raising and arming militia companies for slave-raiding campaigns into Navajo country—an enterprise frustrated by Colonel Sumner. The most moderate voice at the time was that of Theodore Wheaton, speaker of the territorial house of representatives. In a resolution offered when the legislature convened for its first session on June 2, Wheaton declared that it would be both futile and impolitic to make peace with the Navajos unless the tribe first surrendered all New Mexicans held as captives, returned all property stolen during the last five years, and gave up at least fifty of the principal tribesmen as hostages, these headmen to be held indefinitely as prisoners to insure the Navajos' peaceful conduct.[7]

6. December 8, 1851: Backus to McFerran, NA, RAC, RG 393, B-29-1851, LR.
7. Twitchell, *Facts of New Mexican History*, 1963, vol. 2, p. 292.

Against this background, therefore, citizens of the territory could not have been less than surprised when they learned that Colonel Sumner and Governor Calhoun would treat with the Navajos at Jemez on December 25.

Nothing found in the military or civil records relates directly to the cause for the abrupt reversal of their position. Sumner said merely that the Navajos had "sent in word that they wished to make peace, and the Governor and I went to 'Jamez' to meet them in council." [8]

This explanation is less than helpful; the choleric department commander was not given to acceding to Navajo wishes. If Calhoun made any reference to the council at all, it has not been found. However, as early as October 31 he had drawn drafts totaling $2,500 on 1849 treaty funds for presents to be distributed to the Navajos whenever the opportunity seemed right.[9] The drafts give evidence that Calhoun considered taking a softer line than indicated by his position of July 30, but what induced him to follow this course, while deploring "scenes of desolation" left in the path of Navajo war parties, must remain conjectural.

A determining factor, at least in Sumner's case, came with shocking surprise when he learned that Major Backus, without consulting anyone, entered into a preliminary peace agreement with Zarcillos Largos and headmen from Zuni and Hopi pueblos, at Fort Defiance on October 26. No paper formalized the council but Backus advised department headquarters of the terms:

> The following verbal agreement was entered into, and being submitted to the main body of Indians, was accepted and confirmed by them [Backus reported].
>
> 1st The Navajo Indians, shall be at peace with, and shall cease to molest or steal from, the people of the United States—the Mexican people, and our friends the Zunia and Moca [Hopi] Indians.
>
> 2nd The Navajo Indians, shall send three of the principal men of their nation, with an escort of United States troops, to the Department Head Quarters at the Moro [Fort Union], with full powers to enter into, and conclude a lasting treaty of peace, between the people of the United States, and the Navajo nation.[10]

8. January 1, 1852: Sumner to Jones, NA, RAC, RG 393, no. 152, LS.
9. October 31, 1851: Calhoun to Lea, Abel 1915, p. 443. These drafts were upon the firms of D. Waldo & Co. ($1,500) and Alexander Majors ($1,000).
10. November 5, 1851: Backus to AAG, Santa Fe, NA, LR, Box 94, no file mark. Quoted by Hammond, 1957 ("Navajo-Hopi Relations"), vol. 1, p. 16.

Major Backus could not have known that his unauthorized actions would cause Sumner to enter negotiations with the Navajos which he regarded bitterly as a mistake.

At Jemez Pueblo Sumner and Calhoun were met by a detachment of the two companies of dragoons that Sumner some weeks earlier had assigned to temporary duty based at Galisteo. Private James Bennett, fully restored from any ill effects of the recent Navajo campaign and subsequent fandango at Albuquerque, noted that the troopers of his Company I commanded by Major Grier, having once lost the road from Galisteo, reached Jemez after nightfall and that the next morning an elderly Navajo "harangued his people from a sort of rostrum but it was all Greek to me."

Bennett observed that about twenty-five hundred Navajos were gathered early in the afternoon when "a treaty was formed and signed by the various tribes" as well as by Colonel Sumner.[11] Bennett probably overestimated the number of Navajos present, and Sumner no doubt dismissed from mind the Navajo women and children present when he reported that he and Calhoun "met with about 200 and I talked with them very plainly." [12]

From the available eyewitness accounts it is impossible to determine all that happened at the council. The Navajos did agree to remain at peace and to give up New Mexican captives; also, as token of their good intentions, they allowed Sumner to take three hostages (who may or may not have been Navajos). At the end of the proceedings Governor Calhoun distributed the treaty goods he had bought in October. But beyond this, and Sumner's stated displeasure in the whole affair, a great deal remains open to doubt. Sumner mentioned afterward that he had warned the Navajos that unless they remained at peace the troops of Fort Defiance would prevent them from raising a single field of grain —a threat that the one small garrison could not possibly have carried out. Sumner was disgusted that Calhoun had given presents worth two or three thousand dollars. Had it been left to him, he said, he would have put the Navajos on probation for six months "with a rod of iron over their heads."

11. Bennett journal, ed. Brooks and Reeve, 1947, pp. 81–82. In an introduction to the journal Brooks observed that "Bennett apparently copied his notes, after some years had elapsed, and destroyed the original"—thus accounting for numerous errors in dates and occasionally in statements of fact. His entries indicate Company I left Galisteo November 12 and arrived at Jemez the night of November 14. In all probability the actual dates were December 22 and 24.

12. January 1, 1852: Sumner to Jones, cited above.

Although Bennett mentioned that a treaty was drawn and signed by the chiefs of the various tribes, there is evidence that the action was confined to an informal ratification of the verbal agreement Major Backus had entered into on October 26 and to a renewed demand that Navajos comply with Colonel Washington's treaty. A few months later Backus informed Colonel Sumner that Navajos in the vicinity of Fort Defiance "all recognize the Treaty of Octr 26th as binding upon the whole nation, and they seem anxious to carry it into effect. They will be prepared to enter into a detailed Treaty as soon as circumstances permit—but they would prefer meeting, for that purpose, at Cañon Bonito, or at some place west of the Rio Grande, in preference to Santa Fe or Fort Union." His reference to "a detailed Treaty" makes it appear unlikely that new terms of peace were signed by Calhoun and Sumner at Jemez.[13] Some years afterward, James L. Collins, then super-intendent of Indian affairs for the territory, recalled that in the winter of 1851–52 Sumner and Calhoun met a large number of Navajos at Jemez "and proposed another treaty of peace, to the great amusement of the Indians." Many of them refused to consider the idea, but after discussing it among themselves, "they agreed to sign and make binding the treaty made with Colonel Washington."[14]

On his return to Fort Union, a month after the meeting at Jemez, Colonel Sumner advised the adjutant general that "The Navajoes have shown no hostility, since the Governor and I met them in Council at their own solicitation, on the 25th ultimo."[15]

Sumner's guarded comment was in fact an understatement, for on the day he wrote this a delegation of Navajos appeared at the Indian agency in Santa Fe to surrender three captive New Mexican boys and

---

13. January 4, 1852: Backus to McFerran, NA, RAC, RG 393, B-2-1852, LR; September 9, 1854: Kendrick to Nichols, NA, RAC, RG 393, K-12-1854, LR; and enclosure, March 10, 1852: Backus to Governor & People of Zunia. In his letter of September 9, referring to Navajo failure to maintain peace after Mariano and Chapitone signed the 1849 treaty, Kendrick said: "The war substantially continued until the treaty was made with these people, verbally, at this Post, Oct. 26th 1852 [1851], which ignored all claims for past acts." Backus was attempting to adjust a dispute over a Navajo horse stolen by Zunis when, on March 10, he wrote: "It is but a few months since peace was made between the Americans, the Navajoes, the people of Zunia & the people of Moqui. I am sorry to learn that so unimportant a thing as a Horse, is like to disturb the peace. . . ."

14. September 27, 1858: Report of Collins to C.I.A. Mix, *Senate Exec. Docs.*, 35th Cong., 2d sess., no. 1, pt. 1, p. 541.

15. Abel 1915, p. 290. The Sumner letter to Jones quoted here is erroneously dated 1851 and attributed by Abel to Colonel Munroe. The correct date of the letter is January 27, 1852.

give renewed assurances of their desire for peace. Armijo, the headman of the Chusca Valley region, presented himself with Aguila Negra, Barbon (or Barboncito), and Hastiin Miguel—among others—and assumed the role of spokesman. They had come in accordance with their agreement at Jemez, presumably to recover the hostages taken from them at that time and also to appeal for the return of other Navajos held in slavery. Agent John Greiner listened sympathetically as the Navajo spoke of his people's wish to live in peace so that they might raise their crops and hunt for game without molestation.

"I have lost my Grandfather and two other members of my family who were all killed by Mexicans," Armijo said. Now his hair was turning gray, he was getting old, and for himself he wished nothing more than to see his horses and cattle and sheep graze in safety and grow fat. "We like the Americans," he assured Greiner. "We have eaten their bread and meat—smoked their tobacco—the clothing they have given us has kept us warm. . . ."

Greiner interrupted. "Let us talk plain so that we may understand each other—The people living in the Rio Abajo complain that the Navajos have captured their children—stolen their stock—that their fields have to be idle for they cannot work them for fear of your people. Is this not so?"

"My people are all crying in the same way," Armijo replied. "Three of our Chiefs now sitting before you mourn for their children, who have been taken from their homes by the Mexicans. More than 200 of our children have been carried off and we know not where they are. The Mexicans have lost but few children in comparison with what they have stolen from us. Three years ago they took from my people nearly all their caballadas. Two years ago my brother lost 700 animals. How shall we get them again?"

As Greiner remained silent, Armijo continued. "From the time of Colonel Newby we have been trying to get our children back again. Eleven times we have given up our captives—only once have they given us ours. My people are yet crying for the children they have lost. Is it American justice that we must give up everything and receive nothing?"

"You have never told us this before," Greiner said. "The Great Father at Washington shall hear of it, and you shall hear what he says. Hereafter, no more captives must be taken on either side [and] depredations must no longer be committed by either party. Should our people injure you, instead of injuring them you must send one of your young men and let the governor or agent know. Justice will be done, and the offenders shall be punished." In the emotion of the moment Greiner promised even more that was impossible. "If any property is stolen on either side," he said, "it must be restored to the proper owners. The Chiefs will be held responsible for the conduct of their young men."

Armijo nodded agreement and, according to Greiner's report of the meeting, said that it made him happy to hear the agent's talk. The council ended harmoniously, the Navajos promising they would come again to talk in friendship. Presents of blankets, flannel shirts, a few trinkets, and some farming tools were given to the Navajos, and they departed for their homes.

A few days later, informing Calhoun of these proceedings, Greiner commented that he "was so well convinced with the truth of the remarks of Armijo that I confess I had but little to say. If the Indians must return all the Captives & property taken from the Mexicans, is it any thing but just that they should have what has been stolen from them? I think not." [16]

16. A transcript of the council is found in January 30, 1852: Greiner to Calhoun, NA, NMS 234-456. Greiner does not identify him, but his interpreter at the council probably was John Ward, then employed in that capacity at the agency.

11

An Incident at Vallecito

Calhoun's health broke immediately following the council at Jemez. His physician diagnosed his illness as catarrh complicated by jaundice, but something more serious may have afflicted him. In the next two months he became progressively weaker. He was confined to his room when early in February 1852 he observed that Navajos had given no cause for concern since October, but that, because mischievous persons at or near Jemez were meddling and trying to stir up trouble with the Navajos, he had appointed Spruce M. Baird as agent for the tribe. Baird was directed to establish himself with an interpreter at Jemez Pueblo.

Not enough is known of Baird's controversial past; he was a Texan, destined to play a part in the territory's legal affairs and politics. In the months following his appointment as first agent to the Navajos he was found to spend more time at his ranch near Albuquerque than at his agency at Jemez. In the previous December he had applied to Colonel Sumner for permission to open a trading house in Navajo country, preferably at Fort Defiance, but his application was either turned down or subsequently withdrawn.[1]

Colonel Sumner, meanwhile, after finding himself isolated at Fort Union from his scattered command, moved his headquarters in early February to the more centrally placed post at Albuquerque. A small mule train of five wagons had carried emergency supplies of salted meat and clothing to the Fort Defiance garrison in January, covering the distance from Fort Union (about 370 miles) in twenty-five days. Regarding this feat as proof of the superiority of mules to oxen, Sumner

1. December 18, 1851: Baird to Sumner, NA, RAC, RG 393, B-35-1851, LR. His appointment as Navajo agent was dated February 1, 1852. Calhoun referred to him as a major general, presumably a commission dating from the war with Mexico, but his name is not listed by Heitman.

ordered another mule train of eight wagons to make the same trip in March. Each wagon was to haul weight of more than two thousand pounds, the loads comprising bacon, beans, flour, coffee, sugar, rice, salt, vinegar, soap, and candles.[2]

Any doubt Sumner may have entertained of Navajo temper was relieved when Major Backus reported that relations with the tribe continued to be friendly, even though he had been forced to punish a few petty offenders, a course "which seemed to meet the full approbation of the chiefs." Backus observed that although the Navajos professed to be on good terms with Apaches, bands of Apaches in concert with Pueblos of Zuni were exerting pressure from the south. As a result many Navajo families were moving north to plant fields on the San Juan or in the vicinity of Canyon de Chelly. The threat of hostile coalition to the south made the Navajos welcome Fort Defiance as a protective buffer against Apache and Zuni war parties.[3]

Calhoun's health grew worse. On May 5, when he left Santa Fe at the start of his journey home, Sumner moved at once into the governor's quarters and took over the duties of office. His bold seizure of the governorship was entirely without sanction and caused some embarrassment when it became known in Washington. Happily, his tenure in office was brief; William Carr Lane of St. Louis received President Fillmore's appointment to succeed Calhoun and with it a request that he assume the office in all possible haste.[4]

A delegation of Navajos, led by Armijo and including Aguila Negra, Miguelito, and about twenty-five of their people, arrived in the capital not long after Calhoun's departure. They were accorded a friendly reception and given food for their evening meal as well as lodging and forage for their animals. At a council with John Greiner the next day they asked to be compensated for seven horses that they said had been stolen from them by New Mexicans at the pueblos of Jemez and Santa Ana. In support of this they presented a paper signed by Spruce Baird but admitted they had yet to meet the agent in council. They had planted their lands in the northern Chusca Valley and hoped for a good harvest. With most Apaches they were friendly, but one band of Mescaleros had joined with Zunis in raiding them and already had

2. February 15, 1852: Sumner to Sibley, NA, RAC, RG 393, no. 228, LS.

3. May 7, 1852: Backus to McFerran, NA, RAC, RG 393, no file mark, LR.

4. Calhoun did not survive the journey. Two months later, on July 27, mail arriving in Santa Fe brought word to John Greiner that Calhoun had died on the road near Independence, Missouri. Lane, a former mayor of St. Louis, arrived in New Mexico late in August and was inaugurated September 13.

killed a brother of the headman Vestido Colorado, or Red Clothes. Would it be permissible, they asked, for them to send out a war party to take revenge? [5]

Greiner, who had been appointed by Calhoun as acting superintendent of Indian affairs, told them that he could not authorize such action, and then inquired about their relations with other tribes. They were friendly with Jicarilla Apaches, the Navajos said, and wished to be friendly with Utes, although three persons had been killed in a fight with those people not long ago near La Plata Mountains. With the Comanches they always had been at war; with these old enemies they would never make peace.

Greiner evoked the lengthiest response when he asked Armijo and others if Navajos would consent to live in pueblos. Perhaps he had not heard of the century-old experiment at Cebolleta and Encinal.

"They could not live in pueblos," he later noted in his journal, "because they were not Christians, they were wild, their ancient custom had been 'Whenever a head of a family dies to destroy all his property and [burn] the houses. . . .'" For working their fields they would like hoes and spades; for cutting firewood and timber for their hogans they liked American axes. But they would not build houses. Greiner did not press the point. The Navajos then met briefly with Colonel Sumner. Presents were distributed, Greiner noting an expense of more than two hundred dollars for receiving the delegation, which included the favor of repairing their guns, bridles, and saddles.

Major Backus, whose calm good sense and courage had largely been responsible for maintaining peace on the Navajo frontier, departed from Fort Defiance August 3 on extended leave. For a short interval his command was assumed by Captain Joseph H. Eaton. The garrison's strength otherwise remained as before: Companies E and I of the Third Infantry and Company B, Second Artillery, totaling 5 officers and about 170 enlisted men. The period of crisis that had threatened the fort's existence during the previous winter was ended; the problems of supply over the long road to Fort Union were reduced to regular schedules and threatened only by vagaries of weather and occasional thievery.

Construction on the fort continued, but at a less frantic pace. All of the buildings fronting on the rectangular parade ground were of pine logs except the combined guardhouse and smokehouse, built of stone, and all were roofed with heavy layers of earth that in the first summer tended to sprout grass and weeds and even wildflowers. Ten sets of offi-

5. Greiner 1916, pp. 207–9.

cers' quarters lined the north end of the parade ground, each consisting of one room eighteen feet square. Other buildings included five company barracks, each measuring 100 feet long by 20 feet wide, and two of them vacant and in need of repair; five company mess rooms and storerooms of the same size; a storehouse, 130 by 20 feet; laundress quarters, 40 by 20 feet; and a hospital, 50 by 20 feet (half the size it would be when completed). No palisade or wall enclosed the buildings and except for the severity of their arrangement they looked more like a rude frontier village than a fort.[6]

The tranquil appearance was not deceptive, either. Captain Eaton found little to complain about except a faulty mail service that left him and his men yearning to hear from families and friends. In this remote canyon they felt cut off from all life they had known, and forgotten. Before his departure Major Backus had distributed among the Navajos the remaining supplies of tobacco as well as the hoes and spades and other farming tools that had been sent out for their use. Captain Eaton found that the major's policy "has operated most happily in preserving the best relations with the Navajos," and if continued as successfully he saw no reason why trouble should occur again.[7]

On September 8, after his tour with Captain Sitgreaves and an absence from the territory of about a year, Brevet Major Henry L. Kendrick relieved Captain Eaton of command of Fort Defiance.[8] Before a week had passed Kendrick had poked into every corner of the post, acquainted himself with every detail of the garrison's routine, and of-

6. September 1, 1852: Inspection report by Bvt. Maj. E. S. Sibley, *House Exec. Docs.*, 32d Cong., 2d sess., no. 1, pt. 2, pp. 73–77.

7. August 7, 1852: Eaton to Lt. Pleasanton, AAG, NA, RAC, RG 393, E-20-1852, LR.

8. Descended on his father's side from the Englishman John Kendrick, who settled at Newtown, Massachusetts, in the early 1600s, Henry Lane Kendrick was the son of Stephen and Thankful Howe Kendrick. He was born January 20, 1811, at Lebanon, New Hampshire, where he spent most of his youth before entering the U.S. Military Academy at West Point in 1831. After a brief term of service with the 2d Infantry he returned to West Point as assistant professor of chemistry, mineralogy and geology, a position he held until January 1847, when, as a captain of the 2d Artillery, he took part in the war with Mexico. After garrison duty in 1848 at New York Harbor and at Jefferson Barracks, Missouri, he was transferred to duty with Colonel Washington in New Mexico in the spring of 1849. Shortly before he departed for New Mexico, Brig. Gen. Joseph G. Totten intervened in his behalf, writing to Secretary of War Marcy that Kendrick's teaching career at West Point was "highly distinguished," and urging that, in order to encourage his talents in New Mexico, he be given transportation for "some instruments, acids &c for the purpose of making his researches the more productive." Marcy approved the request.

fered a pleasant reception to two visiting headmen who came to take his measure. One of them was Mariano Martínez, whom he remembered from their meeting at Canyon de Chelly three years before during Colonel Washington's campaign. The other, Ish-kit-sa-ne, Kendrick learned, was second in influence to Zarcillos Largos. Both he found to be friendly; both expressed a wish that he in turn should visit them at their rancherias. He assured them that he would. He engaged as interpreter a New Mexican whom he discovered at the fort, identified only as Juan but described as being familiar with all the Navajo country, acquainted with the tribe's principal men, and able to speak their language fluently. Almost certainly this was Juan Anaya, whom he also had met before at Canyon de Chelly (almost certainly again, the captive Calhoun referred to as Josea Ignacio Anañe).

Major Kendrick found that the policies established by Electus Backus in his relations with the Navajos, and continued after by Captain Eaton, had worked too successfully to require change. He saw no reason, either, for increasing the Fort Defiance garrison, but believed that with its present strength of three companies the territory might forget its fear of Navajo raids. Navajos, he observed, were receptive to every effort made to help them as farmers and stock raisers, to the point that "we are fast making ourselves necessary to them." Like others before him, Kendrick predicted that a time would come when Americans might persuade Navajos "to a *considerable* extent" to adopt the Pueblos' way of life. He did not think it necessary to build more military posts in their country, but, if this was to be done, he urged that posts not be built on their best land because it would deprive them of fertile agricultural land and be an unnecessary harassment.

In his desire to start on friendly terms, Kendrick's first request to department headquarters was for a supply of tobacco to give to Navajos when they visited the post. He remembered that among his luggage and personal effects still stored at Albuquerque were such curiosities as music boxes, which he hoped might be sent on with the next supply train; they were not of great value but the Indians might find them amusing gifts.[9]

Colonel Sumner visited Fort Defiance in early October, anxious to determine for himself the attitude of the tribe. His arrival unfortunately coincided with the wounding of the fort's citizen farmer, Jonathan F. Wyatt, by a Navajo. It was the first incident of its kind in

9. September 10, 1852: Kendrick to Sumner, NA, RAC, RG 393, K-6-1852, K-7-1852, LR.

months. Although Wyatt received only a superficial arrow wound, Sumner insisted that Ish-kit-sa-ne be summoned to the post and told that Wyatt's assailant must be surrendered for punishment. Major Kendrick agreed to carry out the order, saying (though he had reason to doubt it) that the Navajo probably would be brought in. Just as tactfully, he then pointed out that it would be a mistake to allow this minor affair to disrupt peaceful relations with the entire tribe; Wyatt, after all, had suffered little harm, and the single action of the man who had attacked him, a Navajo of notoriously bad character and without influence, should not be regarded as anything but the aggressive misconduct of one man.

Sumner was persuaded to drop the matter. His presence at Fort Defiance, he was aware, was regarded with fear by some Navajos. Rumors, said to have originated with Sandoval, convinced some of them that Sumner would have any Indians who visited the fort tied up and their throats cut. The effect of this story on the Navajos, with Kendrick's advice, may have induced Sumner to forget the Wyatt incident. In any case, after meeting with several of the principal men and assuring them that he meant them no harm, the colonel returned to his headquarters at Albuquerque.[10] A civilian who had accompanied Sumner to Fort Defiance informed Governor Lane that other rumors spreading among the Navajos of a citizen campaign to be made against them were so inflammatory as to threaten the peace. Lane accordingly directed Agent Spruce Baird to leave at once for Navajo country to determine the source of the rumors and, if possible, counteract their effect.

Sharing the governor's concern, Sumner declared that the danger most to be feared was not from Navajos but from those who attempted to incite fear among them. He recommended the utmost watchfulness over any dealings that Sandoval's Diné Ana'aii and others on the frontier might have with Navajos. He was convinced that the Navajos would remain at peace if they were not "deceived and tampered with by designing men, white or Indian."

Sandoval of course had denied spreading any rumor regarding Sumner's purpose in going to Fort Defiance, but the throat-cutting lie had been told by someone whose only object was to unsettle good relations with the tribe.[11]

10. October 10 and 13, 1852: Sumner to Kendrick; October 24, 1852: Sumner to Lane; October 13, 1852: Kendrick to Sumner, NA, RAC, RG 393, nos. 678, 679, 686, LS; K-10-1852, LR.

11. November 3, 1852: Sumner to Lane, NA, RAC, RG 393, no. 701, LS.

Whether Spruce Baird accomplished anything on his mission, or whether indeed he made the trip at all, is uncertain. No report by him can be found, but the anxieties and concerns of both sides were stilled with the first snows of winter. Christmas of 1852 and the first day of the new year came and went, and the Navajos remained at peace. The threatened campaign into their country, so urgently rumored, never materialized. The mesa heights and canyon bottom at Fort Defiance were still covered with snow in February when Navajos of that region came to the post to discuss their spring planting with Major Kendrick. It was early, he knew, but he encouraged them to talk of the seeds and fertilizers and farm tools that he hoped might be sent out to them. Even in near-zero weather this talk of turning the earth and planting seed stimulated other ideas. Kendrick began to think of making excursions among these people—to their hogans on the San Juan, perhaps, and to the west through pine forest and over rolling sage prairie as far as the Hopi villages. He wished to learn where and how the people lived, to know how numerous they were, and to see with his own eyes the shape and color of their country.

Another plan materialized sooner. During Colonel Washington's Navajo expedition, Kendrick recalled, the guide Carravahal had spoken of a trail from Cañoncito Bonito to Albuquerque shorter and better than the old road by way of Zuni. Several times in the intervening four years military units had considered exploring Carravahal's trail but for one reason or another had not ventured it. Kendrick felt there had been delay enough. Late in March a survey party went out under command of Lieutenant Armistead L. Long with directions to proceed as far as Cubero before turning back.

By viameter Lieutenant Long measured distances extending south and east from Fort Defiance: to Ojo del Oso, 38.59 miles; to his camp on the Agua Azul, 75.05 miles; to the upper crossing of the Rio Gallo— within a mile or two of the junction with the Zuni road—98.56 miles. Cubero lay 15 miles beyond. This new road, Long observed, was 38 miles shorter than the Zuni road, and with very little labor would be entirely suitable for wagons. There was only one drawback. Between Ojo del Oso and the fort, in dry seasons wagons would travel for two days or more without water.

Major Kendrick personally pioneered the trail when he brought three loaded wagons westward over the Ojo del Oso—or Wingate Valley— route a month later, and in spite of the waterless last stretch recommended that it be used in future after minor improvements were made by a labor detail from the garrison.[12] Not only would there be a saving of two days' time, he pointed out, but also a psychological advantage would be gained from having Navajos see army supply trains crossing their hitherto virgin country. Colonel Sumner gave his approval and soon afterward the new road through Wingate Valley became the commonly accepted route of travel.

Peace had prevailed in most of the territory for so long that a murderous incident in Rio Arriba County excited unusual alarm. Magnified afterward out of all proportion, the affair almost but not quite precipitated war with the Navajo nation. Curiously enough, although he stirred and then fanned belligerent emotions with statements of his own, Colonel Sumner in the end appraised the situation with more insight than any other and forestalled what nearly became bloody, widespread aggression.

As usual, first accounts of the incident were exaggerated and contradictory. Shortly after dark in the night of May 3 at Vallecito on Bear Creek, south of Abiquiu and west of Chamita, five Indians attacked the grazing camp of Ramón Martín without provocation. Two days afterward it was reported in Santa Fe that Martín and one of his sons had been killed and two boys and all of Martín's livestock had been carried away. On the last point there was some doubt; a conflicting story made it appear that the shooting had occurred while Martín was corralling a flock of three hundred sheep and that the Indians had left the sheep penned up but had driven off several horses and a mule. There was evidence that the Indians were Navajos, but, because the sheep were left in the corral, some believed they might have been Pueblos.

12. The "dry" route traced by Lt. Long between Ojo del Oso and Fort Defiance evidently ran to the south of, and so missed, the permanent Rock Springs (the "Ojo de la Trinchera" indicated on the 1851 map compiled for Colonel Munroe by Carravahal and Lt. John Parke). Long's oversight later was corrected and by 1870, if not earlier, Rock Springs was a stopping place on a main-traveled road between new Fort Wingate and Fort Defiance. Water of the springs flows from the base of sandstone cliffs, which, like the face of El Morro, are inscribed with names and dates of scores of passing soldiers and others. The earliest date I have found is 1860, carved by one E. Walsh. C(harles?) Hubbell stopped here in 1870. Fourteen miles northwest of Gallup, New Mexico, Rock Springs in more recent years was the site of a trading post owned first by George W. Sampson and later by George Kennedy. Some say that old Dan DuBois also traded here for a time. Reports relating to the Ojo del Oso route date from March 26 to May 27, 1853 and are found in the NA, RAC, RG 393 series, LR and LS.

Governor Lane immediately asked Spruce Baird to investigate and attempt to recover the captive boys as well as secure the surrender of the murderers. The next day, May 7, he asked John Greiner to go to Vallecito and determine what actually had happened. Greiner, who had only a halting command of Spanish, set out for Chamita with Samuel Ellison, who agreed to serve as interpreter.

Only Ramón Martín had been killed, they were told by an elder son, José María Martín, who at first was believed to have been murdered with his father. They had been herding sheep in the mountainous valley and his father was in the act of lying down to rest, José María said, when a gunshot exploded from behind a brush pen. His ears still ringing, he heard his father cry that he had been hit.

He was about to hang his hat on a pole when the shot boomed out, José María said, and at the very moment his father called to him he heard several arrows whiz past his head. In panic, he ran a short distance in darkness and hid among stones until daylight. (It was then that he found two arrows with iron heads embedded in the pole below his hat.) [13]

From his hiding place he had seen three Indians approach his father and bend over, speaking to him in bad Spanish to determine if he were dead. Satisfied that he was, they moved away. A little later one of the Indians who now carried a blazing torch held it high to cast light into the sheep pen. He was close enough for José María to see that he was wearing his father's coat. José María could see the stain and the hole made by the bullet, in the right breast a few inches below the shoulder.

Miguel Antonio Gonzales, a shepherd boy about ten years old, was lying in the sheep pen with four other youths when the shot was fired. Four of the Indians took the boys from the pen; another took charge of the horses. The captives were carried away—each Indian leading a boy for about a quarter of a mile until they came to a watering place. Here three of the boys were released and told to go back to the grazing camp. The Indians then resumed their flight, taking with them a son and a nephew of the murdered man, José Claudio Martín, eight years old, and José Leonicio Martín, nine.

The children who had been freed told Greiner they could not be sure if the Indians were Navajos or Pueblos, but they were able to describe their appearance in some detail. The men were young, they said; ex-

13. Undated: Greiner to Lane, Enclosure A with May 26, 1853: Lane to C.I.A. George W. Manypenny, NA, NMS 234-546.

cept for one, who was tall and slender and wore a hat, they were of average size and wore woolen cloth around their heads. They wore red shirts and buckskin leggings decorated with "yellow buttons from the knee down," and over these garments, blankets of black and white stripes.

Because Indians of San Juan Pueblo herded their stock near the place where the murder had been committed, Greiner thought it best to question them about the matter. At the pueblo the next morning he was told by those who had been tending the stock that the Pueblo herders had been about two leagues distant when Martín was killed. Word of Martín's murder was brought to them by José Miguel Gonzales, one of the youths released at the spring.

The San Juan Indians immediately went to Martín's camp, where they found the body sprawled on the ground, the sheep safely in the corral, but the camp stripped clean of everything else. Five arrows picked up in the camp, two with iron and three with only sharpened points, the San Juan Indians said were Navajo. It was natural that the raiding party had not attempted to carry off the sheep, the Pueblos said, as there were many herders in the neighborhood and it would have been impossible to drive off the sheep without being discovered. So far as Greiner could learn, the only livestock taken were three horses (one of them abandoned on the trail and later recovered by the San Juan Indians) and a mouse-colored mule.

Greiner's report to Governor Lane indicated that Martín probably had been killed by Navajos and disclosed as well—although neither Greiner nor anyone else seemed to realize it—the motive for the attack.

At the watering place where the Indians first stopped with their captives, the three boys set free were given a message to take back to the sheep camp. They were to tell their people that Tamouche, a war captain of the Capote Utes, recently had stolen a paint horse and a mule from the Navajos. If Tamouche would return the animals to their owners, then the two captive boys—José Claudio and José Leonicio—as well as Martín's mule and horses, would be given up. Perhaps Greiner felt this reference to Tamouche had no material bearing upon the murder of Martín; neither he nor Governor Lane, in any case, appears to have paid it much attention. No mention of it was made again during the growing storm of emotion that soon inflated the Martín incident into a territorial crisis.

More correctly, it should be said that almost no mention was made again. Although he had not been informed by headquarters of the

Martín murder, Major Kendrick reported from Fort Defiance that the wealthy Gordo, a brother of Zarcillos Largos, had come to the post on May 15 and told him that he had heard a small war party had returned after an unsuccessful effort to recover some horses stolen by Utes. On their return, and to compensate for their failure, they had taken two Mexicans as captives from Abiquiu. Gordo also said he had heard there would be a large gathering of Navajos at Ojos Calientes in the Chusca Valley, and that certain of the headmen would demand that the captives be returned to their people, even if it were necessary to buy them from their captors.

Knowing this much of the Vallecito affair, Gordo may be presumed to have known more but concluded it was best to leave it at that. And Major Kendrick—unofficially advised, but told also by Pedro Pino of Zuni "that the Navajoes were dancing on account of it at the *Oso* or *Bear Spring*"—felt the story might be more than a rumor and even have "*some* foundation" in truth.

Immediately upon Greiner's return to Santa Fe two days later, Governor Lane called on the experienced Donaciano Vigil to act as his special agent during the absence of Spruce Baird. Lane had received no reply to his letter to Baird and learned later that Baird was too busy traveling the court circuit and practicing law to attend to affairs of the Navajo agency.

If he did not find the murderers of Ramón Martín at Jemez, Vigil was to carry his search wherever it might lead. He was to recover the captive boys and all stolen property, and if the murderers were found he was to demand that the headmen harboring them surrender them for trial before civil authorities in Santa Fe. Vigil was to have the services of Samuel Ellison as interpreter, and as evidence of the governor's serious intentions Vigil was authorized to warn the Indians that failure on the part of the tribe to comply with his demands would be considered a justifiable cause for war.[14]

Another indication of the governor's mood was noted by John Ward, clerk in the Indian superintendency, who observed that Lane furnished Ellison with horse and saddle, two double-barreled shotguns, a Jäger rifle, and a pistol.[15]

When informed by Governor Lane of all developments in the case, Colonel Sumner said he was fully in accord with the instructions given

14. May 9, 1853: Lane to Vigil, Enclosure B with May 26, 1853: Lane to Manypenny, cited above.
15. Ward Journal, ed. Abel 1941, p. 339.

Donaciano Vigil. If the Indians involved indeed proved to be Navajos, Sumner suggested that Agent Baird be sent to Fort Defiance to act with Major Kendrick in securing Vigil's demands. "Let them assemble all the chiefs immediately," he wrote Lane from Albuquerque, "and say to them plainly, that those captive boys must be restored at once, and the murderers must be given up, or a war will be commenced against the whole tribe." [16] If war must be made against the tribe, Sumner added, he did not believe it would be necessary to raise a large force of volunteers to augment the regular troops, as Lane proposed.

At Jemez Pueblo Vigil was informed that the Indians he sought were Navajos of Aguila Negra's band, and that he might expect to learn more about them in the upper Chusca Valley, where a large number of Navajos were said to be gathering. Baird, of course, was not at the agency quarters at Jemez, but William Keithly, his ailing interpreter, was. He was too unwell to accompany Vigil, Keithly said, but he suggested that in his place Vigil take the agency blacksmith, George C. Carter, who was familiar with all of the mountain and valley country inhabited by Navajos. With Ellison and Carter, and joined by Hosta and ten Pueblos of Jemez, Vigil started on May 13 for Chusca Valley. Four days later, in the vicinity of a place Vigil referred to as "Tunicha Mountain"—probably Cayetano or Beautiful Mountain—he found a camp of about one thousand Navajos. On the same day he held a council with Armijo and Aguila Negra.[17]

The young captive boys were surrendered to Vigil at once, as were three mules offered in partial payment for the animals taken from Vallecito. Vigil, on learning that the five Navajos he sought also were present in the camp, demanded that they be turned over to him, but his demand was refused.

Aguila Negra and other principal men insisted that "they had not sufficient force" to seize the accused men. The leader of the raiding party, identified in later reports as Jasis (Jesús?), said that he and his companions had intended not to kill Martín but only to scare him. His statement, whatever it was worth, could have had no bearing on the outcome, which already was decided. Regardless of what they had done, or had intended to do, he and his companions were not to be turned over to the Bilagáana for punishment. Veteran campaigner that he was, Donaciano Vigil probably was not surprised, even when his

16. May 12, 1853: Sumner to Lane, NA, RAC, RG 393, no. 237, LS.
17. May 25, 1853: Vigil to Lane, Enclosure C with May 26, 1853: Lane to Manypenny, cited above.

warning that war would be made against the entire nation was met with repeated refusal. Aguila Negra and several of his people, who now had reason to fear for their lives, accompanied Vigil's party back to Santa Fe.

John Ward was on hand to observe Vigil's return with the Martín boys in the morning of May 24. He noted that Governor Lane at once directed that the boys be fed well and given new clothing in place of the tattered rags they wore. Aguila Negra and Hosta arrived a few hours later, accompanied by six Navajos and nine Pueblos of Jemez. The day following the Martín boys were sent home in the care of Francisco Tapia.[18]

At a meeting with Governor Lane shortly afterward, Aguila Negra said that he would do all in his power to have the murderers of Ramón Martín brought in, but that he feared his intervention might so excite and divide the Navajos that war would break out among them. Before the council ended Aguila Negra urgently asked that the demand on him be withdrawn; if it were not, he said, lives almost certainly would be lost, including his own. Lane replied that none of Aguila Negra's excuses was acceptable; if the murderers were not delivered to him by the next full moon—July 1—Navajo country would be invaded by soldiers. As an inducement, he said he would offer a $200 reward for the surrender of Jasis—or Jesús—and $100 for each of his companions: Amarillo, Chiquito, Palo de Cochillo, and Asha.[19]

Major Kendrick's interpreter, Juan Anaya, who had been in northern Navajo country, and Henry Dodge, who had been trading among the Navajos thirty miles north of Fort Defiance, both returned to the post at about this time. What they had heard when Navajos spoke of the Vallecito affair and of the recent great gathering in the valley differed in some respects from what Donaciano Vigil had reported to Governor Lane. About the murder of Ramón Martín and the carrying away of the two boys there was no dispute. But it was said that Jesús and his companions had taken three mules (not one) and three horses from Vallecito. It was said, too, as Gordo had said before, that all of these acts "were committed by way of recompensing themselves for losses which they had met with from the Utahs."

More important, Navajos who talked at different times and places with Juan Anaya and Henry Dodge believed that the age-old, customary indemnification had been offered, and the terms agreed to by

18. Ward Journal, ed. Abel 1941, pp. 341–42.
19. May 26, 1853: Lane to Manypenny, cited above.

Vigil. Ten horses had been promised in payment to quiet the hurt of Ramón Martín's family, and the man called Vigil had said he was well pleased with the arrangement.

If Donaciano Vigil had, in fact, agreed to an arrangement quite familiar to him, he disavowed it upon his return to Santa Fe. Major Kendrick, in any event, merely forwarded to headquarters the information he had received from two separate and reliable sources.[20]

Relations with the tribe grew even more strained when word came that in the afternoon of May 22 a party of thirty or forty Navajos had driven off 5,600 sheep that had been brought from the Rio Grande to grazing grounds in the Zuni Mountains. Anastacio García, to whom most of the sheep belonged, had thought he recognized the son of Sandoval among the raiders. Shortly afterward, Zarcillos Largos and Ish-kit-sa-ne told Major Kendrick that "this and other evils are the result of the machinations of Sandoval—that if he were out of the way every thing would be quiet." [21] Kendrick warned the two headmen that war would be inevitable unless the sheep were returned and those responsible for the theft were given up for punishment. He doubted that his demands would be met, although the headmen convinced him of their earnest desire to resolve the difficulties without bloodshed.

Because he was so far removed from the seat of authority, Kendrick recommended that Spruce Baird be sent out with necessary instructions that would help him in negotiating with the headmen. If it were to be decided in the end that a campaign must be made against the Navajos, he urged department headquarters to delay no later than August.

The services of Agent Baird (though Kendrick was not aware of it) were about to be terminated. Even as the major wrote of his need of Baird's presence, Colonel Sumner was congratulating Henry Dodge upon his appointment as Indian agent, adding that he supposed Dodge would be assigned to the Navajos to replace the almost invisible Texan. Sumner then briefly advised Dodge of the circumstances of the Ramón Martín affair and the robbery of García's sheep. He asked Dodge to "impress it upon all the principal men that both these crimes must be atoned for, by giving up the criminals. If they will not do this, we shall

20. May 25, 1853: Kendrick to Sturgis, NA, RAC, RG 393, K-11-1853, LR.
21. May 29, 1853: Ewell to Sturgis; May 25, 1853: Kendrick to Sturgis, NA, RAC, RG 393, E-12-1853, E-13-1853, K-13-1853, LR. Although Sandoval was implicated, the identity of the Navajos was never clearly established. Later reports suggest that García's sheep found their way into the herds of the Aguila Negra and Archuleta bands.

march a large command into their country early next fall, and impel them to do it, or to see their whole country laid waste." [22]

At no time more than now was a contradictory side of Colonel Sumner's nature so exposed. During the first week of June he declared several times that he would make war against the entire Navajo tribe if the murderers of Martín were not surrendered; with as much vehemence, and in the same week, he declared he thought it would be wrong to hold the entire nation accountable for the acts of a few individuals. During a conference with Sumner on June 1, Governor Lane insisted that if the murderers of Martín were not given up by July 1 it would be Sumner's duty to start war against the Navajo nation at once. He again advocated reinforcing Sumner's command with volunteer militia; should Sumner hesitate to commence war with his regulars, Lane said, he would order out the militia.

Sumner at first disagreed with the governor, saying he regarded it as unjust to hold "the whole Navajo tribe responsible for the act of five marauding and ungovernable Indians." In the end he capitulated. Should Lane's ultimatum demanding the murderers fail, Sumner agreed to lay waste to Navajo country by destroying the Navajos' crops and taking their herds. More than that he would not promise. It would be impossible, he said, for his troops to catch the Navajos on their fleet horses.[23]

If a major campaign were to be made against the Navajos, it was essential that the operation be coordinated at once with Major Kendrick's garrison. On his return to Albuquerque after his conference with the governor, Sumner sent an express advising Kendrick of Lane's ultimatum to the tribe. If the Navajos failed to comply by the July 1 deadline, Sumner said, he would lead a force of six or seven hundred troops into their country and inflict as much damage upon them as possible. He warned Kendrick to keep the post cattle herd near the fort and constantly under strong guard, as the beef would be needed for his troops.[24]

22. May 29, 1853: Sumner to Dodge, NA, RAC, RG 393, no. 268, LS. News of Dodge's appointment was received in Santa Fe on May 26, but not until June 26 was it learned that he was assigned to the Navajos. His salary was to be $1,550 a year and he was instructed to take quarters and establish his agency at Fort Defiance. Notification of his appointment, dated May 7, 1853, was first addressed to him at Dubuque, Iowa. He was to be responsible as well for the Pueblos of Laguna, Acoma, Zuni, and the seven Hopi villages (May 7, 1853: Manypenny to Dodge, NA, NMS T-21-1).

23. Ward Journal, ed Abel 1941, pp. 343–45.

24. June 4, 1853: Sumner to Kendrick, NA, RAC, RG 393, No. 279, LS.

Governor Lane believed, as Calhoun had before him, that the department commander needed both prodding and advice. A campaign undertaken by six hundred troops could only lead to a protracted, costly struggle. The Navajo nation could be humbled in a few short months, Lane insisted, if Sumner would only agree to augment his striking force with six hundred to one thousand New Mexican and Pueblo auxiliaries. Lane advised Sumner how these combined forces could best be employed, in conjunction with cavalry and artillery—whose disposal he also outlined—to inflict a speedy and terrible punishment upon the tribe.[25]

Sumner replied temperately and without his usual rancor. He said he would rather coerce the Navajos by peaceful means than force them with guns to give up the slayers of Ramón Martín, but that in the end he feared he might have no other choice. He refused, however, to arm citizens and put them in the field against Navajo men, women, and children. Recalling that Zarcillos Largos and Ish-kit-sa-ne connected Sandoval with the theft of García's sheep "and other evils," Sumner said he had suspected the Diné Ana'aii leader for a long time. Sandoval, he said, "is an unprincipled scoundrel and it is plain that he has everything to gain by a war between the Navajos and whites, for he can then steal from both sides." [26]

A different view of Sandoval was taken by Major Kendrick, who advised Sumner that because the Navajos greatly feared the Diné Ana'aii leader and wished to get rid of him, "we ought to sustain him and to use him as a scourge." Sharing none of Sumner's reluctance to make war on the tribe, for reasons of his own Kendrick bluntly supported Governor Lane's argument for the use of auxiliaries.

"I feel constrained to say," he wrote, "that the most efficient rod in terror to be held over these people is the fear of a permission being given to the Mexicans to make captives of Navajoes and to retain them." Would he shrink from applying the terror of military slaving? Not at all. It would be "a permission at once wise & philanthropic and one which would at an early date settle the question."

Major Kendrick already had threatened Navajos with this brand of philanthropy, and with some effect. During the second week of June, in company with Henry Dodge and Captain Ewell together with a portion of the latter's company of dragoons sent out from Los Lunas on the trail of García's sheep, Kendrick had ridden north toward the

25. June 8, 1853: Lane to Sumner, NA, RAC, RG 393, N-13-1853, LR.
26. June 10, 1853: Sumner to Lane, NA, RAC, RG 393, no. 289, LS.

San Juan and then returned by way of the Chusca Valley. He found Navajos living west of the Chusca Mountains at peace and averse to war. Kendrick was convinced that the recent raids, including a theft of horses from Zuni, were the acts of a few hostile tribesmen living in the valley east of the range, or near Ojo del Oso and the Chacra Mesa.

His party met the Indians in large numbers at various points, and he told them distinctly that war would result unless the Navajos complied with his demands. Kendrick warned that such a war would be the last one ever necessary: that New Mexicans, Pueblos, Sandoval's Diné Ana'aii, and the Americans "would be let loose upon them, their flocks seized, their men killed, their *women and children taken captive*, and ultimately the [Chusca] mountain [range] made their eastern limit."

Navajos with whom he had spoken convinced Kendrick also that only one man was guilty in Martín's murder; thus he had confined his demands to the surrender of this individual and the restoration of García's stock. Navajos who had taken no part in the theft contributed 433 sheep and 14 horses toward meeting this demand. On his return to Fort Defiance Kendrick met in council with a number of the headmen, including Zarcillos Largos, Manuelito, and the son of Juanico, and had Sumner's bellicose letter of June 4 read to them. In response, the Navajos said the five men involved in the Vallecito raid had taken refuge with friends among the Utes, that they feared they could not capture them, but that they would do so if the men could be found. The chances of their doing so, Kendrick believed, were nonexistent.[27]

Kendrick's message, in its ruthlessness unmatched by any of his later expressions, was carried to the river by Captain Ewell, whose troop was accompanied by Henry Dodge. Possibly Colonel Sumner had left his headquarters at Albuquerque by the time they reached there; in any case, Ewell and Dodge continued to Santa Fe.

Five days later, on June 26, mail arriving on the stagecoach from Independence brought word that Governor Lane was shortly to be replaced by a new presidential appointee—a Kentuckian, remembered for an unhappy visit in the distant past, named David Meriwether.

On an outgoing stage the same Sunday, Colonel Edwin Vose Sumner, with few friends present to bid him goodbye, departed for the States—not for a short leave, but relieved of command. He was never to come back. Plans for the Navajo campaign collapsed.

27. June 14, 1853: Kendrick to Sturgis, NA, RAC, RG 393, K-15-1853, LR.

12

Rendezvous on the San Juan

A quiet vacuum settled upon the capital through a hot July as Governor Lane awaited Meriwether's arrival. Sumner's command in this brief interval was assumed by an officer Lane once referred to contemptuously as "a walking sponge, martinet & a ———" (the omission of the epithet not this writer's, but Lane's).

Noted among brother officers for intemperance and a certain windiness of speech, Lieutenant Colonel Dixon Stansbury Miles left his post at Fort Fillmore to move temporarily into Sumner's vacated quarters at Albuquerque. At Fillmore he had had some experience with Apaches, but of the Navajos, and Navajo country, he was the first to admit he knew nothing at all. Not surprisingly, then, and because he was soon to be relieved of department command by Brevet Brigadier General John Garland, he entertained no enthusiasm for the governor's burning cause to war upon the Navajos. He adopted, instead, proposals recently advanced by Major Kendrick for a show of force on the San Juan, with an additional idea or two of his own.

Within a few days of taking command Colonel Miles issued orders for a converging movement of two columns, reminiscent in some degree of Doniphan's 1846 campaign. He directed Captain Ewell to rendezvous with fifty dragoons at Fort Defiance. From there, with such support as Major Kendrick wished to add from the Defiance garrison, the command was to be led by Kendrick to a point near the confluence of the San Juan and Chaco rivers, the vicinity of present Shiprock. Here Kendrick's force would meet a second column of forty dragoons from Abiquiu under command of Second Lieutenant Robert Ransom. It was not his purpose, Miles emphasized, for the troops to make war on the Navajos, but he directed the officers to impress on the Indians once more that stringent measures would be taken against them unless restitution were made for stolen livestock and the thieves among them were turned over for punishment—which he recommended should be lashes with a whip in the presence of either an officer or the Navajo agent.

A demand also should be made for the murderer of Ramón Martín, and for his companions, but Miles indicated he would not press for their immediate surrender. He instructed Lieutenant Ransom to map and make careful notes of the route from Abiquiu to the San Juan and to "block up the pass" that Miles was led to believe formed a narrow gorge between the Carrizo Mountains and the San Juan. After his meeting with Major Kendrick, Miles told Ransom, the major would continue exploring downriver; Ransom was to return to his post at Abiquiu.[1]

Henry Dodge, who left Santa Fe for the Rio Abajo on June 30, was entrusted with delivering the colonel's message to Kendrick at Fort Defiance. He interrupted the journey long enough to carry supplies out to Chupadero, where he made his home and first chose to open the Navajo agency. Two receipts in his handwriting show payment of thirty dollars to a James Sullivan on July 1 and a like amount to José María Amarillo for transporting Indian goods from Santa Fe to "the Navajo Agency Chupadero."[2] Until late fall or early winter of 1853 the affairs of the agency—the first to be located in proximity to Navajo country—were operated from Dodge's stone buildings perched high on a narrow shelf of the mountains above and between Paguate and Cebolleta. Although today it is a lonely and silent place of tumbled walls, the loose cluster of four buildings suggests that in Dodge's time Chupadero was a hacienda rather than a village. Two of the buildings, of Spanish or pueblo style facing each other across a narrow roadway, were of rather massive dimensions, with one-story walls of sandstone blocks mixed with a darker lava rock embedded in adobe and measuring thirty inches in thickness. Such legends as survive postdate Dodge's time: on a knobby knoll close by, a military train "carrying gold bars to old Fort Wingate" was attacked, or threatened with at-

1. July 3, 1853: Miles to Kendrick; July 4, 1853: Miles to Ransom, NA, RAC, RG 393, nos. 309, 311, LS.

2. Files of the Commissioner of Indian Affairs, NA, NMS T21-1. Only these receipts and references contained in a few letters establish the Navajo agency's first location at Chupadero. Such evidence as has been found suggests that Dodge made his home at Chupadero from summer 1850 to early winter 1853. Sandoval was a frequent visitor during the time, and inferentially it may be supposed that very nearly all of his band at one time or another came to Dodge's buildings and were well known by name or sight.

tack, by Navajos in the early 1860s. Soldiers escorting this remarkable train, legend says, buried the gold before all were killed or driven off.[3]

Before either Dodge or Captain Ewell reached Fort Defiance, Navajos brought in and surrendered 280 more sheep, but ten times that number still would have to be turned over before the claims of New Mexican ranchers (Anastacio García remaining the principal claimant) would be satisfied. Several headmen came in offering assurances of their good intentions, but Major Kendrick doubted their ability to secure any effective compliance from the independent and largely uncontrollable bands of the tribe. In the preceding weeks, as his pessimism deepened, he had become resolved that war with the tribe could not be avoided much longer. When the time came, he wrote Colonel Miles, "we ought to have no more small wars with these people," and August should not be allowed to wear away without a strike in force. If troop operations were confined to the range of the offending Navajos—the country east of the Chuscas—Kendrick believed the eastern Navajos would be driven west of the mountains and forced to remain there permanently, an objective that he felt sooner or later was inevitable.[4]

The first phase of Colonel Miles's campaign, in which he personally took no part, started July 12 with the departure from Abiquiu of Lieutenant Ransom and Company I, First Dragoons. One of the privates in Ransom's command, an unofficial chronicler of the events that followed, was James A. Bennett, whose journal also shed casual light on the council held by Sumner and Calhoun with Navajos at Jemez in 1851.

Either Bennett was misinformed about the purpose of the present campaign or he later misinterpreted his own notes, for his journal records that "Reports came to Abiquiu quarters that the Navajos had killed 1 white man and 6 Mexicans who were trapping on the San Juan River. . . . Found the rumor to be true. Reported accordingly. We were ordered to move as soon as practical in that direction."

The facts of this badly confused incident, which had nothing to do with Ransom's march to the San Juan, were these: on a trading expedition the previous May, an American had been killed by a Ute in the

3. The legend was told by Azize Michael of Bibo. Apocryphal as it obviously is, the story has persisted for nearly a century. In May 1965 I found the knoll pitted with fresh diggings of recent treasure hunters. Michael, who in recent years owned the site of Chupadero, sold it in about 1953 to a Dr. Lucius Rice of Albuquerque

4. July 12, 1853: Kendrick to Sturgis, NA, RAC, RG 393, K-18-1853, LR.

vicinity of La Plata Mountains; two New Mexicans who accompanied him had been stripped of all their possessions and then allowed to return to Abiquiu.[5] Subsequent entries in Bennett's journal offer a few helpful observations, but only from a daily record of the march kept by Lieutenant Ransom is it possible to trace the route taken by his column.

After traveling ten miles up the north bank of the Chama River, Ransom turned southwest to the headwaters of the Rio Puerco, thus striking off in a more southerly, direct course to the San Juan than that taken by Major Gilpin in 1846. Camp was made the first night on the Puerco near the present mountain village of Coyote. During the next three days, after fording the Rio Gallinas not far from the site of the Gallina ruins, the troops followed a northwesterly direction toward present Lindrith and then crossed a twenty-mile expanse of Cañada Larga, a nearly level plain dotted with piñon and cedar scrub, before descending into the southern entrance to Largo Canyon. They made a short diversionary march southward to reach a spring; thereafter it is not certain whether they returned to Largo Canyon, as Ransom believed, or proceeded north through Canyon Blanco. In the evening of July 15 the troops halted on the San Juan near the present village of Blanco, thus far having encountered only one Navajo—a man who came to their camp the night before. He said his people were on the river, but having reached there Ransom noted that "None have yet been seen. They probably are frightened at the appearance of Troops in this portion of their country & have left with their stock." [6]

Taking a leisurely pace, the dragoons moved only twelve miles the following day and eighteen or twenty the next, Ransom noting the presence of Anasazi ruins on the river's south bank, before going into camp July 17 near the later Mormon settlement of Kirtland. Here Ransom was approached by several Navajos who told him that their people had been frightened into crossing the river before the troops' advance.

A march of fifteen miles on July 18 brought the column shortly after

5. Bennett journal, ed. Brooks and Reeve 1947, p. 93. Bennett's dates again are faulty, as he indicates the dragoons departed from Abiquiu on June 16. It should be noted, too, that while Colonel Miles directed Ransom to take 40 dragoons on the campaign, Bennett says the company numbered 60. References to the murder of the American trader by a Ute are found in May 25, 1853: Kendrick to Sturgis, NA, RAC, RG 393, K11-1853, LR; and May 25, 1853: Vigil to Lane, NA, NMS 234-546.
6. July 12–30, 1853: "Daily Journal of a march. . . ." enclosure with August 1, 1853: Ransom to Sturgis, NA, RAC, RG 393, R-13-1853, LR.

midday to sandy bottomlands "just above where the Arroya de Tunicha enters" the San Juan. This arroyo was the bed cut by the Chaco River, and Ransom's small command was at rest among cottonwood trees and dense willow brush fringing the San Juan, at this point easily fordable. The dragoons had scarcely put their horses out on picket line when a large number of Navajos appeared over the sand hills. Several of the headmen came forward, among them Archuleta and the very rarely seen Cayetano. Ransom noted later that the headmen said they wished nothing more than to remain at peace; the García sheep had been returned, and the murderer of Ramón Martín would be surrendered "as soon as found." That night about twenty Utes, mingling with Cayetano's Navajos, joined Ransom's camp.

The following morning as Ransom prepared to move his command farther downriver, the Navajos and Utes remonstrated against his proceeding in that direction. Ignoring their protests, Ransom rode on. After traveling fifteen miles he found the fresh tracks of large herds of sheep and other livestock and concluded that the Navajos had hurriedly driven them away that morning. Because he was anxious to join forces with Major Kendrick before all of the stock was spirited away, he pretended he had observed nothing. When a mile or so farther downriver he gave the order to encamp, Navajos again appeared from all directions. They brought him sheep cut out from nearby herds and butchered them for him. Ransom spent an uneasy afternoon. His impulse to force the issue and seize the sheep that all but surrounded his camp gave way finally to a feeling that he should do nothing to alarm the Navajos until Major Kendrick arrived on the scene.

Rising a few miles to the west and south were the foothills and then the shoulders and peaks of the Carrizo Mountains. The river valley where the dragoons were encamped was broad and open and offered nothing in the nature of a pass (as Ransom's orders suggested) that could be blocked off.

Evidently in some reluctance to suspend his surveillance of the grazing herds, Ransom next morning moved his column back one mile upriver and again went into camp. The friendly if watchful atmosphere that until then had prevailed was shattered later in the day when, shortly after Aguila Negra and Miguelito and their people joined his command, Archuleta came in and "created some disturbance." With elaborate care to follow military protocol and avoid mentioning the untidy details of *cause*, Ransom confined his report to the observation, "I made a prisoner of him for some hours & made him furnish me some sheep which he had before refused to do. He seems to day badly disposed & I think is supported by the Utahs."

Although the accuracy of his account may be open to scrutiny, trooper Bennett in more detail relates that about four hundred Navajos gathered about the camp that day as the headmen sat in a semicircle with Ransom, his guide, a New Mexican who served as interpreter for the Navajos, and Bennett himself, who had been asked to translate the New Mexican's Spanish into English. His journal entry continues:

> We demanded the murderers and the stock which had been stolen. In the course of the talk a chief came from quite a distance. Our officer presented him with some flour which was in a sack. It was lying on the ground in the center of the circle. Another chief [Archuleta] became offended because the same favor was not shone him. He sprang to his feet, seized the flour sack by the bottom corners, and giving it a swing, scattered the flour to the four winds. Those seated in the circle were given the appearance of an assemblage of millers. Our officer sprang up, drawing his pistol from his belt. We all seized our arms. The Indians sprang upon their horses with bows in hand. Immediately difficulty was expected.
>
> We took the chief prisoner and directed our guide to say to them that the first move that they made, their chief would be a dead man. They cooled down. We held their chief in custody about two hours. He begged for liberation. We had lost all our fresh meat. Before this happened they had refused to sell any sheep to us. Our officer consented to liberate him on these terms: that he should furnish us with 5 or 6 fat sheep. In 15 minutes time a round dozen of the largest and fat[t]est sheep I have ever seen in any country were brought to us. They refused to take any pay. They left with the chief but promised to come into our camp tomorrow.

Only a few Navajos were seen the next day, and the next. The weather turned intensely hot. Early in the second day the dragoons again went into camp near the point where the Chaco and San Juan rivers converge. An express received during the return march had advised Ransom to expect Major Kendrick's arrival at this place the following day. With improvised hooks and lines the troops whiled away the afternoon at the river, and with luck enough to have fish to fry for supper. Unlike any fish that Ransom, a New York Stater, had seen before, these varied from six inches to two feet in length. Catfish they probably were, and not much to look at, but "of fair eatible quality, being white & firm."

From a distance of about one hundred miles to the south, Major Kendrick meanwhile left Fort Defiance on July 19. His command included Captain Ewell's Company G, First Dragoons, twenty-five troops on foot drawn from the garrison's Third Infantry and Second Artillery, the Diné Ana'aii leader Sandoval with a number of his band—all mounted, painted, and variously armed with bows, lances, shields, and guns—Henry Dodge, and finally the post chaplain, the Reverend John Shaw. Presence of the Diné Ana'aii on such an expedition, with precedent in the past, was accountable now by Kendrick's recent conclusion that Sandoval could be useful to the military's cause as a "scourge"; the inclusion of Chaplain Shaw is nowhere explained. All that is known is that he took genuine interest in the Navajo people and was regarded by Dodge as a good friend.[7]

After leaving Defiance the column marched north to a pass through the Chusca range directly opposite Ojos Calientes, or Bennett's Peak, and reached the valley through Peña Blanca canyon. Once in the valley, Kendrick turned north again, arriving at Lieutenant Ransom's camp on the San Juan early in the morning of July 23. The remainder of that day was spent in rest. Ransom observed that Major Kendrick disabused him of the idea that all of García's sheep had been compensated for and said that less than half the number stolen had been returned. Kendrick makes no reference at all to events of that day and notes only that because he did not regard the support of Ransom's dragoons necessary to his command, he directed the lieutenant to return with his company to Abiquiu.[8]

7. August 15, 1853: Kendrick to Maj. W. A. Nichols, AAG, NA, RAC, RG 393, K-19-1853, LR. Dodge's friendly interest in another frontier clergyman is attested by Clarissa Campbell Gorman, second wife of the Rev. Samuel Gorman, an Ohioan who was assigned by the Baptist Home Mission Society in 1852 to work with the Indians of Laguna Pueblo. With his first wife, Catherine, the missionary tried earnestly to start a school, but each time when a few of the children showed interest, "the governor of the pueblo would order them to stop and not have anything to do with the Gormans in any shape or form. This made it very discouraging. . . . After they had been there about nine months, Captain Henry L. Dodge came, called a council, made a speech an hour long, and succeeded in having [the Gormans] adopted into the Indian community. This gave them permission to remain and enjoy the rights and privileges of the reservation. . . ." (Gorman 1914, pp. 316–20). In months following, Dodge continued to befriend and help the missionary couple.

8. Although he intended to explore up the Animas River, Ransom found on arriving at the river mouth on July 25 that he could not ford the San Juan. His

After parting with Lieutenant Ransom, Kendrick's column moved leisurely westward down the south bank of the San Juan, traveling eighty miles in five days until it reached the mouth of the Rio de Cheille, or Chinle Wash. The arcing course of the river was through open country for the most part, only on the last day raising low bluffs deepening from tan to chocolate hue. At the mouth of the Chinle all suddenly changed. Here the river plunged into a deep canyon of red sandstone—the beginning of a tortuous series of bends named The Goosenecks by some later explorer. The geologist in Kendrick was intrigued. This was, he mused, a "very remarkable cañon, rent in rocks of an ancient date." Sandoval's people told him the canyon continued, much as he saw it, for ten or fifteen days' march until the river finally emptied into the Colorado. From the rim edge looking into the shadowed depths, Kendrick decided he would gain nothing by exploring farther downriver. He turned south, instead, following Chinle Wash, and reached Fort Defiance on August 4.

Henry Dodge, who normally shrank from the pitfalls of placing words upon paper, later was moved to make observations of some importance to the campaign. A letter he submitted to the Santa Fe *Gazette* suggests certain correction by the hand of James L. Collins, the editor and publisher, and contains this extract:

> After leaving the San Juan we returned to the valley of the Chella, which we found to be a wide rich valley, extensively cultivated in corn and some wheat. The wheat grows finely and ripens in June and much of the Indian corn we found well matured and ready for the harvesting the latter end of July. The Navajoes have cultivated much more extensively this year than in any former year, owing perhaps to the supply of hoes and spades furnished them by the government. The plow is now used by them. Their crop consists of wheat, Indian corn, beans, pumpkins and mellons. They have also fine peaches that grow abundantly and of a superior quality. The corn crop from the best estimate that I was able to make exceeds two thousand acres and much of it must give an abundant yield and will doubtless give them a large surplus, which it is my intention to induce them to sell to the troops at Fort Defiance.[9]

column reached Abiquiu July 30—"My men badly off for clothing & my horses weak & much fatigued." Bennett so confused the notes of this return that his journal leads the command errantly off to Fort Laramie and troubles with the Sioux.

9. Santa Fe *Gazette*, September 10, 1853. The entire letter appears in Woodward 1939, pp. 136–38.

Dodge then remarked on a point of interest that Major Kendrick's report failed to mention. From the familiar sand flats on the Chinle where some of these troops once camped with Colonel Washington in the afterglow of burning hogans, they turned into the depths of Canyon de Chelly and traversed the canyon's entire length. They were, as Dodge observed, "doubtless the first Americans that ever passed entirely through the cañon; we were accompanied by about twenty Navajoes" (the last probably was a reference to Sandoval's Diné Ana'aii):

> In the cañon we met Fairweather, a chief who resides there. We were treated with great attention and kindness by the chief and all his people, who feasted us with green corn, mellons, milk and cheese.
>
> Amagoso the principal war captain urged the Rev. Mr. Shaw very hard to pay him a visit when his peaches were ripe. Mr. Shaw is quite popular with the Indians, and has an extensive vocabulary with them, he has made a couple vocabularies of their language and speaks it sufficiently to make himself understood upon almost any subject.

Of his own movements immediately after the return to Fort Defiance, Dodge said nothing. However, because he had had only time enough to deliver supplies to the new Navajo agency before joining the San Juan campaign, it is possible that he returned at once to Chupadero. In his own summary of the campaign, Major Kendrick spoke not of milk and cheese and green corn but of war. He referred again to the advisability of starting operations in late summer if an expedition were to be made this year into eastern Navajo country. And again he repeated that if it came to war, "it should be of the most stringent character—we ought to have no more small wars with the Navajoes." [10] But he thought there was some prospect for temporary peace if two or three more military expeditions, such as the one just concluded, could be made. He proposed as well that as many Navajos as possible be assembled at Fort Defiance and, once gathered, informed that money or goods that otherwise would come to them under 1849 treaty terms would be used instead to recompense New Mexicans for livestock Navajos had stolen.

It was necessary to remember, he added, that all promises and treaties made by or with the Navajos were "utterly worthless unless guaranteed by their interests or their fears."

10. August 15, 1853: Kendrick to Nichols, cited above.

13

Interval of Peace

To David Meriwether and members of his party the rendezvous at Council Grove in late June 1853 may have seemed mildly stimulating but not unusual. In retrospect it was singular. Having progressed this far over the Santa Fe Trail, New Mexico's governor-designate went into camp to await the arrival of Brevet Brigadier General John Garland from Fort Leavenworth.

The timbered bottomlands of the Neosho River had sheltered larger caravans, but perhaps none that ever gathered in the grove was more interestingly diversified. This rendezvous in effect, if briefly, brought together three distinctly separate groups: seven civilians who accompanied Meriwether; a military unit of some two hundred troops, for the moment assigned to escorting the new governor and the general, but thereafter to draw frontier duty out of Fort Union. They were joined on June 28 by General Garland and Major Electus Backus, the latter returning to the Southwest to assume command of Fort Fillmore. With these two officers also came Colonel Joseph King Fenno Mansfield of the Inspector General's Department, with orders to inspect and report upon the condition of all military installations in New Mexico.

Finally were thirty or so members of Captain John William Gunnison's survey party, charged with exploring a rail route to the Pacific along the 28th parallel. With Gunnison—one of eight who would die with Gunnison four months later in willow brush fringing Sevier Lake —was the young artist who had accompanied Colonel Washington's 1849 Navajo campaign—Richard H. Kern.

It was plainly a company of mixed interests that struck westward from Council Grove toward Bent's Fort, where trails would separate. Three of the officers brought their wives and two had children in tow as well.[1] In contrast to Colonel Sumner, Garland, a Virginian and

1. Meriwether 1965, pp. 145–47. While dictating his autobiography in 1886, Meriwether recalled that among General Garland's party was a "Colonel Miles and

veteran of the war with Mexico, avoided publicity and shunned controversy. It was characteristic, therefore, that when he reached Santa Fe in the afternoon of August 7 he diverted attention from himself to the new governor, whose party he had passed in the mountains east of the capital. He let it be known that Meriwether would spend the night at Arroyo Hondo and then went quietly about his own business.

Meriwether had been in the governor's office only two days when he drafted his first report on Indian affairs of the territory. He found the region contained large numbers of roving bands that by long custom depended for subsistence mainly upon wild game or depredations upon the settlements. The government's policy in recent years of moving eastern tribes to open lands on the western frontier, as well as the vast migration to California of gold seekers and settlers, had decimated the game. Buffalo were being slaughtered in great herds or else being driven to such remote regions that it was impossible for Indians of New Mexico to follow; if they were foolhardy enough to try, they were met by warlike tribes of the plains and were either slain or driven back.

Governor Lane had succeeded to some extent in averting raids upon the settlements by drawing heavily from funds allotted to his superintendency to feed the roving tribes and to encourage them to cultivate crops. Now, with responsibility resting in his hands, Meriwether agreed with his predecessor on an almost certain outcome if funds and rations for the Indians were suddenly cut off: "then these Indians must either starve or subsist themselves by depredations committed upon the citizens of this Territory or the trains passing along the roads to and through it."

From this conclusion Meriwether proceeded very nearly to agreement with Lane's policy, which had drawn sharp rebuke from Washington and contributed at least in part to his removal. Meriwether posed the question: Which would be better—to spend a few thousand dollars to feed starving Indians and so prevent them from raiding, or to permit stark necessity to drive them to commit outrages for which they would have to be punished? [2]

For reasons entirely obscure, a few weeks later Meriwether veered a full 180 degrees to an opposite point of view. He found himself entirely in disagreement with Lane's policy, which, he declared, if carried

---

his wife and family." This probably was a slip of memory as the only Col. Miles then serving in the army—Dixon S. Miles—at this time was in Albuquerque waiting for Garland to relieve him of department command.

2. August 10, 1853: Meriwether to Manypenny, NA, NMS 234-546.

out effectually, would cost the government from fifty to one hundred thousand dollars annually. The cost of warring on the tribes—the alternative as he saw it to feeding them—he felt he should not estimate, but he implied it would be less. He could discover little merit, too, in his predecessors' course of submitting to acts of aggression until forced to retaliate with military expeditions, which the Indians usually managed to forestall before damage was done by suing for peace on the promise of offending no more. Treaties resulting from such tactics, Meriwether believed, were signed with no intent of compliance on the Indians' part. Presents or annuities granted to the tribes were regarded by them only as bribes to keep the peace, and every concession or act of kindness was interpreted as fear of the tribes' power.

Meriwether recommended an Indian policy quite simple in concept and relatively inexpensive, a consideration that at once recommended it to a budget-conscious Indian commissioner. Allow him to hold councils with the roving tribes, he advised Commissioner George W. Manypenny; he would obtain their agreement to treaties that would extinguish their title to thousands of acres of land nearest the white settlements, and remove the Indians to lands far distant and remote from white contact. The Indians would be offered annuities for the land they relinquished, but in reality the annuities would be a drawing fund—by treaty an annual fixed amount, but a fund from which the government would deduct any amounts necessary to compensate for property stolen by any band of the tribe. Navajos perhaps better than other Indians would illustrate the wisdom of his policy, Meriwether said. On the authority of Major Kendrick, who twice had traveled through Navajo country, he could assure the commissioner that those Navajos who lived nearest to the whites were lazy, degraded, and warlike, while those farthest removed were peaceful and industrious.[3]

Insofar as his Indian policy affected the Navajos, Meriwether may have been influenced by the commander of Fort Defiance. Major Kendrick took temporary leave from his post between August 6 and September 10 to report to General Garland in Albuquerque, and during the same period it appears that Meriwether talked at length with the major, either at department headquarters or in Santa Fe.

Governor Meriwether did not have long to wait to meet a number of the Navajo tribesmen. For some days, Henry Dodge had been traveling toward the river with a delegation of 104 Navajos headed by

3. August 31, 1853: Meriwether to Manypenny, *Senate Exec. Docs.*, 33rd Cong., 1st sess., no. 1, pt. 1, pp. 429–33.

Zarcillos Largos. To feed his hungry charges, Dodge stopped at Cebolleta to buy seven sheep and six sacks of corn, and again at Isleta Pueblo where he bought a beef cow and two hundred loaves of bread.[4] At Albuquerque the Navajos were courteously received by General Garland, Dodge observing that the department commander's mild and friendly manner impressed the Navajos favorably.[5]

The mounted company rode into Santa Fe in the evening of August 31, their number including twelve women. Some of the Navajos had traveled as far as 250 miles for this chance to talk with the new governor. In addition to Zarcillos Largos, the most influential men composing the delegation were said to be Barboncito of Encino Gordo, the headman of Canyon de Chelly, whom Dodge identified only as Fairweather, Juan Lucero of the Chusca Valley, Gordo de Pesqueso of Ojo del Oso, Colorado and Colas from the San Juan, a brother of Mulas Muchas from Ojos Calientes, Cabras Blancas from the vicinity of Chacra Mesa, and Juanico from Cienega Grande on the eastern approach to Canyon de Chelly.

For three days and four nights the Navajos remained with Dodge in Santa Fe, making their camp on the outskirts of town. They were dressed for this confrontation with the new governor in their finest buckskins and blankets; without ostentation but yet so that it might be seen, they carried their best war gear. They made so striking an appearance that Meriwether was led to observe that they were the healthiest and best-clothed Indians ("in fabricks of their own manufacture") he had seen west of the Arkansas. Their behavior, unlike that of their Bilagáana counterparts on numerous similar occasions, was so restrained that Meriwether further noted they "were never known to drink a drop of sperits of any kind during their stay nor even to ask for it but conducted themselves in an orderly and peacible manner." [6]

Several meetings were held with the governor, the first reported briefly by Dodge in a letter of September 1 published in the Santa Fe *Gazette*. At this council Meriwether told the Navajos firmly that he would expect them to comply with the conditions of the treaty of 1849 —significantly making no reference to the December 1851 council of Sumner and Calhoun at Jemez. He said that any departure from the

4. Receipts signed August 22 at Cebolleta by Francisco Sandoval for $20 and August 30 at Isleta by Ambrosie Beity for $45, NA, NMS T21-1.

5. Dodge letter of September 1, published September 10, 1853, in the Santa Fe *Gazette*.

6. September 17, 1853: Meriwether to Manypenny, NA, NMS 234-546.

stipulations of the 1849 treaty would bring down upon the Navajos the severest punishment. For his part, he said he would not hold the Navajos accountable for any offenses committed by their people before the present date, September 1.

Reference was made to the affair of the previous spring that had so agitated the territory, Dodge remarking that the Navajos promised to deliver the murderer of Ramón Martín as soon as possible, dead or alive. Whether made in good faith or not, it was a promise that was not to be kept. The council ended in a friendly manner, with an understanding that the Navajos would leave the next morning to return home, but they stayed on for two days more.

In conversations held privately with Dodge, Meriwether sought information that he might add to or assess against what he had been told of the Navajos by others. He found that in nearly all matters Dodge and Major Kendrick were rather closely in agreement. Dodge estimated that livestock owned by the tribe (sheep and goats, horses and mules, relatively few cattle) numbered about 250,000 head. He believed that a count of the tribe's population would not exceed 10,000 persons. Corn, wheat, and some fruits and vegetables were grown successfully enough to subsist large numbers of Navajos who rarely if ever had contact with the white settlements or even with a few of the eastern bands said to be most frequently engaged in raiding. Of these last, Meriwether concluded, the band of Archuleta, found on the San Juan and often associated with roving Capote and Wiminuche Utes, gave the most trouble and perhaps was "guilty of most of the mischief attributed to the Navijos." [7]

When the council was reconvened the next day, Meriwether asked what excuse could be made for the tribe's many robberies in the past. Zarcillos Largos admitted that there were some bad men among the people whom the headmen were unable to control. But he denied that any acts of aggression could be charged against the bands represented by himself or the others who were present.

He asked Meriwether to weigh with charges against the Navajos a history of many years of warfare against the Navajos by Spanish and Mexican people, and he referred most bitterly to the imbalance in captives taken, the almost methodical slaving raids of the Spanish, who still held scores or hundreds of Navajo women and children in captivity. Accustomed as he was to practices in his native Kentucky, Meriwether confessed that he was totally ignorant of the application of

7. Meriwether letter of September 17, cited above.

slavery to Navajos. He assured Zarcillos Largos, with sincerity no doubt but with unwarranted optimism, that every Navajo held in bondage would be returned to the tribe.

As evidence of his intentions, Meriwether said if members of Zarcillos Largos's party would identify Navajos held captive in Santa Fe, or give information of others held elsewhere, he would have them restored instantly to their people. At the same time, Navajos must release any captives they had taken from the settlements. Zarcillos Largos replied that among his party were two or three Mexicans who had been captured as children, and who had since taken Navajo women as wives. They were quite free to remain on the river if they chose to do so, he said. Juan Anaya, the interpreter, may have been one of them. When asked their choice, Meriwether observed that the few Mexicans in the Navajo delegation expressed a strong wish to return to Navajo country, and he assented to their decision.[8] The council ended shortly afterward with mutual agreement that captives would be exchanged, Zarcillos Largos saying that four New Mexicans then held by his people would be released to Agent Dodge upon his return and restored to their homes.

In an impromptu ceremony the same evening, Meriwether presented medals to six of the headmen, saving until last the medal most handsomely festooned with ribbons. This, after a flourish of oratory, he handed to Zarcillos Largos. He explained that the medals symbolized the leadership and responsibility of each of the six headmen, and his own trust in their loyalty and willingness to bring any offenders within their bands to Agent Dodge for punishment. The exceptional medal signified the governor's recognition of Zarcillos Largos as "captain over all the others"—a title that the governor's New Mexican advisers may have persuaded him to adopt. The late Governor Calhoun, it was observed, on a previous occasion had presented a cane to Zarcillos Largos in similar recognition of his position of leadership, but this was the first time Navajos had received medals.

The mood of good feeling was not diminished the evening of the

8. Ibid. Evidence of Meriwether's intentions at this time is found in a letter he addressed next day, September 3, to Dodge, saying in part, "you will hasten to return to your agency without unnecessary delay. In addition to the usual duties of your office, you will take steps to have such Navijo captives, as may be found with our people, and may come under your observation, or to your knowledge, speedily returned to their people, when such returne is desired by such captive. You will also hasten to demand from the Navijos, all of our people who may be in captivity with them, and have such captives returned to their relatives, when desired by such captives" (NA, NMS T21-1).

next day when Meriwether invited the Navajo delegation back to distribute presents among them. These, he reported later, were "such articles as they most needed which they received with thanks and protestations of friendship." From lamplit rooms of the Palace of the Governors the company then moved out into the night air of the plaza where, as a throng of citizens gathered to watch, the Navajos "gave us a grand dance." When morning came they started for home.

If the impression he conveyed to Commissioner Manypenny of this first encounter with Navajos indicated a favorable optimism, Meriwether admitted as well to reservations and prejudices. He doubted if it was good policy to welcome these Indians into the settlements; to begin with, it was expensive, and it freely afforded information that could be useful to them and damaging to the whites in any future action of war.

Furthermore, although Henry Dodge had acted only in conformity with custom by bringing this delegation to meet the new governor, Meriwether believed it would be best for Indians as well as whites if in future they had "as little promiscuous intercourse as possible with each other." [9]

How far on the return journey Henry Dodge traveled with the Navajos is not certain, although possibly he went no farther than his agency at Chupadero, from which point his activities in the summer of 1853 appear to have both started and ended. Even less certain is whether Meriwether's views on racial intercourse may have referred obliquely to him, for either at this time or soon afterward Dodge is said to have married, in the custom of the Navajo tribe, a kinswoman of Zarcillos Largos.[10]

There is better evidence that between early July and late September —except for time consumed in the meeting at Santa Fe—Dodge was principally engaged in recovering sheep stolen by Navajos. He was aided in this effort by Sandoval of the Diné Ana'aii, who traveled with him as guide and interpreter for a consideration of forty dollars a month.[11] Dodge's willingness to remain in the saddle for days at a time, as much as his easy way in dealing with Indians, usually produced good results. By fall, an incipient clash that had threatened since August to bring

9. Ibid.
10. Van Valkenburgh 1941.
11. Receipt for $120 paid September 30, 1853, to "Sebolla Sandobal Navijo" by Dodge "at Chupadero Navijo Agency" for "services as interpreter and guide in the recovery of sheep stolen by the Navijo Nation. . . ." (NA, NMS T21-1).

Jicarilla Apaches in raiding reprisal against Navajos was averted when Dodge, again after hard travel, effected the return of five horses stolen from the Jicarillas.

Colonel Mansfield, meanwhile, last found at the Council Grove rendezvous on June 28, reached Fort Defiance in mid-September and stayed for five days. The red rock mesas and pinnacles rising immediately to the east and north of Cañoncito Bonito moved him to comment, "This is the most beautiful and interesting post as a whole in New Mexico." Elsewhere he said, "The buildings are good and mostly of logs and mud, but some good stone store houses have recently been completed." He observed also that Navajos who remained after evening tattoo were required to spend the night in a building reserved for them.[12] This was a small structure set apart by itself at the far north end of the canyon, separated by four stables and then an open area from the row of officers' quarters. During the day the Navajos were permitted to move freely to all parts of the post.

Colonel Mansfield remarked that grazing land was excellent and hay in the region abundant, but he failed to note that for days there had been no rain. It was, in fact, an unusually dry autumn, a season of drought followed by a series of killing frosts. Fear that a large share of the hay crop would be lost was confirmed in the first week of November when the temperature dropped one night to nineteen degrees below zero.

Under these circumstances Major Kendrick made plans to move the post's beef herd to lower winter grazing ground near Ojo del Oso or even farther east to the Agua Azul. At the same time and for the same reason he was forced to decline General Garland's proposal to strengthen the Defiance garrison with a company of dragoons. As an alternative, Kendrick recommended that a detachment of sixteen dragoons be sent out to guard the post's wintering cattle. The presence of even so small a force might have a restraining influence on any Navajos tempted to raid, he felt, and the dragoon horses could be supplied with corn from Laguna or Cebolleta at less cost than if they were subsisted on the Rio Grande. At the same time, in apparent reference to the Navajo whom Dodge identified as Amagoso, Kendrick advised the department commander that "The principal war chief on this side of the mountains is not expected to live; he has the last two years been our firm friend, and has used his influence in our favor. His death will probably not affect our relations favorably." [13]

12. *Mansfield on the Condition of the Western Forts, 1853–54*, ed. Frazer 1963, pp. 21–22, 48.

13. November 6, 1853: Kendrick to Nichols, NA, RAC, RG 393, K-29-1853, LR.

Spanish horsemen trail in ghostly procession high across a cliff face at Standing Cow ruin in Canyon del Muerto—an eloquent Navajo record attributed to Dibé Yázhí Nééz (Little Long Lamb). The subject of the painting, never clearly substantiated, may depict Colonel Narbona's 1805 invasion of the canyon. Long cloaks worn by the horsemen suggest a winter campaign. The central dark-caped figure astride a mule follows in the tracks of what may be an Opata Indian auxiliary. This rendition of the panel was made by the author from a series of closeup photographs, taken on a narrow ledge forty feet above the canyon floor, by Dr. Stephen C. Jett of the University of California.

Scattered bones of Navajo dead, mainly women and children killed by ricocheting Spanish bullets, are viewed in Canyon del Muerto's Massacre Cave by Alfred Vincent Kidder, left, and Charles Avery Amsden.—*Earl H. Morris Photograph, courtesy of Joe Ben Wheat*

Barboncito (Little Whiskers) in the 1860s became eminent as peace leader and principal spokesman for the Navajos. To those of his nation he was known as Be'ats'os Dihi (Black Feathers), and Hozhoonzhi Naat'aanii (Peace Chief). At the time of his death, March 16, 1871, he was regarded as the Navajos' principal headman.—*Smithsonian Office of Anthropology*

Manuel A. Chaves, who dedicated the active years of his life to conducting forays against the Navajos, is pictured here as a young man. A portrait made in later years showed him with hawklike visage in dark profile above a full gray beard.—*Courtesy of the Museum of New Mexico, Santa Fe*

An unusually rare cache of Navajo utility vessels of the Dinetah period was discovered in a cave on Chacra Mesa, east of Chaco Canyon and not far from Pueblo Pintado. Taken to the site by a Navajo friend, archaeologist Gordon Vivian in June 1956 photographed the cache of four conical bottom pots and two water baskets, the latter once coated on interior and exterior with pitch and apparently made of sumac. The basket appearing at the right of the two large pots measures 16½ inches in height, with a maximum diameter of 15½ inches. Vivian tentatively dated the cache as some time prior to 1775.—*Photograph by Gordon Vivian*

Brevet Major William Thomas Harbaugh Brooks, a native of Ohio, was graduated 46th in his 1841 class at the U.S. Military Academy. Under his inept command of Fort Defiance, the once friendly relations with Navajos worsened steadily. Eventually, his order for the destruction of Manuelito's livestock caused the retaliatory murder of his Negro slave, Jim, and this in turn precipitated the first major U.S. campaign against Navajos.—*The United States Military Academy Archives*

Characterized by Navajos as *Nahondzod*— The Fearing Time—a period of eight years of warfare and misery in exile was ushered in by the 1860–61 expedition conducted by Lieutenant Colonel Edward Richard Sprigg Canby. Canby's insistence that Navajos either surrender unconditionally or be exterminated was the initial formulation of a harsh policy later executed by Brevet Brigadier General James H. Carleton.—*The National Archives, U.S. Signal Corps*

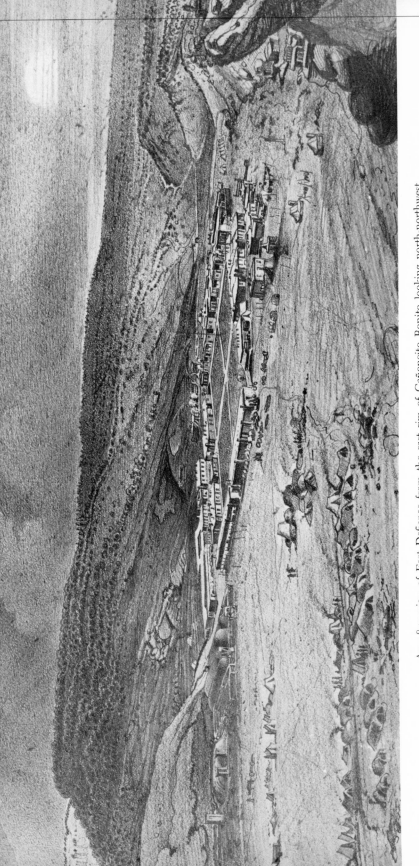

An 1859 view of Fort Defiance from the east rim of Cañoncito Bonito looking north-northwest shows haystacks and corrals at left, a flagpole at the north end of the parade ground in front of officers' quarters. The drawing was made by Joseph Heger, a private in Lieutenant John Van DuBois' Company K, RMR. Born in Hesse, Germany, Heger came to the United States with his parents, was trained as a lithographer, and was living in Jefferson, Wisconsin when he enlisted at the age of twenty, in 1855.—*Arizona Pioneers' Historical Society*

Brevet Major Henry Lane Kendrick served longest in command of Fort Defiance (from 1852 to 1857), and of commanders of New Mexico's frontier unquestionably was the most competent and effective in determining relations with the Navajos. After leaving New Mexico to return to West Point he held a professorship at the Military Academy until his retirement from service in 1880. Always a bachelor, he died in New York City on May 24, 1891.—*The United States Military Academy Archives*

Manuelito, as he appeared in the decade following the Navajos' release from Fort Sumner. The portrait by Eldridge Ayer Burbank was painted during the early 1900s when Burbank worked in a room of one of the original buildings of Lorenzo Hubbell's trading post at Ganado, Arizona. The painting remains at Ganado, a part of the Hubbell Collection.—*From a photograph by the author.*

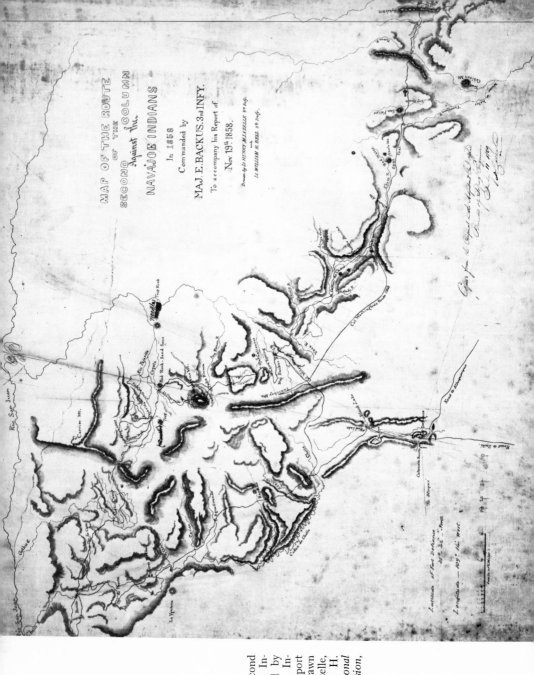

Map of the route of the Second Column against the Navajo Indians in 1858, commanded by Major Electus Backus, 3rd Infantry, to accompany his report of November 19, 1858. Drawn by Lieutenants Henry M. Lazelle, 8th Infantry, and William H. Bell, 3rd Infantry.—*The National Archives, Cartographic Division, Record Group No. 77*

Zuni dancers impersonate an ancient enemy in this reenactment of an attack upon their pueblo by Navajos. Undated, the photograph was taken at Zuni in the 1870s by William Henry Jackson. Dancers for the most part brandish muskets, although a few hold lances and one man (lower left) menacingly gestures with a cavalry sabre. Partially visible at upper right is the abandoned Spanish mission church, burned in 1680, rebuilt in 1699, and restored again in 1972.—*State Historical Society of Colorado*

The best camera lens in the most competent hands is defeated by the depths, the distances, the singular awesomeness of Canyon de Chelly. This wet plate view of 1873 by Timothy H. O'Sullivan may be one of the two or three best photographs of the canyon ever made. For comparative scale, note the tents of the Wheeler Expedition at lower left.—*Denver Public Library Western Collection*

Early winter was closing in when, a week later, Kendrick reported that relations with the Navajos continued to be friendly. He saw no reason why this situation should not prevail indefinitely, provided that the garrison of Fort Defiance was maintained at its present strength of about two hundred troops.

Sometime between late September and the end of 1853 Henry Dodge moved the Navajo agency from Chupadero to a location deep in Navajo country. The first evidence of this is found in a good conduct pass issued to Francisco Terrasino, a Navajo, whom Dodge was pleased to recommend to the kind attention of all Americans. Above an ornate seal and his own signature Dodge wrote, "Given under my hand and Seal at Pass Washington Navijo Agency this first day of January A.D. one thousand eight hundred and fifty four." [14] The exact location of the agency may never be known and there is no certainty, either, whether Dodge operated from a tent, a log dwelling, or something more substantial. There are indications only that Dodge's contemporaries shared this writer's present uncertainty.

Thus, three months later, Major Kendrick admitted that he did not know whether Dodge was in Santa Fe or elsewhere, but he hoped that on the agent's return "to Tunicha" Dodge would get in touch with him. In August, in the space of three days, Governor Meriwether addressed three letters to Dodge at his agency "near Pass Washington," at "Pass Washington," and "near Fort Defiance."

A suggestion that Dodge enjoyed a movable feast of humble fare might be supported by the observation of Senator Henry Dodge, his father, that the senator was deeply impressed with the need for some sort of houses for Indian agents in New Mexico. Commissioner Manypenny would greatly oblige the senator if he would furnish an estimate of the cost of such buildings.[15]

14. NA, NMS T21-2. On the same day, Dodge issued a license to James Conklin to trade with Navajos at Jemez, where Conklin resided. On December 29, 1853, Dodge licensed Jarvis Nolan to trade with Navajos "on the San Juan, Rio Colorado, Chaye, Tounicha, and Chusci."

15. May 1, 1854: U.S. Senator Henry Dodge to Manypenny, NA, NMS 234-547. Van Valkenburgh and McPhee (1938) say that Dodge "wisely and bravely established his agency near the eastern approach to Washington Pass above Sheep Springs," where he "created a stone house. . . ." Though this is entirely possible, the location was not permanent but, at best and for a limited time, seasonal. Conjecturally, the site "above Sheep Springs" may have been in the high forested glade —frequented by Navajos in spring and summer—about one-half mile below the summit of the pass. Sheep Springs, the site of a trading post built in the early 1900s, did not exist as a place name or appear on maps of the time treated here.

With the approach of fall 1854, Dodge asked Major Kendrick if he might establish his agency at Fort Defiance for the winter. Kendrick replied that he had always regarded it as bad policy to provide no fixed time or place for Navajos to receive presents. For this reason he was willing to afford Dodge every accommodation within his power, but he was not certain of demands that might soon be made upon his officers' quarters and therefore could not promise to provide room for the agent. He urged Dodge to come to the fort anyway, so that they might discuss the matter. Dodge evidently moved to the post soon afterward. He may have been established there when Kendrick wrote department headquarters in February 1855 that, for the time at least, "I think it advisable . . . that the Indian Agent should reside at this post; & I respectfully request permission to cause commissary supplies for the *use of his family* [Kendrick's italics], to be sold to him at contract prices so long as he resides here." Although this was a consideration usually denied a civilian, General Garland gave his consent.[16]

As remarked earlier, Dodge is said to have married a kinswoman of Zarcillos Largos, but in the official correspondence this is the only occasion when reference is found to Dodge's Navajo family. Dodge remained at Defiance at least until April 17, but on May 2 was writing from his agency at "Tounicha." [17] A few months later, as will be seen presently, there is reference to Dodge operating from his agency at Laguna Negra (or Red Lake).

If anything certain is to be determined from this, it is that the Navajo agency was located at Fort Defiance in late winter and early spring of 1855, and that in the months immediately before and after— except for the initial period at Chupadero—the agency was to be found moving about with Dodge, from Washington Pass to Chusca Valley, and north of Fort Defiance to the vicinity of Laguna Negra, where Zarcillos Largos is said to have lived in his late years. In early August 1855, Dodge was writing again from Navijo Agency Pass Washington,"

16. February 14, 1855: Kendrick to Nichols, NA, RAC, RG 393, K-1-1855, LR. Garland's endorsement reads: "The Ind Agent, Capt. Dodge, is authorized to purchase sub: stores at Fort Defiance during his residence at or near that post. The quantity to be limited to the immediate wants of his family and at the prices charged to officers of the Army."

17. May 2, 1855: Dodge to Meriwether, NA, NMS 234-547. At about the same time, Dodge reported those employed at the Navajo agency as Juan Anaya, interpreter; Manuel Gallegos, herder; and George C. Carter, blacksmith. Carter first joined Dodge in the third quarter of 1853, moving his forge and tools to Chupadero from Jemez. It is likely that some of the first Navajo smiths learned iron working from him.

but from September 20 of that year until the time of his death, all of his agency correspondence was directed from Fort Defiance.

Coinciding with Dodge's move from Chupadero, an outbreak of smallpox raged through Zuni and pueblos of the Hopis, its effects being most seriously felt in the latter villages. Early in February 1854, Major Kendrick reported the epidemic at an end. During its peak, however, with disease confronting them on one side, the Hopis had faced a warring band of Navajos on the other. Trouble had started when a Navajo was killed after committing a theft. Navajos killed five Hopis in retaliation, but further conflict was averted and the Navajos expressed a willingness to leave the Hopis in peace. From another quarter more disturbing news came soon afterward. Large flocks of New Mexican sheep were being grazed deep into Navajo country and even to the west of Zuni, their owners expressing indifference to Navajo and Zuni complaints of this intrusion upon their grazing lands.

Major Kendrick was infuriated by this encroachment, which he regarded as endangering all of his and Dodge's efforts at the very moment when there was hope of consolidating peaceful relations with the Navajos. He was amazed by what he termed the criminal recklessness of sheep owners in so dangerously irritating the Indians and at the same time providing them an almost irresistible temptation to steal. A few of the encroaching herders already had been "maltreated" by angry Indians, but the owners, who lived far off on the Rio Grande, appeared indifferent to this and seem to care only that if any of their sheep were stolen they would be recompensed for their loss by the government in Washington.[18]

Meriwether shared Major Kendrick's concern that the grazing dispute could erupt into a renewal of hostilities, but he confessed there was very little he could do in the matter. His hands were tied by a ruling of the territorial U.S. District Court, which denied the existence in New Mexico of anything that could be defined, under the laws of Congress, as "Indian country"; and since there was no Indian country under his jurisdiction, it was impossible for Meriwether to invoke federal regulations governing trade and intercourse with Indian tribes. Although New Mexican stock raisers might be unaware of it, the governor could no more prevent their encroachment upon Indian lands than he could authorize payment by the government to recompense the same New Mexicans for any losses in stock suffered in Indian raids.[19]

18. February 10, 1854: Kendrick to Meriwether, NA, NMS T21-2.
19. February 27, 1854: Meriwether to Manypenny, NA, NMS 234-547.

The governor was absent from the capital and William S. Messervy was acting in his place when Henry Dodge appeared with a delegation of twelve Navajos at the end of March 1854. Messervy regarded their presence as something of an embarrassment, as they had come expressly to receive farming tools that Meriwether previously had promised to them, and the Indian superintendency neither had on hand nor could afford to buy.

Because he was unwilling to let the Navajos go home empty-handed, Messervy by some means provided tools for them, at the same time informing Commissioner Manypenny that Governor Meriwether for the last several months had maintained the superintendency with his own private funds.[20] The importance of keeping Meriwether's promises to the Navajos was recognized by Major Kendrick, then in Albuquerque but preparing to return at once to Fort Defiance in light of outbreaks, threatened or real, by Utes and Jicarilla Apaches.

"I have serious fears that the Utahs will tamper with the Navajoes," he informed Messervy, "to prevent wh[ich] at *this time* is of the highest importance. Should Capt. Dodge be in Santa Fe or elsewhere than in the Navajoe Country, I deem it of great importance that he should return to his agency as soon as possible since he will hear of any intended outbreak sooner than we at the Fort. . . . It would be well if Capt. Dodge could take out with him some farming tools & tobacco for presents to the Indians. No effort should be spared to induce the Navajoes to remain friendly, in order that the more attention can be bestowed on the Utahs and Apaches." [21]

If there was no basis to a reported alliance between Capote Utes and eastern bands of Navajos, Major Kendrick was given cause for renewed concern over New Mexican encroachment upon Indian grazing lands. Zarcillos Largos brought word to him in May of a rumored raid by Navajos upon sheep somewhere to the west of Jemez. The aging headman's motives were above suspicion, but the information he could give this time was either contradictory or lacking in detail. It was not certain whether there had been one raid or several, whether the stock had been driven off from the vicinity of Jémez or Laguna, or whether the Indians

20. March 31, 1854: Messervy to Manypenny, NA, NMS 234-547.
21. April 1, 1854; Kendrick to Messervy, NA, NMS T21-2. Kit Carson, then agent for Moache Utes at Taos, reported that in an engagement with Jicarillas March 30 in the Embudo Mountains, Lt. John W. Davidson's company of 60 dragoons lost 22 men killed and 21 wounded—a staggering blow. A force of 200 men was being raised at Taos by Col. Cooke to take the field on April 4 in pursuit.

involved were members of Armijo's band from the Chusca Valley or were Sandoval's Diné Ana'aii near Cebolleta.

In mounting frustration over continued provocations by New Mexican stock owners, and deepening uncertainty over rumored Navajo reprisals, Kendrick vented his anger against Henry Dodge, from whom he had heard nothing for nearly two months. Now well into the season of year when Navajos were most likely to give trouble, with situations arising on all sides that seemed inevitably calculated to invite hostilities, the Navajo agent was unaccountably, and in Kendrick's eyes unforgivably, absent.

With flaring temper, Kendrick observed that at so critical a time in Navajo relations it was a sorry matter for the Navajo agent to go off to the settlements leaving the Indians uncertain whether he was ever coming back. Someone would do Captain Dodge a favor, he thought, by informing him that his influence with the Navajos was suffering. Stories were spreading to the effect that Dodge was afraid to remain, and in Cubero it was said in the bars that he had been run out of Navajo country.[22]

Although from this one might assume that Dodge may have remained in Santa Fe after meeting with Messervy, or returned there again afterward, there is no evidence that he did. There is no evidence, either, aside from the major's implications, that Dodge was anywhere but in Navajo country attending to the affairs of his agency.[23] And despite the drunken gossip of Cubero's barflies, as Kendrick had reason to know, Dodge had a reputation for not running from trouble.

Kendrick's irritation may have been due in part to his feeling obliged to investigate personally the reports of Navajo raids upon New Mexican sheep—a thankless task and one that he might reasonably have thought was the agent's, not his. In any case, soon afterward, he was at Laguna on an illusive trail. His own path, he informed General Garland, had not yet crossed that of Dodge, "whose return to the Navajoe country was more prompt than I had anticipated." [24] Zarcillos Largos and other headmen on the west side of the Chuscas were attempting to collect sheep from western tribesmen to replace sheep stolen by ladrons of the

22. May 13, 1854: Kendrick to Messervy, NA, RAC, RG 393, K-5-1854, LR.

23. Indian Office and military files offer no trace of Dodge's whereabouts between April 1 and May 23, when Kendrick reported Dodge's presence in Navajo country. On April 1, Dodge received a receipt from Simon Delgado, in Santa Fe, for his purchase of "20 lbs. Indigo, 2 Bales Peloncillo, 1 Doz Red Sashes, 1 Hat for the son of Narbona" at a cost of $129 (NA, NMS T21-2).

24. May 23, 1854: Kendrick to Nichols, NA, RAC, RG 393, K-5-1854, LR.

east, but Kendrick doubted if their efforts would amount to much. If the words of Zarcillos could be believed, no more than three hundred sheep had been stolen from the flock of a certain Rafael "Miers" (Miera?), and the marauders were said to be of Armijo's band. Kendrick thought he might proceed from Laguna to seek out Armijo at Ojos Calientes, but if he should meet with Dodge first it might not be necessary for him to go there, as he assumed that Dodge already had warned Chusca Navajos that reparations would be demanded of marauding bands.

From this point forward there is nothing to indicate that relations between Kendrick and Dodge were other than friendly and, during this tense period of maintaining peace, mutually cooperative. From the middle of June until the middle of July, Dodge was away from his agency traveling with Juan Anaya and his herder, Manuel Gallegos, on the trail of sheep stolen from Rafael Miera in May. It appears that he recovered few if any of the Miera stock but instead collected contributions of sheep from the tribe to make up the number of seven hundred (not three hundred) that Miera claimed he had lost. Neither Dodge nor Kendrick reported further on the incident, so it is not known whose band was responsible for the theft, or where the sheep were grazing when run off—a point of some interest in light of Kendrick's charges of New Mexican encroachment upon lands west of Zuni.

With the same companions, in search of horses said to have been stolen by Navajos, Dodge next proceeded from his agency at Washington Pass to the San Juan and from there westward to The Goosenecks and the river's junction with the Chinle Wash. On July 10 he was in Santa Fe briefly on agency business. A part of this business may have been to turn over to Messervy a New Mexican boy named Sisto Martín, who had been stolen by Utes from his home near Abiquiu eight years before and sold to Navajos. The child's recovery at Fort Defiance, where Major Kendrick fed and clothed him, together with arrangements for sending him back safely to the river, coincided with Dodge's trip.

The summer of 1854 passed quietly on the Navajo frontier without further incident. Early in August an agreement that would serve to their mutual advantage was worked out when Dodge requested that half of the tobacco allotted to him by the Indian superintendency in Santa Fe for the Navajos should be shipped directly to Major Kendrick, so that the latter might distribute it to Navajos who from time to time visited the post. In turn, Kendrick was to provide transportation in army wagons for Indian goods sent from the river to the Navajo agency.

In this way, Dodge explained, he would be able to get the Indian supplies out "to my residence in the Navajoe country better & cheaper than as heretofore." [25] The arrangement soon proved better than Dodge might have guessed. On July 31 Congress had authorized a further appropriation of $5,000 for the Navajos in fulfillment of 1849 treaty pledges, and Governor Meriwether, following his return to Santa Fe at the end of July, informed Dodge that he might draw upon these funds in the amount of $1,000 each quarter. At least for a time, therefore, supplies brought out to the Navajos in Kendrick's wagons would increase from a trickle to a small freshet.

A small labor detail from Fort Defiance was cutting hay in a field two miles from the post on October 7 when an arrow struck one of the soldiers. Presence of the Navajo may or may not have been observed in advance, but his flight was marked well when the soldier collapsed to the ground. Private Nicholas Hefbiner, of Company B, Third Infantry, died of the wound next day. His assailant, according to Major Kendrick, was presumed to live in the vicinity of Canyon de Chelly. No motive for the murder was suggested; one might suppose it was irrational and unprovoked. On the other hand, with equal reason, one might suppose that Hefbiner had raped his assailant's wife. No one today knows. In light of certain contradictions that developed later, the official version of the incident, perhaps in most respects accurate, invites a skeptical approach to the entire aftermath.

Major Kendrick did not regard the murder of Hefbiner as an indication of widespread Navajo hostility, and reported it to be the act of a man who, like a few others, was tired by the restraints of a long peace and anxious for excitement.[26] But unofficially, because of what emerged long afterward, he may have regarded it quite differently. The murder, indeed, may have been provoked by the victim.

The Ramón Martín affair was fresh enough in mind that Kendrick was sensitive to his chance of failure, but he nevertheless assembled the headmen and formally demanded the surrender of Hefbiner's murderer. No matter how anxious for peace a majority of the Navajos might be, he was aware that from either a real or a professed inability to do so, they had never surrendered a tribesman for civil court action and public lashes or hanging. This they always insisted was impossible. Kendrick

25. August 5, 1854: Dodge, Fort Defiance, to Superintendent of Indian Affairs, NA, NMS T21-2.

26. October 8, 1854: Kendrick to Nichols, NA, RAC, RG 393, K-15-1854, LR.

now took a position that to maintain his authority he could accept nothing short of absolute compliance. The murderer must be brought in.

As he had both during and after the Martín incident, Kendrick urged that if a military campaign were to be launched (and he appeared to advocate it), General Garland should place an overwhelming force in the field, and soon. A winter campaign would be possible, but milder fall weather offered advantages of movement. A large force of cavalry would be advisable, but at the very least he proposed sending out two companies of dragoons and one of infantry. To these columns he would add the strength of the Defiance garrison: Companies B and H, Third Infantry, and Company B, Second Artillery. There was no advocacy this time of savaging Navajo women and children with auxiliary slave raiders.

General Garland agreed that the murderer must be surrendered. And he was willing, even though much of his command was committed to operations in the north against the Jicarillas, to order troops out to Major Kendrick's support should they be needed. For the time, however, this was as far as he would go; he made no reply to Kendrick's proposal for an immediate campaign in crushing strength.[27]

At Fort Defiance, Major Kendrick used some appropriate term to convey to all Navajos the idea that the hammer of Thor was poised to strike. After preliminary talks the major held with small groups of headmen at the post, Henry Dodge gathered a larger council of Navajos several days later in the vicinity of the Carrizo Mountains some sixty miles to the north, Dodge being accompanied to that place by Second Lieutenant John W. Alley and an escort of twenty men. As before, the Navajos were told they must capture and surrender the murderer; if they failed to do so, a devastating war would be unleashed upon them. The headmen expressed the tribe's desire for peace and asked that the grievance be adjusted by traditional custom—by payment in an equitable number of horses and sheep—but their proposal was rejected. Those who took part in the talks are not identified, but the council was held in a region occupied by or adjacent to the bands of Cayetano, Armijo, Miguelito, Archuleta, and Aguila Negra. Conceivably, Major Kendrick may have referred to one of the last three when he reported that Dodge, in the end, had persuaded "a chief who resides on the San Juan, with eight Navajos" to go in pursuit of the wanted man. Dodge

27. October 18, 1854: Garland to Kendrick, NA, RAC, RG 393, no. 271, LS.

was hopeful of success, but Kendrick was unable to share his optimism.[28]

A few days later, no doubt in response to some word carried to the fort, Dodge started across the mountains for Armijo's camp in the Chusca Valley accompanied by Lieutenant Alley again and twenty-five soldiers. On arrival at Armijo's hogans near the Ojos Calientes they were met by the headman, who informed Dodge that Hefbiner's murderer would be surrendered at this place within seven days. If for any reason his people should fail to bring the man in, Armijo said, he would turn over his own son as hostage pending the murderer's eventual delivery at Fort Defiance.

A badly wounded man who was identified by Navajos as the murderer was turned over to Lieutenant Alley on November 5. He had resisted capture to the end, it was said, and had been taken only after an arrow pierced his groin. The Navajo who shot him, a nephew of Armijo, said the captive owed his life to a rawhide shield; when the man had been seized, his shield, like a veritable porcupine, bristled with thirty-eight arrows. Two days later the prisoner was brought back to Fort Defiance. Here, according to Dodge, he was identified again as the murderer by a sergeant and two soldiers of the garrison. Then, "at the urgent request" of Armijo and Zarcillos Largos, as well as one hundred other of the principal Navajos, Major Kendrick and Dodge "had him hung untill he was *dead dead dead.*" [29]

Major Kendrick noted that on the agent's return with the prisoner, Dodge was accompanied by "many of the better class of Navajoes" who seemed anxious that the prisoner should not escape. Upon the recommendation of Dodge, whose opinion was shared by officers of the garrison and by the Navajos themselves, Kendrick determined to hang the man in the presence of as many Navajos as were willing to witness the execution. The major remarked that this was the first time in the tribe's history that such a course of justice had been taken; he believed that relations with the tribe might again be regarded as satisfactory.[30]

28. October 23, 1854: Kendrick to Nichols, NA, RAC, RG 393, K-17-1854, LR.

29. November 13, 1854: Dodge, Fort Defiance, to Meriwether, NA, NMS, T21-2. Dodge was not exulting over the man's death but borrowing from a famous death sentence uttered in 1847 by Judge Joab Houghton, when he directed that Antonio María Trujillo—accused of treason—be "hanged by the neck till you are dead! dead! dead!"

30. November 11, 1854: Kendrick to Nichols, NA, RAC, RG 393, K-19-1854, LR.

If the hanging did not greatly impress the Navajos (and there is evidence that their version of it was to be dramatically different), Kendrick had other means for making the occasion unforgettable. A shipment of twenty-four rockets, requisitioned from stores at Fort Union, had just arrived. The timing could not have been better. Kendrick wished "to exhibit their flight before these Indians when they congregate here," and the hanging provided the opportune moment.

Governor Meriwether forwarded a copy of Dodge's report of the capture and hanging to Commissioner Manypenny, commenting that "The hanging of this Indian in this summary manner, without a legal trial is to be regreted, but there is no jails or other means of confining such a prisoner in this Territory until next spring, when our civil courts are holden, and it became necessary that an example should be made to impress other bad Indians of New Mexico." [31]

How effective an example the hanging really was, to repeat, is open to question. Officially at least the case was closed and would remain so, but it was reopened unofficially four years later when Brevet Major William T. H. Brooks, then commanding Fort Defiance, reported that the man "given up to Major Kendrick they say was a peon"—not a Navajo at all but a Mexican captive—"which makes a great difference with them." [32]

Only two other minor incidents threatened during the closing months of 1854 to disturb Navajo relations. Concern over the murder of Private Hebfiner was at its height when Sandoval, with his son and a small party of Diné Ana'aii followers, turned up far to the east on the high grazing lands bordering the Pecos.

At the grazing camp of Preston Beck, Jr., they inquired contemptuously of several New Mexican herders if the miserable animals they were tending could possibly be the fine American sheep of which they had heard so much. Perhaps the reply of one of the pastors displeased him, but in any case Sandoval's son lunged for the sheepherder and attempted to snatch the hat from his head. When the man resisted, the young Diné Ana'aii hurled a lance at him, the blade glancing from his arm and drawing blood.

As if this had been a prearranged signal, the Sandoval band fanned out among the grazing sheep and methodically began to slaughter them. The killing was quickly halted, however, and the Diné Ana'aii galloped off when told that Major Carleton with a company of dragoons was al-

---

31. November 30, 1854: Meriwether to Manypenny, NA, NMS 234-547.
32. July 22, 1858: Brooks to AAG, NA, RAC, RG 393, B-45-1858, LR.

most within hearing beyond a distant rise of land.[33] The closeness of Carleton's dragoons was not exaggerated. He was then on the Pecos making a second survey down the river to determine a site for a military post (a survey that resulted eventually in the establishment of Fort Sumner).

At almost the same time, a party of Indians was said to have stolen about sixty-five mules and several horses belonging to Don Antonio José Otero of Peralta from the wealthy rancher's fields or corrals on the Rio Grande. It is unlikely that Sandoval and his people were involved this time, as the mules were driven in a nearly opposite direction, toward Manzana, while the Diné Ana'aii were hastening away from the incident on the Pecos. It was while they were camped on the Puerco a few days later that it was learned that Sandoval planned to follow Major Carleton's column down the Pecos and make a strike against Comanches supposedly in the vicinity. Some concern was expressed in Albuquerque that such a raid would result in Comanche reprisals that could only be harmful to the settlements.[34]

The year ended with a re-echoing warning. Don Ramón Luna of Bernalillo, said to be one of several offending stock raisers, was advised by Major Kendrick that his sheep had been identified among other flocks from the Rio Grande that were being grazed on Navajo land near El Morro. The Navajos were angry over this continuing encroachment; Don Ramón and his fellow ranchers would be wise to withdraw their sheep before the herds were run off and another unhappy incident— for which the government would not pay—was allowed to occur.[35]

33. October 16, 1854: Preston Beck, Jr. to Meriwether, NA, NMS T21-2. The incident described is said to have occurred October 15. Beck and James H. Giddings, as partners, owned a ranch just north of the junction of Agua Negra and the Pecos.

34. October 22, 1854: Capt. J. H. Eaton, commanding Albuquerque, to Nichols, NA, RAC, RG 393, E-19-1854, LR, with three enclosures. No further reference to Sandoval's movements is found and the outcome of his planned raid is not known.

35. December 18, 1854: Kendrick to Luna, NA, NMS T21-2.

14

The Treaty of Laguna Negra

Henry L. Dodge in early February 1855 accompanied two hundred
Navajos to a three-day feast at Jemez. His blithe reference to the affair,
offhanded enough to suggest that he regarded his participation as a
normal part of his duties as agent, unfortunately reveals nothing at all
about the nature of the festivities. Instead, he observed more soberly
that Utes ranging north of the San Juan were making overtures designed
to induce Navajos to join them in war against the settlements.

With only a few exceptions, he said, the Navajos showed no taste
for such an alliance. He had sent runners out among those living on the
San Juan asking them to withdraw southward fifty or sixty miles, and if
possible to prevent Utes from crossing the river, regarded as a boundary
between the two tribes. The more prosperous families, those he would
term *ricos*, already had moved south with their livestock, but Dodge
feared that those who were poor would remain and some might join
the Utes. To prevent such an eventuality he asked that two companies
of troops be sent from Abiquiu to make a show of force in a march
down the north bank of the river.[1] Governor Meriwether, to whom the
proposal was made, doubted if General Garland would find such a
campaign feasible at this time, as all of his disposable command was
operating in the field against Utes and Jicarillas.

Once more at his agency at "Tounicha" on March 27, Dodge found
no ground for his recent concern; overtures by the Utes had been
rejected and the Navajos remained at peace. A heavy snowfall over the
Chusca range had left the mountains white, but already soft winds and
a warming sun promised spring freshets to moisten planting slopes and
thus a good cropping year. On the strength of such favorable signs,
Dodge sent George Carter, his blacksmith, to Santa Fe for farm tools.

1. February 13, 1855: Dodge, Jemez, to Meriwether, NA, NMS T21-2.

Late in April Carter returned with a hired teamster and wagon, bringing 150 hoes and a dozen axes. Before his return, however, anxious that the Navajos not wait to start their spring planting, Dodge went to Fort Defiance with Armijo to obtain such farming tools as Major Kendrick would permit him to borrow from the quartermaster's stores. Kendrick was cooperative to a point. Hoes and spades he let Dodge take, but when Armijo asked if he might borrow a Defiance plow and three yoke of oxen, the major refused. He was sorry, they could not be spared.

Reports were continuing to arrive at the fort of engagements between troops and bands of Utes and Jicarillas in country north and west of Taos, and with these came word of renewed Ute efforts to win Navajos to their side. Major Kendrick and Dodge used such persuasion as they could in talking with the headmen and employed every inducement to encourage the Navajos to remain at work in their fields. Thus far they had been successful.

Late in April 1855, Governor Meriwether was informed by the Indian Office in Washington that he had been designated an officer of that department to negotiate with Mescalero and Mimbres Apaches and with Utes and Navajos. A sum of approximately twenty-five thousand dollars, provided by Congress in the preceding July, was at his disposal for treaty goods and other expenses. Officials concerned in this new endeavor were not unaware that the tribes either had been recently engaged in hostilities or were now at war, and the authorization to treat with them was not in any sense naïve altruism—rather the opposite. Meriwether was instructed to establish tribal boundaries in each of the treaties he made; in other words, to induce these tribes for the first time to accept prescribed reservations.[2] And more than that, the tribes would be asked to give up thousands of acres of land, so that the nearest reservation limits would be far removed from the settlements.

In this there was no element of surprise; the government proposed to implement a policy that Meriwether himself had advocated soon after he became governor of the territory.

Henry Dodge was still preoccupied with farming activities when he learned that Meriwether would meet the Navajos in council in either June or July after he had concluded treaties with the Apaches. A month later the governor informed Dodge that he would leave Santa Fe within a few days to meet with the Mescaleros and expected to meet with the Navajos about July 10. The council was to be held at or near Fort

2. March 16, 1855: Manypenny to Meriwether, NA, NMS T21-2.

Defiance and Dodge was to spare no effort in assembling a large number of the tribe.[3]

Word of the forthcoming visit spread rapidly through Navajo country. Even before he was instructed to bring the Navajos together it was clear to Dodge that this would be unnecessary; of their own volition, out of intense curiosity, hundreds of Navajos were preparing to attend the council. On the other hand, an ugly rumor threatened to keep others away. It was said that the Bilagáana intended the council to be no more than a decoy, and that once gathered at Fort Defiance the Navajos would be killed. To still this rumor (which persisted anyway) as well as for other reasons, Major Kendrick informed Meriwether that it would be unwise to hold the council at the fort. He pointed out that probably a thousand horses would be brought to the place of gathering as well as the many flocks of sheep that the Navajos would have to drive with them to prevent their loss or theft. If the meeting concentrated at Fort Defiance, all of these animals would forage over the garrison's grazing and haying grounds, a disaster that could be averted only by forcibly driving the animals off. Lastly, an atmosphere of coercion might be felt by some, an atmosphere that he said had prevailed to some extent at Canyon de Chelly in 1849, if the treaty were to be made under the guns of the fort.

For these reasons, Major Kendrick explained, he and Dodge had agreed—and had so advised the Navajos—that the treaty council would be held at Laguna Negra, twelve or fourteen miles north of the fort and within easy communication of the garrison's facilities. Here the governor would find a fresh lake continuously fed by Black Creek, a lush meadow of abundant grass, and plentiful wood for campfires from the hilly slopes close by. "It is the prettiest and most eligible locality in the Navajoe Nation," Kendrick wrote, "and is nearer the wealthy Indians than we are."

Meriwether left Santa Fe accompanied by his son Raymond and his private secretary, the territory's former United States attorney, William Watts Hart Davis. Because of a private journal in which Davis made daily entries during the trip, and several pages of notes hastily written during the council with the Navajos, a record of the Laguna Negra meeting survives that matches in freshness of observation Lieutenant

---

3. May 24, 1855: Meriwether to Dodge, NA, NMS T21-2. Treaties were made with the Mescaleros and Mimbres in June, but, as in the case of Meriwether's treaty in August with the Capote Utes, were not ratified by Congress.

Simpson's account of the proceedings six years before at Canyon de Chelly.[4]

Although they had expected to meet General Garland and an escort of Captain Ewell's dragoons at a junction of the Los Lunas road west of Albuquerque, the general was unavoidably detained. Unaware of this and thinking he would find Garland and Ewell's company with a government train some distance ahead, Meriwether pressed forward. The driver of his carriage and a teamster at the reins of a following baggage wagon made up the balance of his party and his only protection. At Laguna they stopped to breakfast at the home of the Reverend Samuel Gorman before continuing to Cubero where they halted again "to fill our keg and canteen, and water the horses. The good people came out to look at the Governor," Davis observed, "and we purchased chickens and eggs for supper. The town contains some two hundred inhabitants, living in mud houses. . . . Here we found two fine springs, which in this country are as important as in the wilderness of Palestine." [5]

With the slopes and peaks of Mount Taylor ahead of them and to their right they entered the Wingate Valley and at once crossed the Gallo, "a beautiful & clear stream of sweet water." Soon afterward the horses picked their way nervously through malpais—porous black rocks and chunks of lava covering the valley bottom for five miles or more, which at one point, Davis thought, "looks like water rippled or ridged in an eddy." They stopped that evening at or near the hay camp where Ownby's men had been shot down by Navajos in 1851. Here they were joined by the Pueblo alcalde of Laguna, who was to serve as guide, and shortly afterward by Juan Anaya, Henry Dodge's interpreter. Encamped close by on the Gallo, their campfires a cheery reassurance in the night, was an army train carrying corn from Laguna to Fort Defiance. The clear sweet stream, Davis noted in closing that day's journal entry, "was filled with fish but we had no lines, nor hooks."

4. Davis later drew extensively from his "Private Journal" when writing chap. 13 (1962 reprint) of *El Gringo*. The pocket-sized, leather-bound diary was presented in 1936 by Davis's son to Senator Clinton P. Anderson of New Mexico. Davis was 35 years old when the hitherto unpublished journal entries quoted here were written. During the Civil War he was a colonel of the 104th Pennsylvania Infantry, returning afterward to his home in Doylestown, Pennsylvania, where he published the weekly *Democrat*. He died in Doylestown at the age of 90.

5. Davis Journal. Unless otherwise noted, Davis's observations (usually modified or softened in *El Gringo*) will be from the same source.

Two days later, on July 12, fifty miles farther to the west, they paused to rest and graze their horses at Ojo del Oso. The majestic palisading of red cliffs that for much of that distance enclosed their valley route to the north somehow escaped Davis's comment, but he did observe that "in the northern ridge of the headlands there rose up a peak that much resembled a church tower with turrets"—a reference to the sandstone formation later to be known as Church Rock. "We had it in sight for two hours & more. . . . Caught a prairie dog which I carried in my hand to the spring and then confined him in the lantern." It was here that Doniphan had come on a similar mission nine years before, to this same wide silent valley; to the same spring that Davis now found "strongly impregnated with iron, but clear and cool"; to the same slopes of piñon and juniper where the "country is covered with wild sage and short dry grass." Davis failed to remark it, but late snows on the Chuscas had not reached Wingate Valley and the season had been dry; the grass usually was tall, very green, waving its tops in west wind.

With nearly forty miles more to travel, Meriwether's party nooned at the spring and continued on. Light was fading over the Cienega Amarilla when they passed the looming red rock domes later dubbed the Haystacks. It was nine o'clock when they reached Cañoncito Bonito, the low buildings of Fort Defiance in darker silhouette against dark canyon walls, some few small rectangles and squares of orange light showing where men were up and moving about. With little formality they were greeted by Major Kendrick, who with officers of his staff welcomed them to the log and adobe outpost.

Early the next day Meriwether visited the planned council site in company with Kendrick, Davis, and the fort's assistant surgeon, Jonathan Letterman. A ride of fourteen miles brought them to the high green valley and sparkling lake that Vizcarra had visited during his campaign of 1823. Two volcanic plugs of great age stand as twin sentinels at the southern approach to the valley; from the west, a dark cover of piñon and juniper descends in gentle slope to a grassy clearing along the laguna shore. The northern gateway to Vizcarra's "Cienega del Peñasco Colorado" (the area known to Navajos as Bee'ek'id Halchíí, or Red Lake Valley) offers narrow passage between mesas and mountains; enclosing the valley to the east, and separating it from the main branch of Black Creek, are cliffs of deep pink and red sandstone. Probably it was to a point among these cliffs that Davis referred when he noted, "Agent Dodge here has his agency, at which we stopped.

. . . The Agent's tent was on an eminence overlooking the lake."

Fewer than one hundred Navajos could be seen in the valley, some engaged in the hoop and lance game or other sports, some riding about or reined in and quietly observing the activity around Dodge's tent, where a Navajo woman soon set about preparing a noon meal of mutton spitted on a stick. Before leaving to return to the fort, Meriwether talked briefly with a number of headmen. It was agreed that the council should be assembled three days after.

A salute by the field battery of six-pound guns greeted the arrival of General Garland and Captain Ewell at Fort Defiance at noon the following day. This and a parading of the entire garrison under arms on Sunday for review and inspection were normal recognition to be accorded a visiting department commander and governor, but in the minds of some Navajos present the military display was an ominous reminder of another day, across the Chuscas, when a field gun had been turned on Narbona and his people. A rumor spread: the council was to be no more than a trap, an ambush.

Governor Meriwether possibly was unaware of this undercurrent of alarm when he returned to Laguna Negra the morning of July 16. The valley swarmed with Navajos, their number ranging from Meriwether's estimate of fifteen hundred warriors to a figure of two thousand reported by Davis and Henry Dodge. The governor observed that few women and children were present but "every man was mounted on his horse and well armed." A tent for the governor was pitched in an open area near the lake while camp was made and a picket line set up close by for Ewell's dragoon escort. No reference was made to the presence of Major Kendrick; it may be presumed he remained temporarily at the fort with General Garland. At one o'clock Meriwether met with a number of headmen in an enclosure of cedar branches arranged for the occasion.

He had come to talk with the Navajos about a country that they and the whites each might have, Meriwether began. He hoped they could agree upon boundaries that would prevent each from grazing their flocks upon the other's lands. If they were to agree to a dividing line so that they knew the limits of each other's country, it would keep them at peace. He then explained the terms of the treaty he had brought with him, asking the headmen to discuss his proposals among themselves and then meet with him again the next morning.[6]

6. Davis's "Notes of a talk between Governor Meriwether and the Chiefs, Head Men, and Captains of the Navajo Indians, held at Laguana Negra the 16th and

"They were a dirty crowd," Davis later noted in his journal, "and could hardly be kept out of our camp. . . . When the Gov came to that part that referred to the giving up of those who committed offences, Sarcos Largo remarked that it was their custom, and they would rather pay a remuneration for offences than surrender the offenders, which of course was not agreed to."

Meriwether was disturbed to find that Navajos actually had taken possession of his camp during his talk with the headmen, and that his own tent had been preempted by warriors. An earlier effort to turn them out was abandoned when one of the Navajos notched an arrow to his bowstring and threatened to shoot point-blank the sergeant of the guard. A noisy, raucous scuffle flared up before the intruders withdrew, some evidence indicating the trouble may have been planned and carried out by Delgadito, a man of some influence and in the recent past known to have been unfriendly to the Bilagáana.[7] A rumor reached the governor's camp that evening that a dissident element among the Navajos feared the council was designed only to screen a plan to kill them. General Garland, who waited at Fort Defiance, was expected to arrive next morning with a light battery of artillery. The dissident Navajos were aware of this, it was said, and were planning to attack the governor's party and escort that night.

Davis noted in his journal, "They said we were only keeping them there until we had time to bring up the big guns and some soldiers to attack them, and that they had better wipe us out before they arrived. The night passed away without any incident. A large part of the Indians remained all night and were fed at the Agency." The rumor finally subsided and there was no further difficulty after General Garland's ar-

---

17th of July 1855, through the medium of two interpreters" (NA, NMS 234–547). The notes were compiled and written by Davis upon his return to Santa Fe on July 27.

7. Neither Davis nor Meriwether connected Delgadito by name with the incident, but on February 25, 1856, Maj. Kendrick informed Gen. Garland, "On our way to the Bear Spring we met with Delgadito, the Chief that the General will remember made himself conspicuous at the Treaty of Laguna Negra in July last. He now proclaims himself friendly and there seems to be a reasonable prospect of his remaining so for the present" (NA, NMS 234-548). In May 1852 the trader Auguste Lacome reported that Delgadito "appeared to be inclined not to give his people advice to keep peacible." Van Valkenburgh and McPhee (1938) say that Delgadito (Chach'osh nez, or Tall Syphilis) was a member of Sandoval's Diné Ana'aii who informed the Navajos of a planned attack upon them in 1858 by a party of New Mexicans and Diné Ana'aii then approaching Cienega Amarilla, and that Delgadito thereafter remained with the tribe.

rival in the morning of July 17. The field battery accompanied him but its presence no longer seemed to be regarded as a menace.

Some concern was felt earlier that day when Zarcillos Largos sent his staff of office and medal—the same beribboned medal presented to him by Meriwether nearly two years before—to the governor's tent with the explanation that he wished to be relieved of responsibility because he felt he was too old and no longer could exert control over his people. Meriwether accepted his resignation and asked the headmen to meet together and choose a man who could speak for the whole tribe. Returning a short time later, the Navajos said that Manuelito, a son of Cayetano, would succeed Zarcillos Largos. A momentary impasse arose when Manuelito declared he would lose the Navajos' respect if he were to accept Zarcillos Largos' official cane; nor would he wear the medal about his neck, as the cord by which it had been suspended about his predecessor's neck would rob him of his influence. The problem was solved when Meriwether presented his own steel cane to Manuelito and had a new thong attached to the medal.

The Navajos began to gather early in the morning of July 17, Davis noted, and by eleven o'clock two thousand warriors had assembled about the agency and Governor Meriwether's camp. "They held a long junta near the Agency and about noon the Chiefs and head men came to our camp to hold another talk with the Gov and give their answer to the Treaty. Some twenty of them sat upon the ground back of our tent, when a long council was held. . . . It required some two hours to explain to them the terms fully and to sign. . . . While the treaty was being made the Indians sat around us on their horses, and some of the time were very noisy, and once or twice their horses got into a stampede. The artillery drilled during the afternoon."

Davis observed that when the council opened Manuelito said the headmen were content with the governor's proposals and would agree to his terms. Meriwether thereupon asked Davis to make a written copy of the treaty, "so that we cannot forget what it contains." Remarking that he had been appointed as successor to Zarcillos Largos (and so now was the principal spokesman for his people), Manuelito told Meriwether the headmen were sorry that some of the Navajos had treated him badly the day before.

Meriwether accepted this apology for the brief seizure of his camp, saying that he knew the principal men were not involved and that only the boys, or younger men, had behaved badly. He then turned again to the interpreters, Davis noted in his journal, and said, "Ask them if they are willing Manuelita shall have the staff of office & medal that Largas delivered me. Thereupon one in four held up their hands."

In transcribing his notes later, to accompany Meriwether's official report of the council, Davis changed the line to read, "They all held up their hands." But the original line in his journal remains legible and unchanged.

Because the treaty of Laguna Negra was not ratified by the United States Senate it has escaped attention in recent years or been regarded as significantly less important than Colonel Washington's treaty of 1849. This is a serious error of judgment, failing as it does to take into account how Navajos felt about the proceedings and how the meeting at Laguna Negra—with or without Senate ratification—affected relations with the tribe.

At the beginning it must be realized that at no time was the treaty of Canyon de Chelly looked upon by Navajos as more than a meaningless charade, a set of impossible conditions presented at gunpoint by Colonel Washington and—to avert further bloodshed—agreed to by two of the nation's lesser headmen. The Meriwether treaty meant vastly more to Navajos because the principal leaders of their nation were persuaded, again in the silent presence of artillery, to accept terms equally undesirable; because the treaty was the first to raise the spectre of tribal confinement within drastically reduced boundaries; and because it marked the emergence of Manuelito as an increasingly influential tribal leader who would become, as his father consistently had been, an advocate of resistance to further encroachment upon Navajo lands. Finally, it must be emphasized that refusal by the Senate to ratify Meriwether's treaty went almost unnoticed at the time in New Mexico. Civil and military authorities appeared to assume that even if the United States remained uncommitted, Laguna Negra morally and legally was binding upon Navajos: they would, in months ahead, be compelled to submit to land seizure and other conditions imposed upon them by Meriwether.

The Laguna Negra treaty set apart a reservation estimated by the governor to be about seven thousand square miles in area.[8] Possibly he was right; as the land had not been surveyed, his figure was an estimate. Possibly he was right, too, when he said Navajos occupied a country of twenty-five thousand square miles. The eastern boundary of his proposed reservation, in any case, deprived the Navajos of Chaco

8. The complete text of the treaty, hitherto unpublished, appears in Appendix C.

Canyon, the Mount Taylor region, grazing lands of the Agua Azul, nearly all of the Wingate Valley, and the plateau and mountainous country north and south of the valley—more than one-fourth of their country east of the Chuscas—while the western boundary chopped off a nearly equal amount of land traditionally theirs north and south of the Hopi mesas.

In return for taking more than two-thirds of their country, or an area roughly corresponding in size to Massachusetts, Connecticut, and Rhode Island, Meriwether proposed to pay the tribe a total of $102,000 in graduated annuities through 1876. The proposal, however, was conditional: the president, at his own discretion, could determine what amount, if any, should be paid in money and what proportion should be expended less directly for the Navajos' "moral improval" and education. Also, the president might draw upon the annuities to satisfy claims arising from Navajo depredations—real, as in the case of Anastacio García, or unreal, as in the cases of Nesbit and Parker and Don Francisco Sarracino. The Navajos, however, could not use any part of the annuities to pay either personal or tribal debts.

Manuelito protested twice during the council, first to the loss of so great an area of country with its several places traditionally sacred to the Navajos, and then to the demand for the surrender of any Navajo sought in connection with any actual or alleged crime. Both times Meriwether insisted that his conditions must be accepted exactly as he presented them, and both times he prevailed.

The treaty was signed at once by twenty-seven of the headmen, Meriwether observing that "the Indians became so impatient to depart to their homes as to render it impossible to detain them long enough to enable us to make a more perfect copy. . . ." A duplicate copy was written the following night during a heavy rainstorm and in Meriwether's tent after he had left Fort Defiance on the start of his return to Santa Fe. Although the original document was signed by the Navajos and Meriwether on July 17, the treaty copy sent to Washington was dated July 18 and all references to the treaty have since perpetuated that error of date.[9]

Davis noted that immediately after the council ended the treaty goods brought out in the governor's baggage wagon were given to the headmen, who in turn said they would distribute them equally to their people. This in a manner of speaking they did, indiscriminately tossing bales of cloth or packages of indigo or knives high into the air and

9. July 27, 1855: Meriwether to Manypenny, NA, NMS 234-547.

into the thick of the milling crowd of mounted Navajos. The scene soon became a riotous scramble. A warrior lucky enough to catch a bolt of cloth at once quirted his horse out of the shouting mob to be pursued by grabbing hands and flashing knives that sent the cloth trailing off in billowing streamers. These banners of white and brilliant red and blue were dashed about at a gallop until knives or the clutching hands of pursuers ripped them to shorter lengths, when they were stuffed into belts or wrapped around the heads of the captors. Into this yelling pandemonium any article light enough to hoist was tossed. All, that is, but one especially solid object. "The tobacco keg caused the most strife," Davis observed, "being harder to get into."

Three days later, on approaching the Agua Azul, the governor's party and escort surprised a large number of Indians, still far in advance, who hurriedly withdrew driving a caballada of horses before them.[10] In the belief that this might be a band of raiders, General Garland directed Captain Ewell to take a detachment of dragoons in pursuit. Upon his return Ewell reported that the Indians were Sandoval's Diné Ana'aii, and that they had given every appearance of being friendly.

Governor Meriwether regarded the results of the Laguna Negra council with some optimism. He was satisfied that the headmen who had signed the treaty were authorized to speak for their people, and he was satisfied, too, that the terms he had proposed had met with favorable response. He had been particularly alert to any objection that might be raised. One dissenting voice in fact had been heard, he said, but "that proved to be on the part of a man of but little note or consequence" —a most curious statement, as the firmest voice of dissent was that of Manuelito.[11] The reservation lands, he informed Washington, had been chosen by the Navajos themselves; they embraced the tribal planting grounds, and ought to be adequate to the tribe's future needs. In addition to their large herds of livestock the Navajos had about four thousand acres of land under cultivation, he explained, so that their condition might be regarded as prosperous; they should be able to cultivate enough more in another year to feed all in the tribe—a number he estimated to be from eight to ten thousand—plentifully.

Only one thorn was observable in the council bower. Every division of the Navajo nation except Sandoval's Diné Ana'aii had been present and represented in the treaty signing. But Meriwether was philosophi-

10. Davis's journal entry for July 20. In *El Gringo* the encounter is moved to Ojo del Gallo.

11. July 27, 1855: Meriwether to Manypenny, cited above.

cal: after all, the Diné Ana'aii numbered only about one hundred, they had separated from the tribe some years before, and "the two parties are decidedly hostile to each other. . . ." This bad feeling, Meriwether went on to report, arose from the refusal of the Diné Ana'aii to join with the rest of the tribe in hostilities against the whites. For some years Sandoval's people had lived apart in the vicinity of Cebolleta, and unless the village could be purchased by the government as a reservation for the Diné Ana'aii—a plan that Meriwether said he strongly recommended—it would be necessary to provide land for them elsewhere. Otherwise, he said, "if these Indians are required to move west of the mountains [the Chuscas] few will survive long."

Henry Dodge, who had every reason to know better, indulged in hyperbole: the reservation provided for the Navajos was amply sufficient for their needs; it was, in fact, larger than they had anticipated, "which caused them to returne to their homes very much delighted with the liberal treatment in Territory and presents [given] them by the Governor." [12]

No serious incident disturbed the quiet of the Navajo frontier during the remaining days of summer and fall. A few minor thefts of livestock occurred, nothing more. Dodge was away from his agency, in Santa Fe, for nearly all of September. His prolonged stay is unexplained; nothing about it is certain except that he stopped frequently at the stores of Webb & Kingsbury and Henry Mercure to spend nearly five hundred dollars on purchases for himself and his family or for Indians of his agency. His selection seems random, including three hats (a boy's size), two packages of hawk bells and a quantity of coral beads, a bar of soap, a trunk and a pocket knife, five pieces of manta, several sides of leather, brass wire, and indigo.

For himself he bought a pair of buckskin gloves, a black beaver hat, and a red flannel shirt.[13] His partiality for the color had been noticed; the Navajos called him Red Shirt, or Bi'éé łichii.

By the end of September Dodge was again at Fort Defiance, where he was to conduct affairs of his agency through the winter, and looking hopefully to a ratification of the Laguna Negra treaty and benefits that he thought then might be gained for the tribe. While in Santa Fe he had heard much criticism from those who felt Governor Meriwether

12. August 2, 1855: Dodge, "Pass Washington," to Manypenny, NA, NMS 234-547.
13. Statement of purchases by Dodge, NA, NMS T21-2.

had been too liberal and had given the Navajos too much land. Dodge would not agree. Much of the land set apart for them was mountainous and of little use to them; not more than one hundred square miles of the entire reservation could be turned to cultivation. The drawing of the eastern boundary, which had met strenuous objection from Manuelito, Dodge regarded as both fair and sensible; in effect it created a buffer zone assuring the Navajos a "country free from the in rodes of New Mexicans which has been from time immemorial one of the causes of difficulty between them." [14]

If the Senate should confirm the treaty, Dodge hoped that funds might then be provided to give the Navajos four sets of blacksmith tools and one thousand pounds of iron. For this there was good reason. To his knowledge there were now eighteen Navajos who had learned to use the hand bellows and primitive tools of the New Mexican silversmiths. Already they had attained enough skill to hammer out creditable bridle bits and rings and buckles of iron; with time and encouragement a new trade might be developed. Navajo talent for working with metal was latent, but emerging. No one, of course, knew then, but there was to be endless delay and disappointment before these simple things could be provided, and the Senate of the United States was not to confirm Meriwether's treaty.

14. September 30, 1855: Dodge to Meriwether, NA, NMS 234-548.

Part Three

Henry Dodge "possessed unbounded influence over the Navajo Chiefs, and was fairly worshipped by them. Had he lived, I am of the opinion that the subsequent Navajo Wars would never have occurred."

—Charles W. Wentz, Company G, First Cavalry, New Mexico Volunteers, to Augustus Caesar Dodge

May 1, 1864

15

Raids on the Puerco

As subtle and disturbing as a shift in an accustomed wind, a difference in mood made itself felt in early weeks of the new year 1856. A glance, a gesture, a tone of voice gave first expression to this change. At his winter quarters at Fort Defiance something more tangible soon made Henry Dodge aware of growing disaffection among some Navajos.

Not then but later was the change in attitude traced to a reduction in strength of the Defiance garrison. Early in the previous December, Brevet Major Oliver L. Shepherd had been ordered to withdraw his grenadier company to Albuquerque. From a force of 174 enlisted men, Major Kendrick's garrison was cut to 114 troops present for duty. A handful more remained on short rations in the guardhouse, but their number was unimportant. The departure of Company B, Third Infantry, was noticed at once; from August 1853 the unit had been accepted by Navajos as a potentially threatening fact of life. Suddenly the troops of Company B were gone and Navajos interpreted their withdrawal as a sign of the military department's weakness.

Winter still darkened the skies and covered the mesa tops with snow when the consequences were first felt. Bands of Navajos in the north on the San Juan and others across the mountains to the east, not waiting for spring, were raiding again. The thrusts at first were tentative, a probing and minor harassment—small thefts of livestock, inconsequential in themselves, but symptomatic.

Henry Dodge was on a mission to the Hopi villages in the evening of February 5 when a sergeant and small escort arrived at Fort Defiance from Major Carleton's post headquarters at Albuquerque. The sergeant and his men were in only slightly better condition than their mounts. So hard had they traveled that the horses would be unfit to ride for three days. In view of the long months of nearly unbroken peace, the news was disturbing.

Major Kendrick was informed that seven days before, at a point somewhere on the Puerco, a band of Navajos had disarmed and stolen the guns of Manuel Barela's peon herders and then run off fourteen of Barela's animals, most of them mules. Barela himself had led a pursuit, tracking the raiders to a camp in the hills beyond Cebolleta. There he had found a part of the animals and there also encountered Miguelito with some of his band. As Barela explained it to Major Carleton later, Miguelito had returned the captured firearms and then assured Barela that the mules and the Navajos who had stolen them would be given up also, provided that Barela returned with a force strong enough to take them. If the words seemed to convey a taunting challenge, Major Carleton understood that, rather to the contrary, Miguelito had spoken in a not unfriendly spirit; he would not assume the authority (and its possible consequences) himself, nor would he stand in Barela's way if the latter wished to force the issue.

Major Kendrick immediately made a copy of Carleton's express for Dodge. In a covering message he asked the agent to return to the fort at once and, if possible, to bring Miguelito with him. He feared that ladrons of the tribe were thinking again of spring raids, and the quicker such thinking was stopped the better. He had no idea where Miguelito would be found but presumed that Dodge, from his old acquaintance with the headman, could find him and persuade him to give up the stock. Ganado Mucho, one of the younger Navajo headmen whose people lived to the west on Pueblo Colorado Wash, and who had demonstrated his friendship for the Bilagáana, agreed to carry the messages and accompany Dodge on his return.[1] Shortly after Ganado Mucho started out to find Dodge, Major Kendrick persuaded Armijo and several other influential Navajos to go in search of Miguelito.

Heavy snow made travel almost impossible, but a council was arranged at Bear Spring with a number of headmen whose bands had

1. February 5, 1856: Carleton to Maj. W. A. Nichols, AAG, with two enclosures, NA, RAC, RG 393, C-3-1856, LR; (same date) Kendrick to Dodge, NA, NMS T21-2; February 15, 1856: Kendrick to Nichols, NA, RAC, RG 393, K-1-1856, LR. Miguelito, found previously with Aguila Negra and Archuleta on the San Juan, served as Dodge's interpreter in August 1855. A Miguelito "claiming to belong to Sandoval's band" of Diné Ana'aii in May 1859 informed military authorities of a Navajo raid upon sheep in the vicinity of Cebolleta. In March 1861, Bvt. Lt. Col. E. R. S. Canby reported that Miguelito was "no longer regarded as a chief by the Navajos themselves," and in October 1866, while in captivity at Fort Sumner, he was referred to by Carleton as then "an old Navajo" and the father-in-law of Manuelito. How long this relationship had existed is uncertain; Manuelito is known to have taken a daughter of Narbona as his first wife.

been involved in recent depredations. Dodge, who had returned to Fort
Defiance in the meantime, accompanied Major Kendrick to the meeting place February 16. Their effort seemed justified when the Navajos
promised full restitution for all losses. Only a few pelados, or nobodies,
whose actions were hard to control, were responsible, Kendrick was
given to understand; a majority of the Navajos, as before, wished to
remain at peace. Other encouraging news awaited them at the fort.
Armijo had been entirely successful. He had found Miguelito's camp
and talked with him. Even now Miguelito was traveling with Manuel
Barela toward the river, and with them they were driving Barela's
mules.[2]

At department headquarters, which he now maintained at Santa Fe,
General Garland received assurances that peace on the Navajo frontier
was secure. With the approach of spring, dispatches from Fort Defiance came less frequently—in itself a reassuring sign—and, although
there were a few troops that could be spared, Garland found no need
to restore the garrison's strength to the 200-man minimum Major Kendrick once had advocated.

This sense of security lasted a short time longer. Henry Dodge came
to Santa Fe on agency business, but with no news of special concern,
and left again April 6 to return to the fort. Two days later an express
rider was sent off to overtake him, carrying two dispatches. One, addressed to Dodge by Acting Governor W. W. H. Davis, was badly
garbled; the other, written by General Garland, he was instructed to
deliver to Major Kendrick at Fort Defiance. The import of Garland's
message was this: somewhere on grazing plains west of the Puerco, Navajo raiders on March 27 had attacked the camps of Antonio José Otero
and Juan Andreas Romero. Three of the herders had been killed and
eleven thousand sheep, it was claimed, had been driven off.

A familiar note sounded. Unless the murderers were surrendered and
the sheep given up, war was inevitable. And if war ensued, Garland declared, he would muster into service every New Mexican booty seeker
who volunteered.[3]

Word of the incident outdistanced the usual means of communication. Navajos informed Major Kendrick of the affair on the eve of his

2. February 25, 1856: Kendrick to Nichols, NA, RAC, RG 393, K-2-1856, LR.
3. April 8, 1856: Garland to Kendrick, NA, RAC, RG 393, LS; and (same
date) Acting Governor Davis to Dodge, "En route to Fort Defiance," NA, NMS
T21-2. Garland's brief report of the raid was accurate. Unaccountably confused,
Davis informed Dodge that only one herder had been killed and that the stolen
sheep belonged to "José Antonia Parea"—José Antonio Perea.

departure for the Hopi villages (where he expected to purchase corn for his garrison) and before Dodge reached the fort. Their stories varied in certain details, but as best he could determine, two, or possibly three, flocks of sheep had been stolen from the Puerco and it seemed certain that two pastors had been killed. Knowing that Dodge was then returning to the fort and no doubt would be fully advised of the raid as well as the action contemplated by authorities in Santa Fe, Kendrick started for Hopi country. General Garland's message reached him at his camp the first night out. He sent his wagons westward with Lieutenant Henry C. Symonds and returned immediately to Fort Defiance.

At the fort next day, in an atmosphere of intense foreboding, Major Kendrick and Henry Dodge met with as many of the headmen as could be assembled on such short notice. Words that had been spoken before were spoken again, but perhaps with less hope. The Navajos' response adhered equally to gloomy formula. Much of the stolen sheep had been scattered—given away or sold—so the Otero and Romero flocks never could be recovered intact. But already, on their own initiative, Armijo and Ganado Mucho had taken perhaps half of the sheep from the thieves, and these, and more to be contributed by Navajos innocent of any wrong, would be given up. To appease the families of the murdered men the Navajos would comply with an old custom: they would give three captive peons or pay to the relatives a satisfactory number of horses and sheep. But they would not, under any threat, agree to surrender the murderers. Here it ended, the Navajos' offer of peons or livestock rejected at once.

No one during the council distinguished between the Navajos wanted for murder in the past and those who were presently accused, although there was, from a white man's point of view, a difference. The Navajos who had killed Ramón Martín and Private Nicholas Hefbiner were unexceptional; they were men of no rank or position in the tribe. The murderers General Garland wanted now, on the other hand, were Navajos of very considerable position. This distinction, emphasized here, apparently was not an issue of importance to Navajos.

Rich and influential Navajos were involved this time—the son of Narbona, two sons of Archuleta, and two sons-in-law of Cayetano. For some time before the raid they had been staying in the lodges of Capote Utes north of the San Juan, Dodge learned, and their attack upon the Otero and Romero camps, inconceivable as it might be in the logic of war-ways of the Bilagáana, had been made to revenge their Capote friends for the theft—*by Navajos*—of eight Ute horses earlier in March.

The friendship and sincere desire of many Navajos for a continuing peace, so clearly demonstrated in recent days by Armijo and Ganado Mucho, Dodge would not question, but among others, and by no means only the pelados Major Kendrick had referred to, there was evidence of growing unrest and hostility. During his recent visit to the Hopi villages Dodge had encountered Navajos of that western region who carried fine rifles mounted with silver, which, together with blankets and tobacco and other things, they had obtained in trade with Mormons. With blunt candor these Navajos told Dodge that the Mormons had asked them questions about Tséhootsooi, or the place called Fort Defiance, and asked them why they did not drive the Bilagáana away from there, because if the soldiers were allowed to stay it would not be long before they took all of the Navajos' land. Dodge found evidence of enough disaffection among the Navajos to convince him that "it would be madness in the extreme to attempt to effect anything with the small force at this post at present as any small party going out to collect sheep or attempt to capture the murder[er]s could be surrounded by a thousand warriors before going twenty five miles." [4]

Major Kendrick was convinced that unless authorities in Santa Fe backed down in their demand for the surrender of the murderers war would result. The sooner extensive preparations were made for it the better, he advised General Garland, because the Navajos would never give up the wanted men until the most stringent war brought them to their knees. The Navajos must be made to comply or there would be no end to their aggressions. Any repetition of the ineffectual and abortive expeditions made in the past would do more harm than good, and probably would result in drawing the Utes in upon the Navajos's side. He recommended that six separate columns of 150 troops in each command be sent against the tribe, and that as many of the troops as possible be mounted. He repeated a dictum for which, in time, he would be remembered: "We had better have a large and short war than a small and long one." [5]

With the limited forces at his command, General Garland found the major's war proposals sound enough but a bit more than he had bargained for. Because the Navajos could mount two thousand warriors against him the general felt it would be unwise to invade their country with fewer than eight hundred troops, more men than could be spared at the moment from the defense of other sections of the territory. Garland believed that his best course was to ask Major Kendrick to recover as many of the stolen sheep as he could, and to temporize with the

4. April 19, 1856: Dodge to Davis, NA, NMS T21-2.
5. April 21, 1856: Kendrick to Nichols, NA, RAC, RG 393, K-5-1856, LR.

headmen in his demand for the murderers until Garland was in a better position to launch an effective campaign. In the meantime, an alternative solution to the impasse might be provided if the Senate should ratify the treaty of Laguna Negra.[6]

Governor Meriwether, who had returned to Santa Fe from Washington only a few days before, could offer the general no more than faint hope with respect to the last point. His trip to the capital had been for the purpose of securing approval of his treaties of the previous year, but senators had given him little encouragement and he had come away with no promise of favorable action. He was further pained to learn that during his absence a portion of the Navajos had broken one of the provisions of the Laguna Negra treaty. Whether he consulted Garland is uncertain, but shortly after his return Meriwether directed Henry Dodge to insist upon the surrender of the Navajos who had killed the three herders.[7] General Garland at almost the same time was informing Major Kendrick that he deemed it best "to temporize a little, for we are not ready to strike. . . . Do not press too hard upon them your demand for the murderers, but give them to understand that you have referred that part of the difficulty to the Governor, and the Department Commander." [8]

In spite of the conflicting orders received from Santa Fe, Major Kendrick and Dodge worked closely in concert; both continued to press hard for the return of stolen sheep and arranged to meet with the Navajos at Laguna Negra on the last day of May, when it was agreed that livestock would be given to them for return to the Otero and Romero families. They continued to insist upon the surrender of the wanted Navajos, who were reported to have returned to the lodges of the Capotes, but carefully refrained from threatening the alternative of war. At the same time they induced as many of the Navajos as they could to turn their attention to planting. From his post supply Major Kendrick provided them with spring seedlings for a potato crop; Dodge distributed packages of seed, sent out to him by Governor Meriwether, that should produce a harvest of corn, peas, cabbage, turnips, and cauliflower. The response was encouraging enough to make Kendrick believe the summer's yield would equal any of the years past.

Dodge, meanwhile, had taken time to visit the scene of the March 27

6. April 30, 1856: Garland to Lt. Col. Lorenzo Thomas, AAG, New York, NA, RAC, RG 393, LS.
7. May 2, 1856: Meriwether to Dodge, Fort Defiance, NA, NMS T21-2.
8. May 3, 1856: Nichols to Kendrick, NA, RAC, RG 393, LS.

raid. Bodies of two of the slain herders were shown to him, but he did not doubt there had been a third; the Navajos themselves agreed that there had been three. He examined the ground where the Otero and Romero sheep had grazed, and poked about the pens and enclosures where they had been kept at night. He studied as well the tracks left when the sheep were run off. Experience told him that in such matters some New Mexican owners exaggerated, while some Navajos underestimated, the numbers of sheep stolen. He was certain in the present instance that six thousand sheep would be a generous estimate of the number taken.[9]

Peace efforts stemming outward from Fort Defiance received a setback about ten days before the meeting at Laguna Negra was to be held, when Navajo raiders appeared in the vicinity of Peña Blanca, on the Rio Grande between the pueblos of Cochiti and Santo Domingo, and drove off four hundred sheep owned by José Ignacio Montoya. Three New Mexican pastors were wounded in the attack, two of them dying later.

The incident appears to have stirred General Garland from his position of temporizing. Almost at once he informed Governor Meriwether that he contemplated making an expedition against the Navajos in either July or August. In all probability he would call upon the governor to raise three companies of volunteers to serve with the regular troops. Meriwether indulged in a fanciful notion that when the time came he would ride out with the expedition and, before any shooting started, persuade the Navajos to turn over to him those who were guilty of depredations.[10]

Realities rather than daydreams confronted Henry Dodge and Major Kendrick when they rode to the council site at Laguna Negra on May 31. No throng of two thousand warriors milled about in the valley this time; a quiet and downcast group that numbered scarcely a score more than one hundred awaited them. Their mood was neither compliant nor unfriendly but resigned. At the urging of Armijo and Ganado Mucho they had collected and brought in four hundred sheep and thirty horses, all contributed by Navajos willing to give this much from their own herds to keep the soldiers away. But these sheep, with one

9. May 16, 1856: Dodge to Meriwether, NA, NMS T21-2; (same date) Kendrick to Nichols, NA, RAC, RG 393, K-7-1856, LR. Capt. Ewell, commanding Los Lunas, reported May 24 that inquiries he had made at Garland's order indicated that 10,000 sheep had been stolen.

10. May 31, 1856: Meriwether to Manypenny, NA, NMS 234-548.

thousand more of the Otero and Romero flocks already recovered and returned, were as much as the Navajos would contribute unless forced to do so at gunpoint.

They brought also to Laguna Negra three sorry-looking and bedraggled peons, and when Dodge and the major again refused to accept them, the captives were sent on anyway to Cebolleta with a headman named José Miguel (the second to sign the Laguna Negra treaty), who spoke Spanish well enough to negotiate for their acceptance by the families of the murdered pastors. The families of the dead men, it was reasoned, might not be so stubborn.

More than Major Kendrick, who now spoke of foregoing further demand for the murderers, Henry Dodge gave evidence of fatigue and dejection. At the end of a cheerless return to Fort Defiance he felt so unwell that he doubted if he could make a planned trip to Santa Fe.[11] He was forty-six years old, no alarming matter, but during recent weeks his traveling about to collect sheep had made heavy demands on his stocky frame. He was tired.

With a few exceptions, most of the Navajos who had been friendly became openly defiant when they learned that of four Navajos who had taken part in the recent Peña Blanca raid two were said to have been killed in an ensuing engagement with New Mexicans at the Valle Grande, in the Jemez Mountains. When Major Kendrick and Henry Dodge pointed out that the raiders had been acting in open violation of the Laguna Negra treaty, the headmen said they were tired of such arguments; it was enough that Mexicans had killed two of their people. For this reason, they would do nothing more in compensation for the Otero and Romero losses.

Manuelito, whose leadership of this new hostile element seemed indisputable, spoke more bluntly. Navajos always had raided upon and killed Mexicans and there was nothing the Bilagáana could do to prevent it. The Americans, he said, "were too fond of sleeping, eating

11. June 2, 1856: Dodge to Meriwether, NA, NMS T21-2; (same date) Kendirck to Nichols, NA, RAC, RG 393, K-8-1856, LR. Well or not, Dodge was asked almost at once to investigate new minor aggressions: a June 6 theft of eight horses owned by Antonio Baca of Peña Blanca, stolen at "the Ranch of Sile" (near Zia Pueblo?), and a June 8 incident of San Ysidro when a band of 30 Navajos said to be with Aguila Negra, returning from a visit to Jemez, were reported to have wounded a mayordomo of Q. A. Sandoval and stolen three cattle. The Indians were said to "live near the point of the Sebolleta Mountains," which suggests a possible confusion of Aguila Negra's people with Diné An'aii (June 17, 1856: Meriwether to Dodge, NA, NMS T21-2).

[and] drinking, and had white eyes and could not see the road" to catch the Navajos.

During the treaty council at Laguna Negra, Manuelito and other headmen had agreed that Navajo livestock would be kept away from the haying and grazing grounds north of Fort Defiance and necessary to the support of the post. What now of that agreement? In response Manuelito's tone became harsher. All of that land had belonged to him since he was a boy. Major Kendrick had wagons and also he had soldiers; let him decide which he would use. Let him send his wagons thirty miles south to the Calites to gather hay, or let him use his soldiers—if he thought his force was sufficient—to drive the Navajos away from the disputed land. He was a powerful war leader, Manuelito declared, and he could quickly call about him one thousand warriors.

Dodge gloomily attributed the Navajos' new mood of hostility in part to reaction against the recent loss of the two Navajo raiders but also to rumors that he said had been started in the previous December by Zarcillos Largos to the effect that Fort Defiance had proved too costly and would be abandoned.

"That the dreadful scourge of war should not be visited upon them," he advised Governor Meriwether, "I have laboured and suffered many privations, but I fear to little purpose." Of similar mind, Major Kendrick reported to the department commander that each passing day made it more clear that war with the Navajos was inevitable.

In comparison with Indian tribes in the east, Kendrick believed, Navajos had little cause for complaint against Americans. Even in the present difficult situation Manuelito and others based their defiance on what they regarded as superior Navajo power, not on alleged wrongs done them by Americans. Kendrick said that he and Dodge had used every possible means to impress upon the headmen an understanding of the government's strength and ability to punish the Navajos, but at the same time had taken pains to demonstrate the government's good intentions toward them. He had hoped, but often with misgivings, that he and Dodge could make them see they had everything to lose and nothing to gain from a war. But now he was discouraged. He had no idea of the disposable force at General Garland's command, but for operations against the Navajos the general could scarcely increase it too much.[12]

12. June 13, 1856: Kendrick to Nichols, NA, RAC, RG 393, K-9-1856, LR; (same date) Dodge to Meriwether, NA, NMS 234-548.

Major Kendrick was given cause to reconsider his earlier advocacy of Sandoval as a useful ally a few days later when it was learned that four Diné Ana'aii had killed Juan de Dios Gallegos of Cubero, and severely wounded his sheepherder. The attack, which occurred in the mountains above the Laguna village of Encinal, was not inspired by the current disaffection of the Navajos controlled by Manuelito but may have reflected the same low esteem to which the major's reduced garrison had fallen in the Indians' regard. Juan de Dios and his herder had both been shot in the back, the former twice—a musket ball entering low near his spine and emerging at the left side, and an arrow planted high and firmly between the shoulder blades. Juan de Dios lived long enough for the less seriously injured pastor to escape and then return to the scene with help. The Cubero man was carried to the house of Don Marcos Vaca where he died the next day, June 26.

So well were Sandoval and his people known in the vicinity that the identity of the assailants as well as their motive were learned almost at once. The four Diné Ana'aii were said to be peons—probably half-bloods—owned by a lesser headman than Sandoval known as Mariana.[13] The attack was said to have been made to avenge Mariana for the killing of his sister some four weeks earlier by Comanches.

Before news of this incident reached Albuquerque, General Garland had issued orders for Major Shepherd to march with his company of infantry to rejoin the Defiance garrison. He was cautioned about the danger of encountering Navajos in numbers superior to his own, and was directed to avoid any show of hostility that might lead to a collision. If attacked, he was to defend himself but no more, "the object of the presence of your company in the Navajo Country being to reinforce the garrison . . . not for aggressive measures." [14]

With nothing worse to report than heat and long stretches between springs, Major Shepherd brought his company into Fort Defiance on July 10. The garrison was thus increased by sixty-nine rank and file to a total strength of just under two hundred men, almost all of them present for duty. Five of the arriving privates were at once locked in the guardhouse for various offenses during the march.

Another meeting with the Navajos that was to have been held two

13. "These are the things told us every few hours by different parties who come in from different places. . . ." June 27, 1856: the Rev. Samuel Gorman, Laguna, to Dodge, NA, NMS T21-2.

14. June 26, 1856: Nichols to Shepherd, Albuquerque, NA, RAC, RG 393, no. 108, LS.

days before the arrival of Shepherd's company was postponed at the request of the headmen. By means of their own, which never ceased to amaze officers at the frontier posts, the Navajos had advance knowl-edge of the beefing up of the garrison, and its effect upon the belli-gerent element of the tribe was immediately apparent. On the same day that Company B reached the fort Henry Dodge was given posses-sion of three hundred sheep and twenty-two horses as additional pay-ment for losses to the Otero and Romero herds. As many more as might be demanded of them would be surrendered, he was assured, before the Navajos could be made to fight the Bilagáana. On the day following, more Navajos than had ever before been seen in Cañoncito Bonito assembled about Fort Defiance for the proposed council.

Manuelito again was the principal spokesman, but his manner now was conciliatory. The interpreters at their last meeting had misstated both his words and his intentions, he told Dodge and Major Kendrick. Proof of this they would find in the Navajos' recent actions. Navajos had removed their livestock from the fort's grazing grounds, and it was their intention to comply with all terms of the Laguna Negra treaty but one: they would not surrender any of their people now implicated in the death of seven New Mexicans and the wounding of two others. If they were to do so, the headmen said, it would cause war among themselves and the Capote Utes would join the conflict on the side of the offending Navajos.

Confronted with this sudden softening of attitude, and uncertain of what response it would draw from Santa Fe, Kendrick and Dodge said little but were careful to give no assurance that the tense situation was in any way eased or changed. Until they received further instructions there was little they could do. Two days after the council, his illness preventing him from going himself, Dodge turned over the livestock recently surrendered to his New Mexican herder and the Navajo José Miguel to be driven to Cubero and left there temporarily in the care of the alcalde, Juan Durrán.[15] Any claim the Romero family may have had was not mentioned when Dodge in effect closed the case at the end of summer, reporting,

"I have succeeded in getting part payment from the tribe. . . . The Nabajoes have paid Mr Otero two thousand sheep fifty 2 horses & three

15. July 13, 1856: Dodge to Meriwether (unsigned, but in Dodge's handwriting, addressed only to "Sir," but delivered to Meriwether by Post Sutler John Weber). Two drafts of the same letter, both breaking off without ending, further attest to Dodge's illness (NA, NMS T21-2 and NMS 234-548).

servants, and all the principal men say they are willing to pay him until he is satisfied." [16] Whether Otero accepted the three captive peons as payment for the murdered herders, or as compensation for stolen sheep, remains unclear. What is quite clear is that the Navajos responsible for the series of murders and stock thefts were not turned in.

Any plan General Garland may still have entertained for military action in Navajo country was modified in late July when he learned of a drastic change in the makeup of his command. All units of the First Regiment of Dragoons, including those of Major Carleton and Captain Ewell, were to be transferred at once, most of them to duty in California and the balance to the small adobe outpost at Tucson. They would be replaced, but not immediately, by a regiment of mounted riflemen. In advising Major Kendrick of this development, Garland suggested that the major again temporize with the Navajos "and arrange matters in such a way that the necessity may not be forced upon us to take up arms at once." [17]

The general's hesitant preparations for a Navajo campaign, which never really got beyond the talking stage, were forgotten entirely when he was temporarily relieved of command by the somewhat legendary Colonel Benjamin L. E. de Bonneville. There was an aura about the new but aging department commander, in some part earned but also in part a literary amplification of his achievements by the pen of Washington Irving; an aura real enough but its light an afterglow of yesterdays. Nothing he was to do this year, or next, would enhance it. He assumed command October 11 almost, it might be said, with the sigh of a man settling down to a deserved rest. If there was to be trouble with the Indians on this frontier, he was not the man to start it.[18]

Meriwether's conduct of Indian affairs was subjected to an increased attack shortly after Bonneville replaced Garland. The critic was James L. Collins, editor and owner of the Santa Fe *Weekly Gazette*, long known as a voice in territorial politics and now interested in a role more active than that provided by the editorial columns of his news-

16. September 30, 1856: Dodge, Santa Fe, to Manypenny, NA, NMS T21-2.
17. July 26, 1956: Nichols to Kendrick, NA, RAC, RG 393, no. 140, LS.
18. ". . . . a silly old man already in his dotage," was the acid characterization of him by a lofty junior officer during the Apache campaign of 1857 (Lazelle Diary, ed. Reeve 1948, p. 288). Benjamin Louis Eulalie de Bonneville was born in France in 1796, came to the United States at an early age, and was graduated from West Point after two years, in 1815, as a second lieutenant in the light artillery. During the remainder of a long career (glamorized by Washington Irving's treatment of Bonneville's own faulty journal), he served also with the 3d 4th, 6th, 7th, and 8th Infantry. He died in 1878 at Fort Smith, Arkansas.

paper. Specifically, Collins aspired to the governor's secondary office of superintendent of Indian affairs—an office soon to be established as a separate entity under presidential appointment.

The Democratic party, to which Collins professed to be partisan, at its summer convention had switched its allegiance from President Pierce to James Buchanan. With Buchanan's victory in the coming election almost assured, Collins hoped that he might gain Buchanan's favorable attention. The folly of Meriwether's Indian policy had been amply exposed by the *Gazette* in his previous editorials, Collins wrote, but the governor had shown no tendency to benefit from the criticism. There was no need to dwell on past mismanagement, but since the duties of the superintendency would soon pass to other hands, it would not be amiss to apprise New Mexico's delegate to the Congress of what his constituents would like to see done by the new superintendent.[19]

First, Collins went on to say, he proposed that the various bands of Apaches be colonized and settled on the Gila River in distinct pueblos, but not exceeding ten or fifteen miles apart, provided good farming land could be obtained within those limits. The Gila or Coyotero bands might be confined to one pueblo, unless it was thought best to divide them because of their numbers. The Mescaleros, Mimbres, and Jicarillas should be confined in separate pueblos. The Utes should be "pushed further west" until they were not less than forty miles distant from the nearest New Mexican settlement and they, too, should be discouraged from future roaming by confinement in pueblos. Military posts and agencies should be established near the pueblos, and at each agency there should be a council house where the superintendent, from time to time, could come to talk with the Indians, thus eliminating the need for any of the tribes to visit the settlements in large parties as they were now permitted to do. Each agency would be furnished a blacksmith, farmer, and carpenter to teach the Indians those useful trades.

For reasons which he neglected to explain, Collins did not advocate placing Navajos in pueblos, but did recommend that "new limits" be set apart for the tribe "so as to give more room to our citizens to graze their stock. There is no necessity for those Indians to have grazing grounds east of their settlements, for they have better pasture lands west of them. . . ." Agencies should be provided for them, as for

19. The Collins editorial (Santa Fe *Gazette*, October 18, 1856) was forwarded by Delegate Miguel Antonio Otero, with a note expressing his full approval of its contents, to Secretary of the Interior Robert McClelland.

Apaches and Utes. All of this, Collins admitted, might look very well on paper, but would the Indians agree to it? In response to this rhetorical question, and employing the editorial writer's plural personality, he added:

"We . . . take the ground, that whether they agree to it or not, they should be *compelled* to submit to it. We no more admit their *right* to live as they are now living, than we admit the right of the thief to pursue his calling."

As he so clearly presumed to do, James Collins may have expressed the views of a majority of Delegate Miguel Antonio Otero's constituents. As merely one editor's viewpoint the proposals had a certain fascination; they assumed greater and more immediate relevance a few months later when President Buchanan, after his inauguration, appointed Collins superintendent of Indian affairs for New Mexico.

From the time of the reinforcement of the Defiance garrison on July 10 the Navajos had remained at peace with the whites. Dodge and Major Kendrick together drew up a formal agreement intended to protect the garrison's unchallenged right to haying and grazing grounds north of the post, at Cañon del Trigo, and La Joya—the same grounds recently claimed by Manuelito to have been his own since boyhood.

The agreement was made solely with El Gordo (the Fat One), referred to on several occasions as a brother of Zarcillos Largos and said to be a headman of considerable wealth, as well as inclined to be good natured and friendly. Gordo agreed that between early April and autumn of each year the grazing lands should be used exclusively by the military; during that period he would keep his own animals and those of his people away. In return, Gordo would be paid each fall one vara (about thirty-three inches) of manta cloth for each load of hay cut for the fort. If the amount of hay should exceed fifteen wagonloads, his payment in manta would be doubled. And if twenty loads of hay should be cut in any season, Gordo would receive an additional bonus of one rawhide, one ax, one hoe, and "two planches of Tobacco." Should an occasion arise when other Navajos claimed that the land belonged as much to them as to Gordo, the latter agreed he would adjust any dispute by dividing his payment with them.[20]

20. November 7, 1856: Agreement signed at Fort Defiance by El Gordo, Kendrick, and Dodge, NA, NMS T21-2.

The understanding thus arrived at was a new approach to one of the sensitive terms of the previous year's treaty at Laguna Negra. Its importance to the maintenance of a garrison at Fort Defiance, and thus to peace on the frontier, was regarded as indisputable and, as time was to show, was not overestimated.

16

Haashk'aan Silah Mesa

An Apache raid on Zuni in October prompted Major Kendrick to plan a scout in the vicinity of the pueblo a few weeks later. He would lead the patrol personally and his small detachment of troops would have the services of Armijo and a few other Navajos as guides. Henry Dodge was asked to join the party, apparently in no official capacity but so that he could take a brief rest from the pressures of the Navajo agency. Dodge undoubtedly welcomed the chance to get away. Since occupation by General Kearny's forces ten years before, the territory had been his home, and circumstances had afforded him little leisure.

The years, he might reflect now, had been hard and with little to show of material gain, but it had been a free life of his own choosing. How he regarded the period spent at Cebolleta and Chupadero would be impossible to say, but something may be read from the silent testimony of stone ruins. The foundations and walls of stone dwellings he left at Chupadero are haunting reminders of the massive stone structures built at a later time at Ganado and Chinle by the trader Lorenzo Hubbell. No motive has been found to explain Dodge's apparent abandonment of his family in Wisconsin. Of his Navajo wife and children hardly more is known, but it is more revealing. In terms of the time Dodge would have been called a squaw man, an intended denigration to be shrugged off. As well as any white man and better than most, perhaps, excepting only Rafael Carravahal of San Ysidro, he knew the Navajo country. Better yet, he knew the Navajos as few men ever did, and his liking for them was returned in kind. If they had met again now, General Kearny might have found Dodge's appearance little changed: three inches short of six feet, probably a little darker and less florid in the face, the eyes gray, the hair still dark but thinner. In ten years he had learned nothing at all about conserving money; as a part of this problem there had been no improvement, either, in his skill at gambling. On this point something more may be said. Always observant in such matters, the Navajos knew him not as El Jugador (the Gam-) bler) but as Red Shirt.

Such Henry Dodge was, a bit more or less, when he left Fort Defiance with Major Kendrick's detachment November 16, 1856. At Zuni a few days later they were joined by Salvador, war captain of the pueblo, and several of his warriors. From a place called Cedar Spring, the patrol's camp thirty miles south of Zuni, Dodge and Armijo left early in the morning of the nineteenth, before anybody else was moving about, to hunt for deer.

The country immediately surrounding them, powdered with snow, normally was a dun-colored plain traversed from east to west by a dry wash, with here and there an outcropping of dark rock and occasional clumps of scrub cedar—nothing in the way of cover or forage to encourage wild game larger than a rabbit. Looming nearby to the west, however, was the forested top of Haashk'aan Silah Mesa, and to this more promising elevation Dodge and Armijo made their way. Not long after they reached the summit they saw a deer; Dodge's first shot killed it. As the hour was still early, Armijo agreed to remain with the carcass while Dodge went on in search of other game. Much later, Armijo rejoined Kendrick's column, believing that Dodge had hunted so far down the mesa that he would not backtrail but would meet the patrol somewhere below on its march toward Zuni Salt Lake.

By the time camp was made near the lake that evening, however, Dodge still had not returned. No particular importance was attached to this, Major Kendrick commented later, as "knowing his intelligence as a good woodsman & having during the march seen no signs of Indians other than the friendly Navajoes & Zuñis who accompanied us, his absence from camp gave . . . no other anxiety than the fear that he might suffer from the cold before finding us." Nevertheless, on the chance that Dodge might try to find their camp that night, Kendrick directed that gunshots be fired at intervals and a bonfire maintained through the night.[1]

1. November 26, 1856: Kendrick to Nichols, NA, RAC, RG 393, K-18-1856, LR. Charles W. Wentz of Company G, 1st Cavalry, New Mexico Volunteers, nearly eight years later wrote to Augustus Caesar Dodge that "Maj. Kendrick sent up some men to the highest peaks of the surrounding hills to make a Fire, thinking that if your Brother had missed his way and was lost he would be attracted by the blazing light at night. The Major after dark also ordered 12 men to go up on top of the adjoining hills and fire off their Rifles, so that in case he should not see the light of the Fires, he might perhaps hear the report of the guns" (May 1,

In the open country that separated the patrol's camp from Haashk'aan Silah Mesa Dodge could have had little trouble in locating Kendrick's position, but by morning he had still not come in. There was cause for concern in this, but soon there was actual reason to fear for his safety. A number of the patrol's horses and mules, most of them hobbled and turned loose to graze the evening before, were traced out on the plain to a point where a confusion of new tracks clearly indicated they had been stolen. Major Kendrick at once asked Armijo to return to the place on the mesa where the deer had been shot and from there follow Dodge's tracks until he was found.

The detachment then separated, Salvador and the other Indians going in advance with Armijo while the main column prepared to follow later. Not until noon the next day was the end of Dodge's trail discovered, among trees and brush and only four or five miles from the previous camp at Cedar Spring. Such evidence as could be found suggested that Dodge had walked unsuspectingly into a trap and been captured by possibly five or six Indians. When Kendrick arrived on the scene with Second Lieutenant Richard V. Bonneau, the mingled prints left by moccasins and Dodge's shoes were pointed out to them. Armijo and Salvador assured the officers that Dodge's captors were Apaches—not Coyoteros, but either Mogollones or Gileños. After examining the signs carefully Major Kendrick concluded that Dodge had been seized without a struggle or other violence, and that after some moments of conversation he had been taken off by the Apaches in a southeasterly direction.

As nearly as he could tell, Major Kendrick estimated that forty-eight hours had passed since Dodge had fallen into the Apaches' hands. The length of time was handicap enough, but darkening skies threatened heavy snow and made any effort at pursuit seem hopeless. Soon the storm came in a thick gray shroud, so enveloping the command that Kendrick's Zuni guide became lost in country he knew well.[2]

As though time itself had come to a standstill and become meaningless, Kendrick in some bemusement later referred cryptically to an encounter with a Mexican—a Mexican captive from Galeana, in Old

---

1864: Wentz, Fort Canby, to A. C. Dodge, Burlington, Iowa, the State Historical Society of Wisconsin, file 1860, Oct. 13). Wentz was not present during these events. This and his letters of May 10 and 16 informed Dodge's brother of what the old dragoon could glean of the agent's fate from enlisted men and officers then attached to Col. Kit Carson's Navajo Expedition.

2. November 26, 1856: Kendrick to Nichols, cited above.

Mexico, "who made his escape from another party of Apaches," and who told him that if the Apaches had not killed Dodge at once they most probably would spare his life and hold him for ransom. The encounter with the Mexican, it would be learned, had occurred after the night-long vigil at the Zuni Salt Lake, in the morning when some of the patrol's horses were discovered missing. Twelve men sent out by Kendrick to track the animals found the Mexican captive—a mere boy—hiding among rocks. At the time Dodge had been seized, he was being held prisoner by a large party of Mogollon and Coyotero Apaches. Some hours after Dodge's captors rejoined the main party, the youth had escaped; attracted by the bonfire and gunshots intended for Dodge, he had made his way to the hiding place close to Kendrick's camp.[3]

Upon reaching Zuni on November 22, Major Kendrick sent a special express to Major Jefferson Van Horne, commanding the post at Albuquerque, informing him that Dodge had been taken captive by Apaches and carried off southward. From all appearances, he said, Dodge had been treated kindly. He added that a Mexican youth who had escaped from the same Apaches believed that the Mimbres chief Mangas Coloradas, or his brother, would learn of Dodge's capture, and that in such event it was possible Dodge would be ransomed. Kendrick asked Major Van Horne to relay the information as quickly as possible to Dr. Michael Steck, agent for the Mescaleros and southern Apache bands at Fort Thorn, "by whom it is presumed Capt. Dodge's liberation can be effected," and to Governor Meriwether and Colonel Bonneville as well.[4]

The express rider either was unimpressed by the need to hurry or had to make his way through deep snow, for it took him five days to reach Albuquerque and he did not deliver Kendrick's message to Governor Meriwether until late afternoon of the sixth day. Within two hours of receiving the express Meriwether sent a special messenger to advise Agent Steck that Dodge had been captured and was being taken toward the Gila River by a party of either Mogollon or Gila Apaches. Steck was instructed to send out without delay one or more parties—either Mimbreños of Mangas Coloradas's band or others—to locate Dodge's captors. Any Indians willing to go would be "reasonably compensated" and an unspecified ransom would be paid for Dodge's release.[5]

3. January 27, 1857: Meriwether to Manypenny, NA, NMS 234-548; May 1, 1864: Wentz to A. C. Dodge, cited above.

4. Enclosure with November 27, 1856: Van Horne to Nichols, NA, RAC, RG 393, V-23-1856, LR.

5. November 28, 1856: Meriwether to Steck, NA, NMS 234-548.

For the moment there was nothing more that anyone in Santa Fe could do. Both the governor and Colonel Bonneville took note of the fact that if Dodge indeed were being held by Mogollones his captors may have been part of the same Apache band against which Lieutenant Colonel Daniel Chandler had campaigned in the previous March. If this were true, Meriwether suggested, there might be unpleasant consequences for the Navajo agent. Bonneville kept any inferences he may have drawn to himself, but vowed that if the Apaches harmed Dodge in any way, "if necessary the whole strength of the Department shall be used to punish and break up this people." [6]

Agent Steck was away attending to the Mescaleros' interests at Fort Stanton when Meriwether's express rider reached Fort Thorn. In his absence the post commander, Captain Thomas Claiborne, undertook to carry out the governor's instructions. With Ammon Barnes, a civilian, he sent Costates and two other Mimbres in search of Mangas Coloradas, who was said to be fifteen or twenty miles west of the fort in the vicinity of the Copper Mines. They were asked to prevail upon the Apache leader, upon finding him, to do everything within his power to find Dodge's captors and arrange for his release. Mangas himself was to be paid liberally, and he was to be authorized to offer a ransom not exceeding one thousand dollars. Captain Claiborne unintentionally added to the doubt surrounding Dodge's fate when he remarked that Delgadito, who with other Mimbreños was then at the fort, "seems to think it probable the Indians will ransom Dodge, but thinks they are Pinal Linas or Coyoteros, in which last event it will be hard to get Dodge." [7]

Major Kendrick was serving on a court martial board in Santa Fe, early in December, when word came to Fort Defiance that a party of Apaches had brought Henry Dodge to Zuni and were prepared to deliver him over to military authorities. Hoping that Dodge would be

6. November 29, 1856: Meriwether to Manypenny; (same date) Bonneville to Thomas, NA, NMS 234-548. Returning from a campaign deep into Mogollon country, and when near the Rio Grande, Chandler ordered his troops to fire on the friendly Mimbres camp of Delgadito and Costates. One woman was killed and another woman and three children were wounded. The Chandler campaign unquestionably touched off a series of Apache reprisals, the death of Henry Dodge being one of nearly a score that resulted.

7. December 1 and 2, 1856: Claiborne to Barnes, and Claiborne to Meriwether, NA, NMS T21-2. Fort Thorn was located on the west bank of the Rio Grande, a few miles north of the present town of Hatch. Ammon Barnes operated the government ferry at the San Diego crossing, a short distance north of the fort.

released immediately, Brevet Major William H. Gordon, temporarily in command, sent a small detachment to the pueblo. The rumor proved to have been a cruel mistake; the Zunis greeted the soldiers in blank surprise. They had neither seen nor heard of the Navajo agent.[8]

About a week later and shortly after his return to Fort Thorn, Agent Steck was informed by Delgadito, who came at the behest of Mangas Coloradas, that the Mogollones and Coyoteros had joined forces to make war on the whites. Already they had committed extensive robberies, and late in November they were said to have raided eastward as far as Acoma. It was believed, too, that the same warring bands were preparing to attack the Navajos. Governor Meriwether should be advised that these Apaches would refuse to make peace, and it would be well if all settlers in the Rio Abajo placed a strong guard over their livestock. Of Henry Dodge's capture and present whereabouts, Mangas Coloradas knew nothing, but he had sent his brother to learn what he could.[9]

Nothing further was heard in the final days of 1856 from others who had gone out. Then in the evening of January 2, José Mangas, the brother of Mangas Coloradas, appeared at Fort Thorn with a Mimbres called Tinaja. As they related to Captain Claiborne and Steck everything they had been able to learn, it became painfully clear that Henry Dodge had been killed, probably immediately when found by the Apaches. The sequence of events, as confirmed later, briefly was this:

The raiding party that had struck at Zuni in October (and occasioned Kendrick's patrol to the Zuni Salt Lake) had come off rather badly. Zuni warriors swarming in pursuit not only recovered most of the sheep the Apaches had stolen but also killed one Coyotero. To avenge their companion the Mogollones and Coyoteros—their number now increased to one hundred or more—were returning to attack Zuni in November when five or six of their party accidentally surprised Dodge near the main war camp on Haashk'aan Silah Mesa. Dodge was shot with a carbine, whether by a Mogollon or a Coyotero is not certain. After his body was disposed of the entire party of Apaches, led by Cautivo and Isano and including some of those who had been attacked in March by Colonel Chandler, moved off to the southeast. Shortly afterward the war party divided into two groups, moving separately for the next month through the sheltering cover of the mountains below

8. December 11, 1856: Gordon to Nichols, NA, RAC, RG 393, G-14-1856, LR.
9. December 18, 1856: Steck to Meriwether, NA, NMS 234-548.

Wingate Valley. In ensuing raids on Laguna and along the Puerco they captured two large herds of sheep; near Zuni, on December 22, they killed ten persons of that pueblo and ran off about one hundred horses and cattle. The fallen Coyotero and the victims of Chandler's campaign thus avenged, they withdrew, uniting again near the headwaters of the Rio San Francisco to divide the booty, then separating once more, the main party moving in the direction of the White Mountains and the others going to the Gila and then to the Dos Cabezas Mountains. Here, near the later site of Fort Bowie, José Mangas found their camp and learned of Henry Dodge's death.[10]

Late in January, at Meriwether's request, Colonel Bonneville directed Major Kendrick to send a detachment of troops to search for Dodge's body, and if successful to return it to Fort Defiance for burial. Bonneville at the same time let it be known that as soon as weather permitted he would lead a punitive expedition against the Apaches. All of the troops that could be spared from the territory's garrisons would be put in the field and would remain there through summer and fall and longer if necessary.

This time there was no delay. On February 3, four days after Bonneville's express left Santa Fe, Orders No. 5 were posted at Fort Defiance. First Lieutenant J. Howard Carlisle of the Second Artillery and Second Lieutenant John W. Alley, Third Infantry, with a mounted party of forty men and rations for twenty-six days, were detailed to proceed as soon as possible in search of Dodge's body. Two additional privates were to accompany the column as far as Zuni and remain there with the detachment's supply wagons. Lieutenant Carlisle was to select a few Navajos to assist him as guides and might engage a limited number of Zunis upon reaching that pueblo.

10. January 2, 1857: Claiborne to Nichols; January 3, 1857: Steck to Meriwether, NA, NMS 234-548. As noted before, Armijo and Salvador were positive that Coyoteros were not present when Dodge was shot. Months afterward, and after Bonneville's summer campaign against the Mogollones and Coyoteros, Agent Steck, reporting the arrival of three Coyoteros at his agency, said: "Chino Peña the spokesman of the party . . . [was] told that they were implicated in the murder of Agt. H. L. Dodge and others. . . . The evidence we had before together with the admissions of Chino Peña dont leave a doubt as to their culpability. He admits that some of their bad men may have been engaged in stealing and that the murderer of Agent Dodge was in his camp when attacked by Col. Bonneville and that he was one of the killed. . . ." (NA, NMS T21-3). Steck's report suggests the possibility that Dodge was killed by a Coyotero, but does not prove it.

Cañoncito Bonito was blanketed with old snow, and it was snowing hard again, when Carlisle led his command away from Fort Defiance at noon of February 5. Snow continued to fall through the afternoon, forcing the mounted column and wagons to a plodding, dragging walk. A bleak camp was made in the narrowing valley above Calites Canyon. All through that night and the next day the snow came down. On the third day, having traveled sixty miles, the command reached Zuni. Here their welcome cooled abruptly when Carlisle explained his mission. In the end, having been refused guides and additional supplies of corn, in the morning of the second day Carlisle started his column southward on what he hoped might be (if it could have been seen) the Salt Lake trail. For guides he would depend now only on Armijo and a few other Navajos. Below Zuni the snow was more than a foot deep, and for eighteen miles it became increasingly deeper.

Leaden clouds were threatening more snow when Carlisle reached Major Kendrick's Cedar Spring camp at noon on February 10. Leaving fifteen men there to prepare a base camp, Carlisle took the Navajos and the balance of his command over the level approach to Haashk'aan Silah Mesa. On reaching the place on the summit where it was believed Dodge had been captured, they spent the remaining hours of the afternoon searching among snow-laden brush and trees. Nothing was found but the heel from one of Dodge's shoes.

The party worked north from there, or back the way they (and presumably Dodge) had come, fanning out over the rough tableland. They found the summit drained by a series of deep arroyos leading off into immense ravines where drifted snow reached a depth of several feet, but patches of ground at the top scoured bare by the wind. On ground clear of snow they picked up the tracks of Dodge's horse, but the tracks seemed to wander in confusion. Armijo suggested that Dodge might have become lost while hunting. (Or did Carlisle, protesting that Dodge was much too good a woodsman to lose himself in this way, miss a glint in the Navajo's eye?) But so it stood, with nothing more than a leather heel and meandering horse tracks to go on, when fading light made them give up the search.

When morning came, returning to the mesa, Carlisle employed a different tactic. Dividing the Navajos between them, he left Lieutenant Alley with fifteen men, afoot, at the point where Dodge had parted from Armijo after shooting the deer. With the same number of men in his own party Carlisle plodded south to the place where Major

Kendrick thought Dodge had been captured. Both parties then spread out and began advancing toward each other. What followed was related by Carlisle afterward.

> We arranged our command so as to cover as much ground as we could search thoroughly & proceeded towards each other. . . . about 11 o'clock A.M. a portion of his remains were found in an arroyo about one mile North West of the point where it appeared [to Major Kendrick] Capt. Dodge had been captured & about one mile nearly west from the place where Armijo parted with him—
>
> The snow at the place was stained with blood & on the reverse side of the arroyo where the snow was melted, were distinct prints of Capt. Dodge's shoes as though he or some one wearing his shoes had stood there for some moments.
>
> Although we had found sufficient to identify the remains as those of the late Capt. Dodge we searched all the vicinity for miles & even had the snow shovelled over in the immediate vicinity without making any further discovery—if any more of his remains are near that place they are undoubtedly buried under several feet of snow in some of the ravines in which that section of country abounds—From all we could see & learn from the tracks &c we were led to believe that Capt. Dodge was waylaid, murdered & *scalped* & deprived of his clothing at or near the place where the snow was stained with blood; that one of his murderers put on the clothes & shoes of Capt. Dodge & that his tracks were mistaken for those of Capt. Dodge—& that it is probable that subsequent to Capt. Dodge's death his horse was lead or ridden in various directions to render it difficult for any who might come in search of him to trail the horse back to where Capt. Dodge was killed.[11]

Lieutenant Carlisle, whose persistence against heavy odds was unusual, claimed no credit for himself. He reserved his praise for Armijo, who "was invaluable to me as a guide in that broken country . . . [and] the only one with me who could follow the track of the Apaches under such unfavorable circumstances." Armijo's tenacious purpose had itself been unusual. As they had left Zuni on the way to Haashk'aan Silah Mesa, Armijo had remarked that he doubted very much if his horse would last out the march. Carlisle had glanced at him in alarm.

11. February 17, 1857: Carlisle to Kendrick; enclosure with February 18: Kendrick to Nichols, cited above.

But that would not matter too much, Armijo continued—he would stay and guide the column even if he had to walk.

A military funeral and burial service were held after the detachment's return to Fort Defiance February 16. The post cemetery occupied a sandy, rocky slope near the head of the canyon. A wooden headboard placed over the grave (no trace of which remains today) was said to have been inscribed

To

The Memory

of

H. L. Dodge

aged 45 years,

agent for the Navajos,

killed by Apache Indians

on the 15th [*sic*] of Nov. 1856

A portion of his remains

rest beneath this spot [12]

The question then remained of the disposition to be made of Dodge's affairs, a subject Major Kendrick approached with reluctance. An administrator would be needed to settle the estate but at Fort Defiance there was no one "who knows anything of the duties or would like to assume them." Although Henry Dodge had lived at the post for some months before his death, his quarters were found to contain very little if anything in the nature of personal property. Kendrick was informed that about all he had owned of value were a few horses, but it would be difficult to determine how many and harder to identify them. The major made no reference at all to Dodge's Navajo family, and their fate remains unknown. His comment on these matters to Governor Meriwether suggests he would have welcomed any assistance the governor could offer that would spare him further involvement.[13]

12. Santa Fe *Gazette*, November 13, 1858. Samuel M. Yost, then editor of the *Gazette*, copied the headboard inscription while visiting Fort Defiance. Post Sutler John Weber gave an accurate account of the circumstances of Dodge's death, which Yost summarized briefly and then disparaged by adding: "It remains with me a question of doubt whether the Navajos themselves did not kill him." Dodge was 46 years old at the time of his death.

13. February 18, 1857; Kendrick to Meriwether, NA, NMS T21-3. In editing the journal of Lt. James H. Simpson (1964, p. 182, n. 20), I repeated a commonly held view that the late Henry (Chee) Dodge, first chairman of the Navajo Tribal Council, was the son of a Mexican father, Juan Cosinisas, who was agency interpreter, and a Navajo mother "of mixed Jemez blood, the oldest daughter of Clah Tsosi (Slim

Late in February Meriwether journeyed once more to Fort Defiance. All he found at the Navajo agency worth mentioning were three dozen farm tools—axes, hoes, and spades—which he distributed among the Indians. John Weber, the post sutler, informed him that in the weeks before his death Dodge had run up a large bill, all purchases for the Navajos, that had not been settled. Among Dodge's effects Meriwether could find no papers confirming the purchases or proving that the things Dodge had bought actually were turned over to the Navajos. Meriwether had no doubt that they were—he simply had no means of furnishing the proof that he knew the clerks of the treasury office in Washington would insist upon having before authorizing payment. From Dodge's last quarterly returns Meriwether knew the agent had owned three horses at the time of his death. One of these—the horse he had been riding—had been taken by Apaches who killed him. What had become of the other two, no one knew.

It was, Meriwether may have reflected, a gloomy business. Of the two sons of an illustrious father, one at this moment was serving as United States Minister to Spain; the other, hacked to pieces, his remains left for wolves, had come to this end at this lonely place, leaving behind nothing but debts to cloud his memory. Meriwether recalled that when he had seen Henry Dodge last, in the previous September in Santa Fe, he had bought and turned over to Dodge, because he did not trust him with the money, a considerable number of farm tools and other things for the Navajo agency. He had, at the same time, given Dodge an

---

Lefthand)." Two documents that have recently come to light discredit this belief and make it appear that the father in fact was Henry L. Dodge. Writing to C.I.A. Edward P. Smith on February 1, 1875, Augustus C. Dodge remarked that he had learned "that my brother Capt. Henry L. Dodge . . . left a son born of a Navajo woman. This boy now some 18 years of age is at, or near, Fort 'Defiance.' . . . He is represented to be a youth of more than ordinary promise . . . [and] speaks the Navajo, Spanish, & English languages with fluency. I was greatly gratified to learn . . . that Gov. [W. F. M.] Arny feels a deep interest in this boy and would be willing to aid in reclaiming him from the quasi condition of slavery in which he is now held by some 'herder,' so called, who is said to treat the boy cruelly. . . ." (NA, Microcopy 234, Roll 13, file mark D48). According to the earlier version of Chee Dodge's parentage, he was raised at Fort Defiance in the post–Bosque Redondo days by a Navajo aunt who married a white man named Perry H. Williams, who was variously employed as agency butcher, herder, and issue clerk. In an affidavit sworn to March 10, 1888, at Fort Defiance, Chee Dodge said, in part: "I am about 30 years old I was born on *this Plaza* at Fort Defiance My Father was a white Officer in the U S Army. My mother was a Navajo Woman. . . ." (NA, RG 75, LR, 8271-1888 Incl. #38).

advance in cash of $500; the same night Dodge had lost it all playing cards.[14]

Charles Wentz, who not long afterward campaigned against the Navajos with Kit Carson, may have been right when he said the Navajo wars of the next eight or nine years would not have occurred had Henry L. Dodge survived. The imponderables are too many for anyone to say what might have been. But of this there is no doubt whatever: Dodge lived the last years of his life for the Navajo people. They in turn gave him their respect; many, and among them would be Armijo, gave their devotion. In the century after his death the tribe would know two, possibly three, other agents who were actually and intelligently concerned with their peaceful survival and their progress, as Navajos, in the often rapacious ways of white civilization. But first of all, and longest, they would remember Henry Dodge.

14. March 27, 1857: Meriwether to Manypenny, NA NMS 234-548. A year later the money owed to Weber, an amount between $500 and $600, remained unpaid. James L. Collins, then superintendent of Indian affairs, advised Commissioner Charles E. Mix, "These purchases were made, I have no doubt, in good faith, and I am well assured that the Indians received the goods, and I think the debts should be paid. . . . Be kind enough to instruct me in the premises" (March 7, 1858: Collins to Mix, NA, NMS 234-549).

17

Seeds of War

A small flurry of Navajo raids on livestock early in 1857 stirred the legislative assembly to renewed criticism of the territory's Indian policy. Governor Meriwether, on whom the blame fell first, prevailed on the legislators to withdraw a memorial critical of himself and in its place substitute another appealing to Congress to limit roving tribes of Indians to the boundaries of reservations as set forth in his treaties of 1855. Because the Senate had failed to ratify the treaties, the memorial declared, a large portion of the most valuable land in the territory could not be opened to settlement until the Indians had been forced to withdraw.

Removed as he was from the political cockpit of the capital, Major Kendrick took a cooler view of the situation and found different causes for concern. Navajo theft of livestock appeared of small moment to him in comparison with recent murders and robberies committed by Mogollon and Coyotero Apaches.

As long as those Indians remained hostile, Kendrick thought there was enough trouble on the frontier without inviting more. For that reason he recommended again that New Mexican owners be persuaded to graze their livestock a safe distance from Navajo country. He noted, too, something that had escaped the attention of legislators in Santa Fe: in continuing warfare between the two tribes, Utes were said to have killed eight Navajos somewhere between the Carrizo Mountains and the mouth of Canyon de Chelly. The Navajos had killed five Utes in retaliation. There were rumors, which Kendrick was inclined to doubt, that Navajos were preparing to make a campaign against these traditional enemies. If the rumors proved to be true, however, and the Navajos should be successful, Kendrick thought, "it will be all *very well*, but otherwise they *may* make up their losses from the Mexicans— another reason for these people being on their guard." [1]

1. February 11, 1857: Kendrick to Nichols, NA, RAC RG 393, K-1-1857, LR.

A few weeks earlier Kendrick had offered another proposal in relation to the Navajos. The tribe numbered twelve thousand, he advised
Governor Meriwether, of whom three thousand were warriors, armed
for the most part with bow and arrow, who always fought mounted.
Navajos, who would believe only what they could see, were increasing
in wealth and numbers and increasing rapidly, too, in the conviction
that they could overpower the Americans whenever they cared to do
so. It would soon be essential to change their minds about this, and to
this end he recommended that a delegation of six Navajos, accompanied
by a few men from Zuni and the Hopi villages of Shipaulovi and Oraibi,
be sent on a tour of the States so that they could judge for themselves
the size of the country and its vastness of resources.[2] He would include
Pueblos, Kendrick explained, not because any danger was to be feared
from them, but because of the influence that they could exert upon warlike tribes with whom they came in contact.

Colonel Bonneville, meanwhile, was planning his expedition against
the Apache bands responsible for the murder of Henry Dodge and
others in the previous fall. The start of the campaign would wait until
May, but as early as February 24 Major Kendrick was informed that
Lieutenant Richard Bonneau of his command would receive orders
from department headquarters to enlist one hundred Navajos as spies
and guides. A similar force of Pueblos was to be recruited by Lieutenant
Alexander McCook of the Santa Fe garrison.

In anticipation of its required service in the campaign, Company B,
Third Infantry, aggregating sixty men, was detached from Fort Defiance
on February 23 with orders to proceed to Albuquerque. The Defiance
garrison again was reduced to one company of infantry and one of
artillery, a thin force of one hundred troops.

The idea of engaging Navajos and Pueblos as auxiliaries, it soon developed, had originated not with Bonneville but with Governor Meriwether, who evidently had arranged to pay for their services from reserve
funds. Meriwether may have been dismayed, therefore, when he learned
that the Navajos refused all of Lieutenant Bonneau's blandishments and
promises of reward. Offering neither excuses nor reasons, all of the
headmen with whom he talked declined to go. Bonneau then went to
Zuni, where the principal men spoke vaguely of spring planting and

2. January 23, 1857: Kendrick to Meriwether, NA NMS T21-3. Meriwether approved Kendrick's proposal, but thought that Utes and Apaches should be sent with
Navajos, instead of Pueblos. The decision rested with the Indian Office in Washington, which took no action in matter.

then, more vaguely still, of a separate, short campaign they might make with Navajos into Apache country at some later time. In the end, like the Navajos, they said they would not go.

At this juncture Major Kendrick ordered Bonneau to find Sandoval and attempt to recruit the services of the Diné Ana'aii.[3] This time Bonneau was successful; Sandoval and a number of his band agreed to join Bonneville's campaign. Together with the Diné Ana'aii, the spies and guides who joined the expedition included fifty warriors from Laguna and sixteen New Mexicans from Cubero and Cebolleta. Two others who were to serve effectively in the same capacity were Blas Lucero and, with the rank of captain, Manuel A. Chaves, in name if not in fact a professional Indian fighter. The three columns of Colonel Bonneville's expedition remained in the field from early May until the middle of July, departmental command reverting to General John Garland. Considerable punishment was dealt the Mogollon, Coyotero, and Gila Apaches. As the campaign did not involve the Navajo tribe, it need not engage further attention here.

Nearly coinciding with the start of the Apache campaign, Major Kendrick informed department headquarters that he would relinquish command of Fort Defiance to accept an appointment as professor of chemistry, mineralogy, and geology at the Military Academy at West Point. Following by six winter months the death of Henry Dodge, the departure of Major Kendrick on May 17 was of far greater consequence to Navajo relations than anyone at the time could have imagined. After coming to the territory seven years before, he had been in command of Fort Defiance since September 1852, a considerably longer time than served by any officer who preceded or followed him. Serious conflict with the Navajo nation had been averted again and again during these years—not because Major Kendrick opposed conflict, for he did not—but more probably because of the Navajos' response to the usually cool, always firm approach to tribal problems that Kendrick, in concert with Henry Dodge, pursued tirelessly. Aside from Armijo and perhaps a few others it is doubtful that many regarded him as more than an aloof figure of authority, but with each new post commander who followed him the Navajos had cause to remember him with ever deepening respect. The first of these successors was Brevet Major William H. Gordon, Third Infantry, a Virginian who had served on Major Kendrick's staff since July 1854.

3. April 12, 1857: Kendrick to Nichols, NA, RAC, RG 393, K-10-1857, LR, with enclosure.

The change in civil government that marked the end of David Meriwether's administration and the beginning of James L. Collins's first term as superintendent of Indian affairs was attended with all of the courtesy and decorum one might expect if a pack of dogs broke up a cockfight staged simultaneously with a band concert in the plaza center at high noon. Record books of the superintendency were filched by the departing governor; the sheriff served a writ of replevin on Meriwether as he was about to board an eastbound stage; and, as obbligato in the background, Secretary Davis piped shrill notes on the theme of Collins's perfidy, inadequacy, and gross moral turpitude.

In his small neat hand Davis filled pages of a letter to President Buchanan, outlining the many reasons why Davis found Collins unsuitable for the office to which Buchanan had appointed him. Although he addressed the president in his capacity as secretary of New Mexico, Davis for six months after Meriwether's departure served also as acting governor, holding that office until the arrival of the new appointee, Abraham Rencher, in November. One of the least known of the territory's governors, Rencher was a Democrat of unquestioned loyalty. A lawyer and former member of Congress from North Carolina, he had served for a brief time as minister to Portugal. With his wife and daughters he occupied the Palace of the Governors without fanfare.[4]

Major Kendrick, stopping in Santa Fe for a few days on his journey east, conferred with Collins at some length about relations with the Navajos. What measures he may have advocated are not known, although Collins later said the major had concurred in his own view that it would be best, for the time being, to prevent traders from entering Navajo country. The first to be affected by this policy would be Auguste Lacome, against whom Collins made no specific complaint; by implication, Lacome was included among those Collins accused of carrying arms, ammunition, and whisky to the pelados most inclined toward raiding. Lacome's license accordingly was temporarily suspended. Notifying J. W. Denver, President Buchanan's new Indian commissioner, to this effect, Collins wrote, "The principal men of the nation are disposed to live at peace with the whites, but a large majority of the 'palados,' or men of less influence are not so disposed, and are frequently committing small depredations upon the herds of our people." [5]

An unusually dry spring combined with other factors precipitated an ugly confrontation that in some ways may be regarded as a rehearsal for,

4. Waldrip 1953, p. 274.
5. May 26, 1857: Collins to Denver, NA, NMS 234-548.

or prophetic warning of, the incident that ultimately plunged the Navajo nation into warfare with the whites. In disregard of the agreement made by Kendrick and Dodge the previous November with El Gordo, Navajos in June moved large numbers of their livestock onto the reserved grazing grounds north of Fort Defiance. A withering drought that left lower pasturage bare was the immediate cause for this, but no doubt there were other reasons. Perhaps the Navajos who moved in on the grass of Cañon del Trigo and La Joya questioned the right of Gordo to bargain away their land. Possibly, too, they found nothing in the weakened garrison and its hard-drinking new commander to deter them. In any case, the Gordo pact of the previous November 7 was ignored.

If Major Gordon's sobriety at the moment might be assumed, the wisdom of his action is open to serious question. He ordered Lieutenant Carlisle to proceed to the grazing grounds at once, remove the animals, and drive off any Indians found there. To accomplish this, the lieutenant was permitted to take thirty men and a battery of field guns. Carlisle's courage had been demonstrated before, but this time he had been ordered to do the impossible. Word of his mission inevitably preceded his column. When he arrived at the grazing grounds his small detachment was confronted by what may have been as many as five hundred mounted, well-armed Navajo warriors. Obedient to his orders, Carlisle told the Navajos that they must remove their animals and withdraw.

The Navajos' exact response is not recorded, although Superintendent Collins later was informed that "They stated . . . that they had lost their agent [Henry Dodge] and Military commandant, Mjr Kendrick, and that they care for no one else."

When their attitude became threatening and it was clear they were about to attack, Carlisle turned his column about and "was able to make good his retreat to the fort." [6] Collins doubted if the time was propitious for a major campaign against the Navajos, but on the following day he informed Commissioner Denver that marauding Indians had caused the territory trouble enough. "I feel an ambition to reduce these tribes to subjection," he wrote, "and have no doubt of success if the proper measures are adopted." [7]

This debacle, following so soon upon Major Kendrick's departure, emphasized the critical condition into which Fort Defiance had fallen.

6. Ibid., June 29, 1857.
7. Ibid., June 30, 1857.

Although Bonneville was still busily engaged against the Apaches, General Garland felt the situation was serious enough to warrant reducing Bonneville's command by one-third; he accordingly ordered Colonel William Wing Loring's column of 300 troops, then somewhere west of the Mogollon Mountains, to move in support of Fort Defiance. In the meantime, he directed that Company G, Third Infantry, march at once for Navajo country from its station at Cantonment Burgwin, near Taos. As these orders were being put into execution, Major Gordon reported himself sick and relinquished command of the Defiance garrison to Lieutenant Carlisle. Gordon remained indisposed for two weeks but was well enough to resume command July 19—the same day, by coincidence, that Lieutenant Henry B. Clitz reached the fort with Company G after a dusty march of more than three hundred miles. His contingent of 50 men raised the garrison's strength to 145 troops present for duty.

Colonel Loring was believed to be on or near the Gila when instructions supplementing earlier special orders were dispatched, directing him to take command of Fort Defiance upon his arrival there. Further, he would "inform [himself] of the temper and disposition of the Indians, and give them distinctly to understand that trespassing upon our grazing grounds, as established by treaty will not be tolerated—that if they continue to do so, they will not only be driven off by force of arms, but that we will retaliate upon them by taking possession of their wheat and corn fields." [8] He was advised that a copy of the Laguna Negra treaty was on file at the fort together with instructions given at various times to Major Kendrick, and upon the basis of this information he should determine his course of action. General Garland either forgot or overlooked the fact that the treaty had not been ratified.

As before, the arrival of fresh troops at Fort Defiance almost at once had a calming effect. Any warlike sentiment that may have survived the appearance of Clitz's infantry evaporated entirely on August 25 when Colonel Loring bivouacked his veterans of the Apache campaign in the valley directly south of the post. Loring immediately relieved Major Gordon of command and brought the garrison to full strength by assigning the only barracks remaining unoccupied to Major Shepherd's Company B, Third Infantry, and a small detachment of Company E of the same regiment. As quarters could not be provided for the balance of his column, Loring established a tent camp near the fort. Troops thus

8. July 1, 1857: Nichols, Santa Fe, to Loring, NA, RAC, RG 393, LS.

sheltered under canvas made up Companies A and I and detachments of Companies C and D, Mounted Rifles. At no time in its previous six years had Fort Defiance harbored such sprawling strength.[9]

This force was still building when Zarcillos Largos, who may have reflected the attitude of older headmen of the tribe, brought to the post and turned over eight mules, stolen some weeks before by a brother of Delgadito. More clearly than words his action demonstrated a new veering of the war vane.

Other harbingers of hopeful promise appeared at the same time. A sizable quantity of Indian goods purchased at St. Louis (the bulk of the shipment being allotted to the Navajos) was received in Santa Fe, and Collins was informed that the vacant post of Navajo agent had been filled with the appointment of William R. Harley, a native of Hernando, Mississippi. Of Harley's qualifications nothing was known or said and no more could be guessed until this gentleman should arrive in the territory.

Colonel Loring, meanwhile, found that the general disposition of Navajos he talked with was for peace. This, too, was the attitude of Manuelito, who impressed Loring as being the most influential of the tribe's headmen. There was no talk of white eyes when Manuelito visited him at the post; on the contrary, Manuelito gave assurances of his desire to remain friendly with the Bilagáana. He promised that the soldiers should have free use of the grazing grounds that he claimed as his own—the place long known to the garrison as Ewell's Hay Camp—and he said he would use his influence with Zarcillos Largos, Gordo, and other headmen to secure for the post similar use of La Joya grazing grounds.[10] But some note of uncertainty in Manuelito's reference to

9. Post Returns for August 1857 show 5 officers and 180 men of the garrison present for duty. Two officers and RMR troops of the attached tent camp brought the total strength to about 435. Prior to this time the former peak strength (295) was in September 1851, when the post was established. After averaging about 150 troops present—rarely more than 200 or fewer than 100—the garrison reached its lowest point (89) in June 1857.

10. August 31, 1857: Loring to Nichols, NA, RAC, RG 393, L-34-1857, LR. Ewell's Hay Camp, at an elevation of 7,200 feet, was two miles southwest of Laguna Negra. The name is traced to a similar critical lack of pasturage in November 1851, when Maj. Electus Backus reported that Capt. Richard Ewell "is now at Laguna (12 miles north) grazing the animals of both companies" of dragoons. La Joya meadows, in highlands to the west, were described in February 1853 by Maj. Kendrick as "ten miles to the north of the Post." Capt. Henry B. Schroeder's 1859 map of Navajo country traversed by his command shows La Joya south and to the west of Laguna Negra, reached by a left fork of the Laguna Negra road—in meadow-lands just south of present Sawmill.

La Joya made Loring wonder if other headmen would agree as easily to letting it go.

Manuelito explained that the withering drought had forced his people to seek grass for their herds wherever they could find it, so they had moved back to the grazing grounds reserved for the fort. This, Loring believed, in addition to the weakness of the Defiance garrison, was the cause of all the trouble. He believed that Manuelito's promises were made in all sincerity, but to ensure pasturage for the several hundred horses of his command he directed two of the rifle companies to move north to Ewell's Hay Camp and another company into camp at Cienega Amarilla, while the fourth remained close to the post.

Informed previously by General Garland that he might withdraw his command as soon as the Navajos agreed to surrender the disputed grazing lands, Colonel Loring decided early in September that his objective had been accomplished. He had talked with Zarcillos Largos, Manuelito, Gordo, and Ish-kit-sa-ne, and all in the most friendly way had assured him that the post's rights to grazing lands would be respected in the future. In his conversations with them he had become convinced that the unexpected appearance of his large command had alarmed the Navajos and persuaded them to take a more friendly course. Their attitude made him believe he could safely reduce the size of the Defiance garrison, but he would send the mounted rifle companies away one at a time, so that their withdrawal would not appear too sudden.[11]

The withdrawal, which the Navajos of course noticed at once, began September 11 with the departure of Company C, Rifles, and a detachment of Company E, Third Infantry. Three days later, Rifle Companies A and I marched away, followed on September 16 by Company D. Colonel Loring himself left Fort Defiance the next day, hopefully turning over command of the garrison to Lieutenant Clitz. Major Gordon (the senior officer remaining behind) had effectively eliminated himself from command. He was now restricted to quarters—under arrest and awaiting court martial for drunkenness while on duty.

As a side effect of Major Gordon's court martial—and in anticipation of it—Gordon's Company H, Third Infantry, was withdrawn from Fort Defiance in October, and was replaced by Company I, Mounted Rifles, commanded by Brevet Captain John P. Hatch. The transfer was an astonishing example of bungling. Riflemen of Company I had scarcely reached Fort Union after their withdrawal from Defiance in September when they were ordered back again. Worn down by the Apache cam-

11. September 2, 1857: Loring to Nichols, NA, RAC, RG 393, L-38-1857, LR.

paign, horses of the company were rendered even more unfit for service by the march of seven hundred miles to Fort Union and back. And at Fort Defiance, as General Garland had every reason to know, there was hardly enough forage to sustain the animals already attached to the garrison. Upon the rifle company's return it was found that fewer than one-half of the unit's horses were serviceable.

Major Gordon's record of insobriety was so thoroughly established that it surprised no one, when he appeared before a board of officers in Santa Fe, that he was cashiered from the service—a sentence later reduced to suspension from rank and pay while serving six months in confinement. Changes in the military position resulting from Gordon's removal were not reflected at once in the Navajos' actions. For a few months more, as new policies slowly evolved with the appearance of strange new faces, the Navajos engaged once more, briefly, in defense against Ute raiders while remaining watchfully at peace with the whites.

Lieutenant Clitz, although young, had the benefit of a level head and one month's experience during the previous fall in command of Fort Union. Now he was confronted with a harsh reality of nature and the fact that Colonel Loring, whatever his other endowments, was not a rainmaker.

During the colonel's presence at Fort Defiance and after his departure, the skies remained brassily dry. At the end of September, with some alarm, Clitz noted the withering of grass at even La Joya and Laguna Negra. Some meager pasturage remained in the vicinity of the fort, but that was all. Two hundred tons of hay were laid in for the winter, but this was reserve supply and not for now. More acutely and directly concerned than himself, Navajos were offering to sell their sheep—in any quantity—at one dollar to one dollar and a half a head. In the present emergency, Clitz was forced to send the post beef herd far eastward to poor but mainly unused valley pasturage between Agua Azul and the Gallo. Even this could sustain the herd for no more than a few weeks, and Clitz earnestly asked headquarters to take the cattle off his hands.[12]

James Collins had an opportunity to measure the effects of the drought when he traveled to Fort Defiance in October. He was accompanied by William Harley, the new agent, whose every action the Navajos were to observe critically and inevitably compare against their brightening memory of Henry Dodge. Twenty-five hundred Navajos who gathered at the post were happily inclined toward a favorable first impression when Harley proceeded at once to distribute nearly four

12. September 26, 1857: Clitz to Nichols, NA, RAC, RG 393, C-22-1857, LR.

thousand dollars worth of annuity goods that he and Collins had brought out by wagon from Santa Fe. The presents included the usual bolts of cloth, indigo, knives, and farming tools—and notably, this time, as a result of Dodge's interest in fostering this skill, a number of blacksmith tools and 484 pounds of iron to be forged and hammered down by Navajos apprenticed in the blacksmith's trade.[13]

All of the principal headmen were present at the gathering. When Collins mentioned to them Kendrick's proposal that a few of their number make a tour of the States, the headmen agreeably but without much enthusiasm said they would be willing to send a delegation. (Collins may have pressed the matter further when he visited Washington in December, but the plan languished; it would not be revived again for seventeen years.) The headmen expressed their wish to remain at peace and assured Collins that it pleased them to have an agent in their midst once again. Harley, who had found quarters at the post, remained behind when Collins departed for Santa Fe.

From all appearances his trip had turned out unusually well, but the superintendent was troubled throughout his return journey by a nagging worry. The Navajo corn crop of the past summer had been nearly a complete failure; their livestock were wasted down by drought, and the Navajos themselves, or many of them, were gaunt with hunger. As he traveled eastward through the dry country Collins weighed the possibility that starvation would drive Navajos back to raiding, weighed this against the expense of sending out supplies of food, and in the end decided that it would be best to do nothing.

Two weeks after his return to Santa Fe Collins was off again, this time for the East, and was not available when another matter requiring decision was addressed to his office. The question was posed in an appeal directed to Lieutenant Clitz by a delegation of Coyotero Apaches through the medium of their agent, Michael Steck. The Apaches asked the commander of Fort Defiance to intervene in their behalf to secure the release of fifteen Coyoteros taken captive during the Bonneville campaign by Sandoval's Diné Ana'aii and held since as slaves by those people. Lieutenant Clitz referred the appeal to department headquarters, where General Garland relayed it to Superintendent Collins.[14] Already nine days out on the stage for Missouri, Collins was

13. June 4, 1857: Invoice of Walker & Chick, Kansas City merchants, NA, NMS T21-4; and October 31, 1857: Collins to Denver, NA, NMS 234-548. This is the first known specific order of blacksmith tools and iron for the Navajos.
14. November 8, 1857: Clitz to Nichols, with two enclosures, NA, NMS T21-3. Garland's endorsement on Clitz's letter, dated November 23, reads: "It is im-

well beyond reach. No further reference to Sandoval's captives has been found, and their eventual fate is unknown.

Sandoval, curiously enough, was at the same time calling on Colonel Bonneville in Albuquerque for assistance in securing the release of five Diné Ana'aii youths and one woman seized by Utes while Sandoval and his warriors were away on the Apache campaign. In forwarding this information to General Garland, Bonneville frankly expressed sympathy for the Diné Ana'aii leader.

Referring to Sandoval as a chief of the Navajos, Bonneville noted with care that he did not wish to be misunderstood. At least since General Kearny's time Sandoval and his people had joined American troops in campaigns against the Navajos, he pointed out. Sandoval had given him substantial aid during the Apache campaign, he always could be counted upon—even to war on hostile Navajos—and for this Navajos "now look upon Sandoval and his band of 100 warriors not only with jealousy, but even with hate." Bonneville regarded the Diné Ana'aii as no longer a part of the Navajo nation and thus as Indians without an agent. He recommended that they receive particular consideration from the United States "as the only tribe that has never failed us . . . when called upon." [15]

At Fort Defiance, meanwhile, Lieutenant Clitz relinquished his command on November 26 to Brevet Major William T. H. Brooks, who might best and most briefly be described as nearly the perfect opposite of Major Kendrick. Once favorably regarded by Colonel Sumner, Brooks had held command of Fort Union for a few months in 1852, being called from that post to command the Fort Marcy garrison at Santa Fe. He had been stationed in or about the capital ever since. There had been little chance for him to learn anything of the Navajos or of their country.

From the capital's relative quiet—and his own obscurity—Major Brooks had emerged once, long enough to propose that Henry Dodge was a Navajo lover and a liar. The affair, which had all of the substance if not the ferocity of Colonel Sumner's quarrels with Calhoun and Lane, had occurred three years earlier when Dodge brought a delegation of Navajos to Santa Fe. Brooks had detected a U.S. brand on the

portant that the Coyoteros get back their people taken in the campaign and the subject is therefore referred to the Supt. of Indian Affairs." Collins left Santa Fe November 15.

15. November 24, 1857: Bonneville to Nichols, NA, RAC, RG 393, B-43-1857, LR.

rump of a Navajo's mule and was about to reclaim the animal when Dodge advised him to back off, explaining at the same time that the mule was one of several captured by Navajos during Colonel Washington's campaign. He and Major Kendrick had long known of this and regarded the mules, by custom, if not precisely by the Articles of War, as rightfully the Navajos' property. Brooks challenged the truth of Dodge's explanation but allowed the matter to drop when Major Kendrick assured the department commander that Dodge's story not only was true but in resisting Brooks's effort to seize the mule Dodge had his complete support.[16]

A native of Ohio, Brooks ranked low scholastically when he was graduated in 1841 from West Point, but he was twice brevetted for gallantry and meritorious conduct during the Mexican War. A photograph of him at about this time reveals a handsome high-domed forehead, the features in profile a bit ambiguous behind a luxuriant dark beard. His arrival at Fort Defiance, accompanied by a detachment of forty-seven recruits and his personal servant, a black slave named Jim, might fairly be termed the final and fateful turning point in relations with the Navajo nation. Not at all at once, but by a process of blunder compounded by erosion of communication and understanding, all of the positive accomplishments of Major Kendrick and Henry Dodge were wiped away. Four days after assuming command, Brooks advised department headquarters,

"So far as I am able to discover, everything pertaining to the discipline of the command is in good order, and the Indians in the Nation are generally quiet—Some complaints have been heard of petty depredations on the frontier towns, to the effect of stealing some provisions, Corn &c, induced I have no doubt by the almost starving condition of the tribe." [17]

The drought of 1857 was one of the worst in memory. Two weeks after the year's end Major Brooks was directed to send all but fifteen of the rifle company horses, and all but four of the garrison's wagon teams, to Albuquerque where forage still was obtainable. The savage spectre of starvation, that in the end would defeat the Navajo nation, was about to drive the young and reckless element, who followed Manuelito, over the edge and into war.

16. August 28, 1854: Brooks to Easton, NA, RAC, RG 393, B-60-1854, LR; and September 9, 1854: Kendrick to Nichols, NA, RAC RG 393, K-12-1854, LR.

17. November 30, 1857: Brooks to Nichols, NA, RAC, RG 393, B-45-1857, LR.

18

The Alienation of Manuelito

Agent William Harley found the winter climate of New Mexico Territory rather more, and less, than he had bargained for. A map he had consulted before leaving home for this bleak wilderness showed Albuquerque to be almost within the same latitude as his native Hernando; what his map did not show was the more than mile-high difference in elevation between Fort Defiance and Hernando. If he had hoped to enjoy again the scent of magnolia blossoms borne on zephyrs, he was sorely disappointed. From early November, one snowstorm followed hard upon another. Blasts of polar air howling through Cañoncito Bonito left the Mississippian with knees knocking and teeth chattering, yet he wanly assured Superintendent Collins that "My health is tolerably good considering . . ." and that "[I] only regret that I have nothing new or interesting to communicate, [because] at this isolated point news is a rare thing."

Although to Harley the news was not interesting, Navajo headmen had complained of bothersome raids by Utes who had used the powder and lead given to them at their Abiquiu agency not for hunting game, as it had been intended, but for shooting Navajos. Hungry Navajos who had plundered a Zuni cornfield had been roughly handled by the Pueblos—one Navajo woman left dead and her companions' horses captured—but this little dispute had been settled with mutual reparations, as had a similar disturbance at one of the Hopi villages.

Some Navajos had expressed their gratitude for blacksmith tools he had given to them in October, but Harley found the headmen "when visiting the agency expect to be treated as they were by Capt Dodge— that is, to sleep and eat with the agent," and that was more than Harley was willing or able to do. Major Brooks, as a matter of fact, was so chary in supplying him with food from army stores that Harley thought it likely he would have to move the Navajo agency to Albuquerque or

Santa Fe.[1] Late in January 1858 he did appear in Santa Fe long enough to draw a draft upon Collins for a bit more than one thousand dollars before boarding the next stagecoach traveling east.[2]

James Collins was still in Washington at the time, but the defection of the agent probably did not go unnoticed by Samuel M. Yost, who was serving in the dual role of editor of Collins's *Gazette* and acting superintendent of Indian affairs. Yost, a Texan, previously had been editor of the Staunton, Virginia, *Vindicator* and later, in Lexington, Missouri, of the *Expositor*. This background, weighed in consideration with his political battle scars as a proslavery Democrat, no doubt had appealed to Collins when Yost arrived in Santa Fe the previous fall, tubercular but aggressively self-confident and looking for work.[3] As bluntly outspoken as his publisher, often hot-tempered, Yost became the *Gazette's* editor in November 1857.

The crisis occasioned by Harley's departure, if crisis is not too strong a term, was overshadowed almost at once by word of the murder of an old Mexican committed by seven young Navajos in the vicinity of Jemez during the first week of February. John Ward, sent out by the superintendency in Santa Fe as a special agent to investigate the affair, returned five days later accompanied by some thirty headmen of the Navajo tribe as well as by Sandoval and possibly other members of the Diné Ana'aii. Ward explained that he quite unexpectedly had met this imposing delegation on his way to Jemez; the Navajos, who were traveling to Santa Fe to sue for peace with the Utes and express "their grievances and wants and to ask for aid and counsel," had waited for him to return, possibly at Santo Domingo, and then accompanied him to the capital.[4]

Grievances of the headmen centered on the episode at Zuni so tersely

1. January 1, 1858: Harley to Collins, with two enclosures, NA, NMS T21-3. Ute raids on Navajos continued, Maj. Brooks reporting that in January 40 Utes "evidently from the Great Salt Lake" came as far as Canyon de Chelly "and there killed Pelon, a chief of considerable property."

2. Nothing more was heard from Harley until the following August 30 when, from the town of Wall Hill, Mississippi, he notified Secretary of the Interior Jacob Thompson of his resignation, effective June 30, 1858.

3. Ganaway 1943, p. 235.

4. February 14, 1858: Acting Superintendent Yost to C.I.A. Mix, NA, NMS 234-549. Yost's version of Ward's report indicates the Navajos killed the man without provocation after persuading him to give them some food. Villagers (of San Ysidro?) organized in pursuit but they were left afoot when the Navajos entered their camp that night and drove off their horses and mules. These animals the marauders soon afterward surrendered to another party of Navajos—presumably those met by Ward—and they were restored to their owners.

related by Agent Harley and on the more recent murder of two Diné Ana'aii, one of them a sixteen-year-old niece of Sandoval. Three or four people of his band (including the girl) had gone to Albuquerque about a week before and there had sold a captive girl to a man named Wheeler for $150. Their afternoon had been spent enjoying this sudden wealth in the chance company of some New Mexicans, evidently met with in one of the town's bars. Still in a festive mood, as during the day "liquor was used pretty freely," the Diné Ana'aii had started for home in night's early darkness. Sandoval's niece and one of the men of the party had been wading across the Rio Grande when at midstream they were overtaken by several of the New Mexicans and instantly stabbed to death. When the bodies were recovered from the water that of the man was found to have been pierced in nine places by a knife, and fifty dollars had been stolen from his person. A companion of the murdered pair, more fortunate, was expected to survive; he had managed to ride his horse across the river before one of the thugs caught up with him, clubbed him on the head from behind, and left him sprawled senseless on the riverbank.

Sandoval's demand that he receive payment for his niece's death was countered with assurances that he probably found unsatisfactory. The principal assailant, he was informed by Yost, had been arrested and awaited trial in the Bernalillo County jail. Some of the stolen money had been found in his pockets and his clothing had been covered with blood. Yost did not name him, but said the prisoner previously had been regarded as a respectable citizen. If his promise that the man would stand trial and be punished was not enough, Yost told the Diné Ana'aii leader, the circumstances would be reported to Washington where possibly, in view of Sandoval's record as a steadfast friend of the Americans, some indemnification might be agreed upon.

More important to the Navajos than these past grievances was their concern over consistent and repeated attacks by Utes. The drought of the previous year having reduced many of them nearly to starvation, they could not survive another cropless year without raiding the property of the whites. This they explained to Yost as forcefully as they could, saying that a continuation of warfare by Utes would, for the Navajos, be disastrous as their best planting grounds were close to the borders of Ute country and would lie fallow in the coming spring unless Ute raids ceased.

"They are earnestly solicitous for peace," Yost observed, "and confidently expect it will be brought about." How this was to be accomplished was another matter. A policy lately enunciated in Washington advised that tribes remaining hostile to the government should be encouraged to make war upon each other.[5] Yost therefore told the Navajos that he would discuss their proposal with General Garland, and that if he and the department commander should agree that peace between the two tribes was "desirable at this time," Agents Kit Carson and Diego Archuleta would be summoned to Santa Fe with some of the principal Utes of the Moache and Capote bands. In the meantime, he would send John Ward as a special agent to Navajo country in an effort to alleviate the conditions of hunger, but "in a judicious and economical manner."

Garland was agreeable to the plan of bringing the tribes together; as the Navajos lingered in Santa Fe word was sent to the Ute agencies at Abiquiu and Taos advising the agents that a peace council was to be held. Diego Archuleta, who was seldom to be found at his Abiquiu agency, did not respond. Kit Carson replied that he had spoken with some of the head warriors of the Moaches at Taos and that although "they have no particular desire to make peace," they were willing to come in. Judging from their attitude, Carson believed that "even if peace is made it will not be of long duration." [6]

Carson's pessimism was well founded. Although he was not invited to attend, Governor Rencher understood that both tribes were well represented when peace talks were held on March 11, but that an air of mutual mistrust and hostility continued throughout the meeting. The council lasted all day and well into the night. Early the next morning the Utes departed, declaring they would make no treaty of peace because the Navajos would not observe it in good faith.[7] Rencher believed there was a strong possibility that the territory was on the verge of an Indian war, an eventuality which he thought would greatly aggravate the suffering of the Indians, especially the Navajos who already during the past winter had suffered much from famine. He advised Secretary of State Lewis Cass that Navajos were the most numerous of the tribes,

5. "Should you fail in your efforts to keep the Indians in a state of peace and quiet, then your aim should be to array them against such other Indians as may be found on the side of the enemies of the Government. . . . The object of the Government is to keep them quiet if possible, but if that cannot be done, then control them in such a manner as to direct their attacks upon those savages who may take up arms against our people" (November 24, 1857: C.I.A. Denver to Collins, NA, NMS T21-3).

6. February 28, 1858: Carson to Yost, NA, NMS T21-1.

7. March 13, 1858: Rencher to Secretary of State Cass, NA, no. 5483, Territorial Papers (hereafter, TP), T-17, roll 1.

but Utes were said to be the most warlike, being well provided with rifles, which they handled with skill.

Kit Carson took a more pragmatic view of the peace council's failure, suggesting that in prosecuting their war against the Navajos, the Utes—to their own ultimate advantage—would be so preoccupied that they would not join with the Mormons in hostilities against the government.[8] In any case, he informed Yost upon returning to Taos, the Utes really had no desire to make peace. They said the Navajos, while asking for peace, at the same time were stealing stock, murdering people in the settlements, and raiding into Ute country.

An incident that occurred about one week before the peace council met explains in part the Ute taunt and at the same time illustrates the aggressive relationship between the two tribes. At almost any other time the Utes would not have considered it their affair, but when a small party of Navajos descended upon Abiquiu and drove off two thousand sheep, forty Ute warriors volunteered at once to accompany some New Mexicans in pursuit. When he was informed of this, Major Brooks expressed surprise—but for the wrong reason. The news was startling, he wrote from Fort Defiance, "for the dread, exhibited by the Navajoes, of the Utahs would make it seem impossible that they would venture so near the Utah country." Having been stationed so long at Santa Fe, Major Brooks should have known that Navajos—as peaceful visitors or as raiders—were no strangers to Abiquiu. He might have known as well that it was not the Utes alone that Navajos feared, but a reported combination of forces that the Navajos believed was forming against them.

John Ward expressed more indignation than surprise when he learned the outcome of this affair. Engaged as he was upon his duties as special Navajo agent, Ward discovered that the pursuing party of Utes and New Mexicans had soon abandoned the trail left by the marauders and the stolen sheep—a trail so broad a child could have followed it—and instead had stalked and fallen upon an unsuspecting camp of Navajos who, Ward said, "had *nothing* to do with the robbery and who were at peace with the whites." Without warning, the Abiquiu avengers with

8. March 31, 1858: Carson to Yost, NA, NMS T21-1. Brigham Young's proposals that Mormon colonies of Utah Territory declare themselves independent of the United States so disturbed the seat of government in Washington that Bvt. Brig. Gen. Albert Sidney Johnston in 1857 was ordered with a small army to the trouble area. Often prejudiced and nearly always exaggerated accounts of the time built a Western myth of Mormon efforts to draw Navajos and Utes into war against the United States. It was to this that Carson referred. At the time he wrote, Johnston's army was quietly based at Camp Floyd, south of Salt Lake City.

their Ute allies killed five Navajos of this party, took two or three captives, and seized a number of animals. The captives later were sold to
New Mexicans. Ward pointed out that under such circumstances Yost
could imagine how the Navajos felt at the time of the peace council.[9]

Whether their feeling was justified or not, Ward found the Navajos
nearest the eastern frontier in great fear of impending invasion. Since
his assignment as special agent late in February he had talked with Indians at Jemez and with villagers of Cebolleta and Cubero and then
had visited two bands of Navajos. He found them excited and fearful
over a rumored expedition that was to be made against them by Utes,
Pueblos, and whites. The season for planting their fields was nearly
over but the seed was not in, and in their anxiety many of the Navajos
had abandoned their homes and fled.

At Cubero he was told that Indians of Jemez, Zia, Santa Ana, and
Laguna—who expected to be joined by Utes—were banding together
at Laguna and within three days would advance into Navajo country.
Ward immediately proceeded to Laguna; upon arriving there he found
evidence that the report was true.

What they proposed to do, Ward warned the people of Laguna,
would be considered by the government as unlawful, and they would
be held responsible for their actions. How well he succeeded in dis-
suading the Pueblos, Ward was not sure; if the planned foray in fact
was made, no report of it reached military or civilian authorities. At
the time of writing, Ward was in Albuquerque negotiating with Dr.
Henry Connelly for the purchase and shipment of corn to the Navajos.
As soon as this business was attended to he expected to leave again for
Navajo country, perhaps to go as far as Fort Defiance.

Sandoval and the Diné Ana'aii do not appear to have been threatened during the reported Pueblo-Ute alliance. The Diné Ana'aii had
moved to camps in the vicinity of Laguna, Ward observed; he added
that Sandoval "has always been our friend, even against his own people who have, therefore, expelled him from among the *real* Navajos."

From the remote vantage point of today it is difficult to determine
what the true state of affairs was at that time. After a year of crop
failure and intense hunger, and after four months of intermittent warfare with enemy Utes, the Navajo nation may have appeared weakened
enough to invite attack by allied enemy forces. A large segment of the

9. April 9, 1858: Ward to Yost, NA, NMS T21-3. The Abiquiu raiders later
were identified as six Navajos of Fuentes Azul's band, who were said to have driven
the sheep to the vicinity of Canyon de Chelly.

Navajo people, at least, was convinced that an alliance of whites with Indians living to the north and east of them threatened to do them great harm.

After the death of Henry Dodge and the departure of Major Kendrick, little information of a reliable nature had come out of Fort Defiance; the first four months of Major Brooks's command reveal almost nothing of conditions at that outpost, outside of slight evidence that relations with the tribe had continued to deteriorate.

Early in April 1858, Major Brooks first admitted that all was not well, and that the disposition of the Navajos was "not of a satisfactory kind." He found it hard to determine exactly what the trouble was, he said, but Manuelito's dissaffection would seem to have been at the root of it. Although his rancheria was a scant twenty miles from the fort, Manuelito had waited until the middle of March before he came in, "whilst passing as it were," to introduce himself to the military commander.

Their first meeting, if not unfriendly, had been cool. When the talk turned to the haying grounds, Manuelito said the Navajos would keep their animals off the southern section of Ewell's Camp, and Brooks, who was not then familiar with the locality, replied only that he would expect to have the use of all the ground that Major Kendrick had claimed. Manuelito repeated what he had said before, and at their parting he agreed to return in two weeks for a distribution of farm tools that had been left there by Agent Harley.[10]

In limiting the areas of Ewell's Camp, Manuelito had said the Navajos would respect the government's claim to grasslands "below the spring"—possibly a reference to the spring in the north central portion of the meadows and east of Sterrett Mesa. His curiosity finally aroused, Major Brooks ventured out to the meadows in question and learned that it was Manuelito's purpose to retain nearly half of the haying grounds formerly mowed by Major Kendrick. His reaction upon discovering this is partly conjectural, but there is some reason to believe that an angry confrontation occurred and that it was serious enough to cause his final break with Manuelito. A few days before the date set for the distribution of farm tools, one of the headmen appeared at the fort with a small entourage and handed to Major Brooks the cane and medal of office presented to Manuelito three years before by Governor Meriwether. Some "trivial reason," Brooks noted, was given

10. April 4, 1858: Brooks to Nichols, NA, RAC, RG 393, B-20-1858, LR.

in explanation of Manuelito's action, an excuse to the effect that these symbols of tribal leadership no longer were respected by New Mexicans or Pueblos—or even by Navajos.

With haughty petulance Major Brooks refused to accept the cane and medal, ordering the headman to take them back and say that if Manuelito wished to give them up he should not send them by unimportant messengers but should come in himself. The insignia of office were not carried away but were left in the care of Juan Anaya, and nothing whatever was heard from Manuelito.

The major's insulting treatment soon afterward of Zarcillos Largos was pointed enough, if not as damaging. At the end of March, Brooks noted, some three or four hundred Navajos ("mostly the pelados of the tribe") appeared at Fort Defiance to receive the promised hoes and spades. Navajo headmen were noticeably absent, but before the last of the Indians had departed a few did come in. These included Zarcillos Largos and the son of Juanico (Hijo de Juanico), neither of whom Brooks had met before, although of the former he had of course heard a great deal. Informed that the aging leader of the Navajos had come to his post, Major Brooks did not attempt to welcome him but remained in his quarters because, as he explained later, "I thought it best not to exhibit any desire, until he made some advance, and he left without doing so."

The strength of the Fort Defiance garrison, so often in the past a reliable barometer of Navajo relations, was nearly at peak level, Brooks having at his disposal two companies of Third Infantry and one company of Mounted Riflemen, a complement of 205 officers and men present for duty. Nine more were on sick report and six were held in arrest. And, a remarkable fact, only four of the rifle company's sixty-one horses were deemed unserviceable.

Events of the preceding few weeks had had an unsettling effect, however, and Major Brooks felt that his position was precarious. Having alienated Manuelito and insulted Zarcillos Largos, and having carefully avoided anything that might appear to be a friendly overture to the other headmen, Major Brooks was so nervously uncertain of the temper of the Navajos that he urgently requested General Garland to allow him one more company of troops. General Garland failed to share the major's alarm. Threatened as they were by Utes on the north, Pueblos on the east, and Apaches on the south, he thought the Navajos would remain friendly with the whites and should be regarded as friendly by them. As for the matter of sending out reinforcements, other demands on him made this utterly impossible.[11]

No better barometer of the garrison's queasy state of mind could be found than a curious incident that occurred at this time. Brevet Captain John Hatch was a seasoned officer who already had won one citation for bravery, but upon his return to post after a search for stolen sheep it was apparent to everyone, including himself, that he had been spooked.

The sheep were part of two large flocks said to have been driven off from the Rio Abajo, possibly numbering six hundred, and last reported near Calites Canyon. To intercept them, Captain Hatch had marched to the Cienega Amarilla with thirteen riflemen of Company I; from there they took the western slope into high forested country, on the trail leading toward the Pueblo Colorado Wash and the Hopi villages. Juan Anaya, who had served Henry Dodge and Major Kendrick so faithfully, and the headman called Herrero, or Blacksmith, rode with Hatch as guides. In the tall pines above the cienega they encountered Manuelito and a few of his people, who at once turned over to Hatch more than one hundred of the stolen animals. With three Navajos to herd and guard them, these were sent back to the cienega. More of the Rio Abajo flocks would be found a few miles further on, Hatch was told.

Nothing Manuelito had done was other than friendly, but by Hatch's frank admission it was at this point that the palms of his hands began to sweat. Fearing that some sort of treachery was planned, he ordered the Navajos, who now numbered about twenty-five, to proceed in advance of his party. As they rode on into the forest his apprehensions were heightened when Manuelito turned south off the trail, saying that he would find Zarcillos Largos and perhaps more sheep a short distance beyond. Soon afterward they came upon the old war leader at a place in the pines where, with perhaps fifty or sixty Navajos, he seemed to be waiting for Hatch. Faces of Manuelito's people were recognized among the warriors ringed about Zarcillos Largos.

During the entire march Hatch was so distrustful of Manuelito's assurances of good faith that he ordered his men to be prepared for a surprise attack, their rifles drawn from saddle boots and ready for use. On halting, the troops were directed to dismount and form lines to the front and flanks of their horses. The response of Zarcillos Largos to

11. April 26, 1858: Nichols to Brooks, NA, RAC, RG 393, LS.

this battle formation was impassively mild; if Hatch and his soldiers would remain where they were, the old man said, he would attempt to recover the sheep still missing. With that, he and the Navajos rode off and were gone for nearly half an hour.

Upon their return Captain Hatch was informed that most of the remainder of the sheep had been scattered among the tribe. A few others had been killed after the Navajo captors were warned that soldiers were coming to collect them. Concluding that it would only endanger his small command if he pressed on, Hatch ordered his men to withdraw, returning to Fort Defiance with 117 sheep and goats previously left at Cienega Amarilla. After his first meeting with Manuelito, Hatch said he was sure the Navajos wanted only to decoy him deeper into the forest—"in the hope that I might be thrown off my guard, and a successful attack be made upon my command."

Major Brooks received Hatch's report with mixed feelings. He doubted that Manuelito and Zarcillos Largos had meditated treachery. In the next moment, and nervously, he admitted that Captain Hatch knew more about these Indians than he did and that he, in fact, was in great doubt as to what the Navajos might do next. The Navajos, he decided, were "at a sort of turning point." [12]

The turning point, when it did come late in May, was the beginning of an ultimate breakdown in relations, the cause of eight years of warfare that ended only with the tribe's surrender and finally with Manuelito's bitter acceptance of captivity at Bosque Redondo. His role was equally important at the outset of this rupture, which grew from a flaring dispute over rights to grazing lands neighboring Laguna Negra— lands he claimed as his own, and cattle and horses, mainly his, that two riflemen on routine patrol from the fort had the temerity to drive off. Aided by men of his band, Manuelito at once drove the animals back to the pasturage; then, his people still with him, he accompanied the two troopers on their return to Fort Defiance.

Here, in another bitter confrontation, Manuelito told Major Brooks what he had said before: it was his grass the soldiers trespassed upon, his water, and his grounds; Colonel Loring had admitted Manuelito's

12. April 11, 1858: Brooks to Nichols, NA, RAC, RG 393, B-19-1858, LR, with enclosure: April 6, 1858: Hatch to Lt. William Dickinson, post adjutant. In his report to Gen. Garland, Maj. Brooks suggested that if a strong force was maintained in Navajo country, "it might be hoped to settle them in permanent residences, to puebloize them. . . ."

rights to what was known as the upper camp, between two springs, and
he would never give it up.[13] Uncertain as to what Loring may have
conceded, Major Brooks examined his file of post correspondence and
found that although Loring's report to department headquarters was
somewhat ambiguous, other papers in the post files indicated that the
garrison's grazing rights had been frequently acknowledged and grass
had been cut on the disputed land in three different seasons.

Major Brooks bluntly informed Manuelito of what he had found and
said that he would maintain the fort's grazing rights by force, if necessary. Manuelito replied that he did not want to see war made over
grass, but he would stay on the grounds even if it were at the risk of
his life. Not by alternate threat, cajolery, and bluster could Brooks
shake Manuelito from this position. The discussion ended in anger, as
it had begun, when Brooks told Manuelito and the Navajos with him
that they were no longer regarded as friends and ordered them, as
enemies, out of the fort.

After Manuelito's departure Major Brooks decided he could not ig-
nore the Navajo leader's defiance "without increasing the contempt
they appear to have for us" and encouraging the Navajos to further
acts of hostility. He accordingly ordered Captain George McLane to
march at midnight for Ewell's Camp with a detachment of two officers
and eighty-one troops. Upon arriving there, McLane was to "drive off
by force any Indian *Herds* . . . [but] in firing upon the *Herds* you will
take care not to fire upon any of the Indians, unless they fire upon you."

McLane's riflemen rested for one hour at the lower portion of the
valley and at daybreak continued for three miles until they reached the
disputed upper camp. The troops' advance could scarcely have been a
surprise; during the march forty-eight head of Manuelito's cattle were
shot down by musket and rifle fire, only a few lumbering off before
they could be hit.

At the upper camp the soldiers were engaged in killing a grazing
string of seven or eight horses when a solitary Navajo rode into range
and began shooting at the troops. Only twelve riflemen of McLane's
command were mounted. With the captain and First Sergeant Mc-
Grath at their head, these men started after the Navajo, who was now
galloping away. The pursuers had hardly started before their line was
diverted in another direction by the sudden appearance of twelve or
fifteen Navajos, all mounted on fine horses and armed with pistols or

13. May 30, 1858: Brooks to Nichols, NA, RAC RG 393, B-35-1858, LR, with
two enclosures.

rifles. A running fight ended soon after it started. McLane explained later that his horses were so exhausted that his men could not have overtaken the Navajos, unless one or two troopers managed it alone, and this he quickly checked to prevent their certain death.

One trooper's horse was killed; as far as McLane knew neither side otherwise received any injury. For three hours after the last shot was fired McLane held his position in the field and then, having carried out his orders ("the complete destruction of [Manuelito's] herd"), withdrew to Fort Defiance. With him the captain carried Manuelito's cane of symbolic leadership, which had been found by one of the troopers lying in the grass where the fighting had occurred.

Major Brooks found a certain fascination in the second reappearance of the cane, which now, like an evil omen, somehow seemed to be linked with Manuelito's behavior—which Brooks decided, was inexplicable. Only a short time after the encounter with Captain Hatch's patrol near Cienega Amarilla during which he had turned over stolen sheep, Manuelito had come to the post to reclaim the cane and his medal. He had appeared to be in a friendly, expansive mood. Grass was abundant everywhere and Brooks had understood Manuelito to say that the commandant could cut it wherever he chose. The incident at Ewell's Camp was a complete reversal of Manuelito's position. Admitting his bafflement, Major Brooks advised department headquarters that he was taking every precaution to prevent a reprisal attack upon the post herds or detached detail parties; reprisal under present circumstances might well be regarded as inevitable.

Zarcillos Largos in the meantime had come to the fort in the role of peacemaker, lamenting the shooting affray and what Brooks understood him to say was Manuelito's foolishness for trespassing on the fort's ground. When Brooks said that the time had come for the Navajos to declare whether they wanted war or peace, Zarcillos Largos replied that he could only speak for himself, and that he was for peace.[14]

In the two weeks that followed, Major Brooks was beset by rumors and his own doubts over what might happen next. "We still remain uncertain as to the intentions of the Navajos," he advised General Garland in June. "Thus far they have done nothing that we know of in retaliation for killing their cattle, and they have all gone off from our vicinity." [15] Some signs Brooks regarded as favorable, but more were bad. Zarcillos Largos had returned again, perhaps too willing to

14. May 31, 1858: Brooks to Nichols, NA, RAC, RG 393, B-36-1858, LR.
15. June 16, 1858: Brooks to Nichols, NA, RAC, RG 393, B-39-1858, LR.

say or agree to anything that Brooks wished to hear. If his visits to the fort were not at all what they appeared to be—if, in fact, he may only have been keeping the fort under surveillance—Brooks preferred to believe Zarcillos Largos when he said the Navajos "were satisfied with what I had done, in killing Manuelito's cattle, &c, and . . . that peace should prevail between us."

In the warm feeling that such reassurances produced, Major Brooks presented Zarcillos Largos with Manuelito's cane, saying that hereafter he would regard him as head chief of all the Navajos. Otherwise, the major had little cause for optimism. Manuelito himself pointedly stayed away. From Juan Lucero, "one of Sandoval's people" who did not stay with the Diné Ana'aii but was said to live near Washington Pass, Brooks learned that among the Navajos there were rumors that the next mail train from Santa Fe would bring orders to pay Manuelito for his cattle. There were reports as well that hundreds of Navajos were gathering at Canyon de Chelly, for what Major Brooks referred to as a war-or-peace junta but which may (in Navajo terms) have been an unseasonal Naach'id. One informant, a New Mexican captive, said that four of the principal headmen (including Hijo de Juanico and Chino) were for war at once, but most of the others talked for peace absolutely, or for peace until after the summer crops had been gathered. Although Navajos now stayed away from the disputed haying grounds, this good sign was offset by other news. The trustworthy Juan Anaya, whom Brooks believed to be "entirely in the control of Sarcillos Largos," had quietly announced his intention to quit his position as interpreter, and Brooks regarded this as not a favorable omen.[16]

The signs, as Major Brooks was able to read them, pointed to war. The surest way to prevent a long campaign against the Navajos, he advised General Garland, was to reinforce Fort Defiance at once—"to show them that we are prepared for them." If the general would send

16. This suggests that the Mexican Juan Anaya since his childhood capture was held in some form of kinship-servitude by Zarcillos Largos, but there is other evidence to the contrary. Lt. Col. D. S. Miles soon afterward observed that "This Juan is a shrewd, intelligent man, and has exercised more influence over the principal chiefs (I am told) than any other person in the country: he is the Peon (nominally) of Ierrara [Herrero], one of the richest among the Navijoes, and except only Sacillos Largos, Armijo and Manuellitta the most important man among them. This chief [Herrero] is under the complete control of Juan's brother, Terribio" (October 25, 1858: Miles to Lt. John D. Wilkins, AAAG, Santa Fe, NA, RAC, RG 393, M-74-1858, LR).

him two or three additional companies, Brooks wrote, "it would put an end to all talk about war, or indemnity for dead cattle."

Garland replied that the major's course of action had his entire approval. The Navajos should be made to understand that no payment would be given for Manuelito's cattle and horses, and the garrison at all hazards would maintain its claim to the several grazing grounds. Colonel Loring was serving with his riflemen in Utah with General Johnston's Mormon Expedition and would not return before August, but Garland would heed Brooks's appeal. Lieutenant William W. Averell with forty-nine mounted rifles of Company F were detached from service at Fort Craig and ordered to Defiance.

For several weeks more before the arrival of Averell's company, an atmosphere of calm prevailed. Zarcillos Largos came frequently to the post, each time with assurances of the Navajos' desire for peace. If reports filtering in were true, the council held at Canyon de Chelly had dissolved after general agreement was reached favoring peace, although it was said that a number of headmen who wanted war had stayed away. It was said also that Barboncito, whose people lived at Canyon de Chelly, had gone to Santa Fe to claim payment for Manuelito's animals that had been killed, and that the Navajos appeared to be waiting upon the outcome of his mission with some anxiety.[17] But there was no word at all—and this was disturbing—about Manuelito. The man who now more than any other was recognized as the leader of the Navajos, who more than any other had challenged the authority of Major Brooks, was an invisible but threatening presence, a man shrouded by his people in silence.

Juan Anaya left the fort on July 1, 1858, informing Major Brooks before his departure of renewed fighting between his people and the Utes.[18] In the quiet that had settled over the post his defection was regarded less seriously than before, Brooks commenting, "I don't know that it necessarily portends any evil."

17. June 25, 1858: Brooks to Nichols, NA, RAC, RG 393, B-41-1858, LR.
18. By Anaya's account, a party of 100 Utes late in June killed 2 Navajo warriors and took 2 women captives in an engagement at Bear Spring. Several hundred Navajos pursued the Utes into the Chusca Mountains but when the invading war party offered peace and the surrender of the captive women, the Navajos agreed readily. As the Indians were separating the Utes again opened fire, and in the ensuing fight of some hours' duration 2 of their warriors were killed. Anaya, who was present, said the Navajos sustained no loss (July 1, 1858: Brooks to Nichols, NA, RAC, RG 393, B-42-1858, LR).

Major Brooks was mistaken; trouble developed almost at once. A Navajo discovered on the post target range picking up spent bullets and musket balls was fired upon by a fort sentinel. The shot was aimed at the dirt, intended only to scare the man away. Under normal circumstances the incident might have passed unnoticed, but a haying detail sent out the same day (July 7) to establish camp at the lower approach to Cañoncito Bonito was chosen by Navajos for immediate reprisal. Eight arrows were fired that night at the haying party's tents, one arrow piercing the bed of a man supposed to be standing guard duty, another killing a dog.

Both were minor incidents and so regarded at the time. Major Brooks was willing to overlook the "insult" because no particular damage had been done and because the episode had been triggered when his sentinel fired on a Navajo. He decided that he would not complain about it to Zarcillos Largos—but he would warn him that this sort of thing had better not happen again.[19]

19. July 15, 1858: Brooks to Nichols, NA, RAC, RG 393, B-43-1858, LR.

19

Reprisal

The partially alerted garrison awaited the enactment of a drama that has often been referred to or described, perhaps never accurately, in the years since: the murderous attack on Major Brooks's personal servant, the black slave Jim, on July 12. His assailant was a Navajo, later described as being at least forty-five years old, who came to the fort ostensibly to sell two blankets.[1] The Navajo lingered for three or four hours, his presence arousing no particular interest until shortly after he had sold the blankets to a camp woman who occupied laundress quarters at the rear of one of the company barracks.

It was at about this time that Jim was first seen, about thirty yards from the major's door, walking toward the Navajo and the rear of the laundress huts. As Jim passed him the Navajo jumped upon his horse, shot an arrow into the Negro's back, and then whipped his horse into a run, escaping from the post. Major Brooks reported later that the arrow had entered Jim's back at the shoulder blades and pierced his lungs, adding,

"The boy strange to say never uttered a word or exclamation but attempted to pull the arrow out, in doing which he broke it off near the head. The head of the arrow remains in the body, the Doctor [James Cooper McKee] being unable to extract it. . . . The boy maintains, and all believe his statement, that he never did anything to the Indian, did not speak to him, and thinks he never saw him before." [2] Jim died of the wound four days later.

No one at the fort who had seen the Navajo could identify the man or recall his having been there before, although Major Brooks observed, "It is thought the Indian is not what is called a pelado—but a man of independence," and added that this might explain the hesitancy of the

1. The age of Jim's murderer was estimated by the post surgeon, J. Cooper McKee (September 9, 1858: McKee to Yost, NA, NMS 234-549).
2. July 15, 1858: Brooks to Nichols, NA, RAC, RG 393, B-43-1858, LR.

rich or influential men of the tribe to intervene or give information about him.

Zarcillos Largos, who came in at the major's bidding, was provokingly cool when Brooks demanded that the man be caught and surrendered at once. He was then on his way to Zuni and would see to it upon his return, the old warrior said, and when the major expressed impatience at the delay, Zarcillos Largos replied that Brooks ought not to be in such a hurry: it was six weeks since the major had killed Manuelito's cattle and horses, and he had done nothing yet to pay for them. Brooks responded shortly that no payment would be made to Manuelito but that if Jim's assassin were not brought in, war would be made upon the Navajo people.

The arrival of Lieutenant Averell with his company of reinforcements from Fort Craig nearly coincided with this unsatisfactory interview, but for once the appearance of fresh troops did little to ease the tension. All of the headmen except Zarcillos Largos and Herrero ignored the major's summons to come in for a talk, and when he did appear with Herrero, Zarcillos Largos gave Brooks no reason to hope the Navajos would depart from their usual custom and agree to his demands. Recalling Major Kendrick's predicament four years before after the murder of Private Hefbiner, Brooks ventured one step beyond the point Kendrick had thought it necessary, or wise, to go: he would allow the Navajos twenty days more to deliver Jim's murderer; if in twenty days the man had not been brought in, war would be declared against the tribe. The reception given this ultimatum was not encouraging.

General Garland, far distant from the scene and entirely reliant upon Brooks for his ultimate judgment of the situation, was soon informed that Brooks regarded war with the Navajos as inevitable. They had been threatened so often in the past with punishment never inflicted that threats no longer held terror for them, Brooks believed, and the time for terror had come. He recommended that a large force be put in the field as soon as possible, not later than September. Because his knowledge of the country was limited, he would not suggest routes the troops might follow, but he hoped that the Utes would be given every encouragement to continue their raids. He had no doubt that New Mexicans could be recruited as guides and spies at a very low cost if the general would hold out to them the promise of booty.

The identity of the Navajo who had killed his slave and the motive for the slaying were still uncertain, Major Brooks said, but he had re-

ceived clues that might prove helpful. His informant again was the
Diné Ana'aii Juan Lucero—"a very reliable man I think, for an Indian," who told him that "the murderer belongs to Caetanos band,
that his people say they will die before they surrender him. . . . It
seems the murderer belongs to a family of influence." [3] Lucero told
him where Cayetano's mountain rancherias might be found, but apparently neglected to inform him that Cayetano was the father of
Manuelito; Brooks, at least, did not mention this relationship, nor
did he speculate then or later upon the motive for Jim's murder.

The major once more was assured that his action had the full support of the department commander. Brooks was right in demanding
the surrender of the murderer, and he should persist in this. But he
probably was right, too, in thinking that war could not be avoided.
General Garland said he would make the necessary preparations for a
campaign at the earliest possible moment, which could be about the
first of September when several hundred fresh recruits were expected
to arrive from Fort Leavenworth. This would enable him to send quite
a respectable force against the Navajos, Garland said, but even so he
might augment it further by asking Governor Rencher for two or more
companies of volunteer militia. As for the major's proposal to encourage
the Utes to make war—it was an excellent idea. No time would be lost
in sending the Utes a supply of ammunition.[4]

At the same time, and with only one reservation, Superintendent
James Collins expressed his approval of the position taken by General
Garland and Major Brooks. He agreed that there was almost no hope
of avoiding war with the Navajos, and advised Commissioner Charles E.
Mix that apart from their difficulties with Major Brooks, the Navajos
were acting in bad faith. The outrages they inflicted almost constantly
upon the settlements were impossible to check by any admonition or
threat. As he had said before, Navajos had no respect for authority;
presents given to them as annuities they regarded cynically as bribes
for good behavior.[5] He differed from the present military policy only
in respect to Major Brooks's proposal to involve the Utes. This, he advised the commissioner, "does not meet my entire concurrence, but as
they are already at war with the Navajos, I shall make no objection."

At about the same time, Collins announced the appointment of Samuel Yost as temporary agent for the Navajos, Zunis, and Hopis, with

3. July 22, 1858: Brooks to Nichols, NA, RAC, RG 393, B-45-1858, LR.
4. July 26, 1858: Garland to Brooks, NA, RAC, RG 393, LS.
5. July 31, 1858: Collins to C.I.A. Mix, NA, NMS 234-549.

instructions that he should proceed to Fort Defiance with as little delay as possible. News of the appointment was received in bad humor by Major Brooks, who wanted no civilian meddling or interference. Shortly before, when Collins had thought it might be necessary to go personally to the trouble area (and then had changed his mind), Brooks had told him bluntly, "I think you have well decided not to come out here— although Capt Dodge was of great use to us when we had a similar difficulty in 1854, yet I conceive he was of greater use to the Indians— I think the time for talking to and advising them has passed." Learning that Yost, the editor of Collins's newspaper, was to come instead of the publisher himself, Brooks snorted, "I can see no good to be derived from this step at this time."

Before his departure from Santa Fe, Yost received detailed instructions from Collins to cooperate with Major Brooks in securing the surrender of the Negro's murderer; Collins added, in part, that upon Yost's arrival at Fort Defiance he should immediately summon the principal headmen to a council. In his meeting with them Yost was to explain that he had come to the fort as their agent and would be ready to defend and advise them whenever a Christian spirit so prevailed on them that they were disposed to be governed by reason and the precepts of right.[6]

In suggesting that peace might still be possible, Collins was far out of step with the military department; machinery for making war on the Navajos had at long last, and very quietly, actually, and irrevocably, been set in motion.

On reaching Albuquerque, Yost found that troops were gathering and preparations were very nearly completed for the largest campaign ever to have been made against the Navajos. His arrival in the river town on August 25 coincided with that of Lieutenant Colonel Dixon S. Miles, who had been chosen by General Garland to lead the expedition. If at Fort Defiance some slim hope remained for avoiding war, on the Rio Grande the decision had been made: Miles was gathering his forces to strike, and the only question was when the blow would be timed. On this point Colonel Miles had something of interest (and later importance) to say. He sent orders to Major Brooks by Captain George McLane, commanding an escort of riflemen for a wagon train on its return to Fort Defiance, stating that if Brooks "had not commenced hostilities not to do so until my arrival, and to immediately

6. August 13, 1858: Collins to Yost, NA, NMS 234-549.

commence entrenching and erecting palisades on the intervals of the Fort."

The usually drowsy town was clamped in an atmosphere of confusion and urgent haste. Captain Blas Lucero was there, almost literally pawing the dust of the plaza, with fifty-two New Mexican spies and guides recruited a week before by Colonel Bonneville from Cebolleta and nearby ranches on the river. Upon his arrival at noon, Colonel Miles had at once ordered Captain McLane to leave with his wagons for Defiance. Yost, obliged to find a fresh mount to replace his own horse, which had foundered on the editor's impetuous ride from Santa Fe, rode out with the escort three hours later. Lucero's sombreroed outfit, veteran (if rusty) Indian fighters all, left at the following daybreak to overtake McLane in camp that night at Cubero. A few hours behind Lucero, if an overdue train from Fort Union should show up, the colonel himself was to follow at the head of Company A, Mounted Rifles, and Company C, Third Infantry.[7] His train of six wagons was said to contain medical and subsistence stores and be accompanied by one hundred beef cattle contracted for with Moore & Reese—but where they were, neither the colonel nor anyone else could say. Other contingents of troops and more supplies were to come later. Miles begged the department commander to issue stringent orders to hurry them along.

Sam Yost, given more to damning than to praise, was captivated during what could only be described as a painfully forced march by Captain McLane's buoyant zest and his courteous, polished treatment of this unwanted supercargo—meaning Yost. Only twelve years out of the Military Academy, among the youngest of the officers who had served in the Mexican War, McLane already was noted among his companions for his personal charm and his eager, sometimes headlong bravery. His recent part in the destruction of Manuelito's livestock had not diminished his reputation as an officer who welcomed action. If there was an imperious strain in his usually pleasant nature it might be traceable to family background: Louis McLane, his father, had served in House and Senate of the United States Congress as a member from

7. August 26, 1858: Miles to Nichols, NA, RAC, RG 393, M-42-1858, LR. Twenty-one of Lucero's New Mexicans were enlisted from Cebolleta, and others from ranches near Albuquerque. They furnished their own arms, saddles, and pack horses, and were supplied only with powder and lead. Lucero and a lieutenant were paid $3 a day, the others $1.50 (August 19, 1858: Bonneville to Nichols, NA, RAC, RG 393, B-57-1858, LR).

the state of Delaware; twice, and with distinction, he was minister to England; he was secretary of the treasury in Andrew Jackson's administration.

Whether he was ordered to do so by Colonel Miles or whether it was his own idea is not clear, but from Cubero, where he was joined by Blas Lucero's company, to Bear Spring, McLane pushed his wagons and escort of twelve men to a remarkable clip of fifty miles a day.

On arriving at Bear Spring in the morning of August 29, Captain McLane persuaded himself that Major Brooks's ultimatum to Zarcillos Largos had failed, as in fact it had, and that consequently the garrison at Fort Defiance must now be at war with the Navajos, which it was not. From this conclusion it was at once obvious to McLane that he would be remiss in his duty—in spite of the orders he carried from Colonel Miles to Major Brooks, the substance of which he had been given orally—if he did not immediately attack any armed force of the enemy he chanced to encounter. Not by chance, because Ojo del Oso was their customary dwelling place, a large number of Navajos could be seen among their hogans on the sloping land a half-mile or more beyond the spring. Nothing in the Navajos' conduct could be described as hostile or provocative, but McLane nevertheless immediately prepared to attack.[8]

The approach was uphill over broken ground and, for the last few hundred yards before he ordered the men to dismount, at a gallop. A low cover of piñon and juniper in the vicinity of the spring offered so little concealment that the Navajos would easily have seen the attack forming, but higher on the hillside the taller trees became more dense. Half of the command was left with the wagons and horses near the spring. With McLane were Yost as a noncombatant observer, four riflemen, and Blas Lucero with twenty-two New Mexicans.

If Captain McLane had expected little resistance, his judgment was confirmed. After a harmless exchange of shots the Navajos, who at first moved off to the right and left as though to flank and encircle him while leaving a few in front to meet and absorb the charge, withdrew to higher ground and the shelter of trees and rocks. The wagons were small in the distance and the firing less frequent when McLane gave the order to dismount. At a range of four hundred yards his rifles and Lucero's old muskets would be more effective from the ground, but the men either failed to hear or did not understand him. Only five heeded the command.

8. September 3, 1858: Yost to Collins, NA, NMS T21-3.

Yost himself remained mounted at McLane's side, observing Lucero's people scatter in pursuit and noting that "all seemed anxious for the fight, and equally anxious for booty." He was marveling at the accuracy of the few rifles at such long range when he saw McLane reel and almost fall. A musket ball fired at 150 yards from concealment at the left had penetrated his chest, glanced from a rib, and emerged, leaving a dark hole in the captain's tunic. "The shock was so great that he staggered some 10 paces," Yost noted, "became very pale and sick at the stomach, and in fact gave every outward indication of a speedy death."

The fighting, which had lasted no more than ten or fifteen minutes, ceased when McLane was lifted to his saddle and helped down the hill to the wagons. Here, with the simple means available, the wound was washed and dressed and then the wagons, with only the riflemen as escort, moved off at once for Fort Defiance. Lucero and his company lingered in camp that night on the Rio Puerco of the West, losing two horses to Navajos who stayed about but in turn capturing three Navajos and their ponies.

At Fort Defiance Captain McLane's wound was found to be less serious than first supposed; he might ride to fight again in a few weeks. Losses sustained during the engagement were not determined until Blas Lucero appeared with his company next day, and even then there was some uncertainty. Eight or ten of Lucero's men, not attached to the attacking force but ordered by McLane to surround and drive off the Navajo herd of some forty or fifty horses, had succeeded in capturing about twenty (which might in part explain the Navajo raid on Lucero's camp that night). Yost believed that not fewer than six Navajos had been killed and three or four wounded, while McLane reported that possibly eight or ten Indians had been killed.[9] Four Navajos in all had been captured by the New Mexicans, a number of hogans destroyed, and a quantity of booty taken, including blankets, cooking utensils, bow cases, and quivers of arrows. Of the attacking party, only Captain McLane had been injured.

Yost had scarcely had time to find his way about Fort Defiance when Sandoval and three or four of his band surprisingly turned up on August 31. If this in truth was not the first occasion when Sandoval ap-

9. September 2, 1858: McLane to Miles, enclosure with September 3, 1858: Miles to Nichols, NA, RAC, RG 393, M-48-1858, LR. Juan Lucero of the Diné Ana'aii later told Brooks that two Navajos were killed at Bear Spring. He asked if this would not satisfy the demand for the murderer, and Brooks replied that it would not (Yost to Collins, cited above).

peared at the fort, it was the first time his presence there was officially noted. Yost offered no explanation but observed that the Diné Ana'aii leader "revealed nothing specific on the object of his visit" and that "he said he would not go out among the Navajoes—he seemed afraid."

Surprisingly, also, because no one else had previously expressed interest in this, Yost attempted to explain the assassin's motive for killing Major Brooks's slave. Whether the agent heard the story from Navajos at the post or from the Diné Ana'aii is not clear, but on the day of Sandoval's arrival he informed Superintendent Collins:

> The Indians say that the murderer had had a difficulty some days before with one of his women. He wished her to go some place with him. She refused, and at a dance he tore from her all the clothing that covered her person. She still refused, whereupon, to appease his feelings, he started out (as is the custom of the Navajo Indians) to kill some one outside of his nation. This he succeeded in doing in the person of the negro boy. The Indian returned to the place where his woman was, and she proceeded with him to the place originally desired by the Indian.[10]

There is reason, since the murder of the major's servant was made the principal issue in justifying the declaration of war, to examine again this generally accepted account of why Jim was killed. The "custom" that Yost referred to might be regarded as an exceptionally rare practice among the Navajos. The rarity of such conduct would not be a reason for questioning the plausibility of Yost's explanation, however, as the least reasonable occurrence, like the random strike of lightning, too often displaces the predictable or expected.

Yost's explanation of motive may be questioned instead not only because it runs directly counter to the grain of Navajo behavior but also because it so conveniently relieved both sides of guilt. If, as the Indians told Yost, the murder was an act of self-appeasement by a Navajo husband, the Bilagáana could have no grievance against the Navajo people, but against only one man; at the same time, by accepting this explanation, the Americans could absolve Major Brooks and all other white men concerned of any responsibility or blame.

In offering this explanation to Superintendent Collins, Yost made no reference to the fact that Jim's murderer was a man at least forty-five years old, a man of influential family attached to the band of Cayetano, who remained aloof and usually hostile to white men. And he made no

---

10. August 31, 1858: Yost to Collins, NA, NMS T21-3.

reference, either, to Cayetano's paternal relationship to Manuelito; to the military trespass upon Manuelito's grazing land; to the destruction of Manuelito's cattle and horses; to the personal insults to Manuelito when Major Brooks gave Manuelito's cane to Zarcillos Largos and when the major ordered Manuelito and his people to leave Fort Defiance, telling them he regarded them not as friends but as enemies. Finally, there was no reference to Jim as the recognized personal property of the man responsible for the loss of Manuelito's property, or to the fact that reprisal for any inflicted damage or wrong was most common practice among Navajos as well as whites.

The evidence indicates that Jim's slayer selected his victim not in haste or at random, as any impersonally aggrieved husband would have done, but that he coolly and deliberately waited three or four hours for one particular person—the slave of Major Brooks.

Yost's credibility as a witness need not be accepted without question. He had resided in New Mexico scarcely ten months and owed his temporary appointment as Navajo agent to the favor of his employer, not to any knowledge he had of these Indians; in two months more, not as Navajo agent but again as editor of the *Gazette*, he would write that, with him, it remained a question of doubt if Henry Dodge had not really been killed by Navajos.

During his march westward to Fort Defiance, Colonel Miles had cause for jubilation. Until now his tour of duty in the Southwest had been a disappointment: dreary garrison command at Fort Fillmore, a brief and undistinguished spell as acting department commander, and then field service during the Apache campaign of 1857, his position subordinate to the older (but not so much older) Bonneville, who of course had reaped all of the glory. His sixty years (give or take one or two) weighed heavily, but suddenly weighed less when General Garland picked him for the assignment, after Colonel Miles had feared that all opportunity had forever passed him by. A phrase current among the department's higher echelon of officers may have been running through his mind like a catchy tune. It went like this: Garland had given Bonneville his tour on the Gila, Colonel Loring his on the Mormon Expedition—"and it was but just to allow Colonel Miles his with the Navajoes." [11]

11. October 19, 1858: Bonneville to Lt. Col. Lorenzo Thomas, AAG, NA, RAC, RG 393, LS. A judgment of Miles that would be more revealing as his Navajo expedition developed, was that of Lt. John Van D. DuBois, during the Apache cam-

At Bacon Spring, fifty-three miles from his destination, he found Captain Hatch waiting with bad news for the colonel and with two rifle companies as protective escort for his supply train. Hatch made no pretense of softening the blow. Miles was furious. Captain McLane's unprovoked attack upon the Ojo del Oso Navajos was contrary to the order McLane carried and knew very well. Miles was sorry that McLane had been slightly wounded, but he regretted more "the commencement of the war with the Navijos in this manner. The result: only to make them fly in every direction." [12] Miles immediately ordered his column into forced march and arrived at Fort Defiance on September 2, two days later.

In response to the colonel's summons, Sandoval went out to call the headmen to a council, but with few exceptions they were reluctant or unwilling to come in. At first only Herrero came in, with Juan Anaya. Miles was ferocious with them. If the murderer was not given up at once, Miles told them he would march against the Navajos in five days with only one object in mind: "to kill and destroy all I meet." He threatened frightfulness from all sides. So soon as his troops were started, so soon would they be joined by Utes from the north, by Pueblos and New Mexicans and the Coyotero Apaches, and they would take women and children as their captives and kill and destroy the Navajo flocks and uproot and devastate the Navajo gardens and orchards. For five days more the headmen might come to see him and leave without harm, but after the fifth day he would talk with none of them again.

Juan Anaya answered levelly, saying that Zarcillos Largos had gone out with others to find and bring in the wanted man. Miles expressed disbelief. Zarcillos Largos appeared at the fort soon afterward, accompanied by Armijo, Vicente Vaca, Sandoval, Juan Lucero, and several others, and the colonel repeated the threats he had made to Herrero and Juan Anaya. Following this confrontation, which occurred the day

---

paign: "I don't believe Col. M cares to find Indians. His lukewarm feeling is shown in every thing he does—Energy would show us an indian camp in four days, but we go to the Depot—to talk it over" (DuBois journals, Coe Collection, the Beinecke Library, Yale University).

12. September 3, 1858: Miles to Nichols, cited above. General Garland's reaction, conveyed by Major Nichols, his adjutant, was stronger. "This ill timed attack has not only defeated the General's intentions [Nichols wrote], but has placed in jeopardy the supply trains and re-inforcements now en route for Fort Defiance, and I am further instructed to say that your contemplated offensive operations, based upon Captain McLane's affair, do not meet the approbation of the Department Commander" (September 9, 1858: Nichols to Miles, NA, RAC, RG 393, LS). Miles, of course, already had started his offensive before this letter reached him.

after he reached Fort Defiance—his expedition headquarters and soon to be the focal point for more than one thousand troops—he requested that General Garland send word asking the Utes to start at once on a foray south of the San Juan and give the order for New Mexicans and Pueblos "to strike in, capture and slay."

Time obviously had run out, perhaps even weeks before, but one more scene of the drama yet remained. In a role more difficult than any other to account for, Sandoval for a few fleeting hours emerged as a principal intermediary, not as a tribal renegade and enemy but as one who would go to unusual lengths and perhaps at great personal risk to prevent the onrushing war. With the knowledge and possibly the sanction of Zarcillos Largos, Armijo, and a few others, he disappeared from the post, returning on September 7 to report that the murderer of the Negro had been found in the Chusca Mountains fifty miles from the fort; the man had fled from the Navajos who were attempting to capture him, and when finally caught and desperately resisting, he had been severely wounded. After delivering this message, Sandoval once more departed, saying he would return with the prisoner the next morning.

He was not pleased with Sandoval's manner, nor did he believe he was sincere, Yost observed later. And when Sandoval returned next morning with word that the murderer had died of his wounds during the night, Yost at once suspected him of lying. He suspected as well the stories of those who had accompanied the Diné Ana'aii, but particularly he doubted Vicente Vaca who the evening before had claimed that he had shot the murderer himself with his pistol.[13]

Yost and Colonel Miles gave slightly different accounts of what happened immediately afterward. Yost said that Sandoval asked for a wagon in which the body of the man might be brought to the fort; this was refused, and he was given a blanket for that purpose. Miles remarked that "Sarcillos Largos and a few came in to say, that the murderer . . . had died last night, requesting a wagon to bring the body in—I told Maj. Brooks . . . he should not give the wagon, but might send a mule to pack this dead body, [and] he did so." [14]

As the garrison settled down to wait, groups of mounted and armed Navajos began gathering about the fort until Yost estimated that they numbered between three and five hundred, a milling and anxious but apparently not hostile force that may have equaled the number of troops disposed through the canyon. At eleven o'clock the body was

13. September 9, 1858: Yost to Collins, NA, NMS 234-549.
14. September 8, 1858: Miles to Nichols, NA, RAC, RG 393, M-50-1858, LR.

delivered to Major Brooks, who at once directed Dr. Cooper McKee to perform an autopsy. McKee's post mortem report confirmed what nearly everyone knew already or grimly suspected. The body was not that of the mature Navajo who had killed Jim, but of a captive youth five feet two or three inches tall, not more than eighteen years old. He was probably, but not certainly, a New Mexican, and obviously had died not of wounds inflicted two nights before but of four rifle and pistol bullets fired at close range that same morning.

Yost met with the Navajo headmen later in the afternoon. He told them that this final turn of events left him no choice. For the moment, at least, his function as their agent had ceased and he was turning them over to the disposition of the military. The Navajos then withdrew, among them Sandoval, who indicated that he would not remain with the others but would rejoin his Diné Ana'aii.

Colonel Miles refused to see or speak with them. He let his plans for the Navajos be known the same afternoon when he directed the posting of Orders No. 4:

> Head Quarters Navajo Expedition
> Fort Defiance N. M. 8th Septr. 1858.
> I. Since the arrival of the commanding officer at this post (2nd inst) sufficient time has been given to the Navajo tribe of Indians, to seek, secure, and deliver up, the murderer of Maj. Brooks' negro: to atone for the insult to our flag, and the many outrages committed upon our citizens. They have failed to do so. Our duty remains to chastize them into obedience to our laws—After tomorrow morning war is proclaimed against them.

Captain Blas Lucero with his spies and guides would proceed in advance of the column, followed by two companies of mounted rifles and two companies of infantry, these to be followed by a pack train and drovers and led horses and beef cattle, the rear guard to be a third company of rifles. His command for this initial strike would number only 350 troops, but hundreds more were gathering on the river or would be coming on soon.

> II. At 8 o'clock tomorrow morning the column designated by Order No. 2 will be in readiness to march, with 12 days rations, to fight these Indians wherever found.

The colonel confided privately to General Garland that he was not at all certain where the Navajos would be found. On his departure from Fort Defiance months ago, Major Kendrick had taken with him every map of the Navajo country, leaving not so much as a poor sketch. The uplands of Tibet were as familiar to Colonel Miles as the wastelands that surrounded him. Even Blas Lucero and his New Mexican spies and guides, at this late and critical hour, confessed a certain inadequacy. Some of them had not been in Navajo country for twenty-five years and only one of them in the last seven. In short, they were not quite sure of where they were, or might be going.

> III. Commanders of Companies are cautioned not to place on one mule all of the ammunition but to distribute the same to at least three packs—
>
> **By order of Lt. Col. Miles.**

On further questioning none of his guides would admit to knowing very much of the country west of Laguna Negra. The colonel was therefore troubled but not daunted when he advised department headquarters, "My march will be like an exploration of an unknown region."

He would start, almost blindly, in the direction of Canyon de Chelly.

Part Four

*"From my own observations I am not able to form
an opinion satisfactory to my own mind of the number
of Indians held as slaves or fixed domestic servants
without their being the recipients of wages. Persons
of high respectability for intelligence, who have made
some calculations on the subject, estimate the number
at various figures, from fifteen hundred to three
thousand, and even exceeding the last number. The
more prevalent opinion seems to be they considerably
exceed two thousand.*

—Chief Justice Kirby Benedict, testifying
before the James R. Doolittle committee
on causes of the Navajo wars,

Santa Fe, July 4, 1865

20

The Miles Campaign

The deep gorges of Canyon de Chelly filled Colonel Miles with cold revulsion. "No command," he wrote to Colonel Bonneville upon his return to Fort Defiance, "should again enter it." With cavalry and infantry and the spies and guides of Captain Blas Lucero, he entered the chasm at the head of Monument Canyon, De Chelly's southern branch. Once on the bottom, he found "the men on top . . . looked like figurines and the mules like rats." His most positive achievement was to have traversed the canyon (the first time this was done by American troops) from east to west. But on emerging at the mouth he was overcome with relief he made no effort to disguise. He encamped at once in a cornfield, he informed the department commander, where his men feasted on green corn and peaches. He was "glad enough to get rid of this remarkable hole in the earth." [1]

Gone were the boasts of how he would kill and destroy all Navajos whom he might meet. Back in the haven of the fort the florid gusts of his former bluster were muted. Although he had been provisioned to remain in the field twelve days, he was back in seven. His return, by way of Be'ikid'ha'tsoh Lake and Pueblo Colorado Wash, had been turned into a retreat. For two days his flanks and rear were under nearly constant clawing attack by the same Navajos he had vowed to kill on sight. He was spared the disaster that had befallen a predecessor's cavalry; but unlike Sumner, Miles could not say that his column had been committed to long, dry, and forced marches. The horses of his mounted riflemen came through almost unharmed.

Casualties were suffered on both sides, so there was some licking

1. September 16, 1858: Miles, Fort Defiance, to Nichols, NA, RAC, RG 393, M-51-1858, LR. Bonneville had replaced Gen. Garland in department command on September 15.

of wounds when the command reached Fort Defiance in the afternoon of September 15. The bugler, Ezekiel Fisher, wandering off in Beautiful Valley, was killed by two arrows the day before, his body left stripped of all but gloves and shoes. Before daybreak on September 14 Navajos slipped in among the picket guard and mortally wounded Private Manus Sweeney, three other enlisted men also being wounded at the same time. Flocks of sheep numbering five to six thousand were captured by the troops and herded back to the fort, where, because Miles found them an encumbrance, all but five hundred were slaughtered. (He was censured for not sending the others back to the river.) For the lives of Fisher and Sweeney, Miles claimed six Navajos killed by his riflemen and four more by Blas Lucero's people.

The first Navajo killed had been captured in the morning of the second day out, not far from Ewell's Hay Camp. Miles described him as being well dressed, fully armed, and well mounted—a man "of too much importance to release." He was accordingly shot as a spy by Miles's Zuni guide, José. The manner of the execution was described later, secondhand, for readers of the Santa Fe *Gazette* by Samuel Yost:

> The Navajo was soon placed at a short distance off, when Zuñi raised his old flintlock fusee to do his duty. Navajo appealed— 'O don't kill me, my friend!' Zuñi very gravely responded— 'Porque, porque?'—'Why not, why not?' This very rational and reasonable question not being satisfactorily answered to Zuñi's notions of the ethics of war, he took deliberate aim, and sent a leaden messenger through Mr. Navajo's brain, thus ushering his untutored spirit into the blissful regions of the great hunting ground. Zuñi was much delighted with the amusement, and says he will be made a big chief when he returns home.[2]

Four days after his return to the fort, under the misapprehension that Zarcillos Largos was camped fifteen miles or so to the south, Colonel Miles ordered a mixed command of mounted riflemen and infantry to attack and destroy the headman's rancherias. Command of this force was given to Major Brooks, with orders to make a night march and take the Navajos by surprise. The mission, which placed Brooks for the first time in the field against these Indians, accomplished nothing. Zarcillos Largos was not in the vicinity of Calites Canyon, as Miles believed, and

2. Governor Rencher was moved to send a clipping of the account to Secretary of State Lewis Cass with the comment that Yost's dispatch "discloses a piece of brutality worthy only of the most degraded savages" (October 16, 1858: Rencher to Cass, NA, NMS 234-549).

Navajos who were in the region were alerted in advance and withdrew before Brooks could attack them. Less than a week later, on more reliable information, Miles sent a similar force north toward Laguna Negra under the command of Captain John P. Hatch. Leaving Fort Defiance in the night of September 24, Hatch brought his column by daybreak to the lower approach to the lake and its verdant valley. It was soon found that hogans in the area had been abandoned and livestock driven off some days before.[3]

Hatch was informed by one of his guides, a Zuni, that the rancherias of Zarcillos Largos lay near wheatfields about nine miles to the north. Because the terrain before him was a gently ascending, open meadowland where a slow advance would surely be detected, Hatch left six riflemen with the baggage train and Lieutenant William D. Whipple's company of infantry at the lake and pressed forward as rapidly as possible with the balance of his cavalry. By entering an arroyo that cut through the plain a mile and a half below the wheatfields, Hatch's troops proceeded unseen until within two hundred yards of their objective. In early morning air the hogans were sharply defined, even against the trees in which they stood. It was seven o'clock. Forming his riflemen in column of fours, Hatch rode at a run to within fifty yards of the hogans, where Navajos already were appearing. He ordered his men to dismount and commence firing, the fire at once being returned by about forty Navajos, nearly all of whom were armed, surprisingly, with muskets or rifles.

Zarcillos Largos could be seen riding about among his people, exhorting and encouraging them with complete unconcern for his own safety. Three times the elderly spokesman for peace was struck and thrown from his horse, but each time he managed to remount and continue to fire, first his rifle and then a revolver, until his ammunition was spent. Only then did the Navajos begin a fighting retreat into thickets of oak, taking Zarcillos Largos and one other wounded man with them and discouraging any effort on Hatch's part at pursuit.

Six Navajo dead were counted among the hogans; more might have been found in the brush, but the captain decided not to risk his men in such a search. A rich booty of buffalo robes, blankets, and saddles was thrown upon a stack of wheat and set afire. Captain Hatch was

3. September 25, 1858: Hatch to Lt. William B. Lane, adjutant, Navajo Expedition, enclosure with (same date) Miles to AAG; and October 15, 1858: Hatch to Lane, enclosure with October 14, 1858: Miles to Lt. John D. Wilkins, AAG, Santa Fe, NA, RAC, RG 393, M-60-1858, M-77-1858, LR.

filled with admiration for Zarcillos Largos, who he thought had been mortally wounded.[4]

On his return to Fort Defiance that evening after an unbroken march of fifty miles in twenty hours, Hatch reported that his command was in as good condition as when it had started out. This, paradoxically, he believed was due to the Navajos having had firearms, weapons evidently obtained in anticipation of this war and with which most of them were inexperienced.

"Had they been armed with the bow and arrow," Hatch observed, "I must have had numerous casualties to report, for certainly no man ever behaved with more gallantry and coolness than did Sarcillo Largo."

Late in September, having tentatively probed the Navajos' strength in other directions, Colonel Miles turned toward the lower Chusca Valley. His command comprised four companies of mounted riflemen and two of infantry, with Blas Lucero and a number of his spies and guides in the vanguard. The troops encountered Navajos with large herds of sheep as soon as they entered the broad plain below Chusca Peak. During most of the ensuing three days of the operation the command was divided and in nearly constant movement, Miles remaining with the infantry and out of touch with the action. One of the rare recorded instances of a clash with Cayetano's band occurred shortly after daybreak on October 1. While pursuing three mounted Navajos into one of the southward-reaching valleys of the Mesa de los Lobos, Captain Andrew J. Lindsay with a dozen troopers had the dismaying success of overrunning his quarry in a box canyon—literally springing his own trap. It was said later that Lindsay had stumbled upon the entire band of Cayetano; authority for this was Blas Lucero, who apparently recognized either the headman or some of his people.

"The Indians were very numerous & my party so small," Lindsay observed afterward, "that I determined to take possession of a wooded knoll in the centre of the cañon, and hold it until I could get assistance."

This he did, managing to send word back to Captain George McLane to come on with all possible haste. In column of fours, McLane's Company I appeared within a few minutes at a full gallop. At once dis-

---

4. September 24, 1858: Yost to Collins, NA, NMS T21-3. Noting Hatch's return to the fort, Yost commented that Zarcillos Largos "was there and fought bravely. It is presumed he is dead, which if so, will have a material effect upon the future action of the Indians." The headman's wounds were less serious than believed and within a few months he took a leading part in peace talks.

mounting and deploying as skirmishers, McLane's riflemen succeeded in momentarily clearing the canyon of Navajos while at the same time capturing a part of their livestock—some seventy horses and four thousand sheep. Warriors who had abandoned the canyon on McLane's precipitate arrival gathered on surrounding heights as Lindsay burned their camp equipage, consisting principally of blankets, buffalo robes, and supplies of corn. Fire pouring in on him from above, which he could not effectively return, induced Lindsay to order a hasty withdrawal. During this movement Sergeant John Thompson of the rear guard was wounded and Privates Mauritz Paulman and William Neugent, first reported missing, later were found to have been killed. Seven of Cayetano's Navajos were said to have been killed and several others wounded.[5]

The first in a flurry of Navajo raids in reprisal coincided with Colonel Miles's return to Fort Defiance. A patrol sent out the day before limped back to the post October 2, having failed to recover any of the oxen driven off from a freighters' camp; one private of the detachment had been killed during the foray. Large war parties soon afterward struck boldly in close proximity to the fort. Two hundred warriors attempted to cut loose and stampede the picketed horses of the rifle companies one-half mile below the post on October 6 but were driven off by the fire of a stable guard; three Navajos shot from their horses were carried off by their companions. An attack next morning on the post beef herd west of the fort was beaten off, the Navajos again carrying away two of their wounded. Twenty-five miles south of the fort a camp of riflemen on escort duty with a commissary train was aroused the next night by a gunshot and loud cries. Awakened by the growling of his dog, Lieutenant William W. Averell had stepped outside his tent to investigate, almost collided with a Navajo, and been shot in the leg. Averell's cries that he had been hit brought troopers running, but the Navajo escaped in rain and darkness.[6]

A more determined effort was made by the Navajos early in the morning of October 17 when a party of 300 warriors appeared suddenly at the mouth of Cañoncito Bonito and attacked just as the post herds

5. October 3, 1858: Miles to Wilkins, with three enclosures, NA, RAC, RG 393, M-64-1858, LR. Officers of Miles's command, returning to Fort Defiance October 2, reported killing ten Navajos, wounding seven, and capturing more than 6,000 sheep.

6. October 10, 1858: Lindsay to Lane, enclosure with (same date) Miles to Wilkins, NA, RAC, RG 393, M-69-1858, LR. The following May, Averell was at Fort Union, hobbling about on two sticks and awaiting transportation back to the States.

were being moved, at the accustomed hour, to outlying grazing grounds. The guard of 15 mounted riflemen and 10 infantry was taken by surprise and might have been overwhelmed had it not been joined at the outset by 160 Zuni warriors encamped close by. The Zunis had arrived at Fort Defiance two days before with Mariano, governor of their pueblo, and four war chiefs, to volunteer their services to Colonel Miles.[7]

Daring in its execution, the raid was regarded by the Navajos as a success; at the very gates of an alert garrison they had inflicted casualties and seized sixty-two mules at a price of three warriors killed. One of the riflemen of the guard had been killed outright, another private of the same company mortally wounded, four troopers wounded, and three rifle company horses killed. No mention was made of Zuni losses. Several Navajos at one point were throwing the body of Private Michael Merrion on a horse when Private Alexander Brown rode in among them, killed one of the warriors, wounded another, and managed to secure Merrion's body on his own horse. Riding back to the fort thus burdened, Brown himself was wounded by an arrow.

Plans were advanced, meanwhile, for a major campaign to be launched against the Navajos from a rendezvous in the Chusca Valley. To this place and a meeting with troops under Colonel Miles, Major Electus Backus was preparing to march from San Ysidro with three companies of infantry and one of mounted riflemen. His Second Column included as well a second contingent of New Mexican spies and guides led by Captain José M. Valdez of Mora and about one hundred Capote and Moache Ute warriors with the war chiefs Sobeta and Kaneatchi. When the two columns met, Miles would have an effective striking force of about eight hundred men. It was with this campaign and its aftermath in mind that Colonel Bonneville, at the request of Superintendent Collins, expressed their mutual concern for the safety of the leader of the Diné Ana'aii. Bonneville directed Miles to be certain that while making war on the Navajo nation that "our old friend Sandoval" and members of his band were not molested. Miles received the order with certain reservations. If current reports were true, a party of Diné Ana'aii traveling with Sandoval to Santa Fe had stolen seventy-five mules from ranches near Albuquerque.[8]

The troops with Major Backus were gathering for a westward march

7. October 17, 1858: Miles to Wilkins, NA, RAC, RG 393, M-79-1858, LR.
8. October 16, 1858: Bonneville to Collins, NA, NMS T21-3; October 24, 1858: Miles to Wilkins, NA, RAC, RG 393, M-76-1858, LR.

through Chaco Canyon to the rendezvous when Miles led an attack on
rancherias he believed were those of Manuelito. In conjunction with
Mariano's Zuni warriors, Miles on October 18 rode with a force of
more than four hundred troops toward the broad valleys lying beyond
Pueblo Colorado Wash. The Zunis refused to march with the troops
or obey orders, instead moving on in advance and then building fires
that Miles angrily declared could be seen for thirty miles. When his
column finally caught up with them, Miles found the Zunis camped
among the burning remains of what he claimed were Manuelito's "many
wigwams or *half* cabins." That, and the Zunis' capture of one hundred
Navajo ponies, were about all that the operation accomplished. If the
hogans indeed had belonged to Manuelito's people, the Navajos had
escaped without other harm.[9]

On his return to Fort Defiance Miles learned that Zarcillos Largos
was not dead as reported, but alive and anxious to discuss terms of
peace. The message had been brought in by Juan Anaya, who at once
(by order of Major Brooks) was locked up in the guardhouse. When
Juan's brother, a man known as Torivio, was captured a few days later,
he confirmed reports that the murderer of Major Brooks's slave had
taken refuge with Utes living north of the San Juan. Miles informed
department headquarters that other headmen besides Zarcillos Largos
wished to end the war but that he, Miles, believed the Navajos had not
yet suffered enough. For the coming campaign with Major Backus,
Miles pressed Juan Anaya and Torivio into service as guides. To insure
their loyalty he ordered that their women and children be locked up
as hostages during his absence.

Ice and snow crusted the high valleys of the Chusca Mountains when
the troops of Colonel Miles and Major Backus met in the morning of
November 2. Their camp was among cornfields on Tuntsa Wash, the
craggy outline of Bennett's Peak visible five or six miles to the north.
Early the next day, while waiting for Captain George Sykes to come
up with the Second Column's supply train, Miles outlined his campaign strategy in a report to Colonel Bonneville. He would lead the
First Column over Washington Pass to Cienega Negra and from there
move north along the western base of the mountains. Major Backus

9. October 23, 1858: Miles to Wilkins, with one enclosure, NA, RAC, RG 393,
M-75-1858, LR. Capt. George McLane reported that a detachment he led to the
vicinity of Black Mesa killed one Navajo and wounded another. Two Zuni auxiliaries
were wounded.

at the same time would seek out Cayetano's rancherias at Beautiful Mountain and then proceed to another rendezvous with Miles, either at Cienega Juanico or on the "carissa" or Lukachukai Creek. The entire command then would sweep westward to the mouth of Canyon de Chelly, following the rim route of Colonel Washington in 1849, on to "Calabasha Seirra" (Miles's misnomer for Black Mesa, which is to the south of the calabazas or pumpkin mesas), and then into Hopi country where he was sure the Navajos would be found in large numbers. Rations for fifteen days would be issued from Sykes's train to men of both columns.

"If my communication is inelegible," Miles explained murkily, "you must excuse it, as the The[r]mometer must be several degrees below zero, my ink freezes before I can use it and my fingers [are] so cold that I can hardly hold my pen." [10]

The two columns moved off in opposite directions the morning of November 4, Colonel Miles turning south toward the foot of Washington Pass. His command, numbering 335 men, included four companies of mounted riflemen, two of infantry, and twenty-five of Blas Lucero's guides and spies. Snow was ankle-deep in the pass and the weather bitterly cold. Major Charles F. Ruff with two companies of riflemen scouted front and flanks, but on this day and for the remainder of the march his and other scouting detachments were held within close distance of the main column. Numerous tracks were discovered, in one instance the troops flushing a fresh trail of an estimated ten thousand sheep, but none of the trails was followed. Even the impetuous George McLane, riding at the head of Rifle Company I, was kept on tight rein.

Navajos were not seen until the fourth day, in the vicinity of Wheatfield Creek, and thereafter were encountered frequently in small parties, such meetings usually resulting in brief fire fights. Colonel Miles justified his determination not to divide his column in pursuit by saying he felt obliged to press on to the appointed meeting with Major Backus. However, when he reached the second rendezvous point

10. November 3, 1858: Miles to Wilkins, NA, RAC, RG 393, M-82-1858, LR. Bad washouts encountered from the Puerco through Chaco Canyon slowed the supply train. Sykes reached Miles's camp in the morning of November 3, unloaded his wagons, and began the return march to Albuquerque next day. Men of his Company K, 3d Infantry detachment, and a few riflemen with Backus, are responsible for the mysterious Windsbecker, Stempt et al. inscriptions and martial petroglyphs, cut into boulders east of the Chaco's Chetro Ketl ruin, which for years have baffled archaeologists.

on Lukachukai Creek and found no sign of the Second Column, he decided not to wait for Major Backus (as they had agreed on November 3 that the one who arrived first would do). Instead, he moved on at once the next morning, resolved, he said, to "attack the cañons on the north side of Cañon de Chelly"—a resolution modified by a renewed sense of urgency that hastened him onward to cornfields he knew would be found at the canyon's mouth. The withered cornstalks would provide good fodder for his animals.[11]

The command crossed another large trail of sheep in the morning of November 9, but Colonel Miles considered his horses "too weak to follow, a gallop of any duration they were unable to accomplish." Navajos continually challenged his front and rear guards and made smoke fires to signal his slowing progress. During the day a number of his horses and mules gave out and had to be shot. But even as the initiative passed from his hands to his enemy's Miles persuaded himself that he was frightening the Navajos into a course not of their own choosing:

"I have had all day constant appeals for peace," he observed. "One that was affecting, the erection of a small cross, with a large white leaf tied on it. It must have been the work of many, from the many foot-prints around [it]. Many women and children bare foot—On all the trails of the sheep we could distinguish where the ground was not frozen, children[']s and women's bare feet, showing what disturbance the march of my column has given these people." [12]

The air was pleasantly mild when the First Column encamped that evening at the canyon's mouth, the soldiers knocking apart several hogans to provide fuel for campfires. In the afternoon of the next day while he rested in camp, Colonel Miles received a white flag sent by Navajos who were seen in great number gathered on hills to the east. Presently, Barboncito approached the camp and asked to see the commanding officer. During the interview that followed Barboncito said that Major Backus was far to the north on the Rio Chelly (or Chinle Wash) near its mouth, and near also to the mountain where the man who killed the slave Jim had found refuge. Barboncito said that a

11. November 15, 1858: Miles, Fort Defiance, to Wilkins, NA, RAC, RG 393, M-87-1858, LR.

12. At another place the troops found a small cross to which a piece of white muslin was attached, the cloth bearing a yellow powder stain. Questioned about this, Juan Anaya explained that "the white muslin was *our* (the American) symbol of peace—the cross, the Mexican sign—and the stain the Navajoe sign" (November 14, 1858: Yost to Collins, NA, NMS T21-3).

number of headmen had gone to meet Major Backus and offer their assistance in finding the murderer. To Barboncito's request that terms of peace be arranged, Colonel Miles assumed authority in two areas that at no time had been delegated to him by the department commander. He replied that peace terms could be discussed with Agent Yost if Barboncito and as many other headmen as he could bring with him were to meet seven days hence at La Joya, the grazing grounds ten miles north of Fort Defiance. He then gave Barboncito good reason to understand that the rules of this war might shortly be changed: he intimated that the surrender of the man who killed Jim need not necessarily be a condition for ending hostilities.[13]

Having thus decided when and how the Navajo expedition might be ended, Colonel Miles made no further pretense of attempting to join his command with the troops of Major Backus. Early in the morning of November 11, with the excuse that his rations had run short and his animals were broken down, Miles ordered his column to begin the return march to Fort Defiance. He arrived there with little incident two days later.

If Major Backus left personal letters relating to the campaign, or a diary, they have not been found. This is unfortunate because without them, one can only wonder what emotions he experienced in returning to this valley, to these mountains, after six years away. He was an old man now, but tough. If he experienced a few proprietary flashes, no one was better entitled to them. In a sense he could think of Fort Defiance as his own because he had built it in the wilderness, from nothing. He had saved it from disastrous abandonment only by his own dogged will and fortitude—traits not discernible in the officer who commanded this expedition and under whom he now served. What were his reactions to Colonel Miles's conduct of the war, and, if they could be known would they be printable?

He moved with his Second Column only a few miles the first day— November 4—making an early camp at a place he called Cave Springs.[14]

13. As early as October 3 Miles "most respectfully and earnestly" asked Bonneville to drop the demand that the murderer of Jim be surrendered. A study of the voluminous correspondence suggests that Miles was not motivated by any reason other than his deepening desire to extricate himself from the hardships of the campaign. Bonneville replied that "he feels the necessity which compels him to differ with you . . . and cannot but reiterate his former instructions, that the murderer . . . must be sent to Albuquerque."

14. The 2d Column, about 350 rank and file, comprised four companies of infantry (3d and 8th Regiments), two of mounted riflemen, 55 spies and guides, and

He offered no reason for this halting start, but mentioned that his movements were watched by his enemy. The tenacious presence of the Navajos irritated Captain Valdez enough to cause him to suggest a concealed movement against them. Backus assented and during the night Valdez slipped away with six Ute warriors and ten men of his spy company. The main command was moving up to Peña Blanca Creek the next afternoon when they were seen again, small figures in the distance, riding in wild pursuit of three Indians. It was an unequal chase: two of the Navajos were shot from their horses and killed. The third escaped.

Backus halted his troops on the dry creek bed about two miles east and south of the first mouse-colored foothills of Beautiful Mountain. The search for Cayetano and his band could wait until morning—a cold, uninviting prospect. In winter evening light the mountain was dark and featureless, the pivotal barrier in the long range starting in the Carrizos to the north and joining, below, with the Chuscas. As symmetrical as the gable of a house roof, its triangular peak one thousand feet above the valley floor was capped with snow. Lieutenant Milton Cogswell, the major's quartermaster and commissary officer, volunteered to lead the next morning's assault. It was arranged that he might take eighty men and a small party of Utes. By reputation, the warriors of Sobeta and Kaneatchi, most of whom (unlike most Navajos) were armed with good rifles, were known to be very effective auxiliaries. They were known, too, to be utterly restive when associated closely with soldiers. Of the one hundred warriors attached to his column at the San Ysidro rendezvous, only twenty-two remained accounted for; the others were believed to be engaged in the mountains, on their own, but not far off.

With the coming of darkness, Major Backus reflected on a warning that had been given (by Miles?), and perhaps wondered, this second night out, how long his luck would hold. He had been told that a tent could scarcely be raised out here at night without, by morning, bearing the holes or rips of musket balls and arrows. To improve his chance of preventing this Backus waited for full darkness before posting his pickets, and then they were stationed farther out than usual. At the end of the campaign he could report that his tents were unripped by shot.

The command divided at seven o'clock in the morning, Lieutenant

22 Utes. The following account of the campaign is based on the reports of Maj. Backus, Lt. Milton Cogswell, and Capt. Thomas Duncan; November 19, 1858: Maj. Backus to Lt. W. B. Lane, adjutant, with two enclosures; and January 1, 1859: Backus to Wilkins, NA, RAC, RG 393, B-77-1858, B-2-1859, LR.

Cogswell taking his detachment into the lower hills that rise to the southern face of Beautiful Mountain.[15] The troops climbed continuously for three hours, gradually at first through a valley that steepened and narrowed to a canyon. A turn brought them to an opening at the rim of a ravine, across which, at startlingly close range, they were confronted by the mountain's immense bulk. The steep snow-streaked green slopes were trisected laterally by sheer ledges of rock, those nearest tan and pink, but the third and highest a serrated palisades of brown rock rising straight for a hundred feet and so dark as to be almost black. In a profile quite different from that seen in the valley of their last camp far below, the still distant peak, here more round, rested like a white nipple on the nearly flat summit of the dark palisades.

Three foot trails were found on the east face of the mountain, two of them very difficult and only one that would allow horses to reach the summit tableland. The passage up through ledge rock at one point became so hazardous that Cogswell was certain a handful of determined men could defend the pass against any assault. As there was no sign of defenders anywhere on the trail, he concluded that the Navajos were unaware of his approach. On reaching the tableland, and after a short halt, Cogswell deployed his force in an extended line and began a slow-paced sweeping march across the summit, which he found to be about a mile wide and four miles long. Numerous tracks of Indians and livestock were discovered, none fresh. A mounted Navajo, the only one found on the heights, was shot and wounded but escaped. At the west rim the mountain dropped off into a deep valley and there, seven hundred feet below them, the troops could see the tiny forms of sheep and a number of Cayetano's band moving about among several toy-sized hogans. Leaving his mounted riflemen to find another way down, Cogswell began the descent with the footmen on what appeared to be a passable trail.

After descending two hundred feet, he noted later, "I found myself and command on the edge of an immense precipice and I was compelled to return, the men assisting each other up the solid rock with their muskets. If a foot had slipped in clambering up the whole distance, the man would have fallen to the bottom. . . ."

The Utes meanwhile had discovered an easier trail. Before Cogswell's troops could follow and catch up with them, they had descended on

15. Cogswell's detachment comprised 40 troops of 8th Infantry led by Lt. John R. Cooke, 15 mounted riflemen and 15 spies and guides led by Lt. Herbert M. Enos, and 10 Ute warriors.

the rancherias and killed two Navajos. Without waiting for Cogswell they started at once to rejoin the main command with Major Backus, driving off five Navajo horses and one hundred goats. Cogswell, on coming up, ordered the deserted hogans burned and then moved his troops to a high ridge running parallel to the west side of the mountain and there encamped.

From his own camp eight or ten miles to the north, on Salt Creek in the vicinity of the present Red Rock trading post, at seven o'clock that night Major Backus sighted a small bright glow of fire on the ridge. It was a prearranged signal that all was well with Cogswell's detachment. A few moments later the Utes reported to Backus with the captured livestock. Cogswell's return the next morning nearly coincided with the departure of Captain Valdez with his company of spies and guides together with Kaneatchi and his Moache Utes. A fresh trail leading northward toward the Carrizo Mountains had been discovered and Valdez had requested permission to follow it.

After resting for a day on Salt Creek, Major Backus on November 8 moved his column nearly due west for about ten miles to a point on a stream he called the Rio Pajarita, known today as Red Wash. Here, in a high valley slightly north of present Cove, he divided his command into three groups. The largest of these Major Backus left to make camp. Captain Thomas Duncan with fifty mounted riflemen circled to the north and west, starting on a trail of sheep, losing it, and returning late to camp after a fruitless march that left their horses jaded. Another detachment, about fifty men of the Eighth Infantry led by Lieutenant Henry M. Lazelle and accompanied by Major Backus, marched directly north into the rough forested country of the Carrizos' southern slopes. They found a few trails of livestock, crossed streams frozen with ice, and followed on its bottom for two miles a canyon as deep as the deepest gorges of Canyon de Chelly. The aging Backus admitted that it had been a hard day's work with nothing to show for it. The constant scrambling up cliffs and descending into ravines ("where I required the assistance of Soldiers to enable me to progress") left him exhausted. The camp lay in darkness, many of the men asleep, when Captain Valdez and his party returned with more than two hundred head of horses, goats, and sheep. Shortly after leaving the Second Column the previous morning he had shot and killed one Navajo. In the mountains later his men had wounded another, probably fatally. It was there that they had captured the Navajo livestock.

While returning from the mountains the Valdez party crossed a broad trail of unattached Utes traveling north with a drove of horses. A suspicion that the horses were war booty was confirmed soon afterward when they found the trail of Navajo pursuers. Nearby they came upon the scene of what must have been a massive conflict. Three horses lay dead in the field and the ground for a wide area was trampled and stained with blood. These signs of battle and of a Ute victory were unsettling to the warriors with Major Backus. In the morning of November 9 Kaneatchi with eleven of his band left the command. The Moache war leader explained later that he was dissatisfied with the way the soldiers made war. While on their way home they surprised a rancheria of Navajos, defeated them, and captured one woman and forty horses. Their arrival at Abiquiu and Taos followed by some days the return of Sobeta and the Capote warriors, who had brought in a number of Navajo captives.[16]

During the day of the Utes' defection, a short march of ten or twelve miles brought the Second Column over the mountains' ridge and down the western slopes into the valley of Los Gigantes. From this place of red sandstone buttes and buttresses and magnificently arched recesses, Major Backus led the command northwestward over a high crest of land and into another valley of imposing sandstone formations. The troops camped on a tributary of Walker Creek, which Major Backus, in tribute to the architectural qualities of the giant red mesas and buttes looming about him, named Gothic Creek. At a spring called Ojo del Casa, a short distance southeast of present Rock Point, the command next day came upon a fresh trail of sheep and horses. Captain Duncan was placed in command of a detachment mounted upon the best of the horses and started at once in pursuit. He rejoined the column November 13 on Chinle Wash, reporting that during the forced march westward toward Tyende Creek, several Navajos had been seen at a distance too great to permit overtaking them.

The return of Duncan's party marked an important change in plans, Major Backus deciding to break off the campaign and get his troops to Fort Defiance as quickly as possible because of the failure to find forage for his horses, now gaunt and unsteady with hunger. Since emerg-

16. From his Taos agency for the Moache Utes, Kit Carson advised Collins of Kaneatchi's arrival, adding, "I thought it better for the squaw to be with me rather than with Mexicans or Utahs. I therefore purchased her of the Utahs, gave two horses and other articles, the sum of $300 in all." Agent Albert H. Pfeiffer reported from Abiquiu that, of the Navajo captives brought in by Sobeta, "Mansanares bought one boy. Juan Martin one girl. Andres Quintana bought the Woman but he sold her again to one in Moro, the report is she died" (December 8, 1858: Carson to Collins; December 3, 1858: Pfeiffer to Collins, NA, NMS T21-1).

ing from the mountains the column had been marching through arid, barren country; such grass as was found was poor. Moving south on Chinle Wash, the command saw some dry irrigation ditches leading to fields that had not been cultivated for a year. The march of November 15 took the column on a course diverging southeasterly from the Chinle Wash and to the deserted rancherias formerly occupied by Herrero and his people. Camp was made there but again the grass was bad, and Major Backus observed that his horses were nearly famished—at the point of dropping.

In the vicinity of Cienega Juanico next day, Navajos approached the troops of the rear guard with a white flag, saying that they wanted to discuss terms of peace. Lieutenant Lazelle, commanding the guard immediately to the rear of Captain Valdez's spies and guides, told them they would have to wait and see Major Backus at the next camp. A few Utes remaining with the column began talking with the Navajos, Lazelle observing at the same time that the Navajos divided to both sides of the trail as the troops passed through a narrow defile. At this moment shots were fired at close range at Captain Valdez. As his horse stumbled and fell dead, Valdez plunged from the saddle, his face streaming blood. Instantly upon striking the ground he rolled over and fired once in return, while the spies and guides who gathered about him opened a fusillade, driving the Indians off. Valdez was severely, though not mortally, wounded in the forehead. Major Backus learned later that the Navajos had been following Valdez since November 5, waiting for a moment when they could avenge the deaths of the two Navajos whom he had chased and shot down on Peña Blanca Creek.

Near Black Lake, four miles west of present Crystal, Major Backus the next day encountered more Navajos who informed him that "peace is made and Col. Miles has gone back to Cañon Bonito." With no further incident Backus brought his Second Column into Fort Defiance November 19. Most of his troops had marched with him from Albuquerque, a distance of 349 miles. The accounts of casualties inflicted on the Navajos by the combined forces of Colonel Miles and Major Backus differ slightly but prove that the greatest damage was done by the Utes. Twelve Navajos were known to have been killed, "many" more (perhaps fifteen) wounded, and some forty horses and three hundred sheep and goats captured. The troops' casualties were light: Private David Payne, with the First Column, and Captain Valdez, both wounded. Colonel Miles reported that during his march he was compelled to shoot twenty-five of his horses and twenty-three mules.

The Utes, all but ignored in the official reports and operating quietly as they had been doing for many years, had mauled the Navajos savagely. No attempt was made by either their agents or the military officers most closely involved with them to determine just how badly they had hurt the Navajos. As late as November 16, when Major Backus was limping southward to Cienega Juanico and Colonel Miles for three days had been warming himself at Fort Defiance, a large Ute war party swooped down upon the rancherias of Caballada Mucha on the San Juan. A Mexican captive of his band who was wounded and escaped brought the story to Fort Defiance. Within the space of a few hours ten Navajos were killed, six women and children were carried off to be sold in the settlements, and Caballada Mucha's entire horse herd—believed by Juan Anaya to number five hundred head—was captured.

The captive was so badly wounded in one hand by a rifle ball, Agent Yost advised James Collins, that amputation would be necessary. The man "seems to be about 22 years old," he added, "—has been with the Navajos 9 or 10 years. . . . From what I can learn there are but few captives in the Navajoe nation, and none of recent date. Those who are among them, have become so embued with Navajoe habits as not to desire to leave them." [17]

Teamsters arriving at the fort with a supply train from Albuquerque brought news of other violence. Puebloans of Isleta had traced the theft of large flocks of their sheep to members of Sandoval's band. The leader of the raiding party was found to be one of Sandoval's sons, a youth eighteen or nineteen years of age. The boy appeared at the pueblo the night of November 5 and was killed. Superintendent Collins officially attributed the death to a drunken frolic and, "to keep Sandoval's people quiet," he ordered that three men of the pueblo be tried for the murder. In his report of the affair to the commissioner of Indian affairs, Collins made no reference to the theft of Isleta sheep.[18]

Mail between Fort Defiance and Santa Fe in the last two months of 1858 required from seven days to more than two weeks in passage, the storms of early winter making a predictable schedule impossible. Colonel Miles's decision to end hostilities came so abruptly, and events thereafter moved so swiftly, that Colonel Bonneville and Superinten-

17. November 23, 1858: Miles to Wilkins, NA, RAC, RG 393, M-98-1858, LR; and (same date) Yost to Collins, NA, NMS T21-3.
18. November 6, 1858: Lt. J. A. G. Whistler, Los Lunas, to Wilkins, NA, RAC, RG 393, W-27-1858, LR; November 15, 1858: Collins to C.I.A. Charles E. Mix, NA, NMS 234-549.

dent Collins experienced a virtual breakdown of communications; they fell hopelessly behind and out of touch with the developments centering on Fort Defiance. Bonneville's reaction upon learning what Miles was up to was one of ponderous disapproval. Collins, a more volatile man, responded in disbelief and frustration; then, in mounting anger, he disassociated himself from the actions of his former editor, Agent Samuel Yost.

Yost precipitated a feud with his superior early in November. He was in warm support of Miles's desire to bring a quick end to the war. Like Miles, he assumed responsibilities well beyond his authority. Worse, in outlining a treaty policy where his role at most could have been only advisory, he undertook to correct Collins's expressed conviction that the Navajos should be confined within boundaries farther removed from the settlements. His reasoning was sound, but his manner was lofty. Reminding Collins that Governor Meriwether had made the same mistake, he said the Indians "have never paid any regard to those limits, and would not do so, even had the U.S. Senate ratified that treaty. *Necessity* would compel them to violate it." [19]

Before Collins had a chance to study and respond to Yost's comment on the error of his ways, Yost and Colonel Miles on November 20 concluded an armistice with Zarcillos Largos and nine other headmen.[20] Their meeting was at Fort Defiance and it was agreed that upon the expiration of the armistice in thirty days, they would meet again to draw up terms of a lasting peace. If Yost and Miles had left it at that, something of small benefit to both sides might conceivably have been salvaged. Instead, they appended terms that made the armistice appear to be the tentative framework of a final peace treaty.

The stipulations that Miles and Yost incorporated in the armistice so infuriated Collins when he received a copy of the document in early December that he accused his agent of presenting to him, in gross insubordination, an ill-conceived draft of a treaty. This the armistice was not, but the terms on which it was based unquestionably were ill conceived. Navajos, it was stipulated, would return all livestock stolen from Fort Defiance during the present war. (What, Collins was to demand, about livestock stolen in the same period from citizens of the territory?) A principal "chief" would be elected by the headmen; he would be

19. November 10, 1858: Yost to Collins, NA, NMS T21-3.
20. November 20, 1858: Miles to Wilkins, with one enclosure, NA, RAC, RG 393, M-84-1858, LR. Among others who signed the armistice were Armijo, Gordo, Herrero, Barboncito, Cabras Blancas, Ganado Mucho, and Huero.

completely subservient (in the old Spanish concept) to American authority, but in all matters he would be obeyed by all Navajos. The murderer of the Negro slave Jim would be surrendered "as soon as they [the Navajos] can catch him." Lastly, an exchange of prisoners would be made the day the peace treaty was signed: all captives held by Navajos would be given up, and all Navajos held captive *at Fort Defiance* in turn would be set free.

Yost explained to the headmen that since the man who had killed Jim might never be found, the Navajos might be called upon to pay for the value of the slave. When he later informed Collins of what had taken place at the council, Yost commented that "the main consideration which has prompted my efforts in behalf of the Indians . . . was the firm conviction that they had been thoroughly humiliated, and were fully impressed with their own insignificance. . . ." [21]

At department headquarters, meanwhile, it was known only that a few Navajo headmen had made overtures for peace. On November 21, the day after the armistice was signed, Colonel Bonneville wrote to Miles saying that if the Navajos' desire for peace was sincere, he and Superintendent Collins would be willing to meet with a delegation of headmen at Albuquerque. He then added:

"You are not, however, on any consideration, until further orders, to deem this sufficient cause for the cessation of hostilities, but on the contrary, you will continue to press the campaign against them." [22]

A week later an express from Fort Defiance brought the startling news that an armistice had been signed. Almost at once Collins and Bonneville decided they had no recourse but to go to Fort Defiance and, as Collins put it, "conclude the final settlement." A military escort was ordered to be ready to join them from the Albuquerque garrison on their departure on December 16. With Bonneville's concurrence, Collins drew up and sent on to Yost an entirely new set of terms, to which he said the Navajos must agree or face a resumption of the fighting. Although Collins referred to his proposals as a revision of the armistice, the terms eventually became the basis of the treaty. Another copy of the terms was forwarded to Washington, Collins advising Commissioner of Indian Affairs Charles E. Mix that

21. November 20, 1858: Yost to Collins, NA, NMS T21-3.
22. November 21, 1858: Bonneville to Miles, NA, RAC, RG 393, No. 286, LS. Miles, on the same day, wrote Bonneville proposing that Maj. Backus, who shortly would assume command of Fort Defiance, be appointed a peace commissioner. If Bonneville approved, Miles requested that he be relieved of command of the Navajo expedition so that he might return at once to the river.

"If I had believed the time had arrived to *offer* peace to the Indians I would so have instructed Agent Yost, but even then I would not have directed him to take the initiative. That I intended should remain with the Military. I am slow to believe that the Indians are so very humble, as the parties at Fort Defiance would have us believe." [23]

An inconspicuous and all but silent observer, Governor Abraham Rencher shared the opinion, now widely held in the capital, that the authorities had been gulled; that—far from suffering defeat—the Navajos had been little hurt.

"The war, in my opinion, was unwisely precipitated upon the Indians," he wrote Secretary of State Lewis Cass, "and [might] have been avoided by prudence and firmness on the part of the Indian agent. The rendition of the murderer of the Negro boy was improperly made a *sine qua non*. . . ." [24]

At Fort Defiance, Miles was encouraged by signs of Navajo compliance with two of his armistice terms. Zarcillos Largos in early December brought a small delegation of headmen to the fort, introducing one of them, a young nephew of Manuelito, as the "chief" elected to represent the nation. His Spanish name was Huero, meaning fair or blond, and to flatter the old colonel it was said that he would be known hereafter as Huero Miles. The next day Huero came again bringing, in partial restitution, ten mules and four horses. A third clause of the armistice became a source of aggravation, however, when Major Brooks asked if Miles would keep a promise he had made regarding the murdered slave Jim. Although the commanding colonel was no farther distant than a hundred yards or so, Brooks committed his question to writing.

"In order that I may not lose time in presenting my claim for this boy," he wrote, "I respectfully request to be informed whether it is, or not, your intention to make any demand upon the Indians for the payment of this boy?" Miles replied that a decision in the matter was not his to make. However, he did recommend to department headquarters that Brooks be permitted to enter a claim on part of a herd of captured goats then being held at Fort Craig.[25]

The impending arrival of Colonel Bonneville and Superintendent

23. December 3, 1858: Collins to Mix, NA, NMS 234-549.

24. November 29, 1858: Rencher to Cass, NA, TP, microcopy T-17, roll 1, no. 5494.

25. December 1, 1858: Miles to Wilkins, with two enclosures, NA, RAC, RG 393, M-95-1858, LR.

Collins was awaited in an atmosphere of nervous expectancy. The lag in communications left every man of the large garrison in doubt over his own immediate future. If peace were made some of them might hope to return soon to the river; for many, in any case, it looked like a long, difficult winter. Never had Fort Defiance been as heavily garrisoned. More than one thousand troops and a score of officers crowded the post quarters and spilled over into surrounding communities of miserable hovels built into the ground, or into even less comfortable tents, which offered little protection against the weather. The post facilities were further taxed by a small army of 184 civilians, including teamsters and packers, several interpreters, and 133 volunteer spies and guides.

Heavy snowstorms and an unbroken wave of freezing temperatures made the journey of Collins and Bonneville an ordeal. The ambulance in which they traveled would not have gotten through had it not, by luck, been following in the rear of a large supply train that broke trail. As it was, however, one of the four mules pulling their vehicle foundered and was shot and its mate in harness became so exhausted it could not make the return trip. The coldness of the last five days on the road was nearly matched, Collins was dismayed to find, by the reception he received from Colonel Miles and his officers. The cause of this hostility was soon discovered. Only a day or so before, Yost had passed among the officers copies he made of one paragraph from a letter he had received from Collins. In the opening sentence Collins had accused Yost of allowing the war to be started unnecessarily by his failure to protest Captain McLane's breach of orders when he made the unprovoked attack upon Navajos at Ojo del Oso. Collins then went on to say:

"And now when the officers in the field find themselves growing tired of the war, and doubtless in view of the fact Christmas is approaching, the agent allows himself to be put forward to close it. . . ." Collins did not attempt to disclaim the words. Instead, in a note to Miles he asked to withdraw the language found offensive by the officers, adding that it had not been his intention to insult them.

An abrasion of feelings remained, however, darkening further the sense of futility that hovered over the treaty council convened at the fort on Christmas Day. Fifteen headmen were present to hear the treaty read. Like the treaties that had preceded it, the agreement placed all burden of blame on the Navajos and imposed conditions that could not be anything but unacceptable to the Indians.

In summary, the first article established an eastern boundary line beyond which Navajos should not venture to graze, plant, or in any other manner occupy. Beginning at Pescado Springs the line went directly north to Ojo del Oso, then to the "ruins of Escondido on the Chaco," and from there on a direct line to the junction of the Chaco and San Juan rivers. Any Navajo livestock or crops found east of the line might be seized or destroyed by United States authorities.

The Navajos were to indemnify all citizens and Pueblos for thefts of property since the previous August 15. The entire Navajo nation was to be held responsible for every individual depredation by a Navajo, and the United States would seize Navajo livestock, as necessary, to assure full restitution. The usual one-sided treatment of captives was stipulated: all persons held by Navajos "who desire their release" were to be set free, whereas only "the Navajo prisoners in the hands of the United States" would be liberated. The demand for the man who killed the slave Jim was waived; however, the Navajos must agree to exile him from their nation and country and never offer him protection. The United States would retain the right to send troops through Navajo country and establish military posts or agencies wherever it was deemed necessary. Huero Miles would be recognized as the central authority of the nation. Finally, Sandoval and his Diné Ana'aii would be permitted to occupy the country where they now lived, thirty miles west of Albuquerque, but otherwise "are to be considered part and parcel of the Navajo nation."

Collins, who felt he had been maneuvered into making a treaty prematurely, allowed his misgivings to be reflected in the preamble to the agreement. Departing from all traditional form, he eschewed the word "treaty." Only when the terms that followed were complied with by the Navajos, by his careful phrasing, would peace and friendship be restored. Neither he nor Colonel Bonneville signed the document, another calculated omission that—had anyone later troubled to submit the agreement for due process—would have guaranteed refusal by the United States Senate to even consider ratification. Only Major Backus, Captain Gordon Granger, and Agent Yost signed, and they only as witnesses.[26]

26. Two copies of the treaty, both without title or covering letter, are found in the NMS files (NMS 234-549 and NMS T21-3, the former in Collins's handwriting). Navajos who signed were Huero, Armijo, Cabeza Colorada, Gordo, Ish-kit-sa-ne, "Huero 2d," Zarcillos Largos, Herrero, Ganado Mucho, Durando, Huero Backus, Herrero Chiquito, "Guardo," Marcus, and "Utah Chicito or Jose Antonio."

Contrary to the treaty clause relating to captives, twenty-one Navajos who were captured during the nearly four months of Miles's campaigning were held in the guardhouse when Bonneville started back for the river. These prisoners, he explained afterwards, were to be held as hostages until the Navajos complied with the treaty terms. Collins and Miles departed on the same day, December 28, their train including two companies of infantry and four of mounted riflemen. During the next three days, six more companies of troops started for the Rio Grande, leaving Major Backus once more in command of Fort Defiance, his garrison numbering 6 officers and 230 enlisted men. Samuel Yost, in serious difficulties, remained at the post temporarily, pending the arrival of his successor.

Colonel Bonneville, who ultimately would be held responsible as department commander, refrained from censuring Miles's conduct of the expedition; from the moment he learned of the November 20 armistice, he lapsed into stunned silence. Collins also remained silent for three months after his return to Santa Fe. Then, in a letter to his immediate superior in Washington, he surprisingly wrote that he felt some anxiety, as rumors were being circulated back to Washington, and "a shameful and unpardonable exaggeration" in a story appearing in the *National Intelligencer* had been reported in other newspapers in the States. All contributed, he said, to a "fulsome adulation" of Samuel Yost and a misunderstanding of what had occurred during the recent Navajo war. He had nothing to conceal and would hold himself responsible for what he might say, Collins wrote, and he added:

"Col. Miles in his official reports, if I mistake not, gives the number [of Navajos] killed at something over sixty, but the two Mexican Captains who commanded the Spyes and guides, told me that they did not believe there were twenty killed. The number of sheep taken and destroyed may be cut down about two thirds. . . . The truth is, the war was commenced with a foolish precipitancy, and I fear it will be found that it was closed in about the same way." [27] Colonel Miles had in fact exaggerated the Navajos' losses, but Collins in this letter minimized them.

27. March 27, 1859: Collins to C.I.A. J. W. Denver, NA, NMS 234-549.

21

1859–60: The War Makers

Impersonal fate dealt Sandoval a blow just when it seemed that his position in the regard of his American friends was impervious to challenge. He was with members of his band one day in February 1859 when he was thrown from an unbroken horse. Before he could move out of the way the horse kicked and badly hurt him. The accident occurred on the sandy plains near Red Mountain, in the vicinity of the Rio Puerco, and it is said that Sandoval was carried to Herrera Mesa where a healing ceremony was performed. The ministrations he received during the sing failed; after several days Sandoval died.[1]

For more than forty years, from the time Joaquín in 1818 had led his people out of the Navajo nation, only Joaquín and Francisco Baca, before Sandoval, had received the allegiance of the Diné Ana'aii. The band's commitment to a life separate from the Navajo nation was too deep to change. Sandoval is said to have been succeeded by one called Andrés, who was replaced by a man referred to in 1861 as Po-ha-Conta, who in turn was replaced by an exceedingly tough, child-selling renegade named Pino Baca. None of these men achieved more than brief recognition or influence. In the early weeks of Kit Carson's Navajo expedition in 1863 a group of fifty-one captives, among them a number of Diné Ana'aii, was the first contingent to go to confinement at Bosque Redondo. Word of their coming preceded them. Authorities at Fort Sumner were told to prepare for the arrival of Sandoval's band. As "Sandoval's band" they would be known for at least a decade more.

Now, bewildered by the loss of Sandoval and without a leader who could win the confidence of American authorities, the Diné Ana'aii slipped into obscurity. Only occasionally were they to attract notice

1. Correll 1970, pp. 38–39. Descendants of the Diné Ana-aii, today known as Cañoncito Navajos, occupy a small reservation of their own north of U.S. Highway 66 and east of Laguna Pueblo.

again, and then usually in relation to minor instances of cooperation with the Bilagáana.

But even as the Diné Ana'aii dropped from sight, young warriors of the Navajos gradually resumed raiding. Their attacks were launched first against pueblos: against Zuni in March, and then in succession against the Hopi villages, Jemez, and Laguna and Acoma. In May two pastors were killed at Agua Azul, 3,200 sheep were stolen from Jemez, and raids were made twice on Abiquiu. As they had done before, Zarcillos Largos and Ganado Mucho tried to restrain the young men, and when that failed they did what they could to recover stolen livestock and return it to the owners. In spite of increasing infirmities of age, Zarcillos Largos was the most active of his people in trying to preserve peace. Huero was recognized in Santa Fe as the "principal chief," but it was Zarcillos Largos who was spoken of by civil and military officers as the Navajos' most influential and powerful man.

From the time of the treaty of the previous December, the Ninth Military Department had retained responsibility for Navajo affairs. Superintendent Collins observed with frustration the increasing tempo of hostilities and Colonel Bonneville's relatively unperturbed response. The peaceful efforts of Zarcillos Largos and other headmen were of little effect, he informed Commissioner Mix, and accordingly he intended to press Bonneville to demand of the Navajos a compliance with treaty terms. Orders already had been issued to more than double the strength of the Fort Defiance garrison. Troops would begin to move about June 15 and by early July some 650 soldiers would be stationed in Navajo country.[2]

Although Collins continued to talk of the inevitability of war and the need to humble the Navajos, the officer chosen by Bonneville for command on the frontier was the antithesis of Collins, more dove than hawk. Major John Smith Simonson, a Hoosier by adoption who rose in the ranks and had been in uniform since 1814, confessed to no interest in killing Indians. A junior officer who had served with him several years before in the Apache campaign of 1857 observed that Simonson was "a simple, but kind old fellow . . . a more benevolent or honorable heart never beat in sympathetic pulsations to the failings of his fellow man." And, less gently, he "was heard to make several stupid remarks in a very stupid and delightful manner—accompanied with much dignity. Repeatedly tooting his nasal organ—dispensing entirely

2. May 15, 1859: Collins to Mix, NA, NMS 234-549.

with a handkerchief—which is unquestionably a high accomplish-
ment . . ." [3] By his own words and deeds Simonson would soon appear neither simple nor stupid.

With two companies of mounted riflemen and detachments of two
more, Major Simonson left Abiquiu on June 17, following the old
Spanish invasion route northwestward into Dinetah, and emerging on
the San Juan at the mouth of Largo Canyon. Because his orders in
part required him to report on the feasibility of this route for a wagon
road, Simonson's observations during the march were more than usually alert. His report, written on arrival at Fort Defiance, together with
a sketch map and detailed notes by Lieutenant William H. Bell, forms
one of the more literate and informative military commentaries on the
Navajo country.[4]

The San Juan he found in spring flood, too high to permit fording
wagons, but "a beautiful stream, sending forth a volume of water equal
to the Monongahela. . . . It has a broad bottom, the river banks
skirted with cotton-wood. . . ." Discovering old ruins and scattered
potsherds as his column proceeded along the south bank, he found
these relics in some respects similar to those seen on the Gila River.
He remarked the presence of Cayetano's band in close proximity to
Utes on the Animas and La Plata rivers, but it seemed there was no
confrontation with them.

Navajos in large numbers were met with after the column, turning
on Peña Blanca Creek at the base of Beautiful Mountain, ascended
into the Chuscas. All whom he met and talked with seemed friendly,
Major Simonson noted. Armijo, "always friendly to whites," met him
at Cienega Negra, and soon afterward Zarcillos Largos joined the column near Laguna Negra and with scores of followers accompanied the
major on the last miles to the fort. He also professed friendship but

3. Lt. Henry M. Lazalle Diary, ed. Reeve 1948, pp. 276–78. Simonson served for
five months in upper Canada during the War of 1812 with Capt. N. F. Knapp's
company of New York State Volunteers. At the outbreak of the war with Mexico
he was appointed a captain in the mounted rifles and later was brevetted major for
gallantry in the battle of Chapultepec. During the Civil War he came out of retirement to command the Military District of Indiana and Michigan from September 1863 to about June 1864. In 1865 he was appointed a brevet brigadier general
while serving as post commander at Indianapolis. He died the evening of December 5,
1881, at the home of his son-in-law, Judge Howk, in New Albany, Indiana (Service
records, NA, RG 94, ACP 79, box 626).

4. July 5, 1859: Simonson to Wilkins, with two enclosures, NA, RAC, RG 393,
S-37-1859, LR.

at the same time made Simonson aware of his great anxiety over the renewed presence of so many soldiers.

Awaiting him on arrival Simonson found supplementary orders from department headquarters. The object of his troops' presence in Navajo country, he was informed, was to effect a show of force sufficient to "support the Indian Department in any demands they may make on the Nation." Otherwise, Simonson was to divide his command into two columns and make a thorough reconnaissance of the entire Navajo country. Colonel Bonneville asked that the troops visit each band, note their numbers, locations, herds of horses, sheep, and cattle, and their planting and grazing grounds—everything, in short, that would be use ful in case of war. At the same time, Bonneville emphasized that he desired Simonson to pursue "a kind and gentle course" with the Indians.[5]

The orders were anathema to Henry Connelly, the Albuquerque merchant. Long an important figure in the territory, he was to be elected two years later to the governorship. Speaking now in behalf of outraged citizens, he spoke as well from personal interest (his supply trains were carrying tons of flour and other goods regularly to Fort Defiance). Reciting a list of alleged robberies and murders, he called in May for a war of extermination against the Navajos. He angrily informed Superintendent Collins that Collins and Colonel Bonneville would be subject to ridicule if they did not enforce their own treaty stipulations. In July he pressed Collins more closely. The department commander, he said, would not feel authorized to resume the war until Collins advised him officially of what all knew—that the treaty had been broken and Collins could not, without Bonneville's aid, force the Indians into compliance.

"Let us have no more [Colonel John M.] Washington treaties," Connelly added, "and dont let the Indians play the same game of deceit and hypocrisy with you that they have played with other Superintendents."[6] Connelly's insistent demands unquestionably stirred public support and played a major part in persuading Collins (who needed little persuasion) and Bonneville into adopting an inflexibly harsh policy toward the Navajos. For a few months more, however, Major Simonson would operate, without interference, on a kind and gentle course.

5. June 10, 1859: Wilkins to Simonson, NA, RAC, RG 393, no. 106, LS. On July 4, the day after his arrival. Simonson relieved Brevet Maj. Oliver L. Shepherd in command of the fort. Maj. Backus had relinquished command to Shepherd the previous February 9.

6. May 13, 1859: Connelly to Collins, NA, NMS 234-549; July 4, 1859: Connelly to Collins. NA, RAC, RG 393, no file mark.

Bonneville's orders were put into effect on July 18 when two columns of troops moved off in different directions on the first exploring operations. From La Joya grazing grounds north of Fort Defiance, Captain John G. Walker's command moved up to the Cienega Negra and the next day to a camp on the Palo Negro, or Wheatfield Creek, where the soldiers encountered a considerable gathering of Navajos. The Indians appeared decidedly restive when they learned it was the captain's intention to descend next morning into the head of Canyon de Chelly's central gorge (for which all of the canyon complex was named). Walker was uncertain why the Navajos objected to this, although the reason they gave was that the captain's plan was suicidally dangerous and they might be held to blame for any resulting fatalities. Firmly committed to the scheme, Walker seized several of the principal Navajos as hostages and guides. His venture would be the first when American soldiers traversed Canyon de Chelly proper from east to west.[7]

"The descent was truly terrific," Lieutenant John Van D. DuBois noted in his journal that night. "We were four hours getting down the 800 feet depth—Mules fell distances of from twenty to forty feet. Two were killed—& several only saved by their loads which prevented them from striking the rocks in their fall—Looking up it seems as if there was no escape. . . . Tall pines look like bushes. . . . Men and animals on the top as seen from below like mites against the sky. Next to Niagara it is the greatest wonder of nature I have ever seen." [8]

Heavy rains of the last few days made a running stream of the Chinle Wash from the head of the canyon to the bend at the mouth, some

7. The 1st Column, commanded by Maj. Shepherd, returned in 22 days after marching to Oraibi Pueblo and south to within sight of the Little Colorado River. On his return, Shepherd reported that during the six years he had been attached to the Defiance garrison, "I have never known a more pacific disposition manifested by the Navajoes." Walker's column included Company K and a detachment of Company E, Mounted Rifles, and Companies C and G, 3d Infantry. The Walker and Shepherd reports are enclosed with August 8, 1859: Simonson to Wilkins, NA, RAC, RG 393, S-44-1859, LR.

8. DuBois Journal, entry of July 20. After designation of his regiment was changed to the 3d Cavalry (by Act of August 3, 1861), DuBois was promoted captain of the 3d Cavalry in 1862, and major in 1869. Assignments after the Civil War, in which he served on eastern battlefronts with distinction, found him variously at Fort Smith, Arkansas, and—in New Mexico—Forts Sumner, Bascom, and Selden, and at Camp Hualpai in Arizona. Retirement that he requested in 1870 because of illness was granted in 1876 when an inquiry conducted at 1700 Pennsylvania Avenue in Washington by Col. William H. Emory determined that his heart and kidney ailment, accompanied with epilepsy, were in no way due to alcoholism. He died at his home in Hudson, New York, July 31, 1879 (Service records, NA, RG 94, ACP R390 CB70, box 412).

thirty miles to the west. Captain Walker shared the awe of his soldiers, finding the perpendicular walls of red sandstone breaking into "gigantic cathedrals, fortifications, castles . . . or what the fancy might easily convert into such." The canyon bottom was extremely sandy, but still it supported dark green patches of deeply planted corn and also some wheat. At the end of the first day's march the column had progressed more than seventeen miles through the gorge.

Early on July 21 after the march was resumed, Lieutenant DuBois noted that the troops "at the mouth of a branch cañon [came upon] what is called Miles' Column—it is a single shaft from 800 to 1000 feet high. . . . What seems to be a small cedar bush is growing on its summit." The enormous tower of rock stood at the junction of the central gorge and Monument Canyon, through which Colonel Miles had made his uneasy way the previous September.[9] Early afternoon brought Walker's detachment out through the mouth of Canyon de Chelly and to a camp near cornfields raided often in the past by invading troops. No mention of such plunder was made on this occasion, DuBois remarking only that "here we had a talk with some two hundred indians [who] came in—bringing their families."

The balance of Captain Walker's reconnaissance for the most part was a retracing, in reverse, of the route followed six years before by Major Kendrick and Henry Dodge. After striking the San Juan, the Walker column skirted the southern slopes of the Carrizo Mountains and then returned to Fort Defiance through the western valleys of the Chuscas. In submitting his report on August 3, Captain Walker offered conclusions that would not have appealed greatly to war makers on the river:

> . . . I would remark that the Navajoes everywhere evinced the most earnest desire for peace. I am not prepared to say what would be the better line of policy towards them, but there is no doubt that a war made upon them now by us would fall the heaviest upon the least guilty, would transform a nation which has already made considerable progress in civilized arts into a race of beggars, vagabonds and robbers. What consideration such views should have in the settlement of our difficulties with them— difficulties based upon exaggerated demands—which every animal in the Navajo country would scarcely be sufficient to satisfy, it is not for one to suggest, but before severe measures are resolved

9. Now designated officially as Monument Rock, it is known far better as Spider Rock, so called from Navajo parental legend that on its summit dwells a spider who, on summons, will drop down on its gossamer thread to fetch back to the awful nest any Navajo child guilty of incorrigible behavior.

on and a course of policy initiated that would entail poverty and wretchedness upon the entire tribe, it may be that some little forbearance might be the part of true wisdom.[10]

Major Simonson largely concurred with Walker's summation. In a covering report to department headquarters, he observed that the reinforcement of the Fort Defiance garrison doubtless had contributed to the Navajos' plainly obvious desire for peace. Nevertheless, he added, claims for robberies made against the Navajos were unquestionably exaggerated. Navajos themselves had suffered great losses at the hands of citizen raiders and had never once been offered restitution by the authorities in Santa Fe or Washington. The ladrons, he said, were responsible for the acts of thievery and murder, but if war were to be made upon the nation for the acts of these individuals, "the innocent and those most active for the preservation of peace would be the sufferers." Foremost among those active for peace was Zarcillos Largos.

An incident showing how far Zarcillos Largos, on rare occasion, would go in cooperating with the military occurred in August. After informing Agent Alexander Baker of the theft of cattle from Zuni by three Navajos, he offered to take a detachment of soldiers to the place where the thieves would be found. Here the soldiers might either recover the stolen animals or seize an equal number in restitution. Accordingly, in an unaccustomed role as guide, Zarcillos Largos led Captain Henry B. Schroeder and his command into the lower Chusca Valley. Twelve or more Navajos who joined the column acted as advance scouts until, at a point not far from Laguna Grande, the three raiders were found up in the mountains about one-half mile ahead. The terrain was too rough to allow pursuit by mounted troops, so Captain Schroeder asked Zarcillos Largos to go as envoy to the Navajos' camp and persuade them to return with him, whereupon it was Schroeder's plan to seize them. Having brought the soldiers this close, however, Zarcillos Largos refused to do more. The Navajos with him declined as well to deliver the thieves to the captain's trap. Instead, with the headman, they left the troops and returned home. Schroeder remained in the field one week and finally reported back to the fort empty-handed.[11]

10. A native of Missouri, Walker did not attend West Point, but volunteered for service in the Mexican War, during which he was brevetted for gallant conduct at San Juan de los Llanos. He resigned from the army in July 1861 and served as a major general with the Confederacy from 1861 to 1865.

11. August 14, 1859: Baker to Collins, NA, NMS T21-4; (same date) Simonson to Bonneville, with one enclosure, NA, RAC, RG 393, unentered letters received. Laguna Grande, possibly an ephemeral lake, does not appear on modern maps. According to both Schroeder's report and Capt. J. N. Macomb's 1860 "Map of

Bonneville's plan for a systematic reconnaissance of Navajo country culminated in late summer when two columns, each made up of four companies of infantry and riflemen, departed from Fort Defiance on September 5. In Orders No. 14, Major Simonson directed that "the columns will visit all bands of Navajoes on their respective routes. . . . A kind and gentle course will be pursued towards them. . . . Persons and property of all peaceable Indians will be respected—their lodgings and dwellings unmolested."

Brevet Major Oliver L. Shepherd led one column into the lower Chusca Valley and then eastward through Wingate Valley to the vicinity of Mount Taylor. At Cubero, where he obtained a guide, he turned southwest, winding through the ragged lava beds about Ojo del Gallo and then crossing the dry desert plains that led him to Rito Quemado and Zuni Salt Lake. The volcanic formation standing in solitary silence in the hot plain of fine sand and gray ash impressed Shepherd deeply. He examined carefully and later described well an elevated crater pool of densely saline solution, the heavy water hot on the bottom. The pool was higher by 150 feet than its neighboring crater and salt lake, Shepherd said, the lower crater deeply bowl-shaped and perhaps two miles in circumference. Whereas the water of the pool above was clear but salty, the lake below formed whitish encrustations, which, skimmed from the mud banks, gave dry crystals of almost pure salt. Major Shepherd did not fail to observe that well-worn trails converged on the craters from all compass points—trails used for centuries by Indian salt gatherers of many different tribes and tongues. From this point the command turned south, Shepherd remarking that he was retracing the outward route of Major Kendrick in November 1856 that had brought Henry Dodge to ambush and violent death.[12]

Taking a nearly opposite course, the command of Captain John G. Walker started west on the familiar Hopi road, then, turning northwesterly near Steamboat Canyon, traversed the high broken ground of Mesa de la Vaca or Black Mesa. On September 12, emerging suddenly on rimrock of a steep-slanting precipice seven hundred feet above the plain, Walker and his men "obtained a view of a vast range of as desolate and repulsive looking country as can be imagined. As far as the

---

Explorations and Surveys in New Mexico and Utah," Laguna Grande was in the Chusca Mountains about sixteen miles (airline) east and a trifle south of Fort Defiance.

12. September 25, 1859: Shepherd to Lt. J. H. Edson, post adjutant; enclosure with September 28, 1859: Simonson to Wilkins, NA, RAC, RG 393, S-65-1859, LR.

eye can reach . . . is a vast mass of sand stone hills without any covering or vegetation except a scanty growth of cedar. In the northwest and
apparently about fifty miles distant *Sierra Panoche* [Navajo Mountain]
looms up, and beyond this . . . our guide pointed to the junction of
Colorado Chiquito [Colorado River] and Rio San Juan . . ."

Desolation—like beauty—is in the eye of the beholder. The Mis-
sourian Walker stood high on the breathtaking threshhold of Monument Valley and, God help him, was appalled. By a precarious zigzag
trail the troops dropped down to the head of Klethla Valley, there
sandy and scrubby and a mile and a half wide. Crossing the valley to
the west Walker led his troops to "an ancient ruin, like all others in
this country, situated on a hill." Indeed, perched high and dark on a
lower level of a great rolling bank or knob of pitted pink sandstone,
Long House (to archaeologists known also as Ruin A) is approached
over a crackling carpeting of dry sand, grass, and millions of tiny polychrome potsherds. Like an elongated box, the once-two-storied Anasazi
dwelling is eighty feet long and a mere seven feet wide. Here Walker's
men camped for the night, pulling down roof timbers for firewood. A
number of them—Lieutenants Thomas W. Walker and William H.
Bell, most elaborately—carved their names or initials and the date in
the soft, smooth stone blocks of the walls.

Morning and a march of four miles to the north brought the troops
into the narrowing pass Captain Walker's guide called "Puerta Limita,"
known today as Marsh Pass at its junction with the westering and at
that point innocent-appearing Tsegi Canyon. On rounding the head of
Black Mesa soon afterward, the troops could see, due north and rising
darkly ten (or was it twenty?) miles distant, the outlines of "the *Lana
Negra* . . . resembling a vast Gothic cathedral"—a hulking rock of
basalt that may have been Salazar's "Cerro Elevado," and is today's
Aghathla Peak. At this point the column began its return march, traveling southeast to join the Chinle Wash above present Many Farms.
Once more on the Chinle, Walker avoided the depths of Canyon de
Chelly and followed the familiar south rim route into the forests, the
steep slopes, and the valleys leading downward to Fort Defiance. With
no unpleasant incident, he arrived there September 19.[13]

The same day the Shepherd and Walker columns left Fort Defiance,
an episode far to the east all but wiped out the efforts of Zarcillos

13. September 20, 1859: Walker to Edson; enclosure with September 23, 1859:
Simonson to Wilkins, NA, RAC, RG 393, S-57-1859, LR.

Largos and others to maintain peace. A war party said to number about fifty Indians swept down on a herd of cattle grazing west of Albuquerque between the Rio Grande and the Puerco. Bristling with arrows, the bodies of two herdsmen, Domingo Carravajal and his son José, later were found near the Puerco. Families of Candelarias, Corrales, and Atrisco claimed that together they had lost between 75 and 100 cattle. Santiago L. Hubbell reported the incident while in Albuquerque, saying that arrows found in the bodies and "other signs" indicated that the Indians were Navajos.

Some doubt about this was raised momentarily by conflicting reports of Apache raids in the same area, but Hubbell's story was, in part, accurate. At Fort Defiance, Cabras Blancas informed the Navajo agent that a party of five, not fifty, Navajos had murdered the Carravajals and had driven eleven head of cattle back to the Chusca Valley. The raid was carried out, Cabras Blancas said, in deliberate retaliation for the recent murder of a brother of the party's leader by citizens of Atrisco.[14]

Responding to cries of outrage from the river, Agent Silas F. Kendrick and Major Simonson arranged to meet with Navajo headmen at Laguna Negra on September 25.[15] In the meantime, Captain Schroeder with a command of infantry and riflemen was ordered to march in search of the five raiders. All of this, and more, spread a pall of unease about the fort. Huero, on a trip to Santa Fe to talk with Superintendent Collins about indemnification payments required by the December 25 treaty, had been set upon and robbed by Pueblos of either Sandia or San Felipe. Among other valuable trade articles his losses included four horses, two dozen Navajo blankets, four buffalo robes, and fourteen yards of bayeta. To make matters worse, a party of twenty-seven New Mexicans, said to be on a trading expedition, had eluded Agent Kendrick and vanished into Navajo country. Theirs was the third

14. September 7, 1859: Hubbell to Bonneville, NA, RAC, RG 393, H-31-1859, LR; and September 23, 1859: Simonson to Wilkins, NA, RAC, RG 393, S-58-1859, LR.

15. Samuel M. Yost served as Navajo agent until the appointment in January 1859 of Robert J. Cowart. Cowart failed to appear at Fort Defiance until late in February and by April 12 he was back in Albuquerque, having resigned. His successor, Alexander Baker, lasted four months and was replaced by Kendrick on August 23. Kendrick almost at once disqualified himself by admitting he found the Navajos "generous and kind, and [with] many noble traits." Already in his one month of duty he had met with the Navajos twice in Canyon de Chelly, where he "eat, drink, and danced with them, which delited them very much" (September 24, 1859: Kendrick to Collins, NA, NMS, T21-4).

such party known to have come out in recent months; because they spread unsettling rumors among the Navajos, their presence at this precarious moment was regarded as dangerous.

Although his garrison numbered almost seven hundred troops, there was little display of force when Major Simonson accompanied Agent Kendrick to the council at Laguna Negra. The major deliberately took a secondary role in the proceedings and limited the escort to fifty of Captain Walker's mounted riflemen. Navajos who gathered at the council ground outnumbered the Americans three to one; their principal spokesmen were Herrero (lately with "Viejo" added to his name), the older still Zarcillos Largos, and Ganado Mucho.

An unlettered man, handicapped by having to express himself through the words of an interpreter, Kendrick asked the Navajos to gather more closely about him and to listen attentively. He was convinced, he said, that not as before, when they met with suspicion and as enemies, they met now as friends. As their friend he must tell them that they could live at peace and as brothers of the Bilagáana only if they paid in full the debt standing against them—the claims for livestock demanded by citizens and Pueblos of the territory. Their debt was greater, he said, in consequence of the recent murders on the Puerco. If they would make him no definite promise of compliance, he would be compelled to turn them over to the military. Major Simonson spoke briefly, saying that much as he regretted it war would be made upon them if they did not abide by the stipulations of the recent treaty. Then Kendrick arose once more to say he would extend by thirty days the time in which the headmen might meet the demands of the authorities in Santa Fe.

The tone of the Navajo response was sombre. What indemnification, the headmen asked, would be made for the six Navajos murdered in recent months by Pueblos and New Mexicans? Huero would be repaid for his recent losses because the *Tata* in Santa Fe had promised it, but what indemnification would be paid to all of the other Navajos who had lost friends and relatives and great numbers of sheep and horses to their old enemies? And why, it was asked, could not the property stolen from Navajos be acknowledged—and applied against the often unjust or exaggerated claims advanced by citizens?

Before the council ended the headmen discussed for an hour or more Agent Kendrick's proposal to extend the time in which they might gather livestock to be sent to citizens on the river. Finally they agreed to try once more, provided that the agent would go with them. Kendrick agreed, and said he would start the next morning. In his report later to Collins, Kendrick said he was hopeful of success. Should their efforts fail, he would ask the superintendent to propose some other plan, he said, but, "I never can give my consent to wage war on those honest men, [who have] done all in their power to do right." [16]

For the first time in the history of such negotiations, the Navajos found in Major Simonson a military officer who would appear in their support as an eloquent advocate. "Let the murderers on all occasions be punished with the utmost rigor," Simonson urged in reporting to head-quarters, ". . . but we should reflect before enforcing claims under the provisions of the treaty of December last, upon the inoffensive and innocent."

By stipulation of the treaty's fourth article the Navajos agreed to indemnify citizens and Pueblos for all robberies committed since August 15, 1858. However, no claims had been put forward at the time the treaty was signed, Major Simonson pointed out, and the Navajos therefore had reason to believe one of two things: either the demands would not be made, or, if they were made, they would be determined by an impartial or otherwise legal method of proving the accuracy of the claim and the valuation of property lost. But at this time, as the full payment of all claims was pressed as the only acceptable alternative to war, the major added, the claims were being entered unjustly or illegally—"on no better authority than the testimony of interested parties. . . . It is believed this is the first instance on record where men who have had the misfortune to lose property have been allowed to prove their claims by their own testimony, set their own value upon it, and have their pretended losses made good to them upon such testimony or enforced at the point of the bayonet."

Major Simonson had reason to know that this unorthodox reasoning ran directly counter to the policies firmly outlined by Colonel Bonneville and Superintendent Collins, but he pressed on. Another matter of great concern, he wrote, were the raids made upon the persons and property of Navajos by New Mexicans and Pueblos. Beginning with the reinforcement of the Defiance garrison late in June, depredations upon the Navajos had increased "under the supposition that the plundering of the Indians could be done with impunity." Until raiding par-

16. September 29, 1859: Kendrick to Collins, NA, NMS T21-4; and September 28, 1859: Simonson to Wilkins, NA, RAC, RG 393, S-66-1859, LR. At the end of his report Simonson wrote: "The energy [Kendrick] displays will soon give him an influence over the Navajo Indians that no Agent has possessed since the death of Mr. Dodge."

ties from the river could be restrained, it would be almost impossible to prevent Navajos from retaliating:

> And I respectfully request to be informed if it was the intention of Colonel Bonneville and Col. Collins who acted in behalf of the United States, to exclude the Navajo Nation from the benefit of indemnity for depredations committed against them by citizens of New Mexico and Pueblo Indians? The treaty binds the Navajoes to make restitution, but leaves them without redress for injuries inflicted upon them. . . . That the Navajoes understood that restitution was to be mutual is certain, from their constant declarations and their frequent applications to the agents and officers of the United States for such restitution and the omission of a stipulation affording them redress . . . must greatly prejudice the character of our country for justice and fair dealing in their estimation.

His intention to retire from the army may have been a factor in Major Simonson's audacious criticism of the current Navajo policy. Two days before the Laguna Negra council he had requested that he be relieved of command, saying that an affliction of rheumatism made it all but impossible for him to walk. His request was granted and he left Fort Defiance October 10, relinquishing command to Major Shepherd pending the arrival, two weeks later, of Major Charles F. Ruff. Captain Schroeder, meanwhile, returned after a fruitless search for the murderers of the Carravajals. (He attributed his failure largely to his Navajo guide, who explained that he had hired on thinking he was wanted for an exploring expedition "and that it was not fair to ask him to inform on his own people.")

Simonson's appeal for just treatment of the Navajos was brushed aside as unworthy of consideration. On October 22 Bonneville issued orders that the entire available command at Fort Defiance march against the Navajos of the Chusca Valley. Major Ruff at once directed Major Shepherd to take the field with a large detachment of infantry and mounted riflemen. At the same time, with care to avoid an appearance of insubordination, Ruff expressed certain misgivings: he would not attempt to predict what effect this blow would have on other Navajos, he said, but he cheerfully would do his best to comply with Bonneville's every order. Agent Kendrick, who was going to Santa Fe on business of his own, was entrusted with delivering Major Ruff's message. The agent was under orders to return and presumably would do so, but Ruff had his doubts. "Learning of the attack upon the Tunicha Valley indians," he wrote, Kendrick "may take fright; I should consider his return very uncertain & if any communications are transmitted for me by him, please send duplicates. . . ."

Major Ruff's misgivings over the outcome of Bonneville's orders were shared by others. In the night before starting out with Shepherd's command, Lieutenant DuBois noted in his journal that "this time some indians will be killed for it is the intention of Col Bonneville no doubt to bring on a war. His order says kill four or five at least of this tribe as a punishment for their depredations—One cannot fight one band of Navajos without fighting all but he thinks differently–. Nous verrons." [17]

The weather in the morning of November 1 was clear but cold and windy. Shepherd's command of some 280 troops moved northward, leaving the lake and red cliffs of Laguna Negra to enter forested country, the trail climbing and turning toward the western approach to Washington Pass. On the third day they descended to Chusca Valley. Shepherd at once turned north again, holding his column close to the broken foothills. In the lee of Beautiful Mountain he set a trap in the morning of November 6. Before moving from his camp on Peña Blanca Creek the major ordered Lieutenant John McL. Hildt with a detachment of twenty-five infantry and riflemen to conceal themselves in the arroyo and wait. The rest of the command then broke camp with more noise than usual and marched off. The troops had proceeded no more than a mile when they saw five mounted Navajos, small figures in the distance moving slowly in the clear morning light, prodding among the remains of the camp's ashes. Hildt's troops opened fire, knocking two of the Indians from their horses. One Navajo was killed instantly. The other escaped by throwing his arms around his horse's neck, but the trail of blood he left convinced Hildt that the man soon died, and tracks showed that his friends had returned to retrieve the body.

During the next two days Major Shepherd's command searched the silent valley in blowing sand for traces of Cayetano's or Armijo's bands. Striking the Tuntsa Wash, they followed its dry bed to withered, abandoned cornfields at the junction of the Tuntsa and the wider but equally dry Chaco Wash. Here, branching off from a few deserted hogans, mute evidence of a rendezvous point, were broad trails of hoof tracks indicating that the Navajos had gathered and then divided, driving on with their livestock. Major Shepherd found the flight had taken two main directions, one eastward into painted badlands and

17. DuBois Journal, entry of October 31, 1859; October 22, 1859: Wilkins to Ruff, NA, RAC, RG 393, no. 200, LS.

slag-heap canyons north of present Bisti, the other toward the ragged ridge of the Hogback, an incredible dorsal pointing toward the San Juan like some scaly and ancient monster caught in the volcanic crust. Shepherd concluded that the Indians were too far ahead of him to make pursuit worth attempting.

Instead he set his bearings on Bennett's Peak, which he could see over the valley's western horizon, and moved his column back toward the Chuscas. The command divided the next day after regaining the forested summit of the mountains. One column, to which Lieutenant DuBois was attached, followed a high ridge until it sighted several herds of sheep, far ahead and below. The slopes were too steep and wooded, and broken to permit the horsemen any formation. After two hours of strung-out pursuit, Lieutenant Ira W. Claflin's riflemen of Company H met again with DuBois's detachment. Somewhere in the rear, lower on the side of the mountain, Lieutenant William Dickinson held a milling herd of about six hundred sheep and goats. In his journal entry relating this episode DuBois lost his customary ready flow of expression:

"Every man came in," he wrote tautly. "We Killed three, captured a woman (wounded in the heel) and about six hundred sheep." The usually communicative young officer had nothing more to say about it.

Major Shepherd's column meanwhile moved through the mountains in another direction. Near a cluster of deserted hogans two old women were flushed from their hiding places, but they and their pitfully small bunch of sheep later were turned loose. On his return to Fort Defiance November 12, Shepherd reported that his command had succeeded in mauling such of the Navajos as could be found. It may have fulfilled DuBois's statement of what Colonel Bonneville wanted.[18]

DuBois himself made at once for the sutler's store. Here, over a toddy, he received confirmation of a rumor he had heard. The riflemen would be withdrawn from Fort Defiance the next day—the familiar

---

18. November 13, 1859: Shepherd to Ruff; enclosure with (same date) Ruff to Wilkins, NA, RAC, RG 393, R-53-1859, LR. As so often in such operations, Shepherd was not certain about Navajo casualties. He reported two killed and left on the ground, and six badly wounded—three so severely that they no doubt died. The actual circumstances are important, as the Navajos regarded this action as a clear declaration of war against their nation. From the Ute agency at Abiquiu, Albert H. Pfeiffer several weeks later noted that Sobeta had come in with a band of Capotes and informed him that "the troops had an engagement with the Navahoes [in which] five of them & one Woman got killed" (December 3, 1859: Pfeiffer to Collins, NA, NMS T21-4).

strike-and-withdraw strategy that guaranteed an intensification of Navajo reprisals. "I was half sorry," DuBois wrote in his journal. "The war had commenced and the prospect was good for an active campaign."

The order withdrawing Major Ruff with two companies of mounted riflemen and two of infantry was issued not by Bonneville but by his successor, Colonel Thomas T. Fauntleroy, freshly arrived from the States.[19] The decision was reached largely on the advice of Superintendent Collins, who allowed Fauntleroy to believe that Bonneville's action had not reopened the war, as in fact was the case. Collins misled the new department commander further by saying that *if* and *when* war with the Navajos was resumed, the choice would be Fauntleroy's. In the meantime, Collins argued, the season was now too far advanced to make war operations advisable. In consequence of this and his own inexperience in Navajo affairs, Fauntleroy reduced the Defiance garrison at a most critical time from eight companies of 645 officers and men to four companies of infantry: 6 officers and 280 men.

Colonel Fauntleroy explained that the reduction also was influenced by his desire to gain time in which to acquaint the army's commanding general with the military situation in New Mexico Territory, and to obtain Winfield Scott's instructions. This would allow him to determine when, "with propriety," he should make war or withhold troops from interfering in the settlement of Indian difficulties. However, in the case of the Navajo nation, Fauntleroy found that "the greatest embarrassment arises from the fact that many of the claims set up against [them] for plundering and stealing stock &c are either wholly fabricated or to a considerable degree exaggerated, and if war is to be commenced upon the simple presentation of these claims, the cause for war becomes interminate"—without end.[20]

Despite the pessimism of Major Ruff, Silas Kendrick returned to his agency at Fort Defiance before the end of December. His return coincided closely with two incidents that deepened the Navajos' commit-

19. The change in command actually occurred November 2, although officially the date is October 25 while Fauntleroy was still en route from Independence, Missouri, to Santa Fe. A Virginian, Fauntleroy did not attend West Point. He entered service in June 1836 as a major of 2d Dragoons. At the outbreak of the Civil War he resigned from the army and served the Confederacy as a brigadier general of Virginia Volunteers, 1861–65.

20. November 6, 1859: Fauntleroy to Lt. Col. Lorenzo Thomas, AAG, New York, NA, RAC, RG 393, no. 211, LS.

ment, in self-defense, to making war. As Kendrick was leaving Albuquerque a war party left Abiquiu bound for another part of Navajo country. The party was a curious mixture of about one hundred Moache and Capote Utes, a number of Jicarilla Apaches, and, expected at a rendezvous somewhere to the west, "a large Mexican force" from the vicinity of Taos. Although he must have been aware that authorities in Santa Fe officially maintained that peace existed with the Navajos, Ute Agent Albert H. Pfeiffer sanctioned the slave-raiding foray, saying he "thought best to let them go it, if they want[ed] to." The raiders came drifting back in small groups before the new year, their combined booty reported as 280 sheep, 35 goats, about 80 horses, and 23 Navajo children—all but two of them described as little girls. Four Navajos had been killed.[21]

A second incident, seemingly minor but important psychologically, occurred shortly before Kendrick's return to the fort. Major Shepherd, once more in command of the garrison, had ordered a Navajo seized and whipped, presumably in public on the parade ground as was the custom. On inquiring what the Navajo had done to deserve such punishment, Kendrick was unable to get an answer. "From what I can learn," he reported, the whipping was ordered "without any *cause* whatever."[22]

Navajo reprisals followed with increasing intensity, even as a few headmen—Barboncito among them—in a desperate last effort to preserve peace, brought in bunches of horses and some cattle to be sent to settle claims on the river. Their effort was futile. Between January 5 and March 16, 1860, settlements on the Rio Grande from near Fort Craig to Albuquerque and north to Abiquiu were struck repeatedly. Four shepherd boys were taken captive near Los Lunas and it was claimed that Navajos had run off 18,500 sheep, 500 mules, and 30 head of cattle. Superintendent Collins remarked on January 7 that public feeling against the Navajos was so high that "it is venting itself in the organization of guerrilla parties to invade the Navajo Country." While he doubted the "propriety" of such expeditions, he said he could not

21. December 18, 1859: Pfeiffer to Collins; and December 27, 1859: John Pumisano Valdes, Abiquiu, to Pfeiffer, NA, NMS T21-4.

22. January 6, 1860: Kendrick to Collins, NA, NMS T21-4. Later it was learned that the Navajo, a member of Ganado Mucho's band, had turned over two army rifles to a military escort on its way to Albuquerque. The officer in command gave the Navajo a note to carry back to the fort. Because he was slow in delivering the message the Navajo received "a severe flogging on his bar[e] back" (ibid., February 25, 1860).

blame the citizens for organizing them. Two days later Agent Pfeiffer remarked that citizens of Rio Arriba County were planning another slave raid, a large one, to start in two days.

Stock thefts by small war parties were merely a prelude to the Navajos' more ambitious plan: to force the abandonment of Fort Defiance and, they hoped, the complete withdrawal of soldiers from their country. A few minutes after sunrise on January 17, Navajos led by Huero and the former interpreter Juan Anaya attacked the post beef herd, which was vital to the garrison's subsistence. The first blow was aimed from ambush at a wagon party as it started from the grazing camp in the Cienega Amarilla, eight or nine miles south of the post, to gather wood. Taken completely by surprise four hundred yards from the corral, the four soldiers of the wood detail were able to fire only two shots before they were overrun. When he came on the scene with a relief party that afternoon, Silas Kendrick counted no fewer than 130 arrows in three bodies; the fourth soldier had managed to escape. Six oxen attached to the wagon had been cut from their traces and driven off.[23]

The entire force of the Navajos, estimated at between 250 and 300 warriors, then swept on toward the grazing cattle. Far outnumbered but with superior firepower, the herd guard of thirty-five enlisted men stood their ground and drove off the first attacking wave. Before the Navajos rallied to strike again the troops drove the cattle into the more defensible position of the camp and corral. Twice more the Navajos charged the cattle herd, coming to within 125 yards of the soldiers' rifles before turning away. Two warriors were shot from their horses, probably mortally wounded, and were carried off by their companions. Sergeant Gable of Lieutenant Hildt's Company C tied a message calling for help around the neck of a dog and started the animal toward the fort at a run.

Shortly before noon a Navajo approached the guard in the hillside blockhouse overlooking Fort Defiance and said he wanted to talk with the agent. With Lieutenant William D. Whipple, Kendrick made his way to the outpost. Here, he later reported, the Navajo was telling them of the morning attack when Sergeant Gable's dog trotted into the fort with the message confirming the Indian's story.

Stripped of cavalry since the previous November, the Defiance garrison was slow-moving. A detachment of seventy-five infantry was on

23. January 23, 1860: Kendrick to Collins, NA, NMS 234-550; and January 17, 1860: Shepherd to Wilkins, NA, RAC, RG 393, S-5-1860, LR.

the point of marching for the Cienega Amarilla when a runner arrived with word that the Navajo war party, having veered off into the mountains, was attacking a lumber detail three miles away. Major Shepherd split the relief force into two parties, setting out himself with fifty men for the wood camp and sending Lieutenant Alexander N. Shipley with the balance of the troops to the Cienega Amarilla. Kendrick elected to go with Shipley. The post's lumber camp, it was learned afterward, had been under Navajo surveillance for some time, but Huero's warriors missed or ignored completely three wagons, still loading, under a guard of eleven soldiers; they attacked three mule teams moving loaded wagons back toward the fort. Major Shepherd arrived to find the Navajos gone. One teamster had been severely wounded; the soldier detailed as escort was bleeding so profusely that he died in the wagon on the way back to Fort Defiance.

Another attack on the beef herd came three weeks later, Huero leading a force said to number more than five hundred warriors, about half of them mounted. This time there was no element of surprise; Navajos had been seen in the vicinity the day before and the guard accordingly had been increased to forty-four enlisted men. Instead of fighting in the open, as at Cienega Amarilla. Huero's warriors as well as the soldiers had the partial covering of belts of forest, the camp being in a mountain glade seven miles west of the fort. The attack began soon after sunrise and lasted about two hours. It was ended abruptly upon the arrival of a mountain howitzer and its gun crew of a corporal and eleven men. As on the first occasion, the cattle herd was drawn back to the corral and came through without loss. Ten Navajos, according to Major Shepherd, "were shot helpless" but were carried off. One of the guard, Private Peter Agnew of Company G, Third Infantry, was slightly wounded in the hand.[24]

Agent Kendrick's usefulness to the Navajos and to his own government came to an end at this time. The end was hastened when Major Shepherd informed him on January 20 that a state of war existed with the Navajo nation and that the agent hereafter, on pain of expulsion from the fort, must refrain from any form of communication with the tribe. Kendrick retorted that he would let the order pass "unnoticed as the ox would the passing fly." But his continued presence at the fort was made virtually impossible when Shepherd cut off most of the sup-

24. February 14, 1860: Shepherd to Wilkins, NA, RAC, RG 393, S-27-1860, LR.

plies and services upon which the agent's support depended. On February 4 he wrote Collins, "My health is not good. I wish verry much to come up to Santa Fe. Can I do so?" Three weeks later he departed for the river.

The moon had set and Cañoncito Bonito lay in predawn darkness when the Navajos gathered to attack Fort Defiance. Before a sound was heard to disclose their presence they had occupied three strategic points. One group of warriors moved to the heights of the mesa rising steeply and within close range directly east of the post. A second party moved up through a covering ravine toward the hay corrals and magazine situated forty yards outside the southwest corner of the post quadrangle. The third and largest force gathered in the gardens and among woodpiles at the northwest corner near Post Sutler John E. Weber's store. One thousand warriors, outnumbering the garrison five to one, waited for the prearranged first blow. It came at four o'clock in the morning of April 30.[25]

A sentinel stationed at No. 2 post over the hay corrals drew the opening fire. He was not hit. With two men assigned to picket duty close by, he found cover at the corner of the nearest fort building—the commissary storehouse. From that point the three returned a raking fire that prevented the Navajos from seizing the corrals and setting fire to the hay.

Navajos holding the eastern heights, if armed with better weapons, would have had the garrison utterly at their mercy. As it was, in the darkness and with bows and arrows and only a few old muskets, their steady fusillade caused concern but no reported damage. The worst they could do was to pin down Lieutenant Dickinson with Company B, whom Shepherd had placed at the foot of the mesa with orders to prevent any possible attempt by the Navajos to descend. The real strength of the

25. May 7, 1860: Shepherd to Wilkins, NA, RAC, RG 98, S-50-1860, LR; and Fort Defiance Post Returns, April, 1860. Warnings of such an occurrence had caused Maj. Shepherd to post orders for a plan of defense as early as February 7. The number of Navajo warriors was estimated as more than 1,000 by Maj. Shepherd, and in the Post Returns summary account as "not less" than that. Either way, if the estimates were accurate, this would have been the largest war party of Navajos of which there is any record. The post garrison, totaling 206 officers and men, was all of the 3d Regiment, U.S. Infantry: Company B—Maj. Shepherd, Lts. Whipple and Dickinson, and 63 enlisted men; Company C—Capt. Johns, Lt. Hildt, and 66 enlisted men; Company E—67 enlisted men; and Company G—a detachment of 5 enlisted men.

assault came from the opposite side of the canyon. Lieutenant Hildt and a part of his company tested it in attempting to clear the gardens and were forced back to the sheltering walls of the bakehouse and laundress quarters.

At about the same time a sharper fight flared at the sutler's store. Navajos had broken through a rear window, rousted out one of Weber's two clerks (men named Kennon and McBride), and were attempting to cut their way into a storeroom. Major Shepherd sent four of Hildt's company through the front doors with orders to clear the place, while six others directed a covering fire against Navajos holding a log building twenty yards distant. The six were too few. Between shooting and loading their rifles they were stormed with arrows. Three of them were hit; Corporal Joseph McCourt and Private John Gibson had minor wounds, but Private Sylvester Johnson, with a shaft deep in his chest, died within three minutes.

Upon Lieutenant Hildt's appearance at this moment, Major Shepherd directed him to clear the log building (Company E bakehouse) of the Navajos who had killed Johnson, and then made his way at a run toward the fire point below the commissary storehouse. Here Lieutenant Whipple and troops of Company E had gained possession of the critical magazine, driven the Navajos from the stables and hay corrals, and were concentrating their fire to force them out of the ravine.

Graying light of morning brought a turn in the battle. Navajos who had been engaged almost hand-to-hand with troops in the canyon now began to withdraw, many of them climbing through the rocks and brush that covered the slopes to the west. With the initiative at last his, Major Shepherd ordered Lieutenant Hildt and Captain William B. Johns to pursue and clear the Navajos from the north and west rims of the canyon. Lieutenant Dickinson was ordered to lend support. Before he could clear the Indians from the east rim, however, he would have to scale the stone precipice of the east mesa while under fire. After brief fire fights at all points, resistance by the Navajos ended.

Two hours after the battle started Fort Defiance remained in the hands of Major Shepherd's troops. The garrison's only casualties were the three taken in the fight for the sutler's store. Navajo losses remained uncertain for some days afterward until, under a flag of truce, Cabras Blancas came to the fort to say that other headmen joined with him in wanting peace. Shepherd's interest lay elsewhere. Under questioning, Cabras Blancas said no count had been made of Navajo wounded, but nine warriors and three headmen had been killed—in addition to some pelados whose number he could not say. A nephew of Zarcillos Largos was said to have been among those killed.

In the weeks that followed, Major Shepherd's report of the attack moved upward from department command to the office of the army's adjutant general, then to the attention of General Scott ("an interesting report . . . does great credit to Major Shepherd, his officers & men"), and finally to Secretary of War John B. Floyd. Rather late, in terms of events occurring in New Mexico, the Secretary on July 9 appended his endorsement to the letter enclosing Shepherd's report:

> Active operations will be instituted against the Navajos as soon as the necessary preparations can be made. A winter campaign *with Infantry*, if inaugurated with secrecy and prosecuted with vigor, will prove the shortest and most effectual plan of operations. However it is not meant to restrict the discretion of the Department commander, except that his measures must not interrupt the summer campaign of the Mounted troops against the Indians of the plains; and that *none other than the regular troops under his command will be used. No volunteers will be employed* [italics added].[26]

Until the extension of telegraph lines to Colorado and then to New Mexico, still nearly a decade in the future, a hopeless communications delay often rendered such orders from Washington inoperable. The order above, critical to the Navajo interest, is a case in point.

26. One of four endorsements with May 20, 1860: Fauntleroy to AAG Lorenzo Thomas, NA, RAC, RG 393, no. 34, LS.

22

Nahondzod

Beginning in late winter of 1860 and continuing well into the warm weather of spring, the Navajos carried their war of reprisal far beyond the limits of Fort Defiance. They swept the land from the Hopi villages to Zuni and on eastward to Acoma and the river settlements, spreading a fearful loss. Superintendent Collins's newspaper, which could mirror his views passively or be used aggressively as a potent instrument to support his policies, distorted a situation already serious enough. In the first six months of the year, the Santa Fe *Gazette* reported, Navajo war parties had killed three hundred persons and stolen property worth $1.5 million.[1] Divided by five, the figures might still have been high.

Governor Abraham Rencher responded to the prevailing mood of anxiety and outrage by giving his approval late in January to the formation of two companies of citizen volunteers in Socorro County, arming them with two hundred muskets. He justified this action, as though he felt compelled to do so, over the opposition of Colonel Fauntleroy, who refused to supply ammunition. Rencher said he had done no more than he was empowered to do by the laws of the territory. "These people," he explained, "prefer to carry on Indian wars in their own way." He neglected to mention that a recent amendment to the Territorial Militia Law shifted the initiative for raising a volunteer company from the governor to any individual citizen "of experience and good character" and, by its silence in the matter, gave tacit approval to continued slave raiding.[2]

1. Santa Fe *Gazette*, November 10, 1860.
2. February 4, 1860: Rencher to Secretary of State Lewis Cass, NA, TP, 5514, microcopy T-17, roll 1. Article 38 of New Mexico's Militia Law (approved July 10, 1851, by Governor James S. Calhoun) declared that any persons wishing to conduct a campaign must satisfy the governor that the campaign would be made in good faith and be conducted according to the rules and customs of war of the United States. Also, that "all captives taken shall be well treated, and turned over to the

Opinion was divided on how strongly Colonel Fauntleroy opposed Rencher's actions. The governor understood him to say that he would not furnish ammunition to implement the law, and that if Rencher were to authorize a volunteer campaign against the Navajos, Fauntleroy would withdraw his troops from Indian country. On the other hand, Fauntleroy denied having refused the ammunition. "I did say," he later explained, "if the companies raised . . . were the freebooting, plundering parties which I understood from hearsay . . . that I would not lend the means of the government to such purposes." Upon assurances by Rencher that the Socorro companies would be used strictly for local defense, Fauntleroy said, he had ordered the ammunition sent to Albuquerque; if the volunteers failed to receive it, "it was because in their eagerness for plunder they went out before it arrived." [3]

Regardless of his private feelings in the case, Fauntleroy's reluctance to cooperate with the governor was determined by orders he had received from the War Department. In a letter dated February 25, 1860, Assistant Adjutant General Edward D. Townsend informed him that the secretary of war had decided that "such extraordinary expenditures" as calling volunteers into service could not be justified. He was advised that Secretary Floyd did intend to increase the number of troops Fauntleroy could employ in Navajo country, and the presence of an effective force "combined with a just but firm policy towards the Navajoes will . . . render anything like general hostilities against that tribe unnecessary." [4] This, of course, was written before the Navajos attacked Fort Defiance, but the Secretary's opposition to the use of volunteers remained unchanged.

In April, Fauntleroy and the governor clashed again when Rencher applied to Captain William R. Shoemaker, ordnance officer in charge of the Fort Union arsenal, for 276 rifles and 20 pistols as well as ammunition to arm additional volunteer companies. Fauntleroy counter-

---

proper authorities to be disposed of *as the governor shall direct*" (italics added). As amended (January 9, 1860), Article 38 omitted reference to the treatment and disposition of Indian captives. As further departure, it provided that "any man of experience & good character who shall raise and organise a force" was authorized to apply to the governor to make a voluntary campaign against Indians at war with the territory, and "on said application being made, it shall be the duty of the Governor to commission such person." The amendment further directed that the governor should furnish necessary arms as specified in an act passed January 28, 1857, authorizing the loan of public arms.

3. May 7, 1860: Fauntleroy to Cass, NA, TP, 5579.

4. February 25, 1860: Townsend to Fauntleroy, NA, RAC, RG 393, A-19-1860, LR.

manded the requisition and subsequently drew the admonishment from Washington that, so far as the arms were concerned, he had exceeded his authority.

As the breach between the two men widened, most New Mexicans lined up in support of Governor Rencher. Fauntleroy was criticized for his seeming lethargy and inexcusable failure to crush Navajo aggression. What the public did not know was that when Fauntleroy pressed Washington for a summer expedition against the Navajos he was told his plans must yield to permit operations against Comanches and Kiowas marauding on the mail routes to the States. Officialdom in Washington was glacially slow in reacting to New Mexico's mounting tensions. Not before mid-summer of 1860 did Secretary Floyd get around to advising Secretary of State Lewis Cass that there was reason to fear injurious consequences from the use of volunteer troops against the Navajos. Secretary Cass was more dilatory, and the summer campaigns by volunteers already had ended when Rencher finally was informed that the State Department "sees no justification for the unauthorized organization of a volunteer force to make war on the Navajo Indians." [5]

Only in the case of the Socorro volunteers raised in January were citizens actually used for limited local defense. Cooperating with Captain George McLane's mounted riflemen patrolling out of Fort Craig, a group of volunteers took part early in February in the pursuit and dispersal of a Navajo war party raiding from Los Lunas down the Rio Grande Valley. Captain McLane referred admiringly to the leader of the volunteers, Manuel Antonio Chaves, as "an experienced and excellent Mexican guide and soldier." In fact, near Cañon del Muerto, where the Navajos were divested of the greater part of seventeen thousand stolen sheep, Captain Chaves planned the strategy of the combined troop movements. Concerning this encounter, McLane observed that he was "well acquainted" with Chaves's "reputation as a guide and Indian hunter . . . [and] could not be otherwise than governed by his opinion." [6]

5. July 28, 1860: Floyd to Cass, NA, TP, 5522; and October 1, 1860: Cass to Rencher, Santa Fe *Gazette*, November 24, 1860, NA, TP.

6. February 11, 1860: McLane to Bvt. Capt. John P. Hatch, enclosure with NA, RAC, RG 393, P-6-1860, LR. About 25 Navajos were said to have been killed and many more were wounded in these operations, extending from February 2 to 10. Manuel Chaves lost 2 of his company killed and 3 wounded. In his first report of the raid, Superintendent Collins said the Navajos had run off 60,000 sheep. He later reduced the figure, after talking with Chaves, to 30,000. Captain Hatch reported the number of sheep stolen was 17,000.

But the volunteer forays that followed were of quite a different character. On May 7, with eleven of the Diné Ana'aii in their group, a troop of ninety-six armed New Mexicans appeared at Fort Defiance, pausing on their way to Zuni Pueblo. The leader, Ramón Baca of Cebolleta, told of their fight with Navajos in the Chusca Mountains. One of his men was mortally wounded, but otherwise the Cebolleteños were pleased with the results. They had killed six Navajos, taken one woman captive, and seized forty Navajo horses and four hundred sheep and goats.

On June 27 a party of thirteen New Mexicans—survivors of a company recruited from Cebolleta and commanded by Joaquín Candelario —straggled into Fort Defiance with seven wounded. In a desperate fight with the Navajos at Laguna Grande, high in the mountains to the east of the fort, thirty of their companions had been killed and thirteen wounded, as well as five Diné Ana'aii allies killed.[7] Of the Navajos, fifteen were said to have been killed and a large number wounded, among them Henry Dodge's former interpreter Juan Anaya. Seven more New Mexicans came in the next day, all but one wounded and two needing hospital care. The third day a body of about twenty-five more citizen troops arrived at the fort. These were commanded by Ramón Baca and constituted the advance unit of two large parties, the second led by Anastacio García of Los Lunas. These companies were augmented by thirty-five Diné Ana'aii, six of whom carried wounds taken in fratricidal combat, possibly while aiding Joaquín Candelario's people at Laguna Grande. The company rode off and soon returned in triumph. Baca, who said he had been in the field since May, gazed cheerfully upon the combined booty: he and García had captured two thousand sheep, six women (one of them the wife of the headman Juan Lucero), and eight children who would be taken back to the settlements as slaves.

From another direction, Jesús Gallegos of Abiquiu appeared at Fort Defiance on July 9 with an armed entourage of about 125 men. Gallegos reported little success thus far. He had encountered few Indians and flocks of no importance on the march, and had killed only one Navajo.

7. Santa Fe *Gazette*, July 18, 1860. In the same issue, Spruce M. Baird, attorney general of New Mexico Territory, indulged in a bit of rabble-rousing when he wrote that, in the attack on Fort Defiance, Zarcillos Largos "has already rubbed his fist under the Colonel's [Fauntleroy's] nose and slapped at him that part of his person right where the breech-clout ought to be. Yet the Colonel folds his arms and says: Sarcillo . . . if it is a row you are after with me you will not get it."

After resting for three days in camp below the post, the company moved on. A few weeks later, having been as far as Black Mesa, they were back. Great herds of livestock seen west of the mouth of Canyon de Chelly had tempted them to go on, but "they were opposed by a thousand indians, and there being a great want of water . . . they were therefore compelled to return with only four ponies captured." They reported, according to Major Shepherd, that some four Navajos had been "shot helpless," and a few others wounded.[8] Their own losses were light: one man wounded and four horses killed.

Late in July, during a lull in the hostilities, an exchange of captives took place between Navajos and New Mexicans camped near the fort. The Navajos released a woman captured with her four children the previous March. It was intended that the wife of Juan Lucero be exchanged, but during the night before this was supposed to be done she escaped from the New Mexicans. Major Shepherd observed that after negotiations were broken off the New Mexicans "succeeded in killing five Navajoes whose bodies were left on the ground." One of these was said to be a brother of Juan Lucero. Barboncito was shot from his horse but managed to escape.

The forays of spring and early summer of 1860 did nothing to relieve the pressure on the New Mexican settlements but instead added to public unease, anxiety, and discontent. Excitement boiled over on August 12 in Santa Fe when a large group of citizens met and adopted a preamble and resolution calling for action. They declared that because Colonel Fauntleroy refused to use his troops to protect the territory and chastise the Navajos, Governor Rencher should be asked to call a regiment of mounted volunteers into the service of the United States. The next day, Oliver P. Hovey, J. M. Gallegos, Miguel E. Pino, and Felipe Delgado, a strategy committee of four, published a broadside in the Santa Fe *Gazette* aimed at stirring wide public support. "For months," they began, "the bells of your edifices have tolled incessantly the obsequies of your slaughtered citizens; for months have their mangled corpses been crowding your graveyards."

In response to such terms, what could honest citizens do but redeem themselves? The committee offered the means by calling for a force of

8. August 3, 1860: Shepherd to Bvt. Capt. Dabney H. Maury, AAG, Santa Fe, NA, RAC, RG 393, S-97-1860, LR. Major Shepherd's reports are the source of information of the May and June forays mentioned here. It is conceivable that other volunteer companies operated in Navajo country at this time, but, in bypassing Fort Defiance, went unreported.

one thousand volunteers to take the field against the Navajos. It was doubtful that they would receive pay, and certainly they would have to furnish their own subsistence; but Governor Rencher would provide arms and Colonel Fauntleroy would supply ammunition "and accept cordially their cooperation"—a misstatement of fact based solely on hope. Each county of the territory was asked to send delegates to a mass meeting to be held August 27 in Santa Fe.[9]

Before the citizen meeting was held, five companies of the Seventh Infantry, withdrawn from the Mormon campaign in Utah, arrived in Santa Fe on August 17. Colonel Fauntleroy immediately announced that he would launch a full-scale expedition against the Navajos. However, neither this development nor a public statement issued by Governor Rencher shortly thereafter cooled the ardor of those committed to raising a force of mounted volunteers. With surprising ambivalence Rencher declared that Colonel Fauntleroy now had forty companies of regulars at his disposal and would have no need of, nor would he accept the service of, volunteers. In the next breath, the governor said that if the people still desired to raise a volunteer regiment to campaign independently against the Navajos, he would feel it his duty to call them up and appoint suitable officers, "not that I believe them at present necessary, but because they believe it." [10]

Governor Rencher's offer was brushed aside on August 27 when citizens attending the mass meeting took matters into their own hands. Acting without official sanction, they voted to raise a regiment of mounted volunteers and depart September 20 for Navajo country. Manuel Chaves was elected lieutenant colonel and given command. Either at the same time or soon afterward, Marquis Lafayette Cotton was named as adjutant general.

Angered over this outcome, Rencher turned upon the volunteers whose cause until now he had advocated. They had acted in open disregard of the laws of the United States and of New Mexico, he advised Secretary Cass, adding, "I have therefore been compelled, under a painful sense of public duty, to resist this movement." [11] Colonel Fauntleroy, who may have shared similar feelings, made no comment; he was preoccupied with assembling troops at Fort Defiance where the Navajo

9. August 13, 1860: A broadside titled "Address to the people of New Mexico, in relation to their present difficulties with the Navajo Indians," signed by the four committee members, Santa Fe *Gazette*, August 22, 1860, NA, TP.

10. Ibid., "To the Public," undated address by Rencher.

11. September 4, 1860: Rencher to Cass, NA, TP, 5525.

campaign, under the command of Brevet Lieutenant Colonel Edward R. S. Canby, was to be launched in early October.

Instead of a regiment, only a battalion of five citizen companies was raised. The deterrent was not the governor's angry disavowal but the necessity for each volunteer to supply his own horses, arms, ammunition, food, and clothing. Only the mules for the pack train, gathered in the five represented counties on the solicitation of the respective probate judges, were furnished. The village of San Ysidro, below Jemez Pueblo, was the rendezvous point and here the volunteers were mustered-in in late September by Adjutant General Cotton. The battalion included Captain Andrés Tapia and a company from Santa Fe County, Captain Narcisso Santi Esteban and company from Bernalillo County, Captain Juan Gallegos and company from Rio Arriba County, Captain Juan N. Gutierres and company from San Miguel County, and Captain J. Francisco Chaves and company from Valencia County. The command numbered 24 officers and 448 men.[12] Forty warriors from Jemez, led by the pueblo's governor, Francisco Hosta, appear to have accompanied the battalion.[13]

The movements of the citizen companies coincided closely with the gathering of Colonel Canby's forces, fourteen companies in all, at Fort Defiance. Captain Henry R. Selden with four companies of the Fifth Infantry arrived first, on September 4. Three days later he relieved Major Shepherd in command, Shepherd departing for the river with the old garrison of the Third Infantry. Brevet Major Henry H. Sibley started from Albuquerque on September 14, traveling through the Wingate Valley to the new post being constructed at Ojo del Oso, and named Fort Fauntleroy.[14] From there Sibley marched to the lower Chusca Val-

12. Adjutant General Records, Militia Description Book, p. 13, Muster Rolls, nos. 16, 9, 568, 574, 1, NMSRCA. Twitchell (*Facts of New Mexican History*, 1963, vol. 2, pp. 320–21, n. 245) mistakenly said the battalion was formed in August 1859 under the command of Col. Miguel E. Pino. Twitchell confused the formation of volunteers discussed here (August 1860) with the August 1861 appointment of Pino to command the 2d Regiment of New Mexico Volunteer Infantry. The younger man of the two, J. Francisco Chaves, was a fifth cousin of Manuel Chaves.

13. "The Pueblos who went out with the volunteers have, we believe, all returned" (Santa Fe *Gazette*, November 10, 1860. NA, TP). In 1863 Indian Agent John Ward wrote, "I would state further that one of the most successful campaigns made against the Navajos for many years was commanded by Justo [Hosta] of Jemes, three years ago, and that forty of the Indians from that pueblo accompanied it" (September 24, 1863: Ward to Superintendent Michael Steck, enclosure with NA, RAC, RG 393, S-205-1863, LR).

14. Named for the department commander, Fort Fauntleroy was established August 31, 1860, by Bvt. Maj. Nathan B. Rossell. The first garrison included 7

ley with five companies of mounted troops and infantry in the hope of "striking a blow" at Navajos he thought might be concentrated there. At Laguna Negra the headman Agua Chiquita approached Sibley's guides, saying he wished to talk with the commanding officer. Perhaps because of something said to him, Agua Chiquita took fright and turned to flee. He was fired on by the guides, wounded desperately, and afterward put to death at Sibley's order. Sibley's arrival at Fort Defiance on September 28 was followed five days later by that of Captain Lafayette McLaws from Fort Craig, with two companies of mounted riflemen and two of the Seventh Infantry. Canby himself arrived on October 4, after a long march from Fort Garland by way of Abiquiu and Largo Canyon.

With the Chaves battalion following closely in his wake, Colonel Canby within less than one week launched his first campaign against the Navajos. His strategy was determined by information that the eastern bands of Indians were in flight to Canyon de Chelly and beyond, to the Hopi villages and "Puerto Limita" or Marsh Pass. His operation, in simple outline, was this: Major Sibley's Second Column of 270 troops left Fort Defiance on October 10, proceeding to Pueblo Colorado —the vicinity of present Ganado, Arizona. From this point Sibley's orders were to seek out and destroy any Navajos found on the southern approaches to Canyon de Chelly and then join Canby's First Column at the canyon mouth. Canby's command, equal in strength to Sibley's, moved out the next day, marching north to Palo Negro (where Canby joined his troops on October 12), and then pivoted around the north rim of Canyon de Chelly. A third column commanded by Captain McLaws remained behind with orders to patrol the western slopes of the Chusca Mountains, ready to intercept and destroy any Navajos found there and any who might filter back through the Canby-Sibley lines. Again on the basis of information he had received, Canby believed that if the main body of Navajos were to flee toward Marsh Pass, he would have them entrapped, caught in nearly impassable country with nothing on the other side but Paiutes, who were said to be hostile to the Navajos.

The low regard in which citizen campaigns against Indians was held by the military accounts in some part for the scarcity of documentary

---

officers and 240 enlisted men of Companies C, E, F, and K, 5th U.S. Infantry. The post was 126 miles west and a trifle north of Albuquerque, and approximately 40 miles southeast of Fort Defiance (Fort Fauntleroy Post Returns, August 1860).

records of such freebooting operations. Even when winked at or openly sanctioned by civil authorities of the territory, there was a general awareness that slave-raiding forays against the Navajos inevitably resulted in reprisals. From the beginning of the American period of occupation of the territory, therefore, there was a tendency not to encourage the publicizing of such activities. Among the half-dozen or so documents of this nature that have come to light, a partial diary kept by Manuel Chaves's adjutant general holds a position of singular interest. For all its brevity, the Marquis Lafayette Cotton diary deserves attention for two reasons. It is the only known personal record of volunteer operations into Navajo country in 1860—a year unequaled since Spanish rule for frenzied citizen engagement. Secondly, with an accompanying letter, it offers corroborative testimony to the circumstances of the death of Zarcillos Largos.

Cotton's diary, which had the unusual distinction of being printed in the Santa Fe *Gazette* of November 24, 1860, begins as the Chaves battalion converged on San Ysidro. It is reproduced here in its entirety.

1860.

Sept. 19. Left Santa Fe and overtook [Tapia's] Santa Fe Company at St. Domingo.

Sept. 20. Crossed the Rio Grande and marched sixteen miles—camped without water.

Sept. 21. Arrived to-day at San Ysidro—at the same hour the Companies from Valencia and Bernalillo counties.

Sept. 22 & 23. In camp.

Sept. 24. Company from St. Miguel county arrived.

Sept. 25. A portion of command detailed to go round by Fort Defiance with wagons. Balance to go on scout. Provisioned for 20 days. Broke camp at 2 o'clock p. m. We of the scout marched 7 miles—camped on a clear running salt stream. Passed to-day several bubbling salt springs.

Sept. 26. Marched 10 miles to the Ojó Espiuti [Espiritu], (Santo spring) and camped. Broke camp at 3 o'clock p. m.,—marched 6 miles—camped on the Rio Puerco,—very little water, but good grass.

Sept. 27. Broke camp at 3 o'clock p. m., marched 20 miles, and camped at El Roya [Arroyo] de los Torreons—little water, but good grass.

Sept. 28. Marched 10 miles, and camped at the "Bordo," (so called, as here commences the Pacific slope of the Rocky mountains).

Sept. 29. Marched to-day 22 miles. Passed the ruins of an old

Pueblo, situated on a hill, at the head of Raton Canon.[15] Could hear of no tradition regarding it. It is built in a square of about 250 feet of lime-stone rock, blocks about 2 feet in length and breadth, and from 1 to 2 inches thickness—mud used for mortar. The walls on the outside were as smooth and regular as the best masons of the present day could possibly make them.—The whole walls (four altogether) were about 30 feet through, making three rooms, each partition carried to the same height as the outer walls. They are now about 20 feet high in places, and were probably divided into 3 or 4 stories. There is every appearance of having been a running stream by it; but there is now no permanent water.

Sept. 30. Marched to-day 12 miles. Camped on the "Escarbada," water by digging. Passed to-day the ruins of a small Pueblo in the Raton Canon.[16]

Octr. 1. Left camp at 1 o'clock, p. m.; marched 60 miles without water, to the foot of the "Tunicha" range. Expected to find Indians here—but "nary Injin." Camped at daybreak.

Octr. 2. In Camp. One false alarm of Indians.—At night the sentinels shot at two Indians riding past—six more seen on the hills.

Octr. 3. Marched 12 miles, to the top of the "Tunicha"; plenty of cool spring water and good grass.

Octr. 4. Marched 22 miles. Camped at "Sienega Grande," and turned our stock into a wheat field. Every appearance indicates the troops to have been lately here.

Octr. 5. Marched 25 miles, and camped at the "Canon des Conosido" [Cañón Desconocido, or Nameless Canyon]. Followed to-day the trail of an immense herd of stock—horses too much used up to follow faster than our usual gait.

Octr. 6. Marched 15 miles. Camped in the "Canon de Trigo." This Canon is from 200 to 400 feet in width, with precipitous bluffs of 250 feet in height. The spies were fired on by an Indian from the top. Another shot fired into camp just before dark. The Picket Guard, soon after going to their stations, fired at what they said was an Indian. Stock to-night have the remnants of a corn field for fodder.

Octr. 7. Broke camp at 6 o'clock, a. m. Marched about 7 miles altogether, when a portion of us were sent out on a fresh Indian

15. Pueblo Pintado, at the head of Chaco Canyon.

16. Chaves's command was lucky to escape the quicksands that follow heavy rainfall in the Escavada Wash, here at the junction with the Chaco, just west of Pueblo Peñasco Blanco.

trail. After following it about 15 miles, the two men in the lead shot a horse from under an Indian, and severely wounded the Indian, but he managed to escape. Captured 11 fine mares and 7 colts. We continued on in hopes to overtake a party with sheep. After chasing about ten miles further, we were obliged to give it up, as a number of our horses gave out. Camped to-night 15 miles from the "Canon de Trigo," at the "Sienega of the Puebla Colorado." [17] The rear guard were fired on from the Bluffs while leaving camp this morning, by the Indians. The advance guard fired on an Indian at a distance of 20 steps, and missed him and horse. Indian signal fires all around our camp. Seven shots fired by sentinels at night, and one arrow into camp. We are to "wait here for the wagons."

Octr. 8. In camp.

Octr. 9. In camp.

Octr. 10. Went to Fort Defiance with an escort of 30 men, to try and hear from the wagons. All out of Flour. Five companies of troops from Fort Defiance camped to-night just below us.[18]

Octr. 11. Returned from the Fort. No news from wagons. All living on horse and mule meat. Troops still in camp below us.

Octr. 12. 135 men started out on scout, mostly footmen. Troops left this morning.

Octr. 13. In camp.

Octr. 14. In camp.

Octr. 15. The scout sent out on the 12th, returned, bringing 50 sheep, 14 horses and 2 colts.

Octr. 16. Twenty-two men started to go to the wagons.

Octr. 17. Wagons arrived to-day; part of the outfit still back on a scout.

Octr. 18. In camp.

Octr. 19. In camp.

Octr. 20. Another party arrived, bringing four prisoners, and report having killed 5 Indians.

Octr. 21. The balance of wagon party arrived to-day, bringing thirteen horses and one hundred and thirty-three sheep and goats.

17. The volunteers were encamped on Pueblo Colorado Wash, 27 miles west of Fort Defiance and in the vicinity of present Ganado, Arizona.

18. Cotton and his escort arrived at the fort inauspiciously on the opening day of Canby's Navajo expedition. Troops who camped that night "just below us" formed Maj. Sibley's 2d Column—two companies of cavalry, three of infantry, who had marched from Defiance that morning. Sibley's less than jubilant comment was, "Much to my disappointment, I found the Mexican battalion of Volunteers here, and no evidence of its recent occupation by Indians."

Cotton's diary here ends abruptly, but he conveyed further information about the past operations of the battalion in a letter he wrote the next day from camp on Pueblo Colorado Wash and mailed with the diary to Oliver P. Hovey in Santa Fe.[19] Both were printed in the Santa Fe *Gazette* of November 24, 1860. Hovey's name first appears in January 1847 when he served as a volunteer among troops gathered to quell the rebellion at Taos following the murder of Governor Charles Bent. With a press sent out from St. Louis in the spring of that year, and with a partner named Davies, he began publication of the weekly Santa Fe *Republican* on September 10, 1847. A member of the lower house of the legislature, he was active in 1858–59 in helping to enact a slave code for New Mexico. A signer of the August 13 broadside mentioned earlier, at the time of this campaign he was engaged in Santa Fe as a public printer. Cotton's letter, in part, follows:

> We start to-day [Cotton wrote on October 22] with a party of three hundred men for the Mokina [Hopi] Villages and vicinity, where we expect to find a greater part of the Navajo Indians.
>
> They are running all over the country; but the most of the trails, and the larger ones, make in that direction. We have captured four Indians, killed five, and wounded another badly, who was apparently a chief. We are informed by one of the prisoners that the celebrated Navajo chief, Sarcillo Largo, was amongst the killed.
>
> Those killed were probably a portion of those engaged in the late massacre of the Stage party on the "Jornado," as there were several articles taken in the Rancheria, such as leather belonging to the boot of a Stage, buttons, such as used to fasten the curtains of a coach, saddle-bags, &c.[20]
>
> We have taken fifty-nine fine horses and two hundred sheep and goats.

19. In all of the military and New Mexico Indian superintendency correspondence at the National Archives, Cotton's name appears in only one other connection: as leader of a party of 14 or 16 citizen volunteers, he engaged a Navajo war party July 31–August 1, 1860 below Santa Fe in the vicinity of Galisteo. Information of the fight (a bitter and long one) was conveyed in a scribbled note by Cotton and in five reports to department headquarters by Lt. John Pegram, who had been sent out with a troop of mounted riflemen in Cotton's support. Pegram made it clear that Cotton was commanding the small volunteer force, but did not mention him by rank. No record of Cotton is found, either, at the NMSRCA.

20. Where on the Jornado del Muerto the attack occurred is not certain. Unless the Navajos struck at the lower extremity of the dry route, which is not likely, the coach would not have been operated by the Butterfield Stage Line, but by another stage and/or mail company running between Santa Fe, Mesilla, and El Paso.

On account of the wagon party not meeting us at the appointed time. we were forced to eat ten of our captured horses and
four Navajo dogs.

We thus far have had a great number of serious difficulties to
surmount; but we have now our headquarters established, and are
prepared to carry on a vigorous war. . . .

Cotton makes it clear that Zarcillos Largos was killed by members of
the volunteer battalion, but he leaves other points of concern in doubt.
The implicit presence of the headman "amongst the killed" and the
reference to "articles taken in the Rancheria" suggest that the Navajos
were surprised in a camp of some permanence, as opposed to a fugitive,
overnight camp. Followers of Zarcillos Largos, as Cotton suggests, may
have taken part in attacking a stage on the Jornado del Muerto, but because of his advanced age and customary avoidance of aggression it is
extremely unlikely that Zarcillos Largos took part in the raid. Cotton
is even less helpful in saying when the celebrated medicine man was
killed, implying only that it was sometime before October 20. He fails
to state whether Zarcillos Largos was killed by Hosta's warriors or by
New Mexicans, and he is silent on the location of the place where the
encounter occurred.

From another quarter and from nearly the same time partial answers
to two questions are found. On October 17 Lieutenant Joseph G. Tilford, with a detachment of mounted rifles and infantry of McLaws'
Third Column, was patrolling the western slopes of the Chusca-Tunicha
range and the rough woodland and cienegas heading about Canyon de
Chelly. Pursuing a fresh Navajo trail westerly from Cienega Juanico for
four or five hours, Tilford's troop came in sight of its quarry—two men
and a woman—in a side canyon entering the main Canyon de Chelly
from the south. Only the woman was captured. Through an interpreter
she informed Tilford that she and other Navajos had fled westward
from their homes in the Chuscas a few days previously when they had
been told (erroneously, as it turned out) that the headman Mariano
had been killed.[21] Remarking upon this later, Tilford noted that he had
learned from a fellow officer who had recently been in the volunteer
battalion camp that a detachment of one hundred men under Manuel
Chaves was scouting through the Chuscas at the time Mariano was said
to have been killed.

21. Mariano lived to sign Canby's treaty of February 18, 1861. Another headman
of the same name was active between 1880 and 1900 in the vicinity of Mariano's
Lake, a few miles north and east of new Fort Wingate (site of Fort Fauntleroy).

"The Captured squaw furthermore stated," Tilford continued, "that her party had just heard that the Chief Sarcillo Largos, a man of great importance among the Navajos had been killed a day or two previous on the south side of the Cañon de Chelly near the west end of the cañon. . . ." [22]

The death of Zarcillos Largos, which evidently occurred on October 15 or 16, was a sorry triumph. Born probably between 1790 and 1800, he is said to have been a medicine man of the Ta'baaha Clan and known to his people at Naat'allee, Peace Chanter, and also Ké'ntsaa, or Big Feet. [23] Nothing in Mexican documents referring to him as raider or war leader has been found; in the first known mention of his name, in June of 1843, Inspector of Militia J. Sarracino listed him among other Navajo headmen opposed to war with the Mexican people. Again and again thereafter, until near the end when he was generally regarded as the most respected and influential man of his nation, Zarcillos Largos appeared as arbitrator, conciliator, and spokesman for peace.

Beginning with the arrival of Manuel Chaves's citizen and Pueblo forces in Hopi country, and then daily until their return to the river settlements, their loss in horses and mules was heavy. Want of forage and exhaustion were the causes most often cited. The company of Captain Andrés Tapia lost more than half of its horses and thirty-three of the forty pack mules with which it started out. Muster rolls recording date and place of each incident of attrition give a fair picture of the battalion's movements. It would appear that the volunteers turned back from the Hopi villages during the first week of November. No effort was made to preserve a single line of march—impossible anyway with the burden of plunder. Each company fended for itself.

The Valencia County men with J. Francisco Chaves (a young man soon to rise in territorial politics) were in the vanguard. When they reached the eastern side of the Chuscas once more, the columns turned south, herding their captured livestock and prisoners through the

22. October 20, 1860: Tilford to Lt. Edward I. Cressy, enclosure with November 17, 1860: Canby to AAG, NA, RAC, RG 393, C-53-1860, LR. The Navajo woman also told of an earlier attack by an independent war party of Utes led by Agent Pfeiffer of Abiquiu. Her story, less detailed, essentially confirmed Pfeiffer's report that his party killed 6 Navajos in the Chusca Mountains and captured 19 women and children, 5,000 sheep, and nearly 500 horses.

23. Brugge 1970. In a somewhat different account, Brugge (pp. 32–33) says that Zarcillos Largos apparently was returning from a visit to Hopi country when, near Sagebrush Spring, south of Klagetoh, he was set upon and killed by a party of Spanish-American and Zuni raiders.

Chusca Valley and then through the lower hump extension of the San Juan's hogback. After resting at Ojo del Oso they continued eastward into the Wingate Valley, camping variously at Agua Azul, Cubero, and, finally before reaching the river, at Laguna. Officially, all of the men were mustered out on December 3 in the towns where each of the companies was originally formed.

Governor Rencher observed their return with well-controlled enthusiasm. "As these volunteers went out without my authority and against my advice," he commented, "I hear nothing from them. . . . It was one of the conditions of their organization that they should not be subject to the control of the Department commander, or of the Governor." As best he knew—and it was merely an early report—the Chaves battalion had cut swathes through Navajo cornfields, captured thousands of their livestock, and returned with about one hundred Navajo women and children euphemistically referred to as captives. This information, Rencher said, was received from "some Peublo Indians [Hosta's warriors], who were a part of the expedition, and who brought back some five thousand sheep and horses as their portion of the spoils." [24]

If it were known, the great success of Chaves's battalion, sweeping in the wake of Canby's three-pronged troop operations, might prove to have been unparalleled. Unfortunately, although Rencher would receive some additional information, no final accounting by either Manuel Chaves or Marquis Lafayette Cotton has been found. As for losses of men, the muster rolls note only that Private Antonio Domingo Durán died October 24, west of Fort Defiance, of inflammation of the bowels (possibly acute appendicitis) and that First Sergeant Amada García died November 28 from musket-shot wounds received at Ranches of Albuquerque.

The earlier plans of some of the citizen companies to campaign through the winter may have been abandoned when word came of the War Department's disapproval of their activities. At about the time that the companies were mustered out, Colonel Fauntleroy was advised by Secretary Floyd,

> The Department sees with regret the reports of a contemplated organization of volunteers to enter the Navajoe country. The troops in the Department are now sufficient to make such a resort entirely unnecessary, and it must be discountenanced and prevented. Instructions will go from the State Department to the Governor of the Territory to that effect. If nevertheless armed

24. November 10, 1860: Rencher to Cass NA, TP, 5527.

bands should persist in invading the Navajoes, [you] will take efficient but quiet means to dissuade them from it; [you] will afford them no support, or assistance of any description; and if they come to posts, or in the vicinity of bodies of troops, within the Indian country, they will be deprived of their booty and sent out.[25]

As previously planned, Colonel Canby's column joined with Sibley's command at the mouth of Canyon de Chelly on October 18. Canby's troops brought gloomy news to the meeting. The personable, impetuous Captain George McLane—the officer censured in 1858 for ignoring orders and attacking Navajos without provocation at Ojo del Oso—was dead. With his Company I, Mounted Riflemen, he had halted briefly five days before at a spring near Black Pinnacle, north of Wheatfield Creek. The troops were watering their mounts when McLane, catching sight of four or five Navajos, spurred his horse after them, plunging into a thicket of brush. A moment later a gunshot was heard and then McLane's horse reappeared dragging the officer's body by one foot caught in a stirrup.

Almost nothing turned out well after this incident. Traveling north on Chinle Wash, Canby's dragoons and riflemen found adequate water each day for the horses, but no grass or forage to speak of other than dried-out cornstalks from old fields. The infantry fared well enough in the increasingly arid country, but Canby became concerned over his supplies. To insure a safe return he sent an express to Fort Defiance on October 19 ordering Captain McLaws to send one hundred troops with twelve hundred rations to establish a supply depot at Ojo de la Jarra, a well-known spring on the military road to the Hopi villages, sixty-five miles west of the fort. More ominously, however, Major Sibley observed two days later that attrition had set in with the cavalry. The horses had begun to yield "to the heaviness of the road . . . a number have perished." [26]

North of present Rock Point the troops left the Chinle Wash, turning westward to Tyende Creek. Here for the first time in more than a week they found luxuriant grass. The daylight hours of October 23 were spent in camp so that the horses could graze. Canby took advantage of

25. October 29, 1860: Adj. Gen. Samuel Cooper to Fauntleroy, NA, RAC, RG 393, A-82-1860, LR.

26. November 12, 1860: Sibley, Ewell's Hay Camp, to Lt. L. L. Rich, AAAG, Navajo Expedition; one of four enclosures with November 17, 1860: Canby, Fort Defiance, to AAG, NA, RAC, RG 393, C-53-1860, LR. The account of Canby's October 10–November 8 campaign is mainly based on these reports.

the time to review his plans. He held, still, to Marsh Pass as being the important goal of his march; and he believed that upon reaching there he would have the Navajos caught on an anvil of impassable rock canyons—he could hammer them into submission. If any were fortunate enough to filter through, he believed, then they would be shot down by hostile Paiutes. Modifying the original plans somewhat, Canby took the four companies of infantry under his own command and assigned all of the cavalry—Companies G and I, Second Dragoons, and Companies B and I, Mounted Riflemen—to Major Sibley. Sibley was then ordered to proceed southwesterly; to ascend and traverse Black Mesa to a point where he could strike Captain John G. Walker's Long House ruin in the valley on the far side. From here he would turn north and rejoin Canby's column of infantry, who by that time ought to be encamped at Marsh Pass. At sundown, accordingly, the command divided, Canby taking a course designed to skirt the north limits of Black Mesa and bring him down to Marsh Pass.

At daybreak of October 24, with the heights of Black Mesa rising before him, Sibley discovered also to his front and at a distance of several miles a large herd of Navajo horses. Holding the two companies of dragoons in reserve for support, he ordered Captain Thomas Claiborne and Lieutenant John Pegram with the riflemen to surround the livestock and destroy any Navajos they might encounter in the process. A short time afterward the troops were rejoined in the shambles of what had been the temporary camp of Delgadito and his band. Five Navajos were said to have been killed in the fight; three women and two children were held as captives. Blas Lucero with a detachment of his spy company, operating with the riflemen, succeeded in capturing two hundred horses and two thousand sheep. Uncertain now of what problems he might find on the mesa's summit, and reluctant to risk losing his valuable booty to survivors of Delgadito's band, Sibley then abandoned his orders from Canby. In the vicinity of present Chilchinbito, Sibley turned north along the base of the mesa. Near Lolami Point he picked up Canby's fresh trail and followed it up Laguna Creek to Marsh Pass. Here he rejoined Canby on October 26.

Four days were spent in operating out of this camp, time enough to demolish the anvil-hammer theory and convince Canby that large numbers of Navajos who had been fleeing in advance of his troops had eluded him completely, dispersing in the wilderness maze of Tsegi Canyon or southward into the Klethla Valley. "We . . . found to our bitter disappointment," Canby reported later, "that all the statements and reports upon which we had relied were erroneous; that the Pah Utes were not at war with the Navajoes, and that the Sierra Limita [region of Marsh Pass] was no barrier to their further flight." [27] Some of his frustration was transferred to Delgadito when the headman visited his camp under a white cloth of truce to ask for peace. Canby responded by saying there would be war until all Navajos agreed to comply with any peace terms Washington might offer. The Navajos, in other words, must surrender unconditionally.

The acute suffering of the horses led Colonel Canby to discard any effort to pursue the Navajos farther or to reach the supply base he had established at Ojo de la Jarra. Instead, when the command started from Marsh Pass on November 1, Canby determined to lose no time in unknown country to the south but to return to Fort Defiance as quickly as possible. He therefore followed the outward route taken by Major Sibley. While encamped the second night on a stream of bitter water near the place where Degadito's band had been attacked nine days before, a picket guard shot and wounded two Navajos, one of them mortally. A trail of blood led soldiers next morning to the survivor, who was brought back to camp and, on Canby's order, shot dead. The two men were identified as brothers of the headman Gordo; if this was true, then they were brothers also of Zarcillos Largos.

From this point onward the troops were shadowed constantly on flanks and rear. The presence of the Navajos was more a harassment than a dangerous threat; evidently their only desire was to be certain the soldiers were really withdrawing. They made little effort to attack the troops and only one soldier was wounded. During the fourth day of the march, in open country and dragging sand, the command found a natural tank of stale water. The nearly perishing horses and mules were held back by force and watered one by one from camp kettles and the soldiers' caps. The ordeal of the campaign ended finally on November 8, when Colonel Canby brought his staggering column to the fresh water and good grazing ground of Ewell's Camp near Laguna Negra.

From the day the Navajo war officially had been resumed with the shooting of the wounded Agua Chiquita on September 24 until November 8, Canby's troops had killed twenty-eight Navajos (including three women), wounded many others, seized five women and children, and captured 360 horses and 2,000 sheep. Ute auxiliaries led by Albert Pfeiffer and Kaneatchi, operating independently as usual but with full sanction by Colonel Fauntleroy and Superintendent Collins, in the

27. November 8, 1860: Canby, Ewell's Hay Camp, to AAG, NA, RAC, RG 393, C-49-1860, LR.

same period had killed six Navajos, taken nineteen women and children captive, and captured 500 horses and 5,000 sheep. As mentioned previously, no official account of losses inflicted by the Manuel Chaves battalion ever was made, but from what little is known the casualties were probably severe. The combined campaigning that started with the slave raids in the summer of 1860 and that was to be continued with unremitting pressure is remembered still by Navajos as the Nahondzod —the Fearing Time—an eight-year term of death and exile that ended only with their release in 1868 from captivity at far-off Bosque Redondo.[28]

The death of Captain McLane, which evoked sincere mourning among many of his companions, was soon overshadowed by graver realities. The dragoon and rifle companies had been rendered totally useless by the campaign. More than half of the surviving horses and mules would not be serviceable again for at least six months. As a consequence Fort Defiance was stripped to infantry for the remaining six months of its existence under that name as a military post, the dragoons and riflemen were ordered back to the fatter fields about Albuquerque. As for Colonel Canby, his campaigning during the next (and last) five months of the Navajo expedition was to be limited to the exertions of the infantry.

How, with infantry alone, does a commander overcome the mobility of Indians renowned as horsemen? Unlike Colonel Sumner, who in similar straits made dragoonish threats but did little else, Colonel Canby, for twenty-five of his forty-two years an infantryman, forged quietly ahead.

Canby was not quite reduced to infantry alone, however. Waiting for him at the bypassed rendezvous at Ojo de la Jarra was a thirty-two-year-old major named Albert James Myer. Freshly arrived in New Mexico, Myer had reported to Fort Defiance on October 20 and three days later joined the detachment ordered out to the springs with the supply train. During this brief interval Major Myer had become a figure of some curiosity and concealed amusement to older officers of lower rank. An imperious quality in his manner, as when he commandeered the best of the Albuquerque quartermaster's mules for his special wagons and ten-man mounted escort, also made him the butt of barbed witticism. Ruffled feelings spreading in his wake soon calmed, however, on a better acquaintance with Myer's talents.

He graduated from West Point Military Academy to become an as-

28. David M. Brugge, personal communication.

sistant surgeon, and, due to some quirk of nature, continued throughout his career to wear an army doctor's uniform. But it was an affectation. The son of a jeweler, Myer helped to pay his way through the medical department of the University of Buffalo by working as a telegraph operator. This experience, combined with a tour of duty on the Texas plains where, in the clear air, distant objects could be seen in sharp definition, gave him the germ of an idea. Abandoning the surgeon's scalpel for good, he devised a coded communications system employing flags, which he described as "flag telepathy"; at night, torches could be substituted for flags. After four years of Myer's efforts and prodding, Congress had added to the army's staff one signal officer with the rank and pay of major. On June 27, 1860, Myer received the appointment. His assignment to Colonel Canby's staff, granted upon his urgent request, was the first operative step in the founding of the U.S. Army Signal Corps.[29]

Major Myer remained at Ojo de la Jarra until an express arriving on November 10 recalled the supply detail to Fort Defiance. Three days later he reported to Colonel Canby, who assigned twenty-two enlisted men to detached service as recruits for the major's signal crew. In addition, Myer was offered the services of First Lieutenant Lucius L. Rich, Fifth Infantry, and Second Lieutenant Orlando G. Wagner, Topographical Engineers, as acting signal officers. For two weeks, during which Canby completed his preparations to move the expedition's headquarters to Fort Fauntleroy, Myer trained his men to transmit messages by using flags. Not unlike the Morse code system of telegraphic dots and dashes, Myer's "wigwag" device was coded to sending, in series, ones, twos, and threes. For short-range messages, two-foot "action" flags on four-foot poles were used. For distance transmission—to a maximum range of about twenty-five miles—ponderously heavy six-foot flags on sixteen-foot poles were needed. As they learned the basic flag positions, Myer drilled his men in snapping the flags with precision. By the end of the two weeks the flagmen could whip out messages with dazzling

29. Marshall (1965, pp. 8, 16–19); NA, Service records, RG 94, ACP 1873, box 73; and *Dictionary of American Biography*, vol. 13, pp. 374–75. During the Civil War Myer was brevetted colonel in 1862 for gallant services at Malvern Hill. He secured the establishment of the U.S. Army Signal Corps on March 3, 1863, and after its authorization was revoked in 1864 he persisted until the Signal Corps was reorganized July 28, 1866, by an act of Congress that also gave Myer the permanent rank of colonel and chief signal officer. At his suggestion, peacetime activities of the corps were extended in 1869 to include sending out storm warnings. With the aid of others he persuaded Congress in February 1870 to establish the U.S. Weather Bureau under Signal Corps direction.

skill. Only Major Myer and his two signal officers, however, knew the code. Neither the flagmen nor the receivers had the slightest knowledge of what was transmitted.

Colonel Canby's decision to move his winter headquarters to the partially completed Fort Fauntleroy was based on information that Navajos in large numbers had moved southward to grazing lands west of Zuni and near the Little Colorado River. If the prospect of winter campaigning with foot soldiers troubled him, no hint of it is found in his correspondence with department headquarters. His departure from Fort Defiance was quietly arranged and quietly executed. Captain Henry R. Selden, soon to be relieved by Captain John A. Whitall, was left in command. Deprived of cavalry, the Canby expedition numbered thirteen companies, 1,015 enlisted men and officers of the Fifth, Seventh, and Tenth U.S. Infantry. All but about twenty of the New Mexican spies and guides returned to the river with Sibley's dragoons and riflemen.

Major Myer had an opportunity to test his signal crew for the first time under field conditions during the march to Fort Fauntleroy. Reporting on the outcome of the operation, he informed the army's Adjutant General Samuel Cooper that he left Fort Defiance with Colonel Canby on November 25, and

> . . . . the use of signals in the field in active service, commenced the same day; an officer being detached in advance of the column to examine for and report by signal, upon a camp at a distance from the road. These duties . . . were continued upon the two days following. The discovery and report by 1st Lieut. L. L. Rich . . . of a pond of water, a matter of importance in this country, at a distance of three miles from the road while the column was in motion upon the march may be mentioned here. On November 27th the Command arrived at Fort Fauntleroy. On November 30th, today, we have marched upon a scout in the direction of the Colorado Chiquito and are encamped at Los Posas. A signal report has just been made by Lieut. L. L. Rich . . . from a height in the vicinity.[30]

A second campaign, meanwhile, was launched against the Navajos under the command of Captain Lafayette McLaws. At the head of

30. November 30, 1860: Myer to Cooper, NA, microcopy M-567, roll 627, LR by the AGO. Although no other reference is found to a "Camp Los Posas" the name would suggest the breastlike eminences today known as Twin Buttes, located south of Mentmore and about six miles west of Gallup, New Mexico.

three companies of infantry, a force of 183 enlisted men and officers, McLaws left Fort Defiance on November 18. His orders were to search out and capture or destroy any Navajos found during his march through Calites Canyon and then west to the Little Colorado River, country in which Colonel Canby believed the Navajos were concentrating. Eighteen New Mexican spies and guides were attached to the command, as well as a Navajo from the Cebolleta region named Juan Chi, possibly a Diné Ana'aii.[31] Below present Hunter's Point, as the command nooned the second day near cornfields, a youth rode toward McLaws "waving a piece of White Sheep Skin, and shouting in the Mexican language"— saying he had been sent by the Navajos to ask for peace. He identified himself as Jesús Arviso and said he had been raised among the Navajos from his capture as a small boy. During this conversation McLaws learned that several women were to be found digging wild potatoes in the next valley to the south. In the hope of capturing them, he ordered Lieutenant Edward J. Brooks to move forward with a detachment of thirty troops and six of the New Mexican spies.

Not long afterward, the captain believed he heard firing from the direction Brooks had taken. With twenty men, McLaws started off to lend support, the balance of the command following in his rear. Upon entering a high valley sloping southward toward Calites Canyon he met the returning forward detachment. Brooks reported that he had had a sharp skirmish with about fifty Navajos—warriors of the combined bands of Armijo and the late Zarcillos Largos. His troops had killed four men and taken four women as prisoners; among these were a sister and a niece of Armijo.

Although the location was not favorable, the troops encamped here; Jesús Arviso remained with them. A cold rain that started after dark turned to snow, the snow lasting through the night and leaving the ground so boggy that in the morning McLaws decided to remain where he was. In early afternoon he moved from the mud and slush of the open valley to a point two miles south that offered firewood and good water.

On the promise of freedom for herself and her daughter if she could obtain a number of horses from her people in exchange, McLaws, who was anxious to mount at least a small squad of men, released Armijo's sister. Some hours afterward she returned alone and on foot. All she

31. December 16, 1860: McLaws, "Camp at West Spring near Ft. Fauntleroy," to AAG, NA, RAC, RG 393, enclosure marked C-12-1861, LR (covering letter lost).

could say was that several headmen of her band desired to communicate with the Bilagáana commander.[32]

The same evening six mounted Navajos entered the soldiers' camp. Their principal spokesmen were a headman named Hastin-ah and Soldado Sordo (Deaf Soldier), a son of Zarcillos Largos and now the leader of his father's band. They said it was the wish of the entire Navajo nation to make peace. In reply, McLaws commented later, "I told them that I had no authority to make peace, that no peace could be made with *any* single band, that . . . the captains of every band in the nation should join together and go in a body to Colonel Canby and . . . be willing to abide by the terms he might grant them, without attempting to make any for themselves." The Navajos were allowed to leave with the warning that in future they would be met as enemies unless they came in with a white flag.

For the remainder of its time in the field the command accomplished little; the march was uneventful. Following Black Creek through Calites Canyon to its junction with the Puerco, McLaws turned west. Many trails of Navajo livestock, none less than one week old, gave evidence of the Indians' recent presence at Jacobs Well and Navajo Springs. Once more on the Puerco, the troops marched to the south of the Painted Desert and finally struck the Little Colorado near present Holbrook, Arizona. The return march by way of Zuni brought the troops into camp near Fort Fauntleroy on December 9. Jesús Arviso stayed with the command throughout.

"The boy 'Jesus,' " Captain McLaws reported, ". . . was taken from his parents in Sonora, his family name having been 'Alviso'—by the Apaches about ten years ago, and after remaining with them a short time, was sold to the Navajoes with whom he has remained until he came to my camp, in the family of a Chief named 'Kla.' He is a good interpreter in the Navajoe language, and appearing to be a very well disposed youth, I offered him the choice of returning to the Navajoes or accepting service as guide to my command telling him that I had no doubt but that the U.S. would return him to his parents if he desired to

32. Captain McLaws apparently never accomplished this trade, as he later reported: "I kept the women captives because two of them were of rich families and I was desirous to exchange them for horses and equipments to mount some of my lightest men and best riders, being deficient in cavalry force. To effect that more promptly I released the oldest sister of Armijo [once more] at my second camp on the Puerco giving her a horse, saddle and bridle of the captured property. She left early one morning promising to return in five days, but was seen no more." What happened to the three other women captives is not known.

go. Without hesitation he said that he had no desire to be with the Navajoes any longer and would come with me willingly. I employed him accordingly."

Unlike Juan Anaya, whom in other respects he resembled, Jesús Arviso did not elect to join with the Navajos against their enemies, but he did not renounce the Navajos, either, as McLaws suggested. He lived among the Navajos for the remainder of his life, serving as their interpreter during their confinement at Bosque Redondo and afterward at the Fort Defiance agency from 1868 to 1880, when those duties were largely assumed by Henry Chee Dodge. Married twice to Navajo women, Jesús lived many years in the lower Chusca Valley and there raised a large family.[33]

In much the same spirit that motivated the citizen volunteers of the Manuel Chaves battalion, New Mexico's Legislative Assembly late in 1860 attempted to enlarge the scope of its 1859 Act for the Protection of Property in Slaves to include "male or female Indians that should be acquired from barbarous nations." Drafters of the February 3, 1859, act clearly had been thinking only of Negro slaves; present proposals extended that thinking to Navajos and possibly other "barbarous" Indians. The act's purpose, explicitly stated in the title, was spelled out at length in thirty-one sections or articles. These ranged from providing fines for any person caught stealing or aiding a slave to escape from his master, to declaring that any slave convicted of any crime might —in lieu of paying a fine in cash—be given lashes on his bare back or branded with an iron, and prohibiting any slave from testifying in court against a white person.

Governor Rencher expressed opposition to the proposal in his annual address to the legislature, delivered the second Monday in December. He said the proposal could not be enacted legally:

> The act seemed to be based upon the supposition that male or female Indians, acquired from barbarous nations, are slaves, which is not the case; nor is it within the power of the Legislature to make them so. The Legislature can neither create nor abolish slavery. They can only regulate it where it already exists, as any other species of property. . . . The normal or native condition of all our Indian tribes is that of freedom, and they cannot under our laws, be made slaves either by conquest, or purchase. We

33. A more detailed biographical sketch of Arviso appears in Brugge 1968, pp. 157–60.

may hold them as Captives, or peons, but not as slaves. When the Territory shall become a sovereign State, she may, if she choose to do so, exercise powers, in this respect, which she can not do as a Territorial Legislature. . . .

When he forwarded a copy of this message to Secretary of State Cass a few week later, Governor Rencher commented with some distaste on the operations of the Chaves battalion. "That force," he wrote, "has returned, having accomplished nothing, except the capture of property and of some Indian Captives, which they have applied to their own use. Not more than eight or ten Indians were killed by them. This I learn from reliable persons who were in the expedition, no public report having been made by the commanding officer." [34]

34. January 10, 1861: Rencher to Cass, NA, TP, 5538; and "Slavery in the Territory of New Mexico," pp. 1–7, *House Exec. Docs.*, 36th Cong., 1st sess., Report no. 508. Peonage was abolished in New Mexico by a March 2, 1867, act of Congress.

23

Massacre at Fort Fauntleroy

A state of constant warfare was contrary to Navajo nature and totally disruptive of normal Navajo life. Stock raisers and farmers could not live as raiding nomads or fugitives. This generalization would except the relatively few Navajo ladrons and *pobres*, whose raids upon the river settlements continued unremittingly through the winter of 1860–61. Colonel Canby, with no previous experience of Navajos, was aware of this fact, if in a tentative way, when he advised department headquarters that there was a strong disposition on the part of the Navajos to submit unconditionally to his peace terms. Since his departure from Fort Defiance he had kept five or six companies constantly in the field. Their performance resulted in few Navajo casualties, but a dogged quality about the infantry's surprising presence in unexpected places relentlessly kept the Indians on the move and when winter came many of them were close to starvation. The year was nearly out when Armijo, old Herrero, and Delgadito persuaded Canby that most of their people were ready for peace. He asked them to come in for preliminary discussions on January 12.[1]

On the assumption that his judgment might be wrong, Canby at the same time laid plans to continue the war should that be necessary. He advised Colonel Fauntleroy that should the Navajos fail to meet his terms, he would establish a supply depot west of the Hopi villages, request reinforcement by two more companies, and then campaign in the vicinity of the San Francisco Mountains where many Navajos were said to have withdrawn with their livestock. Fauntleroy gave his full assent to all that his field commander proposed. If the Navajos were ready

1. December 23, 1860: Canby, Fort Fauntleroy, to AAG, NA, RAC, RG 393, C-1-1861, LR. Between November 19, 1860, and January 9, 1861, by official account, Canby's troops killed 10 Navajos, took 24 prisoners, and captured 25 horses and 120 sheep. During the same period, 1 enlisted man was killed.

for peace, he would trust Canby's decision in the matter. If the decision, instead, was to continue the war, Fauntleroy would make three companies of the Seventh Infantry available to Canby at once.

In preparation for the preliminary council Canby asked his aides to submit a list of the names of headmen known to favor peace. He found that only five of the fifteen names were familiar to him. The others he marked (shown here with an asterisk) in sending the following list to Colonel Fauntleroy:

* Sarcillo Largo (the son) [Soldado Sordo]
  Armijo
  Delgidito
  Manuelita
  Ganado Mucho
  Gordo
* 2 Herrero (two of this name)
* Hostin-ah
* Kla
* Cayatano
* Chino
* Nalgadida
* Barbon
* Baboncito [Barboncito]

On the day appointed, two weeks later, a small delegation appeared at the fort. Again Canby reviewed the terms he would insist upon in drafting his peace treaty. The headmen offered no objection; February 5 was set as the date for a full meeting, and the parties agreed that until that time a partial armistice would be observed. Before they left, the Navajos offered certain revisions to Canby's December 27 list of headmen—most important, deleting Cayetano's name. Under circumstances entirely unknown at the fort, he had been killed at some time before the list was drawn up. Canby was not aware of Cayetano's great influence in Navajo affairs before and after 1839 when, in another treaty-signing at Jemez, Mexican authorities referred to him as one of the most important men of his nation. For this reason, Canby unfortunately left no account of when or how Cayetano died.[2]

2. December 27, 1860, with one enclosure; January 13, 1861 with one enclosure: Canby to AAG, NA, RAC, RG 393, C-4-1861, C-16-1861, LR. A new list of headmen favoring peace was drawn up January 13, the names appearing in order of the headmen's supposed influence: "Herrero Grande, Herrero Chiquito, Aguas Grandes No. 1 or Totisonisne or Ganados Muchos, Armijo, Manuelito, El hijo de Juanico, Totisonines [sic] No. 2, Tagoje, Cavallada Mucho (el tio de Barbon),

In spite of the winter's extreme cold, troops of six companies were ordered to patrol westward during the early weeks of peace negotiations in 1861. Major Myer and his signal party were attached to a column led by Captain McLaws, who was assigned the task of opening a wagon road from Ojo del Oso down the Puerco of the West to connect at Navajo Springs with Lieutenant Edward F. Beale's 1857–58 wagon road to California.[3] In his first two months in the field Major Myer had won unreserved acceptance of his signaling "apparatus." "The signal party," Canby informed Fauntleroy, "has become so valuable an auxilliary to our operations that I should regret any change that would impair its usefulness." And again, nine days later: "The signal party under Major Myer . . . has largely extended our knowledge of a part of the country of which previously but little was known." [4]

Colonel Fauntleroy, in a contrast to the conflict and turmoil surrounding the 1858 treaty, expressed himself as satisfied with both Colonel Canby's arduous services in the field and the proposed terms of his treaty. Through his adjutant he wrote to Canby on January 27 saying that he earnestly hoped Canby "will be able, either by Treaty of Peace, or an Armistice . . . to notify him at an early day, that he may withdraw all of the Troops from the Navajoe Country except the necessary garrisons of Forts Defiance and Fauntleroy. . . ." [5]

All but the weather seemed to conspire in favor of the council. Twenty-four hours before the scheduled time, some two thousand Navajos were encamped near Fort Fauntleroy; others continued to come in. Possibly as many as four hundred of the Indians were at the point of starving; others were said to have died of hunger and cold in the Chusca Valley on their way to the meeting. Temperatures dropped: to sixteen

---

Tocara (Suhijo), El Flaco [The Feeble One] or Es-kate-si-ne [Ish-kit-sa-ne]." Barboncito, El Sordo, Gordo, and Soldado Sordo were listed among nine others said to be of equal rank. The order of importance, by whomever devised, of course is suspect. Canby himself admitted soon afterward that Ish-kit-sa-ne was now so old that he, like the aging Miguelito, no longer was regarded as an important leader.

3. Beale's famous experimental use of camels on the "American desert" almost overshadowed the results of his wagon road survey along the 35th parallel. His expedition officially started August 27, 1857, from Fort Defiance, but actually it started a few days later from the vicinity of Zuni (Jackson 1965, pp. 241–56).

4. January 5, 14, 1861: Canby to AAG, NA, RAC, RG 393, C-13-1861, C-17-1861, LR. Some months later, Bvt. Lt. Col. William W. Loring, then commanding the department, reported to army headquarters that "The favourable opinions of all officers, who used military signals upon the Navajo Campaign, or who were present at their use . . . have led to the almost unanimous expression of the wish, that they should be made of general use in the Army. . . ." (May 2, 1861: Loring to Townsend, AAG, New York, NA, RAC, RG 393, no. 176, LS).

5. January 27, 1861: AAG Maury to Canby, NA, RAC, RG 393, no. 35, LS.

below zero at Fort Defiance, to thirty below in the Chusca Mountains, and to two below at Fort Fauntleroy, where as protection against the cold the Navajos had, at best, flimsy brush shelters. Old Herrero and Barboncito were among twelve headmen who appeared at the fort on February 5, but Colonel Canby decided he would wait for others he knew were coming in from the direction of the Hopi villages, among them Manuelito and Ganado Mucho. Snow eighteen inches deep delayed their coming. Canby announced that the council would be postponed for ten days.

Twenty-four of the thirty-one headmen whom he expected met with Canby on February 15. Again the colonel temporized, delaying for three days more the formal signing of the treaty. "The conference was satisfactory," he reported, "but I do not propose to do more at present than to enter into a conversation with them. . . ." Before leaving the fort the headmen, evidently to satisfy Canby, "elected Herrero Grande the principal chief of the nation [and] pledged themselves to support him and each other in carrying out their promises. . . ." [6]

Colonel Fauntleroy was unable to be present when the treaty was signed on February 18, and Superintendent Collins apparently was not invited—no doubt because jurisdiction in Navajo affairs had rested with the military, in fact if not in record, since Colonel Bonneville reopened the war in the fall of 1859. Canby, who claimed sole authorship of the treaty, was modestly confident that his sincere desire to make a "permanent settlement of all questions" affecting the Navajo nation had a fair chance of realization. To qualify himself for the peacemaker's role, he observed afterward, he had seized every opportunity to acquaint himself with Navajo character, disposition, and habits.

Never before had as many headmen of the nation gathered to sign a treaty. Their attitude was entirely cooperative. They placed themselves unconditionally in the hands of the government, Canby reported to department headquarters. They made no attempt to extract promises from him, nor did they at any time try to impose conditions or terms of their own. Those provisions that Canby made in their favor, he said later, were only those that he considered it proper to make "with a view to an absolute and permanent peace." To that end, he said, "I have not exacted from them conditions which it is absolutely impossible for them to fulfill." [7]

6. February 15, 1861: Canby to AAG, NA, RAC, RG 393, C-31-1861, LR.

7. February 19, 1861: Canby, Fort Fauntleroy, to AAG, with two enclosures: a signed copy of the treaty, and a copy of General Orders No. 14, dated February 19, NA, RAC, RG 393, C-32-1861, LR.

Canby's treaty was brief and, except for the sixth and last article, its language was clear. The first two articles may be regarded as prefatory. First, it was distinctly understood that any act of hostility by the Navajos against citizens and Pueblos or other friendly Indians of New Mexico Territory would be a breach of faith and regarded as an act of hostility against the United States. Second, the Navajo headmen agreed to submit unconditionally to the United States and, on behalf of the entire nation, pledged to perform faithfully all stipulations of the treaty.

The condition on which most emphasis was placed was then introduced: Navajo headmen agreed to make war at once upon the ladrons "and unruly men" of their nation. They would continue the war until the thieves were destroyed and the others brought into submission. Should the ladrons prove too strong for the Navajos to handle, troops would be sent to their aid. A clause subsidiary to this appeared in the fourth article, which declared that "ladrones or bad men" would be refused refuge by their fellow Navajos; if any of them should be discovered hiding among their people they would be surrendered at once to the commander of the nearest military post. Three supplementary but unrelated terms followed in the same article: (1) headmen would not permit their people to purchase or sell stolen property, but agreed to turn it over to the nearest military post; (2) owners of stolen property would be indemnified by the Navajo nation; and (3) if any robberies should be committed against Navajos, "measures will be taken to see that justice is done." What measures, and when and how and by whom they would be taken, was not stated.

Canby went further than any of his predecessors when he stipulated where, and how, Navajos should be allowed to live. In the fifth article, the headmen were called upon to move all of their people at once to country west of Fort Fauntleroy. Until otherwise ordered, no Navajo would be allowed to live or graze livestock in country east of the fort. Any Navajos found east of the fort could expect, as enemies, to be shot. Further: as soon as necessary arrangements could be made, the headmen must "establish their people permanently in pueblos or settled communities."

The new boundary imposed on the Navajos, perhaps unintentionally on Canby's part, was breathtaking in its harsh implications. Two of the Navajos' four sacred mountains would be lost to them, as well as about one-third of their traditionally held land.[8]

8. In General Orders No. 14 (see note 7 above), with reference to the Diné Ana-aii, Canby stated: "This restriction of territory will not apply to the friendly

Finally—and never had a tossed bone been more tantalizingly meta-physical—Canby's concluding article was offered in the Navajos' favor. When the government was satisfied that the Navajo people had ceased their depredations and were complying in good faith with all of the treaty's stipulations, "measures will be taken to render them any assistance that may be necessary to place them in the same condition with other Nations, under the protection of the Government."

The treaty was signed at the time by forty-nine headmen and, some few days later, by at least five others. What else happened at the council may never be known, as Canby's report of the event, still the only one to come to light, omits even the most meager reference to circumstances surrounding the meeting. It may only be assumed that the treaty was signed at or near the fort; because the terms were unconditional, the articles may have been explained to the headmen by an interpreter, but they were not discussed. When he first drafted the treaty, Canby predated it February 15—the previously arranged date for signing. By an oversight, after weather had forced a delay, the written date went unchanged. Canby's name was mentioned in the preamble to the treaty, but he did not sign the document. Instead, the treaty was signed by eleven officers of Canby's command, and by them only as witnesses to each Navajo headman's mark. One officer, by an interesting coincidence, was Captain Benjamin Wingate, soon to die of wounds received at Valverde in an opening engagement of the Civil War. After a passage of time and many vicissitudes a new fort bearing his name would be built on the site of Fort Fauntleroy.[9]

A good soldier Canby was, but a good peacemaker he was not. There is no question that he sincerely hoped to accomplish what all others had failed to do and bring the Navajos to a lasting peace. Unfortunately, his earnest study of Navajo character, disposition, and habits had taught him nothing. He not only repeated the worst mistakes of other treaty makers, he compounded them and invented others. Furthermore, he adopted none of the few constructive proposals of his

---

Navajoes of Po-ha-Conta's (formerly Sandoval's) band now living in the neighborhood of Covero and Servietta [Cubero and Cebolleta: phonetically—Covero and Sevoyetta] &c."

9. Among the headmen who signed the treaty February 18 were Herrero Grande, Armijo, Herrero Chiquito, Barbon No. 1, Soldado Sordo, El Sordo, Barbon No. 2 (Kla), Mariano, José Pelón, El Chupador, Manuelito, Hijo de Juanico, Huero No. 1, Huero No. 2, Juan Lucero, Cayetanito, Gordo, Huero No. 3, Ganado Mucho, Barboncito, and Vicente Baca. Among the few others who signed afterwards were Caballada Mucha, Ish-kit-sa-ne, and Delgadito.

predecessors; he did not, for example, ask for a reciprocal return of captives desirous of exchange and a rigidly enforced prohibition of all slave raiding; nor did he suggest that indemnification of citizens for stolen property be placed in the hands of courts and balanced against equal indemnification of Navajos for their losses to citizens, Pueblos, and Utes. In four of Canby's six articles, the headmen (under a "principal chief") were held strictly accountable for the actions of the entire nation. Such a logical order of authority, splendid for the disciplined operation of an army, was simply and historically unacceptable under the old Navajo adherence to self-determination. Doomed on this miscalculation alone, the treaty was twice doomed by its major concept and requirement. Historically, again, Navajos (excepting always the Diné Ana'aii) never could be made to fight and destroy other Navajos. To the point of death they had resisted any demand that they surrender one of their own for punishment by white men. Since the middle of the eighteenth century they had resisted all efforts to "puebloize" them or pack them into tight compounds, and after 1800 they had demonstrated again and again that persons who would take their land must pay for it with their blood. For these reasons and others Canby's treaty was one of the most unworkable, and therefore one of the worst, ever made with the Navajo nation.

Only the Navajos who signed the treaty could really have explained why they did so. Their ensuing unbroken silence might only suggest that the answer lay in the word *survival*. Their own word *Nahondzod*—the Fearing Time—implied this. From the summer and autumn slave raids of 1860 onward, they had been pursued and hounded and relentlessly driven far from their homes. Those who once had crops had them no more. Many were without clothing to protect them from freezing. Only those who had been very wealthy still retained enough livestock to provide a minimum of clothing and food. Many had died already, and many more were near the edges of starvation.

"One of the gravest difficulties . . . in maintaining a peace with these people," Canby observed the day after the treaty signing, "is that resulting from the dangers of aggression from their neighbors." Who these neighbors were Canby did not say, but within hours of his statement they would reveal themselves. He added, "The temptation to rob, stimulated as it is with nearly two thirds of this people by the danger of starvation is another difficulty of the most serious character."

With an insight not apparent in his treaty, Canby said the danger could be met only by the greatest vigilance on the part of the troops, "unless the Indian Department is provided with the means of applying the cheaper remedy of furnishing food to this part of the Nation until they are enabled to produce for themselves."

An echo of warning was sounded by Colonel Fauntleroy. On receiving word of the treaty signing he wrote Superintendent Collins, who retained his dual role as publisher of the Santa Fe *Gazette*, that ratification of the treaty might be expected by May 20. He added, "In the meantime, in order to afford the Navajo chiefs a fair opportunity of proving the sincerity of their desire for peace, it will be very important that no further hostilities should be made upon them by the people of the Territory. . . ." [10]

As early as February 24 an omen of the nation's onrushing Civil War reached Santa Fe. Colonel Fauntleroy sent two messages to Canby on that day, the first one official and the second marked "Confidential." In light of the gratifying results of his Navajo expedition, the first letter began, and because of the hostile attitude of Mescaleros and other Apache bands, Canby was ordered—"at the earliest practicable moment"—to strip his command of field troops and return these six companies of infantry to stations on the river. Stores at Fort Defiance were to be moved as quickly as possible to Fort Fauntleroy and Fort Defiance abandoned. Financial embarrassments of the military department, the second, confidential, message began, had resulted from "the disturbed condition of our Country." In consequence, regular troops must be withdrawn from Navajo country, this in turn a compelling reason for abandoning Fort Defiance.

"In order to prevent mischievous excitement," Fauntleroy wrote, through his adjutant, "it is desirable that [these orders] should appear to be the natural consequences of the Apache hostilities and by the Navajoe peace. . . . The latest intelligence from home (of date Washington City—Feby 8) is not calculated to abate the anxiety which now oppresses every mind." [11]

10. March 2, 1861: Santa Fe *Gazette*, enclosure with March 3, 1861: Collins to C.I.A. A. B. Greenwood, NA, NMS 234-550.

11. February 24, 1861: AAG Maury to Canby, NA, RAC, RG 393, nos. 76 & 77, LS. 2d Lt. John F. Ritter was the last officer to command the Fort Defiance garrison —136 officers and men of Companies A & B, 5th Infantry—when the fort was evacuated April 25, 1861. The deserted buildings fell unwanted into the hands of Navajos until the fort was reoccupied and renamed Fort Canby in July 1863 during the opening days of Col. Kit Carson's Navajo expedition.

The country was still in shock from the opening shots on Fort Sumter when the United States Senate declined to ratify Canby's treaty. The stated grounds were brief: the Senate would refuse to approve any treaty drawn in New Mexico that required Indians to give up their land. For the present that also was the policy of the new commissioner of Indian affairs, William P. Dole. In advising him to this effect, Dole instructed Superintendent Collins to encourage the Navajos to maintain friendly relations with the government. Collins was directed as well to use every means in his power to prevent raids against the Navajos by citizens of the territory.[12]

Slave raids against the Navajos were resumed as soon as word of the approaching peace treaty reached the river settlements. A starving company of thirty-one New Mexicans appealed for help at Fort Defiance late in February. After starting out from the vicinity of Taos, they said, they had managed to kill seven Navajos—six of them women and children—and they had captured four women. Then their luck ended. Struggling through deep snow, for days without food, they barely succeeded in reaching the fort. They were deprived of their captives, given food, and allowed to go on their way. Not long afterward they appeared at Fort Fauntleroy, again asking for help. Ten of their number were too weak to go on and were taken in for rest and medical treatment; the others were given enough food to enable them to reach the river. Colonel Canby expressed mingled puzzlement and anger. The raiders, he said, "by their own statement had no complaints to make of the Navajoes," and yet "they openly avow their intention to disregard the treaty . . . and on their return home to organize a new expedition to capture Navajoes and sell them." Citizens of Cubero were known to have announced similar intentions.[13]

An Abiquiu company of fifty-two citizens led by José Manuel Sánchez in early March drove off a bunch of Navajo horses grazing near Fort Fauntleroy. Captain Wingate, who was ordered in pursuit with Company D, Fifth Infantry, followed the trail into the lower Chusca Valley where he overtook the party and recovered the horses (an instance of the effectiveness of Canby's infantry). This encounter occurred in the vicinity of Tohgaii, sixteen miles south of present Tohatchi, where the leader of the party, Sánchez, had been killed by a

12. May 9, 1861: Dole to Collins, NA, NMS T21-5.
13. February 27, 1861: Canby to AAG, NA, RAC, RG 393, no file mark, LR.

Navajo a day or so earlier. Wingate held his troops at the springs long enough to satisfy himself that the Abiquiu citizens were started back in the direction of home.[14]

A week before he announced the termination of his Navajo expedition and departed for the river, Colonel Canby received even more disturbing information. Another company of citizens, striking in the vicinity of Beautiful Mountain, was said to have ravaged the rancherias of old Herrero, Vicente Baca, and El Chupador. Ironically enough, these headmen, together with Armijo and a number of their men, were away at the time, rounding up stolen livestock in order to return it to the owners. Fifteen Navajos were casualties, killed, or carried off as captives.

The headmen of the nation were complying in good faith with the treaty terms, Canby reported, "and I have no doubt of the permanent settlement of these troubles if the inroads of Mexicans can be restrained." [15] Canby may indeed have been right, but with the attention of the army soon to be focused on the devastating effects of the Civil War, the restraining of citizen raiders and their Pueblo and Ute allies became virtually impossible. On April 3, the terminal date after which military reports of such matters ceased, Major Henry H. Sibley—soon to lead an invasion of New Mexico by Texan Confederates, but at this time commanding dragoon forces at Taos—reported:

> Having received information this morning of the return to this place of a party of Mexicans and Pueblo Indians, from a campaign against the Navajoes with a number of captives, I considered it my duty . . . to enquire into the matter. . . . I communicated immediately with Judge Pedro Valdez, and, with him, had an interview with the leader of the party, Aban [sic] Romero. . . . Captain Romero acknowledges that he had captured twelve Navajoes, two children had died *en route,* and the rest with the exception of *three* had been disposed of at various points on the return route. In consideration of the statement of Capt Romero . . . that his expedition had started out in February, anterior to the publication of General Orders No. 6 announcing peace, and his promise to me endorsed by Judge Valdez that he would hold the three prisoners in his possession subject to the decision of the

14. March 15, 1861: Wingate to Rich, enclosure with March 18, 1861: Canby to AAG, NA, RAC, RG 393, C-42-1861, LR. Tohgaii, or Tuye Springs, is also found on some maps as Tohlikai.

15. Ibid. Canby ended his campaign and left Fort Fauntleroy March 26.

Dept. Commander, I have allowed him to keep them and now submit the matter accordingly.[16]

The withdrawal of regular troops from New Mexico Territory continued through the spring and summer, a number of the officers at the same time resigning from the army to enlist with the Confederate forces. Colonel Fauntleroy resigned late in March; his successor, Colonel William W. Loring, himself resigned to be replaced in departmental command June 11 by Colonel Canby. It was a time of great confusion, of spreading suspicion among men who had been friends, and of alarm over rumored invasion from the south by Texans forming under the command of Sibley, by then a brigadier general. Very early on, to Canby's immense relief, it was determined that the majority of New Mexicans would not only remain loyal, but that many would demonstrate their loyalty by fighting for the Union cause. Pressures of organizing a new military force to defend the territory fell most heavily on Canby but were shared by the Fort Union depot ordnance officer, Captain William R. Shoemaker. In the tension and frenzy of these early weeks he informed Canby that he could equip two regiments of volunteer infantry with muskets and rifles, but that there would be odd discrepancies in uniforms and equipment. As military storekeeper he was a tough, unpushable veteran of twelve years at this post—years in which he had been besieged with demands for weapons to put down, legally or extralegally, all sorts of impending insurrections, real or imagined. Ordinarily no man was more matter-of-fact than he, but he succumbed in the excitement, if briefly, to quixotic imagination.

Assuring Colonel Canby that he need have no apprehensions of a shortage of arms, Shoemaker proposed equipping New Mexican volunteers with lances, as "they are probably more expert in the use of them, & it might . . . save the expense of ammunition." While inventorying his stores he had come upon a hundred or so sword bayonets, useless with the arms then in service. He could convert them to lance blades, he said, and then doubtfully added, "there are more than it is at all likely the Cavalry will want, if they want any." [17]

Infantry, rather than cavalry, composed the first two regiments of

16. April 3, 1861: Sibley to AAG Maury, NA, RAC, RG 393, S-20-1861, LR. Sibley was instructed by return mail to send the three Navajo captives to department headquarters in Santa Fe. He replied that if he could persuade Romero to give them up, he would "forward them as instructed."

17. June 18, 1861: Shoemaker to Lt. A. L. Anderson, AAAG, Santa Fe; November 23, 1861: Shoemaker to Lt. W. J. L. Nicodemus, AAG, Santa Fe, NA, RAC, RG 393, S-32-1861, S-103-1861, LR.

volunteers mustered into service. New Mexico's First Regiment was organized in July and August at Fort Union by Colonel Ceran St. Vrain and Lieutenant Colonel Kit Carson, the former soon afterward to retire from command in favor of the younger Carson. The Second Regiment, commanded by Colonel Miguel E. Pino, was mustered in during August at Albuquerque by the post commander, Brevet Major Nathan B. Rossell. Manuel Chaves, last seen in Navajo country with his citizens' battalion, received his commission as lieutenant colonel at his home in Peralta on August 1 and later the same day was mustered in at Albuquerque.[18] At the age of forty-two, Chaves had been fighting Navajos for twenty-six years. His assignment to the command of Fort Fauntleroy brought him into close contact with an old enemy. Canby's judgment in sending this man to the Navajo frontier must have been based on one consideration only: the reputation Manuel Chaves had won as a dedicated Indian fighter. Advance units of his command preceded him with a supply train and a fresh beef herd to the fort at Ojo del Oso. Their arrival permitted the three companies of Fifth Infantry under Captain Henry R. Selden to return to the river for assignment to the eastern war front.

Colonel Chaves reached the stone, stake, and adobe fort on August 8 and the next day took command of a garrison of three companies numbering 7 officers and 203 men. Canby's recommendation of the previous February that food be supplied to those Navajos who were starving appears to have been acted upon; 356 Navajos came in during the day of August 10 to receive rations from the post commissary. Their number was very considerably increased after the arrival ten days later of the new Navajo agent, Ramón Luna, who at once convened a council of 34 of the headmen. An armistice with the Navajos had been in effect since the February 18 treaty signing and, following the failure of ratification, Luna had been sent out from Santa Fe for preliminary discussions of a new treaty.

The appearance of Agent John Ward on August 20, upon his return from the Hopi villages, coincided with the climactic day of Luna's council. A throng of Navajos—Colonel Chaves estimated their number at two thousand—was gathered at Ojo del Oso. The presence of Chaves as a garrison commander, his identity known at once to all Navajos in the region, apparently had no dampening effect. If his assessment of their mood was accurate, the Navajos were nursing no old grievances

18. Muster Roll of the field, staff, and band of the 2d Regiment, N.M. (Foot) Volunteers, NA, RAC, RG 94, AGO.

but were anxious to cooperate with Ramón Luna and John Ward in working out a good peace. During the day, as they had done often in the past to signify good faith, they surrendered four captives, all boys. When the headmen finally dispersed it was agreed that Luna and Ward would meet again with them in forty days.[19]

The end came with the abrupt shock of a desert thunderstorm. All of the elements present made the ending inevitable. Only the direction in which the bolt struck was unpredictable.

Five hundred or more Navajos had remained close to the fort after the departure of the two agents. Many of them drew daily rations of beef and flour from an overblown commissary department that kept six enlisted men steadily engaged. Charges brought against him later and signed by six of his own officers suggest that Colonel Chaves was prodigal in dispensing his post's supplies and remarkably lax in maintaining discipline. Sheep intended to supply the garrison with mutton were brought from the post corrals, either on his order or with his permission, to be wagered against Navajo blankets and buckskins in a series of horse races that began September 10 and continued into the late afternoon of September 13. Each of the four days was noisier and more disorderly than the one before, as Colonel Chaves permitted Post Sutler A. W. Kavanaugh to supply liquor freely to the Navajos.[20]

An unreal carnival mood prevailed. Excitement reached its highest pitch at the start of the third race of the fourth day, when one of the best Navajo ponies came to the line with a thoroughbred owned by the post's assistant surgeon, Finis E. Kavanaugh, and ridden by Lieutenant Rafael Ortiz y Chávez. According to one account, the Kavanaugh horse was beginning to pull ahead when "the Navajo struck his own mount with a rope and deliberately swerved into his opponent's path. Young Ortiz vainly tried to avoid a collision, but the chest of his animal struck the Indian and the sorrel and sent them into the dust. In an instant the place was in an uproar."

19. August 22, 1861: Chaves to Canby: three letters, NA, RAC, RG 393, C-131-132-133-1861, LR. Among the headmen present at the council were old Herrero, Ganado Mucho, Barboncito, Cayetanito, El Chupador, Armijo, Hijo de Juanico, Gordo, Delgadito, and Vicente Baca. The son of Zarcillos Largos was not mentioned. Two "Hermanos [brothers] del Manuelito" were present, but not the war leader himself.

20. "Charges and Specifications against Lieut. Colonel Manuel Chaves of the Second Regiment of N.M. Volunteers." Undated enclosure with Consolidated Service Record of Chaves, NA, microcopy 427, roll 36.

From a different vantage point, Sergeant Nicholas Hodt later told quite a different version: "Large bets, larger than on either of the other races, were made on both sides. The Indians flocked in by hundreds, women and children; some of them mounted on fine ponies, richly dressed, and all appeared to be there to see the race, and not with any hostile intentions. . . . The Indian's horse did not run a hundred yards before it ran off the track. I being at the upper end of the track, could not see the cause of it, but the report was that the Indian's bridle broke." Claiming the race was unfairly won, the Navajos demanded that their wagers be returned, but the soldiers who had bet on the Kavanaugh horse refused. Moments later, over the clamor of voices, a shot rang out, followed by a crackling fusillade.[21]

Colonel Chaves afterward accused the Navajos of a prearranged attack on the fort, suggesting that the horse races were no more than a disarming prelude. "It is with deepest grief," he reported later that day to Colonel Canby, ". . . that about the hour of four o'clock a large meeting of the Nabajo Indians having assembled for the purpose of running their horses; they were within two hundred yards of the Fort, in front of the Guard house. At first they appeared to be very peaceable, but after their race was over, they all approached and stood within a hundred yards of the Guard house, when one of them attacked a sentinel, trying to take his arms from him and cocking his pistol on the Sentinel's breast. At the same time an [Indian] of the name Miguelito, belonging to the peaceable portion of the Nabajo tribe, seeing that the other Indians . . . were making every preparation of war . . . shot and

21. The first version, from "A Horserace in New Mexico in 1861," by an anonymous writer (MS in the Amado Chaves Collection, NMSRCA), appears in Simmons 1970, p. 10. Hodt's account was given to the James R. Doolittle Committee September 7, 1865, when Hodt, then a captain, was stationed at old Fort Wingate, near Ojo del Gallo. His testimony appears in Senate Exec. Docs., 39th Cong., 2d sess., Report no. 156, "Condition of the Indian Tribes," p. 314. The Navajo rider is identified as "Pistol Bullet"—otherwise Manuelito—by Keleher (1952, p. 298) and Frink (1968, p. 78) but neither writer gives a source for the statement. Finis Ewing Kavanaugh, a native of Watkins, Missouri, was graduated from St. Louis Medical College. In 1855, Governor Meriwether appointed him assistant surgeon in a battalion of mounted volunteers stationed at Taos. As distinguished from an army surgeon, Kavanaugh was a private physician serving under contract. His term at Fort Fauntleroy extended from August 1 to October 19, 1861, at $120 a month. Long known as a proslavery advocate, Kavanaugh in March 1862 turned over military stores at Cubero to Confederate troops. His relationship to Sutler A. W. Kavanaugh is not known. He died of consumption in 1866 (Santa Fe New Mexican, May 25, 1866; NA, RG 94, Medical Officers File, box 416).

killed an Indian of a party called the Chays Ladrons [ladrons of Canyon de Chelly], who had come for the purpose of attacking the post. After this happening the Indians of [Canyon de Chelly]—numbering about two hundred, well armed and mounted, advanced towards the Guard, shooting at the men . . . but immediately . . . the companies protected the Guard and fired into them, when they put off in different directions leaving twelve dead bodies and forty prisoners or captives. . . ." [22]

Canby at once ordered Chaves to submit a full report of the occurrence and to furnish with it a list of his prisoners. With Sibley's Texas battalion threatening invasion from the south, and dependent mainly on inexperienced volunteer troops to meet them when they came, Colonel Canby was anxious to avoid another Navajo war. When Chaves neglected to comply, Captain Andrew W. Evans of the Sixth U.S. Cavalry was ordered to proceed at once to the fort, its name, since September 25, changed to Fort Lyon. On arrival there Evans was to take a supervisory role and, with the assistance of John Ward, report fully and frequently. Captain Evans did report frequently and all of the messages of routine import are found in the headquarters file. Not found, however, are his reports bearing on the conduct of Colonel Chaves, most particularly Evans's report of October 13, which Colonel Canby acknowledged receiving. This contained the findings of the captain's investigation of what occurred before, during, and after what Colonel Chaves described as a Navajo attack on the garrison. The report, later lost or removed from the department files, was enough for Canby. Captain Evans was placed in temporary command of the fort and Manuel Chaves, suspended from command, was confined to the limits of Albuquerque pending court martial.[23]

Months afterward, applying to headquarters in Santa Fe for back pay and release from arrest (on other charges), Chaves was questioned by Lieutenant Cyrus H. DeForrest about his command at Fort Fauntleroy. His story of unprovoked Navajo attack on the fort was unchanged:

> Question: During this time did anything occur at the post beyond the ordinary routine of post duties?
> Answer: Nothing. (He here corrected himself as follows) Yes sir, the Navajoe Indians attacked the Fort in the month of October. I don't recollect the day [September 13].
> Question: Relate the occurrences of that time.

22. September 13, 1861: Chaves to Canby, NA, RAC, RG 393, unentered LR, 1851–1862, box 40.
23. December 4, 1861: Canby to Chaves, NA, RAC, RG 393, no. 871, LS.

Answer: It commenced by Dr. Cavanaugh making up a horse race with some Navajoes. After the race was over in which Dr. Cavanaugh was winner I and the Doctor returned into the Fort, when the Indians suddenly attacked the guard of the post. One of my men was wounded and twelve indians were killed on the spot. I took 112 prisoners, the rest ran away. They were 500 in number.

Question: What was the particular circumstance which led to this affair? The word or act particular?

Answer: There was no cause given by us. I was in the house of Dr. Cavanaugh when the indians attacked the guard.[24]

What was, covertly, common knowledge throughout most of the territory did not begin to surface openly until the summer of 1865, when a Congressional committee began to investigate conditions at Fort Sumner, where more than seven thousand Navajos were held in captivity. Testifying before the committee on June 26, Major Herbert M. Enos found himself almost unintentionally talking about the Fort Fauntleroy episode. As departmental quartermaster Major Enos had had occasion to visit the Bosque Redondo reservation the previous October. He told the committee he was present when troops tried to move the Navajos into a large corral in order to count them. "The Indians objected," Enos said, "—afraid they were going to be murdered." A number of them had been at Fort Fauntleroy, he continued, when, after some difficulty over a horse race, they "were fired on with mountain howitzers by the New Mexican troops. Some twenty or thirty were killed. Since then they have been more suspicious of our troops." [25]

James Collins, appearing before the committee on July 4 at Santa Fe, mentioned the aftermath of Canby's expedition: "a band of friendly Indians of about three hundred, increased by the addition of those disposed to be friendly to about six hundred, were greatly wronged. . . . There was some difficulty about a horse race. The Indians, I think, won the race, and the Mexican troops in the service refused to give up stakes, when a quarrel arose, and the troops fired into them." [26]

References to the episode by Enos and Collins were passing side-

24. "Interrogations . . . and replies" of February 9, 1863, enclosure with Consolidated Service Record of Chaves, cited above. The disposition made by Manuel Chaves of his Navajo captives—many of them undoubtedly women and children—is a question that remains unanswered. Very possibly the answer might be found in Captain Evans's missing report.

25. "Condition of the Indian Tribes" (cited above), p. 341. Headed by Sen. James R. Doolittle, the committee that conducted hearings in New Mexico also included Vice President L. S. Foster and Rep. L. W. Ross.

26. Ibid., p. 331.

lights in the body of their testimony, and in this, and in the welter of
hundreds of pages of other testimony, the Fort Fauntleroy episode was
lost again until the committee members had left New Mexico and were
returning to Washington. Someone whose identity cannot be determined then remembered Nicholas Hodt. As a sergeant in one of the
Chaves companies, he had been on the scene in 1861. An inquiry was
sent to Fort Wingate where Hodt, then a captain commanding Company B, First New Mexico Volunteer Cavalry, was found. Hodt's memory of the affair was clear enough and he responded willingly. After describing the protests over the Kavanaugh victory, Hodt remarked that
Colonel Chaves ordered the officer of the day to prevent any Navajos
from entering the fort.

> The [Kavanaugh] horse was taken inside the post, followed by
> the whole winning party, the drums beating, fifes and fiddles
> screeching &c., &c. So the procession went whooping and hallooing
> to receive the part they had won. Finally, whilst thus occupied
> a shot was fired at or near the post. Every man then ran to arm
> himself. Companies did not regularly form, but every man ran
> wherever he thought fit.
>
> The shot was fired [because] Private Morales, sentinel No. 2
> . . . oppos[ed] an Indian's entrance to the post. It was said that
> the Indian was intoxicated and tried to force his entrance past
> the sentinel. At that instant the shot was fired and the Indian
> fell. Who fired is not known. . . . The Navajoes, squaws and
> children, ran in all directions and were shot and bayoneted. I
> tried my best to form the company I was first sergeant of, and
> succeeded in forming about twenty men—it being very hard work.
> I then marched out to the east side of the post. There I saw a
> soldier murdering two little children and a woman.
>
> I hallooed immediately to the soldier to stop. He looked up,
> but did not obey my order. I ran up as quick as I could, but
> could not get there soon enough to prevent him from killing the
> two innocent children and wounding severely the squaw. I or-
> dered his [cartridge] belts to be taken off and [ordered him] taken
> prisoner to the post. On my arrival [there] I met Lieutenant Ortiz
> with a pistol at full cock, saying, "Give back this soldier his
> arms, or else I'll shoot you, God damn you"—which circumstances
> I reported to my company commander, he reporting the same to
> the colonel commanding. . . .
>
> The answer he received from the colonel was, "that Lieutenant
> Ortiz did perfectly right, and that [Colonel Chaves] gave credit

to the soldier who murdered the children and wounded the squaw."

Meantime the colonel had given orders to the officer of the day to have the artillery (mountain howitzers) brought out and to open upon the Indians. The sergeant in charge of the mountain howitzers pretended not to understand the order given, for he considered it as an unlawful order; but being cursed by the officer of the day, and threatened, he had to execute the order or else get himself in trouble.

The Indians scattered all over the valley below the post, attacked the post herd, wounded the Mexican herder, but did not succeed in getting any stock; also [they] attacked the expressman some ten miles from the post, took his horse and mail-bag and wounded him in the arm.

After the massacre there were no more Indians to be seen about the post with the exception of a few squaws, favorites of the officers. The commanding officer endeavored to make peace again with the Navajoes by sending some of the favorite squaws to talk with the chiefs; but the only satisfaction the squaws received was a good flogging.

An expressman was sent shortly after the affairs above mentioned happened, but private letters were not allowed to be sent, and letters that reached the post office at Fauntleroy were found opened but not forwarded. To the best of my knowledge the number of Navajoes killed was twelve or fifteen; the number wounded could not be ascertained. There were only two wounded bucks and one wounded squaw in the hospital. The rest [of the] wounded must have been taken away by the tribe.

Colonel Chaves survived the massacre and abortive measures to bring him to trial with no more than the loss of command, a withholding of pay, and idle months with his family while under arrest, first at Albuquerque and then at his home in Peralta.[27] The Navajos, still in the

27. Chaves never was brought before a court martial. Due to an inability to gather witnesses, his arrest was suspended January 21, 1862; on February 10 he rejoined his regiment at Fort Craig. Following the battle of Valverde he was ordered to spy on the advance of Sibley's columns toward Santa Fe. During the battle of Apache Canyon he was said to have performed valuable service. Efforts to schedule his court martial in May 1862 were delayed again and he was ordered to remain under arrest in Albuquerque. Soon after, accompanying troops to Fort Craig he was detached by Canby at La Joya with orders to take wagons and other property captured from Sibley to Sabinal. Instead of obeying, it was charged, Chaves sold the captured property for his own profit and on this charge was arrested when he reached Fort Craig. Chaves spent the summer of 1862 with his family in Peralta

early period of their Nahondzod, fared much worse. In an assessment of
the situation two months after the massacre Colonel Canby determined
that the Navajo nation was so broken up by the affair that Fort Lyon
no longer served any useful purpose. He accordingly ordered the troops
to be withdrawn as soon as possible and the post supplies transferred to
rented quarters in Cubero. (It was these supplies that Dr. Kavanaugh
soon turned over to Sibley's troops.)

In the two weeks following, between November 16 and December 1,
1861, Colonel Canby formulated the basic Navajo policy of the next
six years. He remained in New Mexico long enough to see his policies
begin meshing into gear. His successor, Brevet Brigadier General James
H. Carleton, would carry them, with some innovations of his own,
faithfully into operation.

At Canby's request, Agent John Ward was sent to Cubero with a
military escort commanded by Captain Julius C. Shaw and, from that
base, moved out among the Navajos in an attempt to persuade any who
might be friendly to the Bilagáana to move to a central encampment
near the village of Cubero where they would be offered the protection
of the government. Ward also was instructed to warn all Navajos who
refused to come in that they would be treated as enemies. Because he
carried more than a little influence with the Navajos, Ward eventually
achieved a moderate success.

Conveying the loose outline of his new policy to Captain Evans, who
was now overseeing the preparations to abandon Fort Lyon, Colonel
Canby observed that the period of talking with Navajos had ended.
Those who had acted in good faith in the past would be allowed to
come in to the camp John Ward was establishing and submit unconditionally; but there would be no discussion or debate about it. Eventually—very soon—they must understand that they would have no alternative other than to colonize in settlements or pueblos. Canby perhaps
deliberately avoided use of the word "reservation," but he mentioned
the region of the Little Colorado west of Zuni as possibly an ideal place
for the Navajos' colonization.

Each passing day further crystallized the new policy. On December 1,
Canby wrote to his immediate superior in St. Louis that "recent occur-
rences in the Navajo country have so demoralized and broken up [the
Navajo] nation that there is now no choice between their absolute

---

awaiting trial on the theft charge, but again the trial was delayed for lack of
witnesses and never was convened ("Interrogations . . . and replies" of February
9–10, 1863, enclosures with Consolidated Service Record of Chaves).

extermination or their removal and colonization at points so remote
. . . as to isolate them entirely from the inhabitants of the Territory.
Aside from all considerations of humanity the extermination of such a
people will be the work of the greatest difficulty." [28]

Late in November Canby had received word that some Navajos were
raiding once more, in the vicinity of the river near Alameda. He directed Colonel Kit Carson, commanding the Central Military District
at Albuquerque, to determine if the report were true. If it were, Carson
would at once organize a campaign against the raiders. "You are directed,"
Canby wrote, "to instruct the commanding officer not to take any male
prisoners, and if any men fall into his hands to execute them at once.
Women and children will be turned loose and ordered to go into their
own country." [29]

Canby's plans for the Navajos—even his very words—foreshadowed
in ominous fidelity the shape of events to come. Two years later and at
the start of the last of the Navajo wars, post and field commanders received orders to "kill every . . . Navajo Indian who is large enough to
bears arms. . . . No women or children will be harmed." [30] The echo-
ing voice was the voice of General Carleton. In nearly every respect but
two the echo was faithful to Canby's plans. Whereas Canby told Carson to turn the women and children loose, Carleton ordered them held
captive. And whereas Canby proposed holding submissive Navajos on
treeless plains of the Little Colorado, Carleton instead chose barren
salt flats and wastelands on the Pecos—the place called Bosque Redondo.

The edge of difference was slight. Navajos will remember Canby as
the man who determined their fate; they will remember Carleton as
the man who forced this fate upon them.

28. December 1, 1861: Canby to AAG, HQ, Western Dept., St. Louis, NA,
RAC, RG 393, no. 858, LS.
29. November 26, 1861: Nicodemus to Carson, NA, RAC, RG 393, no. 825, LS.
30. August 19, 1863: Carleton to Capt. Joseph Updegraff, commanding Fort
Sumner ("Condition of the Indian Tribes . . . ," p. 129). Similar instructions
were contained in Special Orders No. 40, Dept. HQ, Santa Fe, August 17, and in
orders sent August 19 to officers commanding Forts Stanton and Bascom.

APPENDIX A

Lieutenant Colonel Antonio Narbona's Engagement with Navajos at Canyon de Chelly, 1805

Following is David M. Brugge's translation of the text, in Spanish, of Lieutenant Colonel Antonio Narbona's report to Governor Fernando Chacón of his January 17–18, 1805 engagement with Navajos at Canyon de Chelly. The letter was written January 24 upon Narbona's return to his expedition headquarters at Zuni. Permission to use this translation was given by Mr. Brugge, who formerly was with the Land Claim Office of the Navajo Tribe and now is Curator at the Hubbell Trading Post at Ganado, Arizona—a national historic site.

The 17th day of the current month I succeeded in attacking a large number of enemy Indians in the Canyon de Chelly, and although they entrenched themselves on an almost inaccessible point, and they had it fortified, it was gained after having battled all day with the greatest ardor and I vowed to finish it the following morning and our arms remained with the success of killing ninety warriors and twenty-five women and children and making prisoner of three warriors, eight women and twenty-two boys and girls, and capturing three hundred fifty head of sheep and goats and thirty horses; one of the captive warriors being the Chief called Segundo with his wife and two children and the total number of killed and prisoners is one hundred forty-eight.

On our part we came out with the loss of the Lieutenant of the Opata Nation of the Company of Bacoachi, Don Francisco Piri dead from pneumonia, of sixty-four wounded among citizens, soldiers, and Indians, and eighty-five horses that I had killed because they were worn out.

The Canyon de Chelly I scouted from its beginning to its mouth. It is the fort on which the Navajo Indians had based their hopes of making themselves invincible, and as it is inhabited by many people, and fortified by nature with the cliffs that form it, that hope is not without reason, and although on this occasion I disillusioned them of it, in spite of this I can do no less than make known to you in fulfillment of my obligation and without omitting anything, that if it should be necessary in the future to return to attack it, it would be indispensable that it be with more men than I had and a great supply of munitions, for that which I brought from my province exceeded ten thousand cartridges, and in order to get out of the said canyon I was forced to use almost all of them.

Its center is ample, and in it they have sufficient fields that are made fertile by a regular river that runs through the middle, but this does not impede, but that the enemy from the high rocks assault those that go below, and because of this it is necessary that besides those that battle inside, there should go two parties over the rims of the canyon scouting to prevent that the enemy unite in ambush and prepared for that eventuality.

Of the slaves captured I have distributed among little ones and wounded ones, eleven to individuals of this province and of that of Sonora and due to this I conduct as prisoners 24 including the two that were made prisoner on my first excursion.

The Indian Cristóbal with his followers requested peace, which I did not wish to allow him; but I told him if he should happen to treat of it with you, he would verify it thus and also in asking for the liberty of Segundo and his family and that you should resolve whether said Indian Segundo remain in this province. Due to finding myself with little ammunition and my horse herd sufficiently used up, I plan my return by the Pueblo of El Paso, for which journey, if you wish, you will be able to make the preparations for me that might be agreeable.

The sheep and goats that were recaptured were consumed by the prisoners, soldiers, citizens and Indians, and the few horses that arrived at this pueblo were divided among the volunteers of my province and guides with whom you furnished me.

These conducted themselves very well and completed as many tasks as presented themselves to me, for which I beg that you dispense the thanks to them that might be agreeable to you, such as to Antonio Armijo who came voluntarily and who served me so much with the good knowledge that he has of the enemy territory.

The troops of this province as well as the citizens and Indians conducted themselves to my satisfaction; but the Captain of Militia Don Lorenzo Gutiérrez with outstanding spirit, efficiency and terms worthy of recommendation, for in battle he demonstrated gallantry and very much, and so public and notorious that I am not embarrassed in praising it more and more and assuring you that he is worthy of being entrusted with the greatest undertakings of war, for with his even temperament, fine tact and good disposition, there may be expected fortunate results in the commissions with which he is entrusted.

The Lieutenant Don Bartolomé Baca commanded the party that protected my descent into the canyon, and afterward continued along the heights; he discharged this duty with definite valor and gallantry, and he sustained several attacks of the opposition with the success of killing three warriors, and making prisoner one of the Moquino Nation who fled from the canyon; he is a lad of good disposition for war and also worthy of being entrusted with the command of detachments.

The Corporal Baltasar Ribera brings eighty-four pairs of ears of as many warriors and the six that are lacking to complete the ninety of which I told you are not sent to you because the subject that I encharged with them lost them.

The Moquino Indian goes included with the three captured warriors, which news I give to you for your superior knowledge.

The Alcalde of this Pueblo, Don Ignacio Sánchez Vergara, is helping me feed my troops as is necessary, and I will advise you of its amount so that it might serve you to repay him if it is agreeable to you.

May God, our Lord, guard your life many years.

Zuñi, 24th of Jan., 1805—Antonio Narbona—

Señor Political and Military Governor, Don Fernando Chacón.

APPENDIX B

The Origin of the Diné Ana'aii

The fateful defection in 1818 of the headman Joaquín resulted in the formation of the renegade Enemy Navajos (Diné Ana'aii). The tribal division was permanent; descendants of Joaquín's splinter band, known as Cañoncito Navajos, today live apart on a small patch of reservation between Cebolleta and Albuquerque. Alcalde Vergara's report of Joaquín's defection, heretofore unpublished, was translated by Marc Simmons.

> Yesterday at sunset smoke was seen not far from this Pueblo; for this reason I took the most hasty precautions so as not to be surprised by treachery. We were thus prepared, when in a short time arrived the *capitancillo* Joaq^n his brother and two nephews, who I received with the greatest tolerance and without showing the slightest surprise. I tried to guess the reason for his coming which in itself was of such a manner as to leave no doubt of his loyalty and friendly attitude. For his part, he indicated that he had come to make known the preparations [for war] of his nation and the great amount of effort which he had exerted to persuade them to remain at peace. But all of his efforts and those of his people were in vain. He has taken the precaution to separate himself with all his people, whom he represents, and to give up the rebels; convinced as he is that we will punish them severely enough to overcome their haughtiness and insolence.
>
> His reasoning tells him that very soon his Nation will be destroyed by five or six campaign forces that will attack them from various directions and will destroy all their plans.
>
> Those who suffer grave injury for having scorned their good advice will see fulfilled the terrible threats which have been thrown at them, all this being the fate of his Nation which inhabits this frontier [of Jemez] and others.
>
> He set forth the information which had been entrusted to him by his people, and which had to be delivered in haste within four days so that his people could carry out the total separation. He informed us that all the rebels had packed off to Carrizo and that some Utes are accompanying their war parties, and that they have some mesas which serve them as a fort. They maintain

themselves at these points from whence they undertake to commit their robberies and wickedness.

On his journey here he encountered five members of his Nation who had carried out a robbery of sixteen animals. And he tried to retake them but only succeeded in taking five, among them a paint mule. A worn out mare which had been stolen from Abiquiu was left by the road. Should two troops take the field against the rebels, he and his men will accompany them, and he will see to the handing over of the goods. And when the plan is carried out, if he doesn't come as he has promised them, they will suspect he is already a prisoner. For this reason, he will wait here only until he receives the decision of Your Lordship in order that he may return, leaving no uncertainty about the meeting that he had with the envoys coming to give an account of the condition of his Nation. And he does not fail to keep his promises, as he has proven.

As a result, I have provided him with the best treatment and with continued care, the will of Your Lordship will be adequately carried out.

May God guard Your Lordship many years. Xemes, July 21, 1818.

> Ygnacio Maria
> Sanch[ez] Vergara

[To]
Señor Lt. Col. Don Pedro Maria de Allande.

APPENDIX C

Treaty of Laguna Negra

The treaty was made with the Navajos and signed by them at Laguna Negra on July 17, 1855. When a copy was made the following night in Governor Meriwether's tent, the fresh draft inadvertently was misdated and the error has been perpetuated since. The following text is taken from the copy in the handwriting of W. W. H. Davis, whose punctuation, spelling and, capitalization are followed throughout.

Articles of Agreement and Convention made and concluded at Laguna Negra in the Territory of New Mexico this eighteenth day of July, One thousand Eight Hundred and fifty five by David Meriwether sole Commissioner duly appointed for that purpose on the part of the United States and the undersigned Chiefs Captains and head-men of the Navajo tribe or nation of Indians they being thereto duly authorized and acting for and in behalf of their respective bands—

Article 1st Peace friendship and Amity shall forever hereafter exist between the United States of America and the Navajo tribe or nation of Indians and this convention and every article and stipulation thereof shall be perpetual and observed and performed in good faith

Article 2d The Navajos do hereby covenant and agree that peaceful relations shall be maintained amongst themselves and all other bands tribes and nations of Indians within the United States and that they will abstain from committing hostilities or depredations in future and cultivate mutual good will and friendship.

Article 3d The Navajos hereby cede and forever relinquish to the United States all title or claim whatsoever which they have or ever have had to lands within the Territory of New Mexico except so much as is hereinafter reserved to them, And the Navajos further agree and bind themselves to remove to and settle on the lands reserved to them within twelve months after the ratification of this treaty without any cost or charge to the United States whatever for their removal, and that they will cultivate the soil and raise flocks and herds for a subsistence and that the President may withhold the annuities herein stipulated to be paid or any part thereof whenever the Indians shall violate fail or refuse to comply with any provision of this instrument or to cultivate the soil in good faith.

Article 4th The United States agree to set apart and withhold from sale for the use of the Navajos for their permanent homes and hereby guarantees to them the possession and enjoyment of a tract of Country within that portion of the Territory of New Mexico, now claimed by them and bounded as follows—viz— Beginning on the south bank of the San Juan river at the mouth of the Rio de Chelly thence up the San Juan to the mouth of the Canado del Amarillo thence up the Amarillo to the top of the dividing ridge between the waters of the Collirado and Rio Grande thence southwesterly along said dividing ridge to the head of the main bank of the Zuni River thence down the north side thereof to its mouth or entrance into the Collarado Chiquito, thence north to the beginning, excluding the lands owned by the Pueblos of Zuñi and Moqui and reserving to them all their rights and priveliges, and reserving to the United States a tract of Country enclosing fifty square miles around Fort Defiance to be laid off under the direction of the Commanding Officer of the Department and in such manner as he may see proper, reserving to the Navajos the right to gather salt at the salt lake near Zuñi, and the United States is hereby authorized to define the boundaries of the reserved tract when it may be necessary by actual survey or otherwise. And the President may from time to time at his discretion cause the whole or any part thereof to be surveyed, and may assign to each head of a family or single person over twenty one years of age, twenty acres of land for his or her separate use and benefit and each family of three or less than five persons forty acres of land and to each family of five or more persons sixty acres, and he may at his discretion as fast as the occupants become capable of transacting their own affairs issue patents therefor to such occupants with such restrictions of the power of Alienation as he may see fit to impose and he may also at his discretion make rules and regulations respecting the disposition of the lands in case of the death of the head of a family or a single person occupying the same or in case of its abandonment by them and he may also assign other lands in exchange for mineral lands if any such are found in the tracts herein set apart and he may also make such changes in the boundary of such reserved tracts as shall be necessary to prevent interference with any vested rights. All necessary roads highways and Rail Roads the lines of which may run through the reserved tracts shall have the right of way through the same compensation being made therefor as in other cases, but the President may grant the right of way to any road free of charge and establish such Military Posts as he may think proper.

Article 5th In consideration of and full payment for the country ceded and the removal of the Navajos the United States agree to pay to the Navajos the following sums without interest, to wit: The United States will during the year[s] 1856 and 1857 pay to the Navajos ten thousand dollars each year [and] during the year 1858 and the two next succeeding years thereafter the sum of six thousand dollars each And during the year 1861 and the next succeeding fifteen years thereafter the sum of four thousand dollars each year all of which several sums of money shall be paid to the Navajos or expended for their use and benefit under the direction of the President of the United States who may from time to time determine at his discretion what proportion of the annual payments in this Article provided for if any shall be paid to them in money And what proportion shall be applied to and expended for their moral improval and education for such beneficial objects as in his judgment will be calculated to advance them in civilization for building opening farms breaking lands providing stock agricultural implements seeds &c. for employing farmers to teach the Indians to cultivate the soil, for clothing pensions and Merchandise for iron steel, Arms and Ammunition for Mechanics and tools and for medical purposes.

Article 6th The annuities of the Indians are not to be taken to pay the debts of individuals but satisfaction for depredations committed by them shall be made by the Indians in such manner as the President may direct nor shall any part of the amount stipulated to be paid ever be applied by the Chiefs or head men to the payment of tribal debts for obligations to traders or other persons.

Article 7th No spirituous Liquors shall be made sold or used on any of the lands herein set apart for the residence of the Indians and the sale of the same shall be prohibited in the territory hereby ceded until other wise ordered by the President—

Article 8th The laws now in force or which may hereafter be enacted by Congress for the regulation of trade and intercourse with the Indian tribes shall continue and be in force in the country set apart for the Navajos and such portions of said laws as prohibit the introduction, manufacture, use of, and traffic in Ardent Spirits in the Indian country shall continue and be in force in all the country ceded until otherwise provided by law.

Article 9th The Navajoes do further agree and bind themselves to make restitution or satisfaction for any injuries done by any band or any individual to the people of the United States and to surrender to the proper Authorities of the United States when demanded any individual or individuals who may commit depredations to be punished according to law And if any Citizen of the United States shall at any time commit depredations upon the Indians the Navajos agree that they will not take private satisfaction or revenge themselves but instead thereof they will make complaint to the proper Indian Agent for redress And the said Indians do further agree to refrain from all warlike incursions into the Mexican provinces and from committing depredations upon the inhabitants thereof—

Article 10th This treaty shall be obligatory upon the contracting parties as soon as the same shall be ratified by the President and senate of the United States—

In testimony whereof the said David Meriwether Commissioner as aforesaid and the undersigned Chiefs Captains and head men of the said tribe of Navajos Indians have hereunto set their hands and seals at the place and on the day and year herein before written

(Sgd)   D. Meriwether   [L.S.]
Com on the part of the United States

Witnesses present		
(Sgd) Jno Garland	(Sgd) Manuelito	his X mark [L.S.]
Bt. Brig Gen	(") Jose Miguel	his X mark [L.S.]
U.S.A.	(") Cabra Blanco	his X mark [L.S.]
(") H. L. Kendrick	(") Francisco Baca	his X mark [L.S.]
Bt Major U.S.A.	(") Segundo	his X mark [L.S.]
(") O L Shepherd	(") Mariano Martinez	his X mark [L.S.]
Capt 3ᵈ Infy	(") Julian Tenorio	his X mark [L.S.]
Bt Major	(") Jas-tin-a	his X mark [L.S.]
(") R. S. Ewell		his X mark [L.S.]
Capt 1ˢᵗ Dragns	(") Jose Baca	his X mark [L.S.]
(") W. W. H. Davis	(") Jose Antonio	his X mark [L.S.]
Secty Terry	(") Jose	his X mark [L.S.]
New Mexico	(") Antonio Viscara	his X mark [L.S.]
	(") Niz-Nez	his X mark [L.S.]
	(") Bele Thlena	his X mark [L.S.]

True copy,	(") Bitche-de-latche	his X mark [L.S.]
W. W. H. Davis	(") Hijo de Juanico	his X mark [L.S.]
Actng Govr	(") Manuel Huero	his X mark [L.S.]
& Supt of	(") Bick-e-de-stedy	his X mark [L.S.]
Indian Affairs	(") Aguilar Negro	his X mark [L.S.]
	(") Caton Colorado	his X mark [L.S.]
	(") Bele-dee-Zine	his X mark [L.S.]
	(") Salvador Colorado	his X mark [L.S.]
	(") Ozi-nez	his X mark [L.S.]
	(") Jose Paya	his X mark [L.S.]
	(") Sarcillas Largas	his X mark [L.S.]
	(") Pana Hulgehi	his X mark [L.S.]
	(") Manuel Armijo	his X mark [L.S.]

APPENDIX D

The Traffic in Slaves

In an order issued from the Executive Mansion June 9, 1865, President Andrew Johnson advised Secretary of the Interior James Harlan:

It is represented to me, in a communication from [your office], that Indians in New Mexico have been seized and reduced into Slavery, and it is recommended that the authority of the Executive branch of the Government, should be exercised for the effectual suppression of a practice which is alike in violation of the rights of the Indians and the provisions of the organic law of the said Territory.

Concurring in this recommendation, I do hereby order that the heads of the several Executive Departments do enjoin upon their subordinates, agents and employes under their respective orders or supervision, in that Territory, to discountenance the practice aforesaid, and to take all lawful means to suppress the same." [1]

Superintendent of Indian Affairs Felipe Delgado, from Santa Fe, wrote Indian Commissioner William P. Dole on July 16, 1865, that reports "made to the Government upon this subject have been greatly exaggerated" and the object in securing Indian captives "has not been to reduce them to slavery, but rather from a Christian piety . . . to instruct and educate them in civilization. . . . This has been the practice in this country for the last century and a half and the result arising from it has been to the captives, favorable, humane and satisfactory." Nevertheless, Delgado said, "I am always ready to obey the laws and comply with the orders of my superiors [and] with this motive in view . . . I will employ all my vigilance to the end that this practice may be forever discountenanced." [2]

At Conejos, Colorado, where he was agent for the Tabeguache Utes, Lafayette Head early in July received the President's order from Colorado Governor John Evans. Aided by a U.S. deputy marshal, Agent Head at once commenced a survey of all Indians held in bondage in Conejos

1. President Johnson's executive order and the letter and lists of captives addressed by Agent Head to Gov. Evans are found in NA, NMS, microcopy 234, roll 553. Superintendent Delgado's letter to Commissioner Dole is found in NA, NMS, microcopy T-21, roll 6.
2. Ibid.

and Costilla counties. He forwarded the results of this survey to Governor Evans on July 17, commenting that

". . . to the credit of the Citizens here, I would add, that they all manifested a prompt willingness to give up said Captives whenever called upon to do so, and . . . I would most respectfully recommend, that all the Navajo Captives here be returned to their people on their Reservation [then at Bosque Redondo] in New Mexico. . . . I have notified all the people here, that in future no more Captives are to be purchased or sold as I shall immediately arrest both parties caught in the transaction. This step, I think, will at once put an end to this most barbarous and inhuman practice, which has been in existence with the Mexicans for generations." Of all the Navajo captives, Head noted, only Catalina, a woman of 35, said she wanted to be returned to her people. Of the others, "there are captives here who know not their own parents, nor can they speak their mother tongue, and who recognize no one but those who rescued them from their merciless captors; what are we to do with these?" [3]

Agent Head enclosed the following lists:

List of Indian Captives in Conejos County, Colorado Territory, July, 1865

Name of Indian	Age	Tribe	When Purchased	Of Whom Purchased	Where Purchased	Sex
Guadaloupe	25	Navajo	1863	Utahs	Conejos	F
Marie Antonio	16	Utah	1855	Utahs	Conejos	F
Estefana	11	Utah	1856	Utahs	Conejos	F
Miguel	7	Navajo	1862	Utahs	Conejos	M
Guadaloupe	38	Pai-ute	1843	Mexican	New Mexico	F
Dolores	12	Navajo	1861	Utahs	New Mexico	F
Refugio	18	Navajo	1861	Mexican	New Mexico	F
Juan	7	Navajo	1865	Utahs	New Mexico	M
Jose Manuel	5	Utah	1863	Utahs	Conejos	M
Jose Rafael	3	Utah	1864	Utahs	San Luis Valley	M
Antonia Rosa	16	Utah	1864	Mexican	San Luis Valley	F
Guadaloupe	7	Utah	1862	Mexican	San Luis Valley	F
Manuel Rosatin	4	Navajo	1864	Mexican	San Luis Valley	M
Catalina	35	Navajo	1865	Mexican	San Luis Valley	F
Guadaloupe	6	Navajo	1864	Mexican	San Luis Valley	F
Reyes	15	Pai-ute	1853	Mexican	San Luis Valley	F
Quaiatano	7	Utah	1861	Utahs	San Luis Valley	M

3. Ibid.

Name of Indian	Age	Tribe	When Purchased	Of Whom Purchased	Where Purchased	Age
Maria Mᵗᵃ	12	Navajo	1862	Utahs	San Luis Valley	F
Maria Jetrodes	11	Navajo	1860	Utahs	San Luis Valley	F
Jose Antonio	10	Utah	1860	Utahs	San Luis Valley	M
Jose Mᵃ	8	Navajo	1864	Mexican	San Luis Valley	M
Mᵃ Guadaloupe	5	Navajo	1863	Mexican	San Luis Valley	F
Rafaela	25	Navajo	1864	Mexican	San Luis Valley	F
Juan Quaro	15	Navajo	1860	Mexican	Navajoe Country	M
Jose Antᵒ	11	Navajo	1864	Mexican	Conejos	M
Mᵃ Dolores	10	Utah	1858	Utahs	Conejos	F
Guadaloupe	15	Navajo	1864	Utahs	Conejos	F
Juan	11	Navajo	1854	Utahs	New Mexico	M
Lorenzo	9	Navajo	1862	Utahs	Colo. Territory	M
Juan	7	Navajo	1862	Utahs	Colo. Territory	M
Trinidad	10	Navajo	1862	Utahs	Colo. Territory	F
Guadaloupe	8	Navajo	1862	Utahs	Colo. Territory	F
Madelina	8	Navajo	1864	Utahs	Colo. Territory	F
Petrudis	8	Navajo	1863	Utahs	New Mexico	F
Mᵃ Benina	15	Utah	1862	Mexican	New Mexico	F
Vicente	4	Utah	1864	Mexican	New Mexico	M
Lucas	4	Utah	1864	Mexican	New Mexico	M
Ana Maria	14	Utah	1856	Utahs	Utah Territory	F
Maria	16	Navajo	1864	Mexican	Colo. Territory	F
Mᵃ Guadaloupe	10	Utah	1864	Utahs	Colo. Territory	F
Rosalie	10	Navajo	1863	Mexican	Colo. Territory	F
Guadaloupe	15	Navajo	1864	Mexican	Colo. Territory	F
Polito	9	Utah	1861	Utahs	Colo. Territory	F
Jetrudes	24	Pai-ute	1848	Mexican	New Mexico	F
Paula	11	Pai-ute	1858	Utahs	Colo. Territory	F
Luis	9	Half-breed	n.d.	—	Colo. Territory	M
Mᵃ Rosalia	5	Navajo	1864	Mexican	Colo. Territory	F
Mᵃ Cueran	7	Navajo	1864	Mexican	Arizona	F
Jose Antᵒ	6	Navajo	1862	Utahs	Colo. Territory	M
Fᶜᵒ Antᵒ	4	Navajo	1862	Mexican	Colo. Territory	M
Juana	4	Navajo	1862	Mexican	Colo. Territory	F
Catalina	7	Navajo	1862	Utahs	Colo. Territory	F
Ramon	13	Navajo	1864	Mexican	Arizona	M
Rosalia	6	Navajo	1864	Mexican	Arizona	F
Guadaloupe	17	Navajo	1864	Mexican	New Mexico	F
Juana	5	Navajo	1864	Mexican	Colo. Territory	F
Jose Lina	5	Pai-ute	1864	Utahs	Colo. Territory	M
Juliana	12	Apache	1855	Apaches	New Mexico	F

Name of Indian	Age	Tribe	When Purchased	Of Whom Purchased	Where Purchased	Age
Catalina	24	Navajo	1863	Mexican	Colo. Territory	F
Jose Anto	4	Navajo	1864	Mexican	Colo. Territory	M
Enconarcion	16	Navajo	1864	Mexican	Colo. Territory	F
Guadaloupe	11	Navajo	1864	Mexican	Colo. Territory	F
Dolores	10	Navajo	1864	Mexican	Colo. Territory	F
Ramon	12	Navajo	1864	Apaches	New Mexico	M
Margarita	18	Navajo	1864	Utahs	Colo. Territory	F
Seferina	28	Navajo	1853	Utahs	Colo. Territory	F
Gregorio	18	Navajo	1853	Mexican	New Mexico	M
Jose	15	Navajo	1861	Mexican	New Mexico	M
Dolores	15	Navajo	1864	Mexican	Colo. Territory	F
Juliana	15	Navajo	1864	Utahs	Colo. Territory	F
Guadaloupe	20	Navajo	1861	Utahs	Colo. Territory	F
J. M. Rita	9	Navajo	1863	Utahs	Colo. Territory	F
Guadaloupe	16	Pai-ute	1852	Utahs	California	F
Librado	7	Navajo	1864	Utahs	Colo. Territory	F
Mᵃ J. Garcia	60	Navajo	1864	Mexican	New Mexico	F
Mᵃ Guadaloupe	52	California	1831	Utahs	California	F
Filomena	14	Navajo	1857	Utahs	New Mexico	F
Hector	12	Navajo	1864	Capotes	New Mexico	M
Agapita	18	Navajo	1863	Mexican	Colo. Territory	F
Rafaela	10	Navajo	1862	Utahs	Colo. Territory	F
Rita	45	Navajo	1864	Mexican	Colo. Territory	F
Mᵃ Anto	12	Navajo	1864	Mexican	Colo. Territory	F
Catalina	19	Utah	1860	Utahs	Colo. Territory	F
Gabriel	12	Navajo	1860	Utahs	Colo. Territory	M
Andres	10	Navajo	1862	Utahs	Colo. Territory	M
Juliana	22	Navajo	1862	Utahs	Colo. Territory	F
Lucas	18	Navajo	1863	Utahs	Colo. Territory	M
Rafael	15	Navajo	1861	Utahs	Colo. Territory	M

List of Indian Captives in Costilla County, Colorado Territory, July, 1865

Name of Indian	Age	Tribe	When Purchased	Of Whom Purchased	Where Purchased	Sex
Rito	10	Navajo	1865	Utes	Colo. Territory	F
Juan Tomas	8	Navajo	1862	Mexican	Colo. Territory	M
Juan	4	Navajo	1862	Mexican	Arizona	M
Guadaloupe	10	Navajo	1864	Mexican	Colo. Territory	F
Resiona	20	Navajo	1864	Mexican	Colo. Territory	F
Lioner	10	Navajo	1861	Mexican	Colo. Territory	F
Antonio	20	Navajo	1864	Mexican	Colo. Territory	F (sic)
Margarita	15	Navajo	1861	Mexican	New Mexico	F
Maria Antonio	14	Navajo	1863	Mexican	Colo. Territory	F
Maria Refugio	20	Navajo	1862	Mexican	Colo. Territory	F
Juan Miguel	12	Ute	1864	Mexican	Colo. Territory	M
Maria	17	Navajo	1864	Mexican	Colo. Territory	F
Mª Guadalupe	30	Navajo	1864	Mexican	Colo. Territory	F
Maria Lucia	8	Ute	1864	Utes	Colo. Territory	F
Pablo	7	Ute	1864	Mexican	New Mexico	M
Juan Antonio	8	Navajo	1864	Mexican	New Mexico	M
Juliana	12	Navajo	1862	Mexican	New Mexico	F
Nicholas	7	Navajo	1860	Mexican	New Mexico	M
Dolores	10	Navajo	1862	Mexican	New Mexico	F
Maria Alioria	11	Navajo	1859	Mexican	Colo. Territory	F
Juan Antonio	6	Navajo	1860	Mexican	New Mexico	M
Maria Paola	14	Navajo	1862	Mexican	Colo. Territory	F
Pedro	7	Navajo	1862	Mexican	Colo. Territory	M
Maria	40	Navajo	1859	Mexican	Colo. Territory	F
Maria Rosario	7	Navajo	1859	Mexican	New Mexico	F
Jose Antonio	9	Navajo	1858	Mexican	New Mexico	M
Margarita	16	Navajo	1860	Mexican	Colo. Territory	F
Galatana	7	Navajo	1864	Mexican	Colo. Territory	F
Juan Jose	8	Navajo	1862	Mexican	New Mexico	M
Miguel	4	Apache	1861	Apaches	New Mexico	M
Antonio	7	Navajo	1863	Mexican	Colo. Territory	M
Padea	10	Navajo	1863	Mexican	Colo. Territory	F
Mariana	6	Navajo	1859	Mexican	New Mexico	F
Maria Louisa	35	Navajo	1860	Utes	Arizona	F
Carmel	14	Navajo	1864	Mexican	Colo. Territory	F
Jose Rafael	11	Ute	1861	Mexican	Colo. Territory	M
Margarita	12	Navajo	1864	Mexican	Colo. Territory	F

Name of Indian	Age	Tribe	When Purchased	Of Whom Purchased	Where Purchased	Sex
Dolores	15	Navajo	1864	Mexican	Colo. Territory	F
Josepha	8	Navajo	1860	Utes	Colo. Territory	F
Felipe	8	Navajo	1863	Utes	Colo. Territory	M
Hilario	4	Navajo	1861	Utes	Colo. Territory	M
Juan Felipe	12	Navajo	1863	Mexican	Colo. Territory	M
Rosalia	18	Navajo	1864	Mexican	Colo. Territory	F
Guadaloupe	18	Navajo	1864	Mexican	Colo. Territory	F
Antonio	7	Navajo	1864	Mexican	Colo. Territory	M
Dominga	25	Navajo	1863	Mexican	Colo. Territory	F
Margarita	16	Navajo	1863	Mexican	Colo. Territory	F
Margarita	25	Navajo	1863	Mexican	Colo. Territory	F
Guadaloupe	50	Navajo	1863	Mexican	Colo. Territory	F
Maria Antonia	20	Navajo	1860	Mexican	Colo. Territory	F
Maria	30	Navajo	1863	Utes	Colo. Territory	F
Lupito	11	Ute	1856	Utes	Colo. Territory	F
Jose Antonio	12	Ute	1859	Utes	Colo. Territory	M
Santona	7	Navajo	1862	Utes	Colo. Territory	F
Calabria	17	Ute	1857	Mexican	Colo. Territory	F
Maria Tomaso	30	Ute	1864	—	Arizona	F
Miguel	8	Navajo	1864	Mexican	Colo. Territory	M
Juan	6	Ute	1860	Mexican	Colo. Territory	M
Juliana	6	Navajo	1864	Mexican	Colo. Territory	F
Maria	11	Navajo	1864	Mexican	Arizona	F

BIBLIOGRAPHY

Archival Materials

NATIONAL ARCHIVES, WASHINGTON, D.C.

Adjutant General's Office, Old Letter Book No. 1, bound as 5.

Headquarters of the Army, Letter Book 7, LS.

Letters Received by the Office of the Adjutant General, Microcopy 567, rolls 398, 420, 421, 431, 432, 449, 450, 452, 453, 454.

Letters Received by the Office of Indian Affairs, New Mexico Superintendency: 1849–80, Microcopy NMS T21, rolls 1–8; Microcopy 234, rolls 546–50.

Letters Received from the Office of the Adjutant General, Microcopy 567, rolls 318, 319, 396, 397.

Post Returns, Cibolleta, N.M., Records of Army Commands, Record Group 94.

Post Returns, Fort Defiance: 1851–61, Microcopy 617, roll 301.

Post Returns, Fort Fauntleroy: 1860–61, Record Group 94, Records of the Office of the Adjutant General.

Post Returns, Fort Sumner: 1862–69, Microcopy 617, roll 1241.

Post Returns, Fort Wingate: 1862–72, Record Group 94, Records of the Office of the Adjutant General.

Post Returns, Fort Union: 1851–74, Microcopy 617, rolls 1305–06.

Records of Army Commands, Record Group 15, 1817-SC-1772.

Records of Army Commands, Record Group 77.

Records of Army Commands, Record Group 77, Topographical Bureau, LR, Box 69.

Records of Army Commands, Record Group 92, Office of the Quartermaster General, Consolidated Correspondence, File 1794–1915, Box 987.

Records of Army Commands, Record Group 94, AGO Letter Book 23, Supplements 1 & 2, 1847, LR.

Records of Army Commands, Record Group 94, AGO Letter Book 24, 1848, LR.

Records of Army Commands, Record Group 94, LR by Office of the Adjutant General.

Records of Army Commands, Record Group 94, Muster Rolls, Mexican War.

Records of Army Commands, Record Group 94, Volunteer Organizations, Muster Rolls.

Records of Army Commands, Record Group 393, AGO Letter Book 7, LS.

Records of Army Commands, Record Group 393, AGO Letter Book 8, LS.

Records of Army Commands, Record Group 393, LR and LS.

Records of Army Commands, Record Group 393, Dept. of N.M., Unentered Letters Received.

Register of General Courts-Martial, Judge Advocate General's Office, War Dept.

Territorial Papers, Microcopy T-17, rolls 1–2.

NEW MEXICO STATE RECORDS CENTER AND ARCHIVES, SANTA FE

Spanish Archival Materials, 1790–1821. Selected civil and military documents. Translations by M. Baca, David M. Brugge, Rosario O. Hinojos, J. M. Martínez, Marc Simmons, and Claribel Fisher Walker.

Mexican Archival Materials, 1821–46. Selected civil and military documents. Translations by David M. Brugge, Jenkins and Johnson, and Marc Simmons.

Adjutant General Records, Militia Description Book (1860), Muster Rolls.

Unpublished Manuscripts, Theses, Diaries, Journals

THE HUNTINGTON LIBRARY, SAN MARINO.

Kern, Richard H. "Notes of a Military Reconnaissance of the Pais de los Navajos in the months of Aug & Sept 1849." H.M. 4274. 1849.

———, Untitled diaries (vols. 1–2) written while accompanying Sumner's Navajo expedition from Santo Domingo as far as the pueblo of Zuni, and thereafter with the expedition of Capt. Lorenzo Sitgreaves down the Zuni and Colorado rivers. H.M. 4277. 1851.

THE LIBRARY OF CONGRESS, WASHINGTON, D.C.

Davis, William Watts Hart. "Private Journal at a Treaty with the Navajo Indians New Mexico July–1855." Typescript. Original in Clinton P. Anderson Collection. 1855.

THE NATIONAL ARCHIVES, WASHINGTON, D.C.

Cooke, Philip St. George. "Journal of the March of the Mormon Battalion of Infantry Volunteers Under the Command of Lieut. Col. Philip St. George Cooke, from Santa Fe, N.M., to San Diego, Calif." Microcopy 567, roll 319. 1847.

THE UNIVERSITY OF NEW MEXICO LIBRARY, ALBUQUERQUE.

Hammond, George P. "Navajo-Hopi Relations." vol. 1—1540–1882; vol. 2—1882–1911; vol. 3—1911–1956. Typescript in Clinton P. Anderson Room. 1957.

Vivian, R. Gwinn. "The Navajo Archaeology of the Chacra Mesa, New Mexico." Unpublished thesis for Master's degree. 1960

THE PEABODY MUSEUM, CAMBRIDGE.

Madrid, Roque de. "Journal of a campaign which Maestro de Campo Roque Madrid made against the Navajo Indians, by order of Governor Don Francisco Cuerbo y Valdes, Year 1705." 1705.

THE BEINECKE LIBRARY OF YALE UNIVERSITY, NEW HAVEN.

DuBois, John Van D. Journals and Letters. William Robertson Coe Collection of Western Americana. 1850–61.

Pratt, Orville C. Diary of an Overland Journey from Fort Leavenworth to Los Angeles, June 9 to October 25, 1848. 2 vols., 157 pp. 1848.

Documents of Navajo Land Claims

THE NAVAJO TRIBE, WINDOW ROCK.

Littell, Norman M. "Proposed Findings of Fact in Behalf of the Navajo Tribe of Indians in Area of the Overall Navajo Claim, (Docket 229)." 6 vols. Mimeographed. 1967.

THE NEW MEXICO STATE RECORDS CENTER AND ARCHIVES, SANTA FE.

Jenkins, Myra Ellen, and Ward Allen Minge. "Record of Navajo Activities Affecting the Acoma-Laguna Area, 1746–1910." Defendants' exhibit for U.S. Indian Claim Commission, Cases 226–27. Typed manuscript. 1961.

SCHROEDER COLLECTION, SANTA FE.

Schroeder, Albert H. Ethnographic Maps, Defendants' Exhibits nos. S-501 through S-515, showing Navajo site clusters and migrations, Apache and other tribal locales, and intertribal raids and visits, 1668–1866. Docket 229: Navajo vs U.S., Indian Land Claim Commission, Washington, D.C. 1961.

Government Records

1849 *House Exec. Docs.*, 31st Cong., 1st sess., no. 17.
1851 *Senate Exec. Docs.*, 32d Cong., 1st sess., no. 1, pt. 1.
1852 *House Exec. Docs.*, 32d Cong., 2d sess., no. 1, pt. 2.
1853 *Senate Exec. Docs.*, 33d Cong., 1st sess., no. 1, pt. 1.
1855–56 *Congressional Globe.*
1856 *House Misc. Docs.*, 34th Cong., 1st sess., no. 113.
1858 *Senate Exec. Docs.*, 35th Cong., 2d sess., no. 1, pt. 1.
1859 *House Exec. Docs.*, 36th Cong., 1st sess., report no. 508.
1866 *Senate Exec. Docs.*, 39th Cong., 2d sess., report no. 156, "Condition of the Indian Tribes."
Kappler, Charles Joseph, *Indian Affairs, Laws and Treaties*, 2 vols., Washington, D.C.: Government Printing Office, 1904.
Heitman, Francis B. *Historical Register and Dictionary of the United States Army, 1789–1903.* 2 vols. 1903. Facsimile reprint. Urbana: University of Illinois Press, 1965.

Newspapers

Santa Fe *Republican.* January 1, September 10, 17, 24, October 20, November 27, December 25, 1847; January 15, April 2, May 21, July 8, August 9, 1848.
Santa Fe *Gazette.* September 10, 1853; October 18, 1856; November 13, 1858; July 18, August 22, November 10, 24, 1860.
Santa Fe *New Mexican.* October 28, 1864; May 25, 1866.
Navajo Times. (Articles by David M. Brugge) September 9, 1965—"Navajo History"; April 28, 1966—"The Battle of Washington Pass—1835"; May 19, 1966—"Antonio El Pinto, ?–1793"; July, 1966—"Early Navajo Political Structure."

Scientific Articles and Monographs

Bandelier, Adolph F. A. *Final Report of Investigations Among the Indians of the Southwestern United States, Carried on Mainly in the Years from 1880 to 1885, Part I.* Papers of the Archaeological Institute of America, American Series III. Cambridge, Mass.: John Wilson and Son, 1890.
Brugge, David M., *Research Reports No. 1. Navajos in the Catholic Church Records of New Mexico, 1694–1875.* Research Section, Parks and Recreation Department. Window Rock: The Navajo Tribe, 1968.
———. "Zarcillos Largos, Courageous Advocate of Peace." Navajo Historical Publications, Biographical Series no. 2, Research Section, Navajo Parks and Recreation Department. Window Rock, Ariz.: The Navajo Tribe, 1970.
Brugge, David M., J. Lee Correll, and Editha L. Watson. *Navajo Bibliography.* Navajoland Publication Series B. Window Rock, Ariz.: Navajo Tribal Museum, 1967.
Correll, J. Lee. "Sandoval—Traitor or Patriot?" Navajo Historical Publications, Biographical Series no. 1, Research Section, Navajo Parks and Recreation Department. Window Rock, Ariz.: The Navajo Tribe, 1970.
Harrington, John Peabody. *The Ethnogeography of the Tewa Indians.* 29th Annual Report of the Bureau of American Ethnology. Washington, D.C.: Government Printing Office, 1916.
Hill, Willard Williams. "Navaho Warfare." Yale University Publications in Anthropology, no. 5. New Haven: Yale University Press, 1936.

————. "Navajo Salt Gathering." The University of New Mexico Bulletin, Whole Number 349, Anthropological Series, vol. 3, no. 4. Albuquerque: University of New Mexico Press, 1940.

————. "Some Navaho Culture Changes During Two Centuries." Smithsonian Miscellaneous Collections, Essays in Historical Anthropology of North America, vol. 100 (whole volume). Washington, D.C.: Smithsonian Institution, 1940.

Keur, Dorothy L. "Big Bead Mesa, an Archaeological Study of Navaho Acculturation, 1745–1812." Memoirs of the Society for American Archaeology, No. 1. Menasha, Wisconsin, 1941.

Letterman, Jonathan. "Sketch of the Navajo Tribe of Indians, Territory of New Mexico." Extracts from the Correspondence of the Smithsonian Institution. House Misc. Docs., 34th Cong., 1st sess., no. 113, 1856.

Van Valkenburgh, Richard. Diné Bikéyah. Mimeographed. Window Rock, Ariz.: The Navajo Tribe, 1941.

Van Valkenburgh, Richard, and John C. McPhee. "A Short History of the Navaho People." Mimeographed. Window Rock, Ariz.: The Navajo Tribe, 1938.

Vivian, R. Gordon. Gran Quivira, Excavations in a 17th-Century Jumano Pueblo. Archaeological Research Series Number Eight, National Park Service. Washington, D.C.: U.S. Department of the Interior, 1964.

Wall, Leon, and William Morgan. Navajo-English Dictionary. Department of the Interior. Phoenix Press, Phoenix Indian School, 1958.

Wilson, John P. Military Campaigns in the Navajo Country, Northwestern New Mexico, 1800–1846. Research Records no. 5. Santa Fe: The Museum of New Mexico, 1967.

Young, Robert W. The Navajo Yearbook. Report no. 6. Window Rock, Ariz.: The Navajo Tribe, 1957.

————. The Role of the Navajo in the Southwestern Drama. Gallup: The Gallup Independent, 1968.

Published Reports, Journals and Diaries

Abert, James William. "Report of Lt. J. W. Abert on his Examination of New Mexico in the Years 1846–47." Facsimile reprint from Senate Exec. Docs., 30th Cong., 1st sess., no. 23. Albuquerque: Horn & Wallace, 1962.

Bennett, James A. "A Dragoon in New Mexico: 1850–1856." Edited by Clinton E. Brooks and Frank D. Reeve. New Mexico Historical Review, vol. 22, no. 1 (1947).

Bourke, John G. "Bourke on the Southwest, X." Edited by Lansing B. Bloom. New Mexico Historical Review, vol. 11, no. 3 (1936).

Castaño de Sosa, Gaspar. A Colony on the Move, Gaspar Castaño de Sosa's Journal, 1590–1591. Edited and translated by Albert H. Schroeder and Dan S. Watson. Santa Fe: The School of American Research, 1965.

Concha, Colonel Don Fernando de la. "Diary, 1788." Edited by Adlai Feather. New Mexico Historical Review, vol. 34, no. 4 (1959).

DuBois, John Van D., Campaigns in the West, 1856–1861, The Journals and Letters of Colonel John Van Deusen DuBois. Edited by George P. Hammond, from original journals and letters in the William Robertson Coe Collection of Western Americana, the Beinecke Library, Yale University. Tucson: Arizona Pioneers' Historical Society, 1949.

Edwards, Marcellus Ball. Diary, in Marching with the Army of the West. Edited by Ralph P. Bieber. Southwest Historical Series, vol. 4. Glendale: Arthur H. Clark Co., 1936.

Emory, Wiliam H. Notes of a Military Reconnoissance from Fort Leavenworth in

Missouri, to San Diego, in California, including parts of the Arkansas, Del
Norte, and Gila Rivers. Senate Exec. Docs., 30th Cong., 1st sess., no. 7, 1848.
Also published in the same year by H. Long & Brother, New York. Reprint.
Edited by Ross Calvin. Albuquerque: University of New Mexico Press, 1951.

Ferguson, Philip Gooch. Diary, in Marching with the Army of the West. Edited by
Ralph P. Bieber. Southwest Historical Series, vol. 4. Glendale: Arthur H.
Clark Co., 1936.

Greiner, John. "Journal." Edited by Annie Heloise Abel. Old Santa Fe, vol. 3,
no. 11 (1916).

Lazelle, Lt. Henry M. "Puritan and Apache: A Diary." Edited by Frank D. Reeve.
New Mexico Historical Review, vol. 33, no. 4 (1948).

Luxán, Diego Pérez de. Expedition into New Mexico Made by Antonio de Espejo,
1582–1583, as Revealed in the Journal of Diego Pérez de Luxán, a Member of
the Party. Translated with an introduction and notes by George P. Hammond
and Agapito Rey. Los Angeles: The Quivira Society, 1929.

McCall, George Archibald. New Mexico in 1850: A Military View. First printed in
Senate Exec. Docs., 31st Cong., 2d sess., no. 26. Reprint. Edited by Robert W.
Frazer. Norman: University of Oklahoma Press, 1968.

Magoffin, Susan Shelby. Down the Santa Fe Trail and Into Mexico: The Diary of
Susan Shelby Magoffin, 1846–1847. Edited by Stella M. Drumm. New Haven:
Yale University Press, 1962.

Mansfield, Joseph King Fenno. Mansfield on the Condition of the Western Forts,
1853–54. Edited by Robert W. Frazer. Inspection Reports, Records of the
Office of the Adjutant General. Norman: University of Oklahoma Press, 1963.

Read, Rev. H. W. "The Rev. Hiram Walter Read, Baptist Missionary." Edited by
Lansing B. Bloom. New Mexico Historical Review, vol. 17, no. 2 (1942).

Rice, Josiah M. A Cannoneer in Navajo Country: Journal of Josiah M. Rice, 1851.
Edited by Richard H. Dillon. Denver: Old West Publishing Co., 1970.

Robinson, Jacob S. A Journal of the Santa Fe Expedition under Colonel Doniphan.
Reprint of Sketches of the Great West, a Journal . . . kept by Jacob S.
Robinson, published in 1848 by the Portsmouth (N.H.) Journal Press. Re-
print. Princeton: Princeton University Press, 1932.

Simpson, James H. Journal of a Military Reconnaissance from Santa Fe, New Mexico, to the Navajo Country made in 1849. Senate Exec. Docs., 31st Cong., 2d
sess., no. 64. Reprint. Navaho Expedition. Edited by Frank McNitt. Norman:
University of Oklahoma Press, 1964.

Turner, Henry Smith. The Original Journals of Henry Smith Turner with Stephen
Watts Kearny to New Mexico and California, 1846. Edited by Dwight L.
Clarke. Norman: University of Oklahoma Press, 1966.

Vizcarra, José Antonio. "Vizcarra's Navajo Campaign of 1823." Translated and
edited by David M. Brugge. Arizona and the West, vol. 6, no. 3 (1964).

Ward, John. "Indian Affairs in New Mexico Under the Administration of William
Carr Lane: From the Journal of John Ward." Edited by Annie Heloise Abel.
New Mexico Historical Review, vol. 16, nos. 2–3 (1941).

Zúñiga, Don José de. "The Zúñiga Journal, Tucson to Santa Fe." Edited by
George P. Hammond. New Mexico Historical Review, vol. 6, no. 1 (1931).

Articles

Amsden, Charles A. "Navajo Origins." New Mexico Historical Review, vol. 7, no. 3
(1932).

Anderson, Clinton P. "The Adobe Palace." New Mexico Historical Review, vol. 19,
no. 2 (1944).

Bandelier, Adolph F. A. "Documentary History of the Rio Grande Pueblos of New Mexico, Part III—1581 to 1584." *New Mexico Historical Review*, vol. 5, no. 4 (1930).

Barber, Ruth Kerns. "Indian Labor in the Spanish Colonies." *New Mexico Historical Review*, vol. 7, nos. 2–4 (1932).

Bieber, Ralph P., ed. "Letters of William Carr Lane, 1852–1854." *New Mexico Historical Review*, vol. 3, no. 2 (1928).

Bloom, Lansing B., ed. "Historical Society Minutes, 1859–1863." *New Mexico Historical Review*, vol. 18, no. 3 (1943).

Brugge, David M. "Navajo and Western Pueblo History." *The Smoke Signal*, Tucson: Spring 1972, no. 25.

Chavez, Fray Angelico. "Comments Concerning 'Tomé and Father J.B.R.'" *New Mexico Historical Review*, vol. 31, no. 1 (1956).

De Harport, David L. "Origin of the Name, Canon del Muerto." *El Palacio*, vol. 67, no. 3 (1960).

Espinosa, J. Manuel, ed. "Memoir of a Kentuckian in New Mexico, 1848–1884." *New Mexico Historical Review*, vol. 13, no. 1 (1938).

Fisher, Kathy, "The Forgotten Dodge." *Annals of Iowa*, vol. 40, no. 4 (1970).

Ganaway, Loomis Morton. "New Mexico and the Sectional Controversy, 1846–1861." *New Mexico Historical Review*, vol. 18, no. 3 (1943).

Gorman, Clarissa C. "Samuel Gorman." *Old Santa Fe*, vol. 1, no. 3 (1914).

Jenkins, Myra Ellen. "The Baltasar Baca 'Grant': History of an Encroachment." *El Palacio*, vol. 68, nos. 1–2 (1961).

Jones, Oakah L., Jr. "Pueblo Indian Auxiliaries in New Mexico, 1763–1821." *New Mexico Historical Review*, vol. 37, no. 2 (1962).

Matson, Daniel S., and Albert H. Schroeder. "Cordero's Description of the Apache—1796." *New Mexico Historical Review*, vol. 32, no. 4 (1957).

Morris, Earl H. "Exploring the Canyon of Death." *The National Geographic Magazine*, vol. 48, no. 3 (1925).

Parish, William J. "The German Jew and the Commercial Revolution in Territorial New Mexico: 1850–1900." *New Mexico Historical Review*, vol. 35, no. 1 (1960).

Reeve, Frank D. "Navaho-Spanish Wars, 1680–1720." *New Mexico Historical Review*, vol. 33, no. 3 (1958).

———. "Navaho-Spanish Diplomacy, 1770–1790." *New Mexico Historical Review*, vol. 35, no. 3 (1960).

———. "Navaho Foreign Affairs, 1795–1846." Edited by Eleanor B. Adams and John L. Kessell. *New Mexico Historical Review*, vol. 46, nos. 2–3 (1971).

Scholes, France V. "Civil Government and Society in New Mexico in the Seventeenth Century." *New Mexico Historical Review*, vol. 10, no. 2 (1935).

———. "Church and State in New Mexico, 1610–1650." *New Mexico Historical Review*, vol. 11, no. 2 (1936).

———. "Troublous Times in New Mexico, 1659–1670." *New Mexico Historical Review*, vol. 12, nos. 2, 4; vol. 16, no. 1 (1937, 1941).

Schroeder, Albert H. "Navajo and Apache Relationships West of the Rio Grande." *El Palacio*, vol. 70, no. 3 (1963).

Simmons, Marc. "Horse Race at Fort Fauntleroy: An Incident of the Navajo Wars." *La Gaceta*, vol. 5, no. 1 (1970).

Tyler, S. Lyman, and H. Darrel Taylor. "The Report of Fray Alonso de Posada in Relation to Quivira and Teguayo." *New Mexico Historical Review*, vol. 33, no. 4 (1958).

Van Valkenburgh, Richard. "Captain Red Shirt." *New Mexico Magazine*, July 1941.
Waldrip, William I. "New Mexico During the Civil War." *New Mexico Historical Review*, vol. 28, no. 4 (1953).
Woodward, Arthur. "The First American Through Cañon de Chelly, Arizona." *The Masterkey*, vol. 13, no. 4 (1939).
Worcester, Donald E. "The Beginnings of the Apache Menace of the Southwest." *New Mexico Historical Review*, vol. 16, no. 1 (1941).
———. "The Navaho During the Spanish Regime in New Mexico." *New Mexico Historical Review*, vol. 26, no. 2 (1951).

Books

Abel, Annie Heloise, ed. *The Official Correspondence of James S. Calhoun*. Washington, D.C.: Government Printing Office, 1915.
Adair, John. *The Navajo and Pueblo Silversmiths*. Norman: University of Oklahoma Press, 1944.
Adams, Eleanor B., ed. *Bishop Tamaron's Visitation of New Mexico, 1760*. Historical Society of New Mexico, Publications in History, vol 15. Albuquerque: University of New Mexico Press, 1954.
Adams, Eleanor B., and Fray Angelico Chavez. *The Missions of New Mexico, 1776*. Albuquerque: University of New Mexico Press, 1956.
Bailey, L. R. *The Long Walk: A History of the Navajo Wars, 1846–68*. Los Angeles: Westernlore Press, 1964.
Bancroft, Hubert Howe. *History of Arizona and New Mexico, 1530–1888*. Facsimile reprint of 1889 edition. Albuquerque: Horn & Wallace, 1962.
Benavides, Fray Alonso de. *The Memorial of Fray Alonso de Benavides, 1630*. Translated by Mrs. Edward E. Ayer; annotated by Frederick Webb Hodge and Charles F. Lummis. Chicago: privately printed, 1916.
———. *Benavides' Memorial of 1630*. Translated by Peter P. Forrestal, C.S.C.; introduction and notes by Cyprian J. Lynch, O.F.M. Washington, D.C.: Academy of American Franciscan History, 1954.
———. *Fray Alonso de Benavides' Revised Memorial of 1634*. Edited by Frederick Webb Hodge, George P. Hammond, and Agapito Rey. Coronado Historical Series, vol. 4. Albuquerque: University of New Mexico Press, 1945.
Bolton, Herbert Eugene, ed. *Spanish Exploration in the Southwest, 1542–1706*. New York: Charles Scribner's Sons, 1916.
Connelley, William Elsey. *Doniphan's Expedition and the Conquest of New Mexico and California*. Kansas City: Bryant & Douglas Book and Stationary Co., 1907.
Cooke, Philip St. George. *The Conquest of New Mexico and California, An Historical and Personal Narrative*. New York: G. P. Putnam's Sons, 1878. Reprint. Chicago: Rio Grande Press, Inc., 1964.
Davis, William Watts Hart. *El Gringo: or New Mexico and Her People. 1857*; reprint ed., Santa Fe: Rydal Press 1938. Facsimile reprint. Chicago: Rio Grande Press, Inc., 1962.
Dunn, J. P. *Massacres of the Mountains: A History of the Indian Wars of the Far West 1815–1875*. First published in 1886. Reprint. New York: Archer House, Inc., n.d.
Espinosa, J. Manuel. *First Expedition of Vargas into New Mexico, 1692*. Translated and with introduction and notes by J. Manuel Espinosa. Albuquerque: University of New Mexico Press, 1940.
Forbes, Jack. *Apache, Navaho, and Spaniard*. Norman: University of Oklahoma Press, 1960.

Frink, Maurice. *Fort Defiance & the Navajos*. Boulder, Colorado: Pruett Press, 1968.

Gregg, Josiah. *Commerce of the Prairies*, Edited by Max L. Moorhead, from texts of the first and second editions (1844–45). Norman: University of Oklahoma Press, 1954.

Hackett, Charles Wilson. *Historical Documents Relating to New Mexico, Nueva Vizcaya, and Approaches Thereto, to 1773*. Vol. 3. Collected by Adolph F. A. and Fanny R. Bandelier. Edited and annotated by Charles Wilson Hackett. Washington: Carnegie Institution, 1937.

Hammond, George P., and Agapito Rey. *Don Juan de Oñate, Colonizer of New Mexico, 1595–1628*. Coronado Cuarto Centennial Publications, vols. 5–6. Albuquerque: University of New Mexico Press, 1953.

———. *The Rediscovery of New Mexico, 1580–1594*. Coronado Cuarto Centennial Publications, vol. 3. Albuquerque: University of New Mexico Press, 1966.

Hine, Robert V. *Edward Kern and American Expansion*. New Haven: Yale University Press, 1962.

Hodge, Frederick Webb. *History of Háwikuh, New Mexico, one of the so-called cities of Cíbola*. Vol. 1. Publications of the Frederick Webb Hodge Anniversary Publication Fund. Los Angeles: The Southwest Museum, 1937.

———, ed. *Handbook of the American Indians North of Mexico*. 2 vols. Originally published in 1907 as Bulletin 30 of the Bureau of American Ethnology, Smithsonian Institution. Facsimile reprint. New York: Rowman and Littlefield, Inc., 1965.

Hughes, John T. *Doniphan's Expedition; Containing an Account of the Conquest of New Mexico*. Cincinnati: U. P. James, 1847.

Hunt, Aurora. *Major General James Henry Carleton, 1814–1873, Western Frontier Dragoon*. Gendale: Arthur H. Clark Co., 1958.

Jackson, W. Turrentine. *Wagon Roads West*. 1952. Paper reprint. New Haven: Yale University Press, 1965.

Kelly, Lawrence C. *Navajo Roundup*. Boulder: Pruett Publishing Co., 1970.

Keleher, William A. *Turmoil in New Mexico, 1846–1868*. Santa Fe: Rydal Press, 1952.

Kirsch, Robert, and William S. Murphy. *West of the West*. New York: E. P. Dutton & Co., 1967.

Lange, Charles H., and Carroll L. Riley, ed. and ann. *The Southwestern Journals of Adolph F. Bandelier, 1880–1882*. Albuquerque: University of New Mexico Press, 1966.

McNitt, Frank. *The Indian Traders*. Norman: University of Oklahoma Press, 1962.

Marshall, Max L. *The Story of the U. S. Army Signal Corps*. New York: Franklin Watts, 1965.

Meriwether, David. *My Life in the Mountains and on the Plains*. Norman: University of Oklahoma Press, 1965.

Moorhead, Max L. *New Mexico's Royal Road: Trade and Travel on the Chihuahua Trail*. Norman: University of Oklahoma Press, 1958.

———. *The Apache Frontier*. Norman: University of Oklahoma Press, 1968.

Sabin, Edwin L. *Kit Carson Days, 1809–1868*. Vols. 1 & 2. New York: The Press of the Pioneers, Inc., 1935.

Simmons, Marc. *Indian and Mission Affairs in New Mexico, 1773*. Santa Fe: Stagecoach Press, 1965.

———. *Border Comanches*. Santa Fe: Stagechoach Press, 1967.

———. *Spanish Government in New Mexico*. Albuquerque: University of New Mexico Press, 1968.

Thomas, Alfred Barnaby. *Forgotten Frontiers—A Study of the Spanish Indian Policy of Don Juan Bautista de Anza, 1777–1787.* Norman: University of Oklahoma Press, 1932.

Twitchell, Ralph Emerson. *Old Santa Fe: The Story of New Mexico's Ancient Capital.* Santa Fe: New Mexican Publishing Corp., 1925.

———. *The History of the Military Occupation of the Territory of New Mexico from 1846 to 1851.* 1909. Facsimile reprint. Chicago: Rio Grande Press, Inc., 1963.

———. *The Leading Facts of New Mexican History.* Vols. 1 & 2. First published in 1911–12. Facsimile reprint. Albuquerque: Horn & Wallace, 1963.

Underhill, Ruth. *Here Come the Navaho!* Department of the Interior, Bureau of Indian Affairs. Lawrence, Kans.: Haskell Institute Print Shop, 1953.

———. *The Navajos.* Norman: University of Oklahoma Press, 1956.

Utley, Robert M. *Frontiersmen in Blue: The United States Army and the Indian, 1848–1865.* New York: The Macmillan Company, 1967.

Index

1848, by Newby, 128-31; of 1849, by Washington, 137-56, 215, 217, 236-37, 309, 348; of 1850, by Ker, 159-60; of 1851, planned and aborted by Munroe, 175-82; by Sumner, 193-99; of 1853, Ransom and Kendrick to the San Juan and DeChelly, 228-36; of 1856, by Kendrick to Zuni Salt Lake, 286-89; of 1857, by Bonneville against Apaches, 292n., 299-300, 333; of 1858, by Miles against Navajos, 328-56: McLane's attack at Ojo del Oso, 330-31, 334 & n.; Miles' orders of march, 336-37; Miles traverses Canyon de Chelly, 341; into Chusca Valley, 344-45; Navajo reprisals, 345-46; rendezvous in Chusca Valley, 347-48; Miles' First Column, 348-50; Backus' Second Column, 350-56; of 1859, reconnaissance by Simonson, 366-71: Walker's command, 367-71; Shepherd's command, 367n., 370; Walker's command, 370-71; by Shepherd, to Chusca Valley, 375-77; of 1860-61, by Canby against Navajos, 390-92, 397-408, 410 & n. 419n.: Canby's strategy, 392; march to Marsh Pass, 400-402; loss of horses, 402-405; develops Signal Corps, 403, 404 & n., 405, 412 & n.; to the Little Colorado, 405-407
Camp Floyd (Utah): 314n.
Camp Hualpai (Arizona): 367n.
Camp San José (New Mexico): 107n., 115
Cañada Larga (New Mexico): 21-22, 231
Canby, Bvt. Lt. Col. Edward Richard Sprigg: 272n., leads 1860–61 campaign, 391-92, 397-408, 410 & n., 419n.; negotiates 1861 treaty, 410-18; commands department, 420; 421, 424, formulates Navajo policy, 428-29
Candelarias, New Mexico: 372
Candelario, Joaquín: leads slave raid, 388
Cañoncito Bonito (Arizona): site of Ft. Defiance, 151, 153, 176n., 194n., 195, 197-98, 201, 217, 244, 260, 281, 292, 310, 324, 382
Cañoncito Navajos: 363n., 434
Cantonment Burgwin (New Mexico): 303
Canyon Blanco (New Mexico): 231
Canyon de Chelly (Arizona): 36n., Narbona's operations against, 41-44, 44n., 56, 76-77, 79, 431-33; 45, 47; skirted by Vizcarra, 59; 60, 63, 65, 67, 78n., 81, 84, sighted by Gilpin, 116; 118, penetrated by Santa Fe Battalion, 126; 143-44, 147-48, penetrated by Simpson, 149; 151, 153, Luna's men killed at, 167; routes to, 175-76, 176n.; 178-79, Sumner's

campaign to, 196-98; 212, 215, traversed by Kendrick and Dodge, 236; 251, 298, 311n., 315n., peace-war council at, 322-23, 337; Miles traverses via Monument Canyon, 341; 348-49, 353, traversed by Walker's troops, 367-71; 372n., 389, 392, 397-98, 424, 431-33
Canyon del Muerto (Arizona): 43 & n., 44, 147
Canyon del Trigo (Arizona): 116 & n., 284, 302, 394-95
Capote Ute Indians: 106, 200, 220-21, 241, 248, 258n., 274, 281, hold peace talks with Navajos, 312-14; 346, 354 & n., 379
Captives (surrendered by Navajos): 22, 44, 55, 85, 131-32, 150, 208, Armijo's comment on, 209-210; 222, 250, 389, 422
Captives (surrendered by whites): 45, 89, 131, Armijo's comment on, 209-210
Captives (taken by Apaches): 379, 443
Captives (taken by Diné Ana'aii): 67-68, 168, 307-308
Captives (taken by Mexicans): 65, 68 & n., 73-74, 76, 78-79, 79n., 81-83, 241
Captives (taken by Navajos): 12, 17n., 34-35, 38, 46, 70, 75, 95n., 102, 159, 219, Zarcillos Largos' comment on, 241-42; Yost's comment on, 356; 379
Captives (taken by Pueblos): 14, 16, 34
Captives (taken by Spaniards): 12-17 17n., 18, 21, 25, 30, 34, 39, 41, 43, 50-51, 241
Captives (taken by Utes): 13n., 89, 250, 308, 315, 323n., 354 & n., 356, 379, 398n., 402-403, 442-46
Captives (taken by whites, post 1846): 130, 141, 167, 241, 315, 331, 362, 379, 388, 401-402, 406, 410n., 418-20, 420n., 425, 442-46
Captives: treaty (or council) references to, 45, 54, 66n., 80, 84, 88-89, 119, 131, 151, 207, 358, 361
Carleton, Brig. Gen. James H.: 190, 192, 254-55, 271-72, 272n., transferred, 282; 428-29, 429n.
Carlisle, Lt. J. Howard: leads search for Dodge's remains, 292-94; forced to withdraw from La Joya grazing grounds, 302; commands Ft. Defiance, 303
Carravahal, Rafael: guide for 1849 campaign, 140-41; 141n., 144, 146, 175, 217, 286
Carravajal, Domingo: killed in reprisal raid, 372, 375
Carravajal, José: killed in reprisal raid, 372, 375
Carrizo Mountains (New Mexico-Arizona): 36n., 49, 58, 78n., 81, 181, 229, 232, 252, 298, 353, 368

81, 88-89, 168, 183n., 312, threatened by Miles, 334; 339, 354n., slave code, 396; 409, 441-46
Sleeping Ute Mountain (Colorado): Navajo *ricos* join Utes at, 73
Smith, Lt. William Duncan: aids survivors of hay camp attack, 186-88
Sobeta (Capote Ute): 346, 351, 354 & n., 377n.
Socorro, New Mexico: raided by Navajos, 75; 91, 100, 102, 113, 122, 386-87
Soldado Sordo (Navajo): son of Zarcillos Largos, 407, 411 & n., 415n.
Spears, Pvt. Robert: one of first two U.S. soldiers killed by Navajos, 122
Spider Rock: see Monument Rock
Steamboat Canyon (Arizona): 370
Steck, Dr. Michael (Apache Agent): 289-91; 292n., 307
Stevenson, James: names Canyon del Muerto, 44n.
Stewart, Pvt. James: one of first two U.S. soldiers killed by Navajos, 122
Stockton, Capt. David D.: with Newby campaign, 128-29
Stuart, Secretary of Interior Alexander: his aid requested in arming citizen volunteers, 175
Sublette, Lt. Linnaeus B.: 122
Sumner, Col. Edwin Vose: 101, 158n., 182, 186, relieves Col. Munroe, 189; refuses cavalry regiment, 190; quarrels with Calhoun, 190n., 193; search for headquarters site, 191-92; leads Navajo campaign, 193-99; 200, opposes citizen forays, 201, 205; at Jemez council, 206-208; moves headquarters, 211; seizes governor's authority, 212; 215-16, 221-22; opposes calling militia, 222, 225-26; relieved of command, 227; 237, 308, 341
Sykes, Capt. George: with Col. Washington's campaign, 153; with Miles campaign, 347, 348n.
Symonds, Lt. Henry C.: 274

Tabeguache Ute Indians: 441
Tamouche (Capote Ute): 220
Taos, New Mexico: 124-25, 125n., 132, 135-36, 181, 191, Moache Ute agency, 248n., 313, 354 & n., 379, 418-19, 423n.
Taos Pueblo, New Mexico: 6, 9, 16, 18, 20, 22, 33, 53, 76, 113, 396
Tapia, Andrés: with Chaves battalion, 391, 393, 398
Tapia, Francisco: 223
Tapia, Ens. Rafael: 79
Taylor, Lt. Oliver Hazard Perry: 134
Tecolote, New Mexico: 95, 149, 191
Tenorio, Julián: a leader of 1836-37 campaign, 77
Tenth U.S. Infantry: 405
Terribio: see Torivio

Tesuque Pueblo, New Mexico: 20
Tewa Indians: 10, 112-113 & n.
Third Mesa (Arizona): 61
Third Missouri Mounted Volunteers: 124, 128-29, 132
Third U.S. Artillery: 132
Third U.S. Cavalry: 367n.
Third U.S. Infantry: 136, 138, 157-58, 165, 192 & n., 194, 199. 203, 213, 234, 251-52, 271, 282n., 292, 299-300, 303, 305, 317, 329, 350n., 367n., 381, 382n., 391
Thomas, John (guide and interprom): 106
Thompson, Bvt. Maj. Philip R.: 192, 196
Tilford, Lt. Joseph G.: 397-98
Tinaja (Mimbres Apache): 291
Tohatchi, New Mexico: 120, 418
Tohgaii (New Mexico): 418, 419n.
Tolin, Richard: interpreter at Cebolleta, 167
Tome, New Mexico: 81, 97
Tonalea (Arizona): 61
Torez, Lt. Lorenzo: 145
Torivio (Navajo captive): brother of Juan Anaya, 322n.; 347
Torreon, New Mexico; 22, 57, 393
Torreon Wash (New Mexico): 65
Totisonisne: see Ganado Mucho (Navajo)
Treaties: see Navajo treaties
Trujillo, Capt. Diego de: 16
Trujillo, Gregorio: one of donors of Ft. Union property, 192
Tsaile Creek (Arizona): 147
Tsaya trading post (New Mexico): 57n.
Tsegi Canyon (Arizona): 371, 401
Tucson, Arizona: 282
Tullis, John R.: 135n.
Tully, Pinckney R.: partner of H. L. Dodge, 170; 184
Tunicha Creek (New Mexico): 143
Tunicha Valley: see Chusca Valley
Tuntsa Wash (New Mexico): 347, 376
Turkey Mountains (New Mexico): 193
Tuye Springs (New Mexico): 419n.
Two Gray Hills trading post (New Mexico): 110n., 143
Tyende Creek (Arizona): 354, 400

U.S. Army Signal Corps: 404 & n., 405, 412 & n.
U.S. Military Academy (West Point): 134, 214n., 282n., 300, 309, 329, 403
U.S. Topographical Engineers: 96, 135, 404
U.S. Weather Bureau: 404n.
Utah Chiquito (Navajo): 361n.
Ute Indians: 7, 9, as captive slaves, 13; campaign with Spaniards, 18; alliance with Comanches against Navajos, 23ff.; join Navajos to raid Comanches, 35; reported joining with Navajos, 49; 73, join with Navajos, 89;